Louisiana Law of
Obligations

Louisiana Law of Obligations

A Methodological & Comparative Perspective

Cases, Texts and Materials

Alain A. Levasseur
HERMANN MOYSE, SR. PROFESSOR OF LAW
DIRECTOR OF EUROPEAN STUDIES
PAUL M. HEBERT LAW CENTER, LOUISIANA STATE UNIVERSITY

Randall Trahan
LOUIS B. PORTERIE PROFESSOR
PAUL M. HEBERT LAW CENTER, LOUISIANA STATE UNIVERSITY

Sandi Varnado
ASSISTANT PROFESSOR OF LAW
LOYOLA UNIVERSITY NEW ORLEANS COLLEGE OF LAW

WITH THE ASSISTANCE OF
Katherine Hand

CAROLINA ACADEMIC PRESS
Durham, North Carolina

ISBN (paperback) 978-1-5310-2244-0
ISBN (hardback) 978-1-61163-162-3
LCCN 2013936374

Carolina Academic Press
700 Kent Street
Durham, North Carolina 27701
Telephone (919) 489-7486
Fax (919) 493-5668
www.cap-press.com

Printed in the United States of America
2021 printing

Contents

Table of Principal Cases

Preface

This is a new and innovative coursebook on the law of Obligations in General and Conventional Obligations under the Louisiana Civil Code. The book covers not only the law of Contractual Obligations, but also, and most importantly, the General Principles of Obligations that govern all subjects addressed in the Civil Code. Such is the case, for example, of the law of Delicts (Torts) (LSA C.C. articles 2315–2324), the law of Things, Book II of the Civil Code, etc.... It is therefore strongly recommended that a reader of this coursebook have available a Louisiana Civil Code to better understand, and appreciate, the intimate connections that exist between the Books and the Articles in the Civil Code.

Like other works of its kind, it features scores of carefully edited excerpts from Louisiana judicial opinions and scholarly writings as well as citations to pertinent articles of the Louisiana Civil Code, all arranged in a systematic fashion, particularly with respect to the ranking of the sources of law. Following the civil law system's approach to the sources of law, we have first listed, under the title of each Chapter, the relevant Code articles to stress the binding authority attached to legislation as the primary source of law. The suggestion is, therefore, that any and all reasoning in a civil law system must start with an understanding of the written source of law under the form of a statute, which a Civil Code actually is. Additionally, we have included some writings of Louisiana scholars and Louisiana cases.

But this casebook includes features that most others do not. Following each case is a series of questions, some designed to direct students to the significant points of the court's analysis, others designed to deepen students' understanding of civil law methodology, above all the principles and techniques of interpretation as applied to a Civil Code. In addition, the coursebook reproduces pertinent articles of foreign civil Codes, excerpts from foreign civil law scholarship and it provides cross-references to relevant provisions of various Anglo-American works on contract law, including the U.C.C. and the Restatements of Contracts. The result is a work that not only provides students [and lawyers] with a comprehensive introduction to Louisiana's law of Obligations, but it also invites students [and lawyers] to draw comparisons between that law and the complementary law of other legal systems.

References

Louisiana Pocket Civil Code (Alain A. Levasseur ed. 2013); LexisNexis.

Alain A. Levasseur, Comparative Law of Contracts (2008); Carolina Academic Press.

Alain A. Levasseur, Louisiana Law of Conventional Obligations: A Précis (2010); LexisNexis.

Alain A. Levasseur, Louisiana of Obligations in General: A Précis (2009); LexisNexis.

Robert J. Pothier, A Treatise on the Law of Obligations or Contracts (William David Evans trans., 1806).

Marcel Planiol, Treatise on the Civil Law (Louisiana State Law Institute trans., 11th ed. 1939).

Part One

Of the Nature, Division & Kinds of Obligations

Chapter One

Obligations: Principles

Louisiana Sources of Law

Louisiana Civil Code

Art. 1756. Obligations; definition.

An obligation is a legal relationship whereby a person, called the obligor, is bound to render a performance in favor of another, called the obligee. Performance may consist of giving, doing, or not doing something. (Acts 1984, No. 331, § 1, eff. Jan. 1, 1985.)

Art. 1757. Sources of obligations.

Obligations arise from contracts and other declarations of will. They also arise directly from the law, regardless of a declaration of will, in instances such as wrongful acts, the management of the affairs of another, unjust enrichment and other acts or facts. (Acts 1984, No. 331, § 1, eff. Jan. 1, 1985.)

Art. 1759. Good faith.

Good faith shall govern the conduct of the obligor and the obligee in whatever pertains to the obligation. (Acts 1984, No. 331, § 1, eff. Jan. 1, 1985.)

Précis: Louisiana Law of Obligations in General § 1.1.1 to 1.4.2

One can find in Justinian's Institutes the following definition of the concept of obligation:

> *"Obligatio est iuris vinculum, quo necessitate adstringimur alicuius solvendae rei, secundum nostrae civitatis iura."*

> "An obligation is a legal bond whereby we are constrained by the need to perform something according to the laws of our state."

It is this meaning which is reflected in the new LSA-C.C. Art. 1756 where an obligation is defined as a legal relationship, whereby a person, called the obligor, is bound to render a performance in favor of another, called the obligee. Performance may consist of giving, doing, or not doing something....

In the narrower sense of the word *source*, the source of an obligation is the particular juridical act or fact susceptible of creating a legal relationship between an obligor and an obligee. There are, in this respect, two categories of sources of obligations. One can identify formal sources specifically listed and identified in the civil Code and sources which, transcending the Code, can be systematized and labeled as juridical "acts" and juridical "facts" as stated in the last words of **LSA-C.C. Art. 1757**....

[A] juridical act, *stricto sensu*, in the technical sense of the words, is any manifestation of the will of a person meant to have legal effects. By contrast, a juridical fact is an event occurring outside the will of a person which, by itself, brings about legal effects. . . .

The verb *to give,* used in connection with the word obligation, must be understood in the technical sense of its Latin parallel *dare* (to transfer, to grant) and not in its more colloquial sense of *donare* or to give as a present, to transfer gratuitously. Therefore, the verb *to give,* as used in the civil Code, should be understood as meaning *to transfer* to an obligee-creditor the ownership of a thing, for example, or more broadly speaking, to grant to someone a *real right* in a thing. Such a transfer can take place either onerously [see, for example, **LSA-C.C. Arts. 2439 and 2456**] or gratuitously [see, for example, **LSA-C.C. Arts. 1468 and 535**]. . . .

An obligation to do requires that the debtor-obligor perform some positive act, such as physically delivering a thing, providing medical care, building a swimming pool, etc. . . . **LSA-C.C. Arts. 227, 2746, 2756** are codal illustrations of such obligations to do.

The personal and actual involvement or participation of the obligor in the performance of an obligation to do may be either essential (in the technical sense of *the essence of the obligation*) or indifferent to the creditor-obligee.

Practical experience suggests that some obligations to do are of such a nature that their performance would require the personal and exclusive involvement of the obligor. . . .

In other kinds of obligations to do, the obligee might very well be satisfied with the performance of the obligation by a third party where the obligor himself would fail, or be unable, to render the performance required of him. . . .

An obligation not to do requires that the obligor refrain or abstain from doing something which, under normal circumstances, he would have the right to do. An illustration of such an obligation is provided by **LSA-C.C. Art. 2931** which forbids the depositary from making use of the thing deposited unless authorized by the depositor . . .

There exists an obligation of result whenever the performance or object of the obligation is so precisely determined as to amount to a definite result to be achieved. An obligation to give a specific thing and an obligation not to do something would be obligations of result. . . .

There is an obligation of means or diligence when an obligor is expected to use the best possible means available to him, or to act with the utmost care and diligence in the performance of his obligation but without guaranteeing a definite result. . . .

The requirement of good faith on the part of parties to an obligation is not a new requirement although it lost some of its importance over the centuries. The specific inclusion of this requirement in a Code article has the merit of raising it to the status of a general principle which, as such, ought to guide the jurist in his analysis of the law of obligations. Coming from Roman law and developed by Canon law, this fundamental theory of *good faith* inspires and pervades the entire law of the civil Code and the law of obligations in particular. Its underlying presence should never be forgotten. . . .

Actually, this general principle or duty of good faith can be considered as including two sub duties which are incorporated in a great variety of Code articles. One such sub-duty could be called the duty of loyalty and the other the duty of cooperation. . . .

Comparative Law Perspective

On "good faith" *see* Part II, Chapter Three — Effects of Obligations, page 293.

Chapter Two

Natural Obligations

Louisiana Sources of Law

Louisiana Civil Code

Art. 1760. Moral duties that may give rise to a natural obligation.

A natural obligation arises from circumstances in which the law implies a particular moral duty to render a performance. (Acts 1984, No. 331, § 1, eff. Jan. 1, 1985.)

Art. 1761. Effects of a natural obligation.

A natural obligation is not enforceable by judicial action. Nevertheless, whatever has been freely performed in compliance with a natural obligation may not be reclaimed. A contract made for the performance of a natural obligation is onerous. (Acts 1984, No. 331, § 1, eff. Jan. 1, 1985.)

Art. 1762. Examples of circumstances giving rise to a natural obligation.

Examples of circumstances giving rise to a natural obligation are:

(1) When a civil obligation has been extinguished by prescription or discharged in bankruptcy.

(2) When an obligation has been incurred by a person who, although endowed with discernment, lacks legal capacity.

(3) When the universal successors are not bound by a civil obligation to execute the donations and other dispositions made by a deceased person that are null for want of form.

(Acts 1984, No. 331, § 1, eff. Jan. 1, 1985.)

Précis: Louisiana Law of Obligations in General § 1.3.1 to 1.4.1

[A] natural obligation, although it expresses the existence of a right in a person, cannot be a ground for an action to have the natural obligation enforced. The creditor-obligee of a natural obligation has no right of action against the *natural obligor....*

LSA-C.C. Art. 1762 is only illustrative of the different kinds of natural obligations that may exist....

The use of the adjective *moral* to describe the inherent value of a natural obligation is broad enough to bring under the label of natural obligations any duty *binding ... in conscience and according to natural justice....*

A natural obligation, because it is defined in part as an obligation, necessarily creates a right in an obligee. That right, however, is deprived of any action for the enforcement of the obligation which is its counterpart. In this respect, the natural obligation is to be distinguished from the civil obligation....

is well settled in the jurisprudence of Louisiana. *Montgomery v. Chaney*, 13 La.Ann. 207; 73
Succession of Maltry, 161 La. 1032, 109 So. 827. 74

There could be no doubt that there is a moral obligation resting upon a parent to do 75
equity between his children by equalizing his gifts to them during his lifetime. This is not 76
seriously disputed by respondent, but a distinction is sought to be made between a moral 77
and a natural obligation. As to this the contention is that the obligation of a parent to 78
equalize his gifts to his children is not embraced in the four classes of natural obligations 79
enumerated in article 1758, Civ. Code, and that they are exclusive. 80

The administration of the law of Louisiana is not hampered by technical and unsub- 81
stantial distinctions. In the absence of a positive statute, it is the duty of her courts to 82
apply the principles of equity, appealing to natural law and reason and received usages in 83
support of those principles. Civ. Code, art. 21. And the maxim 'inclusio unius est exclu- 84
sio alterius' is not always applicable in construing the articles of the Civil Code. As a rule 85
of construction, announced in 1838, and followed ever since, the Supreme Court said in 86
Ellis v. Prevost, 13 La. 230: 87

'The court cannot be ignorant of the mode in which our Codes were prepared and 88
became laws. They were written by lawyers, who mixed with the positive legislation de- 89
finitions seldom accurate, and points of doctrine always unnecessary. The legislature 90
modified and changed many of the provisions relating to the positive legislation, but 91
adopted the definitions and abstract doctrine, without material alteration; from this cir- 92
cumstance, as well as from the inherent difficulty of the subject, the positive provisions 93
of our Code are often at variance with the theoretical part, which was intended to eluci- 94
date them; and whenever that occurs, we deem it a sound rule of interpretation, to dis- 95
regard the doctrine, and consider the definitions modified by the clear intent of the 96
positive enactments.' 97

A reasonable construction of article 1758, Civ. Code, is that the four classes of natural 98
obligations mentioned therein are illustrative, and not intended to be exclusive, and that 99
any natural obligation is sufficient consideration for a new contract. 100

Apparently there is no Louisiana decision expressly holding that the obligation of a 101
parent to equalize his gifts to his children is sufficient consideration for a new contract; 102
but this, perhaps, may be because the doctrine is so well understood that no one has 103
heretofore raised the question in the settlement of an estate. That a natural obligation is 104
sufficient consideration for a note is well settled by the following analogous cases: *Matthews* 105
v. Williams, 25 La.Ann. 585, where a son gave his note in place of his father's note, which 106
was prescribed; *Barthe v. Succession of Lacroix*, 29 La.Ann. 326, 29 Am.Rep. 330, where 107
a note was given as a gratuity beyond his wages to an old and faithful servant, in which 108
case the court used the expressions 'moral' and 'natural' obligations interchangeably; and 109
Interstate F. & B. Co. v. Irwin, 138 La. 335, 70 So. 313, where a note was given by a bank 110
director as a donation to make good the impairment of the capital of his bank. [. . .]. 111

[. . . .] 112

Applying the law of Louisiana to the facts as found by the board, the conclusion is ir- 113
resistible that a natural obligation rested on the decedent to equalize his gifts to his chil- 114
dren; that in executing and delivering to his sons the promissory notes here in question 115
he fulfilled that obligation; that under the law of Louisiana, which is controlling, re- 116
gardless of decisions to the contrary in other states, there was sufficient consideration for 117
the notes, and they were deductible from his gross estate in the payment of estate taxes. 118

[. . . .] 119

Questions

1. Lines 38–62: After you have read the three articles carefully, try to formulate, in your own terms, the reason, i.e., the legal reason or *ratio legis* that you see as a justification for each one of the three kinds of obligation. Focusing on the natural obligation, is the legal reason (*ratio legis*) or justification that you see behind Louisiana Civil Code article 1757-2, i.e., the definition of a natural obligation, allowing you to identify more or fewer examples of natural obligations than those examples listed in Louisiana Civil Code article 1758? Read now the new Louisiana Civil Code articles (since 1984–1985) 1760 and 1762 on natural obligations. How do these latter articles match with your legal reason as you formulated it when considering the former articles on natural obligations? What comment(s) can you make as to the role of legislation and the role of the courts in creating law, if 'creating' is the proper word to use as contrasted with 'interpreting' the law?

2. Lines 63 *et seq.*: Here is an example of civil law methodology: can you identify the *ratio juris* on which the court will be building its reasoning from now on?

3. Lines 65 *et seq.*: There is a reason why the court is referring to a series of Code articles. That reason can be found in the *ratio legis* of the different sets of articles. Do you see any connection between these sets of articles?

4. Line 75: Where do you place a moral obligation in the Louisiana Civil Code?

5. Lines 75 *et seq.*: Considering that this case long preceded the revision of the Law of Obligations in 1984–1985, why should the defendant argue that Louisiana Civil Code article 1758 (Code of 1870) is 'exclusive'?

6. Line 101: What is the Court actually saying in the beginning of the sentence and why do you think the Court is making this statement? Could you relate the court's statements in this paragraph to a type or kind of source of law mentioned in articles 1 to 4 in the Louisiana Civil Code? Is the Court resorting to an *in pari materia* reasoning (*see* La. Civ. Code art. 13)? Do you see any *a pari ratione* reasoning?

Succession of BURNS et al.

Supreme Court of Louisiana
March 2, 1942
7 So.2d 359

FOURNET, Justice.

This case is before us on an appeal from a judgment dismissing the oppositions filed by the widow of the late A. Sidney Burns and certain ordinary creditors of his estate to the first and final account of the testamentary executor of the succession.

A. Sidney Burns died in Lake Charles, Louisiana, on March 16, 1938, leaving an olographic will dated June 28, 1937, in which he bequeathed to his son, A. Sidney Burns, Jr., issue of his first marriage, to Linnie Mai Locke (hereinafter referred to as the claimant), the disposable portion of his estate, and named S. M. DeBakey as his testamentary executor. DeBakey qualified as the executor and sold all of the property Burns died possessed of. On December 5, 1938, he filed his first and final account and plan of distribution, from which it appears that the succession was insolvent. On December 13, following, Mrs. Lois Fussel Burns (hereinafter referred to as the opponent), widow of Burns by his third marriage, as the natural tutrix of her minor child, issue of that marriage, filed an opposition to the account, attacking principally the validity of three mortgage notes listed

therein as being due the first wife, aggregating the principal sum of $7,050, plus interest 19
and attorney fees. These mortgage notes are claimed to have been given as collateral se- 20
curity for an alleged balance of $8,000 due by the deceased to his first wife as the result 21
of the settlement of the community formerly existing between them. 22

In the opposition it is alleged that prior to her marriage to decedent, opponent, hav- 23
ing learned that the community formerly existing between the decedent and the claimant 24
had not been settled and there remained a balance of $15,000 due the claimant by the 25
decedent, refused to accept decedent's proposal of marriage until he settled this claim 26
with his former wife; that such a settlement was made in writing on November 22, 1933, 27
the deceased turning over to the claimant practically all of the property he then possessed, 28
both real and personal, including a furnished home occupied by the claimant in Pon- 29
chatoula, Louisiana, certain vacant property, building and loan stock, an automobile, 30
etc., the claimant accepting the property in full satisfaction of her claim and completely 31
absolving the decedent from any further liability with respect to her claim to the community 32
formerly existing between, the opponent, as a result thereof, marrying the deceased on 33
the 29th of the same month; and that subsequently, during a temporary separation from 34
the opponent, the decedent, together with the claimant, in furtherance of a scheme to 35
defraud opponent and the issue of her marriage to the deceased, executed an instrument 36
on June 18, 1934, setting aside their agreement of November 22, 1933, appraising the 37
property previously transferred to the claimant in accordance with the agreement of No- 38
vember 22, 1933, at $6,000, transferring an undivided 6/10ths interest in the Tangipa- 39
hoa Abstract Company to the claimant for a recited consideration of $1,000, and declaring 40
that there remained due the claimant by the decedent from the community formerly ex- 41
isting between them the sum of $8,000. The opponent further alleged that the notes held 42
by the claimant were not only issued without consideration, but in fraud of her rights 43
and those of her minor child, and, further, that the claimant, by her execution of the in- 44
strument of November 22, 1933, is estopped from asserting any interest in this succession 45
resulting from any claim which she may have as to the former community existing between 46
her and the decedent. She further opposed the account in [**other respects.**] 47

[....] 48

[**By supplemental and amended opposition, filed by opponent,**] in her individual ca- 49
pacity and as the tutrix of her minor child on April 1, 1939, [...] she[, **among other** 50
things,] [...] amplified certain allegations in [... **earlier**] opposition[**s**], alleging that the 51
execution of the mortgage notes and the transfer of the interest in the Tangipahoa Abstract 52
Company were in the nature of 'gratuitous alienations' of the movables and immovables 53
of the community, constituting dispositions of the common property in contravention 54
of the prohibitory provisions of Article 2404 of the Revised Civil Code [...] and that in 55
the event the executor fails or refuses to take the necessary steps to recover [...] the in- 56
terest in the Tangipahoa Abstract Company, that he be held liable for the value thereof. 57

The claimant made herself a party to these proceedings, filing, on December 13, 1939, 58
an answer in the nature of a general denial to [...] oppositions. A similar answer was 59
filed by the testamentary executor. 60

[....] 61

The first question for our determination is whether or not Mrs. Linnie L. Burns, the 62
claimant, did in fact execute an instrument on November 22, 1933, whereby she agreed 63
to and did accept certain property from the decedent in full settlement and satisfaction 64
of her claim against him, absolving him from any further liability thereon; and, second, 65
if so, the effect of such a release. 66

The record unmistakably shows that such an agreement was executed, even though the claimant denied having executed the same in her answer to the oppositions and testified accordingly under oath on the witness stand, for, in addition to the testimony of the opponent, who was acquainted with the claimant's signature, to that effect, we have the corroboration of her testimony in the persons of her mother, her brother, and her sister-in-law — in all respects other than the recognition of claimant's signature, with which they were unfamiliar — as well as the unimpeachable evidence reflected by the instrument dated June 18, 1934, signed by the claimant and the decedent, and upon which her (claimant's) entire claim in this succession is based, that such an instrument did exist. In the document dated June 18, 1934, it is stipulated that '*The parties hereto do hereby mutually agree and declare that a certain agreement, termed a compromise and release, made and entered into between them, dated November 22, 1933, is grossly unfair and unequitable, and the same is hereby set aside, annulled and rescinded.*' (Italics ours.) The parties then proceed to appraise the real estate transferred to the claimant in pursuance to the said agreement of November 22, 1933, at $4,000, to value the 20 shares of capital stock in the Ponchatoula Homestead Ass'n. at $2,000, to transfer to claimant decedent's undivided 6/10ths interest in the Tangipahoa Abstract Company for the recited consideration of $1,000, and to declare that of the original claim of $15,000 which claimant had against decedent as the result of the dissolution of the community by divorce in 1931, there remained due her the sum of $8,000.

The decedent, having given practically all of his personal and real property to his first wife, who was willing to receive it in full payment and satisfaction of the amount due her as the result of the dissolution of their community, obtained thereby a valid release and the debt became extinguished. Articles 2655 and 2656 of the Revised Civil Code. See, also, *Webster v. Hartman*, 148 La. 1080, at page 1093, 88 So. 462.

But counsel for claimant and the testamentary executor argued in brief that inasmuch as the claimant had accepted from the decedent property of the approximate value of $6,000 or $7,000 in satisfaction of an indebtedness to her of $15,000, there remained a *natural obligation* on the part of the deceased to right the wrong and that this was sufficient and valid consideration for the execution of the document of June 18, 1934, and his discharge of the same. In support thereof they rely mainly upon the case of *Jamison v. Ludlow*, 3 La.Ann. 492, in addition to those cases in our jurisprudence holding that a *natural obligation* is a sufficient consideration to support a contract.

None of these cases are analogous to the case under consideration here, and, in our opinion, are inapposite. The Jamison case, in which language was used which appears to support the contention of the claimant, is only authority for the proposition that 'The rule which forbids oral evidence to contradict or vary the terms of a written contract, is not infringed by the admission of oral evidence to prove a new and distinct agreement,' or to prove that a written contract was fraudulently procured. In that case the plaintiff appealed from a judgment dismissing his suit, on the trial of which he was not permitted to prove by parol evidence that a written compromise agreement — releasing upon the payment of half of the debt in installments the obligation due plaintiff by the defendants — had been procured by fraud, and also refusing to permit him to prove, by oral evidence, a subsequent and new agreement to pay the balance of the old debt.

In *Succession of Miller v. Manhattan Life Insurance Co.*, 110 La. 652, 34 So. 723, 725, it was pointed out that 'our Code, art. 1757, draws sharply the line between mere *moral obligations* and such as it calls '*natural obligations,*' and denies to the former not only a right of action, but also 'any legal operation'; the court holding that the four categories of natural obligations enumerated in Article 1758 of the Revised Civil Code are exclusive in

their scope.' (The italics are ours.) Into none of these categories can the obligation in the 116
instant case be fitted. 117

The giving of a *thing* in payment of an obligation under the provisions of Article 2655 118
of the Revised Civil Code, extinguishes, in our opinion, the obligation in toto, the same 119
as if the full amount had been paid with cash. Consequently, any obligation that could 120
arise as the result of the fact that the property transferred is of less value than the amount 121
of the claim, in discharge of which it was accepted, is a moral one, which, under the ex- 122
press provisions of the Revised Civil Code, will not support a contract. Article 1757, and 123
the *Succession of Miller*, supra. 124

The contract for the giving of a thing in payment of an obligation provided for in our 125
Civil Code resembles very closely what is known in the common law as an 'accord and sat- 126
isfaction,' defined in Corpus juris Secundum as follows: 127

'An 'accord' is an agreement whereby one of the parties undertakes to give or perform, 128
*and the other to accept, in satisfaction of a claim, liquidated or in dispute, * * * something* 129
other than or different from what he is, or considers himself, entitled to; and a 'satisfaction' 130
is the execution, or performance, of such an agreement.' 1 C.J.S., Accord and Satisfac- 131
tion, p. 462, § 1. To the same effect is 1 Cyc. 307 and 1 C.J. 523, Section 1. 132

'When an accord is performed or executed, there is an accord and satisfaction and, from 133
the standpoint of consideration, the transaction is *fait accompli. An accord and satisfaction* 134
* * * *extinguishes, discharges, and supersedes the original demand* and bars or prevents any 135
action or proceeding thereon * * *.' 1 C.J.S., Accord and Satisfaction, p. 548, § 45. 136

'It was apparently first laid down by a case in the time of Coke (Pinnel's Case, 5 Coke 137
117a) and has subsequently been treated by most authorities as settled law, that *an accord* 138
*and satisfaction of a claim or demand, * * * where the parties so intend or agree, is effected* 139
*by the transfer and acceptance of property * * * regardless of the actual or intrinsic worth of* 140
*the property so transferred or conveyed * * * provided it is of some value.* So the fact that the 141
property transferred is apparently of less value than the demand, or that it is of small 142
value as compared with the amount of the claim in discharge of which it is accepted, is 143
immaterial * * *.' *The reason for this rule is that '* * * a debtor is under no obligation to de-* 144
liver, or a creditor to accept, anything other than money, in discharge of a debt or demand, 145
and when they do so, there is such a giving and acceptance of something other or differ- 146
ent from that which is claimed or owed as to bring the transaction within the definition 147
of accord and satisfaction * * *.' I C.J.S., Accord and Satisfaction, pp. 487, 488, § 20. To 148
the same effect is 1 Cyc. 335. (All of the italics in these excerpts are ours.) 149

We are therefore of the opinion that the document dated June 18, 1934, declaring that 150
a balance of $8,000 is due claimant, is without legal effect and unenforceable and that the 151
three mortgage notes given claimant as collateral thereto fall with it. Articles 1771, 3133, 152
3136, 3138, of the Revised Civil Code. Consequently, they must be disallowed on the tableau 153
and plan of distribution of the testamentary executor. The undivided 6/10ths interest in the 154
Tangipahoa Abstract Company, transferred to the claimant by the same instrument, was 155
without consideration. It, therefore, belongs to the succession, and must be accounted for. 156

[....] 157

Questions

1. Lines 1–22: The Court, although a Louisiana Court, uses the word 'settlement' (*see*
    line 22) and the verb 'settle' (*see* line 25). This word is common law terminology and
    will not be found in the Louisiana Civil Code. *See* the civil law equivalent under

"Compromise", La. Civ. Code arts. 3071–3083; *see also* "Of Giving in Payment", La. Civ. Code arts. 2655–2659.

2. Lines 67–91: What ought to be the ultimate effect of a giving in payment as regards the debt? Should the debt be fully extinguished or should a natural obligation remain in existence? *See* the plaintiff's claim, lines 101–108. Can you make a solid legal argument for either side or should there be only one answer under the law? For example, can you reason by analogy, *a pari ratione*, between an obligation extinguished by prescription (and not fully paid, obviously) and an obligation extinguished by a giving in payment although not fully paid? *See also* lines 129–34.

3. Lines 118 *et seq.*: For the Court, a giving in payment fully extinguishes a debtor's obligation; not even a natural obligation remains in existence. What do you think about that from a legal point of view? What about from an equitable point of view? Remember that although a debt is extinguished by prescription, there remains in existence a natural obligation (*see* La. Civ. Code art. 1762(1)). In this instance, is the law rewarding a debtor because the time given to the creditor for bringing an action has prescribed? Or is the law punishing a creditor for failing to look after his rights of action? In the case of a giving in payment, why should the law deny the benefit of a natural obligation to a debtor whose giving in payment did not fully extinguish his debt and who wishes to make an additional payment to soothe his conscience or his moral duty to fully pay his debt?

SUCCESSION OF Emanuel HARRISON

Supreme Court of Louisiana
Jan. 16, 1984
444 So.2d 1191

MARCUS, Justice.

Emanuel Harrison died on February 17, 1960 without issue. He was survived by his second wife, Aria Day Harrison, and by his legal heirs: a sister (Ida Harrison Knox), a brother (Daniel Harrison), ten children of a predeceased brother, Minor Harrison, and three children of a predeceased sister, Ada Harrison George. Emanuel Harrison was also survived by his foster son, John D. Harrison, whom he never legally adopted.

A few days after Emanuel's death, John D. Harrison found, in the glove compartment of Emanuel's car, a document which appeared to be Emanuel's will. The document was entirely written, dated and signed in the handwriting of someone other than Emanuel Harrison,[1] then was signed at the bottom in pencil by Emanuel Harrison. The document provided as follows:

Liberty, Miss.

Dec. 15, 1955

I, Emanuel Harrison, of East Feliciana Parish Louisiana, do make this my last will and testament, revoking all others, namely:

(1) I want all my just debts paid;

(2) I give and bequeath my 100 acres in East Feliciana Parish to John D. Harrison and his children;

---

1. John D. Harrison testified at trial that the handwriting was that of William Kline, Emanuel's attorney.

(3) I also give and bequeath lot # 12 in sq. # 2 of North Baton Rouge to John D. Harrison and his children

(4) I futher [*sic*] give and bequeath 1/2 of all my personal property to John D. Harrison and his children.

Thus written, dated and signed in my own handwriting, at Liberty, Miss. Rt. ### 2, in East Feliciana, State of Louisiana, on this the 15 day of Dec. 1955.

Emanuel Harrison

John D. Harrison brought this will to his attorney and was told that the will was invalid. However, the attorney drew up an instrument whereby Emanuel's legal heirs could confirm the donations made in the invalid will. Within a month of Emanuel's death, John D. Harrison obtained the signatures of twelve of the fifteen intestate heirs on the instrument. On February 11, 1972, one more heir (Ada Harrison Johnson) added her signature when John D. Harrison purchased her interest in Emanuel's succession. The instrument provided as follows:

March 21, 1960

The undersigned presumptive heirs of Emanuel Harrison, deceased, are fully aware of the contents of a purported last will and testament made by Emanuel Harrison dated December 15, 1955; that same is not in the handwriting of Emanuel Harrison, but was signed by him and represents his wishes with regard to his estate. We, therefore, desire that the Court give full effect to said will as though it was fully written, dated and signed by Emanuel Harrison as his legal will and testament, in consideration of the fact that John Harrison looked after him as his own child.

Aline George	Annie Belle H. Wallace
Thelma G. Payne	Catherine H. Vernon
Wilbert George	E. M. Harrison
Cheles Price Harrison	His
James Harrison	Bro. Daniel X Harrison
(Sister) Ida Knox	Ada Harrison Johnson
Viola H. Faulkner	Feb. 11
Benjamin F. Harrison	72

John D. Harrison filed a petition in the district court to open the succession of Emanuel Harrison on March 10, 1960[. **Edward Knox was eventually appointed administrator of the succession.**]. [....]

On May 7, 1980, Edward Knox, as administrator, filed a petition to sell the land bequeathed to John D. Harrison in the invalid will at private sale in order to pay the debts of the succession and to facilitate a partition of the estate. The purchasers were to be Minor Harrison, Jr., his sister, Annie Belle Wallace (who had signed the March 21, 1960 instrument), and five of Edward Knox's siblings. After publication in accordance with law, the court on August 25, 1980 authorized Edward Knox, as administrator, to sell the property at private sale to those persons for $51,750.

On February 26, 1981, before the sale took place, John D. Harrison filed a petition opposing the sale on the ground that he should be recognized as transferee of the interests of thirteen of the fifteen legal heirs in the property. He also alleged that the sale should be stopped because the property was worth "substantially more than the $51,750.00 sales price" and because the sale of the property was unnecessary to pay the "very small" debts of the succession. By amended petition filed September 9, 1981, John D. Harrison additionally asked that he be recognized as transferee of the interest of Ada Harrison Johnson in the succession pursuant to a recorded notarized act of cash sale. Edward Knox, in his capacity as administrator of the succession, answered denying that John D. Harrison had any interest in the succession property.

After trial, the district judge rendered judgment in favor of Edward Knox, as administrator of the succession, and against John D. Harrison declaring the purported transfer dated March 21, 1960 invalid, null and without legal effect. However, judgment was rendered in favor of John D. Harrison and against Edward Knox (as administrator) recognizing him as the transferee of the interest of Ada Harrison Johnson in the succession. The judge also set aside his previous order authorizing the sale of the property for $51,750, finding that price to be wholly inadequate, and authorized the administrator to put the property up for sale to pay debts of the succession.

John D. Harrison appealed seeking a reversal of that part of the judgment holding the instrument of March 21, 1960 unenforceable. The court of appeal reversed, finding that the March 21, 1960 instrument was given in fulfillment of a natural obligation imposed upon the legal heirs of Emanuel Harrison and was legally binding. In all other respects, the judgment of the district court was affirmed. The court remanded the case to close the succession.[2] On the administrator's [....] application, we granted certiorari to review the correctness of that decision.[3]

The issues presented for our consideration are whether a natural obligation on the part of the legal heirs of Emanuel Harrison arose from the invalid will and, if so, did the March 21, 1960 instrument have the effect of discharging that obligation.

The December 15, 1955 document clearly is invalid as the will of Emanuel Harrison because it fails to meet any of the forms for wills recognized under Louisiana law. The document does not qualify as an olographic will because such a will must be entirely written, dated and signed by the hand of the testator. La.Civ.Code art. 1588. Except for testator's own signature at the end of the will, the document in question was entirely written in the hand of another. Nor does the document meet any of the other forms for testaments in Louisiana.[4]

However, this invalid will does create a natural obligation on the part of the intestate heirs of Emanuel Harrison under La.Civ.Code art. 1758 which provides:

Natural obligations are of four kinds:

1. Such obligations as the law has rendered invalid for the want of certain forms or for some reason of general policy, but which are not in themselves immoral or unjust.

2. Such as are made by persons having the discretion necessary to enable them to contract, but who are yet rendered incapable of doing so by some provision of law.

3. When the action is barred by prescription, a natural obligation still subsists, although the civil obligation is extinguished.

4. There is also a natural obligation on those who inherit an estate, either under a will or by legal inheritance, to execute the donations or other dispositions which the former owner had made, but which are defective for want of form only.

---

2. 431 So.2d 1060 (La.App. 1st Cir.1983).

3. 438 So.2d 569 (La.1983).

4. The will is also invalid as a holographic will under the laws of the State of Mississippi, the place of execution according to the heading of the will. Miss.Code Ann. §91-5-1 (Supp.1983).

Strictly applying the language of this code article, we find that the natural obligation of the heirs of Emanuel Harrison fits precisely into section four of the article. First, the heirs clearly fall into the category of "those who inherit an estate ... by legal inheritance." Next, we find that the invalid will constituted a donation "which the former owner had made." Edward Knox contends that there is doubt as to whether Emanuel Harrison believed or intended the prepared form to be his will. However, we believe that the record supports the trial judge's finding of fact that Emanuel Harrison "attempted to make a will" which "was intended to be valid pursuant to the rules on olographic wills." Therefore, we concur in the trial judge's finding and reject Knox's contention that Emanuel may not have made the will.

Finally, article 1758(4) requires that the decedent's donation be "defective for want of form only." This element is also met by Emanuel Harrison's will. It contains no prohibited donations or any other substantive defects; it is invalid merely because it fails to satisfy the requirements of testamentary form. Knox argues that the formal invalidity is so severe that it amounts to a substantive defect. This argument is without merit; the defectiveness of the will in question is plainly one of form only no matter how severe the formal deficiencies.

Hence, we hold that Emanuel Harrison's legal heirs have a natural obligation to execute the donations made in his will. This holding is consistent with the result reached by this court on rehearing in *Breaux v. Breaux*, 218 La. 795, 51 So.2d 73 (1951), in which we found a natural obligation on the part of a legatee to carry out the disposition made in an invalid oral will even though that disposition constituted a *fidei commissum*.

A natural obligation, although it cannot be legally enforced, does have certain legal effects. La.Civ.Code art. 1759 provides:

Although natural obligations can not be enforced by action, they have the following effect[s]:

1. No suit will lie to recover what has been paid, or given in compliance with a natural obligation.

2. A natural obligation is a sufficient consideration for a new contract.

The natural obligation of Emanuel Harrison's heirs acted as the cause for a new contract. That new contract was the March 21, 1960 instrument.

This court must now determine the effect of that instrument. A new contract for which a natural obligation acts as "consideration" cannot be fitted into any one accepted legal category and should not be subject to any particular form. The juridical act may embody any contractual obligation the obligor sees fit. Martin, *Natural Obligations*, 15 Tul.L.Rev. 497, 511–12, 515 (1941). To discern the intended effect of the instrument, we will first look to its actual terms. The document asks that "the Court give full effect to said will." Knox argues that, since the instrument contains no language translative of title, it cannot be given the effect of transferring to John D. Harrison any interest in the succession of Emanuel Harrison. Instead, Knox urges, the instrument requests the court to probate an invalid will, an act which does not transfer title in the land to John D. Harrison. We reject this construction of the contract. The Louisiana Civil Code provides the following rule for interpretation of contracts: When there is anything doubtful in agreements, we must endeavor to ascertain what was the common intention of the parties, rather than to adhere to the literal sense of the terms. La.Civ.Code art. 1950. *See also* art. 1945(2). We find that the clear intent of the thirteen heirs who signed the instrument was to discharge their natural obligation and carry into effect the dispositions made in the will. Accord-

157 ingly, we hold that the effect of the March 21, 1960 instrument was to transfer to John
158 D. Harrison and his children[5] the interests of the thirteen heirs[6] who signed the instru-
159 ment in the property bequeathed in the will to John D. Harrison and his children. Hence,
160 we will remand the case to the district court with instructions to the trial judge to recognize
161 John D. Harrison and his children as transferees of the signing heirs' interests in the prop-
162 erty and to place them into possession thereof and to close the succession.

163   [....]

164 WATSON, Justice, dissenting.

165 The majority creates a new method of transmitting property in Louisiana, that is, or-
166 dering probate of an invalid will. The instrument of March 21, 1960, is not a donation.
167 LSA-C.C. art. 1536. If it were a donation, then the natural obligation brought about by
168 the will, which is invalid because of a deficiency of form, would constitute *cause* for the
169 donation and it could not be attacked or set aside for lacking cause. The act is certainly
170 not a sale; in fact, it is a creature unknown to the law. Owners of property—who under
171 the principle of *le mort saisit le vif* became owners the instant their ancestor died are held
172 to transfer land by signing an instrument which asks the court to honor an invalid will.
173 Here, the court is leap-frogging in the guise of pursuing the spirit of the 1960 instrument
174 and ordering transfer of the property to John D. Harrison by a device not found in the
175 Louisiana Civil Code.

176 Therefore, I respectfully dissent.

Questions

1. Lines 38 *et seq.*: Can you explain why all of these statements on and about Emanuel
    Harrison might be relevant as regards the existence or not of a natural obligation? What
    about those about John Harrison?

2. Lines 63 *et seq.*: Is "transferee" a proper legal term under the Louisiana Civil Code?
    What more specific and proper legal word should the Court have used in light of the
    nature of the transfer? A donation? If so, what kind? *See* La. Civ. Code arts. 1526–1527.
    A giving in payment? *See* La. Civ. Code arts. 2655–2659.

3. Lines 98 *et seq.*: Compare La. Civ. Code art. 1758 (Code of 1870) with La. Civ. art.
    1762 (current Code). Is the letter of those two articles supported by the same lawful
    reason (or *ratio legis*)? Can the paragraph found on lines 120 *et seq.* help in identi-
    fying that reason? Are there reasons of form and substance vying with each other?

4. Lines 141 *et seq.*: Notice the phrase "juridical act" on line 143. What does that phrase
    mean? *See* La. Civ. Code art. 395 and La. Civ. Code art. 3471. What do the first four
    lines of this paragraph suggest about the law of contract at civil law and the court's
    task or responsibility to properly identify and classify a contract? What would you say,

---

5. Edward Knox, in brief to this court, specified as error the appeals court's decision that "apparently gave all of the signing heirs' portion of the property to John D. Harrison when the 'purported
will'... bequeathed certain specified items [of] the decedent's property to John D. Harrison *and his
children*." [Emphasis in original.] The appeals court held "the [March 21, 1960] instrument and the
transfers made thereby to be legally valid and enforceable." We construe that language to uphold the
instrument as written, which enacts the bequests in the will to John D. Harrison and his children.
Hence, the appeals court's holding does not omit the children and is without error in this regard.

6. However, Ada Harrison Johnson's entire interest in the succession was transferred to John Harrison in the February 11, 1972 sale of that interest.

now, about Justice Watson's referring to this "act ... as a creature unknown to the law" (on lines 169–70)? What do you think that form can add to a juridical act?

STATE of Louisiana   1
v.   2
Allan L. PLACKE, et al.   3
Louisiana Court of Appeal   4
Second Circuit   5
May 9, 2001   6
786 So.2d 889   7

PEATROSS, J.   8

This appeal arises out of the State of Louisiana's overpayment of a damage award in   9
an underlying medical malpractice suit. The State filed suit naming as defendants Ms.   10
Conerly and her counsel in the original medical malpractice action, Allan L. Placke, Don   11
H. Johnson and Johnson & Placke (collectively referred to herein as "Defendants"), seek-   12
ing return of the overpayment. The parties filed cross motions for summary judgment.   13
The trial court granted the State's motion for summary judgment and denied Defendants'   14
motion. Defendants now appeal and the State has answered the appeal. For the reasons   15
stated herein, we affirm.   16

FACTS and PROCEDURAL BACKGROUND   17

Timothy (now deceased) and Claudia Sue Conerly ("Conerlys") sued E.A. Conway   18
Memorial Hospital (referred to herein as the "State"), a state-owned medical institution,   19
for damages for injuries sustained by their infant daughter, Christina, during and im-   20
mediately prior to her birth. After trial of the medical malpractice claim, the State was found   21
solely liable for Christina's "catastrophic" injuries;[1] and, in its opinion, the trial court   22
stated that actual damages were $3,041,833.75, with legal interest due from date of judi-   23
cial demand until paid. This amount was then reduced to a single award of $500,000, ex-   24
clusive of custodial care and interest, due to the statutory cap on recoveries in medical   25
malpractice cases under La. R.S. 40:1299.39. On appeal, this court affirmed on the issue   26
of liability, but held that each plaintiff's claim was distinct and subject to separate caps.   27
Timothy Conerly, et al., v. State of Louisiana, et al., 29,236 (La.App.2d Cir.3/3/97), 690   28
So.2d 980, *writ denied,* 97-0804 (La.3/13/98), 712 So.2d 864, *writ granted,* 97-0871 (La.3/   29
13/98), 712 So.2d 859, *and rev'd by, Timothy Conerly, et al., v. State of Louisiana, et al.,* 97-   30
0871 (La.7/8/98), 714 So.2d 709. The supreme court reversed on the cap issue alone, ap-   31

---

1. Ms. Conerly was pregnant and at full term with Christina, her sixth child, when she began he-
morrhaging and was rushed to E.A. Conway Memorial Hospital. She was left unattended from her arrival at 11:15 p.m. until 6:00 a.m. the following morning. When she was examined, the baby was in
fetal distress and it was determined that an emergency C-section was necessary. Rather than performing the section immediately, however, the doctors started her on a pitocin drip, which is a drug
used to induce labor. Approximately an hour and a half later, the C-section was performed. Christina
was born alive, but in poor condition. She suffered severe brain damage, seizure disorders, right-
sided tension pneumothorax, chronic renal failure, microcephaly and other complications due to a
lack of oxygen prior to birth. Christina lived to age five, at which time she weighed only 30 pounds.
She could not feed herself, use the bathroom, hold her head up or sit unaided or make any sound
other than to cry or coo. She had seizures, wore braces on her legs and underwent hip surgery. She
died from aspirating vomit because she was unable to roll herself over. Ms. Conerly took care of
Christina on a daily basis and tried to give her some quality of life.

32 plying a single cap (liability and amount of damages affirmed). *Timothy Conerly, et al.,*
33 *v. State of Louisiana, et al., supra.*

34   Prior to the supreme court's decision, the Conerlys' counsel wrote a letter advising
35 the State's counsel that his calculation of the amount due to The Conerlys was
36 $1,174,994.26 (including interest until March 31, 1998), and that, from March 31 for-
37 ward, legal interest would accumulate at $108.27 per day. The State accepted the fig-
38 ures as correct and responded that payment would be delayed pending the decision of
39 the supreme court. In July, after the supreme court's decision, and at the State's request,
40 a second copy of this letter was furnished to the State's counsel with an updated figure
41 of $1,199.147.47 (including interest through July 31, 1998). On August 20, 1998, the
42 State tendered a check in the amount of $1,888,973.99 along with a "Satisfaction of
43 Judgment" to Ms. Conerly. According to the State, the correct figure was $1,188,973.99;
44 in the processing of the request for the check, an "8" was inadvertently placed in the
45 hundred thousandth position instead of a "1." This mistake amounted to an overpayment of $700,000.

46   On receipt of the incorrect check, Ms. Conerly's attorney disbursed the proceeds to
47 her and filed the Satisfaction of Judgment into the record.[2] Subsequently, the State dis-
48 covered that it had paid more than the amount judicially enforceable against it by statute.
49 As previously stated, the State brought the present action to recover the amount it had
50 overpaid and the parties filed cross motions for summary judgment. The trial court
51 granted the State's motion and denied Defendants' motion, finding that the State was en-
52 titled to return of the overpayment because it lacked the "capacity to feel the sort of strong
53 moral duty or duty of conscience that is required to create a natural obligation." The trial
54 court further found that both attorneys, the law firm and Ms. Conerly were jointly and
55 severally liable for return of the overpayment. Finally, finding that the attorneys did not
56 act in bad faith in retaining the funds, despite their knowledge of the overpayment,
57 the trial court required that they pay interest from the date of judgment only, rather than
58 from the date of judicial demand. Defendants appeal and the State has answered the ap-
59 peal requesting additional interest under La. C.C. art. 2303.

60   *DISCUSSION*

61   Defendants argue that the trial court's judgment finding the State liable for in excess
62 of three million dollars created a natural obligation supporting the payment of damages
63 above the $500,000 statutory cap. According to Defendants, the trial court's conclusion
64 in this case implicitly holds that the existence of a natural obligation depends on the sub-
65 jective intent of the debtor, which is not the appropriate inquiry in making such deter-
66 mination. In addition, Defendants assert that the Satisfaction of Judgment drafted by the
67 State and executed by the parties signified the finality of all litigation between the parties;
68 and, therefore, the State's action for recovery of the overpayment should be dismissed. The
69 State argues that it is not capable of forming the subjective intent necessary to support a
70 natural obligation and, in fact, chose to limit its duty to pay injured plaintiffs in medical
71 malpractice actions by enacting the statutory cap on recovery in such cases. In addition,
72 as previously stated, the State has answered the appeal seeking interest from the date of
73 judicial demand pursuant to La. C.C. art. 2303, rather than the date of judgment as or-
74 dered by the trial court.

75   [....]

---

2. The State also notes that the disbursement statement indicates deductions for attorney fees in the amount of $632,401.92 (1/3 of $1,897,205.77) and $40,000 for case costs.

Satisfaction of Judgment

Since Defendants argue that the Satisfaction of Judgment should operate to preclude the action by the State for overpayment of the judgment, we will address this argument first. The judgment rendered in the underlying medical malpractice action on May 7, 1996, including interest, was in the amount of $541,833.75. The Satisfaction of Judgment executed by the parties reads, in pertinent part:

THE JUDGMENT rendered and recorded in favor of Timothy Ray Conerly, Individually and as Administrator for the Estate of his Minor Child, Christina Lea Conerly and Claudia Sue Conerly, rendered and recorded against defendant State of Louisiana through the Department of Health and Human Resources, E.A. Conway Memorial Hospital, Dr. James Waddill and Dr. Charles Anderson, has been fully satisfied and paid. This satisfaction of judgment is authority for the Clerk of Court to cancel and erase from the records of Ouachita Parish that certain Judgment dated May 7, 1996 and filed in favor of Timothy Ray Conerly [et al] ... in the amount of FIVE HUNDRED FORTY ONE THOUSAND EIGHT HUNDRED THIRTY THREE DOLLARS AND 75/00 ($541,833.75); together with interest allowed by law and all court costs....

The State argues that the above language does not speak to the issue presented in this case and does not amount to a waiver of its right to further legal action to recover an inadvertent overpayment of the May 7, 1996 judgment. We agree. The document expressly states that it applies to the judgment rendered on May 7, 1996. As the trial court noted, the satisfaction of judgment was filed prior to the State's learning of the overpayment and does not contain any language suggesting that the State intended to prospectively waive any right to seek recovery in the event of an overpayment. There simply is no evidence that the document constitutes a compromise of anything other than the May 7, 1996 judgment itself. In fact, in a letter dated October 23, 1998, Defendant Allan Placke acknowledged that the May 7, 1996 judgment had been overpaid, writing "[i]t does appear that the State paid more than the value of the judgment...." This argument is without merit.

Natural Obligation

The first inquiry in determining whether a natural obligation exists on the part of the State in the case *sub judice* is to decide if, in fact, a juridical person such as the State of Louisiana can *ever* satisfy the requirements of a natural obligation. In answering this question, we begin with the premise that no Louisiana court has ever found a juridical person to be the obligor of a natural obligation.[3] Our analysis, therefore, begins with the treatises on the origin and development of the law on natural obligations. After an exhaustive review of the literature, we conclude that a juridical person such as the State of Louisiana is incapable of forming the conscious moral feeling required to have a natural obligation.

The Civil Code articles on natural obligations are as follows:

Art. 1760. Moral duties that may give rise to a natural obligation.

A natural obligation arises from circumstances in which the law implies a particular moral duty to render a performance.

---

3. Defendants rely on *Muse v. St. Paul Fire and Marine Insurance Company,* 328 So.2d 698 (La.App. 1st Cir.1976), in support of the proposition that feelings sufficient to support a natural obligation are imputed onto the State. Defendants misinterpret the holding of *Muse.* In *Muse,* the court determined that, while a charity hospital does not have an action for payment of medical services rendered to an indigent, the indigent, nonetheless, owes a natural obligation to the charity hospital for payment of medical services rendered. There was no finding in *Muse* regarding whether the State is capable of feeling the requisite moral duty required to owe a natural obligation.

116   Art. 1761. Effects of a natural obligation.

117   A natural obligation is not enforceable by judicial action. Nevertheless, whatever has
118   been freely performed in compliance with a natural obligation may not be reclaimed.

119   A contract made for the performance of a natural obligation is onerous.

120   Art. 1762. Examples of circumstances giving rise to a natural obligation.

121   Examples of circumstances giving rise to a natural obligation are:

122   (1) When a civil obligation has been extinguished by prescription or discharged in
123   bankruptcy.

124   (2) When an obligation has been incurred by a person who, although endowed with
125   discernment, lacks legal capacity.

126   (3) When the universal successors are not bound by a civil obligation to execute the
127   donations and other dispositions made by a deceased person that are null for
128   want of form.

129   Nowhere in the Civil Code is the term "natural obligation" precisely defined and our
130   courts have construed the listing of examples of such obligations as illustrative and not
131   exclusive. *Gray v. McCormick,* 94-1282 (La.App. 3rd Cir.10/18/95), 663 So.2d 480; *Muse*
132   *v. St. Paul Fire & Marine Insurance Company,* 328 So.2d 698 (La.App. 1st Cir.1976). The
133   determination of whether a natural obligation exists, therefore, depends on the facts of
134   each particular case.

135   The concept of natural obligations subsumes the "reality" of a moral duty. Litvinoff,
136   The Law of Obligations § 2.3, 5 Louisiana Civil Law Treatise (1992). In other words, there
137   must exist a moral duty, described as a duty of conscience, in order for a natural oblig-
138   ation to arise. The moral duty is "the imperative feeling that something ought to be done
139   or not done or given" and must be "so strongly felt by a person that his conscience will
140   not be appeased unless he renders to another a certain performance." *Id.* Once such a
141   duty is felt with such a compelling force, it becomes part of the "structure" of the natural
142   obligation. *Id.*

143   We do not believe that a juridical person such as the State of Louisiana is capable of
144   feeling a moral compulsion so intense that it can only be appeased by satisfaction of the
145   duty.[4] The trial court was correct in concluding that the State of Louisiana is not capable
146   of having a natural obligation.

147   Assuming, *arguendo,* that there exist circumstances which would support a natural
148   obligation on the part of a juridical person such as the State of Louisiana, such circum-
149   stances are not present in the undisputed facts of this case. Our courts have set forth
150   four requirements which must be present in order for a duty to be considered a natural
       obligation:

151   (1) The moral duty must be felt towards a particular person, not all persons in
152   general.

153   (2) The person involved feels so strongly about the moral duty that he truly feels he
154   owes a debt.

---

4. There is also a question of whether or not the State's overpayment of the judgment may have
constituted an *ultra vires* act, i.e., an act beyond the powers granted to the agency. In other words, we
question whether the agency had the authority to pay more to Ms. Conerly than the amount for which
the State was cast in judgment.

(3) The duty can be fulfilled through rendering a performance whose object is of pecuniary value.

(4) A recognition of the obligation by the obligor must occur, either by performing the obligation or by promising to perform. This recognition brings the natural obligation into existence and makes it a civil obligation.

Litvinoff, § 2.4; *Terrell v. Nanda,* 33,242 (La.App.2d Cir.5/10/00), 759 So.2d 1026; *Thomas v. Bryant,* 25,855 (La.App.2d Cir.6/22/94), 639 So.2d 378. All four requirements must exist to support a natural obligation. In the case *sub judice,* we find that at least the first two of these requirements have not been met. These two requirements provide the focus of our discussion and we begin with the second of the two requirements regarding the strength of the feeling of the moral duty by the alleged natural obligor, or, in this case, the State.

Defendants argue that the trial court's focus on the subjective intent of the alleged natural obligor was incorrect. While we agree that it is not the sole criterion on which the finding of a natural obligation should be based, we do agree with the State that the intent of the alleged natural obligor is relevant to the determination of whether the alleged natural obligor felt the moral compulsion necessary to transform his moral duty into a natural obligation. In this regard, Litvinoff states that "the person's [alleged natural obligor's] belief in the existence of the moral duty is ... as important as its reality...." See also *Thomas v. Bryant, supra.* In the present case, the State has clearly expressed its intent not to have a moral duty to pay any judgment that exceeds $500,000. This intent was expressed by the State in the passage by the legislature of La. R.S. 40:1299.39, which contains the statutory cap on recovery in medical malpractice actions against the state. We can find no support in the record for the conclusion that the State experienced strong, forceful moral compulsion to pay Ms. Conerly an amount greater than it had decided to pay all other successful plaintiffs in medical malpractice cases.

Defendants emphasize that voluntary payment of a natural obligation through error or mistake does not allow recovery of the payment. The Civil Code makes this clear.[5] This rule of law, however, is never reached if there is, in fact, no natural obligation in the first place; and, in order to find a natural obligation, as previously explained, there must exist a moral duty to pay. This is a separate and distinct inquiry from the later determination (after a natural obligation is found to exist between the two parties) of whether the erroneous payment was voluntary, although in error, and, thus, not recoverable. Litvinoff explains:

If the conclusion is that no natural obligation arose from a certain situation, that is so because, for the lack of a clear object, the moral duty involved is not sufficiently precise to allow the court's conviction that it was the force that prompted the alleged debtor to act.

Litvinoff, § 2.6 at p. 36. Applying this logic to the present case, we conclude that a natural obligation did not arise from the trial court's assessment of actual damages in this case. This is so because there is no moral duty owing from the State to Ms. Conerly in particular that is "sufficiently precise" to support our conviction that it was the moral duty or compulsion on the part of the State which prompted the overpayment of the judg-

---

5. Comment (b) to article 1761 states that "... this Article means that the performing party must have acted without outside compulsion by fraud or violence. It does not mean that his performance cannot have been induced by error...."

198 ment. With no underlying natural obligation, the fact that the payment made to Ms.
199 Conerly was made in error is irrelevant.

200   The scenario in the case *sub judice* is different from the scenario envisioned by article
201 1761 and the principle that a payment on a natural obligation, even if made in error or
202 by mistake, is not recoverable. The object of the "no recovery if paid in error" principle
203 is to prevent a debtor who is bound by a natural obligation, i.e., feels a strong moral duty
204 to pay a debt which is not enforceable against him, and makes payment on the debt, from
205 later deciding that he wants the payment back. This is the situation which article 1761 is
206 designed to prevent. See also Litvinoff, § 2.22 at p. 41.

207   Litvinoff next explains that not every moral compulsion transforms into a natural
208 obligation. The moral duty must be owed to a particular person and not to a class of
209 persons in general. This is the basis for the first requirement. In the case *sub judice,* we
210 believe it clear that, assuming the State owed a moral duty under the circumstances of
211 this case, it would be a duty to the class of persons, generally, who are awarded actual
212 damages in excess of the amount which the legislature has deemed can be judicially
213 enforced against the State in a medical malpractice action. It would not be a moral
214 duty felt by the State for the specific loss sustained by Ms. Conerly, or any other par-
    ticular plaintiff.

215   Since we find that the first two requirements for the existence of a natural obligation
216 are not met under the undisputed facts presented in this case, we conclude that the trial
217 court correctly granted the State's motion for summary judgment. [....]

[....]

Questions

1. Lines 1–217: Read Louisiana Civil Code articles 2299–2305. Could some of these ar-
    ticles have been used by the court in this case? If you answered this question in the
    affirmative, would the State have recovered the same amount it paid in excess be-
    cause of a mistake?

2. Lines 135–150 *et seq.*: What do you think of these statements by the court: (1) "We do
    not believe that a juridical person such as the State of Louisiana is capable of feeling
    a moral compulsion...."; (2) "The concept of natural obligation subsumes the 'real-
    ity' of a moral duty"; (3) "Assuming, arguendo, that there exist circumstances which
    would support a natural obligation on the part of a juridical person such as the State
    of Louisiana, such circumstances are not present in the undisputed facts of this case"?

3. Lines 149 *et seq.*: What do you think of the court stating: "Our courts have set forth
    four requirements which must be present ..."? Shouldn't the requirements be set by
    the Code, as legislation? Since the courts' duty is to apply the law, is there not a dan-
    ger on the part of the courts to create their own requirements? Is the court, in this
    case, relying too much on prior cases and doctrine (Professor Litvinoff), which are
    merely persuasive sources of law, and overlooking the law of the Code? Has the court
    carved an exception for the State out of Louisiana Civil Code article 24 and carried
    that exception over into "Natural Obligations" (La. Civ. Code arts. 1760–1762) when,
    in fact, no exception is made in the latter articles?

4. What lesson should be drawn from this case for individuals who have dealings with
    the State?

See also *Succession of Jones*, 505 So.2d 841 (La. 2nd Cir. 1987).

Comparative Law Perspective

Natural Obligations

Marcel Planiol & Georges Ripert, Traité Pratique de Droit Civil Français

vol. 7, n° 979, at 314, & n° 982, at 316–18 (Paul Esmein rev., 2d ed. 1954)

979. Juridical foundation. The natural obligation incontestably constitutes a juridical anomaly. The lack of a sanction [for its enforcement], whatever efficacy it may have otherwise, places it at the extreme limit of the law and on the boundary of morality....

* * *

982. The theory of natural obligation founded on the duty of conscience. In the most diverse and the most certain cases of natural obligations (prescribed debt, annulment for incapacity, ...), one finds a common element: the existence of a duty of conscience of the debtor toward the creditor. The natural obligation ... is tied ... to a moral duty in which the law recognizes a certain value up to the point of making of it an obligation deprived of the normal sanction, but without, however, adopting it fully. It is a rule of conscience that penetrates into the domain of the law while remaining yet at the law's frontier.

* * *

If there is a progressive assimilation of natural obligation and moral duty, there is, nonetheless, no complete concurrence between them. The separation of law from morality ought to be maintained. It follows that not every duty of conscience constitutes a natural obligation.... Only those duties of conscience that are judged, at a given moment, by the legislature or the courts to be, at once, the most conformed to the general interest and the most [widely] acknowledged in the current general opinion of individuals are transformed into natural obligations. There are some moral obligations that are of such a nature that they are not and can never be clothed with any juridical efficacy whatsoever: the benefits that inspire thoughts of charity, of devotion, of love, even though these thoughts may be commanded by morality, can be analyzed in relation to the law only as liberalities. To the contrary, other moral obligations can, upon the refining of the public conscience, end up being recognized as natural obligations some day, even though they have not theretofore been so recognized.

Jacques Ghestin & Gilles Goubeaux, Traité de Droit Civil: Introduction Générale

n° 669, at 644, & n° 672, at 648 (3d ed. 1990)

A natural obligation is a moral duty that rises to the level of juridical life. The act of him who was held to this duty gives it access to the juridical world. The court must investigate the motives that led this person to act and must take into consideration whether he was inspired by the desire to accomplish his duty. Not every moral duty can be transformed into a civil obligation. But when the obligor himself recognizes the existence of the duty that weighs on him, it's a matter thereafter of helping him to accomplish this duty and also of protecting him against a return to immorality by maintaining the effects of the accomplished duty. The natural obligation ... is born by the recognition by the obligor of his moral duty. Still, it's also necessary … that this duty be among those that the legislature or the courts judge to be the most imperious and the best conformed to the general interest.

Henri Mazeaud et al., Leçons de Droit Civil: Introduction à l'Étude du Droit
n° 362, at 473 (François Chabas rev., 10th ed. 1991)

But it is difficult to specify on what conditions a moral duty is called to the rank of natural obligation. Not every duty of conscience is a natural obligation. The perception remains that one who shows himself to be charitable does not accomplish a juridical obligation: he makes a liberality. Thus, a natural obligation presupposes in the person who accomplishes a duty of conscience a imperious sentiment that he *had* to submit himself to it, that he really was *indebted*, that he wanted to free himself from a veritable debt, and not to make a liberality. Pothier wrote: "One calls a natural obligation that which, *in the name of honor and of conscience*, obliges him who has contracted to the accomplishment of that which the contract contains."

It is necessary, then, that the person who performs consider himself to be bound.

Chapter Three

Heritable, Personal & Real Obligations

Louisiana Sources of Law

Louisiana Civil Code

Art. 1763. Definition.

A real obligation is a duty correlative and incidental to a real right. (Acts 1984, No. 331, § 1, eff. Jan. 1, 1985.)

Art. 1765. Heritable obligation.

An obligation is heritable when its performance may be enforced by a successor of the obligee or against a successor of the obligor.

Every obligation is deemed heritable as to all parties, except when the contrary results from the terms or from the nature of the contract.

A heritable obligation is also transferable between living persons. (Acts 1984, No. 331, § 1, eff. Jan. 1, 1985.)

Art. 1766. Strictly personal obligation.

An obligation is strictly personal when its performance can be enforced only by the obligee, or only against the obligor.

When the performance requires the special skill or qualification of the obligor, the obligation is presumed to be strictly personal on the part of the obligor. All obligations to perform personal services are presumed to be strictly personal on the part of the obligor.

When the performance is intended for the benefit of the obligee exclusively, the obligation is strictly personal on the part of that obligee. (Acts 1984, No. 331, § 1, eff. Jan. 1, 1985.)

Précis: Louisiana Law of Obligations in General § 2.1.1 to 2.1.2

On the basis of the Latin origin of this concept, LSA-C.C. **Art.** 1763 defines a real obligation as a **"duty correlative and incidental to a real right."** ...

Thus a real obligation is an obligation, or a duty, owed to a person who can claim a performance because that person is the holder of a real right, *i.e.,* a right to make a direct and immediate [fictitiously without the involvement of an intermediary person] use of a thing.

The greater or lesser use the holder of a real right can make of a thing suggests that a distinction be made between principal real rights and accessory real rights....

27

The effects of real obligations flow from two fundamental prerequisites: A) there can be no real obligation unless there is a thing in existence; B) the real obligation is transferred with the thing as its accessory....

The second type of obligations or rights are those held or owned by a person *vis-à-vis* another person. The creditor or holder of such an obligation holds a right *in personam*, a right against the person of the obligor who may be under an obligation to give, to do or not to do something. The nature of the performance owed by the obligor leads to draw a distinction between heritable obligations, on the one hand, and strictly personal obligations, on the other hand....

Every obligation is thus presumed to be heritable as to both parties which means that, being part of one's patrimony, an obligation can be transferred or passed on to one's heirs. This presumption, however, is rebuttable and can be defeated either by the terms of a contract or by the circumstances if they are such as to suggest that the nature of the legal relationship binding the parties dictates that one or both obligations are to be considered as strictly personal. (**LSA-C.C. Art. 1766**)....

LSA-C.C. Art. 1766 defines a strictly personal obligation ...

An obligation which is classified as strictly personal is, therefore, an obligation which can be performed only by the obligor or exclusively for the benefit of the obligee-creditor. Such obligations are said to have been entered into *intuitus personae* or in contemplation of the person of either party or both of them....

Cases

JOHNSON   1

v.   2

LEVY et al.   3

Supreme Court of Louisiana   4
Jan. 7, 1907   5
43 So. 46   6

[....]   7

MONROE, J.   8

Plaintiff alleges that in 1901 she became engaged to be married to Lazare Levy, and,   9
whilst so engaged, was seduced by him; that he repeatedly promised to fulfill his engage-   10
ment, but failed to keep his promises, and, on June 29, 1903, was put in default by formal   11
demand, with which he refused to company; that, thereafter, plaintiff gave birth to a child,   12
issue of her connection with said Levy, and, as a consequence of his refusal to marry her,   13
is condemned to a life of social ostracism, disgrace, and poverty, and is injured and dam-   14
aged in the sum of $20,000. She alleges that said Levy died on June 29, 1903, and that the   15
three parties made defendants herein (who reside in the parish of Terrebonne), with six   16
others (who reside elsewhere), brothers and sisters of decedent, have accepted his succes-   17
sion unconditionally, and are liable to her jointly, for the damages so sustained. Where-   18
fore she prays for judgment against said defendants, each, for his virile share of the amount   19
stated. [....] When the case was called for trial plaintiff offered certain testimony in sup-   20
port of the allegations of her petition, whereupon 'counsel for defendants objected to the   21
evidence, and to any and all other evidence to be offered on behalf of plaintiff, in support   22

23 of the allegations of her petition, upon the grounds and for the reasons: First. The plain-
24 tiff sues for the breach of a marriage contract, and the same petition shows the death of
25 the promisor, Lazare Levy, and an action instituted against his heirs. This being shown on
26 the face of the petition, no cause of action lies against the heirs, since the action for breach
27 of promise is an entirely personal action, and not heritable. Second. If it could be con-
28 tended that the action of breach of promise of marriage can be instituted against the heirs
29 of Lazare Levy for a recovery of pecuniary or specific damages to the person or property
30 of the plaintiff in this case, there is no averment of damage to property, but a simple aver-
31 ment of damage to the feelings of the plaintiff herein, therefore * * * no evidence what-
32 ever is admissible to support the demand of the plaintiff.'

33 The court having sustained this objection, counsel for plaintiff announced that it was
34 'impossible for them to proceed any further, inasmuch as they could not introduce any
35 evidence to sustain the allegations of their petition,' and, after some discussion as to the
36 proper course to be pursued, the court 'discharged the jury from any further considera-
37 tion of the case, and ordered the plaintiff's demand dismissed, as in case of nonsuit,' and
38 from the judgment so rendered, plaintiff has appealed.

39 Opinion.

40 It has been argued here that, plaintiff having declined to proceed, the judgment ap-
41 pealed from is to be regarded as having dismissed the suit for want of prosecution. We are,
42 however, of opinion that the dismissal of the suit was the logical and inevitable consequence
43 of the exclusion of the testimony offered and to be offered, in support of plaintiff's de-
44 mand, and that the appeal from the judgment of dismissal brings up that ruling for review.

45 The obligation resulting from a marriage engagement, or promise of marriage, is per-
46
47 sonal, and not heritable, because no one but the obligee can enforce its performance, and
48 it can be enforced against no one but the obligor. Civ. Code, art. 1996 et seq. The obliga-
49 tion to respond in damages for the breach of such contract springs from the contract it-
50 self, as one of the incidents of its obligations. Civ. Code, arts. 1763, 1930. Unless time be
51 made of the essence of the contract, the obligor may comply with his obligation thereun-
52 der at any seasonable moment until he is put in default; from which it follows that, if the
53 obligor die before compliance and before he is put in default, no action will lie to enforce
54 compliance or to recover damages for noncompliance. In such case the obligation to re-
55 spond in damages retains its status as a mere incident of the obligation to comply with
56 the promise of marriage, and, as the principal obligation ceases to exist, its incidents cease
57 likewise. The obligation to respond in damages may, however, lose its incidental charac-
58 ter, and assume a new and independent form. Thus the obligee may obtain judgment
59 against the obligor for the damages, in which event the judgment could be enforced against
60 the heirs of the obligor should be die before satisfying the same; or the obligor may aban-
61 don his right to comply with his promise, and voluntarily bind himself to pay the dam-
62 ages resulting from his noncompliance, and the obligation thus assumed could be enforced
63 against his heirs. Or (and we now come to the position of the plaintiff before the court),
64 the right of the obligor to comply with his promise of marriage may be forfeited, and his
65 liability for damages fixed, by certain legal proceedings. The law provides that a contract
66 may be violated 'possively by not doing what was covenanted to be done, or not doing it
67 at the time or in the manner stipulated or implied from the nature of the confract [sic].'
68 Civ. Code, art. 1931. And that, in such case, 'damages are due from the time that the debtor
69 has been put in default,' etc. Civ. Code, art. 1933. And specific provision is made as to
70 manner of putting in default. Civ. Code, art. 1911 et seq. 'The object of the putting in de-
71 fault [this court has said] is to secure to the creditor his right to demand damages, or a dis-
72 solution of the contract, so that the debtor can no longer defeat this right by executing, or

Questions

1. Lines 9 *et seq.*: According to the plaintiff, "she became engaged to be married to Lazare Levy…." Where does engagement finds its source if it creates an obligation? *See* La. Civ. Code arts. 1756–1757. What about Louisiana Civil Code articles 1 through 4? How does engagement fit under Louisiana Civil Code articles 1906–1908? What about Louisiana Civil Code articles 1914–1915?

2. Lines 45/46–48: Explain why, in your opinion, a marriage engagement or promise of marriage creates a personal and not heritable obligation. How important do you think is the fact that "no one but the obligee can enforce its performance and it can be enforced against no one but the obligor"? If the obligation itself, because of its personal nature, cannot be enforced, do you think that it would be lawful or fair/equitable to consider the existence of an alternative obligation as a substitute for the promise of marriage, which is personal?

3. Lines 48 *et seq.*: Read Louisiana Civil Code articles 1989–1993 on "Putting in default". Do you give these articles the same meaning as the court gave? Do you read anywhere in those Louisiana Civil Code articles that an obligor has until he is put in default to "comply with his obligation" but that beyond a putting in default, an obligor can no longer carry out his principal obligation and must now pay "compensatory damages"? Isn't the first sentence of Louisiana Civil Code article 1989 actually saying that an obligation can be performed after the obligor has been put in default? Under Louisiana Civil Code article 1991, why would an obligee put his obligor in default and request performance if such performance were no longer possible according to the Court in *Johnson v. Levy*? How much did the death of the promisor, Lazare Levy, weigh, if at all, in the opinion of the Court? Could you use Louisiana Civil Code articles 1873, 1875, and 1876 with some success? Do you think that the fact that the plaintiff gave birth to a child had any bearing on the court's legal analysis and, ultimately, its decision?

4. Lines 81 *et seq.*: What impact did the putting in default have on the nature or kind of obligation created by the promise of marriage or engagement? Should a 'putting in default' have this impact on all personal obligations? What if one promised another that he would divorce his or her spouse and then failed to do so? In that situation, could the promisee put the promisor in default and seek damages?

BOGART

v.

CALDWELL

Louisiana Court of Appeal
Second Circuit
April 30, 1953
66 So.2d 629

GLADNEY, Judge.

[….]

Appellant [**Fannye Mae Bogart**] is the widow of Harry Dalton Bogart, Jr., who died intestate on October 1, 1951. During the existence of the community between appellant and her late husband, the latter purchased from defendant the property known as the Strand Theater in Farmerville, paying as consideration therefor $60,000 of which $30,000

14 was paid in cash and the remainder payable in monthly installments. The act of sale was
15 authentic in form and contained stipulations which gave rise to the issues that must be
16 determined.

17   [....]

18   From the date of its purchase the Strand Theater has been in continuous operation, first
19 by Bogart, and, after his death by his widow. The entire ownership of said property is
20 presently in appellant, she having acquired the one-half interest that became part of the
21 Henry D. Bogart, Jr. estate by reason of inheritance from her husband and through pur-
22 chase from the decedent's father and mother of the interest inherited by them, decedent
23 being without issue. Appellant, of course, as a partner of the community with her hus-
24 band, owned a one-half interest in said theater in her own right after June 30, 1951. On
25 January 30, 1952, after being informed defendant was preparing to commence the oper-
26 ation of a motion picture show business in the Union Theater building in Farmerville, ap-
27 pellant, through her attorney, wrote defendant a letter calling to his attention provisions
28 in the contract between him and her deceased husband, wherein it was agreed Caldwell
29 would not open a motion picture theater in said building, and warning him she would
30 take legal action to prevent him from doing so. The defendant, however, did on March
31 2, 1952, open and commence the operation of a picture show business in the Union The-
32 ater building and the operation thereof by defendant is, we presume, presently continu-
33 ing. Because of this, this lawsuit was filed.

34   In her petition appellant alleged that by reason of such competition defendant has
35 caused her serious injury and damage, and the continued operation of such a business will
36 result in future injury and damage by reducing the attendance at the Strand Theater with
37 material reduction in her income and profits; and, further, that unless defendant be re-
38 strained she will suffer irreparable injury and damage. Upon trial of the case evidence
39 was adduced disclosing [sic] that after Caldwell had re-opened the Union Theater there
40 was a substantial falling-off in the attendance of the Strand Theater.

41   The defense urged is fully stated in the answer wherein it is urged that the agreement
42 of defendant and Harry Dalton Bogart, Jr. was that defendant's use of the Union Theater
43 building should be restricted only so long as the said Harry Dalton Bogart, Jr. should
44 himself own the Strand Theater building and that such restrictions should terminate
45 when the said Harry Dalton Bogart, Jr. ceased to own the Strand Theater, whether such
46 cessation of ownership by Harry Dalton Bogart, Jr. was by sale, death or in any other
47 manner. Appellant insists, on the other hand, that Caldwell's obligation was not one
48 strictly personal,—that it was heritable, and inured to the benefit of the widow and heirs
49 of Harry Dalton Bogart, Jr.

50   The act of sale between Caldwell and Bogart, bearing date of June 3, 1950, being in the
51 form of an authentic act, unless ambiguous, may not be explained or altered by parol ev-
52 idence. Articles 2236 and 2276, LSA:Civil Code. Brenard Mfg. Company v. M. Levy, Inc.,
53 1926, 2 La.App. 577, affirmed 161 La. 496, 109 So. 43; Brenard Mfg. Company v. Levy,
54 Inc., (App. 1926), 4 La.App. 279, affirmed 161 La. 496, 109 So. 43; Hafner Mfg. Com-
55 pany v. Lieber Lumber & Shingle Co., 1910, 127 La. 348, 53 So. 646; Hartsfield v. Green,
56 La.App., 1952, 62 So.2d 180.

57   The seller within the terms of the act of sale is bound to explain himself clearly re-
58 specting the extent of his obligation and an obscure or ambiguous clause must be con-
59 strued against him. Article 2474 LSA:Civil Code. Frost-Johnson Lumber Company v.
60 Salling's Heirs, 150 La. 756, 91 So. 207; Hicks v. Griffith, 10 La.App. 442, 121 So. 328; Krauss
61 v. Fry, 209 La. 250, 24 So.2d 464.

To be found in the act of sale between Bogart and Caldwell are the following provisions: 62

> 'The parties hereto agree that this vendor, John L. Caldwell, is the owner of   63
> another theater building in the Town of Farmerville, Louisiana, known as the   64
> Union Theater, and, as a part of the moving consideration for this sale, it is   65
> agreed that this vendor will not open or operate another moving picture show   66
> or theater in said building.   67
>
> 'The parties hereto agree that the agreement contained herein with reference   68
> to the operation or non-operation of a picture show in the Union Theater build-   69
> ing by the vendor herein, shall be binding for so long as this vendee owns the prop-   70
> erty herein conveyed to him, but shall terminate in the event said vendee sells the   71
> property.'   72

The provisions plainly imply the vendor would not open or operate another motion   73
picture theater in the Union Theater building so long as the vendee should own the prop-   74
erty conveyed to him, and that Caldwell's obligation would terminate in the event the   75
vendee should sell the property. However, the latter proviso is of no consequence since   76
defendant has admitted in his answer Bogart during his lifetime did not sell the Strand   77
Theater. The legal issue is thus narrowed to a resolution of the question whether the death   78
of Bogart resulted in a cessation of his ownership, and the termination of the obligation.   79

Defendant's covenant was an obligation not to do. The contract of which the condi-   80
tion forms a part is, like all others, complete by the assent of the parties; the obligee has   81
a right of which the obligor cannot deprive him and its exercise is only suspended, or   82
may be defeated according to the nature of the condition. This right is heritable, if it is   83
not one of those that result from an obligation designated in law as a personal one. Ar-   84
ticles 2028, 2029, LSA:Civil Code. An obligation is strictly personal when none but the   85
obligee can enforce its performance, or when it can be enforced only against the obligor.   86
It is presumed to be personal as to the obligee in a contract to do or to give, when that   87
which is to be done or given is exclusively for the personal gratification of obligee, and   88
could produce no benefit to his heirs. Articles 1997, 2201 LSA:Civil Code. The nature   89
and effect of a personal obligation is further explained in Ferguson v. Thomas, 3 Mart.,   90
N.S., 75, at pages 80, 81:   91

> 'The general rule is that all the obligations of the ancestor pass to his heirs,   92
> active as well as passive. The exceptions to this rule are those obligations, which   93
> result from agreements, in which the personal qualities of the person promising   94
> are to be supposed the leading motive of the contract, and where the want of   95
> them cannot be supplied by any other, or compensated by pecuniary damages.   96
> Such is the confidence we repose in our physician, who assists us in sickness; the   97
> painter whom we may desire to make family portraits; and in case of their de-   98
> cease, their heirs cannot demand that they shall be permitted to supply their   99
> place or perform their contract. But an engagement to ship cotton may be per-   100
> formed by any one, the qualities of mind are not the leading consideration that   101
> induced the contract. Pecuniary responsibility is the moving cause, because the   102
> nonperformance can be compensated in damages and no objection can be made   103
> to the heirs, on that score, where they are the creditors of the person whose en-   104
> gagement they seek to enforce.'   105

The heritable obligation is one from which there arises the right of the heirs and as-   106
signs of one party to enforce the performance against the heirs of the others. Heritable   107
obligations and stipulations give to and impose upon heirs, assigns and other represen-   108
tatives the same duties and rights that the original parties had and were liable to, except   109

that beneficiary heirs can only be liable to the amount of the succession. Every obligation shall be deemed to be heritable as to both parties, unless the contrary be specially expressed or necessarily implied from the nature of the contract. Articles 1997, 2008, LSA:Civil Code.

Manifestly, the obligation not to operate a competitive picture theater can by no stretching of the imagination be said to exist for the personal gratification of the obligee and it is productive of financial benefit to the heirs of the obligee. It is not the sort of personal obligation that ends with the death of the obligee. It is a heritable obligation the right to which is enforceable by the heirs of the obligee.

In the confection of the act of sale there was inserted a provision the vendee was purchasing with his separate and paraphernal funds. This statement is refuted by other provisions in the act of sale, that is to say the vendee is declared to be living with his wife, and that half of the consideration was to be paid under terms of credit. The funds used, therefore, were not obtained from the separate property of Bogart. Counsel for the defendant concede that the property acquired entered the community of acquets and gains, but they argue that the clause is material as evidence of limitation upon the obligation of Caldwell as existing only for Bogart and not for his wife or his heirs. The argument, we think, is untenable. Though there was a brief separation between appellant and her husband prior to the execution of the deed, the inference is not warranted that he intended to use this means to circumscribe his property rights to the disadvantage of his heirs upon his own death. It is conceivable that the non-operation of a rival motion picture show in a town of the size of Farmerville could make the difference between profit and loss in the operation of the Strand Theater. Caldwell in first offering the Strand Theater for sale to Bogart realized this and himself proposed that if Bogart purchased one of the shows owned by him, he would not keep the other open.

The codal provisions heretofore referred to clearly show the subject obligation was not strictly a personal obligation that ceased upon the death of the obligee, but being a heritable obligation it continued in existence under the ownership of Bogart's surviving widow.

Where, as in this instance, the obligation be not to do, the obligee may demand the obligor be restrained from doing anything in contravention of it in cases where he proves an attempt to do the act covenanted against. Article 1929, LSA:Civil Code. Algiers Ry. & Lighting Company v. New Orleans Ry. & Lighting Company, 1915, 137 La. 579, 595, 68 So. 960, 962. In the latter case it was said:

> 'Plaintiff bases its suit for injunction to prevent the defendant from doing an act which it contends may be injurious to it (plaintiff) or impair a right which it claims. And it argues that the respondent judge had no discretion in the matter, and should have issued a preliminary injunction when applied for by it, and supports its argument by reference to article 1929, C.C., which reads:

> "If the obligation be not to do, the obligee may also demand that the obligor be restrained from doing anything in contravention of it, in cases where he proves an attempt to do the act covenanted against."

> 'The foregoing article explicitly states the law with reference to obligations 'not to do'; that a remedy by injunction will lie; and in the case of Levine v. Michel, 35 La.Ann. 1121 (1127), we hold it to be the legal duty of the obligor to comply with the terms of the contract, and the legal right of the obligee to exact compliance; in other words, the obligee may enforce a contract not to do by specific performance. And that a violation of said contract is injurious to plaintiff

and impairs a right which he claims, and is therefore a proper subject for in-   157
junction, within the very terms of article 296, C.P.'   158

Plaintiff's reservation of her right to sue defendant for damages already suffered is   159
proper.   160

For the foregoing reasons the judgment is in error. It is, therefore, ordered, adjudged   161
and decreed that the judgment from which appealed is avoided, annulled and reversed,   162
and it is ordered that there be judgment in favor of plaintiff, Mrs. Fannye Mae Bogart   163
and against the defendant, John L. Caldwell, Sr., permanently enjoining, restraining and   164
prohibiting said defendant from the further operation of a moving picture show or the-   165
ater in the Union Theater building located in the Town of Farmerville, Louisiana.   166

It is further ordered that plaintiff's right to sue defendant for all damages suffered by   167
her as a result of defendant's opening and operation of a picture show in the Union The-   168
ater building be reserved.   169

It is further ordered that defendant, appellee, pay all costs incurred in this suit, in-   170
cluding costs of the appeal.   171

Questions

1. Lines 1–171: What was the obligation 'not to do' created in the contract between
   Harry Bogart and John Caldwell? Could such an obligation not to do be personal?
   Heritable? Why is the selection of the proper nature of the obligation not to do
   important?

2. Lines 41 *et seq.*: Why is the defendant arguing that his obligation was restricted to
   Harry Bogart? To what kind of obligation is the defendant referring? Explain how
   the plaintiff, Fannye Mae Bogart, can make the argument that Caldwell's obligation
   to her husband was not strictly personal. Does the Louisiana Civil Code provide for
   a presumption regarding the nature of an obligation? *See* La. Civ. Code art. 1765.
   Which party in the case could rely on the benefit of such a presumption? What procedural consequence does such a presumption have?

3. Lines 68 *et seq.*: How do you read this provision of the contract with respect to the
   kind of obligation that was to be created? Do the phrases "this vendee" or "said
   vendee" have any legal meaning? What if, instead of selling the theater, the vendee,
   Harry Bogart, had created a mortgage on the theater? *See* La. Civ. Code arts.
   3278–3337. What about a usufruct? *See* La. Civ. Code arts. 535–629. Under either
   of those situations, would the vendor, Caldwell, be relieved of his obligation not to
   open his own theater?

4. Lines 119–126: What would be a legal effect of the theater "having entered the community of acquets and gains ..." resulting from the marriage of Harry and Mae Bogart? *See* La. Civ. Code arts. 2334–2369.8.

5. Assume that Harry Bogart is alive and that Caldwell, in turn, wants to sell his own
   theater to a third party. Can he do it or not? Explain why or why not. What if Caldwell had actually sold his theater to a third person? Could Bogart then go against the
   third person and prevent him or her from operating the theater he or she purchased
   from Caldwell? Be sure to properly identify, for the benefit of Bogart, the kind of
   obligation on which he should be basing his argument. What if Caldwell had died before Harry Bogart: would Caldwell's heirs be bound, if at all, by Caldwell's obligation to Bogart not to open his theater as long as vendee, Bogart, owned his theater?

ST. JUDE MEDICAL OFFICE BUILDING
LIMITED PARTNERSHIP

v.

CITY GLASS AND MIRROR, INC., et al.

Supreme Court of Louisiana
May 24, 1993
619 So.2d 529

WATSON, Justice. [....]

FACTS

In 1983, the St. Jude Medical Office Building Limited Partnership contracted with
Spaw Glass, Inc. for construction of the St. Jude Medical Office Building, a seven-story
medical office and retail complex in Kenner, Louisiana. Spaw Glass contracted with
various sub-contractors. The building was completed in February of 1985. Approximately two months later, the Partnership applied to Travelers for permanent financing.
On October 10, 1985, Travelers advanced $25 million on the Partnership's promissory
note. The note was secured primarily by a real and chattel mortgage on the building,
the underlying property, and all related land and improvements. The note and mortgage contained *in rem* language limiting Travelers' default remedy to judicial sale of
the property.

After closing the loan with Travelers, the Partnership discovered defects in the building's construction, including water leakage through the second floor windows, leakage
through the building's skylights and ground settling damage to the sidewalks and drive-
ways. The Partnership asked Spaw Glass and the sub-contractors to voluntarily repair
their allegedly defective work. The requested repairs were never performed. At an im-
passe, the Partnership filed suit against Spaw Glass and the sub-contractors in February
of 1988.

In its original and amended petitions, the Partnership alleged that defects in the materials and workmanship of the building breached express and implied warranties of the
contractor and several sub-contractors. Damages were estimated at $10 million.

In March of 1990, the Partnership defaulted on its note. On June 1, 1990, Travelers
filed suit in the United States District Court for the Eastern District of Louisiana. Among
other relief, Travelers requested recognition of its *in rem* mortgage on the building, a judgment for the amount due on the note, and seizure and sale of the building. On November 24, 1990, the federal court entered a partial final judgment in favor of Travelers,
recognizing its mortgage and awarding damages of approximately $26 million. Travelers
executed on the judgment with a writ of fieri facias directing the marshal to seize and sell
the building. Travelers acquired the building at a judicial sale on October 18, 1991, for
$7.5 million.

[In 1991, Travelers intervened in the Partnership's state court lawsuit against the building's contractor and subcontractors,] [....] alleging that it was subrogated to the Partnership's claims for construction breaches of express and implied warranties. The
Partnership and several of the defendants filed exceptions of no cause of action and no
right of action. The trial court sustained both exceptions and dismissed Travelers' petition with prejudice. In a well-reasoned opinion, the court of appeal affirmed the trial
court judgment. 608 So.2d 236 (La.App. 5th Cir.1992). A writ was granted to review the
court of appeal judgment. 613 So.2d 959 (La.1993).

LAW AND ANALYSIS

[....]

The general Louisiana rule is that a purchaser cannot recover from a third party for property damage inflicted prior to the sale. *Prados v. South Central Bell Telephone Company*, 329 So.2d 744, 750 (La.1976); *Gumbel v. New Orleans Terminal Co.*, 197 La. 439, 1 So.2d 686 (1941); *Taylor v. New Orleans Terminal Co.*, 126 La. 420, 52 So. 562 (1910); *McCutchen v. Texas & P. Ry. Co.*, 118 La. 436, 43 So. 42 (1907); *Bradford v. Richard, et al.*, 46 La.Ann. 1530, 16 So. 487 (1894); *Clark v. Warner & Co.*, 6 La.Ann. 408 (La.1851).

Travelers relies on the decision in *Aizpurua v. Crane Pool Co., Inc.* 449 So.2d 471 (La.1984), for its right to intervene in the Partnership's suit. In *Aizpurua*, the purchasers of a residence brought suit against the company that had constructed a swimming pool on the property prior to plaintiffs' purchase. At that time, LSA-C.C. art. 2011 provided:

Not only the obligation, but the right resulting from a contract relative to immovable property, passes with the property. Thus, the right of servitude in favor of immovable property, passes with it, *and thus also the heir or other acquirer will have the right to enforce a contract made for the improvement of the property by the person from whom he acquired it.* (Emphasis added.)

Relying on LSA-C.C. art. 2011, now repealed, *Aizpurua* decided that a subsequent purchaser was subrogated to the implied warranty of materials and workmanship in a building contract. Despite lack of privity, the purchaser of immovable property was allowed to enforce a property improvement contract made by the previous owner.

In 1984, LSA-C.C. art. 2011 was repealed and was replaced by LSA-C.C. art. 1764. LSA-C.C. art. 1764 now provides:

A real obligation is transferred to the universal or particular successor who acquires the movable or immovable thing to which the obligation is attached, without a special provision to that effect.

But a particular successor is not personally bound, unless he assumes the personal obligations of his transferor with respect to the thing, and he may liberate himself of the real obligation by abandoning the thing.

Official Comment (D) to this article states that Civil Code Article 2011 (1870) was suppressed because its provisions were conceptually inconsistent with other provisions of Louisiana law. It was, of course, in derogation of the general rule of non-recovery.

Aizpurua was based on the now repealed provisions of LSA-C.C. art. 2011. The substantive changes made by LSA-C.C. art. 1764 have superceded *Aizpurua*. Travelers cannot rely on *Aizpurua*. In addition, important distinctions exist between the facts in *Aizpurua* and those in this case. In *Aizpurua*, plaintiffs purchased their residence by a conventional sale and the alleged defects in the pool's construction were hidden from them at the time of the sale. Here, Travelers purchased the building at a judicial sale and knew of the defects in the building. Under LSA-C.C. arts. 2537 and 2619, Travelers would have had no redhibition claim for hidden defects because the property was purchased at judicial sale.

Applying LSA-C.C. art. 1764 to the facts of this case, the central issue is whether an action for defective construction of a building is based on a real or a personal obligation.

Official Comment (f) to LSA-C.C. art. 1764 provides in pertinent part:

89   Louisiana courts have held that … damages due to the owner of a thing for its partial
90 destruction or for an interference with the owner's rights, belong to the person who was
91 the owner at the time of the … destruction or interference. *These are personal rights that*
92 *are not transferred to a successor by particular title without a stipulation to that effect.* (Em-
93 phasis added.)

94   The underlying obligation here is personal and not real. As a successor, without stipu-
95 lation or assignment, Travelers has no right of action to intervene in the Partnership's suit.

Questions

1.   Lines 10 *et seq.*: After you have read the "Facts" carefully, draw a diagram of the different legal relationships or bonds of law that have been created. Can you identify some of these bonds of law as being principal and others as being secondary or accessory?

2.   Lines 48–49: What is, in your opinion, the *ratio legis*, the reason or policy, for this rule? Could your choice of a *ratio* or policy have an impact on the legal nature of the obligations created by the rule? Read now lines 67–74: Are there any differences in the legal identification of the kinds of obligations created before and after the revision of the law of Obligations in 1984?

3.   Lines 86–87: In light of the above questions and your legal analysis, what would be your answer to the kind of question the court is posing here, that is, "Is an action for defective construction of a building based on a real or a personal obligation?" Do you agree with the Court's ruling in lines 91–93?

See also Breaux v. Laird et al., 65 So.2d 907 (La. 1953).

Chapter Four

Obligations of Result & Means

Louisiana Sources of Law

Précis: Louisiana Law of Obligations in General § 1.2.2

There exists an obligation of result whenever the performance or object of the obligation is so precisely determined as to amount to a definite result to be achieved. An obligation to give a specific thing and an obligation not to do something would be obligations of result....

There is an obligation of means or diligence when an obligor is expected to use the best possible means available to him, or to act with the utmost care and diligence in the performance of his obligation but without guaranteeing a definite result....

Cases

Miss Lula Mae JOHNSON

v.

NEW ORLEANS PUBLIC SERVICE, INCORPORATED

Louisiana Court of Appeal
Fourth Circuit
March 8, 1974
293 So.2d 203

SAMUEL, Judge.

This is a suit for damages for personal injuries sustained by plaintiff as a result of a fall on a New Orleans Public Service, Inc. bus. Following trial on the merits judgment was rendered in favor of defendant, dismissing plaintiff's suit. Plaintiff has appealed.

Plaintiff, a fare paying passenger on the bus, had boarded the vehicle at Orleans Avenue and Roman Street in the City of New Orleans. Shortly before the bus arrived at the stop at which she desired to get off, plaintiff got up from her seat and pulled the cord to indicate to the driver she intended to alight. She started to walk to the rear exit door. Before she reached the door she fell and injured herself. Being notified by another passenger that an accident had occurred, the driver brought his vehicle to a stop and went to plaintiff's assistance. He then resumed driving and called the police and his supervisor from the first stop at which a telephone was available. Plaintiff was taken to a hospital for examination and treatment.

Testimony relative to the occurrence of the accident was given by plaintiff, Louis Hancock (an independent witness who was a passenger on the bus at the time of the acci-

dent), Joseph Reed (the defendant's driver), and a defendant claims representative who [23]
had interviewed plaintiff concerning the accident. [24]

Plaintiff testified: In traveling its regular route the bus had to make a left turn from [25]
Orleans Avenue onto Treme Street. Just before her stop she pulled the signal cord and [26]
began to walk to the rear. As she did so, the bus started into the turn and struck a curb, [27]
causing her to fall to the floor and injure her knee and her leg. A passenger 'hollered' and [28]
the driver came to her assistance after he had stopped the bus somewhere in the next [29]
block or so. Later the supervisor arrived and she was taken to the hospital. Plaintiff ad- [30]
mitted surgery had been performed on both of her knees several years before the acci- [31]
dent but said she had experienced no trouble with the knees since recovery from that [32]
surgery.

Joseph Reed, the driver stated: Orleans Avenue is a four lane street with a neutral [33]
ground running from the river to the lake. Treme is a two lane street, but wider than the [34]
ordinary street. He was traveling about 3 or 4 miles per hour as he neared the turn onto [35]
Treme. He looked in his rear view mirror and saw no traffic. As the bus turned onto [36]
Treme it crossed railroad tracks which were embedded in the street. Shortly after mak- [37]
ing the turn he heard a passenger 'holler' that someone was hurt. He went back to help [38]
plaintiff after stopping the bus at the first convenient place and assisted her to a seat. He [39]
carefully examined the bus to determine what had caused her fall, but he could see noth- [40]
ing. He testified the bus had not hit the curb. [41]

Louis Hancock, called by the defendant, testified: He was the passenger who called [42]
the driver's attention to the fact that plaintiff had fallen and injured herself. He saw [43]
plaintiff get up from her seat, pull the signal cord to indicate to the driver she desired [44]
to alight, and proceed to walk toward the rear of the bus. She 'slipped some kind of [45]
way' and fell as she was walking to the rear. He did not know what caused her to fall, [46]
although he did notice a worn piece of metal on the floor in the area in which she fell. [47]
At the time of the fall the bus was proceeding at a normal rate of speed just after mak- [48]
ing the turn and there was no unusual jolt or jerk with the exception of some bounc- [49]
ing across the railroad tracks. This witness further stated that 'to my knowledge' the bus [50]
did not hit the curb. [51]

The defendant claims adjuster testified only regarding conversations he had with the [51]
plaintiff at the hospital and at his office following the occurrence of the accident. [52]

Applicable here are the following jurisprudential rules: A public carrier, while not an [53]
insurer, is required to exercise the highest degree of care for the safety of its passengers, [54]
and a mere showing of injury to a fare paying passenger establishes a prima facie case of [55]
negligence against the carrier.[1] Once a prima facie case has been established, the burden [56]
of proof is then on the defendant to show there has been no disregard of its duties and [57]
that the damage resulted from a cause which human care and foresight could not pre- [58]
vent.[2] In the operation of transit vehicles there is a certain amount of jerking or jolting [59]
consistent with the operation which is to be expected, should be anticipated, and for [60]
which the carrier cannot be held liable.[3] [61]

---

1. Wise v. Prescott, 244 La. 157, 151 So.2d 356; Green v. Taca International Airlines, La.App., 293 So.2d 198, handed down this date; Alfred v. Benoit, La.App., 253 So.2d 797.
2. Wise v. Prescott, Supra, footnote 1; Jones v. New Orleans Public Service, Inc., La.App., 254 So.2d 652; Walker v. New Orleans Public Service, Inc., La.App., 245 So.2d 763; Hurst v. New Orleans Public Service, Inc., La.App., 235 So.2d 103; King v. King, 253 La. 270, 217 So.2d 395.
3. Harris v. Shreveport Railways Company, La.App., 83 So.2d 517; Rhodes v. New Orleans Public Service, La.App., 75 So.2d 549.

62   In the instant matter plaintiff clearly has established a prima facie case. There is no
63 question that Mrs. Johnson fell on the bus and suffered injuries. However, the evidence
64 shows the bus was traveling at a normal and reasonable rate of speed and that there was
65 no unusual jolting as it crossed the railroad tracks, an operation which is expected and
66 should be anticipated by passengers. We are satisfied the bus did not hit a curb and thus
67 cause the fall in suit. The only evidence indicating the bus had hit a curb was the testi-
68 mony given by the plaintiff herself, but the other testifying passenger and the bus driver
69 effectively denied such an incident. Nor do we feel plaintiff fell as a result of slipping on
70 worn metal on the bus floor. The only evidence to that effect is the testimony of the other
71 passenger and, from our reading of all of his testimony, we are of the opinion he was
72 merely speculating in an effort to find some reason for plaintiff's fall. Neither in her plead-
73 ings nor in her testimony did the plaintiff complain about any jolting as the bus went
74 over the tracks or about any slip because of the condition of the bus floor; her only com-
75 plaint was that she fell because of the single jolt caused by the bus hitting a curb.

76   Under these circumstances we agree with the trial court's conclusion that the defen-
77 dant has carried its burden of proof showing it exercised its required degree of care for
78 the safety of its passengers. [....]

Questions

1.   Lines 9-78: Having read the pages given here, you have read the whole case: what do
     you think of the sources of law used by the Court in this case? What about reading
     the first four articles of the Louisiana Civil Code? Does that help in grounding your
     opinion or evaluation of the Court's use of sources of law?

2.   Lines 53 *et seq.*: Is there not in the Louisiana Civil Code a kind or type of contract
     that would fit a carrier and its liability? *See* La. Civ. Code art. 2754.

3.   In which category would you place the obligation of a carrier towards its passenger:
     result or means? If you ever have travelled by plane, or bus, or boat with other pas-
     sengers, what would be their likely answer to your question about the obligation of
     an airline, bus company, or ship company towards their passengers?

1
2
3

Warner Max ALEXANDER

v.

ALTON OCHSNER MEDICAL FOUNDATION et al.

4
5
6
7

Louisiana Court of Appeal

Fourth Circuit

April 3, 1973

276 So.2d 794

8 SCHOTT, Judge.

9   The plaintiff appeals from a judgment dismissing his suit against Alton Ochsner Med-
10 ical Foundation, Ochsner Clinic and three physicians associated with those entities, Dr.
11 Kenneth Meyer, Dr. Hurst B. Hatch, Jr. and Dr. Joseph K. Bradford. The case was tried
12 to a jury resulting in a unanimous verdict for the defendants.

13   In his petition, plaintiff alleged alternatively that the defendants, including the three
14 physicians named, as well as other physicians associated with them, in the period be-
15 tween April 20, 1967, and May 5, 1967, violated an agreement made with him in that the

treatment afforded him was not performed in accordance with the standard of profes- [16]
sional skills and care prevailing in the community and were negligent in that they failed [17]
to exercise ordinary care and skill required of them. In this Court, plaintiff contends that [18]
the defendants failed to use various processes and facilities to minimize his pain during [19]
the course of their treatment, thereby failing to render to him treatment which the com- [20]
munity has a right to expect and thereby violating an implied warranty existing between [21]
plaintiff as a patient and defendants. [22]

[....] [23]

On April 20, 1967, plaintiff was admitted to the defendant hospital by defendant, Dr. [24]
Hatch, who had found that the plaintiff was suffering from a spontaneous pneumotho- [25]
rax, a condition in which air has escaped from the lung into the space between the lung [26]
and the chest wall as a result of the rupture of a blister on the surface of the lung. This [27]
condition had first manifested itself on April 13, 1967, when plaintiff complained to Dr. [28]
Hatch that two days prior thereto he had an onset of stabbing pain in the mid sternal re- [29]
gion, aggravated by breathing and by changing his position from lying prone. The doc- [30]
tor, on the basis of X-ray studies, diagnosed a 10% Pneumothorax and prescribed bed rest [31]
and medication. Plaintiff was told to return in a week or sooner if his condition worsened. [32]
When he returned on April 20, 1967, and X-ray studies revealed that the condition had [33]
worsened Dr. Hatch consulted with defendant, Dr. Kenneth Meyer, of the Surgery Department [34]
of Ochsner, whereupon the two physicians concurred that it was necessary to conduct a [35]
surgical procedure known as a thoracotomy. [36]

This procedure performed by Dr. Meyer consists of the insertion of a catheter through [37]
the wall of the chest and into the space between the lung and the interior chest wall so [38]
that air can be aspirated from that pleural space. As the air is removed the lung re-expands [39]
and becomes sealed with the result that the leakage of air from the lung is gradually elim- [40]
inated. The insertion of the tube is accomplished by means of a local anethesia [sic] being [41]
administered, followed by an incision in the chest, the slant of which controls the direc- [42]
tion to be followed by the catheter. A steel trocar or needle tube containing the catheter [43]
itself is then used to penetrate the chest muscle and chest wall. When the desired posi- [44]
tion is reached the trocar is removed leaving the catheter in place with the outside end of [45]
the catheter then connected to a suction apparatus. [46]

This procedure was carried out at 4:30 PM on April 20, 1967. The nursing notes show [47]
that on April 21 at 12:45 PM plaintiff was complaining of severe pain above the site of the [48]
insertion in the chest and 'cannot move legs, arms or head without pain.' Dr. Meyer tes- [49]
tified that when this report came to his attention he examined the plaintiff, finding that [50]
he was able to turn and move with ease as he was requested to do in order for him to [51]
carry out his examination. A chest X-ray was taken and thereafter the position of the [52]
catheter was changed. The doctor explained that by this time most of the air in the pleural [53]
space had been removed but there was still fluid on the periphery of the space. The tube [54]
had to be repositioned in order to place one of the holes in the tube in the particular [55]
space where the fluid was located. He explained that in addition to the hole on the end [56]
of the catheter additional holes were placed in the catheter so as to make the removal of [57]
the air more effective. Plaintiff was seen by Dr. Hatch daily while in the hospital until [58]
May 1. By April 30 he felt that there was no more leakage from the lung so that the catheter [59]
could be removed, but on consultation with Dr. Meyer it was decided to leave the catheter [60]
in place for a short while longer. On May 1 Dr. Hatch's responsibility for the plaintiff was [61]
assumed by defendant, Dr. Bradford, to whom it was apparent by May 2 that plaintiff's [62]
lung had re-expanded completely, so that it was time for the catheter to be removed from [63]
his chest, and this was confirmed by X-ray examination. The catheter was removed on May [64]

65 4 and plaintiff was discharged from the hospital on May 5 with no problems of mobility.
66 Dr. Meyer and Dr. Bradford both testified that the procedure followed, and the treat-
67 ment administered, was in accordance with standard medical practice in the City of New
68 Orleans. Dr. Bradford further testified that Drs. Hatch and Meyer both have the neces-
69 sary training and skill to have treated plaintiff.

70 [....]

71 With respect to plaintiff's position that the defendants committed a breach of con-
72 tract, we are guided by the following principles enunciated in Phelps v. Donaldson, 243
73 La. 1118, 150 So.2d 35:

74 'We think the general rule universally obtaining on the subject matter is that:
75 'When a physician undertakes the treatment of a case he does not guarantee a cure,
76 nor is any promise to effect a cure or even a partial healing to be implied, nor
77 does the law raise from the fact of employment an implied undertaking to cure,
78 but only an undertaking to use ordinary skill and care. For this reason a physi-
79 cian cannot be held up to a standard of civil responsibility similar to that of en-
80 gineers, mechanics, and shipbuilders. of course a physician might contract
81 specifically to cure and he would be liable on his contract for failure, but, in the
82 absence of such a special and peculiar contract, the fact that treatment has re-
83 sulted unfavorably does not even raise a presumption of want of proper care,
84 skill, or diligence. * * *' 21 R.C.L. Sec. 36, p. 391. Also, see 70 C.J.S. Physicians
85 and Surgeons s 57, pp. 981, 982 'A dentist, like a physician or surgeon, is not an
86 insurer or guarantor or results, in the absence of express agreement.' 41 Am.Jur.,
87 Physicians and Surgeons, Sec. 104, p. 219.'

88 There is no evidence of any expressed contract to cure. The testimony of defendant physi-
89 cians standing alone is sufficient in this case with respect to implied warranty to show
90 that they did use ordinary skill and care and their testimony is corroborated by the tes-
91 timony of every other physician who reviewed their procedures and approved of same.
92 Plaintiff attempts to contradict this testimony by suggesting that X-ray photographs taken
93 by Drs. Hatch and Meyer were inadequate in that they did not reveal the depth into the
94 chest cavity which the catheter reached. He speculates that this caused his suffering. But
95 Dr. Leon thoroughly discredited this theory as a cause for plaintiff's problem. Plaintiff's
96 argument that additional X-ray photographs should have been taken and that additional
97 procedures, such as fluoroscoping and other tests, should have been implemented is not
98 supported by any testimony, medical or lay. The real nub of the plaintiff's position seems
99 to be that he was in pain at the beginning and continued to be in pain at the time of the
100 trial; therefore, a breach of contract was committed by defendants who had undertaken
101 to treat him, but the law does not exact upon the physician a guarantee to cure anyone.
102 Furthermore, the pain and discomfort described in the nursing note of April 21 are fully
103 explained by Dr. Meyer who testified that a thoracotomy necessarily causes a patient to
104 be uncomfortable as long as the catheter remains inserted and discomfort continues even
105 after the patient is discharged from the hospital because of the incision and irritation to
106 the lining of the lung and chest wall. Finally, the testimony of almost every physician who
107 appeared at the trial, as well as numerous consultants to whom reference was made by those
108 physicians, compels a conclusion that plaintiff's pain was not the result of defendants'
109 actions but was psychogenic or emotional requiring psychiatric treatment for a cure.

110 As to the allegations of negligence on the part of defendants, their conduct must be
111 judged on the basis of whether they exercised that degree of skill and care which is usu-
112 ally possessed and exercised by practitioners of the profession in the same community, it

cisions reached by the courts in both France and Quebec. The Work of the Louisiana Appellate Courts for the 1974–1975 Term Contracts in Particular, 36 La.L.Rev. 417, 421––426 (1976). It is also consistent with the rule of this circuit in attorney malpractice cases. Jackson, above. The decision of the Third Circuit appears to be an importation from the common law. See 70 C.J.S. Physicians and Surgeons s 57. It has no theoretical foundation in the civilian law of obligations. In Steel the court relied on Phelps v. Donaldson, 243 La. 1118, 150 So.2d 35 (1963) to sustain its position. However, that case does not support the proposition asserted. In the case, although an exception of prescription was sustained as to the tort claim, trial was conducted on the contractual claim. The trial court found that a contract to straighten the plaintiff's daughter's teeth had not been proved. The Court of Appeal affirmed on the basis that the action was essentially in tort and that it had prescribed. Phelps v. Donaldson, 142 So.2d 585 (La.App. 3rd Cir. 1962). The Supreme Court, in its affirmance, followed the trial court rationale rather than that of the Court of Appeal. It was never found as a fact that the doctor performed in a substandard fashion. Apparently the plaintiff attempted to rely on the fact that her daughter's teeth were not straightened to sustain her breach of contract action. Absent proof of a contract to cure, such proof was found to be insufficient. We believe that this is the actual holding of Phelps plaintiff simply failed to prove a breach. Our decision here is not inconsistent with that holding. If plaintiff succeeds in proving a contract to cure, he will be relieved of his burden of proving substandard conduct. But if he does not prove such a contract he can still recover by proving Dr. Peden has violated his obligation of due care.

We next move to the assertion that Henson's contractual claim has prescribed. In support of this contention defendant relies on R.S. 9:5628 (added by Act 808 of 1975 and amended by Act 214 of 1976). Although the alleged negligent act of defendant's insured occurred prior to September 12, 1975 (the effective date of Act 808), suit was instituted after this date. Defendant asserts that prescription statutes are remedial and procedural in nature and that they therefore are to be applied retroactively. It is true that prescription statutes may be applied to causes of action arising prior to their enactment, at least so long as a reasonable time is given for the assertion of rights, if the legislature so intends. Cooper v. Lykes, 218 La. 251, 49 So.2d 3 (1950). This is well illustrated in Mire v. Hawkins, 177 So.2d 795 (La.App. 3rd Cir. 1965), affirmed at 249 La. 278, 186 So.2d 591 (1966). There a statute specifically provided for retroactive effect and included a saving clause allowing those who would be cut off by retroactive application to have one year to bring their action. Such a provision was held to be valid. However, in Act 808 the legislature did not specifically address this problem. Therefore it is our duty to ascertain the presumed legislative intent as to retroactivity.

The general rule is that when a prescriptive period is changed "the time which preceded the change of legislation or altering the period of prescription, should be reckoned according to the ancient law, and that which followed according to the new law." Goddard's Heirs v. Urquhart, 6 La. 659, 674 (1834), accord 1 Planiol, Treatise on the Civil Law, s 248 (translation by the Louisiana State Law Institute, 1959). This solution is very equitable. In the absence of an express legislative intent to the contrary, we believe it is the rule to be followed.

In applying this proportionate method to the facts of this case we find that Henson's contractual claim has not prescribed. He filed suit within six months of the effective date of Act 808. Therefore over one-half of the prescriptive period under C.C. Art. 3544 would have had to elapse before Act 808's effective date in order for his claim to be prescribed. It had not done so.

The finding by the trial judge that plaintiff's tort action had prescribed was correct. However, the plaintiff has sufficiently alleged a timely breach of contract action. We therefore

117 reverse and remand the case to the trial court for further proceedings in accordance with
118 law. Costs in this court are to be borne by appellee. All other costs are to await a final de-
119 termination on the merits.

Questions

1. Lines 38 *et seq.*: Is the court saying that, in the absence of a contract creating an oblig-
    ation of result on the part of a physician, the latter can only be bound by an obliga-
    tion of means? If you conclude that this is what the court is saying, can you give
    some reasons in support of the court's statement? Is the distinction between an oblig-
    ation of result and one of means only a matter of procedure/evidence?

2. Lines 65 *et seq.*: Since the civil law system of Louisiana is one of many other civil law
    systems, it is logical and helpful to learn from these other civil law systems, i.e. to do
    some comparative law research. Notice that the court is also looking at the common
    law (*see* lines 70–71).

3. Lines 115–119: This paragraph in the opinion of the court conveys a most impor-
    tant instruction to lawyers and judges: Identify clearly, in legal terms, of course, first
    and foremost, the source of the obligations that may have been created. These sources
    of obligations are legislation and custom (*see* La. Civ. Code arts. 1–4), juridical acts
    (mostly contracts but not exclusively) and juridical facts (such as torts/delicts). Note
    here that the trial judge identified the source of obligations as being a tort, whereas
    the court of appeal saw a contract. Is there any difference in the legal effects of one
    source versus the other, with respect to prescription, for example? *See* La. Civ. Code
    arts. 3492 & 3499.

Comparative Law Perspective

Obligations of Result & Means

France

2 Henri et Léon Mazeaud et al., Leçons de Droit Civil: Obligations,

Vol. 1: Théorie Générale n° 21, at 13–15 (François Chabas rev., 9th ed. 1998)

    *21. — Determinate obligations (or obligations of result) and general obligations of pru-
dence and diligence (or obligations of means).* — This classification rests on the following observation: *Sometimes the obligor is bound to accomplish a determinate result; the
obligation is strictly specified and the obligor must attain that result; at other times, on the
contrary, the obligor is bound only to act with diligence and to conduct himself with prudence in order to attempt to achieve a desired result.* [For example,] whereas a transporter
is bound to deliver the merchandise at the agreed-upon time and place, a doctor is bound
only to conduct himself *with prudence and diligence* in view of obtaining the healing of
the patient.

    The practical interest of the distinction is most significant on the plane of proof.

    It suffices for the obligee of a determinate obligation to establish that the result has
not been attained. The obligee thereby demonstrates that the obligor has not performed
his obligation. In order to exonerate himself, the obligor must then prove that the non-

performance proceeded from a cause that was foreign to him. For example, the transporter must establish the fault of the sender or an event of *force majeure*.

If the obligation that weighs on the obligor is only to conduct himself with prudence and diligence, an examination of the obligor's conduct becomes necessary. In fact, when the anticipated result is not attained, the obligee, in order to demonstrate that the obligation has not been performed, must prove that the obligor has not comported himself with the prudence and diligence to which he was held—fault in the classic sense. Proof of the imprudence or negligence of the obligor is at the charge of the obligee. For example, the patient must establish the imprudence or negligence of the doctor.

Thus, in determinate obligations, it suffices for the obligee to prove that the result has not been attained, and it is up to the obligor to demonstrate a foreign cause. In obligations of prudence and diligence, the obligee must put on proof (which is [more] difficult) of some negligence or imprudence of the obligor. Given the practical importance of the burden of proof, the classification is of primordial interest …

It is not always easy to determine if one is in the presence of a determinate obligation or a general obligation of prudence and diligence. *What is the criterion for the distinction?*

On contractual terrain, it is necessary to search out the will of the parties. Has the obligor taken the engagement of achieving the result in view of which the parties contracted? Then the obligation is determinate. Has the obligor only engaged himself to try, by prudent and diligent conduct, to achieve the result in view of which the parties concluded the contract? Then the obligation is a general obligation of prudence and diligence. In the absence of other circumstances that might permit one to discover this will, one should seek to ascertain *whether the realization of the end pursued through the contract entails some risk (alea)*. When this realization is aleatory [contains an element of risk], one must suppose that the obligation which the obligor assumed is only of prudence and diligence, for an obligor normally does not engage himself to attain a result that he knows is aleatory. It is so with the doctor *vis-à-vis* his client: the healing is aleatory. It will therefore be admitted that, unless the parties have expressed a will to the contrary, the doctor does not engage himself to heal the patient, but to give him prudent and diligent care in order to try to heal him. When, on the contrary, the realization of the result in view of which the contract was made is not aleatory, one can normally conclude that the obligor has promised this realization. It is so with the transporter as to the delivery of the transported thing in good condition within the fixed delay. *Thus, the aleatory or non-aleatory nature of the realization of the end to be attained permits one to discover the unexpressed will of the parties.*

On extra-contractual terrain, there is no question of searching out the will of the parties. Because the obligation is imposed by law, it is the *will of the legislators* that must be detected when they have not expressed it.

––––––––––

Québec

Jean-Louis Baudouin, Les Obligations
n° 36, at 26–27, & n° 37, at 27–28 (4th ed. 1993)

An obligation of result is that for the satisfaction of which the obligor is bound to furnish to the obligee a specific result, fixed in advance. Such is, for example, the obligation of a seller (or that of a transporter) to deliver the merchandise.

An obligation of means is that for the satisfaction of which the obligor is bound to employ the best possible means and to act [27] with prudence and diligence in view of obtaining a result, but nevertheless without making himself a guarantor of that result. Such is, for example, the obligation of a doctor toward his patient, that of a lessee to use the leased thing as a reasonable person, ... that of an employee, ... that of a mandatary [agent], [and] that of a borrower or depositary of a thing to stand watch over the conservation of the loaned or deposited thing. In the same fashion, the general [tort] obligation not to cause damage to another is an obligation of means.

...

37.—*Consequences of the distinction*—This classification has great importance on the practical plane, both as to the prerequisites for the responsibility [liability] of the obligor and as to the proof [of that responsibility]. Regarding the prerequisites for the responsibility of the obligor, if it's a matter of an obligation of means, only fault in the utilization of the means can engage his responsibility [make him liable]. For example, the simple fact that a surgical operation fails does not automatically lead to [28] the doctor's responsibility. The patient must demonstrate that the doctor has committed fault in the means that he has utilized in order to care for him. In the same way, the occurrence of some harm, standing alone, does not, in principle, render the author of the damage responsible, if he has proved he was reasonably prudent and diligent. If it is a matter of an obligation of result, the fact that the promised result has not been attained results in the obligor's responsibility being presumed....

In the case of an obligation of means, the obligee, in order to cause the obligor to be held responsible, must prove that the obligor has not exercised reasonable prudence and diligence in pursuit of the end fixed [by the parties or the law]. The absence of that result does not, then, cause the fault of the obligor to be presumed. The burden of proving this fault rests on the obligee. To the contrary, in the case of an obligation of result, the simple ... absence of the result or of the harm experienced suffices to cause the fault of the obligor to be presumed, once the very fact of nonperformance or of the occurrence of the damage has been demonstrated by the obligee. At that point, the obligor, in order to escape his responsibility, must go beyond proof of a simple absence of fault, that is, must demonstrate that the nonperformance or the harm experienced proceeded from a *force majeure*. He could not be permitted to escape his responsibility solely by putting on proof of an absence of fault....

This classification, to which the courts are appealing more and more often, has the merit of being simple and of permitting one to measure exactly the intensity of the obligor's obligational duty.

Chapter Five

Terms & Conditions

Louisiana Sources of Law

Louisiana Civil Code

Art. 1767. Suspensive and resolutory condition.

A conditional obligation is one dependent on an uncertain event.

If the obligation may not be enforced until the uncertain event occurs, the condition is suspensive.

Art. 1770. Condition that depends on the whim or the will of the obligor.

A suspensive condition that depends solely on the whim of the obligor makes the obligation null.

A resolutory condition that depends solely on the will of the obligor must be fulfilled in good faith. (Acts 1984, No. 331, § 1, eff. Jan. 1, 1985.)

Art. 1771. Obligee's right pending condition.

The obligee of a conditional obligation, pending fulfillment of the condition, may take all lawful measures to preserve his right. (Acts 1984, No. 331, § 1, eff. Jan. 1, 1985.)

Art. 1775. Effects retroactive.

Fulfillment of a condition has effects that are retroactive to the inception of the obligation. Nevertheless, that fulfillment does not impair the validity of acts of administration duly performed by a party, nor affect the ownership of fruits produced while the condition was pending. Likewise, fulfillment of the condition does not impair the right acquired by third persons while the condition was pending. (Acts 1984, No. 331, § 1, eff. Jan. 1, 1985.)

Art. 1776. Contract for continuous or periodic performance.

In a contract for continuous or periodic performance, fulfillment of a resolutory condition does not affect the validity of acts of performance rendered before fulfillment of the condition. (Acts 1984, No. 331, § 1, eff. Jan. 1, 1985.)

Art. 1778. Term for performance.

A term for the performance of an obligation is a period of time either certain or uncertain. It is certain when it is fixed. It is uncertain when it is not fixed but is determinable either by the intent of the parties or by the occurrence of a future and certain event. It is also uncertain when it is not determinable, in which case the obligation must be performed within a reasonable time. (Acts 1984, No. 331, § 1, eff. Jan. 1, 1985.)

Art. 1779. Term presumed to benefit the obligor.

A term is presumed to benefit the obligor unless the agreement or the circumstances show that it was intended to benefit the obligee or both parties. (Acts 1984, No. 331, § 1, eff. Jan. 1, 1985.)

Art. 1781. Performance before end of term.

Although performance cannot be demanded before the term ends, an obligor who has performed voluntarily before the term ends may not recover the performance. (Acts 1984, No. 331, § 1, eff. Jan. 1, 1985.)

Art. 1785. Performance on term.

Performance on term must be in accordance with the intent of the parties, or with established usage when the intent cannot be ascertained. (Acts 1984, No. 331, § 1, eff. Jan. 1, 1985.)

Précis: Louisiana Law of Obligations in General § 2.2-A.1 to 2.2-B.2

LSA-C.C. Art. 1767 defines a conditional obligation as **one dependent on an uncertain event.** In this limited context one can also define a condition as being an uncertain event which may or may not occur. The contrast can now be clearly marked with the *term* which is defined in **LSA-C.C. Art. 1778** as a period of time either certain or uncertain but, in all circumstances, as a period of time bound to occur in the course of nature....

Suspensive and Resolutory Conditions.

An obligation is subjected to a suspensive condition when it may not be enforced until the uncertain event occurs (LSA-C.C. Art 1767) Although this description of the effects of a suspensive condition states that the obligation **may not be enforced**, actually a suspensive condition has a much more drastic effect: it suspends the existence of the obligation between the parties until the uncertain event occurs and, therefore, suspends the enforcement of that same obligation. Although the bond of law has been formed, no obligation is yet in existence....

Whether suspensive or resolutory, a condition can be expressed in a stipulation or implied by the law, the nature of the contract, or the intent of the parties (LSA-C.C. Art. 1768)....

A condition may be implied by the law as, for example, in **LSA-C.C. Arts. 2604 and 2605** which give a buyer a reasonable opportunity to inspect the things and to reject nonconforming things within a reasonable time....

A condition may also be implied from the intent of the parties whenever the circumstances are clearly indicative of consent (**LSA-C.C. Art. 1927**)....

A condition would be unlawful or immoral whenever it would violate **LSA-C.C. Art. 7** and as is otherwise illustrated throughout the civil Code in **Articles 1519, 1968, 2030, etc.**...

An impossible condition would contemplate the occurrence of an event which could absolutely not take place....

The principle governing the fulfillment or occurrence of the condition is that of the retroactivity of the effects of the condition....

LSA-C.C. Art. 1775 expresses the general principle in these terms: **"Fulfillment of a condition has effects that are retroactive to the inception of the obligation ..."**

The essence of a suspensive condition is to *suspend* the effects of an existing legal relationship and, *a fortiori,* all performances flowing from the effects of that legal relationship. Through the fiction of retroactivity, there will take place a sort of creation *ab initio* or *ex tunc* of the effects of the relationship and the resulting obligation....

There are, obviously, some limitations to the retroactive effect of the condition. On the basis either of the good faith principle or the public records doctrine, **LSA-C.C. Art. 1775** stipulates, in part, that **"fulfillment of the condition does not impair the right acquired by third parties while the condition was pending."** ...

Another limitation to the retroactive effect of the condition is stated in these terms in **LSA-C.C. Art. 1775.**...

The retroactive effects of a resolutory condition are basically the same as those of a suspensive condition. An interesting illustration of the impact of these effects can be found in the contract of sale with the right of redemption. Under **LSA-C.C. Art. 2567, 2572 and 2588**, the vendor and original owner of the thing sold receives it back, in theory, as if the sale had not taken place....

LSA-C.C. Art. 1778 describes the *term*....

A term is, therefore, a future and certain event which will definitely occur and which may either delay the performance of an obligation, as suggested by an *a contrario sensu* reasoning on **LSA-C.C. Art. 1777-2** or bring an end to the performance of an existing obligation, such as put an end to a lease, for example....

A term is *suspensive* whenever it suspends or delays the right to demand the performance of an obligation until the term occurs. It means, therefore, that as long as the term has not occurred, the performance of the obligation cannot be demanded by the obligee, even though the obligation itself does exist....

An extinctive term is one which, when it occurs, brings an end to a binding commitment to perform an obligation. Once the event selected as the term occurs, the obligation which existed until then ceases to exist *ex nunc,* or prospectively....

A term is *certain* whenever the period of time preceding the occurrence of the event has been fixed. **LSA-C.C. Art. 1778.**...

A term is said to be *uncertain* only when the period of time preceding the occurrence of the definite event or term "is not fixed but is determinable either by the intent of the parties or by the occurrence of a future and certain event. It is also uncertain when it is not determinable, in which case the obligation must be performed within a reasonable time....

A conventional term is a term or certain event expressly or impliedly agreed upon between the parties to a contract (**LSA-C.C. Art. 1777**)....

A legal term is a term granted or imposed by law....

A judicial term, also called a period of grace, is a term granted by a court to a debtor who is sued by his creditor seeking performance of the obligation. The court may grant or deny this term of grace in consideration of the particular situation of the debtor....

The function of an extinctive term is to bring an end to the performance of an existing obligation. Therefore, before the happening of the extinctive term, the obligation is immediately enforceable as any pure and simple obligation would be....

The function of a suspensive term is to delay the performance or execution of an existing obligation until a certain time after that obligation has come into existence. It follows that the parties are subjected to a dual legal status: one which relates to that period of time before the occurrence of the suspensive term and the other which concerns the period of time that follows the happening of the term....

It is most important to stress that, although the execution or performance of the obligation is delayed until the term occurs, the obligation itself is born and does exist in the sense that it has created rights and obligations in the parties....

Upon occurrence or happening of the suspensive term, the obligor's performance becomes due, and the obligee may then demand that performance. It is important to state again that the occurrence of a term has no retroactive effect; in other words, the past relationship between the parties is unaffected by the occurrence of a term....

Cases

In re Liquidation of HIBERNIA BANK & TRUST CO.
In re INTERVENTION of D. H. HOLMES CO., Limited

Supreme Court of Louisiana
March 7, 1938
189 La. 813

FOURNET, Justice.

D. H. Holmes Company, Limited, intervened in the liquidation proceedings of the Hibernia Bank & Trust Company to have its note dated March 13, 1933, for $100,000, payable to the order of the bank on June 12, 1933, declared offset against its deposit in the bank and to have the said note returned to it marked paid.

The defense is that the two debts were not equally due and demandable at the time the bank was placed in liquidation on May 20, 1933, and, in reconvention, the Hibernia Bank & Trust Company, in liquidation, prayed for judgment for the balance due on the note, $57,000, with interest and attorney's fees.

[....]

It is provided by the Revised Civil Code that, 'when two persons are indebted to each other, there takes place between them a compensation that extinguishes both the debts,' * * * article 2207, and that 'compensation takes place * * * by the mere operation of law, even unknown to the debtors; the two debts are reciprocally extinguished, as soon as they exist simultaneously, to the amount of their respective sums,' article 2208, but '*compensation takes place only between two debts, having equally for their object a sum of money, * * * which are equally liquidated and demandable,*' article 2209. (Italics ours.) See, also, Brock et al. v. Pan American Petroleum Corporation, 186 La. 607, 173 So. 121; People's Bank in Liquidation v. Mississippi & Lafourche Drainage District, 141 La. 1009, 76 So. 179.

We deem it unnecessary to narrate the facts, in detail, of this case following the 'banking holidays,' because we have done so many times in other cases. Suffice it to say that beginning with the morning of March 2 to the time the State Bank Commissioner took over the affairs of the bank for liquidation, on May 20, 1933, it remained on a restricted basis whereby 5 per cent. of the intervener's deposit was made available and the remaining 95 per cent. frozen and unavailable. In the interim, on March 13th, intervener's note for $100,000 matured and was renewed by the execution of a new note for the same amount, payable on June 12, 1933.

The status of intervener's rights, both as a creditor by virtue of its deposit with the bank and as a debtor by virtue of its note due the bank, became fixed from the moment

35 the bank was placed in liquidation and its affairs taken over by the State Bank Commis-
36 sioner. Thomas v. Marine Bank & Trust Co., 156 La. 941, 101 So. 315; Brock et al. v. Pan
37 American Petroleum Corporation, supra; People's Bank in Liquidation v. Mississippi &
38 Lafourche Drainage District, supra.

39   But counsel for intervener contend [*sic*] that the obstacle to the compensation in this
40 case—the maturity date of the obligation—was removed by its letter of April 3, 1933,
41 wherein it requested that its note be offset by its frozen account. It is their contention
42 that the term of an obligation is in favor of the debtor and may be waived by him.

43   In support of their contention, counsel for intervener, in their brief, quote from arti-
44 cle 2053 of the Revised Civil Code as follows: '*The term is always presumed to be stipulated*
45 *in favor of the debtor.*' But this is qualified by the following: '*Unless it result from the stip-*
46 *ulation, or from circumstances, that it was also agreed upon in favor of the creditor.*' In the
47 instant case all the stipulations in the body of the note are expressly stated to be in favor
48 of the bank, and the evidence conclusively shows that that right has not been waived by
49 the bank. (Italics ours.)

50   In Daniel on Negotiable Instruments, 7th Ed., it is stated that 'payment (of a note)
51 can only be made before maturity by consent of both debtor and creditor,' Vol. 3, § 1416,
52 p. 1461; § 1418, p. 1464; and in Corpus Juris, that 'the maker of a note has no right to
53 pay the same before maturity without the consent of the holder,' Vol. 8, § 840, p. 603.

54   We therefore conclude that the two debts were not equally due and demandable at the
55 time the bank was placed in liquidation, and compensation did not take place under the
56 express provisions of articles 2207, 2208, and 2209 of the Revised Civil Code.

57   But it is argued by counsel for intervener that because the note was indorsed in blank
58 by William F. Tutt, assistant cashier, that 'the negotiation must have been made by the bank
59 itself, and not by the liquidators. As an endorser, by the terms of the note, it became a
60 party thereto, and the note provides that when any party goes into liquidation, the note
61 automatically matures.'

62   It is evident from a reading of the provisions of the note that the stipulations con-
63 tained therein and relied upon by counsel were not intended for the benefit of the mak-
64 ers or indorsers, etc.—in the instant case, the maker—but expressly for the bank's.

65   For the reasons assigned, the judgment of the lower court is affirmed; appellant to pay
66 all costs.

[....]

Questions

1. Line 9 *et seq.*: Please read the Code articles on "Compensation" (La. Civ. Code arts.
    1893–1902), "Loan" (La. Civ. Code arts. 2891–2913) and "Deposit" (La. Civil Code
    arts. 2926–2945).

2. Line 9 *et seq.*: Is D. H. Holmes a creditor of Hibernia Bank to the extent that Holmes
    has deposited money in the bank? What is the status of Holmes vis-à-vis its deposit
    account? Conversely, what is the legal status of the Bank vis-à-vis Holmes?

3. Lines 43–49: Why is Holmes claiming to be a debtor? A debtor of what? What legal
    ground could the court have cited (what Code article) in support of its statement: "all
    the stipulations of the note are expressly stated to be in favor of the bank" to the ex-
    tent it could apply to a term? Since a term is attached to the performance of an oblig-

ation, which party to a contract of loan above could claim the benefit of a term? If a term is a benefit to a party, could that party waive that term? Is there any legal support for your opinion in the Louisiana Civil Code?

4. Lines 54–56: Explain why the "two debts were not equally due and demandable at the time the bank was placed in liquidation...." Is Louisiana Civil Code article 1894 at all relevant? Going back to the Code articles on deposit, was the Court correct in writing about "two debts"? Were there really two debts or only one? If only one debt exists, can compensation take place?

HOUSING AUTHORITY OF THE TOWN OF LAKE ARTHUR, La.

v.

T. MILLER & SONS et al.

Supreme Court of Louisiana
April 25, 1960
120 So.2d 494

SIMON, Justice.

This is a suit by plaintiff, the Housing Authority of the Town of Lake Arthur, Louisiana,[1] against defendant, T. Miller & Sons, Contractor, seeking the recovery of $8,875.41 plus 10% Attorney's fees, for damages allegedly sustained by plaintiff arising from defendant contractor's refusal to comply with its bid and to execute a public construction contract for which defendant was the low bidder in response to plaintiff's invitation for bids.

The facts, as revealed by the record, show that in 1952, in order to construct the housing project and in order to be guaranteed the necessary funds therefor, plaintiff, in cooperation with the Government of the United States, in due and legal form advertised or invited bids on this project.

After a thorough examination of all conditions and specifications defendant partnership submitted a bid in the amount of $223,777.77, and simultaneously supplemented its bid by a notation on the envelope under the signature of David B. Miller reading:

'Deduct from our base bid the sum of $11,000.00. T. Miller & Sons by David Miller.'

Thus the final net bid submitted by defendant amounted to $212,777.77.

Conformably with the terms of the invitation and advertisement on April 22, 1952, at 2:00 o'clock P.M. plaintiff received, opened and read aloud defendant's bid, along with others. In accordance with the advertisement, as well as the invitation to bid and the specifications set out in the project, the local Housing Authority had thirty days subsequent to the opening of the bids within which to accept or reject any and all that had been submitted. The fact that this right of thirty days within which to accept or reject was well within the knowledge of defendant and that this privilege was part of the terms and conditions to the proposed contract is made evident by the provisions of the bid[2] submitted by the defendant.

---

1. A duly established public organization created and existing under the provisions of LSA-R.S. 40:381 et seq., and domiciled in Jefferson Davis Parish, Louisiana.

2. '1. The undersigned (T. Miller & Sons) having familiarized themselves * * * with the specifications including invitation for bids * * *.

It also appears that the invitation for bids expressly stipulated the following pertinent provision:

> 'No bid shall be withdrawn for a period of thirty (30) days subsequent to the opening of bids without the consent of the Housing Authority of the Town of Lake Arthur.'

The record further discloses that after the opening and reading of all submitted bids, and it appearing that the defendant had submitted the lowest, a resolution was proposed and unanimously adopted by the local Housing Authority authorizing its director to accept defendant's bid and to proceed with the execution of the contract, but subject to the following pertinent condition, viz.:

> 'Section 4. That the foregoing action and the contract to be executed is expressly declared to be subject to the approval of the Public Housing Administration.'

It further appears that by letter dated May 12, 1952, C. J. Stenzel, Director, Fort Worth Field Office of the United States Public Housing Administration, well within the thirty-day period, notified the local director that plaintiff had full power and authority to execute the construction contract with the defendant in accordance with the latter's bid, the construction to be limited to the parcels to which plaintiff had title. It also appears that this letter constituted an unqualified approval of defendant's proposed contract. For reasons not disclosed by the record, the local director failed to notify the defendant immediately of plaintiff's acceptance of the former's bid, other than is hereafter shown. However, it is shown by the testimony of the local director that prior to May 22, 1952, he made several unsuccessful telephone attempts to so notify the defendant.

It is also shown that on May 22, 1952, shortly after 2:00 P.M. defendant wired the plaintiff that it was withdrawing its bid which had been submitted at 2:00 o'clock P.M. on April 22, 1952. Knowledge of the contents of this telegram was first obtained in a telephone conversation had between the local director and the defendant and before its actual receipt later that day. As a consequence of this 'phone conversation, the local director wired the defendant notifying it of the local Housing Authority's acceptance of its bid, which telegram was received at its offices the same afternoon at 3:35 P.M. on May 22, 1952.

Upon defendant's refusal to execute the contract, the Housing Authority accepted the next lowest bid, which was submitted by the Lewis Lumber Company of Crowley, Louisiana, in the sum of $221,653.18. The Lewis Lumber Company constructed the housing units and was paid in full for its services in accordance with the terms of its bid. Whereupon the Housing Authority filed suit against defendant and its insurer and bondsmen to recover the difference between the bid of T. Miller & Sons and that of Lewis Lumber Company, namely $8,875.41 plus 10% Attorney's fees, the latter under the provisions of LSA-R.S. 22:658.[3]

---

2. 'In submitting this bid, it is understood that the right is reserved by the Housing Authority of the Town of Lake Arthur to reject any and/or all bids. If written notice of the acceptance of this bid is mailed, telegraphed or delivered to the undersigned (defendant) *within thirty days after the opening thereof,* or at any time thereafter before this bid has been withdrawn, the undersigned agrees to execute and deliver a contract in the prescribed form and furnish the required bond within 10 days after the contract is presented to him for signature.' (Italics ours.)

3. 'All insurers issuing any type of contract other than those specified in R.S. 22:656 and 22:657 shall pay the amount of any claim due any insured including any employee under Chapter 10 of Title 23 of the Revised Statutes of 1950 within sixty days after receipt of satisfactory proofs of loss from the insured, employee or any party in interest. Failure to make such payment within sixty days after receipt of such proofs and demand therefor, when such failure is found to be arbitrary, capricious, or without probable cause, shall subject the insurer to a penalty, in addition to the amount of the loss,

The trial judge rendered judgment in favor of defendant, assigning as his reasons the   70
following: 71

'The Court is of the opinion that the inserting of Section 4 of the contract by   72
plaintiff changed the terms of the bid of defendant partnership in that it made   73
it conditional upon its approval by a third party and was, therefore, unenforce-   74
able. See Fontenot v. Huguet (230 La. 483), 89 So.2d 45.   75

'However, should the above conclusion be wrong, the Court is still of the   76
opinion that plaintiff cannot recover for the reason that the defendant partner-   77
ship withdraw its offer timely and before an acceptance by plaintiff. The bids   78
were opened at 2:00 P.M. on April 22, 1952. Shortly after 2:00 P.M. on May 22,   79
1952, defendant partnership withdrew its bid prior to acceptance by plaintiff.   80
The 30 day period had expired.'   81

Plaintiff perfected its appeal.   82

Two principal defenses are here involved. [....] The first defense is that there was no   83
acceptance of the contractor's bid as the alleged acceptance was qualified and conditioned   84
upon the approval of the Public Housing Authority, a third party. The second defense, urged   85
in the alternative, is that defendant's bid was legally withdrawn after the expiration of   86
thirty days and prior to notification of acceptance of the bid or award of the contract.   87

The first question presented by this appeal is whether the acceptance of defendant's bid   88
by the Housing Authority was conditional and unenforceable as found by the trial judge.   89

LSA-R.S. 38:2211–2217 prescribe the manner in which contracts may be let for con-   90
struction by any public corporation or political subdivision. Section 2212 thereof pro-   91
vides for the designation of the time and place that the bids will be opened and the contract   92
let, and it further provides that the governing authority 'shall at the place and time spec-   93
ified open the bids and let the contract. The governing authority may reject any and all   94
bids.' Hence, defendant contends that on the day the bids were opened it was mandatory   95
that the Housing Authority, under the provisions of said Section, unconditionally accept   96
the lowest bid or reject all the bids; that by including in the resolution of acceptance the   97
condition that the acceptance was to be subject to the approval of the Public Housing   98
Administration, there was neither an unqualified acceptance of the lowest bid nor a re-   99
jection of all the bids as required by law; and that any action taken by the Public Hous-   100
ing Administration, or anyone else, not directly a party to the advertisement and reception   101
of bids, cannot be used as a substitute for the specific mandate statutorily prescribed.   102

It is manifest that under the plain and unmistakable terms and conditions of the ad-   103
vertisement and invitation for bids, plaintiff had the unquestioned right of either ac-   104
cepting or rejecting defendant's bid within the period of thirty days from the date (April   105
22, 1952) of the opening of the bids. The defendant expressly recognized and bound it-   106
self accordingly in submitting its written bid as hereinabove referred to. It is common   107
knowledge that a reasonable delay, in this instance a thirty-day period, is usually included   108
in all bidding for public construction or works preceding the formal acceptance or award   109
of the contract. This delay thus affords the parties an opportunity to investigate, among   110
others, the moral attending risks, an adequate opportunity to investigate the ability, fi-   111

---

of 12% Damages on the total amount of the loss, payable to the insured, or to any of said employees, together with all reasonable attorney's fees for the prosecution and collection of such loss, or in
the event a partial payment or tender has been made, 12% Of the difference between the amount
paid or tendered and the amount found to be due and all reasonable attorney's fees for the prosecution and collection of such amount. * * *'

nancial, workmanship or otherwise, of the bidder or offerer to perform the contract in an acceptable manner, not excluding the preparation of the formal contract. It must be borne in mind that this public work was being done with financial aid from the Public Housing Administration, and needless to say, the Federal Government, through its Housing Agency, would necessarily insist that the submitted bid, with all heretofore mentioned factors, be first approved by it during the thirty-day period prescribed.

There can be no doubt that defendant was cognizant of the fact that the proposed contract was being financed through local and Federal public funds and that the formal approval of the proposed contract by both agencies was indispensable. This approval by the federal agency is fully established by its letter of May 12, 1952, well within the thirty-day period. Conceding the proviso of Section 4, supra, subjecting the execution of the contract to the approval thereof by the federal agency, to be a suspensive condition, it follows that once the proposed contract was approved, as it is shown to be, the condition became fulfilled, and may be deemed eliminated, thus affording plaintiff the right to accept or reject defendant's bid so long that affirmative action in either instance was exercised and accomplished within the thirty-day period mutually recognized.

Our Codal Articles wisely provide that conditional obligations are such as are made to depend on an uncertain event, and is suspensive when the obligation is not to take effect until the happening of the event.[4] It is further provided that when an obligation has been contracted on condition that an event shall happen within a limited time, when the time he expired without the event having taken place, the condition is considered as broken.[5] Manifestly, by analogy and equal reasoning, when the condition is one performed within the limited time the condition becomes fulfilled and is binding and enforceable.

[....]

We now consider the second defense, whether the acceptance of plaintiff was timely. Defendant contended, and was upheld by the district court, that the thirty-day period during which plaintiff could accept or reject its bid began to run at 2:00 o'clock P.M. on April 22, the day the bids were received and opened, and ended at 2:00 o'clock P.M. on May 22. If we accept this view, plaintiff's acceptance by telegram to the defendant at about 3:30 o'clock P.M. on May 22 came too late as defendant had already withdrawn its bid at 2:02 o'clock P.M. that same afternoon. While counsel for defendant has devoted a large portion of the argument in his brief to this proposition, the authorities relied on are inapposite from a legal and factual standpoint. It cites Ratcliff v. Louisiana Industrial Life Ins. Co., 185 La. 557, 169 So. 572; and Richardson v. American Nat. Ins. Co., 18 La.App. 468, 137 So. 370, both involving insurance policy claims in which the contract provided that the policy was to be effective on the date on which it was written. Naturally, the date on which the policy was written, by the very provisions of the contract itself, would be counted in determining its enforceable term. Counsel for defendant also cites election contest cases, namely Smith v. Fitch, La.App., 194 So. 435, and Brown v. Democratic Parish Committee, 183 La. 967, 165 So. 167, in which the courts held that the delay for

---

4. LSA-C.C. Article 2021: 'Conditional obligations are such as are made to depend on an uncertain event. If the obligation is not to take effect until the event happen, it is a suspensive condition; if the obligation takes effect immediately, but is liable to the defeated when the event happens, it is then a resolutory condition.'

5. LSA-C.C. Article 2038: 'When an obligation has been contracted on condition that an event shall happen within a limited time, the condition is considered as broken, when the time has expired without the event having taken place. If there be no time fixed, the condition may always be performed, and it is not considered as broken, until it is become certain that the event will not happen.'

filing suit begins at the time of the promulgation of the election, not the day after. Clearly these cases are inapplicable and not controlling as to contracts, which are peculiarly governed by Articles 2057[6] and 2058[7] of the LSA-Civil Code.

In the case at bar it is obvious to us that the provision that 'If written notice of the acceptance of this bid * * * within thirty days after the opening thereof, or at any time thereafter before this bid has been withdrawn, the undersigned agrees to execute and deliver a contract in the prescribed form and furnish the required bond within ten days after the contract is presented to him for signature,' shows that the parties clearly contemplated that both periods of time alluded to therein meant, and was intended to mean thirty full days, or in the latter instance ten full days, and not a fraction of a day. It is equally clear to us that the fact that a meeting called for the hour of 2:00 o'clock P.M., after which hour the bids would be opened, read and publicly announced, was not intended as the specific time in which the thirty-day period would begin to run, this hour being one to satisfy the convenience of all interested parties and at which time the meeting would be called to order and thereafter proceed with the orderly process of business. We cannot say that because the meeting was called for 2:00 P.M. necessarily means the actual opening of the bids at that exact hour.

We think, and we are supported in that view by the great weight of modern authority, that in the construction of contracts and statutes, when an act is to be performed within a specified period from or after a day named, the rule is to exclude the first day and to include the last day of the specified period.

In the case here the word 'after' is used. Generally, when computing time 'after' an act, the day on which the event took place is excluded. American Jurisprudence, Vol. 52, Sections 17 and 27, pages 342 and 352.

Our Code of Practice, Articles 180 and 318, in the computation of time for delays in filing pleadings, do not consider fractions of a day.

Hence, the Housing Authority had thirty full days subsequent to the opening of the bids to accept or reject defendant's low bid. In effect, it had until sunset of May 22, 1952, and its telegraphed acceptance of the proposed contract between 2:00 and 3:00 o'clock P.M. on that day, which defendant admits was received by it, constituted a legal and enforceable acceptance of the contract within the thirty-day period to which defendant bound itself.

In oral argument before this Court, both parties agreed that it [*sic*] plaintiff is entitled to recover in this suit, the amount of $8,875.41 sought in its petition to the district court is correct.

[....]

Questions

1. Lines 24 *et seq.* and footnote 2: What kind of term, if any, would you say is the Court referring to? What legal adjectives would you use to describe whatever term may

---

6. 'Where a term is given or limited for the performance of an obligation, the obligor has until sunset of the last day limited for its performance, to comply with his obligation, unless the object of the contract can not be done after certain hours of that day.'

7. 'When the contract is to do the act in a certain number of days, or in a certain number of days after the date of the contract, the day of contract is not included in the number of days to be counted, and the obligor has until sunset of the last day of the number enumerated for the performance of his contract, with the exception contained in the last preceding article.'

exist? Explain your answer in proper legal language. Assuming a term exists, in whose favor is it? Does the Louisiana Civil Code lay down a presumption? What is the legal nature of the obligation entered into by the defendant, Miller & Sons? What is, in turn, the legal nature of the obligation binding the Housing Authority?

2. Lines 38–54: Could you provide some important legal details on what the Court refers to summarily as "the following pertinent condition"? Do you think that the Court meant 'condition' in the sense of Louisiana Civil Code articles 1767–1776 or, instead, in the sense of a charge or duty? Under the facts of this case, was a condition to happen within a term? Explain.

3. Lines 55–61: Does the defendant's argument based on its computation of the time make sense? Could the defendant have found support for his argument in the Louisiana Civil Code? Note that the trial judge "'rendered judgment in favor of defendant....'" *See* lines 70–81. Besides citing a case, is there any other legal authority for the trial judge's ruling?

4. Lines 103–127: In your opinion, does the Court give a fair/good explanation of the interaction between a suspensive condition and a term? Could the Court have made the distinction clearly by quoting specific Louisiana Civil Code articles? What is the Court actually saying in the following statement (found on lines 122–127): "Conceding the proviso of Section 4, subjecting the execution of the contract to the approval thereof by the federal agency, to be a suspensive condition, it follows that once the proposed contract was approved ... the condition became fulfilled, and may be deemed eliminated, thus affording plaintiff the right to accept...."?

5. Lines 136 *et seq.*: Read again Question 3 above. What was your answer? Why is the Court, in this paragraph (in lines 142–154) saying that "while counsel for defendant has devoted ... the authorities relied on are inapposite from a legal and factual standpoint...."? Can it be said that counsel for defendant did not do his homework in not referring to the Louisiana Civil Code to begin with? Remember the Court stating that "our Codal Articles wisely provide ..." on line 128?

6. Lines 155 *et seq.*: Read footnotes 6 & 7 and read Louisiana Civil Code article 1784. Do you see any major difference? Is the Court making a wise/proper application of then-existing Louisiana Civil Code articles 2057–2058? Would the application of Louisiana Civil Code article 1784 lead to a different result?

HOLMES BRICK & SALVAGE CO., Inc.

v.

REO CONSTRUCTION, INC.

Louisiana Court of Appeal

First Circuit

Sept. 2, 1971

253 So.2d 562

BLANCHE, Judge.

This matter involves a controversy over a default judgment taken by plaintiff. [....] [T]he following evidence was presented at the confirmation of the default:

'The evidence presented by plaintiff on confirmation consisted of the original contract which was the subject of the suit, the testimony of Mr. Philip H. Holmes, President of the plaintiff corporation, and the affidavit of Mr. Holmes previously filed in the record. The testimony of Mr. Holmes was as follows:

'According to Mr. Holmes, defendant, Reo Construction, Inc., had been hired as general contractor by the Wilberts to construct a new funeral home on the site of Wilbert's Funeral Home in Plaquemine, Louisiana. At the request of the architect for the project, plaintiff examined the Wilbert's property in Plaquemine and gave an estimate setting the price at which plaintiff would demolish and remove the two existing buildings on the Wilbert's property. Plaintiff did make an estimate which consisted of two parts, first, the charge for demolishing and removing a certain smaller building on the rear of the Wilbert property, and second, the charge for demolishing and removing the large building on the front of the Wilbert property which housed the old funeral home. Defendant was not present at this examination. The witness further stated that subsequent to the examination he sent his son, Michael Holmes, to meet with the architect, the Wilberts, and defendant, at which time Michael Holmes made it quite clear to them that any contract entered into by plaintiff would have to provide for plaintiff demolishing and removing both of the buildings.

'Mr. Holmes then explained how such an estimate is made for demolition work. According to his testimony, the usual contract entails the demolition contractor acquiring (ownership) to all or a part of the salvaged materials. It is first necessary to determine the value of the salvage to be realized from a particular building before setting any additional charge for the demolition and removal. The actual charge will then be smaller, if the value of salvaged materials is large, and vice versa.

'Mr. Holmes then identified and explained the contract which he drafted pursuant to his understanding with the parties and pursuant to the estimate, whereby plaintiff agreed to demolish and remove the two buildings in question in two designated phases. Phase #1 involved demolition and removal of the smaller building at the rear of the Wilbert property at a charge of $1,500.00, the salvaged materials to become the property of the plaintiff. Phase #2 involved the demolition and removal of the large building on the front of the Wilbert property at a charge of $4,000.00, the salvaged materials to become the property of the plaintiff. The witness explained that the second phase of the contract was to be performed at a time designated by defendant, which stipulation was included in the contract. Mr. Holmes signed the contract on behalf of plaintiff and forwarded same to Mr. Ray Roussel, who signed on behalf of defendant.

'The testimony of Mr. Holmes further indicated that Phase #1 of the contract was performed by plaintiff and payment in full was received therefor. However, he then stated that defendant never called upon plaintiff to perform Phase #2 of the contract, and that someone else demolished the large building on the front of the Wilbert property.' (Narrative of Facts, Record, pp. 15-A, 15-B)

The contract was offered into evidence and under the date thereof is the following notation:

'Re: Demolition of two buildings at Wilbert's Funeral Home; Plaquemine, La. Work to be done in two phases numbered one and two.' (Exhibit P-1, Record, p. 6)

Phase 2 of the contract referred to above provides:

'* * * At a time designated by you, we will demolish and remove the large building on the front of the property. Our charge for this part of the demolition is $4000.00 (four thousand dollars) payable to us upon completion.' (Exhibit P-1, Record, p. 6)

Plaintiff's suit against the defendant alleges a breach of contract as a result of plaintiff's failure to call upon him to demolish the building called for in Phase 2 of the contract and by permitting the building to be removed by someone else. Damages were sought totaling $7,500 and consist of $4,000 as the agreed contract price and $3,500 as the value of the salvage materials to be derived from the performance of Phase No. 2 of the contract. The Court accepted the estimate of Mr. Holmes as to the value of the salvage material and gave plaintiff judgment as prayed for. From the default judgment in favor of plaintiff, the defendant took this appeal.

The defendant contends that the setting of a time for the plaintiff's performance of Phase 2 was a suspensive condition of the contract. In support of this contention defendant cites the following articles of the Civil Code:

> 'Art. 2021. Conditional obligations are such as are made to depend on an uncertain event. If the obligation is not to take effect until the event happen, it is a suspensive condition; if the obligation takes effect immediately, but is liable to be defeated when the event happens, it is then a resolutory condition.'

> 'Art. 2043. The obligation contracted on a suspensive condition, is that which depends, either on a future and uncertain event, or on an event which has actually taken place, without its being yet known to the parties.

> 'In the former case, the obligation can not be executed till after the event; in the latter, the obligation has its effect from the day on which it was contracted, but it can not be enforced until the event be known.'

The future and uncertain event in this case is alleged to be the defendant's designation of a time for the demolition of the building described in Phase 2 of its contract with plaintiff. We reject this interpretation in favor of plaintiff's argument that the words 'at a time designated by you' constitute the term for the performance of the contract.[1]

In this case the parties had reached an agreement which was complete in all respects except for the time of performance. The 'event' of demolition was certain. The only element of uncertainty was that pertaining to When the demolition would become necessary. Obviously, it was to occur when the defendant's progress on the contract with Wilbert's Funeral Home reached the point where the building described in Phase 2 of the contract was available for demolition and removal.

The words 'at a time designated by you' cannot be construed to mean that the defendant reserved the right to refrain from Ever designating a time. This is not a case of a contract that leaves the defendant the option of requesting the plaintiff's performance. In other words, the contract does not read 'at a time designated by you If you decide to set a time,' nor does it read 'at a time designated by you If you decide to choose us as the demolition company for Phase 2 of the contract.' Instead, the contract called for the plaintiff's performance of Phase 1 immediately and Phase 2 at a date to be determined in the

---

1. Articles 2048–2051 of the Civil Code are pertinent to this interpretation:

'Art. 2048. The time given or limited for the performance of an obligation, is called its Term.'

'Art. 2049. A term may not only consist of a determinate lapse of time, but also of an event, provided that event be in the course of nature, certain; if it be uncertain, it forms a condition.'

'Art. 2050. When no term is fixed by the parties for the performance of the obligation, it may be executed immediately, unless, from the nature of the act, a term, either certain or uncertain, must be implied. Thus, an obligation to pay money, without any stipulation for time, may be enforced at the will of the obligee. But a promise to make a crop of sugar is necessarily deferred, until the uncertain period when the cane shall be fit to cut.'

'Art. 2051. The term differs from the condition, inasmuch as it does not suspend the engagement, but only retards its execution.'

future. Phase 1 was completed as contemplated by the parties; however, the plaintiff's 98
performance of Phase 2 of the contract was never sought by the defendant. Defendant should 99
have sought plaintiff's performance when defendant's progress of the contract with 100
Wilbert's Funeral Home reached the point where the building described in Phase 2 was 101
available for demolition and removal. This event was to occur, and did occur, in the 102
course of defendant's work for Wilbert's. 103

Since defendant did not designate a time for plaintiff's performance, we hold that plain- 104
tiff is entitled to damages for defendant's breach of Phase 2 of the contract described herein. 105

[....]

Questions

1. Lines 11 *et seq.*: Describe in legal terms the kinds of obligations created, for example, to do v. not to do; result v. means; personal v. heritable; etc.

2. Lines 51 *et seq.*: Read carefully the two short excerpts from the contract. What is your
   understanding of the phrase "at a time designated by you"? Does that phrase signify
   that the contract contains a term and/or a condition? If you answered "term", what
   kind? If you answered "condition", what kind?

3. Line 68–69: What do you think of the defendant's argument? If there exists a suspensive
   condition, what other adjective could you add to better describe that condition? Is
   the defendant wise in making this argument? *See* La. Civ. Code art. 1772.

4. Lines 81 *et seq.*: Do you agree with the Court endorsing the plaintiff's argument? Can
   you describe in proper legal terms why "the event of demolition was certain"? Does it
   matter whether it is the obligee or the obligor of the obligation who designates the time?

5. Lines 91 *et seq.*: Can you identify the kind of obligation or obligations the court might
   be considering when it states, basically, that the defendant had no option but to designate a time?

6. Lines 104–105: Shouldn't this statement of the Court have been grounded in at least
   one Louisiana Civil Code article? If you answered in the affirmative, which one?
   Couldn't the outcome of the case have been the same had the Court held that there
   existed a suspensive condition (instead of a term)? Consider Louisiana Civil Code
   article 1772 carefully.

F. J. DeMARY   1
v.   2
Louis A. FONTENOT   3
Louisiana Court of Appeal   4
Third Circuit   5
Feb. 18, 1964   6
161 So.2d 82   7

FRUGE, Judge.   8

This suit was brought to enforce an agreement made between plaintiff and the defen- 9
dant for the sale of certain race horses. 10

On August 21, 1959, at Orange, Texas, plaintiff and defendant entered into an agree- 11
ment whereby plaintiff did 'sell, transfer, assign and deliver' to the defendant six partic- 12

ular horses. The total consideration was stated as $9,200 which, according to the agreement, was to be paid in the following manner:

'THE TOTAL CONSIDERATION for all of the above named Race Horses is NINE THOUSAND TWO HUNDRED ($9,200.00) DOLLARS which is payable in the manner as set out, expressly stipulated and fully agreed on as follows:

"IN THE EVENT either of the above named Race Horses is Sold outright or is Claimed in a Race known and termed as a Claiming Race, the entire Sale Price or the Claiming Price, whichever applies, is to be surrendered to and delivered to the Seller, F. J. DeMary, at his office in the City of Orange, Orange County, Texas, and the amount so paid or surrendered to F. J. DeMary shall be applied by him on the full Purchase Price of NINE THOUSAND TWO HUNDRED ($9,200.00) DOLLARS. ON ALL EARNINGS at various Race Tracks where these Race Horses might be raced, the Seller, F. J. DeMary, is to receive and is to be paid an amount equivalent to Forty (40%) Per Cent of the Net Purse, meaning the Track Winning Purse, whether the Purse be for Winning, Placing, Showing or Placing Fourth, or such percentage fully applies to the winnings as commonly termed 'Across the Board' and it is understood that such payments are to be continued until the Seller, F. J. DeMary, has been paid the full Selling Price of NINE THOUSAND TWO HUNDRED ($9,200.00) DOLLARS."

Plaintiff brought suit in St. Landry Parish praying for a judgment for the amount of the purchase price and that his vendor's privilege be recognized and maintained against the property. The defendant filed an untitled exception which was maintained by the district judge. From this ruling plaintiff appeals.

[....]

Defendant contends that since the total consideration is not to be paid until the horses are either 'claimed' or have won a race or races, such operates as a suspensive condition to the completion of the contract until the horses are raced. Plaintiff argues that this is merely a method of paying the purchase price.

In considering the exception we must accept the pleaded facts of the plaintiff. In his pleading plaintiff alleges that defendant is indebted to the plaintiff, that the plaintiff received no payment whatsoever despite amicable demand for payment, and that defendant has actively breached the contract. Whether these alleged facts are true or not is a matter for the trial court to decide when trying the case on the merits. Regardless of whether the agreement contains a suspensive condition or is merely a method of payment, the facts pleaded by plaintiff show that there was an agreement and are sufficiently set forth to entitle plaintiff to a trial on the merits.

[....]

Defendant also contends that the agreement contains a potestative condition because the performance of the agreement is conditioned solely upon the horses being raced.

'Every obligation is null, that has been contracted, on a potestative condition, on the part of him who binds himself.' LSA-Civil Code art. 2034. 'The last preceding article is limited to potestative conditions, which make the obligation depend solely on the exercise of the obligor's will; but if the condition be, that the obligor shall do or not do a certain act, although the doing or not doing of the act depends on the will of the obligor, yet the obligation depending on such condition, is not void.' LSA-Civil Code art. 2035. In Long v. Foster & Associates, Inc., 242 La. 295, 136 So.2d 48, 53, the Supreme Court stated that 'Article 2034, because of the limitations placed on it by

Article 2035, is applicable only to the Purely potestative condition, that is, one which is subject only to the Whim or pleasure of the promisor and would involve no detriment, disadvantage or inconvenience to him if he brings about or hinders the happening of the event on which the obligation depends.' (Emphasis added.) Thus, we must determine in the present case whether the condition imposed for the payment of the price was purely potestative, depending merely on the whim or pleasure of the promisor. Actually, the issue is whether or not the legal freedom of the plaintiff was limited in any way. Here, if defendant sold the horses or if they were claimed, he had to pay the plaintiff. If defendant raced the horses a portion of the earnings would have to be paid to the plaintiff. Certainly this was a limit on defendant's legal freedom to use the property. There was therefore no purely potestative condition involved in the agreement.

For the foregoing reasons the maintaining of the exception by the district court is reversed and the case is remanded for proceedings not inconsistent with this opinion.

Reversed and remanded.

CULPEPPER, Judge (dissenting).

I respectfully dissent from the majority decision that the exception of no cause of action must be overruled. It is my opinion that the exception of no cause of action should be sustained, because the contract contained a suspensive condition, as to a future and uncertain event, which is not alleged to have taken place. However, I think this case should be remanded to the district court, for the purpose of allowing plaintiff to amend his petition, so as to allege that the suspensive condition has been fulfilled.

LSA-C.C. Art. 2043 provides that if an obligation is contracted on a suspensive condition, as to a future and uncertain event, the obligation is not due until after the event has taken place. Under the contract in question, plaintiff sold the defendant six race horses for the price of $9,200. The contract expressly states that this purchase price is not to be paid unless or until the horses either: (1) are sold outright by the defendant or (2) are claimed in a 'claiming race' or (3) win money in a race. It seems clear to me that these are suspensive conditions, the effect of which is that the purchase price does not become due unless or until one of these events takes place.

Plaintiff's petition alleges only the contract and that plaintiff has not been paid the purchase price for the horses. The petition does not allege that the horses have ever won any money in a race or that they have ever been claimed in a 'claiming race' or that they have been sold outright by the defendant. Thus, under the contract, which is the law between the parties, the plaintiff has failed to state a cause of action in that he has failed to allege that any of these suspensive conditions, on which the obligation to pay the purchase price depends, have taken place.

These suspensive conditions cannot be lightly brushed aside, as the majority has done, by simply stating that, regardless of whether the agreement contains a suspensive condition, the facts pleaded show that there was an agreement by the defendant to pay the purchase price. In my view, the express stipulation for payment, only in the event of certain events taking place, was of the very essence of the agreement. Horse racing is a most precarious business. The parties to this contract didn't know whether these horses would ever win money or be claimed in a claiming race. It appears to me they clearly intended that unless and until one of these events occurred, defendant would not have to pay anything on the purchase price. (It is not disputed that a contract can provide for payment only from certain specified sources. Williams v. Ligon, La.App., 144 So.2d 131 and the cases cited therein; 40 Am.Jur. 734, Verbo Payment, Section 33.)

108 I agree with the majority that there was no purely potestative condition in this contract.
109 I do not think it was left entirely within the power of the defendant to determine whether
110 or not he ever paid the purchase price. LSA-C.C. Art. 2024. I think there was an implied
111 condition that the horses would be raced in an effort to win money or have the horses claimed.
112 LSA-C.C. Art. 2026. However, if it is the contention of the plaintiff that there was an im-
113 plied obligation on the part of the defendant to race the horses, and that defendant has
114 prevented the fulfillment of the suspensive conditions by failing to enter the horses in a
115 race, then in order to state a cause of action under the contract he must certainly allege
116 such facts. (Plaintiff's counsel stated to us in oral argument that the horses actually have
117 been raced but counsel did not state whether the horses have won any money or been
118 claimed in a claiming race.)

119 In his brief filed in this court, counsel for the plaintiff has, in the alternative, asked
120 that in the event we conclude the exception of no cause of action must be sustained, we
121 remand this case to the district court for the purpose of allowing him to amend his pe-
122 tition so as to allege that the suspensive conditions have taken place. I think the case
123 should be remanded to the lower court for this purpose, in accordance with the provi-
124 sions of LSA-C.C.P. Art. 934 which provides for amendment within a delay allowed by
125 the court.

[....]

Questions

1. Lines 9–139: After you have read the case, please read carefully Louisiana Civil Code article 2439 defining the contract of sale. In the instant case, was a price agreed upon? Was there an agreement as to the object of the sale, i.e., the horses and their number? Without going into any detail, was there a sale in your opinion? Look now at Louisiana Civil Code article 2456. On the basis of these two articles, where was the ownership of the horses: with the seller or with the buyer?

2. Lines 15–31: Describe in legal terms the modalities of payment of the price. Remember that the buyer is bound to pay the price, but the modalities of payment of the price may vary.

3. Lines 37 *et seq.*: What do you think of the defendant's exception based on the existence of his suspensive condition theory? Would a suspensive condition affect, in this case, the formation of the contract or the performance of its obligations to pay the price by the buyer? Remember that under Louisiana Civil Code article 2456, the ownership of the horses had passed to the buyer. What, then, is your answer?

4. Lines 50 *et seq.*: Why would the defendant argue that the agreement contains a potestative condition? What kind of potestative condition? What kind of condition is the court referring to: suspensive or resolutory? Considering that the defendant had the ownership of the horses and was to pay the price, if the condition affects the buyer's performance of having to pay the price, what should happen if the buyer does not pay the price? Is the condition, now, still suspensive or not?

5. Lines 9–125: Including the dissenting opinion in this question, is it conceivable that the judges failed to draw the proper line between an uncertain suspensive term and a suspensive condition? Can you explain the difference(s) between the two?

See also *Turner v. Watson*, 912 So.2d 391 (La. 2nd Cir. 2005).

Comparative Law Perspective

Robert J. Pothier, A Treatise on the Law of Obligations or Contracts
vo. 1, n°s 227-232, at 130-32, & n°s 198-201, at 111-12 (William David Evans trans., 1806)

Article III
Of a Term of Payment

[227] An obligation is either contracted with a term for discharging it, or not: when it is contracted without a term, the creditor may require it to be discharged immediately; when it includes a term, he cannot require it until the term is expired.

§ I *What a Term of Payment is, and the different Kinds of it.*

[228] A term is a space of time granted to the debtor for discharging his obligation: there are express terms, resulting from the positive stipulations of the agreement; as where I undertake to pay a certain sum on a certain day; and also terms which tacitly result from the nature of the things which are the object of the engagement, or from the place where the act is agreed to be done. For instance, if a builder engages to construct a house for me, I must allow a reasonable time for his fulfilling his engagement. If a person at *Orleans* undertakes to deliver something to my correspondent at *Rome*, the engagement tacitly includes the time necessary for taking the thing to *Rome*....

§ II. *Of the Effect of a Term, and in what Respect it differs from a Condition*

[230] A term differs from a condition, inasmuch as a condition suspends the engagement formed by the agreement: whereas a term does not suspend the engagement, but merely postpones the execution of it....

[231] A term defers the right of requiring payment until it is fully completed. Therefore if I promise to pay this year, no demand can be enforced on the last day; for that day is comprised within the term.

[232] This effect of a term, in postponing the right of requiring payment until it is expired, is common to a term of right, and to a term of grace.

A term of right has another effect which is peculiar to itself, viz. that it prevents the debt being opposed by way of compensation or set-off, until it is expired....

Article I
Of Suspensive Conditions, (a) and Conditional Obligations

[198] A conditional obligation, is that which is suspended by the condition under which it was contracted, and which is not yet accomplished....

§ I. *What a Condition is, and its different Kinds.*

[199] A condition is the case of a future uncertain event, which may or may not happen, and upon which the obligation is made to depend.

[200] Conditions upon which an obligation may be suspended, are divided into positive and negative.

A positive condition consists in the case where a thing that may or may not happen, shall happen, as *if I marry.*

A negative condition is that, which consists in the case where something, that may or may not happen, shall not happen, as *if I do not marry.*

[201] Conditions are also distinguished into potestative, casual, and mixed.

A potestative condition is that, which is in the power of the person in whose favor the obligation is contracted; (a) as if I engage to give my neighbor a sum of money, in case he cuts down a tree which obstructs my prospect.

A casual condition is that, which depends upon accident, and is no wise in the power of the creditor, as *if such a ship shall arrive safe.*

A mixed condition is that, which depends upon the concurrence of the will of the creditor, and of a third person; as if you marry my cousin.

———————

Impossible Conditions: Meaning of "Impossible"

Robert Pothier, Traité des Obligations

vol. 1, n° 204, at 211 & 212 (2d ed. 1825)

The condition of an impossible thing ... under which someone promises something renders the [juridical] act [from which the promise springs] absolutely null when that impossible thing is *in faciendo* [i.e., when it involves doing something]. No obligation is born from such an act.... [A]s if I have promised you a sum under this condition: *if you make a triangle without angles.*...

...

When the impossible condition is *in non faciendo* [i.e., when it involves *not* doing something], as if I have promised you a sum *if you do not stop the sun in its course*, it does not render null the obligation under which it is contracted. This condition has no effect, and the obligation is pure and simple.

———————

C.-B.-M. Toullier, Le Droit Civil Français

vo. 3, n° 481 & 482, at 307 (J.-B. Duvergier rev., 6th ed. c. 1846)

481. A condition is impossible when the accustomed order of nature is an obstacle to its accomplishment. Roman legislation gave as examples of it [i] if you touch heaven with your finger, [ii] if you drink all the water in the sea, [iii] if you give me a centaur, etc. This is a natural impossibility.

A condition that's possible in itself can become impossible by reason of some circumstance that gets added to it. For example, the condition of building a house *in three days.* This is what one calls impossibility of fact.

...

Finally, there are some impossibilities that are absolute and others that are only relative and personal. It is impossible *for me* to make a painting or a statue as Girodet or Canova could do it.

...

482. Because the Code does not explain what it means by an impossible condition, some doubt can arise. There is no doubt, however, in regard to natural impossibility and impossibility in fact. As to relative impossibility, Roman legislation determined that it does *not* annul contracts and that a stipulation is valid, even though a person engages himself to do a thing that is personally impossible for him, if it is possible for another. This determination ought to be continued under the domain of the Code, for it is founded in reason.

———————

Gabriel Baudry-Lacantinerie et Louis Joseph Barde,
TRAITÉ THÉORIQUE ET PRATIQUE DE DROIT CIVIL

tome XII (DES OBLIGATIONS tome II) n°s 809–826, at 34–49 (2d ed. 1902)

[35] ...

809. ... [L]et us determine the bearing of the principle formulated in the first part of Article 1179 ["A condition, once fulfilled, has effects that are retroactive to the day on which the engagement was contracted."]: after the occurrence of the conditional event, the situation is the same as if the obligation had arisen at the moment of the contract and had been immediately perfected....

[39] ...

The retroactive effect of a fulfilled condition ... is ... [a] fiction.... [S]ince this retroactivity is a fiction, it is appropriate to use a restrictive interpretation in cases in which it is doubtful that retroactivity should be applied.

810. Inasmuch as Article 1179 is conceived in the most general terms, the principle of retroactivity is applied in the system of our Civil Code regardless whether the condition is suspensive or resolutory....

815. From the point of view of conditional ownership, here are the principal consequences of retroactivity:

1° When an obligation to give a certain and determined thing has been contracted subject to a suspensive condition, the creditor, once the condition is fulfilled, will been deemed to have become the owner from the very day of the contract. It follows from this that all real rights to which the alienator consents in the interval between the making of the contract and the realization of the condition will be effaced, not simply for the future, but also for the past, in such a fashion that, in the eyes of the law, they will have never existed. In fact, these real rights turn out to have emanated from a person who, at the moment at which he granted them, was not the owner.

816. 2° In an inverse sense, again in a case involving the accomplishment of a suspensive condition, the real rights granted on the thing by the acquirer *pendente conditione* turn out to have existed starting from the moment at which they were granted....

[42] ...

817. 3° In the case of an alienation under a resolutory condition, real rights constituted on the thing by the acquirer, while the condition was in suspense, are reputed, once the condition is realized, never to have arisen.... (l) Thus, contracts whereby the acquirer under a resolutory condition has granted real rights on the alienated immovable to third persons are annihilated by the occurrence of the condition....

818. 4° In an inverse sense, in the same hypothetical case [an alienation subject to a resolutory condition], ... real rights granted on the thing by the alienator *pendente conditione* turn out to have been granted by the owner and, as a result, to have been acquired from the moment of the making of the contract....

819. 5° When an immovable sold under a suspensive condition is seized and judicially sold at the request of one of the creditors of the seller, this seizure and this judicial sale, in the even that the condition should be realized, cannot be asserted against the conditional acquirer, if the title of the seizing creditor and those of all the other inscribed creditors are posterior in date to the transcription of the conditional sale....

[43] ...

820. If an immovable alienated under a resolutory condition has been seized and judicially sold *pendente conditione,* what will become of the seizure and the judicial sale if the event occurs? When all the mortgages that burden the immovable are for the benefit of the acquirer, the seizure and judicial sale [are as if they] did not happen. On the contrary, the seizure and sale subsist if there is one or there are several mortgage creditors of the alienator or of a previous owner, even if the seizing party was a creditor of the acquirer. Thus, in order for the seizure and judicial sale to be maintained, it suffices if only one of the mortgage creditors was able to effect the seizure in regard to the alienator....

821. 6° When an immovable sold under a suspensive or resolutory condition is possessed by a third person who is in the process of acquisitive prescription, the prescription, once the contemplated event is realized, must be assessed in relation to the contracting party for whose benefit the condition was fulfilled. It is yet another necessary consequence of the retroactive effect [of the fulfillment of a condition] that this effect is pro[44]duced in regard to third persons as well as in regard to the parties. It follows from this that this contracting party [the one benefitted by the fulfillment of the condition] could invoke the causes of suspension or interruption of prescription that would have existed as to him. But he could not, on the other hand, avail himself of those that would have existed as to the other contracting party.

823. We have seen that acts of disposition are effaced by the retroactive effect of a fulfilled condition. Should this conclusion be extended to acts of administration, in particular, to leases?

Are leases granted *pendente conditione* by him who has alienated a thing under a suspensive condition retroactively annihilated by the occurrence of the condition?

Is it the same with leases passed *pendente conditione* by the acquirer under a resolutory condition?

In our opinion, these questions must be answered in the negative. The contrary [45] solution has the consequence of rendering very difficult, if not impossible, the administration of the thing that forms the object of the contract. If leases granted by the intermediary possessor [the alienator, in the case of a suspensive condition; the acquirer, in the case of a resolutory condition] should fall in the event of the fulfillment of the condition, then no one would deal with him. Is it conceivable that the legislature has accepted a solution that is, from an economic point of view, so bad as this?....

Finally, when there is doubt as to whether Article 1179 should be applied, must we not pronounce ourselves in favor of the more restrictive interpretation, inasmuch as retroactivity has the character of a fiction?

[47] **825.** Should one make an exception to the principle of retroactivity when the condition is suspensive and is potestative for the debtor? Clearly this question can be posed only in relation to a condition that is *simply* potestative, that is to say, when the condition consists of an event that the debtor has the power to cause to occur or to prevent. The question could not include *a purely* potestative condition—a condition *si voluero*—since that kind of condition renders the obligation that it affects null. Art. 1174. Such being the bearing of the question, it is necessary to respond that a condition that is potestative on the part of the debtor has, when it is fulfilled, the same retroactive effect as every other condition....

Chapter Six

Conjunctive, Alternative & Facultative Obligations

Louisiana Sources of Law

Louisiana Civil Code

Art. 1807. Conjunctive obligation.

An obligation is conjunctive when it binds the obligor to multiple items of performance that may be separately rendered or enforced. In that case, each item is regarded as the object of a separate obligation.

The parties may provide that the failure of the obligor to perform one or more items shall allow the obligee to demand the immediate performance of all the remaining items. (Acts 1984, No. 331, § 1, eff. Jan. 1, 1985.)

Art. 1808. Alternative obligation.

An obligation is alternative when an obligor is bound to render only one of two or more items of performance. (Acts 1984, No. 331, § 1, eff. Jan. 1, 1985.)

Art. 1809. Choice belongs to the obligor.

When an obligation is alternative, the choice of the item of performance belongs to the obligor unless it has been expressly or impliedly granted to the obligee. (Acts 1984, No. 331, § 1, eff. Jan. 1, 1985.)

Art. 1812. Impossibility or unlawfulness of one item of performance.

When the choice belongs to the obligor and one of the items of performance contemplated in the alternative obligation becomes impossible or unlawful, regardless of the fault of the obligor, he must render one of those that remain.

When the choice belongs to the obligee and one of the items of performance becomes impossible or unlawful without the fault of the obligor, the obligee must choose one of the items that remain. If the impossibility or unlawfulness is due to the fault of the obligor, the obligee may choose either one of those that remain, or damages for the item of performance that became impossible or unlawful. (Acts 1984, No. 331, § 1, eff. Jan. 1, 1985.)

Art. 1814. Obligor's liability for damages.

When the choice belongs to the obligor, if all the items of performance contemplated in the alternative obligation have become impossible and the impossibility of one or more is due to the fault of the obligor, he is liable for the damages resulting from his failure to render the last item that became impossible.

If the impossibility of one or more items is due to the fault of the obligee, the obligor is not bound to deliver any of the items that remain. (Acts 1984, No. 331, § 1, eff. Jan. 1, 1985.)

Précis: Louisiana Law of Obligations in General § 4.1.1 to 4.3.1

CONJUNCTIVE OBLIGATIONS

An obligor may bind himself to **"multiple items of performance"** (LSA C.C. Art. 1807) in such a manner that he cannot be said to have performed his obligation and extinguished it until all items have been fully carried out. The obligation thereby created may involve either several different or identical items of performance which are bound in such a way as to form a universality of things....

A conjunctive obligation is therefore an obligation comprised of multiple performances. Fictitiously each performance could be looked at as the object of a constituent obligation ...

According to **LSA-C.C. Art. 1807-2, "The parties may provide that the failure of the obligor to perform one or more items shall allow the obligee to demand the immediate performance of all the remaining items."** ...

ALTERNATIVE OBLIGATIONS

An alternative obligation requires that a choice be made between two or more items of performance so that the obligor will be released from his obligation whenever he will have carried out one of those items of performance. The essence of an alternative obligation is to place two (or more) items of performance on the same plane so that they are all *principal* items. No single item is an accessory to another. If the obligation deals with two objects, they are equally due and the performance of either one will be sufficient to extinguish the whole obligation....

It is possible to see in an alternative obligation a sort of insurance granted to an obligee-creditor, a kind of guarantee of payment assuring him that at least one item of performance out of two or more will be conveyed to him....

It is a presumption of the Louisiana law of obligations that, in an alternative obligation, **"the choice of the item of performance belongs to the obligor."** ...

The presumption that the choice belongs to the obligor is a rebuttable legal presumption since it merely protects the interest of private parties. Consequently, it is conceivable that the choice of the object of the obligation be **"expressly or impliedly granted to the obligee."** ...

Either party who is given the choice must make that choice in good faith....

Whenever the choice of one item of performance has been made by the proper party and in due time, that item is owed in its entirety. Once selected, the item becomes the only object of an obligation which, from alternative, has now become pure and simple. The exercise of the choice extinguishes the alternative feature of the obligation....

An obligation is facultative when an obligor owes one particular principal item of performance and when, at the same time, he may be released of that performance by tendering another item as a substitute item which will take the place of the principal item of performance. The facultative obligation is thus characterized by the existence of a principal item which is the only one truly due under the obligation (this item is said to *in obligatione*) but, to that item the obligor, at the moment of performing may, of his own volition, substitute another item for his performance (this item is said to be *in facilitate solutionis*)....

LSA-C.C. Art. 234 offers an example of a facultative obligation. Under this article a father, or a mother, who owes alimony to a child **"may offer to receive, support and**

maintain the child, to whom he or she may owe alimony, in his or her house ...” The principal obligation imposed on the father or mother is to pay alimony for the support of the child; the substitute facultative obligation available to the father or mother is to receive the child in his or her own home. This facultative obligation is available to the father or mother in response to the child's only right to alimony payments....

Cases

Mrs. Estelle Polmer RABIN

v.

Margaret S. BLAZAS and Harry Frisch

Louisiana Court of Appeal
Fourth Circuit
Sept. 16, 1988
537 So.2d 221

ARMSTRONG, Judge.

The defendant, Harry Frisch, appeals from a judgment rendered against him for breach of an agreement to purchase real property. Frisch argues that the judgment of the trial court should be reversed because 1) the court erred in failing to rescind the agreement on the ground that he was incapable of contracting due to his age and infirmity; and 2) the court erred in awarding an amount in excess of that stated in the liquidated damages clause of the agreement. For the reasons that follow, we affirm the judgment of the trial court as to the breach of contract claim against Frisch and modify as to the amount of damages awarded.

On April 11, 1986 Margaret S. Blazas and defendant Frisch signed a Gertrude Gardner Realtors, Inc. document entitled "agreement to purchase or sell." They signed on the lines beneath the word "offeror" for the purchase of real property located at 801–03 Desire Street and 3401–03 Dauphine Street in New Orleans. The purchase offer was for $55,000.00, all cash. Lines 34 through 37 of the agreement provide:

> Upon acceptance of this offer, seller and purchaser shall be bound by all its terms and conditions and purchaser becomes *obligated to deposit* with seller's agent not later than 48 hours from acceptance, *10% of the purchase price* amounting to $_____ and *failure to do shall be considered a breach* thereof, *and seller shall have the right,* at sellers option, to reinstate said property for sale and *to demand liquidated damages equal to the amount of the deposit* or specific performance, *and purchaser shall,* in either event, *be liable for the agents commission, attorneys fees and costs.*

(Emphasis added.) On the line provided for the amount reflecting 10% of the purchase price, the figure $5,500.00, and the word "chek" (sic), are hand written. Alex Seidenfield is listed as both the selling and the listing agent and Gertrude Gardner is listed as the Broker. The offer was accepted by the seller, plaintiff Estelle P. Rabin, on the same date, April 11, 1986.[1]

Neither Frisch nor Blazas tendered $5,500.00 to Seidenfield within forty-eight hours of the offer's acceptance as was required in the agreement. Rabin then filed this action

---

1. *See* plaintiff's Exhibit No. 2.

against Frisch and Blazas alleging breach of contract as a result of their failure to deposit the same. [....]

After a bench trial, judgment was rendered against Frisch in the principal amount of $12,450.00, plus costs, allocated as follows: $5,500.00 for breach of contract; $5,500.00 for liquidated damages; $450.00 for lost rent on the property subject to the sale, and $1,000.00 for attorney's fees.[2, 3]

By his first assignment of error defendant Frisch, an eighty year old man with hearing difficulty, argues that the contract as to him should be rescinded because, due to his age and mental infirmity, he did not have the mental capacity to contract. In support of this contention, Frisch points to the testimony of Dr. Jack C. Castrogiovanni, his internist. Dr. Castrogiovanni's deposition was admitted into evidence over the plaintiff's objection.[4] Dr. Castrogiovanni stated that Frisch suffered from organic brain syndrome. Dr. Castrogiovanni described this disease as "characterized by recent memory loss, inability to have introspection frequently into the acts of one, progressive inability to care for one's own needs, and it's more or less like sliding scale (of degree)." However, this diagnosis was not made until September 19, 1986, more than five months after Frisch entered into the agreement in question. Moreover, although Dr. Castrogiovanni also testified that organic brain syndrome develops over a period of time (so that it could have existed six months earlier), he did not testify that Frisch had organic brain syndrome at least six months before the diagnosis was made. In any case, it is clear that Frisch has never been interdicted.

Article 1925 of the Louisiana Civil Code provides:

> A noninterdicted person, *who was deprived of reason at the time of contracting, may obtain rescission of an onerous contract upon the ground of incapacity only upon showing that the other party knew or should have known that person's incapacity.*

(Emphasis added.) Thus, because Frisch has failed to prove, in the first instance, that he was deprived of reason *at the time of contracting,* the trial court was correct in not rescinding the contract as to Frisch. Moreover, even if Frisch were incapacitated he has, nevertheless, failed in his second burden of proving that "the other party", i.e., Seidenfeld, knew or should have known of such incapacity.

Our review of Seidenfeld's testimony with respect to Frisch's reasoning capacity both before, as well as at, *the time of contracting,* bears this out. Seidenfeld testified that, although Frisch had difficulty hearing, he did appear to understand what he, Seidenfeld, was saying. Seidenfeld also portrayed Frisch, who owned several properties, as a man knowledgeable in real estate transactions and as having asked many questions with respect to the property he was about to purchase on April 11, 1986, the date of the sale.

Before April 11, 1986, Seidenfeld met Frisch on only one other occasion, April 8 or 9, 1986. On that day, Seidenfeld met with Blazas to show her the property. According to Seidenfeld, Frisch drove Blazas to the site of the property, rolled down the car window and had a discussion with Seidenfeld about interest rates and financing and the advantage of paying cash. In short, there was nothing to put Seidenfeld on notice that Frisch suffered from any mental infirmity either before or on the day Frisch signed the agreement.

---

2. On September 12, 1986 a default judgment was rendered against Blazas in the principal amount of $5,500.00 plus attorneys' fees in the amount of $2,000.00 and all costs. That judgment is not before us for review.

3. The trial court's judgment approved a $3,000.00 attorney's fee, but reduced it by $2,000.00, the amount assessed against Blazas in the September 12, 1986 default judgment.

4. We need not decide the correctness of the trial court's decision to admit this testimony because, even assuming its admission was in error, our result would be the same.

80 By his second assignment of error, defendant contends that the court erred in award-
81 ing plaintiff damages in excess of the contractual liquidated damages provision.

82 It is clear under the terms of the contract that, upon failure to make the required
83 $5,500.00 deposit, the buyer becomes liable for $5,500.00 in liquidated damages "or" spe-
84 cific performance—not both. This is consistent with La.Civ.Code art. 2007. Rabin opted
85 to exercise the liquidated damages provision rather than to demand specific performance.
86 However, in awarding Rabin $5,500.00 liquidated damages *plus* $5,500.00 for breach of
87 contract, the trial court was awarding liquidated damages *and* partial specific perfor-
88 mance. That was error.

89 The trial court's award of $450.00 for lost rent also was error. The $5,500.00 liquidated
90 damages clause fixes the amount of *all* damages that may be recovered under the con-
91 tract. By contract, the parties substituted the liquidated sum of $5,500.00 for actual dam-
92 ages with the result that, upon breach, *actual* damages need not be determined and may
93 not be awarded. Thus, in opting to exercise the liquidated damages clause, Rabin was en-
94 titled to recover $5,500.00, but no more.

[....]

Questions

1. Lines 22–29: How do you read the words 'terms' and 'conditions' in this sentence?
    What kind of obligation is an obligation to deposit? *See* La. Civ. Code arts. 2926 *et
    seq.* Is failure "to do" a term or a condition? Can you fully characterize your choice
    in proper legal terms? Do the words "at seller's option" suggest that the seller will be
    the only one with the right to choose among two or more obligations that will have
    to be performed by the obligor-buyer? From the point of view of the latter, is that op-
    tion of the seller like a suspensive condition?

2. Lines 82–88: In a prior paragraph on lines 57/58–61, the Court referred specifically
    to Louisiana Civil Code article 1925 in support of its legal analysis. Likewise, what
    Louisiana Civil Code article(s) should the Court have cited in this paragraph (lines
    82–88), particularly where the Court uses the preposition "or"?

Editor's Note: *See* Walter J. Wadlington III, *Conjunctive, Alternative and Facultative Obligations in Louisiana*, 37 Tulane L. Rev. 67 (1962).

1   ## Stanford LATTER and Robert L. Yuspeh

2   ### v.

3   ## STATE of Louisiana

4   Louisiana Court of Appeal
5   First Circuit
6   March 12, 1993
7   621 So.2d 1159

8   PITCHER, Judge.

9   [....]

10 ### BACKGROUND

11 According to the petition, on June 15, 1981, petitioners, Stanford Latter and Robert
12 L. Yuspeh, submitted a bid for leasing the 13,000 square feet of their property at 2025

Canal Street, New Orleans, Louisiana, to the State of Louisiana, Department of Health   13
and Human Resources, Office of Family Security. Subsequent thereto, petitioners were no-   14
tified on August 17, 1981, that their bid had been accepted, were requested to execute the   15
lease, and were informed that the bid would be forwarded to the Assistant Commissioner   16
of the Division of Administration for approval.   17

On September 1, 1981, petitioners and R.P. Guissinger, Secretary of the Department of   18
Health and Human Resources, executed the lease of the Canal Street property. The lease   19
provided for a term of five years commencing on November 1, 1981, and ending on Oc-   20
tober 31, 1986. The consideration of the lease was the payment of $552,499.80, payable   21
in sixty equal installments of $9,208.33 each. The first installment under the lease was   22
due on November 1, 1981, and the remaining installments were due on the first day of   23
each month thereafter.[1] The lease also provided that the lessee would pay for all public util-   24
ities such as gas, water, and electricity. On April 13, 1982, the Division of Administration   25
approved the lease, and occupancy of the leased premises began on July 15, 1982.   26

FACTS   27

On November 18, 1985, petitioners filed a suit for declaration judgment, "declaring the   28
State of Louisiana to pay Seventy Three Thousand Six Hundred Sixty-Six and 64/100 Dol-   29
lars ($73,666.64) for past due rentals and Eight Thousand One Hundred Eighty-Nine and   30
58/100 Dollars ($8,189.58) for utilities petitioners paid on behalf of defendant between   31
November 1, 1981, and July 15, 1982."[2] The State of Louisiana answered the petition,   32
denying the allegations set forth therein and alleged that petitioners' action for past due   33
rent had prescribed by the passage of three years and that petitioners' action for wrong-   34
ful or intentional acts or abuse of right had prescribed by the passage of one year. Peti-   35
tioners subsequently amended their petition on May 19, 1990.   36

On June 29, 1990, the State reurged the peremptory exception raising the objection of   37
prescription. After a hearing, the trial court sustained the State's peremptory exception   38
raising prejudice.   39

From this adverse judgment, petitioners appeal, assigning as error the trial court's sus-   40
taining of the objection of prescription. Petitioners argue that prescription does not com-   41
mence to run until the end of the lease term and that, if prescription commenced to run prior   42
to the end of the lease term, then the rental payments from July 15, 1982, through October   43
31, 1986, suspended or interrupted the running of prescription as to the unpaid amounts.   44
45

---

1. The lease also provided as follows:

[I]n the event occupancy by Lessee occurs subsequent to the first rental payment date Lessor waives any rights to rental payments for a period of thirty (30) days after Lessee actually occupies the leased premises.

Should the Lessee be unable to obtain possession of the leased premises within sixty (60) days after Division of Administration approval of the lease, whether or not said delay is caused by the Lessor, the Lessee shall be entitled to the remission of rent for such term during which the Lessee is deprived of possession, and to reimbursement for any damages which the Lessee may suffer as a result of said deprivation of possession. In addition, should the Lessee be deprived of possession of the leased premises for a period of more than sixty (60) days, then this lease may be cancelled at the option of the Lessee.

2. Thereafter, the State of Louisiana filed a dilatory exception pleading the objection of prematurity on the grounds that petitioners failed to exhaust their administrative remedies under the Louisiana Procurement Code, as set forth in LSA-R.S. 39:1673. By judgment, dated May 7, 1986, the State's exception pleading the objection of prematurity was overruled.

The State of Louisiana also filed a peremptory exception raising the objection of no cause of action. By judgment dated September 10, 1986, the trial court overruled the State's exception raising the objection of no cause of action.

PRESCRIPTION

Although petitioners filed a petition for declaratory judgment as opposed to a petition for damages, the allegations of the petition determine the true nature of the action and the applicable prescriptive period. *Starns v. Emmons,* 538 So.2d 275, 277 (La.1989); *Hampton v. Hibernia National Bank,* 598 So.2d 502, 503 (La.App. 2nd Cir.1992); *Arceneaux v. Courtney,* 448 So.2d 197, 198 (La.App. 1st Cir.1984). The petition filed by petitioners clearly requests payment for past due rentals.

LSA-C.C. article 3494(2) provides that an action for arrearage of rent is subject to liberative prescription of three years. LSA-C.C. art. 3495 provides that prescription begins to run from the day payment is exigible. *See Montiville v. City of Westwego,* 592 So.2d 390, 391 (La.1992).

Petitioners argue that prescription did not begin to run until the end of the lease term. However, LSA-C.C. art. 1807 provides that an obligation is "conjunctive" when it binds the obligor to multiple items of performance that may be separately rendered or enforced. In such case, each item is regarded as the object of a separate obligation. *See Gardiner v. Montegut,* 175 So. 120, 122 (La.App.Orleans, 1937). The parties may provide that the failure of the obligor to perform one or more items shall allow the obligee to demand the immediate performance of all the remaining items. Comment (b) to LSA-C.C. art. 1807 provides that when a sum is owed in installments or rent is paid periodically, the running of prescription starts separately for each installment or rental payment in the absence of an acceleration clause.

In the instant case, the State was to pay a lump sum of $555,499.50 for the occupancy of petitioners' premises. This amount was divided into sixty (60) equal installments of $9,208.33 plus utilities. The lease provided that "the first installment [was] due and payable on the first day of November, 1981, and the remaining installments [were] due and payable, respectively, on the 1st day of each month thereafter." Additionally, there was no acceleration clause.

Therefore, the obligation was conjunctive, and each installment was a separate obligation. Prescription began to run separately for each installment as it became due. Accordingly, the past due rents from November 1, 1981 through July 15, 1982, had all prescribed by the time petitioners filed the instant suit on November 18, 1985.

[....]

Questions

1. Lines 18 *et seq.*: What kind of obligation is created by a lease: real, heritable or strictly personal? *See* La. Civ. Code arts. 2668–2729. Can you identify a term or multiple terms and their kind in this contract of lease? Was the lessee, the State of Louisiana, bound by one or more than one obligation? Can you characterize it or them? Assuming that there is more than one obligation, how do these obligations relate one to another? Are they related by "and"? By "or"? Read Louisiana Civil Code articles 1815–1820 on divisible and indivisible obligations. Would you characterize the State's obligation to pay the rent in sixty installments as a divisible obligation? Is a divisible obligation the same thing as a conjunctive obligation? *See* La. Civ. Code art. 1807.

2. Lines 40–44: Why is the plaintiff, petitioner on appeal, making this argument? Is the plaintiff arguing that there was only one obligation created by the contract of lease and only one object (the full amount of the rent) and, therefore, there was only one term to consider? Is the lessor arguing here that the term is in his favor? Is the

lessor an obligor? An obligee? Or both simultaneously? In whose favor, the lessor or the lessee, would the presumption of art. 1779 operate?

3. Lines 53–56: What is the legal connection between Louisiana Civil Code articles 3494(2)–3495 and a term?

4. Lines 57–66: Does this paragraph help you, now, to answer Question 1 above: "Is a divisible obligation the same thing as a conjunctive obligation?" Do you see the important legal effect of a term being attached to a conjunctive and divisible obligation? What benefit did the State derive from the fact that an action by the lessor to collect the rents on the first two years of the lease had expired? Aren't all prescriptive periods subject to a term? What kind? Since the State was no longer bound by any civil obligation to pay the first two years of rent, would you hold the State liable under a natural obligation? *See* La. Civ. Code art. 1762(1).

Comparative Law Perspective

Robert J. Pothier, A Treatise on the Law of Obligations or Contracts
vol. 1, nᵒˢ 245–47, at 136–37 (William David Evans trans., 1806)

ARTICLE VI
Of Alternative Obligations (b).

[245] An alternative obligation is contracted where a person engages to do, or to give several things in such a manner, that the payment of one will acquit him from all: as if I engage to give you a particular horse, or twenty guineas to build you a house, or pay you a hundred pounds.

Where a person is obliged in the disjunctive to pay one sum of money or another, he is only debtor to the amount of the least.

[246] In order to constitute an alternative obligation, it is necessary that two or more things should be promised disjunctively. Where they are promised conjunctively, there as many obligations as the things which are enumerated, ... and the debtor cannot be wholly liberated without discharging them all; but where they are promised in the alternative, though they are all due, there is but one obligation which may be discharged by the payment of any of them....

[247] The choice belongs to the debtor ... unless it is expressly agreed that it shall belong to the creditor. This is a consequence of the rule of interpretation.... But though the debtor may elect to pay which he pleases, he cannot pay part of the one and part of the other. Therefore if the obligation is to pay ten pounds or six measures of corn, or a hundred pounds or an acre of land; he cannot give fifty pounds and half of the land, or five pounds and six measures of corn; he must either pay all the money or give the whole land, or the whole quantity of corn; so where the creditor has the choice he cannot require part of the one and part of the other....

Chapter Seven

Joint, Solidary, and Divisible Obligations

Louisiana Sources of Law

Louisiana Civil Code

Art. 1787. Several obligations; effects.

When each of different obligors owes a separate performance to one obligee, the obligation is several for the obligors.

When one obligor owes a separate performance to each of different obligees, the obligation is several for the obligees.

A several obligation produces the same effects as a separate obligation owed to each obligee by an obligor or by each obligor to an obligee. (Acts 1984, No. 331, § 1, eff. Jan. 1, 1985.)

Art. 1788. Joint obligations for obligors or obligees.

When different obligors owe together just one performance to one obligee, but neither is bound for the whole, the obligation is joint for the obligors.

When one obligor owes just one performance intended for the common benefit of different obligees, neither of whom is entitled to the whole performance, the obligation is joint for the obligees. (Acts 1984, No. 331, § 1, eff. Jan. 1, 1985.)

Art. 1789. Divisible and indivisible joint obligation.

When a joint obligation is divisible, each joint obligor is bound to perform, and each joint obligee is entitled to receive, only his portion. When a joint obligation is indivisible, joint obligors or obligees are subject to the rules governing solidary obligors or solidary obligees. (Acts 1984, No. 331, § 1, eff. Jan. 1, 1985.)

Art. 1790. Solidary obligations for obligees.

An obligation is solidary for the obligees when it gives each obligee the right to demand the whole performance from the common obligor. (Acts 1984, No. 331, § 1, eff. Jan. 1, 1985.)

Art. 1794. Solidary obligation for obligors.

An obligation is solidary for the obligors when each obligor is liable for the whole performance. A performance rendered by one of the solidary obligors relieves the others of liability toward the obligee. (Acts 1984, No. 331, § 1, eff. Jan. 1, 1985.)

Art. 1795. Solidary obligor may not request division; action against one obligor after action against another.

An obligee, at his choice, may demand the whole performance from any of his solidary obligors. A solidary obligor may not request division of the debt.

Unless the obligation is extinguished, an obligee may institute action against any of his solidary obligors even after institution of action against another solidary obligor. (Acts 1984, No. 331, § 1, eff. Jan. 1, 1985.)

Art. 1796. Solidarity not presumed.

Solidarity of obligation shall not be presumed. A solidary obligation arises from a clear expression of the parties' intent or from the law. (Acts 1984, No. 331, § 1, eff. Jan. 1, 1985.)

Art. 1799. Interruption of prescription.

The interruption of prescription against one solidary obligor is effective against all solidary obligors and their heirs. (Acts 1984, No. 331, § 1, eff. Jan. 1, 1985.)

Art. 1800. Solidary liability for damages.

A failure to perform a solidary obligation through the fault of one obligor renders all the obligors solidarily liable for the resulting damages. In that case, the obligors not at fault have their remedy against the obligor at fault. (Acts 1984, No. 331, § 1, eff. Jan. 1, 1985.)

Art. 1801. Defenses that solidary obligor may raise.

A solidary obligor may raise against the obligee defenses that arise from the nature of the obligation, or that are personal to him, or that are common to all the solidary obligors. He may not raise a defense that is personal to another solidary obligor. (Acts 1984, No. 331, § 1, eff. Jan. 1, 1985.)

Art. 1802. Renunciation of solidarity.

Renunciation of solidarity by the obligee in favor of one or more of his obligors must be express. An obligee who receives a partial performance from an obligor separately preserves the solidary obligation against all his obligors after deduction of that partial performance. (Acts 1984, No. 331, § 1, eff. Jan. 1, 1985.)

Art. 1804. Liability of solidary obligors between themselves.

Among solidary obligors, each is liable for his virile portion. If the obligation arises from a contract or quasi-contract, virile portions are equal in the absence of agreement or judgment to the contrary. If the obligation arises from an offense or quasi-offense, a virile portion is proportionate to the fault of each obligor.

A solidary obligor who has rendered the whole performance, though subrogated to the right of the obligee, may claim from the other obligors no more than the virile portion of each.

If the circumstances giving rise to the solidary obligation concern only one of the obligors, that obligor is liable for the whole to the other obligors who are then considered only as his sureties. (Acts 1984, No. 331, § 1, eff. Jan. 1, 1985.)

Art. 1806. Insolvency of a solidary obligor.

A loss arising from the insolvency of a solidary obligor must be borne by the other solidary obligors in proportion to their portion.

Any obligor in whose favor solidarity has been renounced must nevertheless contribute to make up for the loss. (Acts 1984, No. 331, § 1, eff. Jan. 1, 1985.)

Art. 1815. Divisible and indivisible obligation.

An obligation is divisible when the object of the performance is susceptible of division.

An obligation is indivisible when the object of the performance, because of its nature or because of the intent of the parties, is not susceptible of division. (Acts 1984, No. 331, § 1, eff. Jan. 1, 1985.)

Art. 1816. Effect of divisible obligation between single obligor and obligee.

When there is only one obligor and only one obligee, a divisible obligation must be performed as if it were indivisible. (Acts 1984, No. 331, § 1, eff. Jan. 1, 1985.)

Art. 1818. Effects of indivisible obligations between more than one obligor or obligee.

An indivisible obligation with more than one obligor or obligee is subject to the rules governing solidary obligations. (Acts 1984, No. 331, § 1, eff. Jan. 1, 1985.)

Art. 1820. Solidarity is not indivisibility.

A stipulation of solidarity does not make an obligation indivisible. (Acts 1984, No. 331, § 1, eff. Jan. 1, 1985.)

Précis: Louisiana Law of Obligations in General § 3.1.1 to 4.4.2

[A]n obligation is several on the part of obligors whenever each one of them is independently bound to a separate and distinct performance not owed in any manner by the other obligors. The item or items of the respective obligor's performance(s) may be to do different acts or give different things or abstain from doing something, etc.. . . .

The analysis of the effects of several obligations does not require any extensive treatment since a several obligation must be considered as being merely the gathering under one source of multiple but separate obligations creating as many different bonds of law as there are parties.. . .

There exists a joint obligation on the part of different obligors when these obligors are bound **together** to **one** performance arising from one and the same obligation. Likewise, an obligation is joint on the part of different obligees when, together, they are entitled to just **one** performance from the obligor. As **LSA-C.C. Art. 1788** states.. . .

The joint obligation is considered as the common rule or as the general principle of the law of obligations with multiple persons.. . .

A joint obligation on the part of obligors is created whenever multiple obligors are bound **together** to perform **one** obligation. However, each one of them is bound to perform only his individual share of the whole obligation; each one of them is bound *pro numero virorum*.. . .

The plurality of links or bonds of law between the obligee and the joint obligors has this consequence that the joint obligors will not necessarily be bound to the obligee under the same legal regimes. Each bond of law may be vested with a particular legal identity so that, for example, some defenses available to one obligor may not be available to others.. . .

Whenever a joint obligation is indivisible in its performance, in the sense that the item of performance owed by the joint obligors is not susceptible of being divided in parts (**LSA-C.C. Art. 1789**), the rules of solidarity (**LSA-C.C. Arts. 1790** *et seq.)* and those of indivisibility (**LSA-C.C. Arts. 1815** *et seq.*) will apply.. . .

Solidarity must be understood both as a legal fiction and as a practical necessity. In essence, solidarity is an obstacle, a bar to the division of an obligation as a result of a particular feature attached to the bond of law binding together multiple persons. These persons can be, either multiple obligees [and we have then an instance of active solidarity], or multiple obligors [and we have then an instance of passive solidarity]....

The far-reaching, harsh and aleatory effects of solidarity are the reason why "**solidarity of obligation shall not be presumed. A solidary obligation arises from a clear expression of the parties' intent or from the law**" (**LSA-C.C. Art. 1796**). The two sources of solidarity are, thus, the law and contract. The fact that there may be two different sources of solidarity of an obligation is not an obstacle to two or more obligors being held solidarily bound for that same obligation. One solidary obligor could be bound solidarily on account of a contract whereas another solidary obligor could be bound for the same obligation because of an existing legal disposition....

The practical effects of active solidarity are many. First of all, each one of the solidary obligees may demand the whole performance and when that performance has been rendered to any one of them it extinguishes the obligation and releases the obligor even though the benefit of the obligation is to be divided among the multiple obligees. A second effect is that, should a solidary obligee interrupt prescription of the action against the obligor, the other solidary obligees will benefit from such an initiative. Thirdly, and reasoning *a pari ratione* on **LSA-C.C. Art. 1793**, should a solidary obligee put the obligor in default, the benefit of this action will be shared with the other solidary obliges....

As far as the relationship between the obligees is concerned it can be said that, in general, they divide among themselves, according to their respective rights, the performance received from the obligor....

LSA-C.C. Art. 1794 states that "**an obligation is solidary for the obligors when each obligor is liable for the whole performance. A performance rendered by one of the solidary obligors relieves the others of liability toward the obligee.**" This article suggests that there is, at the same time, only *one item* of performance owed, that is to say *the whole performance,* and a plurality of obligors held personally and individually for that performance regardless of whether the object or item of performance is divisible or indivisible in its performance. Thus, solidarity creates a personal bond between the obligee and each one of the solidary obligors.

This multiplicity of bonds between the solidary obligors and their obligee carries with it many important consequences....

Once the obligee has received the full performance of the obligation from one of the solidary obligors, the benefit of solidarity disappears with the extinction of the debt. The principle which now governs the relationship between the solidary obligors is that solidarity is not heritable, it cannot be claimed by that solidary obligor who, through his performance, extinguished the obligation....

The division of the debt among the obligors is not necessarily made on an equal basis. It may exist some exceptions to an equal distribution....

LSA-C.C. Art. 1815 states in very simple terms that:

> "**An obligation is divisible when the object of the performance is susceptible of division.**
>
> **An obligation is indivisible when the object of the performance, because of its nature or because of the intent of the parties, is not susceptible of division.**"

Absolute natural indivisibility is dictated, first of all, by the law of nature and appears as the only authentic and unquestionable kind of indivisibility of an obligation. It can also be created by law making the indivisibility "fictitiously" natural. Whether actual or fictitious, absolute natural indivisibility refers to an object of an obligation which, in its performance, cannot possibly be divided in parts....

An obligation is relatively indivisible whenever its object, although susceptible of material or intellectual division, must be considered as being indivisible in relation to, or in light of, the *natural* objective pursued by the parties. The goal intended to be achieved by the obligor's performance is the fulfillment of an indivisible object....

By their contract, parties may provide for an *artificial* or *fictitious* indivisibility of an obligation which, otherwise, would be naturally divisible. The intent of the parties may be to make the *object* of the obligation or *item of performance* indivisible in its fulfillment. Conventional indivisibility strives to conceptually and artificially attach to an object a legal feature which only nature would normally impose. Regardless of the number of parties involved, the item of performance cannot be divided between them because their will has made it indivisible....

Cases

Jimmie WILKS et ux.
v.
ALLSTATE INSURANCE COMPANY et al.

Louisiana Court of Appeal

Third Circuit

Feb. 15, 1967

195 So.2d 390

TATE, Judge.

[....]

[**At the trial court,**] the plaintiffs recovered judgment on the merits against the two defendants, a garageman (Jacobs) and an insurer (Allstate). The defendants now appeal this adverse judgment. [....]

There is no serious dispute with regard to the negligence or to the amount of the award. The chief issue of this appeal is raised by the contention of Allstate, the defendant insurer, that the award against it should be reduced by one-half because of its policy provision allegedly limiting its liability if there is other valid and collectible insurance. (The alleged other insurer was not brought into this action, either by the plaintiff as a defendant to the principal demand or by the defendants by a third-party demand.)

Facts.

The plaintiff wife was driving the family car when it was struck by a vehicle which negligently ran a stop sign. An employee of the garageman Jacobs was driving the other vehicle. It belonged to a customer (Calhoun) to whom Allstate had issued a liability policy. Allstate was held liable as the omnibus insurer of the garageman Jacobs or his employee, who were using the car with the consent of Calhoun, Allstate's named insured. See 177 So.2d 790 (opinion on first appeal).

Allstate contends, however, that its liability is limited to one-half of the amount for which cast. Allstate relies upon an 'other insurance' clause of its policy, which provides for the

apportionment of its liability when there is other insurance covering the same loss.[1] All-   28
state contends that immediately before the accident the garageman Jacobs himself had   29
applied for and been granted an oral binder for a garage liability policy, which — being   30
valid and collectible insurance — had the effect of reducing Allstate's liability propor-   31
tionately under its 'pro rata' clause.   32

We may say that the showing in support of this contention indicates its probable weak-   33
ness. According to this showing: 34

A local agent had issued garage liability policies to Jacobs which covered periods in   35
1961–62 and 1962–63, the last of which had expired nineteen days before the accident of   36
December 3, 1963.[2] On December 3rd, the day of the accident, Jacobs appeared at his local   37
agent's office, paid up arrearages on his expired policy, and requested further coverage.   38

The agent testified, and the agent's correspondence indicates, that Jacobs did apply for   39
insurance, but a couple of hours After [sic] the accident. An affidavit from Jacobs states that   40
he telephoned the agent in the morning of the day and received assurance of coverage   41
then,[3] although he did not pay the arrearages until later in the day, presumably after the   42
accident in the afternoon. The agent actually forwarded an Application for coverage to a   43
new company which had never previously insured Jacobs, merely recommending that the   44
insurer issue and forward a policy, which further complicates the coverage question.[4]   45

[....]   46

'Pro rata' liability of both insurers: Treatise and decisional references.   47

For purposes of summary judgment, we will therefore assume that at the time of the   48
accident the tortfeasor's automobile was insured by one policy issued by Allstate to the ve-   49
hicle's owner (Calhoun) and also by another policy issued to the garageman (Jacobs). We   50
further assume that each policy had a bodily injury limit of $5,000 per person and that   51
each contained a pro rata 'other insurance' clause. We further assume that both of these   52
policies were applicable as 'primary' insurance. Since the recovery from Mrs. Wilks's per-   53

---

1. The applicable clause of Allstate's policy reads: 'Other Insurance. If the insured has other insurance against a loss covered by Part 1 of this policy (automobile liability insurance) the company
shall not be liable under this policy for a greater proportion of such loss than the applicable limit of
liability stated in the declarations bears to the total applicable limit of liability of all valid and collectible insurance against such loss; provided, however, the insurance with respect to a temporary
substitute automobile or non-owned automobile shall be excess insurance over any other valid and
collectible insurance.'

2. If These policies has [sic] been in effect, they plainly provide that they were excess insurance only,
if there was other insurance. Allstate's own 'other insurance' clause provides that only with respect to
a 'non-owned' automobile was the Allstate policy excess when other insurance is applicable; and here
the vehicle insured by Allstate was an 'owned' vehicle, i.e., owned by the named insured. There is thus
no conflict between the clauses, and so therefore Allstate alone is liable as the primary insurer, with
its 'pro rata' clause not coming into play so as to reduce its own liability just because there is a secondary insurer. See Peterson v. Armstrong, La.App. 3 Cir., 176 So.2d 453, 458 (footnote 2). The general rule in fact is that the owner's policy then provides the primary insurance, with the non-owned
coverage provided by the other policy being excess insurance only available after the primary policy's
limits are exhausted, despite any pro rata clause in the primary policy. Annotation, Liability Insurers-
apportionment-'excess' versus 'pro rata', 76 A.L.R.2d 502; 16 Couch on Insurance 2d, Section 71-72;
8 Appleman, Insurance Law and Practice, Section 4914; 7 Am.Jur.2d Automobile Insurance, Section
202.

3. The suggestion is thus made on Jacobs's behalf that, although a new policy was not actually issued, there was an oral binder or estoppel to deny continued coverage. 1 Couch, Section 14:32 and 4
Couch, Sections 26:189–91; 12 Appleman, Section 7192 and 16 Appleman, Section 9202.

4. See Couch, Section 26:198, regarding inception of coverage and preliminary contract of insurance.

sonal injuries was approximately $5,000, or within the limits of both policies, each insurer would be liable proportionate to its limits, i.e., for one-half of this amount (see pro rata clause set forth in footnote 1) If both insurers were joined as parties to this action. See State Farm Mutual Auto. Ins. Co. v. Travelers Ins. Co., La.App. 3 Cir., 184 So.2d 750.

The defendant Allstate's position is, essentially, that, where recovery is within policy limits and two policies with pro rata clauses are each applicable, then each insurer can never be liable for more than its proportionate share of the recovery, even though the other insurer is not a party to the suit. In the present case, then, assuming the facts to be as stated previously, it is contended that the injured plaintiff can recover only $2,500 against Jacobs's insurer Allstate although the judgment against Jacobs himself is $5,000 for Mrs. Wilks's injuries, even though Allstate had issued and received premiums for policy protection up to $5,000 per person injured.

In making this contention, Allstate's counsel particularly relies upon the statement in the Annotation, Insurers-Apportionment of Losses, 21 A.L.R.2d 611: 'The authorities uniformly hold that such an insurance contract, in the absence of statute to the contrary, is valid, and creates a liability that is several and not joint. Consequently, such a contract will not justify a recovery by the insured against the insurance company for more than the pro rata amount stipulated therein.'[5] See also to similar effect, 16 Couch on Insurance 2d, Section 62:7.

As we will shortly illustrate, this principle was for the most part applied in decisions where both insurers were parties, where at issue was primary-versus-pro rata liability of the insurers or the right of contribution of one insurer from another.

A different principle may be applicable when the litigation concerns the claim of the insured (or the injured person under the Louisiana Direct Action Statute, LSA-R.S. 22:655) to enforce against either one of the insurers that insurer's full policy limits. This differing principle is stated at 8 Appleman, Insurance Law and Practice, Section 4913, p. 387, as follows:

> 'The liability of the co-insurers to the insured is several, and not joint, so that the policyholder may collect the full amount from either insurer, leaving the latter to its right of contribution from the other.'[6]

In support of the Appleman statement are cited sixteen decisions, including the 1966 pocket parts. In support of the Couch statement to apparently opposing effect are cited twelve decisions, including two of those cited by the cited A.L.R. annotation (see footnote 5). Examination of the decisions cited in support of either view indicates that most of

---

5. The uniform authorities referred to are only four decisions: Globe Indem. Co. v. Sulpho-Saline Bath Co., C.A.8 Neb., 299 F. 219 (1924); Ranallo v. Hinman Bros., D.C.Ohio, 49 F.Supp. 920 (1942); Consolidated Shippers v. Pacific Employers Ins. Co., 45 Cal.App.2d 288, 114 P.2d 34 (1941); Grabenstatler v. Rock Asphalt & Constr. Co., 215 App.Div. 257, 213 N.Y.S. 216 (1926). As the text of this opinion indicates, these cited decisions concern the division of the liability where both insurers are joined as parties, see text at footnote 7 (Ranallo, Consolidated Shippers), or the right under equity or common law principles of one insurer to obtain contribution from another, see text at footnote 9 (Globe Indem. Co. case). The cited Grabenstatler decision is completely inapposite; it involved the statutory authority of a workmen's compensation board to apportion a judgment between two compensation insurers, both of which were parties to the litigation.

6. It is to be noted that Appleman states the liability to the insured of each insurer is 'several and not joint', so therefore the insured can collect the full amount from either. The ALR annotation, to the exact contrary, states that each insurer is bound only for its pro rata portion because the liability is 'several and not joint'! 21 A.L.R.2d 611. The common law concept of a several obligation will be discussed under a separate heading below.

them are inapplicable or else authority merely by way of dicta or implication. Very few of the decisions touch the actual issue of this litigation, which concerns the insured's right to collect the full policy limit against the sole insurer which is a party and before the court.

For instance, many of the decisions arose from litigation in which both of the insurers were parties, where the court was simply fixing the liability between the insurers without there being any issue as to the solidary liability vel non of the insurers with regard to the insured himself.[7] (Similarly, some of the cases relied upon by the appellant State Farm concern the fixing of proportionate liability between insurers, both of whom were before the court.[8])

Again, another group of the treatise cases concerns the right of one insurer who has paid the judgment to obtain contribution from another, with the earlier cases tending to disallow contribution for reasons found upon common law technicalities of pleading or definition,[9] and the later cases tending to permit it for a variety of reasons.[10] See also 46 C.J.S. Insurance, s 1207; 7 Am.Jur.2d Automobile Insurance, Section 203. Yet other of the cited decisions concern whether the liability of the insurer is primary or pro rata.[11] Others concern the proportionate liability of fire insurance under particular valued-policy statutes.[12] Yet others involve issues so tangential to the present as not to warrant classification or citation.

After eliminating the foregoing decisions, there does remain a residue of cited opinions, to divided effect, in which the present question was directly at issue. Two decisions hold that an insured may recover against his insurer for a liability within its policy limits, despite the application of other insurance and applicable pro rata clauses. Clow v. National Indemnity Co., 54 Wash.2d 198, 339 P.2d 82 (1959); Commercial Casualty Ins. Co. v. Knutsen Motor T. Co., 36 Ohio App. 241, 173 N.E. 241 (1930). Under similar circumstances, two decisions limited the insured's recovery to the proportionate liability of the defendant insurer. Vrabel v. Scholler, 369 Pa. 235, 85 A.2d 858 (1952); Traders & General Ins. Co. v. Hicks Rubber Co., 140 Tex. 586, 169 S.W.2d 142 (1943).[13]

---

7. Hospital Service Dist. No. 1 v. Delta Cas., Inc., La.App. 4 Cir., 171 So.2d 293 (1965); Case v. Fidelity & Cas. Co., 105 N.H. 422, 201 A.2d 897 (1964); Celina Mutual Cas. Co. v. Citizens Cas. Co., 194 Md. 236, 71 A.2d 20, 21 A.L.R. 20, 21 A.L.R.2d 605 (1950); Kenner v. Century Indem. Co., 320 Mass. 6, 67 N.E.2d 769, 165 A.L.R. 1463 (1946); Ranallo v. Hinman Bros. Const. Co. (D.C. Ohio) 4. F.Supp. 920 (1942), aff'd. Buckeye Union Cas. Co. v. Ranallo, 6 Cir., 135 F.2d 921; Employers Liability Assurance Corp. v. Pacific Employers Ins. Co., 102 Cal.App.2d 188, 227 P.2d 53 (1951); Consolidated Shippers, Inc. v. Pacific Emp. Ins. Co., 45 Cal.App.2d 288, 114 P.2d 34 (1941); Lamb v. Belt Cas. Co., 3 Cal.App.2d 624, 40 P.2d 311 (1935); Employers Mutual Liability Ins. Co. of Wis. v. Indem. Ins. Co. of N. Am., 37 Misc.2d 421, 234 N.Y.S.2d 839 (1962).

8. Guin v. Commercial Cas. Ins. Co., 224 La. 44, 68 So.2d 752, 753 (and companion case of same title, 224 La. 59, 68 So.2d 757); Milan v. Providence Insurance Co., 227 F.Supp. 251 (D.C.La., 1964).

9. Globe Indemnity Co. v. Sulpho-Saline Bath Co., C.A. 8, 299 F. 219 (1924); Commercial Standard Ins. Co. v. American Emp. Ins. Co., (D.C., Ky.) 108 F.Supp. 176 (1952).

10. Clow v. National Indemnity Co., 54 Wash.2d 198, 339 P.2d 82 (1959), and summary of recent cases cited therein; Liberty Mutual Ins. Co. v. Standard Acc. Ins. Co. (D.C., N.Y.) 164 F.Supp. 261 (1958); Central Surety & Ins. Corp. v. New Amsterdam Cas. Co., Mo.App., 216 S.W.2d 527 (1948).

11. Commercial Casualty Ins. Co. v. Hartford Acc. & Indem. Co., 190 Minn. 528, 252 N.W. 434, 253 N.W. 888 (1934); New Amsterdam Cas. Co. v. Hartford Acc. & Indem. Co., (D.C., Ky.) 18 F.Supp. 707 (1937).

12. Walker v. Queen Ins. Co., 136 S.C. 144, 134 S.E. 263, 52 A.L.R. 259 (1926); National Fire Insurance Co. v. Dennison, 93 Ohio St. 404, 113 N.E. 260, L.R.A. 1916F, 992 (Ohio S.Ct. 1916).

13. Three other decisions limited an insured's recovery against his insurer to the insurer's proportionate liability under the pro rata clause. Baysdon v. Nationwide Mutual Fire Ins. Co., 259 N.C. 181, 13 S.E.2d 311 (1963); Friedfeld v. Royal Indemnity Co., Fla.App., 167 So.2d 586 (1964); Air Transport Mfg. Co. v. Employers Liability Assur. Corp., 91 Cal.App.2d 129, 204 P.2d 647 (1949). However, the result in each of these decisions can be explained under the principle that the liability

115 The two lines of decisions cannot be reconciled. The Clow decision, specifically citing
116 the latter two cases, simply states that they are the minority view, citing five decisions al-
117 legedly contrary (but four of which actually concern distinguishable questions).

118 The source of much of the confusion in the field, both in the decisions cited immedi-
119 ately above and in the conflicting dicta in many of the decisions earlier cited, is the vari-
120 able meaning attached to the common-law concept of a 'several' obligation. (See footnote
121 6 above.) It may therefore be advisable to discuss briefly this common-law concept and
122 the civil law concepts most nearly equivalent.

123 A 'several' obligation in the common law.

124 Under the Louisiana Civil Code, 'Several obligations are produced, when what is
125 promised by one of the obligors, is not promised by the other, but each one promises
126 separately for himself to do a distinct act * * *.' Article 2078.

127 By this definition, the obligors bound severally cannot have agreed to perform the
128 same act. On the other hand, 'When several persons obligate themselves to the obligee
129 by the terms In solido, or use any other expressions, which clearly show that they in-
130 tend that each one shall be Separately bound to perform the whole of the obligation,
131 it is called an obligation In solido on the part of the obligors.' Article 2082. (Italics
132 ours.) The solidary obligation to pay the entire debt can result from different instru-
133 ments, or although the obligors be obliged differently to pay the same debt, Article
134 2092; Hidalgo v. Dupuy, La.App. 1 Cir. 122 So.2d 639. Both of these types of obliga-
135 tions are to be distinguished from the 'joint' obligation of our Civil Code where sev-
136 eral persons join in the same contract to do the same thing, Articles 2080, 2081, where
137 all joint obligors must be joined in any suit to enforce the obligation, Articles 2085,
138 2087, and where each joint obligor is held liable only for his proportion of the obligation. Article 2086.

139 See also Comment, Solidary Obligations, 25 Tul.L.Rev. 217 (1951).

140 The 'joint and several' obligation of the common law is quite similar to the solidary oblig-
141 ation of the civil law in that either or both of the obligors may be sued for enforcement
142 of the whole obligation. 4 Corbin on Contracts, Section 937 (1950); 17A C.J.S. Contracts
143 s 355; 17 Am.Jur.2d Contracts, Section 299. However, the common-law concepts of 'joint'
144 and of 'several' obligation differ distinctively from the Louisiana concepts denoted by the
145 identical terms.

146 The several obligation of the common law could not only be the legally independent
147 promises of two obligors to perform separate and distinct acts (as with the several obligor
148 of the Louisiana civil law); it could also denote separate promises by two obligors for the
149 same performance (as in the Louisiana solidary obligation). Corbin, Section 925; 17A
150 C.J.S. Contracts s 352. The joint obligation of the common law referred primarily to the
151 ancient necessity to join all joint obligors in the same suit to enforce the obligation (as with
152 Louisiana joint obligors); but it also included the concept that all joint obligors could
153 each be bound for the entire performance to the obligee (rather than only for his proportional
154 part, as with the Louisiana joint obligor). 4 Corbin, Chapter 52 ('Joint and Several Oblig-
155 ations'), especially Section 925; 17A C.J.S. Contracts § 353.

---

of an insurer may be reduced proportionately to the extent that an insured has destroyed that insurer's right to contribution from another insurer by relieving the latter of liability through failure to
give a requisite notice of claim—somewhat similar to the principle of Louisiana law that a creditor
who remits the debt due by one solidary codebtor discharges the other codebtor pro tanto, cf., LSA-
Civil Code Articles 2101, 2103, 2203, Harvey v. Travelers Ins. Co., La.App. 3 Cir., 163 So.2d 915.

Thus, with regard to the old common law distinctions the classification of an obliga- 156
tion as 'several' or 'joint' is not significant for the determination of the real question be- 157
fore us: Can either insurer be held for its full policy limits owed to the insured, even 158
though another insurer has issued a policy covering the same liability? (That is, leaving 159
the insurers to fight out between themselves any right one may have to enforce contribution 160
from the others.) Under the common law definitions the obligation could be either joint 161
or several and still be enforceable in full against either obligor. For purposes of the instant 162
case, the question of whether the insurers' obligations would be termed 'joint' or 'several' 163
by the common law judges is irrelevant. 164

The ultimate test of whether the obligor could be held for the whole or for only a pro- 165
portionate part of the obligation is essentially whether the two obligors each promised the 166
same (i.e., the full) performance or else whether each had promised only a different per- 167
formance (i.e., to pay only its proportionate part of the liability). Corbin, Section 925.[14] 168
In this regard, decision of this essential question is determined by an interpretation of 169
the intention of the parties in the light of the language used and of the surrounding cir- 170
cumstances. 4 Corbin, Section 926; 17A C.J.S. Contracts s 350; 17 Am.Jur.2d Contracts, 171
Section 299. 172

The insuring agreement of a liability insurance contract. 173

Under the insuring agreement, the defendant Allstate agreed 'to pay on behalf of the 174
insured all sums which the insured shall be legally obligated to pay as damages * * * aris- 175
ing out of the ownership, maintenance, or use of the owned automobile * * *.' This in- 176
suring agreement creates a solidary obligation with the insured, although the insured and 177
the insurers are bound differently to perform the same obligation. LSA-C.C. art. 2082; Hi- 178
dalgo v. Dupuy, La.App. 1 Cir., 122 So.2d 639, certiorari denied. Under the respective 179
insuring clauses, each of the insurers are solidarily bound for the same debt, namely the 180
tort liability of the insured, although of course the policy provisions limiting liability 181
limit respectively the recovery against each insurer. 182

Allstate persuasively argues that the pro rata clause limits the solidary liability of the 183
insurer to and for the insured, just as the policy limits do. Allstate in effect contends that, 184
where there is other valid and collectible insurance, the pro rata clause, where applica- 185
ble, has the effect of converting its liability to its insured into joint Or several (i.e., only 186
for the insured's proportionate share of the insured's liability) rather than joint And sev- 187
eral (i.e., solidary with its insured's tort liability up to policy limits). 188

We must reject this forceful argument. We hold instead that by reason of the solidary 189
liability of each of the two insurers with the insured, the policyholder may collect the full 190
amount from either insurer, leaving the latter to its right of contribution from the other 191
insurer, in accord with what Appleman, Section 4913, and Clow v. National Indemnity 192
Co., 54 Wash.2d 198, 339 P.2d 82 (1959) state is the majority rule. We thus conclude that 193
the liability of each insurer with the insured continues to be solidary, Hidalgo v. Dupuy, 194
cited above, and is not transmuted by the pro rata clause into only partial coverage which 195
may be less than the policy limits for which premiums were charged. 196

We so conclude by reason of our interpretation of the presumed intent of the parties 197
to the insurance contract. In doing so, we take into consideration that otherwise the in- 198

---

14. This treatise section contains an interesting discussion noting the distinction between the common-law concepts is largely irrelevant under modern statutory and jurisprudential law, since based chiefly on ancient analytical and procedural doctrines, now nearly extinct, relating to survivorship, discharge, and joinder of parties.

sured may be forced to pay a portion of the recovery against him even though (as here) such recovery is within the policy limits. We are also influenced to conclude this intent by other practical consequences resulting from the opposing interpretations:

a. Proof of existence of other 'valid and collectible' insurance:

Under the pro rata clause (see footnote 1), the company's liability is shared proportionately with the policy limits of another company which has also provided 'valid and collectible insurance against such loss'. If this other alleged insurer is not impleaded in the suit, any holding that this other insurance is 'valid and collectible' is not binding upon the other company in different proceedings by the insured against such other company to enforce such other alleged coverage. Thus a defendant insurer's protection of its insured might be reduced to below policy limits in present litigation, but the insured nevertheless denied recovery against the other insured in subsequent litigation. To effectuate the policy intention we believe that ordinarily the other insurance cannot be regarded as 'valid and collectible' so as to reduce an insurer's liability below policy limits, unless the validity and collectibility[15] of the other insurance is determined by proceedings to which the alleged other insurer is a party.[16]

b. Purpose of liability policy and relative resources of the insurer and the insured

An automobile liability policy is issued to protect the insured against claims arising out of automobile use. Under the insuring agreement, the insurer agrees to pay on behalf of the insured damages within policy limits and to provide him with a legal defense against damage suits so arising. The insurer has readily available legal counsel and nationwide investigative resources, the benefits of both of which the insured contemplates receiving when covered by a valid policy.

If we adopt Allstate's present contention, then where other insurance is potentially available, even under farfetched circumstances such as the present (see Facts above), the insured would be required to retain counsel independent of his insurer's in order to implead the alleged other insurer or else to prove the invalidity or uncollectibility of such coverage. Within the contemplation of the parties and of the purpose of the insurance contract, this burden should instead be on the insurer, which can more readily and efficiently investigate the potential liability of the other insurer and, if so indicated, implead it as a party to the litigation.

(We will use the present litigation as an illustration of the possible harsh results if Allstate's construction of the policy provision were adopted:

(The record shows that the potential claim against Employers, the other insurer, is tenuous; recovery against it is far from assured, if indeed possible at all. The record further shows that the insured garageman (Jacobs) was so impecunious that his own counsel withdrew from the case because of nonpayment of legal fees.

(With its investigative resources, Allstate is better able than Jacobs to produce a showing of coverage by Employers, which showing might even preponderate in the present proceedings since Employers is not impleaded and will not directly oppose such showing with its own resources. Should Allstate by this ad hoc preponderance of evidence in

15. For instance, an insolvent company does not provide 'collectible' insurance within the meaning of the clause. 8 Appleman, Section 4911, text at footnote 2.

16. We pretermit the further suggestion that such a nebulous claim of coverage against the 'other' insurer as the present (see Facts above) should not be regarded as 'valid and collectible', since it is obviously suggestive of litigation and not collectible, if at all, until after suit. See Clow v. National Indemnity Co., 54 Wash.2d 198, 339 P.2d 82 (1959).

These proceedings succeed in reducing its liability below its policy limits (i.e., to $2,500 of the $5,000 judgment rendered against it and Jacobs), then Jacobs would have the burden of suing Employers for the allegedly insured difference; but, now directly opposed by Employers's own investigative resources, he might then be unable to produce evidence that still preponderates that Employers's coverage is valid. (That is, even assuming this impecunious insured could retain counsel and proceed to attempt to collect this problematical claim.) The $2,500 portion of the judgment—allegedly insured by Employers—would of course be executory against him during the pendency of any proceedings by him against Employers, whether or not he eventually prevailed.

(Further, to avoid such possible results, the insured might be required to retain counsel and assert claims against a potential 'other insurer' which both the insured and the counsel he retains feel to be almost groundless.)

c. Procedural consequences of the opposing constructions

Under our interpretation of the pro rata clause, the liability of both insurers with the insured and with each other is solidary. If so, any insurer sued can implead any other alleged insurer by third party demand. LSA-C.C. Art. 2103; LSA-C.C.P. Art. 1111. A defendant insurer is generally far better able to do so than is the insured (see illustration above).

On the other hand, if the obligation of each insurer is only for a proportionate part of the recovery against the insured, then the defendant insurer may not implead the other alleged insurer in order to have the validity of this other coverage finally determined in the present suit. A principal defendant may implead as third party defendant only a party 'who is or may be liable to Him for all or part of the Principal demand.' LSA-C.C.P. Art. 1111; Lanza Enterprises, Inc. v. Continental Insurance Co., La.App. 3 Cir., 129 So.2d 91 (syllabus 2), certiorari denied. Thus, the insured might not have the legal or investigative resources to institute a third party demand against some other insurer potentially liable (see illustration above), but nevertheless the defendant insured itself would be legally unable to implead such other insurer to have determined finally the validity of its coverage.

Placing the duty upon the insurer (rather than the insured) to investigate, to attempt to secure contribution from, and to implead any other alleged insurer is in accord with the insured's fiduciary responsibility to protect the interests of its own insured in matters of settlement and litigation. Cf., Younger v. Lumbermen's Mutual Cas. Co., La.App. 3 Cir.,174 So.2d 672. By a contrary construction of the pro rata clause, the insurer—if unable to directly implead the alleged other insurer—is forced to raise such defense by instead using its superior investigative and legal resources against its own insured in order to exculpate itself from liability for a portion of the policy limits set forth by the policy.

The insuring agreement of the liability insurance contract: Conclusion.

In summary, we conclude that, with respect to the interests of the Insured, the pro rata clause does not entitle an automobile liability insurer to reduce below policy limits its coverage of the liability of the insured. Within the intent of the parties, the pro rata clause is simply designed to regulate contribution As between insurers which may have provided coverage which happens to apply to the same loss.

As stated in a similar context, with citations from numerous jurisdictions in support: '* * * the rights of the insured must be fully protected and, hence, the pro rata clause must not be so applied as to diminish his protection under any circumstances. The reason generally advanced for this principle is that since usually the insurer fixes the amount of his premium regardless of other insurance, and if, after the loss, he happens

287 to find other insurance which relieves him in part from his liability, it is a piece of pure
288 good fortune for him, his principal engagement having been to pay the loss in full up
289 to the face of his policy and that the insured, having given no promise to take out or to
290 keep up other insurance, should not suffer by a windfall of the insurer.' Annotation,
291 Apportionment or contribution as between specific and blanket insurance policies, 169
    A.L.R. 387, 397–98.

292   Our interpretation of the insurance policy to this effect is in accord with the usual
293 rules of policy construction.

294   As shown by the divided jurisprudence of other states, it is at least ambiguous
295 whether the pro rata clause is intended to apportion liability only as between the in-
296 surers with coverage applicable, rather than being intended also to reduce a particu-
297 lar insurer's liability to its insured to a sum less than the policy limits. In cases of
298 ambiguity, policy provisions are construed most favorably to the insured and against
299 the insurer; of the permissible constructions, the courts will adopt that which effec-
300 tuates coverage over that which defeats it. Schonberg v. New York Life Ins. Co., 235 La.
301 461, 104 So.2d 171, Wilks v. Allstate Insurance Co., La.App. 3 Cir., 177 So.2d 790. Fur-
302 thermore, limitations of and exceptions to the coverage of a policy must be clearly ex-
303 pressed and in case of doubt are construed unfavorably to the insurer who, after all,
304 drafted the policy. Kendrick v. C. N. Mason Co., 234 La. 271, 99 So.2d 108, Wilks v.
    Allstate, cited above.

[....]

Questions

1. Lines 26 *et seq.* and footnote 1: What kind or form of liability is Allstate claiming to be bound by? What should be the effect of a pro rata clause? *See* lines 47–90. Note that the Court is making extensive references to cases from federal courts as well as from other states. *See also* footnote 7. What weight should be given to these cases?

2. Line 123–172: Read with attention the comparative analysis made by Judge Tate of "a several obligation in the common law", "the joint and several obligation of the common law", and "the several obligation of the common law". How similar or different are these obligations of common law from the corresponding obligations of the Louisiana civil Code? Does terminology matter? Was Judge Tate correct when he wrote "The source of much of the confusion in the field ... is the variable meaning attached to the common-law concept of a several obligation"? *See* lines 118–122.

3. Lines 174–188: What difference is there, if any, between "joint and several" and "joint or several"? Which form of liability is Allstate claiming to be bound under? Why?

4. Lines 197 *et seq.*: Judge Tate "so conclude[s] [his] interpretation of the presumed in-tent of the parties to the insurance contract". Is this conclusion supported by Louisiana Civil Code article 1796?

5. Lines 215 *et seq.*: Remember the first question? Was your answer similar to or different from Judge Tate's policy statement? Do you agree with Judge Tate's views or policy as to the *raison d'être* of an insurance contract? How far does the Court extend its un-derstanding of its policy? *See* lines 252–256. Should a court be allowed to make legal decisions on policy grounds? Could there exist a legal ground available to the Court to hold the two insurers solidarily liable or liable *in solido* "with each other"? *See* lines 253–254. What do you think of Louisiana Civil Code articles 1815-2 and 1818?

William HOEFLY & Joann C. Hoefly

v.

GOVERNMENT EMPLOYEES INSURANCE COMPANY, et al.

Supreme Court of Louisiana
June 21, 1982
418 So.2d 575

DENNIS, Justice.

The question presented by this case is whether an automobile accident victim's uninsured motorist carrier is solidarily obliged with the tortfeasor so that the victim's timely suit against the latter interrupts prescription with regard to the insurer. The court of appeal affirmed the trial court's judgment sustaining the insurer's plea of prescription, holding that the plaintiffs' timely suit against two tortfeasors, one uninsured and another underinsured, failed to interrupt prescription because the uninsured motorist insurer and the tortfeasors were not solidary obligors. We reverse. An obligation is solidary among debtors when they are obliged to the same thing, so that each may be compelled for the whole, and when payment by one exonerates the other toward the creditor. When these characteristics result from provisions of law, as in the case of the obligation of the tortfeasor and uninsured motorist carrier, an obligation in solido exists without requiring an express declaration. Consequently, the plaintiff's timely and properly filed suit against the tortfeasors interrupted prescription as to his uninsured motorist carrier.

This suit arises out of an automobile accident which occurred on November 1, 1976, when Mrs. Joann C. Hoefly was struck and injured by an automobile driven by Kim Lewiston, a minor, as Mrs. Hoefly was getting out of her own vehicle. On October 12, 1977, Mrs. Hoefly and her husband filed this suit against Neftali Rodriquez, the owner of the automobile driven by Kim Lewiston, Mrs. Margaret C. Lewiston, the mother of Kim Lewiston, and Government Employees Insurance Company, Mrs. Lewiston's liability insurer. In their original and amended petitions the plaintiffs alleged that Kim Lewiston was negligent in operating the vehicle without an operator's license, failing to maintain proper speed and control of the vehicle, and in failing to discover a defective condition in the vehicle. Plaintiffs also alleged that Rodriquez was negligent in allowing an unlicensed minor to operate the vehicle, failing to maintain the vehicle in proper working condition and in seizing the steering wheel from the minor just before the accident. On September 5, 1980, plaintiffs filed an amended and supplemental petition naming Allstate Insurance Company, the Hoeflys' uninsured motorist carrier, as a defendant and alleging that Rodriquez was an uninsured motorist and that the insurance provided by Government Employees to Mrs. Lewiston was insufficient to pay for all of the damages sustained by plaintiffs. Allstate filed a peremptory exception of prescription which was sustained by the trial court. Plaintiffs appealed and the court of appeal affirmed. 403 So.2d 853 (La.App. 2d Cir. 1981). We granted certiorari to review the appeals court's holding that "[a]n uninsured motorist carrier is not liable in solido with the tort-feasor; therefore the filing of suit against the tort-feasor and/or his liability insurer does not interrupt prescription against the uninsured motorist carrier of the injured party." Id. p. 854–855.

Allstate's plea of prescription is based on the circumstance that the accident occurred on November 1, 1976, whereas the amended and supplemental petition naming it as a defendant was not filed until September 5, 1980. It is thus urged that the action for recovery of damages sustained in a motor vehicle accident brought pursuant to uninsured motorist insurance coverage has prescribed, having been filed more than two years after

48 the date of the accident in which the damage was sustained. La.R.S. 9:5629 (Supp.1977).
49 The plaintiffs, however, rely upon the timely institution of their suit against Mr. Ro-
50 driquez, Mrs. Lewiston and her insurer as an interruption of prescription.

51 In our opinion, the trial court and the court of appeal incorrectly decided that All-
52 state's plea of prescription should be sustained. The timely and proper filing of the suit
53 against Mr. Rodriquez, Mrs. Lewiston and her insurer prevented the accrual of pre-
54 scription against them. La.R.S. 9:5801 provides: "All prescriptions affecting the cause of
55 action therein sued upon are interrupted as to all defendants, including minors or inter-
56 dicts, by the commencement of a civil action in a court of competent jurisdiction and in
57 the proper venue. * * * "Since the original filing of the suit interrupted prescription against
58 Mr. Rodriquez, Mrs. Lewiston and her insurer, it also interrupted prescription against
59 Allstate. "A suit brought against one of the debtors *in solido* interrupts prescription with
60 regard to all." La.C.C. art. 2097. Although the court of appeal held, and Allstate contends,
61 that the filing of suit against the tortfeasor and his liability insurer does not interrupt pre-
62 scription against the uninsured motorist carrier of the injured party, we are constrained
63 to disagree.

64 Under Civil Code Article 2091, "[t]here is an obligation *in solido* on the part of the
65 debtors, when they are all obliged to the same thing, so that each may be compelled for
66 the whole, and when the payment which is made by one of them, exonerates the others
67 toward the creditor." When an obligation fulfills this definition and contains these ingre-
68 dients, the obligation is in solido. *Sampay v. Morton Salt Co.*, 395 So.2d 326 (La.1981);
69 *Foster v. Hampton*, 381 So.2d 789 (La.1980); *Pearson v. Hartford Accident & Indemnity*
70 *Co.*, 281 So.2d 724 (La.1973); *Thomas v. W. W. Clarklift, Inc.*, 375 So.2d 375 (La.1979) (Den-
71 nis, J., concurring); *Wooten v. Wimberly*, 272 So.2d 303 (La.1972) (Tate, J., concurring and
72 Barham, J., dissenting); *Kern v. Travelers Insurance Co.*, 407 So.2d 2 (La.App. 4th Cir.
73 1981); *Granger v. General Motors Corp.*, 171 So.2d 720 (La.App. 3d Cir. 1965); *Hidalgo v.*
74 *Dupuy*, 122 So.2d 639 (La.App. 1st Cir. 1960); The Work of the Louisiana Appellate Courts
75 for the 1973–1974 Term-Obligations, 35 La.L.Rev. 280, 297 (1975). As we analyze the
76 obligation in this case, it satisfies the prerequisites for a solidary obligation.[1]

77 The tortfeasor and the uninsured motorist carrier are obliged to the same thing. A
78 tortfeasor is obliged to repair the damage that he has wrongfully caused to the innocent
79 automobile accident victim. La.C.C. art. 2315. Subject to conditions not granted the tort-
80 feasor, the uninsured motorist carrier is independently obliged to repair the same dam-
81 age. By effect of the uninsured motorist statute, La.R.S. 22:1406(D)(1)(a), and its insuring
82 agreement, the plaintiffs' uninsured motorist carrier is required to pay, subject to statu-
83 tory and policy conditions, amounts which they are entitled under other provisions of law
84 to recover as damages from owners or operators of uninsured or underinsured motor ve-
85 hicles. By effect of law and the terms of the insuring agreement, therefore, both the unin-
86 sured motorist carrier and the tortfeasor are obliged to the same thing. The Work of the

1. Since this court has rejected the distinction between "perfect" and "imperfect" solidarity, *Foster v. Hampton, supra* at 791, we need not analyze the nature of the present obligation from this stand-point, although the exercise may prove interesting from an historical and academic perspective. See 2 M. Planiol, Civil Law Treatise, pt. 1, nos. 777–779 (11th ed. La.St.L.Inst. trans. 1959); 4 C. Aubry & C. Rau, Droit Civil Francais, §298b (6th ed. Bartin) in A. Yiannopoulos, 1 Civil Law Translations 20–21 (1965); The Work of the Louisiana Appellate Courts for the 1967–1968 Term-Insurance, 29 La.L.Rev. 253 (1969); The Work of the Louisiana Appellate Courts for the 1973–1974 Term-Obligations, 35 La.L.Rev. 291 (1975); The Work of the Louisiana Appellate Courts for the 1974–1975 Term-Obligations, 36 La.L.Rev. 375 (1976); Comment, Solidary Obligations, 25 Tul.L.Rev. 217 (1951); Comment, Pre-scribing Solidarity: Contributing to the Indemnity Dilemma, 41 La.L.Rev. 657 (1981).

Louisiana Appellate Courts, 1974–1975 Term-Obligations, 36 La.L.Rev. 375, 379–380 at   87
n. 23; The Work of the Louisiana Appellate Courts for the 1967–1968 Term-Insurance,   88
29 La.L.Rev. 253, 257 (1969); The Work of the Louisiana Appellate Courts for the 1966–1967   89
Term-Insurance, 28 La.L.Rev. 372, 373–374 (1968).   90

The tortfeasor and the uninsured motorist carrier each may be compelled for the whole.   91
The principal result of solidarity is to prevent the division of the debt and to obligate   92
each debtor for the whole, as if he were alone. 2 M. Planiol, Civil Law Treatise, pt. 1, no.   93
745 (11th ed. La.St.L.Inst. trans. 1959). This essential element of solidarity, that each   94
debtor may be compelled for the whole, means simply that the debtor who has been sued   95
cannot plead the benefit of division, which was invented for the benefit of sureties whereby   96
the creditor is required to divide his action between them. This is covered expressly in   97
Article 2094 because under the ancient law several attempts had been made to extend   98
benefit of division to solidary co-debtors. That each debtor is held for the whole, i.e., un-   99
able to plead the benefit of division, is solidarity's most direct consequence. 2 M. Plan-   100
iol, *supra*, no. 746.   101

This requisite of solidarity is satisfied in the case of the uninsured motorist and the   102
tortfeasor because neither may plead the benefit of division, as if each were alone. To per-   103
mit the tortfeasor or uninsured motorist carrier to plead the benefit of division would be   104
inimical to the legislative aim of the uninsured motorist statute. The object of that leg-   105
islation is to promote full recovery for damages by innocent automobile accident victims   106
by making uninsured motorist coverage available for their benefit as primary protection   107
when the tortfeasor is without insurance and as additional or excess coverage when he is   108
inadequately insured. *Bond v. Commercial Union Assur. Co.*, 407 So.2d 401, 407 (La.1981)   109
(on rehearing); *Booth v. Fireman's Fund Ins. Co.*, 253 La. 521, 218 So.2d 580, 28 A.L.R.3d   110
573 (1968). The statute is to be liberally construed to carry out this objective of provid-   111
ing reparation for those injured through no fault of their own. *Niemann v. Travelers In-*   112
surance Co., 368 So.2d 1003 (La.1979); *Elledge v. Warren*, 263 So.2d 912 (La.App. 3d Cir.   113
1972); *Valdez v. Fed. Mut. Ins. Co.*, 272 Cal.App.2d 223, 77 Cal.Rptr. 411 (1969). The leg-   114
islation cannot be construed, therefore, to benefit the insurer and the tortfeasor by requiring   115
the accident victim to divide his action between them.   116

The uninsured motorist carrier is obliged differently from the tortfeasor because its   117
liability is conditioned by the tortfeasor's total or partial lack of liability insurance, the type   118
of damage he has caused and any limits in the insurer's policy that are permitted by law.   119
Contrary to Allstate's arguments, however, the terms and conditions which have been al-   120
lowed the uninsured motorist carrier by law and by contract, while the tortfeasor is bound   121
pure and simple, do not prevent the uninsured motorist carrier and the tortfeasor from   122
being obliged to the same thing or being unable to plead the benefit of division. "The   123
obligations may be *in solido*, although one of the debtors be obliged differently from the   124
other to the payment of one and the same thing; for instance, if the one be but conditionally   125
bound, whilst the engagement of the other is pure and simple, or if the one is allowed a   126
term which is not granted to the other." La.C.C. art. 2092. See, *American Bank and Trust*   127
Co. v. Blue Bird Rest. & Lounge, Inc. 290 So.2d 302 (La.1974); *Pearson v. Hartford Acci-*   128
dent & Ind. Co., 281 So.2d 724 (La.1973); *Hidalgo v. Dupuy*, 122 So.2d 639 (La.App. 1st   129
Cir. 1960).   130

For similar reasons, the fact that the uninsured motorist carrier is bound by the com-   131
bined effect of the tortfeasor's wrongful act, the uninsured motorist statute, and the car-   132
rier's delivery or issuance for delivery of automobile liability insurance, while the tortfeasor   133
is obliged merely because of his delict, does not prevent there being an obligation in solido   134
on the part of the debtors. The obligation may be in solido even though the obligations   135

136 of the obligors arise from separate acts or by different reasons. La.C.C. arts. 2091, 2092.
137 *Pearson v. Hartford Accident & Ind. Co., supra. Granger v. General Motors Corp., supra;*
138 *Hidalgo v. Dupuy, supra; Finance Security Co. v. Williams,* 42 So.2d 310 (La.App. 1st Cir.
139 1949); *Kirtland v. J. Ray McDermott & Co.,* 568 F.2d 1166, 1171 (5th Cir. 1978); *Avon-*
140 *dale Shipyards v. Vessell Thomas E. Cuffe,* 434 F.Supp. 920, 932 (E.D.La.1977); Develop-
141 ments in the Law, 1979–1980-Obligations, 41 La.L.Rev. 355, 357 (1981).

142   When payment is made by either the tortfeasor or the uninsured motorist carrier the
143 other is exonerated toward the creditor as to the solidary obligation. This is a direct con-
144 sequence of each debtor being obliged to the same thing so that each may be compelled
145 for the whole, as if he were the sole debtor. 4 C. Aubry & C. Rau, *supra*, p. 27. Moreover,
146 the underlying purpose of both delictual responsibility and uninsured motorist coverage
147 is to promote and effectuate complete reparation, no more or no less. Accordingly, as to
148 the debt to which the tortfeasor and uninsured motorist carrier are solidarily obliged,
149 payment of it by one exonerates the other toward the creditor.

150   When an obligation by effect of law contains the requirements or fulfills the defini-
151 tion of Article 2091, the obligation is in solido and the law from which it results need not
152 state that the obligation is solidary. "Article 2093 provides that '[a]n obligation *in solido*
153 is not presumed; it must be expressly stipulated.

154   This rule ceases to prevail only in cases where an obligation *in solido* takes place of
155 right by virtue of some provisions of the law.'" The first paragraph of Article 2093 deal-
156 ing with conventional solidarity, requires that it be expressly stipulated. But it is other-
157 wise with regard to the second paragraph of the same article which, dealing with legal
158 solidarity, admits it in all cases where it results from a provision of law, without requir-
159 ing an express declaration. 4 C. Aubry & C. Rau, Droit Civil Francais, § 298b note 13
160 (6th ed. Bantin) in A. Yiannopoulos, 1 Civil Law Translations 24 (1965); *Cline v. Cres-*
161 *cent City R. Co.,* 41 La.Ann. 1031, 6 So. 851 (1889); *Hidalgo v. Dupuy, supra; Finance Se-*
162 *curity Co. v. Williams, supra.* The previous expressions to the contrary by this court in
163 *Wooten v. Wimberly,* 272 So.2d 303 (La.1973) and *Cox v. Shreveport Packing Co.,* 213 La.
164 53, 34 So.2d 373 (1948), which have received scholarly criticism, *Wooten v. Wimberly,*
165 *supra* (Tate, J., concurring and Barham, J., dissenting); The Work of the Louisiana Ap-
166 pellate Courts, 1972–1973-Obligations, 34 La.L.Rev. 231 (1974); Note, The Nonsolid-
167 ness of Solidarity, 34 La.L.Rev. 648 (1974); Comment, Prescribing Solidarity: Contributing
168 to the Indemnity Dilemma, 41 La.L.Rev. 657, 674–676, and have been substantially un-
169 dermined, *Sampay v. Morton Salt Co., supra; Foster v. Hampton, supra; Kern v. Travelers*
170 *Insurance Co., supra,* are now expressly overrruled.

171   The solidary obligation in the present case results primarily from provisions of law,
172 viz., the general rules of delictual responsibility, La.C.C. arts. 2315, et seq., and the unin-
173 sured motorist statute, La.R.S. 22:1406(D). Although an insurer must deliver or issue for
174 delivery automobile liability insurance in order to be bound, the basic ingredients of the
175 obligation are provided and required by law. Under these circumstances, the obligation
176 is solidary by operation of law, without requiring an express declaration.

177   Allstate argues that the conclusion we have reached will cause all effects of solidarity
178 to be applied in uninsured motorist cases. Care should be taken by civilian attorneys and
179 jurists to be on guard against applying one segment of the code in isolation from others.
180 Neither the Civil Code nor the revised statutes were intended to be applied in this man-
181 ner. A full delineation of the relationship between the tortfeasor and the uninsured mo-
182 torist carrier after payment of the debt owed by them solidarily is beyond the scope of this
183 case. However, it is clear that the Civil Code recognizes that debtors, although solidarily

bound for the creditor's benefit, may have differing relationships among themselves. The 184
conclusion that debtors are solidarily bound does not alone determine the rights and 185
obligations of the debtors in relation to each other. La.C.C. arts. 2103, 2104, 2106; 2 M. 186
Planiol, *supra*, nos. 767–771; *Wooten v. Wimberly, supra* (Tate, J., concurring). The Work 187
of the Louisiana Appellate Courts for the 1972–1973 Term-Obligations, 34 La.L.Rev. 231, 188
233 (1974). 189

For the foregoing reasons, the judgment of the court of appeal is reversed and the case 190
is remanded to the district court for further proceedings. 191

REVERSED AND REMANDED. 192

CALOGERO, J., dissents and assigns reasons. 193

MARCUS, J., dissents and assigns reasons. 194

BLANCHE, J., dissents and assigns reasons. 195

MARCUS, Justice (dissenting). 196

There is an obligation *in solido* on the part of the debtors, when they are all obliged to 197
the same thing, so that each may be compelled for the whole, and when the payment 198
which is made by one of them, exonerates the others toward the creditor. La.Civ.Code 199
art. 2091. An obligation *in solido* is not presumed; it must be expressly stipulated. This 200
rule ceases to prevail only in cases where an obligation *in solido* takes place of right by 201
virtue of some provisions of the law. La.Civ.Code art. 2093. I do not consider that an in- 202
jured party's U/M carrier is liable *in solido* with the tortfeasor. U/M coverage is a con- 203
tract whereby the insurer agrees to indemnify the insured in the event that the insured is 204
injured by a tortfeasor who is uninsured or underinsured. There is no relationship, con- 205
tractually or otherwise, between the U/M carrier and the tortfeasor. The obligation of the 206
tortfeasor to repair the damage that he has caused is not the same as the obligation of the 207
U/M carrier under its insurance contract. Moreover, there is no provision of law which 208
makes the U/M carrier liable *in solido* with the tortfeasor. Compare La.Civ.Code art. 2324 209
which makes joint tortfeasors "answerable *in solido.*" Accordingly, I respectfully dissent. 210

CALOGERO, Justice, dissenting. 211
212

I dissent from the majority opinion because in my view the requirements for solidar- 213
ity expressed in La.C.C. art. 2091 are not met in this case; the payment by one of the 214
debtors (uninsured motorist carrier) does not exonerate the other (tortfeasor). 215

La.R.S. 22:1406(D)(4) does not grant the uninsured motorist carrier, which pays its in- 216
sured in the appropriate case, the right of legal subrogation. To the contrary, the provi- 217
sion only gives the uninsured motorist carrier a right of reimbursement from "the proceeds 218
of any settlement or judgment resulting from the exercise of any rights of recovery of 219
such person [the insured] against any person or organization legally responsible for the 220
bodily injury for which such payment is made." Thus, under this provision, there is no 221
exoneration of the tortfeasor because of payment by the uninsured motorist carrier. The 222
victim/insured may assert his claim against the tortfeasor with a right in the uninsured 223
motorist carrier to be reimbursed from the insured out of any recovery. 224

Insofar as the insured and the insurer may contract in the policy to give the insurer a 225
right to conventional subrogation [See *Niemann v. Travelers Ins. Co.*, 368 So. 1003 (La.1979) 226
and *Bond v. Commercial Union Assur. Co.*, 407 So.2d 401 (La.1981), on rehearing], the 227
tortfeasor is not exonerated toward the claimant by the *payment* by the uninsured mo- 228
torist carrier. At best it can be said that the conventional subrogation effects an assign- 229
ment of the claimant's right against the tortfeasor to the uninsured motorist carrier. 230

231   BLANCHE, Justice (dissenting).

232   Louisiana law requires all insurers to extend uninsured motorist coverage to their
233 insureds, unless such coverage is explicitly waived by the insured. Under the unin-
234 sured motorist portion of an insurance policy, the uninsured motorist carrier con-
235 tracts to indemnify the insured, in the event the insured is injured by a tortfeasor who
236 is unable to fully respond in damages. The *sole* basis of the uninsured motorist carrier's
237 liability to the insured remains the contract of insurance, to which the tortfeasor is
       not a party.

238   The majority opinion correctly notes that "[a]n obligation *in solido* is not presumed;
239 it must be expressly stipulated. This rule ceases to prevail only in cases where an obliga-
240 tion *in solido* takes place of right by virtue of some provisions of the law." Civil Code Art.
241 2093. In erroneously concluding that the relationship between the uninsured motorist
242 carrier and the tortfeasor is one of legal solidarity, the majority completely ignores the ab-
243 sence of a most vital element present in all other cases of legal solidarity. There must be
244 *some* relationship between the two parties who are to be held solidarily liable. The solidary
245 relationship between an employer and his employees is premised upon the employment
246 relationship which exists between these parties. A principal becomes solidarily liable with
247 his agent by virtue of their unique relationship. The solidary relationship of a liability
248 insurer and its insured is founded upon the vital contract of insurance which binds these
249 two parties.

250   In all other cases in which legal solidarity arises, there exists *some* relationship between
251 the parties who are held solidarily liable. By contrast, there is *no* relationship, contrac-
252 tual or otherwise, between the uninsured motorist carrier and the tortfeasor. A solidary
253 relationship between the uninsured motorist carrier and the tortfeasor does not exist by
254 virtue of some provision of the law;[2] rather, it is purely the creation of the majority opin-
255 ion. Such judicial legislation is beyond the bounds of our authority. By the express pro-
256 visions of C.C. art. 2093, we cannot presume a solidary relationship where none is intended
       to exist.

257   For the foregoing reasons, I respectfully dissent.

Questions

1. Line 10 *et seq.*: What is the main issue raised in this case?

2. Lines 77–90: Notice the first line or statement. It is a heading which is developed in
    the following paragraph. The whole legal analysis is based on the last two words of
    that sentence, "same thing". Consider the role of the persuasive authority cited by
    the Court.

3. Lines 131–141: What matters the most, if at all? The fact that two obligors owe the
    same thing, hence they can be held solidarily liable? Or that the sources of solidar-
    ity between these two obligors can be different?

4. Lines 142–149: What is the real foundation or reason for solidarity between two
    obligors?

5. Lines 193–257: On what grounds did the dissenting Justices dissent? What is their
    main concern? Do they share the concern expressed by the majority on lines
    142–149?

---

2. Compare C.C. art. 2324, which establishes a solidary relationship between joint tortfeasors.

LOUISIANA BANK AND TRUST COMPANY, CROWLEY, Louisiana
v.
Mrs. Jewel B. BOUTTE et al.
Supreme Court of Louisiana
Feb. 24, 1975
309 So.2d 274

DIXON, Justice.

Louisiana Bank and Trust Company of Crowley sued Rex Rice Company, Inc. and Lake Rice Mill, Inc., claiming a balance due on promissory notes in the amount of over $600,000, and joined in the same suit defendant Matthew L. Hanagriff and three other persons under 'continuing guaranty' agreements, alleging that the defendants were liable for the debts of Rex Rice Company, Inc., the principal debtor.

While the case was pending, a compromise agreement released the parties defendant with the exception of Hanagriff, who did not join the compromise agreement, and against whom the plaintiff bank reserved its rights.

There was judgment in the trial court in favor of plaintiff and against defendant, which judgment was amended and affirmed in the Court of Appeal. Louisiana Bank & Trust Co. v. Boutte et al., La.App. 298 So.2d 884 (1974).

We granted writs on the application of defendant Hanagriff to determine the effect of the 'continuing guaranty' agreement. Before us the defendant argues that his obligation under the contract of guaranty had prescribed; that the release of the principal debtor released the defendant, who was a surety; that the plaintiff creditor received immovable and other property in the payment of the principal debt, resulting in the full discharge of the surety under C.C. 3062; and, finally, that defendant's property had been illegally subjected to attachment.

The record reveals that Rex Rice Company, Inc. was indebted to the plaintiff bank in 1962. On May 18 of that year the 'continuing guaranty' agreement was executed and signed by the four shareholders and directors of the Rex Rice Company, Inc., including the defendant Hanagriff. The complete agreement is reproduced in footnote.[1] This suit was filed March 25, 1969, and a writ of attachment was issued, seizing Hanagriff's home.

---

1. 'CONTINUING GUARANTY': In consideration of the LOUISIANA BANK AND TRUST COMPANY, CROWLEY, LOUISIANA, at our request, giving or extending terms of credit to REX RICE COMPANY, INC. hereinafter called debtor, we hereby give this continuing guaranty to the said LOUISIANA BANK AND TRUST COMPANY, CROWLEY, LOUISIANA, its transferees or assigns, for the payment in full, together with all interest, fees and charges of whatsoever nature and kind, of any indebtedness, direct or contingent, of said debtor to said LOUISIANA BANK AND TRUST COMPANY, CROWLEY, LOUISIANA, up to the amount of TWO HUNDRED THOUSAND DOLLARS Dollars, [sic] whether due or to become due, now existing or hereafter arising. The Bank may, in its judgment, grant extensions, take and give securities, accent compositions, grant releases and discharges, make changes of any sort whatever in the terms of its contract or manner of doing business with the debtor and with other parties and securities in relation thereto. The Bank may also apply all moneys received from the debtor and others or from securities as it may think best, without in any way altering, affecting, limiting or lessening the liability of the undersigned under this Guaranty; the whole without any notice to or consent from us. The Bank shall not be bound to exhaust its recourse against the debtor or other persons or upon the securities it may hold before being entitled to payment from the undersigned of the amount hereby guaranteed. We do furthermore bind and obligate ourselves, our heirs and assigns, in solido with said debtor, for the payment of the said indebtedness precisely as if the same had been contracted and was due or owing by us in person hereby agreeing to and binding

Release of the Principal Debtor

In the interval between the filing and the trial of the suit, three compromise agreements had been executed, the effect of which was to convey property from Rex Rice Company, Inc., Jack R. Smith, Mrs. Louie F. (Hattie F.) Broussard and Mrs. Jewel B. Boutte, the other three shareholders and directors of Rex Rice Company, Inc., to the plaintiff bank. Those parties were released from further liability. The bank reserved its rights against Hanagriff. Numerous other parties were involved in the compromise agreements, including another bank and other creditors of Rex Rice Company, Inc. Judgment was rendered against Hanagriff alone on June 7, 1973, following a trial on the merits on April 10, 1973. At the trial, it was shown that the balance due on Rex Rice Company, Inc. indebtedness to the plaintiff bank was $477,021.46, all of which had accrued following the execution of the 'continuing guaranty' agreement. Since the 'continuing guaranty' was for a sum of $200,000, the trial court rendered judgment against Hanagriff for one-fourth of that amount, because he was one of four signers. The Court of Appeal reduced the amount of the judgment against Hanagriff to $40,000 because Rex Rice Company, Inc. was also a solidary obligor, making Hanagriff's virile share one-fifth of the total, under C.C. 2103.[2]

Defendant's argument that the release of the principal operated to discharge his, the surety's, liability depends upon classifying the instrument of 'continuing guaranty' as a contract of suretyship. Defendant relies on the following cases for the proposition that a surety bound In solido is a surety nevertheless: Jones v. Fleming, 15 La.Ann. 522 (1860); Lee v. City of Baton Rouge, 243 La. 850, 147 So.2d 868 (1963); Keller v. General Motors Acceptance Corp., 233 La. 320, 96 So.2d 598 (1957); Elmer Candy Co. v. Baumann, 150 So. 427 (La.App.1933); Brock v. First State Bank & Trust Co., 187 La. 766, 175 So. 569 (1937).

Jones v. Fleming supports the position of the defendant; the court there disregarded the surety's liability In solido and released him under C.C. 3063 when the principal debtor was granted a prolongation of term for payment. The substance of the holding in Jones v. Fleming, However, was disapproved in Jones v. Fleming, however, was disapproved, [*sic*] La. 970, 76 So. 166 (1917), and was criticized in a comment at 39 Tul.L.Rev. 85 (1964–65), where the cases on solidary suretyship are collected and analyzed.

The other cases cited in defendant's brief do not support his position. Lee v. City of Baton Rouge involved the compromise of a tort claim, and held that the release of joint

---

ourselves, our heirs and assigns, by all terms and conditions contained in any note or notes signed or to be signed by said debtor, making ourselves a party thereto; hereby waiving notice of any such indebtedness and of demand, presentment, protest or notice of any act to establish the liability of any party or any commercial or other paper, indebtedness or obligation covered by this guaranty; we do further waive all notice and all pleas of discussion and division and we agree to pay upon demand at any time to said Bank, its transferees or assigns, the full amount of said indebtedness up to the amount of this guaranty, together with interest, fees and charges, as above set forth, becoming subrogated in the event of payment in full by us to the claim of said Bank, its transferees or assigns, together with whatever security if any they may hold against said indebtedness.'

'It is expressly agreed that this continuing guaranty is absolute and complete, and that acceptance and notice of acceptance thereof by the Bank, are therefore unnecessary and they are hereby expressly waived, and the same shall continue in force until written notice or its discontinuance shall be served upon one of the executive officers of the said Bank, but such discontinuance shall not affect our liability on any debts and/or obligations of the debtor then existing nor the liability of any other party liable in the premises. In faith whereof we have hereunto signed our name on this the 18th day of May, 1962. S/ Jack R. SmithS/ Matthew L. HanagriffS/ Mrs. Louie F. BroussardS/ Mrs. Jewel B. Boutte'

2. Plaintiff has not complained of this ruling, and the question is not before us whether the contractual terms of the 'continuing guaranty' would have permitted a judgment against Hanagriff for the entire $200,000.

tort feasor with reservation of rights against the tort feasor who was primarily liable did
not release the tort feasor who was primarily liable. The case has no application.

Keller v. GMAC, is not applicable. This was an action by a guarantor to recover the amount
paid by an endorser and guarantor for negligently marking the note paid and returning
it to the maker.

The Elmer Candy Co. case is not applicable. It merely held that the release of one solidary surety, or guarantor, without reservation released the other solidary guarantors.

Brock v. First State Bank, although containing language that 'a contract of guaranty in
this state is equivalent to a contract of surety,' (175 So. 569, 570) held that guarantors, bound
unconditionally and In solido for the payment of a note could be sued at the same time
as the principal, and that the creditor could not be required to exhaust his remedies against
the principal before suing the surety.

Like so many legal classifications, those of surety and solidary obligor are not mutually exclusive. Provisions for Solidary sureties are found in the Civil Code, and can be
traced to Roman law. Planiol, Traite Elementaire De Droit Civil, translated by Louisiana
State Law Institute, Vol. 2, No. 2351.[3]

Civil Code 3045[4] provides that the obligation of the surety toward the creditor, when
the surety is bound In solido with the debtor, is 'regulated by the same principles which
have been established for debtors In solido.'

Civil Code 2106,[5] with reference to the case in which there is a principal debtor, for whose
benefit the principal obligation was incurred, provides that with regard to the principal
debtor, the solidary codebtors 'are considered only as his securities.' As Planiol explains
in Vol. 2, No. 768:

> 'Art. 1216 (C.N. 1216; C.C. 2106) has taken care of this situation by provid-
> ing that in such a case the debt should be entirely borne by the debtor who is di-
> rectly concerned, and that the others are to be considered in relation to him as his
> Sureties only; they have merely bound themselves in the interest of another. How-

---

3. 'Sureties resemble solidary co-debtors, in their relations with the principal debtor, and in their relations between themselves: there is no division between them, and each one of them can be sued before
the debtor. However this is not true solidarity, since the law accords to them the benefits of discussion and
of division, benefits which are the negation of solidarity and which are refused to real solidary co-debtors.'
This contradictory explanation is explained by the historic development of suretyship. Under the Roman
Fidejussio, the surety was originally a debtor as firmly bound as the principal obligor: Then there was a
reaction in favor of debtors, and various benefits were accorded which provisionally improved the position of the surety. But they went too far. By relaxing the liability of the surety they injured borrowers
whose credit was destroyed. Capitalists demand serious security; if not, they do not loan; and in fact, although our laws have retained the favors accumulated by the Roman law for the benefit of sureties, the
practice has regulated itself otherwise and has passed them by. *It employs the very simple method of requiring
the sureties to renounce, by a special clause, all their benefits which has the effect of re-establishing the ancient
solidarity affaced by the Roman legislation.* In our day simple suretyship tends to become more and more
rare; almost always the sureties engage themselves solidarily with the principal debtor or between themselves. There has been a return thus, to the primitive rigor of the law.' (Emphasis added).
4. 'The obligation of the surety towards the creditor is to pay him in case the debtor should not
himself satisfy the debt; and the property of such debtor is to be previously discussed or seized, unless the security should have renounced the plea of discussion, or should be bound In solido jointly
with the debtor, in which case the effects of his engagement are to be regulated by the same principles which have been established for debtors In solido.'
5. 'If the affair for which the debt has been contracted In solido, concern only one of the coo blig-
ors, [sic] In solido, that one is liable for the whole debt towards the other codebtors, who, with regard to him, are considered only as his securities.'

ever, this assimilation with the surety is not true except in the relations of the co-debtors among themselves: 'with relation to him,' says Art. 1216, and not in their relations with the creditor. It is, in fact, an entirely different thing to obligate one-self as a solidary co-debtor and as a surety; the surety enjoys, against the credi-tor, various benefits which the solidary debtor does not enjoy.' (Emphasis added).

The effect of the application of these articles is that, as between the creditor and the sol-idary surety, the obligations of the surety are governed by the rules of solidary obligors.

The solidary surety waives the pleas of discussion and division. C.C. 3045; Brock v. First State Bank, supra, Hibernia Bank & Trust Co. v. Succession of Cancienne, 140 La. 969, 74 So. 267 (1917); Home Ins. Co. v. Voorhies Co., 168 So. 724 (La.App.1936); 2 Planiol, No. 2352. A remission to a simple surety does not discharge his co-sureties. C.C. 2205. As to solidary sureties, a remission by the creditor was held, in Elmer Candy Co. v. Baumann, supra, to have discharged the solidary co-sureties because the creditor failed to reserve his rights against the remaining sureties; otherwise, C.C. 2203[6] provides that a discharge of one solidary co-debtor discharges the others.

Among the co-obligors, however, bound In solido, the legal relationships may be gov-erned by the rules of suretyship. Both the simple surety and the solidary surety who pay the debt have a right of recourse against the principal debtor.[7] C.C. 2106; Marfese v. Nel-son, 10 Orl.App. 288 (1913); 2 Planiol, No. 768, No. 2352.

There are exceptions, and sometimes the relationships among solidary sureties are not governed by the rules of suretyship. A simple surety who pays the whole debt can enforce contribution against the other sureties, but Only when he has paid 'in consequence of a lawsuit instituted against him.' C.C. 3058. But a solidary surety need not await suit be-fore paying, in order to preserve his right of contribution. There is no reason to require such a delay, since pleas of discussion and division are not available to him. Ferriday v. Purnell, 2 La.Ann. 334 (1847); Bond v. Bishop, 18 La.Ann. 549 (1866).

We hold, therefore, that the compromise[8] and release of the principal debtor, Rex Rice Company, Inc., did not operate to release the solidary surety, Hanagriff.

---

6. 'The remission or conventional discharge in favor of one of the codebtors In solido, discharges all the others, unless the creditor has expressly reserved his right against the latter. In the latter case, he can not [sic] claim the debt without making a deduction of the part of him to whom he has made the remission.'

7. The right of subrogation of the surety who pays the creditor is not the only source of the solidary obligor's action against the principal debtor when he pays the creditor. A compromise and discharge of the principal debtor by the creditor might leave the simple surety, if he were forced to pay the creditor any balance, without any subrogation rights against the principal debtor because of the accessory na-ture of the suretyship obligation. C.C. 3035. If the principal creditor could discharge the debtor and proceed against the surety, the creditor's rights against the principal debtor having been extinguished, there would be nothing left to which the surety might become subrogated, should he become forced to pay the creditor. The other source of the solidary surety's right of recourse against the principal debtor is 'one which is personal to him arising from the contract of suretyship ...' 1 Planiol, No. 2354, No. 2355. It is this remedy, says Planiol, which is referred to in C.N. 2028 and C.N. 2030 (2029), the sources of our C.C. 3052 and 3053. C.C. 3053 refers to the right of subrogation granted to co-debtors In solido, a different source of the paying solidary surety's right of recourse against the principal debtor. Therefore, when, under a contract a solidary suretyship, one is forced to pay the creditor a debt of the principal obligor, even after the creditor has discharged the principal obligor, the surety does not lose this right of recourse against the principal debtor, which has arisen from the nature of the contract of suretyship.

8. Compare 2 Planiol, No. 761: 'If one only of the co-debtors compromises with the creditor, the compromise does not bind the others and cannot be opposed by them to the creditor. (Art. 2051).' Our C.C. 3077 differs in phraseology from C.N. 2051, its source.

The judgment of the Court of Appeal is therefore affirmed and amended, awarding plain- 117
tiff, Louisiana Bank and Trust Company, Crowley, Louisiana, judgment against defen- 118
dant, Matthew L. Hanagriff, in the sum of $40,000, and there is further judgment in favor 119
of Matthew L. Hanagriff, plaintiff in reconvention, and against Louisiana Bank and Trust 120
Company, Crowley, Louisiana, defendant in reconvention, dissolving the writ of attach- 121
ment and awarding plaintiff in reconvention damages in the sum of $100.00, all at the cost 122
of defendant, Matthew L. Hanagriff. 123

SANDERS, C.J., concurs with written reasons. 124

BARHAM, J., concurs with reasons. 125

SANDERS, Chief Justice (concurring). 126

In the present case, the plaintiff compromised its suit against Rex Rice Company, Inc., 127
and others, reserving its rights against the present defendant, Hanagriff, who had exe- 128
cuted a continuing guaranty. The main question is whether the release of Rex Rice Com- 129
pany discharged the defendant. I think not. 130

Article 2203 of the Louisiana Civil Code provides: 131

'The remission or conventional discharge in favor of one of the codebtors In 132
solido, discharges all the others, unless the creditor has expressly reserved his 133
right against the latter. 134

'In the latter case, he can not [*sic*] claim the debt without making a deduction 135
of the part of him to whom he has made the remission.' 136

Since the compromise contained an express reservation of rights against the present 137
defendant, he was not discharged in accordance with the exception set forth in the above 138
article. 139

For the reasons assigned, I respectfully concur in the decree. 140

BARHAM, Justice (concurring). 141

I concur in the majority opinion under the simple finding that as between the Plain- 142
tiff-creditor and All of the original defendants, Rex Rice Company, Inc., and the four in- 143
dividuals who signed the continuing guaranty (including the present defendant, Hanagriff), 144
all the defendants were Principal co-obligors. 145

I differ from the majority in my opinion that having been presented Only with the 146
question of the relationship between The plaintiff and The single defendant, Hanagriff, 147
we are obliged to confine ourselves to a discussion of the law pertinent to resolving the 148
legal rights and obligations betweeen [*sic*] them. Significantly, we do not have before 149
us the proper parties for determining the legal relationship between the rice company 150
and the four continuing guarantors. That must be resolved in another lawsuit in the 151
absence of agreement among those parties. We cannot here decide whether the five 152
original defendants are solidary obligors as between themselves to the extent that each 153
is responsible for a virile portion of the debt or whether one of the five is a principal 154
obligor who must indemnify the other four under a surety agreement. We should not 155
even decide in this lawsuit whether, in relation to each other, the four continuing guar- 156
antors are solidary obligors or solidary sureties with a right of virile contribution 157
among themselves. 158

The majority opinion quotes doctrinal authority which in fact is a correct analysis of 159 the position I have stated above. The difficulty is that the majority opinion does not clearly set forth the result which should be obtained in this suit under that doctrinal statement. The quote from 2 M. Planiol, Traite, e le mentaire de droit civil No. 768 (La.St.L.Inst. trans. (1959) is a correct statement of the law applicable to the issue between the parties to this lawsuit. However, the following translation of 7 M. Planiol and M. Ripert, Traite pratique de droit civil francais 466–67 (2me e d. Esmein, 1954) may more clearly state the position of the French in interpreting their Code Napole on Article 1216 (our Civil Code Article 2106):

> '§ 1091. Case where one of the debtors is totally liberated. The inequality in the debtors' share of the common debt may be very large. Carrying this conclusion to the farthest extreme it may even be, as it is in fact in the most recurring cases, that, given two solidary debtors, only one must fully pay the debt without the other having any share thereof.

'Article 1216 (of the Code Napole on [sic]) has foreseen such a situation in asserting that, in such a case, the debt must be entirely borne by the debtor in whose interest the debt was contracted while the other debtors, In their relation to the first one, are regarded as his sureties. They occupy such a position for having bound themselves for the full amount of the debt for the benefit of their co-debtor. This assimilation of the position of a solidary debtor to the one of a surety, however, is only valid insofar as the relation between solidary co-debtors is concerned. It is not valid concerning the relation between such debtors and the creditor. As a matter of fact, One thing is to bind oneself as Solidary debtor, and another is to bind oneself as Surety, since, From the viewpoint of his relation with the creditor, a surety enjoys certain privileges which are refused to a solidary debtor.' (Emphasis here and elsewhere supplied.)

See also 1 C. Aubry & C. Rau, Droit civil francais 33 (La.St.L.Inst. transl.1965). See also 3 C. Toullier, Le droit civil francais 588 (1833).

The point to be made is that the majority is wrong to conclude in this limited action we consider between the plaintiff-creditor and one continuing guarantor, Hanagriff, that Rex Rice Company, Inc., one of the defendants, is the principal debtor and that Hanagriff is a solidary surety with the three other guarantors. That relationship is to be determined between Those parties and has no bearing upon the decision we make; it is actually an intrusion by this Court into another legal relationship not yet litigated. The majority concedes from the law it cites that there may be solidary sureties who, as to third parties, may also be solidary obligors with a principal debtor. However, this occurs only when, as between the solidary sureties and the creditor, the sureties become principal debtors along with someone else.

A. Weill, Droit civil, les obligations, No. 920 at 879, 880 (1971) states that '(w)hen one of the co-debtors has paid the debt, * * *' the law establishes a presumption that co-debtors distribute their responsibility among themselves according to their virile shares, or if it be so agreed, 'according to the interest which each has had in the business.' Weill then says that, '(i)n an exceptional case it can happen that there is no such contribution to be made to a co-debtor who has paid the debt, as when one of the co-debtors who has paid, alone, was directly concerned in the business (was the principal obligor) and the others are engaged Only under the title of Solidary sureties. Art. 1216 (La.C.C. art. 2106) anticipates this hypothesis.'

It is my feeling that we should make very apparent that the instrument we interpret here (footnote 1 in the majority opinion), insofar as the creditor and one of the guarantors are

concerned, is an agreement of co-obligation—a solidary obligation by each of the sign-   207
ing parties to that creditor for the full indebtedness. Their distribution of that debt Among   208
themselves depends upon their agreement as to the interest of each in the business, even   209
to the extent that only one of them may be concerned directly while the others are engaged   210
only as Solidary sureties who are entitled to indemnification from the one who is the   211
principal obligor. We cannot, and we should not, address ourselves to that issue. The   212
continuing guaranty instrument alone on its face does not, without extrinsic evidence, per-   213
mit us to make such a determination, even if it were properly before us. That act of guar-   214
anty does not unambiguously set forth a suretyship, although this is not to say that it was   215
not intended as a suretyship by the parties.   216

I respectfully concur.   217

Questions

1. Lines 9–13: How many obligors are there? Are they all equally bound? How would
    you apply Louisiana Civil Code article 1804 to the type of relationship that may exist
    between all the obligors?

2. Lines 14–16, 32–46: What is a "*compromise* agreement" and what are its effects? *See*
    La. Civ. Code arts. 3071–3083.

3. Lines 32–46: Can you figure out the two different distributions of the continuing
    guaranty of $200.000? The effect of the three compromise agreements was to convey
    property. Thus, what could be this form of payment under the Louisiana Civil Code?
    See La. Civ. Code arts. 2655–2659.

4. Lines 78–95: What important distinction is made here in the context of solidarity
    between sureties and a principal obligor?

5. Lines 96 *et seq.*: What is remission? What are its effects? *See* La. Civ. Code arts.
    1888–1892. On lines 20 *et seq.* the court speaks about release and again on lines
    115–116. Is a release the same thing as a remission?

S & W INVESTMENT COMPANY, Inc.   1
v.   2
OTIS W. SHARP & SON, INC.   3
Supreme Court of Louisiana   4
Dec. 14, 1964   5
170 So.2d 360   6

HAMITER, Justice.   7

In this suit S & W Investment Company, Inc., seeks to recover a sum expended by it   8
for completing a swimming pool which the defendant, Otis W. Sharp and Son, Inc., had   9
originally contracted to build but later abandoned.   10

[....]   11

The swimming pool was to be built by the defendant, at a contracted price of $4725,   12
in the patio area of a motel proposed to be constructed by plaintiff. It was understood by   13
the parties that, in order to permit the use of plaintiff's heavy equipment nearby and to   14
avoid the risk of damaging the pool tiling and appurtenances during erection of the build-   15
ings, the concrete shell of the pool would be provided first and the remaining work (in-   16

17   cluding the installing of tiling, filter, ladders, trim, etc.) would be undertaken following
18   the buildings' completion.

19   The written contract dated September 12, 1961 provided in part:

20   'ARTICLE I. SCOPE OF WORK — The Contractor shall furnish all of the ma-
21   terial and perform all of the work for the construction of a Swimming Pool as
22   described below.

23   'ARTICLE 3. PROGRESS PAYMENTS — * * * Upon completion of shell (which
24   is all but tile, brick, filter, deck eqpt., plum. line to building, and interior finish),
25   amt. due $3000.00. Remainder due upon completion of pool.'

26   Also, the contract obligated the owner to excavate the pool site, to move the excavated
27   material, and to place the backfill around the shell.

28   The excavation was performed by a construction company paid by plaintiff, but the work
29   was under the direction and supervision of the defendant. The shell was completed about
30   October 17, 1961, and on October 22, 1961 plaintiff gave to the defendant the $3000
31   progress payment then due (more particularly hereinafter discussed).

32   Prior to leaving the job temporarily an employee of the defendant closed a hydrosta-
33   tic pressure relief valve (which had been installed in the shell as a safety device) by in-
34   serting a plug in it, and he then commenced filling the shell with water by means of a
35   garden hose. He was sent back to the site at least two more days for the purpose of con-
36   tinuing the water filling and (to quote his testimony) 'to watch that Our plumbing, pipes
37   and the shell of the pool wasn't damaged by the equipment being used to backfill.' (Ital-
38   ics ours.)

39   The evidence is to the effect that the safest method of protecting the shell was to fill it
40   with water rather than to depend on the valve. However, before a sufficient amount of water
41   was placed therein the filling operation was discontinued and the hose was removed from
42   the site by defendant's employee.

43   A heavy rainfall that occurred in early November, 1961 caused the uprooting or 'float-
44   ing' of one end of the shell. Defendant's initial salvage attempts were unsuccessful, and
45   it disclaimed any further obligation when plaintiff refused to augment the contract price.

46   Plaintiff, thereupon, employed the services of J. Stanley Middleton, d/b/a Family
47   Pools, to make the necessary repairs and to bring the work to operational status for the
48   price of $3899.95. Plaintiff's claim in this suit of $2174.95 represents the difference be-
49   tween the amount paid to Middleton and the balance remaining under the contract with
50   the defendant.

51   Plaintiff cites and relies on Revised Civil Code Article 2758 which states: 'Builder fur-
52   nishing materials — Destruction of work before delivery — Bearing of loss. — When the
53   undertaker furnishes the materials for the work, if the work be destroyed, in whatever
54   manner it may happen, previous [sic] to its being delivered to the owner, the loss shall
55   be sustained by the undertaker, unless the proprietor be in default for not receiving it,
56   though duly notified to do so.'

57   Plaintiff contends that this defendant had obligated itself to construct a complete swim-
58   ming pool — an indivisible obligation; that the progress payment of $3000, made for the
59   benefit of the undertaker, did not relieve the latter of the responsibility of preserving the
60   entire work until it was finished, delivered and accepted; and that, consequently, under
61   the aforequoted codal provisions any damage thereto occurring before that time must be
62   borne by the defendant contractor.

The defendant apparently recognizes that generally, in the absence of an agreement of the parties, the risk of loss in a building contract is on the contractor until he has completed and delivered the work. This can hardly be gainsaid in view of the provisions of Article 2758.

It urges, however, that this particular contract was one 'for work composed of detached pieces', to wit: (1) a shell and (2) the completion of a shell into a finished pool, all as is contemplated by Revised Civil Code Article 2761 which reads: 'Delivery of work in separate parts.—If the work be composed of detached pieces, or made at the rate of so much a measure, the parts may be delivered separately; and that delivery shall be presumed to have taken place, if the proprietor has paid to the undertaker the price due for the parts of the work which have already been completed.' It argues that under the provisions of this article there arose a presumption of delivery to and acceptance by the owner when the latter paid for that 'piece' (the shell) already completed; and that, therefore, following such payment, and pending the finishing of the entire work, the risk of loss of such 'piece' was on the owner.

The Court of Appeal (as did the district court) found that, within the contemplation of the parties, the obligation undertaken by this defendant was an indivisible one; and it was inclined to the view that, under the circumstances, the provisions of Article 2758 placed the loss on the undertaker. However, a majority of its members determined that two prior decisions, N. Levy and Son v. Paquette et al., 144 La. 244, 80 So. 269 and Industrial Homestead Association v. Charles A. Junker et al., Orleans Appeal, No. 7402, Unreported (February 13, 1919, cert. den. May 9, 1919-2 Peltier's Orleans Appeals 80) required a different holding, and they felt constrained to follow their interpretation of those decisions which was to the effect that when stage or progress payments are provided for in an otherwise indivisible building contract, and when the owner makes such payments, there arises a presumption of delivery and acceptance of the then completed portion of the work so as to place on the owner the risk of loss thereof pending performance of the entire contract.

We agree with the Court of Appeal's conclusion that the obligation here was an indivisible one and that it did not constitute two obligations to do two different things. Under it, for a stipulated price, the contractor was obliged to construct and deliver a completed swimming pool—not to build a shell for a price and to finish a shell at another price.

Divisible and indivisible contracts are dealt with in the Revised Civil Code Articles 2108–2116. Specifically, the first two of these articles provide: 'Divisible or indivisible—Distinguishing features.—An obligation is divisible or indivisible, according as it has for its object, either a thing which, in its delivery or a fact which, in its execution, is or is not susceptible of division, either material or intellectual.' Article 2108. 'Indivisibility under terms of obligation.—The obligation is indivisible, though the thing or the fact which is the object of it, be by its nature divisible, if the light, in which it is considered in the obligation, does not admit of its being partially executed.' Article 2109.

Clearly the contract under consideration does not admit of its being only partially executed. Neither the shell by itself nor the finishing operation alone is a complete work fit for the use intended as the object of the agreement. The so-called 'detached pieces' (if a finishing operation can be considered as a 'piece') are totally interdependent and such interdependence was the principal motive of the contract. The worth of each component part is increased by its union with the other, and the absence of one renders the other virtually useless or without value.

That such was the understanding of the parties is clearly evidenced by their actions at an unsuspicious time. Thus, when the defendant requested the progress payment, it did not submit a bill for the 'construction of a swimming pool shell'. Rather, the bill read:

"OTIS W. SHARP & SON, INC.
General Contractors
P. O. Box 5164 2401 Rousseau St.
New Orleans 15, La.

"Name	S & W INVESTMENT CO. 7525 Airline Highway New Orleans, La.	Date 10/20/61 Bill No. 1991
"Job	SWIMMING POOL 7525 Airline Hwy. First Request for Partial Payment	$3000.00"

And the inscription on plaintiff's check issued on October 22, 1961 in payment of such bill recited: 'First Partial payment on swimming pool contract.' (Italics ours.)

We consider the above quoted language as evidence of the intention of the parties that neither considered the agreement as constituting two separate and severable obligations to the extent that the progress payment would settle in full one of them. The defendant's obligation, in other words, was indivisible. It was not transformed into a divisible one by the mere provision for the making of partial payments as the work progressed.

Also, for the foregoing reasons, the contract cannot be considered as a conjoint one within the contemplation of Revised Civil Code Article 2063, as urged by the defendant. That article provides that a contract is conjoint when the obligations are severally comprised therein, and that the obligor may, when he wishes, force the creditor to receive them separately. Clearly the obligations undertaken by this defendant were not several and separable. They, as above shown, were totally interdependent. Obviously, for instance, the defendant could not have required the plaintiff to accept only performance of the 'finishing' work.

Inasmuch as defendant's obligation was not divisible, i.e., it was not for work composed of 'detached pieces', Article 2761 is inapplicable. From which it follows that the progress payment cannot form the basis of a presumptive delivery of the work as of the time it was made; and in the absence of such delivery, as well as of an acceptance by the owner, the swimming pool construction remained at the risk of the contractor until its complete performance. Article 2758.

We have carefully examined the decisions relied on by the majority of the Court of Appeal (and cited by the defendant), but we do not find that they conflict with the result reached herein by us.

In N. Levy and Son v. Paquette et al., supra, Paquette had contracted with the Town of Mandeville to build a sea wall for a specified sum, using concrete piles as recited in the contract. The agreement contained a provision that when the piles were made the town would pay to the contractor $10,000. Following completion of the piles they were inspected, approved and Formally accepted by the town council. Under a subrogation agreement between the contractor and the manufacturer of the piles, the $10,000 was paid to the latter (not the contractor) who gave a receipt 'in full acquittance therefor'. The court held the contract to be a divisible one—for the furnishing of the piles and for the building of the sea wall—and that when the town Actually accepted the piles and made payment it became the owner thereof, precluding attachment by a creditor (plaintiff in the suit) of the contractor. Conceding the correctness of this reasoning, it is clear that the court did not hold that a mere progress payment, Without actual delivery and acceptance, would effect a transfer of ownership of a partially completed work.

In Industrial Homestead Association v. Charles A. Junker et al., supra, the defendant   147
agreed to build a house for plaintiff for a stipulated sum, the contract containing a pro-   148
vision for progress payments during the course of the construction. After one payment   149
was made a storm blew down the partially completed structure. Reconstruction was com-   150
menced, but after the making of the second progress payment the building was again de-   151
molished by more violent winds. The defendant was then prohibited from rebuilding by   152
the city architect who found the plans, Furnished by plaintiff, to be defective. In the suit,   153
in which plaintiff sought to recover his two progress payments, the court held that under   154
the mentioned circumstances the contractor refused to finish the work only because it   155
was impossible to do so on account of the owner's defective plans; and that, consequently,   156
such refusal did not constitute an arbitrary abandonment of the contract but was legally   157
justified. As to another aspect of the case the court further found that the collapse itself   158
was the result of the owner's faulty plans, and it held that when a partially completed   159
work is destroyed Due to the fault of the owner the loss is his.   160

However, in the Junker case, despite such two holdings, the court did indulge in spec-   161
ulative observations regarding the effect of the progress payments on the risk of loss, it   162
citing (among others) many common law authorities. Nevertheless, because of its firm   163
holdings resulting from its factual finding that the owner's plans were defective and   164
caused the loss, it is clear that such observations were purely dicta. Consequently, our   165
refusal to grant a writ in the matter did not indicate an approval of the dicta contained   166
in the opinion.   167

[....]   168

For the reasons assigned the judgment of the Court of Appeal is reversed and set aside,   169
and the decree of the district court awarding to plaintiff the sum of $2174.95 is reinstated   170
and made the judgment of this court. The defendant shall pay all costs.   171

Questions

1. Lines 19–27: Can you identify an obligation of result? A personal/heritable obliga-
    tion? An obligation to do? To give? Any term or condition?

2. Lines 46–50: What kind of obligation is created by a contract for services? *See* La.
    Civ. Code arts. 2745–2750 and 2756–2777. Read carefully Louisiana Civil Code ar-
    ticle 2758 as the Court refers to it on line 51. Notice that the Court does take the law,
    the Louisiana Civil Code articles, in consideration to support its opinion.

3. Lines 57 *et seq.*: Is it in the plaintiff's interest to argue that the defendant was bound
    by an indivisible obligation? What benefit(s) is (are) attached to an indivisible oblig-
    ation? Whose obligation was it to make progress payments? What does it mean as
    regards the nature of that obligation, its kind? Can an obligation be divisible on one
    side and indivisible on the other side?

4. Lines 67 *et seq.*: Why is the defendant building its argument on the basis of Louisiana
    Civil Code article 2761? On what kind of obligation, divisible or indivisible, is the de-
    fendant relying?

5. Lines 89 *et seq.*: After stating that it agrees with the Court of Appeal's holding that the
    obligation of the contractor was an indivisible obligation, the Supreme Court cites
    some Louisiana Civil Code articles on the distinction between a divisible obligation
    and an indivisible one. Do you approve of the choice of "all" or "only some" of the words
    used by the Supreme Court on line 93? From where do these "legal terms" come?

Bryan Ardis FRAME, et al.,

v.

SHREVEPORT ANTI-TUBERCULOSIS LEAGUE, et al.,

STATE of Louisiana, Through the DEPARTMENT OF HIGHWAYS,

v.

Bryan Ardis FRAME, et al.

Louisiana Court of Appeal
Second Circuit
Jan. 18, 1989
538 So.2d 684

LINDSAY, Judge.

These are consolidated cases concerning ownership of approximately fifty-five acres of land donated in 1918 to the Shreveport Anti-Tuberculosis League for use as a tuberculosis treatment facility. The heirs of the original donor sought to revoke the donation for failure of the ultimate donee of the property, the State of Louisiana, to comply with the condition of the donation. The condition called for the property to be used as a tuberculosis sanitarium or camp or for some other equally charitable purpose.

The trial court held that the heirs were entitled to ownership of approximately one-half of the property plus a sum of money deposited in the registry of the court pursuant to an expropriation of a portion of the property. The court also held that the State was entitled to retain ownership of the remainder of the tract in question. The State appealed and the heirs answered the appeal, each claiming ownership of the entire property. For the following reasons, we affirm in part and reverse in part the trial court judgment.

FACTS

On May 15, 1918, Colonel J.B. Ardis donated approximately fifty-five acres of land to the Shreveport Anti-Tuberculosis League for use as a tuberculosis sanitarium, subject to the following condition:

> It is agreed and understood that if said property should cease to be used for a tuberculosis sanatorium or camp or some other equally charitable purpose, the same should then revert back to the donor.

Following the donation, a facility for the treatment of tuberculosis was established on the property. The facility was operated by the Shreveport Anti-Tuberculosis League for many years. On May 20, 1948, the Shreveport Anti-Tuberculosis League donated the property to the Pines Sanitoria, Inc. In that same year, the Pines Sanitoria, Inc. donated the property to the State of Louisiana. The State operated the tuberculosis treatment center on the property continuously until 1972. The facility was known as the Pines Tuberculosis Sanitarium.

Due to innovations in the treatment of tuberculosis, the need for hospitalization and isolation of tuberculosis patients became less frequent. Nationally, the number of patients housed in specialized tuberculosis treatment facilities declined. The same was true of the Pines Tuberculosis Sanitarium. In early January, 1972, Governor Edwards ordered the Pines closed as a treatment facility for tuberculosis patients. The patients who were hospitalized at the Pines were transferred to other facilities or were treated on an outpatient basis.

Shortly after the closure of the tuberculosis sanitarium, the State began renovations on one of the residences on the property for use as a halfway house for recovering alcoholics. The halfway house was opened in September or October, 1973.

On June 7, 1973, the heirs of Colonel Ardis filed suit to revoke the donation. Bryan Ardis Frame, Caro P. Mills, Nancy Mills VanHoose and George H. Mills filed suit against the Shreveport Anti-Tuberculosis League, the Pines Sanitoria, Inc., the Louisiana Tuberculosis and Respiratory Disease Association and the State of Louisiana, claiming that the State had abandoned use of the property for any purpose and therefore ownership of the property should revert to the heirs of the donor.

In the alternative, the heirs claimed that any portion of the property not being used by the State for a charitable purpose, in compliance with the donation, should be returned to them.

[....]

On May 6, 1974, the State of Louisiana, through the Department of Highways, filed an expropriation suit against Bryan Ardis Frame, Virginia Frame, Betsey Frame, George H. Mills, Jr., Caro P. Mills, Nancy Mills VanHoose, the Pines Sanitoria, Inc., Shreveport Anti-Tuberculosis League and the Louisiana Tuberculosis and Respiratory Disease Association. The Highway Department sought to expropriate 5.15 acres in the southern portion of the property in order to relocate U.S. Highway 80 and to build the Pines Road interchange onto I-20. [....]

[....]

The trial court, in written reasons for judgment, cited the applicable Civil Code Articles dealing with donations[1] and concluded that the clause contained in the act of donation executed by Colonel Ardis, requiring that the property be used for a tuberculosis sanitarium, camp or other equally charitable purpose, created a right to revoke the donation for noncompliance with the condition. The court went on to cite Civil Code Articles dealing with general obligations and the divisibility of obligations. The court then reasoned that the wording of the condition allowed the donee to make alternate uses of the property and gave the donee a choice as to the method of fulfilling the condition of the donation. The court stated that because the donation provided for alternative uses of the property, the obligation created by the condition of the donation was a divisible obligation. The court resorted to Civil Code articles dealing with equity to conclude that because the obligation was divisible, it could be fulfilled on parts of the property and not fulfilled on other parts.

The trial court then found that through the years the defendants had used the property in Tract 2 for tuberculosis treatment and an equally charitable purpose (the treatment of alcoholism). These uses of the property were sufficient to fulfill the condition of the donation and prevent reversion of that tract of land to the plaintiffs.

The court found that after the tuberculosis sanitarium had closed there had not been sufficient use of Tract 1 to fulfill the condition of the obligation. Therefore, the court held that ownership of Tract 1 reverted to the heirs.

The court also found that the State, by expropriating 5.15 acres of the property for a highway, had ceased to use this portion of the land for a charitable purpose. Therefore, the court ruled that the money paid for the property in the expropriation suit belonged to the heirs of the donor.

The court found that the State, by virtue of the expropriation, separated the 0.6 acre tract and the 3.15 acre tract from the main portion of the property and thereby rendered

---

1. The articles dealing with donations and obligations in effect prior to the 1985 revision are applicable to this case.

90 them unusable for the charitable purposes contemplated by the condition of the dona-
91 tion. The court held these two pieces of property also reverted to the ownership of the
92 plaintiffs.

93   From this judgment, the State appealed, claiming that the trial court erred in finding
94 that the condition was divisible and in failing to recognize that fulfillment of the condi-
95 tion by the use of a portion of the property would constitute fulfillment of the condition
96 as to all the property. The State contends that the trial court should have completely re-
97 jected the heirs' claim for revocation of the donation. The heirs answered the appeal,
98 claiming that the trial court erred in failing to declare them to be owners of the entire
99 property.

100   The issues raised in this appeal are whether the trial court was correct in finding a con-
101 ditional donation to be a divisible obligation, thereby entitling the heirs to a portion of
102 the property, whether the trial court was correct in finding the heirs were entitled to the
103 money from the expropriation suit and whether the heirs were entitled to ownership of
104 the 0.6 acre tract and the 3.15 acre tract separated from the main property by virtue of
105 the expropriation and relocation of U.S. Highway 80.

106 [....]

107 DIVISIBILITY OF THE CONDITIONS

108   The trial court found that even though the State had fulfilled the condition of the do-
109 nation sufficient to prevent a reversion of a portion of the property, the condition was di-
110 visible and had not been fulfilled on other portions of the property. Therefore the court
111 found that the ownership of some portions of the original tract reverted to the heirs of
112 the donor.

113   The trial court reached this conclusion by reliance upon former LSA-C.C. Arts. 2108
114 and 2109[2] dealing with the divisibility of obligations. The trial court reasoned that because
115 the condition of the donation allowed alternate uses of the property and permitted the
116 donee to use the property for other than as a tuberculosis sanitarium or camp, or other
117 equally charitable purposes, the donee had the choice of methods of fulfilling the condi-
118 tion and therefore the condition created a divisible obligation. By implication the trial
119 court further reasoned that the property itself could be divided based upon whether its
120 various parts were being used in compliance with the terms of the donation. The court
121 then cited general rules of equity to reason that the State had fulfilled the condition on a
122 portion of the property donated, but had failed to fulfill it on other parts. Therefore, the
123 court found that the ownership of Tract 1, as shown on the survey map drawn by the
124 heirs' surveyor, reverted to the heirs. The trial court also found that ownership of the two
125 parcels of land separated from the main tract by the highway expropriation also reverted
126 to the heirs because the State had made no use of this property since 1972.

127   For the following reasons, we reverse this portion of the trial court judgment.

128   The trial court erred in finding the condition to be a divisible obligation which al-
129 lowed an arbitrary division of the property along a surveyor's line. In the present case, there
130 is only one general condition, that the property be used for the treatment of tuberculo-

---

    2. Art. 2108. An obligation is divisible or indivisible, according as it has for its object, either a thing which, in its delivery or a fact which, in its execution, is or is not susceptible of division, either material or intellectual.

    Art. 2109. The obligation is indivisible, though the thing or the fact which is the object of it, be by its nature divisible, if the light, in which it is considered in the obligation, does not admit of its being partially executed.

sis or some other equally charitable purpose. Performance of that condition requires the   131
heirs of the donor to allow the donee to remain in possession of all the property which   132
was made the subject of the donation.   133

The condition does not require that every square inch of the property be occupied by   134
buildings or structures used in pursuit of the purposes of the donation. Good faith use   135
of a substantial portion of the property for the purpose intended, as occurred here, is   136
sufficient to fulfill the condition as to all the property and to prevent the revocation of the   137
donation.   138

We find no other case in which a court has revoked a donation as to a portion of the prop-   139
erty for nonfulfillment of a condition, but has upheld the donation as to other portions.   140
In cases dealing with donations containing conditions that the property be used for a par-   141
ticular purpose, fulfillment of the specified condition has been sufficient to prevent revo-   142
cation of the entire donation. *Board of Trustees of Columbia Road Methodist Episcopal Church*   143
of Bogalusa v. Richardson, 216 La. 633, 44 So.2d 321 (1949); *Bonner v. Board of Trustees,* 181   144
So.2d 255 (La.App. 4th Cir.1965), writ denied 248 La. 915, 182 So.2d 664 (1966).   145

We find that the State has fulfilled the condition of the donation. Therefore, owner-   146
ship of the entire property remains with the State, with the exception of the tract which   147
was expropriated for the relocation of the highway[....]   148

[....]   149

[W]e find that the trial court erred in holding that the condition of the donation was   150
fulfilled only as to Tract 2, i.e., that portion of the property upon which the main treat-   151
ment facility is located. Good faith use of a substantial portion of the property for the pur-   152
pose intended, as occurred here, fulfills the condition as to all the property.   153

Therefore, that portion of the trial court judgment directing that ownership of Tract   154
1, the 0.6 acre tract and the 3.5 acre tract be transferred to the heirs is hereby reversed and   155
set aside. The State of Louisiana is hereby recognized as the owner of and entitled to the   156
continued possession of the entire property.   157

[....]

Questions

1. Lines 12–23: Identify and characterize, in legal terms, the obligation(s) created and its (their) modalities. Any divisible/indivisible obligation?

2. Lines 25 *et seq.*: Focusing on lines 28–30, do you see any condition? If you answered in the affirmative, what kind? Is there any legal meaning attached to the word "or"? Was the obligation to use the property tantamount to the granting of a right of use (*see* La. Civ. Code arts. 639 and 645) or a predial servitude (*see* La. Civ. Code arts. 646 and 652)? Was the obligation to use the property as a ... or as a ... a divisible obligation or an indivisible obligation? Look at lines 64 *et seq.*

3. Lines 64–76: Focus on lines 72–76. Is the Court's statement accurate? Do alternative choices create a divisible obligation? Or does an alternative obligation create a divisible obligation? Isn't the Court somewhat or much 'off track'?

4. Lines 81–83: What adjective would you add before the word/concept of 'condition' to properly identify the type of condition referred to by the court?

5. Title on line 107 to lines 112 *et seq.*: What do you think of this title? On line 114, the court uses the phrase "divisibility of obligations". Is this choice of phrase cor-

rect? What should have been the title on line 107? Again, on line 117–118, the court is stating that "the condition created a divisible obligation". Isn't the court confusing "divisible obligation" with "alternative obligation"? Read Louisiana Civil Code article 1808 and compare it with Louisiana Civil Code article 1815. Do you see any difference?

Richard A. BERLIER
v.
A.P. GREEN INDUSTRIES, INC., et al.

Supreme Court of Louisiana
April 3, 2002
815 So.2d 39

JOHNSON, Justice. [....]

We granted a writ in this case involving a settlement of an asbestos-related personal injury and wrongful death claim to determine whether the four settling defendants are solidarily liable. After reviewing the record and the applicable law, we find that the settlement constitutes a joint and indivisible obligation, and each of the defendants are bound for the full $450,000.00.

FACTS AND PROCEDURAL HISTORY

On November 12, 1998, Richard Berlier filed a petition for damages for personal injuries resulting from occupational exposure to asbestos products. After his death on January 30, 1999, his surviving spouse and five adult children amended the petition to assert a wrongful death and survival action, as well as loss of consortium claims.

On December 13, 1999, the day the case was set for trial, the plaintiffs agreed to settle their claims against four of the defendants, GAF Corporation ("GAF") [....], Turner & Newell, PLC ("T & N"), Union Carbide Corporation ("Union Carbide"), and Asbestos Claims Management Corporation ("ACMC"), for a lump sum total of $450,000 to be paid on or before March 13, 2000. At the time of the settlement, all four defendants were members of the Center for Claims Resolution ("CCR"), an organization established in 1988 to handle asbestos claims on behalf of its twenty-one member companies.

The relationship among the various members of the CCR is controlled by the "Provider Agreement Concerning Center for Claims Resolution (the "Provider Agreement")," which was executed on September 28, 1988. The CCR is administered by a Board of Directors, and the Provider Agreement authorizes the CCR "to administer and arrange for the evaluation, settlement, payment, or defense of all asbestos-related claims." By becoming a member the CCR, the member "designates the [CCR] as its sole agent to administer and arrange on its behalf for the evaluation, settlement, payment or defense of all asbestos-related claims against [it]." The Provider Agreement, further provides that liability payments shall be apportioned to each member according to a specific share allocation matrix, that such apportionment shall establish the responsibility of each [member] for a percentage share of liability payments, and that each member shall pay in a timely manner the percentages of liability payments involved. Any disputes between the CCR and the members regarding the allocation or payment of a member's percentage of liability are to be resolved through alternative dispute resolution.

The settlement reached by the parties was announced on the record as follows:

William Harrison for Turner and Newell [T & N plc], GAF Corporation, National 41
Gypsum [which later became ACMC], together with my partner, Janet McDonell for 42
Union Carbide, put on the record on behalf of those four defendants, we have reached a 43
full settlement with all the plaintiffs in this matter, in Berlier versus A.P. Green and that 44
we have discussed this matter with Frank Swarr and Mr. Diaz as well as attorney for 45
Maples and LeBlanc. We understand Your Honor will be signing an order as to the funds 46
and we'll have the check made payable to both law firms, Mr. Diaz, and to LeBlanc, 47
Maples. We'll give it to Mr. Diaz to be deposited and subject to the Court's order. At that 48
point— 49

MR. DIAZ [Attorney for plaintiffs]: 50

Your Honor, that is correct. I understand what I'm going to do is take the 51
check. I'm going to deal with my opponent here. He's going to see that it gets signed 52
on behalf of Maples and LeBlanc right away, negotiate with the plaintiffs what 53
their costs and attorney's fees are, disburse that to them, subject to his prior ap- 54
proval, and take residue of that in a separate trust account and keep it there until 55
further orders of the Court. 56

THE COURT: 57

So talking about the costs, you said attorney fees, costs, and their settlement 58
proceeds, so attorneys fees will be held in trust. 59

MR. SWARR [Attorney for plaintiffs]: 60

The intervention will be tried before you as a bench trial. 61

On the settlement, I don't mind the settlement as long as any and all rights 62
are reserved against any other defendant known or unknown; it will be fine. 63

MR. HARRISON: 64

That's acceptable. 65

(UNIDENTIFIED ATTORNEY): 66

Just for the record, this will be committed to a separate writing in the form 67
of a receipt and release. 68

On December 17, 1999, James McFadden of the CCR sent a letter to plaintiffs' coun- 69
sel confirming the settlement, noting the lump sum amount of the settlement at the top 70
of the letter, and providing as follows: 71

This letter confirms settlement of the above-referenced matter. It is agreed 72
and understood that this settlement fully releases all members whether or not 73
such members are parties to these lawsuits. Furthermore, it is understood that 74
this settlement includes any and all companion actions in this or any jurisdiction 75
for these plaintiffs. 76

Payment will be made in accordance with the terms of the settlement, pro- 77
viding a release has been executed properly and returned to the CCR. Please have 78
the enclosed release request form completed and returned to Denise Loughran 79
at the Center. We, in turn, will prepare the release from the information pro- 80
vided on the release form and send it to you for execution by your clients. 81

The release, executed by the plaintiffs on January 28, 2000, provided in pertinent part 82
as follows: 83

For and in consideration of the sum of One Dollar ($1.00), and other good 84
and valuable consideration, the receipt and sufficiency of which are hereby ac- 85

knowledged, we [plaintiffs] ... release and forever discharge: Amchem Products, Inc.; Armstrong World Industries, Inc.; The Asbestos Claims Management Corporation (formerly known as National Gypsum Company) and The NGC Asbestos Disease and Property Damage Settlement Trust; CertainTeed Corporation; C.E. Thurston & Sons, Inc.; Dana Corporation; Ferodo America, Inc.; Gasket Holdings, Inc. (f/k/a Flexitallic, Inc.); GAF Corporation, J.U. North America, Inc.,; Quigley Company, Inc.; Shook & Fletcher Insulation Co.; T & N, plc; Union Carbide Corporation (f/k/a Union Carbide Chemicals & Plastics Company, Inc.); and United States Gypsum Company ... from any and all rights, ... which Releasors now have or may have in the future for personal injuries, disability, pain and suffering or death ... or any other asbestos-related diseases or condition suffered by RICHARD A. BERLIER, SR.,....

* * *

The parties understand and agree that nothing contained in this agreement shall be construed or deemed an admission of wrongdoing or of liability by any party as to any of the claims or counter-claims which have been made in the litigation....

On March 8, 2000, the CCR sent plaintiffs' counsel a check for $250,028.46, along with a letter containing the following:

Pursuant to the CCR's settlement with you, enclosed is a check for $250,028.46. This check represents the total of the amounts due for each of the claims in the attached listing, subject to payment at this time under the terms of the settlement agreement, less the amounts payable for each of these claims by GAF Corporation—which total $199,971.54. The CCR has billed GAF Corporation for these amounts, but GAF has to date refused to pay such billings. [....]

The plaintiffs refused to cash the check and on March 17, 2000, filed a Motion to Enforce Settlement against all four defendant companies. At the hearing on the motion, GAF was represented by its own counsel. During the course of the hearing, the trial judge inquired about the settlement:

THE COURT:

In the settlement. Each defendant entered into a settlement. When it was being put on the record, at that point, I said unless I have an amount I can't enforce the settlement. And it was agreed between counsel that there would be a written document transferred back and forth which would then make it an enforceable settlement because the amount would be contained in the written document. Did that occur?

MR. SWARR:

Your Honor, yes.

MR. HARRISON:

Your Honor, I believe that there is a letter from the CCR shortly after the December 13 settlement that was placed on the record. It's attached as an exhibit.

It's from a gentleman named Mr. Jim McFadden and sets out the cumulative amount for the four members, one of which is GAF.

MR. DUVAL [Attorney for GAF]:

Your Honor, as follow-up to that, I think you just touched on the heart of the whole matter.

On April 27, 2000, the trial court entered a judgment in favor of plaintiffs, finding   131
that GAF, ACMC, Union Carbide, and T & N are liable, *in solido*, to plaintiff in the sum   132
of $450,000.00. All four defendants appealed. [....]   133

[....]   134

The appellate court then set out to decide "only the single issue presented by the ap-   135
peal filed by the CCR defendants—whether the trial court properly entered judgment   136
against all four settling defendant companies *in solido*, rather than entering judgment   137
against GAF/G-I Holdings alone, as the Berliers orally requested at the hearing on the   138
matter." *Id.* The court of appeal affirmed the trial court's judgment, finding that the four   139
settling defendants were solidarily liable for the settlement as a matter of law, as expressed   140
in *Cole v. Celotex Corp.*, 599 So.2d 1058 (La.1992). *Id.* at 1060. This court granted the   141
writ application filed by T & N and Union Carbide. *Berlier v. A.P. Green Industries, Inc.*,   142
01-1530 (La.9/14/01).   143

DISCUSSION   144

The sole issue before us is whether the four defendants are solidarily obligated to pay   145
the $450,000.00 lump sum settlement.   146

The Louisiana Civil Code provides the framework for analyzing the types of obligations   147
involving multiple persons recognized under Louisiana law, which are several, joint, and   148
solidary obligations. LSA-C.C. art. 1786. In this case, the lower courts found that the   149
four defendants are solidarily liable under the terms of the settlement.   150

Solidary Liability   151

LSA-C.C. art. 1796 provides: 152

> Solidarity of obligation shall not be presumed. A solidary obligation arises   153
> from clear expression of the parties' intent or from the law.   154

The court of appeal found that a solidary obligation arose in this case from the law, re-   155
lying on *Cole v. Celotex, supra,* in which "the Louisiana Supreme Court held that various   156
asbestos defendants are solidarily liable for damages suffered by plaintiffs." 787 So.2d at   157
1060. However, the court of appeal erred in relying on *Cole*, a delictual action wherein cer-   158
tain defendants were found liable after a two-week trial for failing to provide a safe work-   159
place, and the liability of the manufacturers of asbestos containing products, who settled   160
before trial, was stipulated at trial. In this case, there was no trial on plaintiffs' tort claim   161
as the parties settled before trial, and, the release expressly states that "nothing contained   162
in this agreement shall be construed or deemed an admission of wrongdoing or of liability   163
by any party...." Except for the settlement, there would be no liability at all, since this   164
case has not been tried. Whether the defendants in this case would have been solidarily   165
liable in tort has not been, and may never be, determined. Therefore, *Cole* is inapplica-   166
ble to the instant case.   167

Thus, as solidary liability does not arise in this case from law, the only remaining issue   168
is whether it arises from a "clear expression of the parties' intent." A solidary obligation   169
may arise even though the words "solidarity" or "*in solido*" are not used, as long as the par-   170
ties' intent to be solidarily liable is clearly expressed. La.-C.C. art. 1796, Official Com-   171
ment (b). In resolving this issue in a case involving the joint or solidary liability of six   172
makers of a promissory note, this Court explained: 173

> When several persons join in the same contract to do the same thing, it pro-   174
> duces a joint obligation on the part of the obligors. However, where several per-   175
> sons obligate themselves to the obligee by the terms In solido or use any other   176

expressions that clearly show that they intend that each one shall be separately
bound to perform the whole of the obligation, it is called an obligation in Solido
on the part of the obligors. An obligation In solido is not presumed; it must be
expressly stipulated.

It is well settled that, absent additional promissory language, the words '(w)e promise
to pay' in a note signed by co-makers are insufficient "to constitute the express stipulation
of liability In solido required by law.

Johnson v. Jones-Journet, 320 So.2d 533, 536–37 (La.1975). Likewise, albeit in dicta,
this Court explained:

> The coextensive obligations for the "same thing" create the solidarity of the
> obligations. When it is not clear that the parties are all obliged to the same thing
> (as in the case of an agreement by several parties to repay a loan), then an oblig-
> ation in solido is not presumed and must be expressly stipulated. La. C.C. art.2093
> [now La. C.C. art. 1796]. However, when it is entirely clear that the parties are
> all obliged to the same thing (as when the law requires each of two or more par-
> ties to pay tort damages concurrently caused by each party), then there is an
> obligation in solido by definition, as a matter of law, and there is no need to pre-
> sume solidarity. The presumption against solidarity is only designed to be of as-
> sistance when it is necessary to determine whether an obligation is joint or
> solidary.

Narcise v. Illinois Cent. Gulf R. Co., 427 So.2d 1192, 1194 (La.1983).

In this case, there is no evidence of a "clear expression" of the defendants' intent to be
solidarily bound. As stated above, at the hearing on December 13, 1999, when the settlement was announced, Mr. Harrison stated: "William Harrison for Turner and Newell
[T & N plc], GAF Corporation, National Gypsum [later ACMC], together with my partner, Janet McDonell for Union Carbide, put on the record on behalf of those four defendants, we have reached a full settlement with all the plaintiffs in this matter." The
plaintiffs argue that Mr. Harrison's statement that "*we'll* have *the check* made payable to
both law firms" represents the defendants' intent to be bound *in solido* by issuing only
one check. We disagree that the issuance of one check clearly indicates an expression of
solidarity. Secondly, the confirmation letter from the CCR on behalf of the four defendants dated December 17, 1999, wherein a lump sum amount of the settlement was written at the top of the letter, does not contain a clear expression of the parties intent to be
bound in solido. Instead, it is an agent's agreement that his principals will pay the lump-
sum of $450,000 to the plaintiffs conditioned upon the release of all CCR members from
this lawsuit. There is no expression, clear or otherwise, that the four defendants will be
solidarily bound to pay that amount. Finally, the release executed on January 28, 2000,
contains only general release language in favor of all the defendants in the lawsuit, including the four CCR defendants, and can in no way be construed to contain a clear expression that the any of the defendants would be solidarily bound. Therefore, we find
that the lower courts erred in holding that the defendants are solidarily liable for the
amount of the settlement.

Several Liability

The second category of obligations is that of several liability. An obligation is several
for the obligors "when each of different obligors owes a separate performance to one
obligee, ..." LSA-C.C. art. 1787. The comments to this article explain that "if the performance owed by each obligor has a different object, the obligation is several, as when one
obligor owes delivery of a thing and another owes payment of a sum of money." LSA-

C.C. art. 1787, Official Comment (b). For example, if through the same act, two persons each bind themselves to give a different sum of money to another, the obligation is several for the obligors. Litvinoff, Treatise *supra* § 7.11. Professor Litvinoff also notes that in the typical several obligation, the performance promised by each obligor has a different object, which allows each obligor to be regarded as the passive subject of a different and separate obligation. *Id.*

In the instant case, rather than separate performances, the agreement indicates that only one performance was contemplated on the part of the defendants, namely one payment of $450,000 in exchange for the plaintiffs' signing a document entitled "RELEASE," which released from liability fifteen different business entities. Also, the obligors together promised to give to the plaintiffs one sum of money, not each a different sum. It follows that the defendants' performance had only one object, the lump sum payment of $450,000, and each defendant cannot be regarded as the passive subject of a different and separate obligation. Therefore, the obligation at issue is not a several obligation.

Joint Liability

The final category is that of joint obligations. In part, a joint obligation is one where different obligors owe together just one performance to one obligee, or where one obligor owes just one performance intended for the common benefit of different obligees. LSA-C.C. art. 1788. Professor Litvinoff states that an obligation would be joint for the obligors if, through the same act, they promise to give just one sum of money to another, such as in the instant case. Litvinoff, Treatise *supra* § 7.21. In addition, a pre-revision case which the reporter of the revision committee found useful indicated that the classification of an obligation as several or joint depends upon the parties' intentions and understanding, as revealed by the language of their contract and the subject matter to which it refers. *See Nabors v. Producers' Oil Co.*, 140 La. 985, 74 So. 527, 531 (1917); LSA-C.C. art. 1788 cmt. (d). In *Nabors,* this Court stated:

> With regard to the subject-matter, the authorities agree that the contract is entire and not severable, although it embodies a conveyance or delivery of several things, if the consideration is paid in a gross sum and it is impossible to affirm that the party making the payment would have done so unless the rights he acquired should apply to all of the things mentioned.

Nabors, 74 So. at 531. *Nabors* held that a mineral lease created a joint obligation where several lessors disposed of the mineral rights on several tracts of land for a gross price, without stating the amount paid to each lessor and without stating or designating the area of land belonging to each lessor.

Although *Nabors* dealt with an obligation that is joint for the obligees (lessors), it is nevertheless instructive on whether an obligation is joint for obligors, such as in the instant case. The defendants owed one performance to the plaintiffs, namely to pay the plaintiffs a lump sum of $450,000.00, and they bound themselves for this performance through the same act, namely the settlement agreement. It would be impossible to affirm that the defendants would have agreed to pay the plaintiffs unless all the defendants were released, or whether the plaintiffs would have released all the defendants unless all the money were paid. Also, similar to *Nabors,* the plaintiffs released their rights to hold all the defendants, plus others, liable for a gross price, and there was no statement of the amount for which each defendant was responsible. Accordingly, we hold that the four defendant companies, T & N, GAF, ACMC, and Union Carbide, are jointly obligated to the plaintiffs for the full amount of the settlement.

273   Next, to determine the effect of a joint obligation on the obligors, it is necessary to
274 determine whether the joint obligation is divisible or indivisible, because the revision
275 "leans heavily on the notions of divisible and indivisible obligations." Expose, *supra* § 5.
276 If the joint obligation is divisible, neither obligor is bound for the whole performance; rather,
277 each joint obligor is bound to perform only his portion. LSA-C.C. art. 1789. On the other
278 hand, if the joint obligation is indivisible, the joint obligors are subject to the rules gov-
279 erning solidary obligors. *Id.* One of the principal applications of the rules governing sol-
280 idary obligors to joint and indivisible obligors is that the obligee, at his choice, may
281 demand the whole performance from any of the joint and indivisible obligors. *See* LSA-
282 C.C. art. 1795. This notion that all parties who contract an indivisible debt may be li-
283 able for the whole is not new; it appears in art. 2113 of the 1870 Code, art. 2109 of the
284 1825 Code, and art. 122 of the 1808 Code. [....] Revised article 1789 reflects a partial
285 change in the law, but one consistent with general principle, and one that provides a prac-
286 tical approach to situations where theoretical foundations could become insurmountable
287 obstacles to fair solutions, such as in the instant case. Litvinoff, Treatise, *supra* § 7.94.

288   In Louisiana, divisibility of a joint obligation depends on divisibility of the object of
289 the performance, unlike joint obligations at common law. Litvinoff, Treatise, *supra*
290 § 7.94; *Hincks v. Converse,* 38 La. Ann. 871 (1886). This rule is expressed in LSA-C.C.
291 art. 1815:

292   An obligation is divisible when the object of the performance is susceptible
293   of division.

294   An obligation is indivisible when the object of the performance, because of
295   its nature *or because of the intent of the parties,* is not susceptible of division.

296 (Emphasis added.)

297   French doctrine has always held that division of an obligation cannot take place
298 when the object of the performance is indivisible. Litvinoff, Treatise, *supra* § 7.94 (cit-
299 ing 7 Planiol et Ripert, *Traite pratique de droit civil francais* 413 (Louisiana State Law
300 Institute transl., 2d ed.1954)). Combining the ideas of Charles DuMoulin and Andre
301 d'Alciat, Planiol explains that indivisibility is derived sometimes from the nature of
302 the object due (*ex natura*), and sometimes from the intention of the parties (*ex voluntate*).
303 2 Marcel Planiol & George Ripert, Treatise on the Civil Law, pt. 1 no. 782
304 (La.St.L.Inst.trans., 11th ed.1939). Planiol also states that indivisibility is contractual,
305 or *ex voluntate,* when the thing which makes the object of the obligation is in all re-
306 spects divisible, but the parties intend that the obligation should be executed as if it were
307 indivisible. *Id.* at No. 787. Authorities are in agreement that money, which is the ob-
308 ject of the obligation at issue in the instant case, is "in all respects divisible." *See, e.g.,*
309 *Martin v. Louisiana Farm Bureau Cas. Ins. Co.,* 94-0069, p. 5 (La.7/5/94), 638 So.2d 1067,
310 1069 (stating that "[t]he obligation to pay money at issue here is susceptible of divi-
311 sion and thus provides no basis for legal subrogation"); Planiol, *supra* (remarking that
312 nothing is more divisible than money); Saul Litvinoff, The Law of Obligations in the
313 Louisiana Jurisprudence 599 (1979) (stating that a sum of money is divisible as a mat-
314 ter of fact).

315   Although money, by its nature, is divisible, LSA-C.C. art. 1815 provides that an ob-
316 ject can also be indivisible because the parties so intended. Thus, even where an ob-
317 ject by its nature may be rendered in partes (such as a lump sum settlement for
318 $450,000.00), it must be performed as a whole where it is indivisible because of the
319 parties' intent. Saul Litvinoff, The Law of Obligations in the Louisiana Jurisprudence
320 599 (1979).

In this case, it is apparent that the parties to the settlement agreement intended that "the obligation should be executed as if it were indivisible." If the parties had intended for the obligation to be divisible, then one would reasonably suspect that they would have determined each defendant's pro-rata portion, and each defendant would be bound for a sum certain. However, the parties never made such a determination, nor did they discuss such a method of payment. Rather, throughout their negotiations, plaintiffs and defendants proceeded as though their mutual obligations were indivisible. At all times, the defendants acted through a single mandatary, the CCR. On the morning of trial, the four defendants, represented by one law firm, announced on the record that, "on behalf of those four defendants, we have reached a settlement with the plaintiffs." The parties contracted for one lump-sum payment of $450,000.00, and the letter sent by the defendants' mandatary confirmed the object as a single sum, $450,000.00. Plaintiffs were never informed as to how the settlement amount would be apportioned among the four defendants, and there was no indication that the amount would be paid other than by the mandatary in full. Pursuant to the agreement, plaintiffs could not release only those defendants who contributed to the settlement, but had to release, unconditionally, all four defendants, plus fifteen other business entities. Therefore, as this obligation is indivisible because of the parties' intent, it must be performed as a whole even though, by its nature, its object may be rendered in parts. Litvinoff, Obligations, *supra* at 599.

Of course, this is not to say that the obligation in question is indivisible merely because it was incurred in exchange for an indivisible obligation. Aubry & Rau, *Cours de Droit Civil Francais*, Vol. IV-Sixth Edition, *translated in* 1 Civil Law Translations § 301 (La.St. L. Inst.1965) (stating that a divisible obligation does not become indivisible merely because it is correlative to an indivisible obligation from a commutative contract). Rather, it is the sum total of the facts surrounding the defendants' obligation, as discussed above, which reveals that the parties' intent was that their obligation be indivisible.

CONCLUSION

For the reasons stated above, we find that there existed a joint and indivisible obligation which binds each of the defendants for the full $450,000.00.

LOBRANO, J., concurs in the result.

VICTORY, J., dissents and assigns reasons.

TRAYLOR, J., dissents for reasons assigned by VICTORY, J.

VICTORY, J., dissenting.

I dissent from the majority's holding that the settlement in this case constitutes a joint and indivisible obligation, binding each of the defendants for the full $450,000. Initially, however, I must point out that in my view, it is not at all clear that there is a legally enforceable settlement agreement in this case under La. C.C. art. 3071, much less a "settlement agreement wherein the parties contracted for one lump-sum payment of $450,000." Op. at 48.

While I agree with the majority's finding that "there is no evidence of a 'clear expression' of the defendants' intent to be solidarily bound" under La. C.C. art. 1796, I find that, for the same reasons that the majority made that finding, there was also no evidence that the defendants intended to be solidary bound for purposes of creating a joint and indivisible obligation under La. C.C. art. 1815. Based on the same evidence, the majority finds "there is no evidence of a 'clear expression' of the defendants' intent to be solidarily bound," yet then concludes "it is apparent that the parties to the settlement agreement intended that 'the obligation should be executed as if it were indivisible.'" However, the

368 obligation does not meet the requirements for a joint and indivisible obligation under
369 La. C.C. art. 1815 because there is no evidence that it *was the intent of the parties* to treat
370 the object of the defendants' obligation, the payment of a sum of money, as an indivisi-
371 ble obligation. See Saul Litvinoff, *Louisiana Civil Law Treatise: The Law of Obligations*,
372 § 9.5 (defining a conventional indivisible obligation as follows: "When an obligation would
373 be divisible because the object of its performance is susceptible of division, the parties to
374 a contract *may agree* that it shall be performed as if its object were invisible, which makes
375 the indivisibility conventional, rather than natural.") Not only is there no evidence that
376 the defendants intended the payment of the $450,000 to be divisible. The majority opin-
377 ion discusses at some length the arrangements made between the defendants and the CCR
378 clearly showing the defendants did not intend to be bound for the whole, but only for the
379 percentage assigned in the Provider Agreement. Further, there is no evidence the plain-
380 tiffs intended the obligation to be indivisible for the defendants, as this settlement was so
381 loosely structured that no amount was even stated on the record in open court.

382   The reason the code articles require that both parties intend that a joint obligation be
383 either solidary under La. C.C. art. 1796 or indivisible under La. C.C. art. 1815, is be-
384 cause of the onerous effects on the obligors if the obligation is characterized as either of
385 the above. To allow the intent of just one party, the obligee, which in this case is not even
386 discernable, to impose solidary liability on the obligors is unjust. Further, La. C.C. 1818
387 clearly states that "[a]n indivisible obligation with more than one obligor or obligee is
388 subject to the rules governing solidary obligations." La. C.C. art. 1796, requiring that a
389 solidary obligation shall not be presumed and "arises from a *clear expression of the par-*
390 *ties' intent* or from the law" is certainly a "rule [ ] governing solidary obligations." By pro-
391 viding a lower standard in the law for what constitutes a joint and indivisible obligation
392 under La. C.C. art. 1815, which under the majority's holding is an "apparent intent," the
393 majority opinion renders meaningless the requirement found in La. C.C. art. 1796, made
394 applicable by virtue of La. C.C. art. 1818, that a clear expression of intent is need to cre-
395 ate a solidary obligation, and, creates far too much certainty in the law on which contracting
396 parties have relied in this state for years.

397   Therefore, I respectfully disagree with the majority's holding that the parties intended
398 this divisible obligation be treated as if it were indivisible under La. C.C. art. 1815, and
399 I am of the firm view that the defendants are not solidarily liable in this case, neither by
400 virtue of La. C.C. art. 1796 nor 1815.

Questions

1. Lines 321–326: The majority states that the defendants who signed on to the settle-
    ment agreement did not "determine[] each defendant's pro-rata portion" nor even "dis-
    cuss such a method of payment". Is that correct? What of the provision in the
    defendants' collective "Provider Agreement", alluded to in Justice Victory's dissent,
    to the effect "that liability payments shall be apportioned to each member according
    to a specific share allocation matrix, that such apportionment shall establish the re-
    sponsibility of each [member] for a percentage share of liability payments, and that
    each member shall pay in a timely manner the percentages of liability payments in-
    volved"? Does that provision concern (1) the "vertical" relationship between the de-
    fendants, as a group, and the payee or (2) the "horizontal" relationship among the
    defendants or (3) both?

2. By means of what criterion(a) does the majority determine that the defendants "in-
    tended" that the object of their obligation, a monetary payment, be "indivisible"? Is

it anything more than "if multiple parties to a settlement that calls for a lump sum payment do not, contemporaneously with the settlement (or, is it 'in the act of settlement itself'?), apportion the payment among themselves, then they intend that the payment be indivisible"? But wouldn't that be the typical case with a settlement? And, if it is, is there not something to Justice Victory's complaint that the majority's approach to indivisibility effectively undermines the presumption against solidarity?

3.   Imagine that you are the attorney for one of multiple defendants in a pending tort suit, one that the defendants are about to settle. What, in the aftermath of *Berlier*, would you advise your client regarding how the settlement should be worded? Is there not, in fact, a simple way "around" the rule of *Berlier*?

See also *Wooten v. Wimberly*, 272 So.2d 303 (La. 1971), *Steptoe, et al. v. Lallie Kemp Regional Hospital, et al.*, 618 So.2d 1008 (La. 1st Cir. 1993), *Steptoe, et al. v. Lallie Kemp Regional Hospital, et al.*, 634 So.2d 331 (La. 1994), *Hidalgo v. Dupuy*, 122 So.2d 639 (La. 1st Cir. 1960).

Comparative Law Perspective

France

Robert J. Pothier, A TREATISE ON THE LAW OF OBLIGATIONS OR CONTRACTS
vol. 1, n⁰ˢ 287–88, at 171–73 (William David Evans trans., 1806)

§ I. *What is a Divisible Obligation, and what is an Indivisible one.*

[287] A Divisible Obligation is that which may be divided. An Indivisible Obligation is that which cannot be divided. An Obligation is not the less divisible, though it be actually undivided; for it is sufficient to render it divisible if it is capable of being divided.

For instance, if I have singly contract to pay you a thousand pounds, this obligation is undivided; but it is divisible, because it may be divided; and in fact will be divided among my heirs, if I leave several, and die before discharging it....

[288] We are now to see what Obligations can be divided, and what cannot.

An obligation may be divided, and is divisible, when the thing which is the matter and object of it is susceptible of division and parts, by which it may be paid; and on the contrary, an obligation is indivisible, and cannot be divided, when the thing is not susceptible of division and parts, and can only be paid altogether.

The division in question is not a physical division ... but a civil division.

There are two kinds of civil division, the one consisting in real and divided parts, the other intellectual, and undivided parts. When an acre of ground is divided into two parts by placing a fence in the middle, this is a division of the first kind: the parts of the acre, which are separated by this fence, are real and divided parts.

When a man who was proprietor of this acre of ground, or of any thing else, dies, and leaves two heirs, who continue proprietors of it, each having an undivided moiety, it is a division of the second kind; the parts which result from this division, and which belong to each of the heirs, are undivided parts, which are not real and which subsist only *in jure et intellectu.*

Things which are not susceptible of the first kind of division, may be of the second. For instance, a horse, a watch, are not susceptible of the first kind of division; for these things are not susceptible of real and divided parts, without the destruction of their substance; but they are susceptible of the second kind of division, because they may belong to several persons, in undivided parts.

Things are indivisible, when they are neither susceptible of real nor even of intellectual parts; such are for the most part, the rights of predial servitudes (a) *quæ pro parte acquire non possunt.*

The obligation of giving a thing of this nature is indivisible.

Alex Weill & François Terré, Droit Civil: Les Obligations
n° 948, at1013 (3d ed. 1980)

The essential difference between indivisibility and passive solidarity is that, in the event of the death of one of the debtors of an indivisible debt, each of his heirs remains bound for the totality, while the heirs of a solidary co-debtor are bound only for their part. This difference is explained by this idea that indivisibility is connected with or is thought to be connected with the nature of the object.

In addition, indivisibility, inasmuch as it is connected with the nature of the object, does not suppose a community of interests among the debtors. As a result, it is admitted that the notion of a "reciprocal mandate" ought to be excluded and that, in this context, the secondary effects of solidarity are not produced, other than the effect regarding the interruption of prescription.

Charles Demolombe, Cours de Code Napoléon: Traité des Contrats
vol. 26, n° 597, at 534–35 (1880)

[I]n a solidary obligation, there exists, among the co-obligors, a juridical relation of mandate, of suretyship, or of partnership. This relation explains the reciprocal necessity in which each finds himself to advance the parts [of the total performance] that appertain to his co-obligors and serves, in fact, as the basis on which the entire theory of passive solidarity rests....

[I]n a divisible obligation, the obligors ... are not obligated for each other; each of them, on the contrary, is obligated separately only for himself. And the necessity in which each finds himself of advancing the parts [of the total performance] that appertain to his co-obligors does not derive from some juridical relation that makes them reciprocal mandataries of each other; it derives solely from a physical or juridical impossibility [i.e., the impossibility of rendering less than the total performance due].

This difference is of capital importance!

What if one of many solidary co-obligors destroys, by his fault, the thing that forms the object of the obligation? The other co-obligors are not freed, for they respond for the fault of their co-obligor, that is to say, of their mandatary or partner.

But what if, on the contrary, one of many co-obligors of an indivisible obligation, by his fault, causes the thing that forms the object of that obligation to perish? The other obligors are freed, for they do not respond for each other, and the individual fault of one, insofar as the others are concerned, is a fortuitous event.

Belgium

Henri de Page, TRAITÉ ELÉMENTAIRE DE DROIT CIVIL BELGE: LES OBLIGATIONS pt. 2
vol. 3, n° 295, at 298–300 (3d ed. 1967)

Indivisible obligations and solidary obligations have this *common trait*: that both of them ... have the effect of [enabling one party or the other] to escape the inconveniences of a divisible obligation with a plurality of subjects. But for the rest, the *differences* between the indivisible obligation and solidary obligation are important.

The indivisible obligation sometimes has *more intense* effects and sometimes *less intense* effects that the solidary obligation.

1° *More intense effects.* — Indivisibility — natural, but also conventional — is extended to the heirs of the multiple debtors; solidarity is not. When several multiple debtors engage themselves indivisibly, if one of these debtors happens to die, his heirs are bound indivisibly, each of them with the others debtors, as was their author-in-title [i.e., the *de cujus*]. The creditor, then, can act *for the whole* against *any one or more of them*. Such is not the case with solidarity, where the debt of the solidary obligor *is divided* among his heirs, without solidary. From this, one can understand the utility of the clause that one encounters so frequently in practice: "the debtors engage themselves *solidarily and indivisibly*." Though this clause, at first glance, appears to be redundant, the utility of it appears in the case of the *death* of one of the solidary debtors. The heirs will no longer be held *solidarily*, but they will still be held *indivisibly*.

2° *Less intense effects.* — Indivisibility sometimes engenders effects that are less intense than those of solidarity:

a) When the indivisibility is founded on the *nature* of the object, the indivisibility does not subsist beyond this object. When an obligation to do, which is indivisible as such, is substituted, in the event of non-performance, for an obligation to pay a sum of money (damages), this latter obligation becomes divisible.... It is otherwise in the case of solidarity....

b) According to the traditional opinion, solidarity presupposes an idea of *mandate* among the co-debtors, an idea that is lacking from indivisibility. It follows, then, that:

1] Whereas the putting in default of one of the solidary debtors produces an effect in regard to the others, it is not the same among the debtors of an indivisible obligation;

2] Whereas the loss of the thing due to the fault of one of the solidary debtors does not free the others, in the case of an indivisible obligation such a loss is considered to be a *cas fortuit* by relation to the other debtors and leads to their

Part Two

Conventional Obligations

Chapter One

General Provisions

Louisiana Sources of Law

Louisiana Civil Code

Art. 1906. Definition of contract.

A contract is an agreement by two or more parties whereby obligations are created, modified, or extinguished. (Acts 1984, No. 331, § 1, eff. Jan. 1, 1985.)

Art. 1907. Unilateral contracts.

A contract is unilateral when the party who accepts the obligation of the other does not assume a reciprocal obligation. (Acts 1984, No. 331, § 1, eff. Jan. 1, 1985.)

Art. 1908. Bilateral or synallagmatic contracts.

A contract is bilateral, or synallagmatic, when the parties obligate themselves reciprocally, so that the obligation of each party is correlative to the obligation of the other. (Acts 1984, No. 331, § 1, eff. Jan. 1, 1985.)

Art. 1909. Onerous contracts.

A contract is onerous when each of the parties obtains an advantage in exchange for his obligation. (Acts 1984, No. 331, § 1, eff. Jan. 1, 1985.)

Art. 1910. Gratuitous contracts.

A contract is gratuitous when one party obligates himself towards another for the benefit of the latter, without obtaining any advantage in return. (Acts 1984, No. 331, § 1, eff. Jan. 1, 1985.)

Art. 1911. Commutative contracts.

A contract is commutative when the performance of the obligation of each party is correlative to the performance of the other. (Acts 1984, No. 331, § 1, eff. Jan. 1, 1985.)

Art. 1912. Aleatory contracts.

A contract is aleatory when, because of its nature or according to the parties' intent, the performance of either party's obligation, or the extent of the performance, depends on an uncertain event. (Acts 1984, No. 331, § 1, eff. Jan. 1, 1985.)

Art. 1913. Principal and accessory contracts.

A contract is accessory when it is made to provide security for the performance of an obligation. Suretyship, mortgage, pledge, and other types of security agreements are examples of such a contract.

When the secured obligation arises from a contract, either between the same or other parties, that contract is the principal contract. (Acts 1984, No. 331, § 1, eff. Jan. 1, 1985; Acts 1989, No. 137, § 16, eff. Sept. 1, 1989.)

Art. 1914. Nominate and innominate contracts.

Nominate contracts are those given a special designation such as sale, lease, loan, or insurance.

Innominate contracts are those with no special designation. (Acts 1984, No. 331, § 1, eff. Jan. 1, 1985.)

Art. 1915. Rules applicable to all contracts.

All contracts, nominate and innominate, are subject to the rules of this title. (Acts 1984, No. 331, § 1, eff. Jan. 1, 1985.)

Précis: Louisiana Law of Conventional Obligations— Article I to 1.6.2

To a legal concept is associated a legal regime, a set of legal rules which govern a carefully described factual situation matching the proper legal concept....

[T]he Louisiana civil Code has classified "contracts" under a series of "definitions" to which are attached specific legal regimes which are distributed all over the civil Code and which can be fully grasped only as a consequence of an understanding of the structure of the whole civil Code....

A contract, an agreement between two parties at least, is unilateral when only one of the two parties owes an obligation to the other; only one party is a debtor whereas the other party is the creditor of that debtor. We can analogize such a unilateral contract to a "one-way street," the obligation moving in one direction only....

It is most important to distinguish a "unilateral contract" from a "unilateral juridical act." In the latter case only one person is bound by her/his single will; such would be the case of an "offer" which binds the offeror only until it expires or is revoked. If it should be accepted, we will then have a "bilateral juridical act" or contract. That contract will be "unilateral" if it creates obligations on one party only, or it will be "bilateral/synallagmatic" if both parties owe obligations to each other. A bilateral or synallagmatic contract is, therefore, a "two-way street" because the obligations flow in both directions....

"A contract is onerous when each of the parties obtains an advantage in exchange for his obligation." LSA-C.C. Art. 1909. In such a contract, for example a contract of sale, each one of the two parties owes some performance to the other and is entitled to receiving a performance from that other party....

"A contract is gratuitous when one party obligates himself towards another for the benefit of the latter, without obtaining any advantage in return." LSA-C.C. Art. 1910. It is the gratuitous motivation or intent of that party who obliges herself towards another "without obtaining any advantage in return" that actually determines the nature of that contract. The typical and most common example of such a kind of contract is the "donation purely gratuitous ... which is made without condition and merely from liberality." ...

There exist some important legal and practical reasons for this distinction between onerous and gratuitous contracts....

COMMUTATIVE AND ALEATORY CONTRACTS
LSA-C.C. ARTS. 1911–1912

This classification as it exists in the Louisiana civil Code is, we believe, problematic....

Louisiana civil Code of 1870: Art. 1768: "Commutative contracts are those in which what is done, given or promised by one party, is considered as equivalent to, or a consideration for what is done, given, or promised by the other." *Article 1776*, in its first paragraph, stated: "*A contract is aleatory or hazardous, when the performance of that which is one of its objects, depends on an uncertain event.*" ...

[T]he *civil Code of Québec* states in *Article 1382* that "*A contract is commutative when, at the time it is formed, the extent of the obligations of the parties and of the advantages obtained by them in return is certain and determinate. When the extent of the obligations or of the advantages is uncertain, the contract is aleatory.*" ...

It is our position that Article 1911 first does not add to the definition of bilateral/synallagmatic contract and, second, fails to emphasize the difference between a truly "commutative" contract at civil law and an aleatory contract as it is defined in LSA-C.C. Art. 1912.

What does "correlative" mean and how can its meaning fit in the definition of <u>both</u> LSA-C.C. Articles 1908 and 1911? ...

It is inherent in any bilateral/synallagmatic contract that each party owes to the other the performance of the object of her own obligation. ...

In a bilateral/synallagmatic contract, not only the obligations themselves are "reciprocal, correlative" as LSA-C.C. Art. 1908 states, but so are the performances by the very fact that they are inherent to the very nature of any bilateral/synallagmatic contract. Such a contract by itself can only create the reciprocity, the correlation, of the performances which are necessarily engendered by the reciprocity, or correlation of the obligations without which no performance could exist. We believe, therefore, that LSA-C.C. Art. 1911 adds absolutely nothing to Art. 1908. ...

LSA-C.C. Art. 2982 describes in clear legal terms what an aleatory contract is: "**The aleatory contract is a mutual agreement, of which the effects, with respect both to the advantages and losses, whether to all the parties or to one or more of them, depend on an uncertain event.**" The specific legal terms to focus on are that an *aleatory contract* is a *mutual agreement* which *creates effects*, i.e. advantages and losses, *vis-à-vis one or more parties*, and the occurrence of *which effects depend on an uncertain event*. ...

A principal contract is one which can stand on its own; it needs no legal (contractual or otherwise) support than its own to exist; it does not need to *arise* from any other contract. A contract of sale can stand on its own; so can a donation or marriage contract.

On the other hand, when a contract needs the support of another contract (or legislation), when "**it is made to provide security for the performance of [a principal] obligation**" then it is an "accessory" to the principal contract. Article 1913 illustrates this concept of accessory contract with "**suretyship, mortgage, pledge** ..."

The rule is that parties can be bound by a contract which is merely *consensual*, which results from the oral exchange of their wills. The most common *consensual* contract we enter into just about every day, and sometimes more than once, is the contract of sale of a movable thing. Such is very clearly stated in LSA-C.C. Art. 2439 § 2: "**Sale is a contract whereby a person transfers ownership of a thing to another for a price in money.**

The thing, the price, and the consent of the parties are requirements for the perfection of a sale." The binding force of "consent" is such that "**Ownership is transferred between the parties as soon as there is agreement on the thing and the price is fixed, even though the thing sold is not yet delivered nor the price paid.**" (**LSA-C.C. Art. 2456.**)

To the contrary, and as an exception to the rule that contracts are consensual, there are instances of contracts, in the civil Code, which require a "form," a writing, for some contracts to be valid and binding. They are called *solemn* or *formal* contracts. We read, for example, in LSA-C.C. Art. 2440 that "A sale or promise of sale of an immovable must be made by authentic act or by act under private signature, except as provided in Article 1839." ...

As a general rule, contracts are negotiated between two parties who mutually agree on their reciprocal obligations and rights....

Such contracts resulting from a mutual agreement between the two parties are presumed to fully reflect the principles of "autonomy of the will" and "freedom of contract" which are the foundations of the law of contracts at civil law....

However, today, contracts are less and less negotiated on equal basis and more and more either non-negotiable at all or negotiable in part only. Such contracts are often referred to as "contracts of adhesion" or "adhesion contracts." ...

Illustrations abound: insurance contracts, electricity supply contracts, transportation contracts, etc....

With respect to contracts which the courts will qualify and describe as "adhesion contracts," it is the responsibility of the courts to attempt to re-establish some balance between the unequal bargaining powers of the parties, to protect the "weak" against the "strong." ...

Cases

LILLIS

v.

OWENS

Louisiana Court of Appeal
Orleans
Feb. 26, 1945
21 So.2d 185

McCALEB, Judge.

The plaintiff is engaged in the contracting business in New Orleans and conducts his operations under the name of Brandin Slate Company. On November 18th, 1941, he entered into a written contract with the defendant, Mary Owens, under which he agreed to make certain alterations, additions and improvements to the real property of the defendant designated as Nos. 2427–29 London Avenue, New Orleans, in consideration of a price of $1890. This contract, which describes in detail the work to be performed by plaintiff, stipulates that the price of $1890 is 'to be paid in monthly installments' and further that 'Owner gives Brandin Slate Company permission to try and arrange the financing.'

Alleging that, in accordance with his obligation under the aforesaid contract, he has fully performed the work required of him; that he is and has been ready and willing to deliver the building and improvements to defendant free and clear of all liens and claims for labor and material furnished by him which was used in connection with the alteration and repairs to the building and that he has made demand on defendant for the payment of the price due under the contract without avail, plaintiff instituted suit in the Civil District Court to recover from defendant the contract price of $1890.

After filing an exception of no right or cause of action which was overruled by the trial court, the defendant answered plaintiff's petition and denied the allegations of fact contained therein. She further set forth that the contract was void; that the price was exorbitant; that plaintiff's agent obtained her signature to the so-called contract through fraud and deceit and that the court should declare that she was relieved of any and all responsibility in the premises.

The case thereafter proceeded to trial on the issues thus formed by the pleadings. At the outset of the hearing, counsel for defendant objected to the introduction of evidence in the case 'for the reason this contract which we submit to the Court is not a contract upon which one can be sued on for the reason everything is in blank.' After hearing argument on this objection, the court made the following ruling: 'In this so-called contract everything that involves a meeting of the minds is blank. Considering the fact that the alleged contract was in fact no contract at all and there was no meeting of the minds evidenced in that written agreement, and that the petition does not allege any demand to recover on a quantum meruit, the Court must sustain the objection and exclude all evidence. I will dismiss the case as of non-suit, so that there will be no question of res adjudicata in the event of a new suit on a quantum meruit or some other contract growing out of the same transaction.'

In conformity with this ruling, a judgment was rendered dismissing plaintiff's demand as in case of nonsuit. Both parties prosecuted appeals from the judgment, defendant contending that plaintiff's suit should have been dismissed absolutely and plaintiff maintaining that the judge erred in refusing to hear evidence in the case and in dismissing his demand. Since the record has been lodged in this court, counsel representing plaintiff in the District Court has joined the Armed Forces of the United States and other attorneys have been employed. The attorney, who represented defendant in the lower court, has died and, although defendant has been duly notified of the hearing, she has not appeared either in person or through other counsel.

The objection to the hearing of any evidence in the case, which was interposed in the lower court by counsel for defendant, was based upon the theory that there were 'blanks' contained in the written agreement which were required to be filled out in order for the parties to execute a binding contract. The judge, in maintaining this objection, remarked that 'in this so-called contract everything that involves a meeting of the minds is blank.'

An examination of the contract, which is attached to plaintiff's petition, reveals that it was executed on a printed form of Brandin Slate Company. The work which the contractor proposed to perform under the agreement is fully detailed in typewriting, as well as the price of $1890, which the defendant agreed to pay. The only 'blanks' to be found in the document are those contained in that part of the printed form referring to the making of a down payment by the owner and the execution of a promissory note, payable in installments, to be given to the contractor for the balance to become due on the work. Obviously, it was unnecessary for the parties in the instant case to fill in those blanks, as the typewritten portion of the contract, which prevails over the printed matter, did not contemplate any down payment at all or the giving of a promissory note for the price of the work. Hence, it is difficult for us to understand how the presence of the blanks in the printed portion of the contract was pertinent to the judge's ruling that a binding contract did not exist as there was no meeting of minds by the parties.

While the reason given by the judge for his statement that the contract is unenforceable because of lack of mutuality does not clearly appear from his ruling, it is evident that he was of the opinion that, because the parties stipulated that the purchase price was to be paid in monthly installments without stating the amount or the number of such installments, their failure to do so was fatal to the agreement. In other words, it is ap-

parently the view of our brother below that an agreement to do work for a certain price, 74
payable in monthly installments, is not a binding contract because, inasmuch as the par- 75
ties have not agreed upon the amount of such installments, it is impossible for the court 76
to fix the method of payment of the price. 77

We cannot agree with this view. In an agreement to alter, repair or construct a build- 78
ing, where the work to be done is set forth and the price to be paid is fixed, all of the es- 79
sentials of a binding contract are present. The mode of payment of the price, whether in 80
installments or otherwise, is merely an accidental stipulation. Under Article 1764 of the 81
Civil Code, it is provided that all things not forbidden by law may legally become the 82
subject of contracts but that different agreements are governed by different rules 'adapted 83
to the nature of each contract to distinguish which it is necessary in every contract to 84
consider: 85

'1. That which is the essence of the contract, for the want whereof there is ei- 86
ther no contract at all, or a contract of another description. Thus a price is es- 87
sential to the contract of sale; if there be none, it is either no contract, or if the 88
consideration be other property, it is an exchange. 89

* * * 90

'3. Accidental stipulations, which belong neither to the essence nor the nature 91
of the contract, but depend solely on the will of the parties. The term given for 92
the payment of a loan, the place at which it is to be paid, and the nature of the 93
rent payable on a lease, are examples of accidental stipulations. 94

'What belongs to the essence and to the nature of each particular description of con- 95
tract, is determined by the law defining such contracts; accidental stipulations depend 96
on the will of the parties, regulated by the general rules applying to all contracts.' 97

Thus, it will be readily observed that the agreement under consideration contains all 98
of the necessary elements of a binding contract, set forth in Article 1764, i.e., the work 99
to be done by the contractor and the payment by the owner of a fixed price therefor. 100
There is, however, an accidental stipulation contained in the agreement, which refers 101
solely to the manner in which the price is to be paid by the owner— that is, that the par- 102
ties contemplated that the owner would have the right to pay the agreed price in monthly 103
installments. The fact that the amount of these installments is not fixed does not make 104
the price indefinite but merely exhibits that the parties contemplated that the amount to 105
be paid each month would be agreed upon at some future date. This intention is evi- 106
denced by another provision of the contract declaring that the owner grants to the con- 107
tractor permission 'to try and arrange the financing'. In other words, it seems clear to us 108
that, at the time the agreement was made and the price fixed, the contractor believed that 109
he could arrange for a loan on the property whereby he could obtain the price of his work 110
in full and in one payment. If he had been successful in arranging this loan, the covenant 111
respecting the installment payments would hav [sic] amounted to naught. However, if 112
he was unsuccessful (as apparently was the case here), it became necessary for the parties 113
to agree upon the amount of the monthly payments in order for the owner to liquidate 114
the fixed price for the work. If, in fact, no agreement was made concerning the amount 115
of the monthly installments, the owner might have had the right to a rescission of the 116
contract on the ground that she agreed only to become liable for the price, provided pay- 117
ment could be made by monthly installments. But can she now claim that there is no 118
contract at all nor an obligation on her part to pay the fixed price, where she has per- 119
mitted the contractor to execute his part of the engagement, on the theory that she agreed 120
to become liable only if payments were made in monthly installments and that the amounts 121

of said installments were not fixed? Stated in another way, if it be conceded that defendant had the right to prevent performance of the agreement, while it was still executory, on the ground that the amount of the monthly payments contemplated could not be fixed by amicable agreement, can she now make the same defense after she has permitted the contractor to execute his undertaking? We think not.

It is well recognized that the nonperformance of an accidental stipulation does not invariably have the effect of abrogating an agreement forasmuch as such a covenant is not of the essence of a valid contract. See Andrus v. Eunice Band Mill Co., 185 La. 403, 169 So. 449 and Moore v. O'Bannon & Julien, 126 La. 161, 52 So. 253, 255. In the Moore case, which was quoted from with approval in the Andrus case, it is said: 'The stipulations relating to the erection of the mill and the making of the payments thereon pay days to be fixed are quoad the sale of the timber 'accidental,' being neither of the essence of the contract nor necessarily implied from its nature, but depending solely upon the will of the parties, regulated by the general rules applicable to all contracts. Civ.Code, art. 1764, par. 3. Where the parties so agree, or, in some cases, where there is no agreement to the contrary, noncompliance with accidental stipulations may furnish good cause to annul a contract.

The accidental stipulation contained in the contract in this case was obviously inserted for the benefit of the defendant—for, if nothing had been covenanted by the parties respecting payment in installments, the price would become due as soon as the work had been completed by the contractor. See Civil Code, Article 2050. The provision in the contract, respecting the payment in monthly installments, does not contemplate the payment of interest to the contractor on the deferred balance of the price while the work was in progress and, therefore, the stipulation cannot in any sense be regarded as one in his favor. Hence, since the stipulation for installment payments was inserted solely for defendant's benefit, it could be waived by her. If we assume, as we must, that the contractor was unsuccessful in arranging for the financing of the job and if the parties were unable to come to an agreement respecting the amount of the contemplated monthly installments, defendant would have had the right to withdraw from the contract and have had it rescinded. But this right to withdraw from the engagement could be waived by defendant, either expressly, or impliedly by permitting the contractor to fulfill his part of the bargain without protest. In 17 C.J.S., Contracts § 443, pp. 926 and 927, we find the following:

> 'The right to rescind may be lost or waived by delay, or by words or conduct evidencing an intention not to exercise it, such as by accepting its benefits. * * *

> 'There is a waiver of the right to rescind a building contract where the contract is treated, by the party having such right, as still in force. So also a party to a building contract may waive his right to rescind the contract by not exercising such right promptly.'

Hence, we conclude that, since the agreement under consideration contains all of the essential elements of a contract, i.e., the work to be done and the price to be paid, a valid contract subsists, despite the fact that it contains a provision concerning terms of payment which is vague and indefinite because the amounts of the monthly installments are not stated. It well may be that, if the judge had not refused to hear any evidence in the case, plaintiff or defendant could have cleared up the ambiguity as to the amount of the installments by submitting evidence to show that the parties, subsequent to the execution of the contract, agreed to, and fixed, the amounts which should be paid each month. Such evidence would be clearly admissible. On the other hand, if neither plaintiff nor defendant are able to show that an agreement was reached respecting the amounts of the monthly in-

stallments, plaintiff's petition nevertheless states a cause of action for recovery of the en-   170
tire contract price, since he has alleged that he has fully performed his obligation under   171
the agreement. In view of this allegation, the question will be presented on the merits as   172
to whether the defendant, in permitting plaintiff to excute [*sic*] his part of the engagement,   173
has not waived, by her conduct or otherwise, her right to insist that she is not liable for   174
the stipulated price on the ground that the parties contemplated that that price was to   175
be liquidated in monthly installments and that no agreement could he reached concern-   176
ing the amount of those installments. The result to be reached on this question can only   177
be determined by the hearing of evidence.   178

We therefore hold that the objection interposed by defendant to the hearing of any   179
evidence in the case was erroneously sustained and it is now overruled.   180

For the reasons assigned, the judgment appealed from is reversed and the case is re-   181
manded to the Civil District Court for further proceedings in accordance with law and   182
consistent with the views herein expressed. The costs of this appeal are to be paid by the   183
defendant, Mary Owens, other costs to await the final disposition of the matter.   184

Reversed and remanded.   185

Questions

1. Lines 9–16: the court states that the parties "entered into a written contract". Was (were) there a term and/or a condition? If one and/or the other, what kind(s)?

2. Lines 30 *et seq.*: Why is the court saying that the "alleged contract was in fact no contract at all and there was no meeting of the minds"? Would any blank in the contract lead to the court saying there was no meeting of the minds? Should a distinction be made between blanks bearing on essential elements/component parts of a contract and blanks bearing on accessory or secondary or incidental elements/component parts of a contract?

3. Lines 56–68: Isn't the court making a distinction here between the many elements of a contract? Focusing on lines 33–68, isn't the Court of Appeal making such a distinction? From line 98 onward, see what the court is saying about accidental stipulations and the effect or lack thereof of these accidental stipulations not being performed?

4. Lines 98 *et seq.*: Can you identify the essential elements of the contract at issue here (a construction contract, according to the court) and those that are not essential? Are the requirements listed in Louisiana Civil Code article 2756 the essential requirements the Court identified as such in this case?

ORKIN EXTERMINATING COMPANY   1
v.   2
James T. FOTI   3
Supreme Court of Louisiana   4
Oct. 28, 1974   5
302 So.2d 593   6

TATE, Justice.   7

Orkin, the employer, sues its former employee Foti to enjoin him for working for two   8
years in the pest control field in approximately the western half of Louisiana. The cause   9

of action is based upon a clause in the employment contract by which Foti had agreed not to compete for two years in such area after his employment with Orkin was terminated. The employer complains of the grant of only a limited injunction,[1] affirmed by the court of appeal, 287 So.2d 569 (La.App.3d Cir. 1973).

We granted certiorari, 292 So.2d 241 (La.1974), in order to resolve a conflict in the intermediate court decisions interpreting the legality of agreements exacted by employers from their employees not to compete with them after the termination of an employee relationship.

1.

More specifically at issue is the application of La.R.S. 23:921 as amended in 1962.

This statute as originally enacted in 1934 and as incorporated into the 1950 Revised Statutes provides: 'No employer shall require or direct any employee to enter into any contract whereby the employee agrees not to engage in any competing business for himself, or as the employee of another, upon the termination of his contract of employment with such employer, and all such contracts, or provisions thereof containing such agreement shall be null and unenforceable in any court'.

The statute was amended by Act 104 of 1962 to add as a proviso a limited exception to this stringent blanket prohibition of non-competition agreements: 'where the employer incurs an expense in the training of an employee or incurs an expense in the advertisement of the business that the employer is engaged in', then a non-competition agreement was permitted that, at the termination of employment, the 'employee will not enter into the same business that employer is engaged over the same route or in the same territory for a period of two years.'[2]

The conflict in the intermediate courts developed as to what extent the proviso had modified the original basic policy disfavoring non-competition agreements. See Comment, Agreements Not to Compete, 33 La.L.Rev. 94, 103-06 (1972).

One line of decisions holds that, in view of the basic policy of the statute to which the 1962 amendment was a proviso, the terms of the amendment imported sums not usually or customarily expended in the normal course of employment—that the amendment contemplated validating a non-competition agreement only where substantial funds were spent in special training or in special advertisement of the employee himself (rather than generally of the business).

The other line of cases holds that any expense incurred in training an employee, even normal supervisory assistance in breaking him in, and any expense incurred in advertising the employee's connection with the business, however nominal, validated an otherwise-prohibited non-competition agreement.

The leading case in the first line of decisions is National Motor Club of La., Inc. v. Conque, 173 So.2d 238 (La.App.3d Cir. 1965), certiorari denied, 247 La. 875, 175 So.2d

---

1. The defendant Foti was enjoined from soliciting or getting business from customers of Orkin formerly contacted or serviced by him as an employee of Orkin. No appeal was taken from this ruling.

2. The full language added to La.R.S. 23:921 by the 1962 act is: 'provided that in those cases where the employer incurs an expense in the training of the employee or incurs an expense in the advertisement of the business that the employer is engaged in, then in that event it shall be permissible for the employer and employee to enter into a voluntary contract and agreement whereby the employee is permitted to agree and bind himself that at the termination of his or her employment that said employee will not enter into the same business that employer is engaged in over the same route or in the same territory for a period of two years.'

110 (1965). Other decisions of similar import are: Weight Watchers of Louisiana, Inc. v. Ryals, 289 So.2d 531 (La.App.1st Cir. 1973), certiorari granted, 292 So.2d 242 (La.1974) (argued at same time as present case and decided this date, La.App., 302 So.2d 598); Peltier v. Hebert, 245 So.2d 511 (La.App.3d Cir. 1971).

The leading case in the latter line of decisions is Aetna Finance Co. v. Adams, 170 So.2d 740 (La.App.1st Cir. 1964), certiorari denied, 247 La. 489, 172 So.2d 294 (1965). Other decisions of similar import are: National School Studios, Inc. v. Barrios, 236 So.2d 309 (La.App.4th Cir. 1970); World Wide Health Studios, Inc. v. Desmond, 222 So.2d 517 (La.App.2d Cir. 1969). Cf. also Louisiana Office Systems, Inc. v. Boudreaux, 298 So.2d 341 (La.App.3d Cir. 1974).

We resolve the conflict by approving National Motor Club v. Conque and its progeny. Aetna Finance Co. v. Adams and those decisions which follow its rationale or reach its result are overruled.

2.

The basic public policy of this state disfavors non-competition agreement exacted of employees. The basic provision of La.R.S. 23:921 (see above) is a strict prohibition against any employer requiring such an agreement of his employee. Even before the 1934 statutory prohibition, the Louisiana courts had consistently held such agreements to be unenforceable. Cloverland Dairy Products Co. v. Grace, 180 La. 694, 157 So. 393 (1934); Blanchard v. Haber, 166 La. 1014, 118 So. 117 (1928). See: Comment, 33 La.L.Rev. 94 (1972); Note, 27 Tul.L.Rev. 364 (1953). In the absence of an enforceable contract to other effect, an employee has the absolute right to enter the employment of another and actively compete with his former employer. Jones v. Ernst & Ernst, 172 La. 406, 134 So. 375 (1931).

As noted in Conque, 173 So.2d 241, the essential basis of these decisions 'is the right of individual freedom and of individuals to better themselves in our free-enterprise society, where liberty of the individual is guaranteed. A strong public policy reason likewise for holding unenforceable an agreement exacted by an employer of an employee not to compete after the latter leaves his employment, is the disparity in bargaining power, under which an employee, fearful of losing his means of livelihood, cannot readily refuse to sign an agreement which, if enforceable, amounts to his contracting away his liberty to earn his livelihood in the field of his experience except by continuing in the employment of his present employer.'

These fundamental background principles must be borne in mind in interpreting the intent of the 1962 amendment. This provides only a limited exception to the stringent prohibition of the statute against such non-competition agreements, and to the strong and long-established public policy of this state to such effect.

If the 1962 amendment is construed as by the Aetna v. Adams line of decisions, then Any expense incurred by an employer in training or advertisement entitles him to enforcement of a two-year restrictive covenant. If, however, this is the proper meaning of the amendment, then virtually any employer can qualify for the exception. This is contrary to the basic public policy incorporated by the statute. By such a construction, the 1962 amendment, which in terms merely added a proviso to the basic enactment, would in actuality have repealed it.

The purpose of the limited exception permitted by the 1962 amendments could not have been to repeal the fundamental purpose of the prohibition. The basic public policy incorporated was to forbid an employer from effectively tying an employee to his present employment. Such a non-competition agreement may effectively prevent an employee from leaving his present employment in order to earn a better living in the occupation in which experienced and in the area of his livelihood.

97   In view of the fundamental policy of the basic statute, the apparent purpose of the
98   1962 amendment, as stated in Conque, 'is to protect an employer only where he has in-
99   vested substantial sums in special training of the employee or in advertising the employee's
100 connection with his business.' 173 So.2d 241.

101 If an employer extensively advertises a particular employee as the man to go to for
102 the employer's type of services, it is not unfair to protect the employer's investment in
103 this particularized asset by authorizing a limited non-competition agreement to pre-
104 vent the advertised employee from misusing it. If an employer spends a substantial sum
105 affording special training to an employee, it may not be unfair to protect the employer
106 by authorizing a limited non-competition agreement to prevent the employee from
107 using this specialized training for the benefit of another in competition with his former
     employer.

108 However, as the Conque line of cases holds, normal expenses of administration and
109 supervision — such as employee sales and training meetings, the time spent breaking in
110 a new employee, training courses in the administrative needs of the employer itself—
111 cannot be considered the sort of 'training' expense intended to justify the heavily disfa-
112 vored non-competition agreement. Almost any employer could so tie his employees to their
113 present employment by exacting a non-competition agreement. As Conque notes, 173
114 So.2d 241: 'What the legislators must have intended, it seems to us (since they did not re-
115 peal the basic prohibition against such contracts as void as against the public policy of the
116 state), was to protect the investment of those employers who afford special training of a
117 substantial nature to their employees, and to encourage them to do so.'

118   3.

119 Foti was employed almost five years by Orkin. He was first employed in Alexandria in
120 1968 at $500 per month. Non-competition agreements were exacted of him in 1970, when
121 he became manager of the New Iberia office, in 1971 when he became branch manager
122 at Monroe, then again in 1972, when he was transferred to the Louisiana district office
123 in Alexandria at a base salary of $750 per month.

124 Included in the three pages of the last contract, here sought to be enforced, was an
125 agreement not to engage in the pest control business, for two years after his employment
126 terminated, in the cities of Alexandria, Crowley, Monroe, Lafayette, Lake Charles, Natchi-
127 toches, New Iberia, Shreveport, or Ruston, or anywhere within a radius of fifty miles of
128 the official geographical boundaries of each of these Louisiana cities.

129 This injunctive proceeding was brought when Foti left Orkin's employ and then started
130 his own pest control business in Opelousas. Orkin claims that its non-competition agree-
131 ment is validated by sums spent in training Foti as a pest control worker and as a branch
132 manager. (It also claims that its general expenses of advertising to improve its business
133 are sufficient to validate the contract.)

134 We agree with the court of appeal that the one-day service training schools in 1970,
135 1971, and 1972, and the supervisor's leadership conference in August, 1972 represent a
136 type of normal administrative expense not available to validate non-competition agree-
137 ments; they are not special training expenditures of a substantial nature. Likewise (even
138 aside from the fact the expenditure occurred prior to the 1972 agreement here sought to
139 be enforced), the $261.50 expense furnished the employee for attending the Orkin's Man-
140 ager Training School in Atlanta, Georgia, in 1970 cannot justify enjoining the employee
141 from working for himself or another in 1973 and 1974— the employer had long received
142 the benefit of its investment through the employee's two years of managerial service af-

terwards; the amount is insubstantial in relation to the period of service;[3] and the train- 143
ing was primarily to benefit Orkin rather than to add a marketable talent to the employee. 144

Likewise, Foti's on-the-job training through his experience, through the supervisory 145
assistance initially received by him, and through his access to Orkin training manuals and 146
technical bulletins, constitute usual and ordinary expenses of employee-utilization. They 147
are not expenses for specialized training of the nature that could validate a non-competition 148
agreement. 149

As our brothers of the intermediate court correctly observed: '* * * the basic and nec- 150
essary knowledge in the business of pest eradications and control was acquired by the de- 151
fendant, Foti, by everyday exposure to the business during the five years he was employed 152
by the plaintiff. We cannot envision a rule whereby a man who has learned a trade by his 153
own ability and hard work 'on the job' would be restricted by the courts from trying to 154
better himself by starting his own business. This would be contrary to our free-enterprise 155
system.' 156

[....]

Questions

1. Lines 19 *et seq.*: What do you think was the policy or *ratio legis* behind La. R.S. 23:921 of 1934 with respect to non-competition clauses? What about the exception added by Act 104 of 1962? How much should the courts be involved in implementing these policies? Shouldn't the courts be given some outside guidance? *See* lines 62 *et seq.* How should a court look upon an exception?

2. Lines 62 *et seq.*: Isn't it of the essence of a principle to call for exceptions? How can there be a conflict between a principle and an exception to that principle? Could it be because policies rather than rules of law are vying for their particular scope of application? What are then the courts to do?

---

3. Thus, specialized training involving an actual cash expenditure of $400 might be regarded as the investment of a substantial sum if the employee quit soon after receiving it. However, if the termination of the employee's services occurs two or three years later, after the employer had, so to speak, amortized its investment, then the amount so spent can be regarded as insubstantial insofar as sustaining an injunction to keep the employee from working in the field of his experience for years, even though in the interval insubstantial routine training expenditures have been incurred. But see Louisiana Office Systems, Inc. v. Boudreaux, 298 So.2d 341 (La.App.3d Cir. 1974), certiorari granted, 302 So.2d 37 (La.1974).

CELLULAR ONE, INC.

v.

John Brent BOYD

CELLULAR ONE, INC.

v.

Hamilton J. LEMOINE

Louisiana Court of Appeal

First Circuit

March 3, 1995

653 So.2d 30

LOTTINGER, Chief Judge.

This is an appeal by defendants from the granting of a preliminary injunction enforcing a noncompetition agreement executed between plaintiff and defendants.

FACTS

John Boyd and Hamilton Lemoine were employed as sales representatives for Cellular One from 1989 to 1993. During the course of their employment, they signed several noncompetition and nondisclosure agreements. When Boyd and Lemoine left the employment of Cellular One in December of 1993, they had executed identical noncompetition agreements which became effective on September 1, 1993.[1]

Upon leaving Cellular One both defendants went to work for Affordable Cellular, an authorized agent of Bell South Mobility. Cellular One filed this suit for injunctive relief asserting that Boyd and Lemoine were in violation of the noncompetition agreement. Cellular One sought to prevent the defendants from competing against it in the cellular telephone business and from soliciting the business of Cellular One's customers in the parishes of East Baton Rouge, West Baton Rouge, Ascension, and Livingston. The suit also sought protection against disclosure of confidential information.

Following the hearing on the preliminary injunction, the trial court enjoined defendants from engaging in the radio telephone service business in the parishes of East and West Baton Rouge, Ascension, and Livingston, for a period of two years. The court further enjoined defendants from directly soliciting any Cellular One customer to transfer or purchase radio telephone services or equipment. The court also ordered that should any customer of Cellular One initiate contact with defendants, said customer shall be referred back to Cellular one and not to any other radio telephone service. The trial court then suspended that portion of the injunction which prohibited the defendants from engaging in the radio telephone service business.

Defendants appeal, asserting that the trial court erred in:

1. enforcing a noncompetition clause in an employment at will agreement because the agreement lacks mutuality of obligation and the agreement fails to provide sufficient consideration for the employee;

---

1. Boyd was fired from Cellular One whereas Lemoine resigned.

2. failing to find that circumstances involving economic threats were sufficient
to constitute duress;

3. failing to rule that the agreement provided for stipulated damages;

4. finding that the noncompetition clause was sufficient to meet the requirements of La.R.S. 23:921; and

5. granting a preliminary injunction because no evidence was set forth that
defendants in fact violated the confidentiality or nondisclosure clauses of the
agreement.

THE NONCOMPETITION AGREEMENT

The contract at issue in this suit contains several provisions which purportedly comprise the noncompetition agreement. These provisions are:

III. Commissions and Other Incentives

D. Non-Competition Payments (NCPs):

NCPs are payable for the term listed below even if the eligible Sales Representative leaves the employment of the company. The main exception to
this statement is if the former Sales Representative is employed by or is contracted with any Radio/Telephone Service of Baton Rouge Cellular One during the time period that the NCP payments are due as per the Employee
Handbook. In the event that the Sales Representative is employed by or is
contracted with a Radio/Telephone Service, all NCPs are forfeited by the Sales
Representative. The Sales Representative also forfeits all NCPs earned during
his/her employment at Cellular One.

....

VIII. Direct Sales Non-Competition Payments (NCPs)

NCPs are payable at 3% for 3 years for those accounts having monthly bills
over $50 per month. This includes access and airtime. The 3 years is based from
the date of the start of the original contract.

Terms & Conditions: (Eligibility Requirements)

....

6.) Should the Direct Sales Rep leave or be terminated, Cellular One will continue to fulfill its obligation to the employee, but only for as long as the former employee does not engage in business or employment with another Radio/Telephone
Service entity. Also, should any customer cancel, any retractions the former employee
might have qualified to receive will be applied to the noncompetition payment.

....

NON-COMPETITION AGREEMENT

I agree to refrain from carrying on or engaging in a radio telephone service business
similar to that of Cellular One, Inc. and/or from soliciting customers of Cellular One,
Inc. within the parishes of East Baton Rouge, West Baton Rouge, Ascension and Livingston for a period of two years from separation of employment with Cellular One, Inc.

THE STATUTORY PROVISION

Louisiana has consistently had a strong public policy against noncompetition contracts which prohibit employees from competing with a former employer. *Orkin Exter-*

minating Company v. Foti, 302 So.2d 593, 596 (La.1974). Prior to 1989, La. R.S. 23:921 permitted noncompetition agreements only if the employer incurred significant or extensive expenditures in the training of the employee or the advertisement of the business. *Id.* at 597. In 1989, the legislature amended La.R.S. 23:921 and replaced this single exception. However, the public policy disfavoring noncompetition agreements is still reflected in subsection (A) of the amended statute which provides:

> Every contract or agreement, or provision thereof, by which anyone is restrained from exercising a lawful profession, trade, or business of any kind, except as provided in this Section, shall be null and void.

One of the exceptions to this general prohibition is contained in subsection (C) which states:

> Any person, including a corporation and the individual shareholders of such corporation, who is employed as an agent, servant, or employee may agree with his employer to refrain from carrying on or engaging in a business similar to that of the employer and/or from soliciting customers of the employer within a specified parish or parishes, municipality or municipalities, or parts thereof, so long as the employer carries on a like business therein, not to exceed a period of two years from termination of employment.

Subsection (G) lists remedies available to an employer when a former employee breaches a noncompetition agreement.

> Any agreement covered by Subsections B, C, D, E, or F of this Section shall be considered an obligation not to do, and failure to perform may entitled the obligee to recover damages for the loss sustained and the profit of which he has been deprived. In addition, upon proof of the obligor's failure to perform, and without the necessity of proving irreparable injury, a court of competent jurisdiction shall order injunctive relief enforcing the terms of the agreement.

In amending section 921, the Louisiana Legislature expanded the use of noncompetition agreements. The legislature recognized that employers have a right to protect their business investment provided they comply with the exceptions contained in the statute.

COMPLIANCE WITH LA.R.S. 23:921

In assignment of error four, defendants allege that the agreement does not meet the requirements of La.R.S. 23:921(C). Defendants assert that the agreement does not adequately define the geographical location or time limitation within which the noncompetition agreement would apply. They further assert that there is no adequate definition of the business from which they are allegedly prohibited from competing.

To be valid, a noncompetition agreement may limit competition only in a business similar to that of the employer, in a specified geographic area and for up to two years from termination of employment. Public policy requires that the provisions of noncompetition agreements be strictly construed in favor of the employee. *See Pelican Publishing Company v. Wilson,* 626 So.2d 721 (La.App. 5th Cir.1993); *Comet Industries, Inc. v. Lawrence,* 600 So.2d 85 (La.App. 2nd Cir.), *writ denied,* 604 So.2d 1002 (La.1992). Accordingly, noncompetition agreements which fail to specify the "parish or parishes, municipality or municipalities, or parts thereof" wherein the employer carried on a similar business are unenforceable. *Comet Industries, Inc.,* 600 So.2d at 87. Similarly, contracts seeking to extend noncompetition agreements beyond the two year statutory limit are null and void. *Allied Bruce Terminix Companies, Inc. v. Ferrier,* 93-0561 (La.App. 1st Cir. 3/11/94); 634 So.2d 44.

In this case, the contract prevents the defendants from "engaging in a radio telephone   131
service business similar to that of Cellular One, Inc." in the parishes of East Baton Rouge,   132
West Baton Rouge, Ascension and Livingston, for a period of two years after employ-   133
ment termination. The language used in the agreement to define plaintiff's business tracks   134
the statutory language of La.R.S. 23:921(C). This language adequately defines the busi-   135
ness from which the defendants are prohibited from competing. Further, the geographic   136
and time limitations are clearly specified in the contract and comply with the statutory   137
guidelines.   138

For these reasons, we find that the noncompetition agreement meets the requirements   139
of La.R.S. 23:921(C) and accordingly, this assignment of error is without merit.   140

MUTUALITY AND CAUSE   141

In assignment of error one, defendants assert that noncompetition agreements should   142
be unenforceable in employment at will situations because of a lack of mutuality and an   143
insufficiency of cause.   144

Both defendants were at will employees who are now asking this Court to apply prin-   145
ciples of "mutuality" stated in a Kentucky federal district court case, rather than to fol-   146
low the principles and policies set down by the Louisiana legislature.[2] Defendants assert   147
that "the Courts have yet to address the inequities and legal deficiencies involved in an em-   148
ployment agreement which encompasses no term and/or an employment at will clause   149
and a non-competition agreement."   150

To illustrate the potential inequities, defendants present the following example. An   151
employer who has executed an employment agreement which contains no term and a   152
non-competition agreement can fire the employee without cause at any time. However,   153
the employee is restricted from any participation in his established career for two years   154
within a limited geographic area. In the most severe circumstances, an employer may   155
enter into such an agreement with an employee one day, terminate the employee the fol-   156
lowing day, without cause, and thereafter, restrict the employee from participating in his   157
profession.   158

The inequities illustrated through defendants' example are not present in this case.   159
Here, the defendants were employed by Cellular One as successful sales representatives for   160
three and one half years.[3] Throughout their employment, Cellular One periodically re-   161
quested the defendants and all sales representatives to execute employment agreements.   162
These agreements were at will employment contracts containing noncompetition agree-   163
ments. Defendants signed these agreements as a condition of their continued employ-   164
ment. Defendants now complain, after successful careers with Cellular One, that such   165
agreements potentially establish great inequities which must be addressed by this Court.   166

After reviewing the extensive history of noncompetition agreements in Louisiana, we   167
conclude that the Louisiana legislature has adequately addressed the equities and inequities   168
of such agreements. After dealing with this issue for many years, the legislature amended   169
La.R.S. 23:921 in 1989, and expanded the use of noncompetition agreements in Louisiana.   170

---

2. Defendants cite *Orion Broadcasting, Inc. v. Forsythe*, 477 F.Supp. 198 (W.D.Kentucky 1979). In
Orion, the court relied on principles of mutuality in determining that noncompetition agreements
are unenforceable in at will employment situations when the employee is fired. *Id.* at 201. However,
the court went on to note that had Ms. Forsythe, an at will employee, voluntarily severed her employment, the noncompetition agreement would have been enforceable against her. *Id.*
3. Boyd was employed from May 17, 1989, through December of 1993. Lemoine was employed
from April 20, 1989, through December of 1993.

While subsection (A) reflects the strong public policy against noncompetition agreements, the legislature made it clear, in subsection (C), that "any person" may enter into such a contract with their employer provided they follow the specific guidelines. The legislature has already addressed the policy considerations raised by defendants. Therefore, we are compelled to follow the unambiguous language of the statute which allows "any person", including an at will employee, to enter into a noncompetition agreement.

Furthermore, we do not find that the agreement is unenforceable for lack of cause. The Civil Code defines a contract as "an agreement by two or more parties whereby obligations are created, modified, or extinguished." La.Civ.Code art. 1906. No obligation can exist without a lawful cause, which is defined as "the reason why a party obligates himself." La.Civ.Code arts. 1966–67. The defendants signed the agreements as a condition of continued employment. Employment was the valid cause of the contract.

For these reasons, we reject defendants' argument that the noncompetition agreement is unenforceable because of a lack of mutuality or insufficient cause.

DURESS

In assignment of error two, defendants assert that the trial court erred in failing to find that the agreement was vitiated by economic duress. Defendants argue that the threat of termination constituted economic duress.

However, defendants were at will employees subject to termination at any time, for any reason. The threat of doing a lawful act does not constitute duress. La.Civ.Code art. 1962. Thus, the threat of termination, an act which Cellular One had a legal right to do, cannot constitute duress. *See Allied Bruce Terminix Company, Inc. v. Guillory,* 94-319 (La.App. 3rd Cir. 11/2/94), 649 So.2d 652; *Litigation Reprographics and Support Services, Inc. v. Scott,* 599 So.2d 922, 923 (La.App. 4th Cir.1992). Accordingly, we conclude that this assignment of error is without merit.

STIPULATED DAMAGES

In assignment of error three defendants assert that injunctive relief was inappropriate and that the only remedy available to plaintiff was collection of stipulated damages.

In the contract, defendants agreed to forfeit noncompetition payments upon breach of the agreement. Defendants assert that the forfeiture of these payments is stipulated damages and is the exclusive remedy available to Cellular One. Defendants contend that according to La.Civ.Code art. 2007, when stipulated damages are provided for in a contract, no other remedy is available.

Even assuming that the forfeiture of the noncompetition payments constitutes stipulated damages, this case falls under a specific statute, La.R.S. 23:921(G). Subsection (G) specifies that failure of an employee to perform a noncompetition agreement entitles the employer to recover damages and "IN ADDITION, upon proof of the obligor's [employee's] failure to perform, and without the necessity of proving irreparable injury, a court of competent jurisdiction shall order injunctive relief enforcing the terms of the agreement." (Emphasis added.) After reviewing this statute, we conclude that injunctive relief was an appropriate additional remedy available to Cellular One.

PROOF OF IRREPARABLE INJURY UNNECESSARY

In assignment of error five, defendants assert that Cellular One must set forth evidence of irreparable injury in order to obtain a preliminary injunction for the confidentiality, nondisclosure or nonsolicitation clauses of the agreement. Defendants contend there was no evidence whatsoever showing that they disclosed any confidential information or that they solicited customers. Thus, they conclude that the trial court erred in issuing a preliminary injunction on these issues.

Initially, we note that the injunction issued by the trial court does not refer to the confidentiality or nondisclosure clauses. Thus, we need not discuss these issues. The injunction does however, prohibit defendants from directly soliciting any customer of Cellular One. Thus, we will discuss the validity of that portion of the injunction.

The evidence submitted at the hearing shows that 90% of Boyd's Affordable customers and 73% of Lemoine's customers were former customers of Cellular One. Although several Affordable customers testified that they were not solicited by the defendants, the enormous percentage of former Cellular One customers was sufficient evidence for the trial judge to conclude that the defendants had breached the nonsolicitation portion of the agreement.

The nonsolicitation clause falls squarely under La.R.S. 23:921(G), which provides that upon proof of a breach of the agreement, and without the necessity of proving irreparable injury, the court may issue an injunction. Thus, following proof that defendants breached their agreements not to solicit Cellular One customers, the trial court properly issued the injunction without requiring further proof of irreparable injury.

For these reasons, we conclude that the trial court properly enjoined defendants from soliciting Cellular One customers.

CONCLUSION

For the foregoing reasons, we affirm the judgment of the trial court issuing the preliminary injunction against defendants. Costs of this appeal are assessed against defendants.

AFFIRMED.

SHORTESS, J., dissents with reasons.

SHORTESS, J., dissenting.

I do not agree with the result in this case. I would find this noncompetition agreement unenforceable because it lacks mutuality of obligation and because consent was vitiated by economic duress.

The only noncompetition agreement signed by the parties which arguably contained any mutual benefit was the initial one, which was signed in consideration of initial employment. They did not gain anything by signing new more onerous agreements—they were allowed to hold onto what they already had. Plaintiff did not give up anything at all in consideration for a new agreement. In these economic times, continued employment is not sufficient cause for a noncompetition agreement. It is economic blackmail.

The law of Louisiana never favored noncompetition agreements. The legislative permission to engage in voluntary noncompetition agreements that contain mutual benefit and sacrifice for the parties is permissible. Limited permission to make such a contract, however, does not abrogate the strong public policy against contracts which prohibit an employee from competing with a former employer. The basic premise underlying the prohibition stems from the fundamental right of individuals to seek success in our free-enterprise society. *Hawthorn, Waymouth & Carroll v. Johnson,* 611 So.2d 645, 656 (La.App. 1st Cir.1992) (Shortess, J., dissenting); *Winston v. Bourgeois, Bennett, Thokey & Hickey,* 432 So.2d 936 (La.App. 4th Cir.1983). This also is consistent with the policy of at will employment in this state.

I respectfully dissent.

Questions

1. Lines 82 *et seq.*: Why do you think is the Court starting with this express reference to "a strong public policy"? Could the Court want to establish the foundations of the Louisiana Civil Code articles and statutes to which it is about to refer? If so, why?

2. Lines 119 *et seq.*: How do these sentences relate to the questions above? Can you reconcile the statement of the Court on lines 121–122 with the Court's statement on lines 171 *et seq.*?

3. Lines 114–166: How do you understand the defendant's argument that the non-competition agreement lacks mutuality? Mutuality of what?

4. Lines 167–176: On the basis of the public policy the Court referred to above on line 82, was the Court justified in giving a broad meaning to the statutory words "any person"? Did the Court create law or did it merely apply the law and its reason/policy/ratio?

5. Lines 189 *et seq.*: The Court cites Louisiana Civil Code article 1962. Do you agree with the statement that "the threat of termination [was] an act which Cellular One had a legal right to do. . . ."? Read Louisiana Civil Code article 1962, 2nd paragraph. What does it mean that an act can be "lawful in appearance only" and thus constitute duress?

See also *Davis v. Humble Oil & Refining Company, et al.*, 283 So.2d 783 (La. 1st Cir. 1973), *John Jay Esthetic Salon, Inc. v. Woods*, 377 So.2d 1363 (La. 4th Cir. 1979), *Louisiana Smoke Products v. Savoie Sausage and Food Products*, 696 So.2d 1373 (La. 1997)

Comparative Law Perspective

Alain Levasseur, COMPARATIVE LAW OF CONTRACTS
13–35 (2008)

Juridical Acts

Many civil law jurisdictions make a distinction between juridical acts and juridical facts. This distinction, made on the basis of the source of an obligation, has been elaborated mostly by civil law scholars, or doctrine. . . .

The essence of the difference between juridical acts and juridical facts consists in the following: a juridical act is the expression of a person's will manifested with the intention to create specific legal effects by entering willingly into a bond of law. On the other hand, a juridical fact is an event, devoid of human will, which, when it occurs, brings about the existence of an obligation creative of legal effects. A typical illustration of a juridical act is a "contract" . . .

A tort, or delict in civil law terms, would be an example of a juridical fact. . . .

The common law does not know this concept of 'juridical act'. . . .

Institutes of Justinian, Book III, Title XXII "De Consensu Obligatione":

Obligations are formed by the mere consent of the parties in the contracts of sale . . . An obligation is, in these cases, said to be made by the mere consent of the parties, because there is no necessity for any writing ... the mere consent of those between whom the transaction is carried on suffices....

Fr. Civ.C.

Article 1101: "A contract is a convention whereby one or more parties bind themselves towards one or more other parties, to give, to do or not to do something".

Article 1134 § 1: "Conventions legally entered into have the effect of law for the parties ..."

C.C.Q.

Article 1378: "A contract is an agreement of wills by which one or several persons oblige themselves to one or several other persons to perform a prestation...."

William Blackstone: Commentaries on the Laws of England, (1765–1769)

Book II. Ch.XXX. Of Title by Gift, Grant, and Contract.

IX. A contract, which usually conveys an interest merely in action, is thus defined: "an agreement, upon sufficient consideration, to do or not to do a particular thing." From which definition there arise three points to be contemplated in all contracts; 1.The *agreement*: 2. The *consideration*: and 3. The *thing* to be done or omitted, or the different species of contracts.

First then it is an *agreement*, a mutual bargain or convention; and therefore there must at least be two contracting parties of sufficient ability to make a contract; ...

G.H.Treitel, Q.C., The Law of Contract, Seventh Edition, Stevens & Sons, 1987.

A contract is an agreement giving rise to obligations which are enforced or recognized by law. The factor which distinguishes contractual from other legal obligations is that they are based on the agreement of the contracting parties ... [...] the law of contract is concerned with the circumstances in which agreements are legally binding. [...]

United States law

Restatement, 2d

§ 1. Contract Defined.

A contract is a promise or a set of promises for the breach of which the law gives a remedy, or the performance of which the law in some way recognizes as a duty."

§ 3. Agreement Defined; Bargain Defined.

An agreement is a manifestation of mutual assent on the part of two or more persons. A bargain is an agreement to exchange promises or to exchange a promise for a performance or to exchange performances.

UCC

§ 1-201 (3): "Agreement", as distinguished from "contract", means the bargain of the parties in fact, as found in their language or inferred from other circumstances, including course of performance, course of dealing, or usage of trade as provided in Section 1-303

§ 1-201 (12): "Contract", as distinguished from "agreement", means the total legal obligation that results from the parties' agreement as determined by [the Uniform Commercial Code] as supplemented by any other applicable laws.

Bilateral Contracts and Unilateral Contracts

At civil law

Fr. Civ. C.

Art. 1102: A contract is synallagmatic or bilateral when the parties obligate themselves reciprocally towards each other.

Art. 1103: It is unilateral when one or more parties are bound towards one or more parties without any reciprocal obligation on the part of the latter parties.

See: La. Civ. C.: Articles 1907–1908

C.C.Q.

Art. 1380: A contract is synallagmatic, or bilateral when the parties obligate themselves reciprocally, each to the other, so that the obligation of one party is correlative to the obligation of the other.

When one party obligates himself to the other without any obligation on the part of the latter, the contract is unilateral.

At Common law: USA

Restatement, 2d

§ 45. Option Contract Created by Part Performance or Tender

(1) Where an offer invites an offeree to accept by rendering a performance and does not invite a promissory acceptance, an option contract is created when the offeree tenders or begins the invited performance or tenders a beginning of it.

(2) The offeror's duty of performance under any option contract so created is conditional on completion or tender of the invited performance in accordance with the terms of the offer.

Comment: a. ... Such an offer has often been referred to as an "offer for a unilateral contract". Typical illustrations are found in offers of rewards or prizes and in non-commercial arrangements among relatives and friends.

Onerous Contracts and Gratuitous Contracts

At civil law

Fr.Civ. C.

Art. 1105: A contract is gratuitous when one party intends to provide an advantage to the other without receiving an advantage in return.

Art. 1106: A contract is onerous when each of the parties expects to receive from the other an advantage in exchange for the advantage she herself provides.

See: La. Civ. C.: Articles 1909–1910

C.C.Q.

Art.1381: A contract is onerous when each party obtains an advantage in return for his obligation.

When one party obligates himself to the other for the benefit of the latter without obtaining any advantage in return, the contract is gratuitous.

At common law

Wm Blackstone, Commentaries on the Laws of England

[…] gifts are always gratuitous, grants are upon some consideration or equivalent; … A true and proper gift or grant is always accompanied with delivery of possession, and takes effect immediately: as if A. gives to B. 100L, or a flock of sheep, and puts him in possession of them directly, it is then a gift executed in the donee; … But if the gift does not take effect, by delivery of immediate possession, it is then not properly a gift, but a contract; and this a man cannot be compelled to perform, but upon good an sufficient consideration … I. Sale, or exchange, is a transmutation of property from one man to another, in consideration of some price or recompense in value: for there is no sale without a recompense: there must be quid pro quo.

Restatement, 2d

§ 86. Promise for Benefit Received

(1) A promise made in recognition of a benefit previously received by the promisor from the promisee is binding to the extent necessary to prevent injustice.

(2) A promise is not binding under Subsection (1)

(a) if the promisee conferred the benefit as a gift or for other reasons the promisor has not been unjustly enriched; or

(b) to the extent that its value is disproportionate to the benefit.

§ 90. Promise Reasonably Inducing Action or Forbearance

(1) A promise which the promisor should reasonably expect to induce action or forbearance on the part of the promisee or a third person and which does induce such action or forbearance is binding if injustice can be avoided only by enforcement of the promise. The remedy granted for breach may be limited as justice requires …

———

Alex Weill & François Terré, Droit Civil: Les Obligations
n° 36, at 41, n° 465, at 538, & n° 469, at 540 & 541 (3d ed. 1980)

Unilateral v. Synallagmatic Contracts:
Exceptio non Adimpleti Contractus

36. Why the distinction matters. — … In synallagmatic contracts, the obligations created at the charge of each of the parties serve reciprocally as the cause of each other. The notion of cause is altogether different in unilateral contracts. And this notion [cause] has considerable repercussions, not only in the formation of the contract, but also in its execution, when one of the parties does not execute his obligations, as we will see when we study the exception non adimpleti contractus (infra n°s 465 et seq.)….

465. — **Principle.** — In principle, performances promised by the contracting parties must be executed simultaneously. [For example,] the buyer must pay the price at the same time at which he takes delivery of the thing….

It results from this principle that, if one of the contracting parties does not execute his performance at the moment at which he should, the other can himself refuse to execute [his performance]and can oppose to the demand of his fellow contracting party the exception non adimpleti contractus. In this fashion he does justice to himself. But he does so only in a provisional manner, for the exception non adimpleti contractus (or the exception of non-execution) leads only to the adjournment [to a later date] of the execution of the obligations, not to their disappearance.

469.—Origin of the exception *non adimpleti contractus.*

The exception ... was created by the canonists and post-glossators for synallagmatic contracts. Considerations of a moral order, which inspired the former [the canonists], justified, in their eyes, the application in such cases of the principle non servanti fidem non est fides servanda ...[1]

In a bilateral contract neither one of the parties can demand its fulfillment if it is not shown that he himself has fulfilled it or offered to fulfill it, unless his obligation is subject to a term.

---

1. Roughly translated: "He who is not ready to observe good faith is not accorded good faith."

Chapter Two

Requisites to the Formation of a Valid Agreement

Section I—Capacity to Contract

Louisiana Sources of Law

Louisiana Civil Code

Art. 1918. General statement of capacity.

All persons have capacity to contract, except unemancipated minors, interdicts, and persons deprived of reason at the time of contracting. (Acts 1984, No. 331, §1, eff. Jan. 1, 1985.)

Art. 1920. Right to require confirmation or rescission of the contract.

Immediately after discovering the incapacity, a party, who at the time of contracting was ignorant of the incapacity of the other party, may require from that party, if the incapacity has ceased, or from the legal representative if it has not, that the contract be confirmed or rescinded. (Acts 1984, No. 331, §1, eff. Jan. 1, 1985.)

Art. 1921. Rescission of contract for incapacity.

Upon rescission of a contract on the ground of incapacity, each party or his legal representative shall restore to the other what he has received thereunder. When restoration is impossible or impracticable, the court may award compensation to the party to whom restoration cannot be made. (Acts 1984, No. 331, §1, eff. Jan. 1, 1985.)

Art. 1922. Fully emancipated minor.

A fully emancipated minor has full contractual capacity. (Acts 1984, No. 331, §1, eff. Jan. 1, 1985.)

Art. 1923. Incapacity of unemancipated minor; exceptions.

A contract by an unemancipated minor may be rescinded on grounds of incapacity except when made for the purpose of providing the minor with something necessary for his support or education, or for a purpose related to his business. (Acts 1984, No. 331, §1, eff. Jan. 1, 1985.)

Art. 1925. Noninterdicted person deprived of reason; protection of innocent contracting party by onerous title.

A noninterdicted person, who was deprived of reason at the time of contracting, may obtain rescission of an onerous contract upon the ground of incapacity only upon showing that the other party knew or should have known that person's incapacity. (Acts 1984, No. 331, §1, eff. Jan. 1, 1985.)

Précis: Louisiana Law of Conventional Obligations—
Article I to 2.2.1

The concept of "capacity," in its legal sense, must be distinguished, first, from the concept of "personality" and, second, from the notions of "authority or power."

"Personality," in the sense of the civil Code, is the ability to hold rights and owe obligations. Personality is therefore proper to "persons," be they natural persons or juridical persons, i.e. legal entities, because upon birth (and even conception) or incorporation, persons are automatically holders of a "patrimony." "Patrimony" can be described as the sum total of the rights and obligations of a monetary value vested in the person. LSA-C.C. Arts 25 and 26 clearly identify this concept of 'personality" as concerns natural persons....

Natural personality vests in any natural person the legal ability to hold rights and owe obligations as is stated in **LSA-C.C. Art. 27: "All natural persons enjoy general legal capacity to have rights and duties....**

[A] distinction is made between "incapacity to enjoy" and "incapacity to exercise" a right.

As regards the notions of "authority or power," they are related to the concept of "Representation" as this concept is described in LSA-C.C. Arts 2985 and 2986....

There exists an incapacity of enjoyment when a person is deprived of the ability to "enjoy" a particular right. **For example, under LSA-C.C. Art. 941 "A successor shall be declared unworthy if he is convicted of a crime involving the intentional killing, or attempted killing, of the decedent or is judicially determined to have participated in the intentional, unjustified killing, or attempted killing, of the decedent. An action to declare a successor unworthy shall be brought in the succession proceedings of the decedent.**

An executive pardon or pardon by operation of law does not affect the unworthiness of a successor." ...

[I]ncapacities of enjoyment are always, and can only be, special, restricted, limited in scope, because they amount to depriving a "person" of a necessary component of her "personality" which is the ability to be a holder of all rights under the law as from conception or birth....

Incapacities of exercise are much more common than incapacities of enjoyment, so much so that the concept of "incapacity" is used, in general, to refer to incapacities of exercise....

For example, under **LSA-C.C. Art. 28 "A natural person who has reached majority has capacity to make all sorts of juridical acts, unless otherwise provided by legislation."** ...

Under **LSA-C.C. Art. 395: "A full interdict lacks capacity to make a juridical act. A limited interdict lacks capacity to make a juridical act pertaining to the property or aspects of personal care that the judgment of limited interdiction places under the authority of his curator, except as provided in Article 1482 or in the judgment of limited interdiction."** ...

As regards "minors," **LSA-C.C. Art. 1919** lays down the general rule that a contract entered into by **"a person without legal capacity is relatively null and may be rescinded."** ...

LSA-C.C. Art. 1923 states that "A contract by an unemancipated minor may be rescinded on the grounds of incapacity except when made for the purpose of providing the minor

with something necessary for his support or education, or for a purpose related to his business." ...

Case

1 ## FIDELITY FINANCIAL SERVICES, INC.
2 ### v.
3 ## Edward E. McCOY
4 Louisiana Court of Appeal
5 First Circuit
6 Oct. 6, 1980
7 392 So.2d 118

8 CHIASSON, Judge.

9 This is a suit on a promissory note defended successfully by the defendant-appellee, Ed-
10 ward E. McCoy, on the ground of insanity. The trial court also ordered the cancellation
11 of a chattel mortgage which was granted by the defendant at the same time.

12 Plaintiff-appellant, Fidelity Financial Services, Inc., appeals the judgment contending
13 [among other things] that the lower court erred [....] in finding that the defendant had
14 proven the incapacity of the defendant to have existed at the time the contract was made
15 [....]

16 The record establishes that Mr. McCoy was discharged from the U.S. Army in 1960
17 because of his mental condition and that he has been receiving psychiatric treatment and
18 medication at the V.A. hospitals in New Orleans and Gulfport ever since. His wife, his son,
19 and two other persons from the community testified that they knew and that it was com-
20 monly known in the community that defendant was mentally incapable of handling his
21 affairs. Mr. McCoy was interdicted after the filing of this suit by judgment rendered on
22 April 19, 1979.

23 Plaintiff's only witness was its vice president and general manager who negotiated the
24 loan. He testified that a car dealer, for whom he was then handling automobile financ-
25 ing, brought Mr. McCoy to his office to secure a loan for the purchase of a 1973 Chevro-
26 let Malibu automobile; that he obtained all the information contained in the chattel
27 mortgage (another car, a tractor, a T.V., and other household goods) from Mr. McCoy;
28 that the whole transaction took about forty-five minutes; and that Mr. McCoy appeared
29 to be normal.

30 To annul the contract the law requires that the defendant proves he was incapacitated at
31 the time of the contract (La.C.C. art. 1788(2)) and that it was generally known by those
32 who saw and conversed with him or it was known to the person who contracted with him
33 (La.C.C. art. 1788(3)). Louisiana Civil Code Article 402 has basically the same requirements.

34 The trial court found that the defendant had established his mental incapacity; that his
35 condition was common knowledge in the community; and that the incapacity existed at
36 the time of the contract.

37 Plaintiff's first specification of error is no more than an attack upon the court's eval-
38 uation of the credibility of the witnesses. We hold that the determination of the trial court
39 is based upon a reasonable evaluation of credibility and of the evidence presented. Our

review of the entire record convinces us that the trial court was correct in its findings. 40
Arceneaux v. Domingue, 365 So.2d 1330 (La.1978).   41

Plaintiff argues in brief it had carried its burden of proof to establish that the contract 42
was made during a lucid interval. La.C.C. art. 1788(9). Mr. Brown was plaintiff's only wit- 43
ness, although the record establishes that the car dealer was present during the loan prepa- 44
ration and he was available as a witness. Failure of plaintiff to call this witness raises a 45
presumption that his testimony would be unfavorable to plaintiff. Morgan v. Matlack, 46
Inc., 366 So.2d 1071 (La.App. 1st Cir. 1979) and cases cited therein.   47

But even without that presumption, we find that the plaintiff failed to carry its bur- 48
den of proof. Although plaintiff claims it obtained all the information about the other items 49
in the chattel mortgage from Mr. McCoy, its representative testified that he had consulted 50
a "credit bureau" and obtained all of the financial transactions of Mr. McCoy. The record 51
therefore is not clear as to what information Mr. McCoy furnished and what information 52
was furnished by a third person.   53

[....]

Questions

1. Lines 16 *et seq.*: What does it mean "commonly known in the community"? Why
    should this common knowledge be imputed to the plaintiff, Fidelity Financial Ser-
    vices, Inc.? Is there any difference between the phrases "common knowledge" and "it
    was generally known by those who saw and conversed with him ..."? *See* lines 30–33.
    Whose burden should it be to establish that "it was commonly known in the com-
    munity...."? Notice that the Court states, on the one hand, that "two other persons
    from the community" and, on the other hand, that "plaintiff's only witness was its
    vice president...." Wasn't the latter a member of that same community? So, did one
    more witness tilt the scale in favor of defendant?

2. Lines 49 *et seq.*: Is it possible that the Court had its mind made up as regards the de-
    fendant's incapacity?

See also *Skannal v. Bamburg*, 33 So.3d 227 (La. 2nd Cir. 2010), p. 213 herein.

Section II — Consent

Louisiana Sources of Law

Louisiana Civil Code

Art. 1927. Consent.

A contract is formed by the consent of the parties established through offer and acceptance.

Unless the law prescribes a certain formality for the intended contract, offer and acceptance may be made orally, in writing, or by action or inaction that under the circumstances is clearly indicative of consent.

Unless otherwise specified in the offer, there need not be conformity between the manner in which the offer is made and the manner in which the acceptance is made. (Acts 1984,
No. 331, § 1, eff. Jan. 1, 1985.)

Art. 1928. Irrevocable offer.

An offer that specifies a period of time for acceptance is irrevocable during that time.

When the offeror manifests an intent to give the offeree a delay within which to accept, without specifying a time, the offer is irrevocable for a reasonable time. (Acts 1984, No. 331, §1, eff. Jan. 1, 1985.)

Art. 1930. Revocable offer.

An offer not irrevocable under Civil Code Article 1928 may be revoked before it is accepted. (Acts 1984, No. 331, §1, eff. Jan. 1, 1985.)

Art. 1932. Expiration of offer by death or incapacity of either party.

An offer expires by the death or incapacity of the offeror or the offeree before it has been accepted. (Acts 1984, No. 331, §1, eff. Jan. 1, 1985.)

Art. 1934. Time when acceptance of an irrevocable offer is effective.

An acceptance of an irrevocable offer is effective when received by the offeror. (Acts 1984, No. 331, §1, eff. Jan. 1, 1985.)

Art. 1935. Time when acceptance of a revocable offer is effective.

Unless otherwise specified by the offer or the law, an acceptance of a revocable offer, made in a manner and by a medium suggested by the offer or in a reasonable manner and by a reasonable medium, is effective when transmitted by the offeree. (Acts 1984, No. 331, §1, eff. Jan. 1, 1985.)

Art. 1937. Time when revocation is effective.

A revocation of a revocable offer is effective when received by the offeree prior to acceptance. (Acts 1984, No. 331, §1, eff. Jan. 1, 1985.)

Art. 1939. Acceptance by performance.

When an offeror invites an offeree to accept by performance and, according to usage or the nature or the terms of the contract, it is contemplated that the performance will be completed if commenced, a contract is formed when the offeree begins the requested performance. (Acts 1984, No. 331, §1, eff. Jan. 1, 1985.)

Art. 1940. Acceptance only by completed performance.

When, according to usage or the nature of the contract, or its own terms, an offer made to a particular offeree can be accepted only by rendering a completed performance, the offeror cannot revoke the offer, once the offeree has begun to perform, for the reasonable time necessary to complete the performance. The offeree, however, is not bound to complete the performance he has begun.

The offeror's duty of performance is conditional on completion or tender of the requested performance. (Acts 1984, No. 331, §1, eff. Jan. 1, 1985.)

Art. 1942. Acceptance by silence.

When, because of special circumstances, the offeree's silence leads the offeror reasonably to believe that a contract has been formed, the offer is deemed accepted. (Acts 1984, No. 331, §1, eff. Jan. 1, 1985.)

Art. 1943. Acceptance not in accordance with offer.

An acceptance not in accordance with the terms of the offer is deemed to be a counteroffer. (Acts 1984, No. 331, §1, eff. Jan. 1, 1985.)

Art. 1944. Offer of reward made to the public.

An offer of a reward made to the public is binding upon the offeror even if the one who performs the requested act does not know of the offer. (Acts 1984, No. 331, § 1, eff. Jan. 1, 1985.)

Art. 1945. Revocation of an offer of reward made to the public.

An offer of reward made to the public may be revoked before completion of the requested act, provided the revocation is made by the same or an equally effective means as the offer. (Acts 1984, No. 331, § 1, eff. Jan. 1, 1985.)

Précis: Louisiana Law of Conventional Obligations— §§ 3.1.1 to 3.1.2

An offer, in its legal and technical sense, is a firm and definite proposal to enter into a contract, of a <u>kind</u> agreed upon, under pre-arranged precise conditions. Such a definite proposal or offer, when accepted, will bring about the existence of the very contract the parties intended to enter into.

The offer must be <u>precise</u> in the sense that it must contain the "essential" component parts of the nominate or innominate contract to be entered into upon the offeree's acceptance. The civil Code does provide a few examples of the contents of a precise offer to enter into a nominate contract. We can find one in **LSA-C.C. Art. 2439** which defines a sale as "a **contract whereby a person transfers ownership of a thing to another for a price in money. The thing, the price, and the consent of the parties are requirements for the perfection of a sale."** ...

If an offer does not refer precisely to the "essential" component parts of the contract the parties wish to enter into, it will not qualify as an offer. . . .

Under the second paragraph of **LSA-C.C. Art. 1927, "A contract is formed by the consent of the parties established through offer and acceptance.**

Unless the law prescribes a certain formality for the intended contract, offer and acceptance may be made orally, in writing, or by action or inaction that under the circumstances is clearly indicative of consent. Unless otherwise specified in the offer, there need not be conformity between the manner in which the offer is made and the manner in which the acceptance is made." ...

As regards the addressee of an offer, there are at least three possibilities: either the offer is made to a particular person, or to several persons or to the public at large. . . .

If the offeror has specified a period of time for the acceptance then, according to **LSA-C.C. Art. 1928,** such an **"An offer that specifies a period of time for acceptance is irrevocable during that time."** The same Article adds that **"When the offeror manifests an intent to give the offeree a delay within which to accept, without specifying a time, the offer is irrevocable for a reasonable time."** It follows logically that **"An irrevocable offer expires if not accepted within the time prescribed in the preceding Article."** (LSA-C.C. Art. 1929).

In the event an offer is not irrevocable (under LSA-C.C. Art. 1928) then, under **LSA-C.C. Art. 1930** it **"may be revoked before it is accepted."** Furthermore, **"A revocable offer expires if not accepted within a reasonable time."** (LSA-C.C. Art. 1931). . . .

LSA-C.C. Art. 1943 states that **"An acceptance not in accordance with the terms of the offer is deemed to be a counteroffer."** Reading this Article *a contrario*, it is easy to conclude that an acceptance, pure and simple, is one which meets the terms of the offer in such a way that the **"consent of the parties has been established."** (LSA-C.C. Art. 1927).

Such an acceptance is not complete and ceases to be pure and simple, or firm, whenever the offeree expresses some reservations of substance or suggests some conditions to his acceptance. There will be, then, a "counteroffer" by the offeree as stated in LSA-C.C. Art. 1943....

As regards the form of the acceptance, the civil Code contemplates different situations. As a general principle, **"Unless the law prescribes a certain formality for the intended contract, offer and acceptance may be made orally, in writing, or by action or inaction that under the circumstances is clearly indicative of consent."** (LSA-C.C. Art. 1927). Likewise **"A medium or a manner of acceptance is reasonable if it is the one used in making the offer or one customary in similar transactions at the time and place the offer is received, unless circumstances known to the offeree indicate otherwise."** (LSA-C.C. Art. 1936). In other words, like an offer, an acceptance can be *express* or *tacit*....

Acceptance by silence, as a matter of principle, does not meet the requirements of a binding acceptance: silence is not acceptance. However, **"When, because of special circumstances, the offeree's silence leads the offeror reasonably to believe that a contract has been formed, the offer is deemed accepted."** (LSA-C.C. Art. 1942)....

[W]hen an offer is irrevocable, it cannot be revoked by the offeror once the offeree has become aware of the offer. The offeror is bound unilaterally to keep his offer open. However, this same irrevocable offer represents a great benefit for the offeror since the **"acceptance of an irrevocable offer is effective when received by the offeror."** (LSA-C.C. Art. 1934)....

On the other hand, when an offer is revocable, the offeree is given control over the moment of formation of the contract. As **LSA-C.C. Art. 1935** states: **"Unless otherwise specified by the offer or the law, an acceptance of a revocable offer, made in a manner and by a medium suggested by the offer or in a reasonable manner and by a reasonable medium, is effective when transmitted by the offeree."** ...

Cases

WAGENVOORD BROADCASTING COMPANY, Inc.

v.

CANAL AUTOMATIC TRANSMISSION SERVICE, INC.

Louisiana Court of Appeal
Fourth Circuit
June 7, 1965
176 So.2d 188

CHASEZ, Judge.

On the 5th day of May, 1964, a representative of Wagenvoord Broadcasting Co., Inc., contacted the defendant, Canal Automatic Transmission Service, Inc., and discussed with its Mr. Canfield the sale of radio advertising time on Radio Station WWOM. This discussion ended in the defendant signing an authorization order for radio advertising on Station WWOM 5 days per week (Monday–Friday), for a total of 75 periods, commencing May 6, 1964 and expiring August 10, 1964. The following clauses appear in the document signed:

'Oral changes in contract will not be recognized.'

'When signed by the advertiser and accepted in writing by Broadcasting Station WWOM, this order shall become an agreement binding upon the respective parties. Additional amount of twenty-five per cent of balance due shall be paid as attorney's fee if attorney is employed for collection. The rates shown hereon are net and are not subject to any discount other than as set forth above.'

'This contract entitles client to Las Vegas excursions upon payment of this contract. 15 vacations —'

This alleged contract was signed by the defendant and was accepted by the plaintiff. The consideration set forth in the contract for the advertising was $900.00, payable in four monthly payments of $250.00 per month. Several hours after this document was signed by the defendant, but prior to knowledge that its order was accepted by plaintiff, the defendant corporation through, Mr. Canfield, communicated with plaintiff's representative Mr. Sam Zach and advised plaintiff that it was withdrawing and cancelling its offer as it did not desire to go through with the purchase. It was then that plaintiff informed defendant that defendant's offer had been accepted and there was a contract between the parties. Plaintiff insisted that the defendant comply with the agreement and ultimately filed this suit praying for:

1) Specific performance; and alternatively,

2) The sum of $900.00 plus 25% Attorney's fees, interest and costs which it alleges is the damage it sustained as a result of defendant's noncompliance.

The court A qua rendered a judgment in favor of the plaintiff the sum of $250.00, with legal interest from the date of judicial demand until paid, plus 25% Attorney's fees on principal and interest and for all costs. From this judgment the plaintiff-appellant, Wagenvoord Broadcasting Co., Inc., appeals devolutively.

Defendant-appellee, Canal Automatic Transmission Service, Inc., answered the appeal and prayed primarily that the judgment rendered by the court A qua be reversed and that appellant be condemned to pay the costs of both courts; and alternatively, should said judgment not be reversed, it prayed that the cause by remanded for the admission of further evidence bearing on the damages sustained by the plaintiff.

We believe that the questions posed to us for consideration and determination are:

(1) whether the acceptance of an offer must be communicated to the offeror in order to complete the contract;

(2) during what period of time is an offer irrevocable;

(3) was there actually a contract in existence between the parties as a result of the negotiations above described?

There is no doubt that the representative of the plaintiff did contact the defendant and did secure the signature of the defendant through a proper representative to an offer for radio advertising on Station WWOM. The agent of plaintiff, however, was not in a position to complete the contract for he had no authority to accept the contract for and on behalf of his employer, Station WWOM. The evidence indicates that the general manager of the plaintiff corporation, David Wagenvoord, was the only person who could bind the plaintiff to the contract and this officer of the plaintiff corporation testified that at approximately 1:00 p.m., on May 5, 1964, he completed the contract by placing his signature thereon. Notification of this alleged completion of the contract was not given to the defendant, Canal Automatic Transmission Service, Inc., by the plaintiff and the first knowledge that defendant had that its order for advertising time on Station WWOM was agreed to by plaintiff was when its representative called and informed the plaintiff that he desired to cancel the arrangements it had entered into a few hours earlier.

The view that the acceptance must be communicated to the offeree is expressed by Plainoil in the following succinct manner:

> 'It is necessary for the formation of a contract that the acceptance made, outside the presence of the offeror be communicated to him. Of what value is it if the acceptance is made and the offeror knows nothing about it? The offer is a question which requires a response; and the response does not exist until it is known to him who asks for it.' Plainoil, Traite Elementaire deDroit Civil, Vol. 2, pt. 1, Sec. 984.

Moreover, our Civil Code seems to recognize a receipt theory of acceptance. According to LSA-C.C. 1809 the obligation is not complete until either the acceptance itself or circumstances indicating acceptance '* * * are known to the party proposing; * * *' and LSA-C.C 1819 defines consent to a contract as '* * * the concurrence of intention * * * reciprocally communicated * * *'

The receipt theory of acceptance also underlies the rationale of Union Sawmill Co. v. Mitchell, 122 La. 900, 48 So. 317, in which defendant made an offer to sell timber to the plaintiffs; the plaintiff then accepted the offer by notarial act but did not communicate the acceptance to the vendor immediately and before notice of this acceptance, the defendant entered into another contract to sell timber to another party. The court held that because the acceptance was not communicated to the offeree before he signified his change of intention, there was no contract.

We find, therefore, that the withdrawal of the offer in this case was effective because the acceptance was not complete until it had been communicated to the offeror.

However, we must further decide whether or not defendant's withdrawal of the offer was ineffective because it was made during a period of time in which the offer was irrevocable. The general rule is that an offer can be revoked any time prior to its acceptance. National Co. v. Navarro, 149 So.2d 648, 649 (La.App.1963); Miller v. Douville, 45 La.Ann. 214, 12 So. 132 (1893); Leaman v. (Putman) Puttman, Orleans Appeals No. 8742. However, Article 1809 makes the following exception:

> '* * * he may therefore revoke his offer or proposition before such acceptance, But not without allowing such reasonable time as from the terms of his *offer he has given, or from the circumstances of the case he may be supposed to have intended to give to the party, to communicate his determination*' (Emphasis added).

However, the jurisprudence indicates that a strong fact situation would be necessary before the courts would imply that an offer is irrevocable for any substantial length of time.

In R. P. Farnsworth & Co. v. Albert, 176 F.2d 198 (5th Cir. 1949), the Fifth Circuit Court of Appeals considered the question of whether or not a subcontractor's bid was irrevocable during the period that the prime contractor used it to bid on a construction job; and the court, while recognizing that Article 1809 could be applicable to such a situation, found the evidence insufficient to establish the existence of a custom or any other fact that would make the bid irrevocable.

In a recent decision of this court, National Co. v. Navarro, supra, the defendant entered into a home improvement agreement which was conditional upon securing of the necessary financing. The home owner withdrew the offer before it was accepted by the home improvement company. The plaintiff-contractor invoked Article 1809, contending that

the implication was that the offer would be irrevocable during the time in which negoti- [109]
ations for financing were being carried on. The court however, refused to find any such im- [110]
plication and held the withdrawal effective. See also Loeb v. Johnson, La.App., 142 So.2d [111]
518 (in which a similar offer was held revocable without any consideration of Article 1809). [112]

Under these circumstances, for what period of time was defendant's offer irrevocable? [113]

The view that absent of some express or implied time for the offer's expiration the of- [114]
feree only has the time that it takes to present the offer to him and to communicate his [115]
acceptance to the offeree, is properly set out in the following interpretation of Article [116]
1809 in a comment by Robert A. Pascal in the L.S.U.Law Review: [117]

'I. An offer remains open and irrevocable: [118]

A. For the time expressly or impliedly given for the acceptance; or [119]

B. If no time has been given by the proposer in his offer — for the time rea- [120]
sonably necessary for the acceptance and its communication to the proposer; [121]
which is computed by considering: [122]

1. The time required for communication to and from the party to whom [123]
the proposition was made: [124]

a. In face to face offers (or offers by telephone or radio), only an in- [125]
stant is required; [126]

b. In proposals to parties at a distance, *only the time necessary for the* [127]
transmission of the proposal and the acceptance by the authorized or usual [128]
means of communication is required' (Emphasis added). 1 La.Rev. 182 [129]
at 195. [130]

Moreover, in National Co. v. Navarro, supra, and Union Sawmill Co. v. Mitchell, supra, [131]
the courts indicated that the offeree must accept immediately in order to avoid revoca- [132]
tion. In the National Company case the court quoted, with approval from Toullier's Com- [133]
mentaries, as follows: [134]

'For example, in consenting to contract with titles by the agency of third par- [135]
ties, who never had the mandate, I am tacitly obliged to wait for the time suit- [136]
able or sufficient for ratification. I am engaged conditionally. The contract never [137]
existed if T does not ratify. If he ratifies, the ratification goes back to the date of [138]
contract, the same as the contract accomplishes a retroactive effect to the day [139]
on which the engagement has been contracted. * * * This is why the laws say that [140]
ratifications has a retroactive effect. * * * [141]

'But in what time should T ratify in order to prevent a revocation? As soon as he would [142]
have knowledge of the contract.' 6 Toullier, Book 3, Title III, Note 30. [143]

Similarly in Union Sawmill, the court said: [144]

'Under the circumstances, we think no more time was intended to be allowed [145]
to the vendees than what might be required to submit the contract to them for [146]
acceptance or rejection.' 48 So. 317 at 319. [147]

Therefore, we conclude that the plaintiff should upon immediate acceptance of the [148]
offer which its agent submitted to it, have completed the acceptance by promptly notify- [149]
ing the defendant. Instead it waited until the defendant withdraw [*sic*] its offer by tele- [150]
phone. Because defendant's offer was revocable at the time of its withdrawal, no contract [151]
was ever consummated. [152]

[....]

Questions

1. Lines 16–23: Do the following clauses referenced by the court amount to an offer? In the affirmative, was the offer directed at entering into a nominate or innominate contract? Shouldn't the contract to be entered into dictate that the offer include the specific requirements for the intended contract? Was it the case here? Is it important to identify, at the outset, the party who is the offeror? Why or why not?

2. Lines 24 *et seq.*: Was the offer revocable or irrevocable? Explain. Was there any suspensive condition in existence in the relationship between the Broadcasting Co. and the representative? Could there be an issue of capacity on the part of the representative? *See* La. Civ. Code arts. 2985–2986 and lines 52–64.

3. Lines 65–66: The court has used the word "communicated", and will use the word "communication" further down [line 121, citing Professor Pascal]. What does the Court mean? *See* La. Civ. Code art. 1938 and the word "communications".

4. Line 73–77: Under Louisiana law, when an offer is revocable, does receipt (presumed knowledge of the acceptance by the offeror) mark the time of formation of the contract? Or does the formation of the contract result from the mere dispatch of the acceptance? What is the legal regime of the irrevocable offer in the Louisiana Civil Code?

5. Lines 148–152: See question 1 above. How do you understand, now, the statement of the court in lines 148–151? Who is/was the offeror? Was it the defendant, Canal Automatic Transmission Service, Inc.? Was the defendant in control of the "essential elements" of the contract? Was the defendant in a better position than the professional plaintiff broadcasting company to know how their own business works? Did the broadcasting company really fail to accept within a reasonable term? Was there a term to the broadcasting company's acceptance? In whose favor is a term presumed to exist? *See* La. Civ. Code art. 1779.

1   # EVER-TITE ROOFING CORPORATION
2   ## v.
3   ## G. T. GREEN et ux.
4   Louisiana Court of Appeal
5   Second Circuit
6   Nov. 2, 1955
7   83 So.2d 449

8   AYRES, Judge.

9   This is an action for damages allegedly sustained by plaintiff as the result of the breach
10   by the defendants of a written contract for the re-roofing of defendants' residence. De-
11   fendants denied that their written proposal or offer was ever accepted by plaintiff in the
12   manner stipulated therein for its acceptance, and hence contended no contract was ever
13   entered into. The trial court sustained defendants' defense and rejected plaintiff's de-
14   mands and dismissed its suit at its costs. From the judgment thus rendered and signed,
15   plaintiff appealed.

16   Defendants executed and signed an instrument June 10, 1953, for the purpose of ob-
17   taining the services of plaintiff in re-roofing their residence situated in Webster Parish,
18   Louisiana. The document set out in detail the work to be done and the price therefor to
19   be paid in monthly installments. This instrument was likewise signed by plaintiff's sale

representative, who, however, was without authority to accept the contract for and on   20
behalf of the plaintiff. This alleged contract contained these provisions: 21

> 'This agreement shall become binding only upon written acceptance hereof,   22
> by the principal or authorized officer of the Contractor, *or upon commencing*   23
> *performance of the work*. This contract is Not Subject to Cancellation. It is un-   24
> derstood and agreed that this contract is payable at office of Ever-Tite Roofing   25
> Corporation, 5203 Telephone, Houston, Texas. It is understood and agreed that   26
> this Contract provides for attorney's fees and in no case less than ten per cent at-   27
> torney's fees in the event same is placed in the hands of an attorney for collect-   28
> ing or collected through any court, and further provides for accelerated maturity   29
> for failure to pay any installment of principal or interest thereon when due.   30
>
> 'This written agreement is the only and entire contract covering the subject   31
> matter hereof and no other representations have been made unto Owner except   32
> these herein contained. No guarantee on repair work, partial roof jobs, or paint   33
> jobs.' (Emphasis supplied.)   34

Inasmuch as this work was to be performed entirely on credit, it was necessary for   35
plaintiff to obtain credit reports and approval from the lending institution which was to   36
finance said contract. With this procedure defendants were more or less familiar and   37
knew their credit rating would have to be checked and a report made. On receipt of the   38
proposed contract in plaintiff's office on the day following its execution, plaintiff re-   39
quested a credit report, which was made after investigation and which was received in   40
due course and submitted by plaintiff to the lending agency. Additional information was   41
requested by this institution, which was likewise in due course transmitted to the insti-   42
tution, which then gave its approval.   43

The day immediately following this approval, which was either June 18 or 19, 1953,   44
plaintiff engaged its workmen and two trucks, loaded the trucks with the necessary roofing   45
materials and proceeded from Shreveport to defendants' residence for the purpose of doing   46
the work and performing the services allegedly contracted for the defendants. Upon their   47
arrival at defendants' residence, the workmen found others in the performance of the work   48
which plaintiff had contracted to do. Defendants notified plaintiff's workmen that the work   49
had been contracted to other parties two days before and forbade them to do the work.   50

Formal acceptance of the contract was not made under the signature and approval of   51
an agent of plaintiff. It was, however, the intention of plaintiff to accept the contract by   53
commencing the work, which was one of the ways provided for in the instrument for its   54
acceptance, as will be shown by reference to the extract from the contract quoted here-   55
inabove. Prior to this time, however, defendants had determined on a course of abro-   56
gating the agreement and engaged other workmen without notice thereof to plaintiff.   57

The basis of the judgment appealed was that defendants had timely notified plaintiff   58
before 'commencing performance of work'. The trial court held that notice to plaintiff's   59
workmen upon their arrival with the materials that defendants did not desire them to   60
commence the actual work was sufficient and timely to signify their intention to withdraw   61
from the contract. With this conclusion we find ourselves unable to agree.   62

Defendants' attempt to justify their delay in thus notifying plaintiff for the reason they   63
did not know where or how to contact plaintiff is without merit. The contract itself, a copy   64
of which was left with them, conspicuously displayed plaintiff's name, address and tele-   65
phone number. Be that as it may, defendants at no time, from June 10, 1953, until plain-   66
tiff's workmen arrived for the purpose of commencing the work, notified or attempted   67
to notify plaintiff of their intention to abrogate, terminate or cancel the contract.   68

Defendants evidently knew this work was to be processed through plaintiff's Shreveport office. The record discloses no unreasonable delay on plaintiff's part in receiving, processing or accepting the contract or in commencing the work contracted to be done. No time limit was specified in the contract within which it was to be accepted or within which the work was to be begun. It was nevertheless understood between the parties that some delay would ensue before the acceptance of the contract and the commencement of the work, due to the necessity of compliance with the requirements relative to financing the job through a lending agency. The evidence as referred to hereinabove shows that plaintiff proceeded with due diligence.

The general rule of law is that an offer proposed may be withdrawn before its acceptance and that no obligation is incurred thereby. This is, however, not without exceptions. For instance, Restatement of the Law of Contracts stated:

'(1) The power to create a contract by acceptance of an offer terminates at the time specified in the offer, or, if no time is specified, at the end of a reasonable time.

'What is a reasonable time is a question of fact depending on the nature of the contract proposed, the usages of business and other circumstances of the case which the offeree at the time of his acceptance either knows or has reason to know.'

These principles are recognized in the Civil Code. LSA-C.C. Art. 1800 provides that an offer is incomplete as a contract until its acceptance and that before its acceptance the offer may be withdrawn. However, this general rule is modified by the provisions of LSA-C.C. Arts. 1801, 1802, 1804 and 1809, which read as follows:

'Art. 1801. The party proposing shall be presumed to continue in the intention, which his proposal expressed, if, on receiving the unqualified assent of him to whom the proposition is made, he do not signify the change of his intention.

'Art. 1802. He is bound by his proposition, and the signification of his dissent will be of no avail, *if the proposition be made in terms, which evince a design to give the other party the right of concluding the contract by his assent; and if that assent be given within such time as the situation of the parties and the nature of the contract shall prove that it was the intention of the proposer to allow.* * * *

'Art. 1804. The acceptance needs (need) not be made by the same act, or in point of time, immediately after the proposition; *if made at any time before the person who offers or promises has changed his mind, or may reasonably be presumed to have done so, it is sufficient.* * * *

'Art. 1809. The obligation of a contract not being complete, until the acceptance, or in cases where it is implied by law, until the circumstances, which raise such implication, are known to the party proposing; *he may therefore revoke his offer or proposition before such acceptance, but not without allowing such reasonable time as from the terms of his offer he has given, or from the circumstances of the case he may be supposed to have intended to give to the party, to communicate his determination.'* (Emphasis supplied.)

Therefore, since the contract did not specify the time within which it was to be accepted or within which the work was to have been commenced, a reasonable time must be allowed therefor in accordance with the facts and circumstances and the evident intention of the parties. A reasonable time is contemplated where no time is expressed. What is a reasonable time depends more or less upon the circumstances surrounding each particular case. The delays to process defendants' application were not unusual. The contract was accepted by plaintiff by the commencement of the performance of the work

contracted to be done. This commencement began with the loading of the trucks with the   116
necessary materials in Shreveport and transporting such materials and the workmen to   117
defendants' residence. Actual commencement or performance of the work therefore began   118
before any notice of dissent by defendants was given plaintiff. The proposition and its   119
acceptance thus became a completed contract.   120

By their aforesaid acts defendants breached the contract. They employed others to do   121
the work contracted to be done by plaintiff and forbade plaintiff's workmen to engage upon   122
that undertaking. By this breach defendants are legally bound to respond to plaintiff in   123
damages. [....]   124

Plaintiff expended the sum of $85.37 in loading the trucks in Shreveport with mate-   125
rials and in transporting them to the site of defendants' residence in Webster Parish and   126
in unloading them on their return, and for wages for the workmen for the time con-   127
sumed. Plaintiff's Shreveport manager testified that the expected profit on this job was   128
$226. None of this evidence is controverted or contradicted in any manner.   129

[....]

Questions

1. Review in your mind the phase of the negotiations between the two parties here in-
    volved. Are the two parties on a par level when entering the negotiations? Is one more
    knowledgeable than the other and could that have an impact on the inner meaning
    of the stipulations in the contract?

2. Lines 16 *et seq.*: Can you identify the kinds of obligations created by the contract?
    For example, do you see any condition/term? Any conjunctive/alternative obligation?
    Any obligation to give, to do, or not to do? Can you explain why it might be im-
    portant for each party to have a good understanding of the legal effects attached to
    these different kinds of obligations? Who is the offeror under the facts of this case?
    Should it matter? You will read on line 22 the word "acceptance": does it necessarily
    mean that the offeree is "the principal or authorized officer of the Contractor"?
    Shouldn't the offeror, in the legal sense of the term, be that party most knowledge-
    able in the matter?

3. Lines 35–43: Do you see any term and/or condition? If you answered in the affir-
    mative, what kind? Do you see any impact on the revocability or not of the offer?
    When plaintiff "requested a credit report", was it the performance of a separate oblig-
    ation totally unrelated to the roofing contract? Or was it the performance of one
    obligation as a component part of a conjunctive obligation? Would it matter? Or was
    it a form of commencing performance of the work as stated on lines 23–24? Would
    it matter?

4. Lines 44–57: Look back at lines 22 *et seq.* and the question above regarding the ex-
    istence (or not) of an alternative obligation. Was there one and only one method of
    acceptance or more than one? In the latter case, who had the choice of the method
    of acceptance? Had the method of acceptance chosen by the plaintiff been agreed to
    by the Greens? Was that method of acceptance an acceptance of a revocable offer or
    an irrevocable offer? Does it matter if the Greens are the offerors? Consider carefully
    the words of the sentence on lines 56–57: "defendants had determined on a course
    of abrogating the agreement ...". Is the Court saying that there was an agreement, a
    contract in existence? Does the court mean that the contract had been formed, per-
    fected before the trucks reached the Greens' residence? Thus, have the Greens breached

a contract by which they had been bound sometime before they received what they thought was the plaintiff-contractor's acceptance? Would this mean that the Greens' offer was revocable and, therefore, accepted when the trucks were dispatched, unbeknownst to the Greens?

5. Lines 69 *et seq.*: How important is the court's statement on lines 72–73? *See* Questions 1–3 above. Again, how important are the court's statements on lines 72 *et seq.*? Can you now qualify the offer as revocable or irrevocable? How determinant, here, is the concept of term?

6. Lines 109–120: There was acceptance by beginning of performance consisting in "the loading of the trucks ..." and acceptance occurred "before any notice of dissent by defendants was given plaintiff." The consequence is that "the proposition and its acceptance thus became a completed contract." What about checking on the Greens' credit and obtaining credit reports? Wasn't the performance of this obligation by the contractor the acceptance of the Greens' offer as the first and necessary component part of a conjunctive obligation made up of two parts, dispatching the trucks being the second part?

The NATIONAL CO., Inc., d/b/a
The National Roofing and Siding Co.
v.
Fano J. NAVARRO and Anna Mae Navarro

Louisiana Court of Appeal
Fourth Circuit
Feb. 4, 1963
149 So.2d 648

REGAN, Judge.

Plaintiff, The National Company, Inc., conducting its business under the trade name of The National Roofing and Siding Company, instituted this suit against the defendants, Fano J. and Anna Mae Navarro, endeavoring to recover the sum of $1,061.40, representing liquidated damages and expenses incurred by plaintiff as a result of defendants' alleged breach of a contract which involved the application of siding to their residence in Nashville Avenue in the City of New Orleans.

The defendants answered and asserted that the document sued on was not a contract, but was merely a 'proposal', which plaintiff's agents had informed them could be withdrawn at any time by defendants prior to commencement of the work. In the alternative, they insisted that if the document is construed to be an offer, then it was withdrawn before the plaintiff accepted; therefore, there was no contract.

Secondly, in the alternative, the defendants contend that the offer never ripeded [*sic*] into a contract since plaintiff failed to procure a loan for defendants to finance the work, which, under the terms of the document, it was required to do.

Then, assuming the position of plaintiffs in reconvention, they maintain that the contractor was indebted to them for $100, the amount deposited when the offer was signed.

[....]

From a judgment in favor of the defendants dismissing plaintiff's suit, and awarding defendants the amount of $100 prayed for in the reconventional demand [...], the plaintiff has prosecuted this appeal.

The record reveals that at 7 p.m. on October 18, 1961, the defendants signed a document wherein they offered to pay plaintiff $3,488.00 to apply aluminum siding to their residence and deposited $100 on account thereof. Prior to the signing thereof, Milton Loeb, one of plaintiff's salesmen, had visited the defendants at their residence on two previous occasions to sell the job.

When the instrument was signed, there were six persons present, the defendants, their mother, their aunt and plaintiff's two salesmen, Loeb and Amann. The defendants and their relatives all testified, over the objection of counsel for the plaintiffs, that one of plaintiff's agents assured them that the contract was not binding, and it could be cancelled at any time prior to commencement of performance. However, both salesmen deny that any such assurance was given.

The offer, submitted on a form prepared by the plaintiff contractor, provided in part:

'This contract is binding, subject only to acceptance by an executive of the NATIONAL ROOFING & SIDING CO., who reserves the right to reject it without liability on its part.'

The following day, Anna Mae Navarro testified that her brother was informed that the First Homestead would not loan the full amount which was required to pay for the renovation. This fact is disputed by plaintiff's representative, who testified that the First Homestead had approved the loan. In passing, it is of interest to merely note that neither plaintiff nor defendants adduced proof to support their respective contentions concerning the financing, when proof thereof was readily available to either.

In any event, at 11 a.m. on October 19th, Miss Navarro telephoned the plaintiff's salesman, Loeb, to inform him they had changed their minds and desired to cancel the 'contract'. He was not in the office when she called so she left a message with one of plaintiff's employees to the effect that the offer was being withdrawn. Loeb obviously received the message for he returned the call at 2 p.m. Miss Navarro repeated that the offer was being withdrawn; however, Loeb advised her she could not cancel since the materials were on delivery to her home and the contract had been accepted.

At 4 p.m. that same day, a small truck containing a few materials for use in application of the siding arrived at the defendants' home, and Miss Navarro refused delivery thereof.

The following day, October 20th, the defendants received a letter from plaintiff informing them that the offer or contract had been accepted. This letter was postmarked 7 p.m., October 19th, which was eight hours after Miss Navarro initially notified defendant that she was withdrawing the offer.

Predicated on the foregoing evidence, the trial judge reasoned that the offer never materialized into a contract because the defendants revoked their offer before the plaintiff accepted it.

Counsel for plaintiff contends that the trial court erred in concluding as a matter of law that the defendants had a right to revoke their offer.

The general rule relating to offer and acceptance is stated in LSA-C.C. Art. 1800, which reads:

'The contract, consisting of a proposition and the consent to it, the agreement is incomplete until the acceptance of the person to whom it is proposed. If he, who proposes, should before that consent is given, change his intention on the subject, the concurrence of the two wills is wanting, and there is no contract.'

While counsel for plaintiff recognizes the general rule, he insists that the offer submitted by the defendants was irrevocable until the offeree was afforded a reasonable time to accept, and points to the rationale of LSA-C.C. Art. 1809 in support thereof, which reads:

> 'The obligation of a contract not being complete, until the acceptance, or in cases where it is implied by law, until the circumstances, which raise such implication, are known to the party proposing; he may therefore revoke his offer or proposition before such acceptance, but not without allowing such reasonable time as from the terms of his offer he has given, *or from the circumstances of the case he may be supposed to have intended to give to the party, to communicate his determination.*' (Emphasis added.)

This article obviously places a limitation upon the general rule that offers may be revoked any time before they are accepted, and is applicable where the offeror has expressly stated an intention to make the offer irrevocable within a stipulated period of time or where the offer is of such a nature that from its very terminology the implication is present that the offeror intended to make it irrevocable for a reasonable period of time, within which it would be necessary for the offeree to signify his acceptance.

Plaintiff argues that since it was incumbent upon it to arrange for financing the work by obtaining a loan for the defendants, the offer was necessarily irrevocable until it had the opportunity to negotiate such a loan. He points out that the defendants attempted to cancel before a reasonable time elapsed within which to arrange financing.

To support his argument he relies upon the rationale emanating from Ever-Tite Roofing Corp. v. Green.[1] In that case, the defendant submitted an offer to have the roof on his home replaced. This offer contained a provision to the effect that either notification by the plaintiff or the commencement of the job would constitute an acceptance. Several days after the offer was submitted, the plaintiff delivered the materials to the job preparatory to commencing performance, and discovered that the defendants had employed another contractor to perform the work.

In the Roofing case, the defendant at no time withdrew his offer before the offeree accepted by tendering performance in conformity with the very terms of the agreement; therefore, there was a meeting of the minds when the materials were delivered and defendant's refusal of performance constituted a breach of the contract.

In discussing whether the offeree had accepted timely the court stated:

> 'Therefore, since the contract did not specify the time within which it was to be accepted or within which the work was to have been commenced, a reasonable time must be allowed therefor in accordance with the facts and circumstances and the evident intention of the parties. A reasonable time is contemplated where no time is expressed. What is a reasonable time depends more or less upon the circumstances surrounding each particular case. The delays to process defendants' application (which involved obtaining financing) were not unusual. * * *' (Parenthetical material added.)

Plaintiff argues that the ratio decidendi of this case is to the effect that when an offer to perform work, which is contingent upon arranging a loan to pay for the job, is submitted to the offeree, an implication arises that the offeror intended to make his offer irrevocable until the offeree has had a reasonable time within which to negotiate a loan for the offeror.

---

1. La.App., 83 So.2d 449.

We find no merit in this contention. A case is authority for only what it actually de-
cides, therefore we think the case holds that an offer Which has not been revoked is not
revoked by implication when it is accepted within a reasonable time. The above quoted
discussion was included in the opinion to counter the argument that the offer had been
impliedly revoked since it was not timely accepted, because the court quoted and under-
lined LSA-C.C. Art. 1804, as follows:

> 'Art. 1804. The acceptance needs (need) not be made by the same act, or in
> point of time, immediately after the proposition; *if made at any time before the
> person who offers or promises has changed his mind, or may reasonably be pre-
> sumed to have done so, it is sufficient.* * * *' (Emphasis supplied.)

Thus the court refused to supply an implication of revocation when the offer contemplated arranging financing and the arrangement was completed within a week.

We are of the opinion that the matter now before us is not controlled by the rationale
of LSA-C.C. Art. 1809 since we do not think that the necessity for procuring financing is
a circumstance from which we can supply the implication that the offeror intended to
make his offer irrevocable for any period of time before acceptance.

Article 1809 initially appears in the Civil Code of 1825 as Article 1803, and the language
was not changed when it was incorporated in the Revised Civil Code of 1870. The article
provoked our curiosity, and it was of interest to learn that it has no counterpart in the Code
of 1808 or the Code Napoleon. Therefore, the redactors of the Code of 1825 were apparently influenced by Toullier's commentaries. In 6 Toullier, Book 3, Title III, Note 30, the French
commentator, after discussing the general principles of offer and acceptance states that there
is one case where the offer is irrevocable before the acceptance, which is when the one who
had made the offer has set a determined time for the acceptance, either expressly or tacitly.

Toullier cites the following example of the offer which tacitly is irrevocable for a reasonable period:

> 'For example, in consenting to contract with titles by the agency of third par-
> ties, who never had the mandate, I am tacitly obliged to wait for the time suit-
> able or sufficient for ratification. I am engaged conditionally. The contract never
> existed if T does not ratify. If he ratifies, the ratification goes back to the date of
> contract, the same as the contract accomplishes a retroactive effect to the day
> on which the engagement has been contracted. * * * This is why the laws say that
> ratifications has a retroactive effect. * * *
>
> 'But in what time should T ratify in order to prevent a revocation? As soon as
> he would have knowledge of the contract.'

Applying this example to the instant case, an executive of plaintiff who was authorized to accept the offer was apprised thereof but had not accepted before the defendants
revoked. Therefore, the revocation was timely.

A more modern version of the above example might exist when a custom prevails in
the building trade to the effect that a subcontractor's bid to a general contractor, in the
absence of a provision to the contrary, may be considered irrevocable after it has been
used in preparation of the general contractor's bid to the owner, and has been accepted
by the owner prior to the attempted revocation by the subcontractor.

The fact that financing was necessary before the work would be performed does not
raise the implication that the offer was irrevocable until the offeree had time to procure
financing. Had the offer been timely accepted and ripened into a contract, then the ability to procure financing would merely operate as a suspensive condition to suspend per-

168 formance until the loan was procured, or negate the contract if financing was not avail-
169 able.

170   Since the plaintiff failed to establish that the offeror impliedly intended to make the offer
171 irrevocable until the defendant was afforded a reasonable opportunity to accept, we are
172 of the opinion that, in conformity with the provision of Art. 1800, the offeror was enti-
173 tled to withdraw his offer at any time before it was accepted, and the record conclusively
174 establishes that it was withdrawn timely.

[....]

Questions

1. Lines 10–67: Was the document a mere proposal to enter into a contract later on? Or
   was it an offer? If an offer, who was the offeror? Focus on lines 21–23. What would
   be your legal analysis/description? For whose benefit would it be? Here, as in the
   Ever-Tite Roofing case, was there any conjunctive obligation?

2. Lines 41–44: Who is the offeror here? What do you think of the first words of the excerpt: "This contract … acceptance.…"? On line 41 we read the word "offer", but on
   line 42, we read the phrase, "this contract." Which one is the correct one? What legal
   label would you attach to the phrase, "who reserves the right to reject it without liability.…"?

3. Lines 45 *et seq.*: Was the so-called offer revocable or irrevocable? How was the acceptance to be given? Again, as per lines 65–67, who is the offeror and who is the offeree? Does it make sense?

4. Lines 96 *et seq.*: How similar to, or different from, the *Ever-Tite Roofing* case, are the
   facts and circumstances of this case? Focus on lines 116–120. How beneficial to the
   plaintiff is the *ratio decidendi* of the *Ever-Tite Roofing* case?

5. Lines 164–169: After you have read the Louisiana Civil Code articles on conditions
   (*see* La. Civ. Code arts. 1767–1776), what critical evaluation do you make of the
   statement by the court in lines 166–169?

1 **Leland H. JOHNSON**

2 **v.**

3 **CAPITAL CITY FORD COMPANY, Inc.**

4 Louisiana Court of Appeal
5 First Circuit
6 Dec. 30, 1955
7 85 So.2d 75

8 TATE, Judge.

9   This suit is for specific performance of a contractual obligation allegedly resulting from
10 plaintiff's acceptance by act (without negotiation or other discussion) of an alleged offer
11 made by newspaper advertisement to the public by defendant automobile dealer. Defen-
12 dant dealer appeals from judgment of the District Court decreeing specific performance
13 of the alleged obligation; plaintiff Johnson answered this appeal, praying for amendment
14 of the decree.

15   The basic question involved is whether the newspaper advertisement in question con-
16 stituted an 'offer' rather than merely an invitation to bargain. If the former, a secondary

question for determination is whether any act or omission of plaintiff-acceptor-obligee
waived his right to require the defendant-offeror-obligor to perform the obligation resulting from plaintiff's acceptance. If as contended by defendant the newspaper advertisement
was merely an invitation to bargain, then of course defendant's objection to parol evidence as enlarging or varying a certain written contract in evidence was well founded; if,
on the other hand, this newspaper advertisement constituted a continuing offer which
the plaintiff accepted by such purchase, and thus as the District Court found, created a
contemporaneous collateral obligation of defendant to do something in addition to the
obligation embodied in the written contract, then of course such evidence was correctly
admitted to prove the existence of this independent, collateral contract.

When the 1955 models were about to appear, defendant Ford dealer in an effort to
dispose of an excessive supply of 1954 models (which were shortly to be outmoded by
the 1955 Ford cars) engaged in an intensive advertising campaign by newspaper and radio,
the first day's advertisement concerning which is self-explanatory:

'TWO FOR ONE.... For two weeks BUY A NEW '54 FORD NOW TRADE
EVEN FOR A '55 FORD

Don't Wait-Buy a 1954 Ford now, when the 1955 models come out we'll trade
even for your '54. You pay only sales tax and license fee. Your '55 Ford will be the
same model, same body style, accessory group, etc. A sure thing for you — a
gamble for us, but we'll take it. Hurry, though, this offer good only for the remainder of September.

The 1954 car must be returned with only normal wear and tear. Physical damage, such as dented fenders, torn upholstery, etc. must be charged to owner or
repaired at owner's expense. No convertibles or Skyliners on this basis.

CAPITAL CITY FORD CO., INC. 1849 North St.-Dial 31721

A GREAT WAY TO SAY, 'WE TRADE YOUR WAY'"

[....]

It may be added that the 1955 models were expected to arrive within 60–90 days of this
bargain sale of 1954 models.

Plaintiff and his wife testified that in response to these newspaper and radio advertisements they went to defendant's premises on September 21st, 1954. Johnson there purchased a 1954 Ford Sedan with certain accessories; he received an allowance of $974.05
for his old car and paid boot of $1,660 in cash. Johnson executed an act of sale for the
1954 Ford purchased by him, which we will discuss below.

In December, 1954, when the 1955 models were advertised, Johnson appeared at defendant's premises and requested its compliance with the newspaper offer accepted by him. At
this time or soon after, Johnson or his attorney was informed that defendant's newspaper advertisements were not intended as offers, but merely as invitations to come in and bargain;
that by delivery of the 1954 automobile for the consideration expressed in the executed act
of sale, defendant felt it had fully complied with all obligations whatsoever to Johnson.

Detailed discussion of the evidence is unnecessary, for we do not find the District
Court's determination of the facts manifestly erroneous, supported as it is by sworn evidence and certain corroborating circumstances. For instance, defendant urges with considerable effect that Johnson's behavior in buying the 1954 Ford without any discussion
whatsoever as to his right per the newspaper offer to exchange said model for a 1955
model, is not the usual and normal course of behavior.

64   But what we are here concerned with is not the *usual* course of behavior, but what
65 transpired on *this* particular occasion.

66   Basically, when defendant urges that because *usually* and *ordinarily* a person would not
67 behave as Johnson and his wife stated they did, in assuming without further discussion that
68 they acquired the right to a 1955 model Ford upon their purchase of a 1954 Ford per the
69 newspaper offer, defendant is attacking the credibility of the testimony of plaintiff and his
70 wife, which issue the District Court with opportunity to see and hear personally all wit-
71 nesses has resolved in favor of the plaintiff. Because plaintiff's conduct was improbable
72 does not require a holding that it did not occur as testified under oath by himself and wife
73 and believed by the District Court, for human beings do improbable things at times.[1]

74
75   We further do not find manifestly erroneous the District Court's determination that
76 the pencilled [*sic*] notation 'No '55 deal' was not on the contract of purchase of the 1954
77 Ford when executed by plaintiff on September 21, 1954.[2]

78   Accepting the facts so found by the District Court, we believe its application of legal
79 principles thereto was correct.

80   In Louisiana and elsewhere a newspaper advertisement may constitute an offer, ac-
81 ceptance of which will consummate a contract and create an obligation in the offerer to
82 perform according to terms of the published offer; Schreiner v. Weil Furniture Co., Inc.,
83 La.App., 68 So.2d 149; Youngblood v. Daily and Weekly Signal Tribune, 15 La.App. 379,
84 131 So. 604; Kodel Radio Corp. v. Shuler, 171 La. 469, 131 So. 462; Maginnis v. Union
85 Oil Company, 47 La.Ann. 1489, 18 So. 459; Deslondes v. Wilson, 5 La. 397, 25 Am.Dec.
86 187; Corbin on Contracts, Vol. 1, pp. 60 et seq., Section 25.

87   In the Schreiner case very recently our brethren on the Orleans Court of Appeal ob-
88 served: 'It is possible to make offers to anyone, or to everyone, who may perform a spec-

---

1. Although E. J. Daigle, the salesman involved testified that he must have discussed the lack of application of the advertised offer, because he invariably did so, plaintiff and his wife testified un-equivocally and were believed by the District Court, that no discussion whatsoever occurred con-cerning the right to acquire a 1955 model automobile when plaintiff purchased his 1954 Ford. And it is to be noted that by implication defendant's president admitted that the salesmen did not invari-ably discuss with customers whether they were interested in the bargain deal expressed by the adver-tisements, see testimony of J. Theron Brown, President of Defendant at Tr-16: 'Q. Well, now, was it the policy of you and your employees or your salesmen, or anyone connection with these deals, to dis-cuss that with these people and inform them when they bought a 1954 Ford that they might not be entitled to a 1955 Ford?' 'A. *If they came in and referred to the ad* and for the purpose of discussing that particular proposition offered in the paper, yes. But that, as I understand it, was not mentioned in this particular case by the purchaser.' (Italics ours.)

2. To the naked eye this notation appears to be by a different hand and different pencil than the signature of the salesman who allegedly made this notation; on a photostat of this sale, all other pen-cilled [*sic*] notations allegedly made at the same time are legible, but this notation is almost invisible and cannot be read. Plaintiff and his wife testify positively that such notation was not on the con-tract when executed, nor when they returned approximately 2 months later, to receive their 1955 model; and while defendant's salesman testified that it must have been on there because he would not have made such notation after the deal, another representative of defendant whom plaintiff and his wife testified on the latter occasion had examined the contract with them and found no such no-tation, was unable to remember *either to confirm or to deny* this visit of Johnson and his wife or whether or not he saw the contract on that occasion. Some further corroborative force to plaintiff's story is the testimony that such transactions were always stamped with a *rubber stamp* when a 'No 1955' deal was made, and in this instance plaintiff's contract was not so stamped. Of course, defendants testify with allegedly equal effect that these contracts were always likewise noted when a 1955 exchange deal *was* consummated. But it is to be remembered that contracts, including omissions, are to be con-strued against him who prepares them, in this case defendant dealer.

ified act or make a specified promise. * * * There is no doubt that as a result of Mrs. Butscher's success in the contest the defendant must be held bound to his obligation. When plaintiff performed all of the requirements of the offer in accordance with the published terms, it created a valid and binding contract, under which she became entitled to the promised rewards. That there was a serious and mutual consideration is obvious.' 68 So.2d 151.

'In order to constitute a proposal which may be converted into a contract by acceptance, the offer need not be addressed to a particular individual. A binding obligation may even originate in advertisements addressed to the general public,' 12 Am.Jur. 527, Verbo Contracts, Section 28. Whether in any individual instance the newspaper advertisement is an offer, rather than an invitation to make an offer, depends on the legal intention of the parties and the surrounding circumstances; Annotation, 157 A.L.R. 744–751, 77 C.J.S., Verbo Sales, §26, p. 634; 17 C.J.S., Verbo Contracts, §46, p. 389; 12 Am.Jur. 526–527, Verbo Contracts, Section 28.

The advertisement denotes itself as an 'offer', the wording to a reader denotes a bona fide bargain offer, and it was certain and definite enough to constitute a legal offer, Articles 1779, 1886, LSA-Civil Code.

If the automobile dealer had stated on September 17th to a specific customer: 'If you buy a 1954 automobile before October 1st, I will let you trade it even (except for license and sales tax) for a 1955 model of exactly the same model, body style, and accessories when these 1955 models come out in 60–90 days, providing you return the 1954 model with only normal wear and tear'; undoubtedly the offeree's purchase of a 1954 model before October 1st would have been a binding acceptance (without any further discussion) of the dealer's offer, creating in the dealer an obligation to furnish a 1955 model when available according to the terms of the offer.

In light of the legal principles above summarized, this same offer communicated to the general public by a newspaper advertisement has the same legal effect when accepted according to its terms. In the absence of any limitation in the offer solely to cash purchases, we do not feel the situation differs because plaintiff purchased the 1954 Ford by trade-in with cash boot, instead of by cash only.

If appellant-dealer argues it did not actually intend this newspaper advertisement to constitute an offer, and therefore the advertisement did not do so, nevertheless 'The rights of plaintiff and defendant are to be tested by the actual legal consequences flowing from a sale [contract] made under the particular advertisement * * *. These consequences cannot be altered or checked because the agent of the company may have had an erroneous belief as to what the advertisement as written meant, or what it would legally convey. The advertisement controlled the rights and obligations of the parties', Maginnis v. Union Oil Company, 47 La.Ann. 1489 at pages 1495–1496, 18 So. 459, at page 461. In the Maginnis case, the purchaser's acceptance at public sale of the vendor's advertised offer to sell was *held* to require conveyance not only of the land and buildings, but also of the valuable machinery therein (immovable by destination), although it was the *explicit intention* of the vendor in preparing the advertisement not to include this machinery in the offer.

It must further be remembered that the words of the advertisement were of course chosen by defendant-dealer, and if any ambiguity exists as to their meaning, it must be resolved against their composer; LSA-Civil Code, Article 1957; Crummer v. Nuveen, 7 Cir., 147 F.2d 3, 157 A.L.R. 739, holding a newspaper advertisement to purchase bonds at par was an offer, rather than a mere proposal to negotiate, being complete and definite, and if ambiguous, construed against offerer.

137 Defendant urges that plaintiff was under some duty when he appeared on defendant's
138 premises in response to the advertised offer to indicate that he was accepting same, since
139 defendant indicates it would have offered less trade-in value for plaintiff's old car had it
140 known that this was a '1954–1955' deal as advertised.[3] Assuming defendant would not have
141 allowed as much trade-in if it had thought this was a '1954–1955' deal, if there was a bur-
142 den on anyone, it would seem to be upon defendant to inform the plaintiff of any condi-
143 tions or modifications of the apparently bona fide offer contained in the advertisement.
144 'The party proposing shall be presumed to continue in the intention, which his proposal
145 expressed, if, on receiving the unqualified assent of him to whom the proposition is made,
146 he do not signify the change of his intention', Article 1801, LSA-Civil Code. See Loyd Mer-
147 cantile Co. v. Long, 123 La. 777, 49 So. 521; Comment, (now Professor) Pascal, 'Duration
148 and Revocability of an Offer', 1 La.Law Review 182. 'But if the doubt or obscurity [in the
149 agreement] arise for the want of necessary explanation which one of the parties ought to
150 have given, or from any other negligence or fault of his, the construction most favorable to
151 the other party shall be adopted, whether he be obligor or obligee', Article 1958, LSA-C.C.

152 Thus we have here what is denoted both in the common law and in our civil code as
153 a unilateral contract, or an obligation created by an offer accepted by an act: the offer or
154 exchange of a promise for an act. The execution of the act (purchase of the 1954 Ford)
155 by plaintiff in compliance with terms of defendant's published offer constituted plain-
156 tiff's acceptance of said offer, creating defendant's duty or obligation to furnish a 1955 Ford
157 according to the terms of the published offer. See Comment, 'The Unilateral Contract in
158 Civil Law and in Louisiana' 16 Tulane Law Review 456.

159 Plaintiff's *motive* in purchasing the 1954 Ford was not only to receive it for the trade-
160 in and boot given, but also to receive the right to exchange without substantial charge
161 this 1954 Ford for a 1955 model when the latter became available. The *cause* or consid-
162 eration for what plaintiff gave the dealer, included not only the 1954 Ford but also the right
163 to exchange it for a 1955 Ford according to the terms of the published offer. See Civil
164 Code Article 1896: 'By the *cause* of the contract, in this section, is meant the considera-
165 tion or motive for making it.'; also (Professor) Smith, 'A Refresher Course in *Cause*', 12
166 La.Law Review 2.

167 The executed sale which plaintiff signed when he purchased the 1954 Ford contained
168 within a paragraph printed at the bottom of the page:

169   'The front and back of this order comprise the entire agreement pertaining to
170   this purchase and no other agreement of any kind, verbal understanding or
171   promise whatsoever, will be recognized.'

172 Defendant urges with considerable force that applying the rule stated in United Engi-
173 neering Co. v. Durbin, La.App. 1 Cir., 68 So.2d 614, the alleged independent collateral
174 agreement based on acceptance of the newspaper offer was so closely related to the contract
175 for purchase of a 1954 Ford as to be 'naturally and normally' included in the written con-
176 tract; therefore that parole proof should have been barred; or, that, in any event plaintiff
177 waived his right to enforce this obligation as against defendant in view of the quoted clause.

178 However, as pointed out above, in the present case defendant was under a duty to no-
179 tify plaintiff of any modification of the newspaper offer. The omission in this contract is

---

3. Plaintiff's answer is that he would not have bought the 1954 Ford car from defendant, even at
that trade-in value given him by defendant, unless he thought he was to receive the 1955 car in exchange therefor without extra cost (except for sales tax and license) when such later model was available.

construed against defendant. In a very similar situation, construing a similar clause, our Supreme Court held that acceptance of an advertised order completes the contract, which is not subject to further modification by either one of the parties without the consent of the other, Kodel Radio Corporation v. Shuler, 171 La. 468, 131 So. 462. Further, the terms of this proviso limit it as the 'entire agreement pertaining to *this purchase*', which indeed was a complete contract within itself; but this purchase-sale contract, complete within itself, was nevertheless also the acceptance of an offer, creating *another* and a separate obligation.

Acceptance of an offer may of course be made by silent deed as well as by word; consent may be implied from actions under the circumstances, as well as by expressed words; but such acceptance of, founded on such consent to, an offer nevertheless creates a valid contract, and the offerer is bound by the obligation previously offered by him in exchange for the act which the obligee has performed in response to the offer, LSA-Civil Code Articles 1802, 1811, 1816; Shreveport Traction Company v. Mulhaupt, 122 La. 667, 48 So. 144; Lowy v. Builliard, La.App. 1 Cir., 17 So.2d 855; Netterville v. Police Jury, 6 La.App. 512 (1 Cir.).

The record reflects that plaintiff went to defendant's premises with the perhaps naive belief that the advertisement meant just what it said; that as subsequently blazoned by heavy black headlines in large advertisement, 'TWO FOR ONE ... Til September 30th AND THERE'S NO CATCH IN IT' [...]; that *everyone* who bought a 1954 Ford during the 2-week period was ipso facto entitled to exchange it for a 1955 model when such were available, according to the dealer's offer. The published offer without qualification was that plaintiff's acceptance thereof by purchase of a 1954 model entitled him to receive a 1955 model in exchange, which implicitly no more needed discussion or formalized warranty in acceptance than does the assumption of one purchasing a new car that it will be painted rather than naked steel.

If defendant seriously argues that despite the plain wording of the advertised offer, defendant had absolutely no intention of making a bona fide offer but was merely intending to lure customers to defendant's sales lot, or that, if a bona fide offer, the routine signing of a form document by plaintiff amounted to a waiver of substantial property rights because of small print at the bottom, not called to his attention by defendant, it may be well to recall the expression of the Ohio Supreme Court in an almost identical factual situation as reported at Meyer v. Packard Cleveland Motor Co., 106 Ohio St. 328, 140 N.E. 118, at page 121, 28 A.L.R. 986, at page 991:

> 'There is entirely too much disregard of law and truth in the business, social, and political world of to-day. * * * It is time to hold men to their primary engagements to tell the truth and observe the law of common honesty and fair dealing.'

[....]

LOTTINGER, Judge (dissents)

[**After detailing the facts and opining that certain evidence should not have been admitted, Judge Lottinger discussed the legal effect of the content of the newspaper advertisement.**] [...] I still feel that petitioner's case must fail as, under the greater weight of authority, the newspaper advertisement was not an offer but was merely an invitation to enter into negotiations for an agreement. The rule on this particular point is stated in Volume 1, Corbin on Contracts, Section 25, page 60, as follows:

> 'It is quite possible to make a definite and operative offer to buy or to sell goods by advertisement, in a newspaper, by a handbill, or on a placard in a store

window. It is not customary to do this, however; and the presumption is the other way. Neither the advertiser nor the reader of his notice understands that the latter is employed to close the deal without further expression by the former. Such advertisements are understood to be mere requests to consider and examine and negotiate; and no one can reasonably regard them otherwise, unless the circumstances are exceptional and the words used are very plain and clear.

'On the other hand it is very common, where one desires to excite many people to action, to offer a reward for such action by general publication in some form. Some offers must be reasonably interpreted, according to their terms and the surrounding circumstances; but action in accordance with such interpretation will close a contract.'

It is noted that Mr. Corbin, as well as the other writers on the subject, draw a distinction between advertisements to sell merchandise and advertisements for a reward. Advertisements announcing the terms of a prize contest fall into the same category as announcements of rewards because the characteristics of both require that they be addressed to the general public by advertising. As offers of rewards and prizes must of necessity be made by advertisements, it is well settled that they can be withdrawn only in the same manner. Advertisements relating to the sale of merchandise do not have the same characteristics and, consequently, are governed by different legal rules.

In 77 C.J.S., Sales, § 25, p. 634, the rule is stated in similar language as follows:

'Business advertisements published in newspapers * * * stating that the advertiser has a certain quantity or quality of goods which he wants to dispose of at certain prices and on certain terms, are not offers which become contracts as soon as any person to whose notice they may come signifies his acceptance by notifying the other that he will take a certain quantity of them, but are ordinarily construed merely as an invitation for an offer for sale on the terms stated, which offer when received may be accepted or rejected, and which, therefore, does not become a contract of sale until accepted by the seller; and until a contract has been so made the proposer may modify or revoke such prices or terms.'

In 17 C.J.S., Contracts, § 46, p. 389, I find the following language:

'*Proposals to deal.* * * * Whether or not a business circular, a corporate prospectus, a published price list, or other advertisement of like nature is an offer which will, on acceptance form a contract, or is merely an invitation to make an offer, depends on the language used; but generally a newspaper advertisement or circular couched in general language and proper to be sent to all persons interested in a particular trade or business, or a prospectus of a general and descriptive nature, will be construed as an invitation to make an offer.

'*Prize Contests, etc.* An offer of a prize may mature into a binding contract in favor of a successful contestant who has complied with the terms of the offer. However, a response to a proposal for exhibitors to show their wares at a public exhibition has been held not to make an agreement.'

In 12 American Jurisprudence pp. 526–527, Contracts, Section 28, I find:

'* * * A general offer must be distinguished from a general invitation to make an offer. Performance of the conditions of the former makes a legally binding contract, whereas compliance with the requirements of the latter involves nothing more than an offer, which may or may not be accepted by the party who issued the invitation therefor. A mere quotation of price must be distinguished

from an offer. From the nature of the subject, the question whether certain acts   274
or conduct constitute a definite proposal upon which a binding contract may be   275
predicated without further action on the part of the person from whom it pro-   276
ceeds or a mere preliminary step which is not susceptible, without further action   277
by such party, of being converted into a binding contract depends upon the na-   278
ture of the particular acts or conduct in question and the circumstances attend-   279
ing the transaction. It is impossible to formulate a general principle or criterion   280
for its determination. Accordingly, whether a communication naming a price is   281
a quotation or an offer depends upon the intention of the owner as it is mani-   282
fested by the facts and circumstances of each particular case.'   283

Of course throughout the country there are cases pro and con on the subject. Some   284
hold newspaper advertisements by their peculiar wording to constitute offers. Others   285
hold the advertisements to be mere invitations. In Louisiana we have certain cases hold-   286
ing advertisements to be binding offers, however, these cases deal with contests for prizes   287
and with auction sales. In Schreiner v. Weil Furniture Co., La.App., 68 So.2d 149, the   288
Court held the advertisement to be a binding offer, however, this case dealt with an ad-   289
vertisement announcing the rules and prizes to be awarded in a contest. A similar hold-   290
ing was reached in Youngblood v. Daily and Weekly Signal Tribune, 15 La.App. 379, 131   291
So. 604, which dealt with a newspaper subscription contest. In Maginnis v. Union Oil   292
Co., 47 La.Ann. 1489, 18 So. 459, the offer was to sell at auction to the last and highest   293
bidder, under terms and conditions set forth in the advertisement. These particular sit-   294
uations are covered by their own particular rules and statutes, and are not similar to the   295
particular situation which is before us. Actually the question presented in the instant case   296
is res novo in Louisiana.   297

As stated, the greater weight of authority in this country is to the effect that a news-   298
paper advertisement of the nature presented in this case is not an offer, but merely an in-   299
vitation for the customer to make an offer.   300

For the reasons hereinabove assigned, I respectfully dissent from the majority.   301

Questions

1. Lines 15–16 and lines 31 *et seq.*: After you have read the sentence in lines 15–16,
    make a legal analysis of the excerpt from the newspaper reproduced in lines 31 *et seq.*
    The purpose of making your own legal analysis is for you to make up your own mind
    as to the nature of the excerpt, specifically whether it is an offer or an invitation to
    bargain and why. Since a 'sale' could be the named contract you could identify as a
    result of your analysis, read the code articles on the contract of sale, particularly
    Louisiana Civil Code articles 2439, 2448, 2456, 2464. Who, in this case, could be the
    offeror? Why does it matter to identify a party as the offeror?

    NOTE: We call your attention to the fact that the phrases "collateral obligation" (line
    24) and "independent, collateral contract" (lines 25–26) do not exist in the Louisiana
    Civil Code. These are not civil law concepts.

2. Lines 31–42: Identify the kinds of obligations and/or modalities of obligations hid-
    ing behind some of the words used in the excerpt. For example, what kind of legal
    modality should be associated with the phrase "For two weeks...."? What about "two
    for one"?

3. Lines 64–73: The contrast between "usual" course of behavior and "this particular oc-
    casion" illustrates the fundamental distinction between, on the one hand, an objec-

tive standard of behavior (or an *in abstracto* standard), the standard of the average person or bonus paterfamilias (usually, ordinarily, line 66) and, on the other hand, a particular-individual standard (an *in concreto* standard) (*see* lines 71–73). Which one of these two standards would better fit the form of the plaintiff's acceptance? *See* lines 87–118.

4. Lines 114 *et seq.*: On what grounds does the court rely to state that this is an offer? What are some of the legal consequences?

5. Lines 178 *et seq.*: Can the court's statements be easily accepted in these circumstances where we have a well-established, professional corporate entity dealing with an average, naive consumer couple? On lines 178–195, is the Court formulating some policy in the place of the Louisiana legislature?

See also *Succession of Aurianne*, 53 So.2d 901 (La. 1951), *Breaux Brothers Construction Company v. Associated Contractors, Inc.*, 77 So.2d 17 (La. 1954), *Pooler Building Materials, Inc. v. Hogan*, 244 So.2d 62 (La. 1st Cir. 1971), *Marine Chartering (Gulf) Ltd. v. Boland Machine & Manufacturing Co., Inc.*, 273 So. 2d 316 (La. 4th Cir. 1973)

Comparative Law Perspective

Alain Levasseur, COMPARATIVE LAW OF CONTRACTS
37–68 (2008)

Formation of Contracts
Offer and Acceptance

When is an offer, an "Offer" in a legal sense?

A: Civil law

See: La.Civ.C.: Articles 1927–1928

Fr.Civ.C.

Art. 1108: Four requirements are essential for the validity of a convention:

— the consent of the party who binds herself.

C. C. Q.

Art. 1388: An offer to contract is a proposal which contains all the essential of the proposed contract and in which the offeror signifies his willingness to be bound if it is accepted.

Art. 1389: An offer to contract derives from the person who initiates the contract or the person who determines its content or even, in certain cases, the person who presents the last essential element of the proposed contract.

Common law

Restatement, 2d

§ 24. Offer Defined

An offer is the manifestation of willingness to enter into a bargain, so made as to justify another person in understanding that his assent to that bargain is invited and will conclude it.

§ 26. Preliminary Negotiations

A manifestation of willingness to enter into a bargain is not an offer if the person to whom it is addressed knows or has reason to know that the person making it does not intend to conclude a bargain until he has made a further manifestation of assent.

§ 39. Counter-offers

(1) A counter-offer is an offer made by an offeree to his offeror relating to the same matter as the original offer and proposing a substituted bargain differing from that proposed by the original offer.

E. Allan Farnsworth

§ 3.3. Offer and Acceptance.

What is an "offer"? It can be defined as a manifestation to another of assent to enter into a contract if the other manifests assent in return by some action, often a promise but sometimes a performance. By making an offer, the offeror thus confers upon the offeree the power to create a contract.... Offer, then, is the name given to a promise that is conditioned on some action by the promisee if the legal effect of the promisee's taking that action is to make the promisee enforceable. Empowerment of the offeree to make the offeror's promise enforceable is thus the essence of an offer ...

UNIDROIT

Art. 2.1.2: (Definition of offer): A proposal for concluding a contract constitutes an offer if it is sufficiently definite and indicates the intention of the offeror to be bound in case of acceptance.

When is an "Acceptance", an "Acceptance" in a legal sense?

Civil law

See: La. Civ. C.: Articles 1927–1928–1939–1942–1943

C.C.Q.

Art. 1393: An acceptance which does not correspond substantially to the offer or which is received by the offeror after the offer has lapsed does not constitute acceptance.

It may, however, constitute a new offer.

Common law

G.H. Treitel

Acceptance Defined

An acceptance is a final and unqualified expression of assent to the terms of an offer. The objective test of agreement applies to an acceptance no less than to an offer. On this test, a mere acknowledgment of an offer would not be an acceptance; nor is there an acceptance where a person who has received an offer to sell goods merely replies that it is his "intention to place an order....

(3) Acceptance by conduct

An offer may be accepted by conduct, e.g. by dispatching goods in response to an offer to buy ... Conduct will, however, only have this effect if the offeree did the act with the intention of accepting the offer ...

(4) Acceptance must be unqualified

A communication may fail to take effect as an acceptance because it attempts to vary the terms of the offer.

Restatement, 2d

§ 30. Form of Acceptance Invited

(1) An offer may invite or require acceptance to be made by an affirmative answer in words, or by performing or refraining from performing a specified act, or may empower the offeree to make a selection of terms in his acceptance.

(2) Unless otherwise indicated by the language or the circumstances, an offer invites acceptance in any manner and by any medium reasonable in the circumstances.

§ 32. Invitation of Promise or Performance

In case of doubt an offer is interpreted as inviting the offeree to accept either by promising to perform what the offer requests or by rendering the performance, as the offeree chooses.

E. Allan Farnsworth

§ 3.3 Offer and Acceptance ... What is an acceptance? It can be defined as the action (promise or performance) by the offeree that creates a contract (i.e. makes the offeror's promise enforceable). Acceptance, then, is the name given to the offeree's action if the legal effect of that action is to make the offeror's promise enforceable.

UNIDROIT

Art. 2.1.6 (Mode of acceptance)

(1) A statement made by or other conduct of the offeree indicating assent to an offer is an acceptance.

(3) However, if, by virtue of the offer or as a result of practices which the parties have established between themselves or of usage, the offeree may indicate assent by performing an act without notice to the offeror, the acceptance is effective when the act is performed.

Art. 2.1.11 (Modified acceptance)

(1) A reply to an offer which purports to be an acceptance but contains additions, limitations or other modifications is a rejection of the offer and constitutes a counter-offer.

(2) However, a reply to an offer which purports to be an acceptance but contains additional or different terms which do not materially alter the terms of the offer constitutes an acceptance, unless the offeror, without undue delay, objects to the discrepancy. If the offeror does not object, the terms of the contract are the terms of the offer with the modifications contained in the acceptance.

Meeting of the minds: revocable or irrevocable offer

Civil law

See: La. Civ.C.: Articles 1936–1935–1937

C. C. Q.

Art. 1392: An offer lapses if no acceptance is received by the offeror before the expiry of the specified term or, where no term is specified, before the expiry of a reasonable time; it also lapses in respect of the offeree if he has rejected it.

Common law

Restatement, 2d

§ 63. Time When Acceptance Takes Effect

Unless the offer provides otherwise,

(a) an acceptance made in a manner and by a medium invited by an offer is operative and completes the manifestation of mutual assent as soon as put out of the offeree's possession, without regard to whether it ever reaches the offeror; but

(b) an acceptance under an option contract is not operative until received by the offeror.

§64. Acceptance by Telephone or Teletype

Acceptance given by telephone or other medium of substantially instantaneous two-way communication is governed by the principles applicable to acceptances where the parties are in the presence of each other.

§66. Acceptance Must be Properly Dispatched

An acceptance sent by mail or otherwise from a distance is not operative when dispatched, unless it is properly addressed and such other precautions taken as are ordinarily observed to insure safe transmission of similar messages.

§67. Effect of Receipt of Acceptance Improperly Dispatched

Where an acceptance is seasonably dispatched but the offeree uses means of transmission not invited by the offer or fails to exercise reasonable diligence to insure safe transmission, it is treated as operative upon dispatch if received within the time in which a properly dispatched acceptance would normally have arrived.

UCC

§2-204. Formation in General

(1) A contract for sale of goods may be made in any manner sufficient to show agreement, including offer and acceptance, conduct by both parties which recognizes the existence of a contract, the interaction of electronic agents, and the interaction of an electronic agent and an individual.

(2) An agreement sufficient to constitute a contract for sale may be found even if the moment of its making is undetermined.

(3) Even if one or more terms are left open, a contract for sale does not fail for indefiniteness if the parties have intended to make a contract and there is a reasonably certain basis for giving an appropriate remedy.

(4)....

UNIDROIT

ARTICLE 2.1.3:
(Withdrawal of offer)

(1) An offer becomes effective when it reaches the offeree.

(2) An offer, even if it is irrevocable, may be withdrawn if the withdrawal reaches the offeree before or at the same time as the offer.

ARTICLE 2.1.4:
(Revocation of offer)

(1) Until a contract is concluded an offer may be revoked if the revocation reaches the offeree before it has dispatched an acceptance.

(2) However, an offer cannot be revoked

(a) if it indicates, whether by stating a fixed time for acceptance or otherwise, that it is irrevocable; or

(b) if it was reasonable for the offeree to rely on the offer as being irrevocable and the offeree has acted in reliance on the offer.

Section III—Vices of Consent

Louisiana Sources of Law

Louisiana Civil Code

Art. 1948. Vitiated consent.

Consent may be vitiated by error, fraud, or duress. (Acts 1984, No. 331, §1, effective. January 1, 1985.)

Art. 1949. Error vitiates consent.

Error vitiates consent only when it concerns a cause without which the obligation would not have been incurred and that cause was known or should have been known to the other party. (Acts 1984, No. 331, §1, eff. Jan. 1, 1985.)

Art. 1950. Error that concerns cause.

Error may concern a cause when it bears on the nature of the contract, or the thing that is the contractual object or a substantial quality of that thing, or the person or the qualities of the other party, or the law, or any other circumstance that the parties regarded, or should in good faith have regarded, as a cause of the obligation. (Acts 1984, No. 331, §1, eff. Jan. 1, 1985.)

Art. 1951. Other party willing to perform.

A party may not avail himself of his error if the other party is willing to perform the contract as intended by the party in error. (Acts 1984, No. 331, §1, eff. Jan. 1, 1985.)

Art. 1952. Rescission; liability for damages.

A party who obtains rescission on grounds of his own error is liable for the loss thereby sustained by the other party unless the latter knew or should have known of the error.

The court may refuse rescission when the effective protection of the other party's interest requires that the contract be upheld. In that case, a reasonable compensation for the loss he has sustained may be granted to the party to whom rescission is refused. (Acts 1984, No. 331, §1, eff. Jan. 1, 1985.)

Art. 1953. Fraud may result from misrepresentation or from silence.

Fraud is a misrepresentation or a suppression of the truth made with the intention either to obtain an unjust advantage for one party or to cause a loss or inconvenience to the other. Fraud may also result from silence or inaction. (Acts 1984, No. 331, §1, eff. Jan. 1, 1985.)

Art. 1954. Confidence between the parties.

Fraud does not vitiate consent when the party against whom the fraud was directed could have ascertained the truth without difficulty, inconvenience, or special skill.

This exception does not apply when a relation of confidence has reasonably induced a party to rely on the other's assertions or representations. (Acts 1984, No. 331, §1, eff. Jan. 1, 1985.)

Art. 1955. Error induced by fraud.

Error induced by fraud need not concern the cause of the obligation to vitiate consent, but it must concern a circumstance that has substantially influenced that consent. (Acts 1984, No. 331, §1, eff. Jan. 1, 1985.)

Art. 1956. Fraud committed by a third person.

Fraud committed by a third person vitiates the consent of a contracting party if the other party knew or should have known of the fraud. (Acts 1984, No. 331, § 1, eff. Jan. 1, 1985.)

Art. 1958. Damages.

The party against whom rescission is granted because of fraud is liable for damages and attorney fees. (Acts 1984, No. 331, § 1, eff. Jan. 1, 1985.)

Art. 1959. Nature.

Consent is vitiated when it has been obtained by duress of such a nature as to cause a reasonable fear of unjust and considerable injury to a party's person, property, or reputation.

Age, health, disposition, and other personal circumstances of a party must be taken into account in determining reasonableness of the fear. (Acts 1984, No. 331, § 1, eff. Jan. 1, 1985.)

Art. 1960. Duress directed against third persons.

Duress vitiates consent also when the threatened injury is directed against the spouse, an ascendant, or descendant of the contracting party.

If the threatened injury is directed against other persons, the granting of relief is left to the discretion of the court. (Acts 1984, No. 331, § 1, eff. Jan. 1, 1985.)

Art. 1961. Duress by third person.

Consent is vitiated even when duress has been exerted by a third person. (Acts 1984, No. 331, § 1, eff. Jan. 1, 1985.)

Art. 1962. Threat of exercising a right.

A threat of doing a lawful act or a threat of exercising a right does not constitute duress.

A threat of doing an act that is lawful in appearance only may constitute duress. (Acts 1984, No. 331, § 1, eff. Jan. 1, 1985.)

Art. 1963. Contract with party in good faith.

A contract made with a third person to secure the means of preventing threatened injury may not be rescinded for duress if that person is in good faith and not in collusion with the party exerting duress. (Acts 1984, No. 331, § 1, eff. Jan. 1, 1985.)

Art. 1964. Damages.

When rescission is granted because of duress exerted or known by a party to the contract, the other party may recover damages and attorney fees.

When rescission is granted because of duress exerted by a third person, the parties to the contract who are innocent of the duress may recover damages and attorney fees from the third person. (Acts 1984, No. 331, § 1, eff. Jan. 1, 1985.)

Précis: Louisiana Law of Conventional Obligations— §§ 4.1.1 to 4.3.3

Error

LSA-C.C. Article 1949 contains a hint at providing some understanding of this concept of error: "**Error vitiates consent only when it concerns a cause without which the obligation would not have been incurred and that cause was known or should have been known to the other party.**" ...

All in all, an error consists in considering something as true when it is actually false or, conversely, in considering as false something which is actually true....

An error must be serious, as must the intent to enter into a contract. As stated in **LSA C.C. Art. 1949**, **"Error vitiates consent only when it concerns a cause without which the obligation would not have been incurred and that cause was known or should have been known to the other party."** ...

The seriousness of an error can only bear on an essential requirement for a contract to exist. Otherwise the error would bear on an accessory element of the contract and such an error could not bring about the nullity of the contract (unless the parties have made such an accessory element a suspensive condition of their contractual obligations) as long as its essential requirements have been met....

There can be an error made by the parties as to the *nature* or *kind* of contract they wish to enter into....

For example: a party may think she is negotiating a contract of loan when the other party thinks that she will be a party to a contract of deposit ...

The error can bear on the identity of the *thing* as the principal object of their contract. For example, in a contract of sale, the buyer may truly believe that he is buying a certain tract of land, the Laurentine Plantation, when the seller has in mind selling another and different tract of land, the Bayou Bleu Plantation....

Instead of bearing on the identity of the thing itself, an error can bear on **"a substantial quality of that thing"** or the **reasonable fitness** of the thing for its **ordinary use**....

An error can bear also on **"the cause"** of the contract or "reason why a party obligates himself" since "cause" is an essential requirement for the formation of any contract....

LSA-C.C. Art. 5 states that **"No one may avail himself of ignorance of the law."** Once a statute has been promulgated, no party to a contract can argue that she made an error as to the existence of that statute. Yet, one may enter into a contract under some misunderstanding of the statute, such as the nature or extent of one's rights....

However the civil Code provides for instances where an error of law, even though legitimate, cannot be raised as a ground for the nullity of some contracts or juridical acts. For example, under **LSA-C.C. Art. 1761**: **"... whatever has been freely performed in compliance with a natural obligation may not be reclaimed."** Another example of a contract that cannot be rescinded for error of law is the contract of *compromise or transaction*. **LSA-C.C. Art. 3080** states: **"A compromise precludes the parties from bringing a subsequent action based upon the matter that was compromised."** ...

"Error may concern ... the person or the qualities of the other party" (LSA-C.C. Art. **1950**). These are the only words in the Civil Code to address this issue of error as to the person, the other party to the contract. Such an error as to the person must, necessarily, concern a *cause* of the contract as stated at the beginning of **Art. 1950**. Contracts which might be annulled on this ground of error are most likely to be *gratuitous contracts* or, more generally, contracts entered into *intuitu personae* wherein the consideration of the person of the co-contracting party is foremost in the mind of the other party....

Not every error leads to the nullity of a contract. Not every kind of error listed in Art. 1950 will necessarily carry with it the nullity of the contract which is the consequence of an error. Some conditions are attached to the error made by one party in her relation with the other party and some limitations can affect the extent of the effects of the nullity of the contract....

The error can become a ground for nullity of the contract except when that error could be considered so excessive or negligent that it should not be excused: The equities of the situation may indeed favor the other party to the contract and justify that the contract remain binding.

In addition "A party may not avail himself of his error when the other party is willing to perform the contract as intended by the party in error." (LSA-C.C. Art. 1951)....

Fraud

LSA-C.C. Art. 1953 describes fraud in these terms: "Fraud is a misrepresentation or a suppression of the truth made with the intention either to obtain an unjust advantage for one party or to cause a loss or inconvenience to the other. Fraud may also result from silence or inaction." ...

Fraud is not, therefore, in itself a vice of consent. It is, rather, either an action such as a misrepresentation or a false assertion meant to hide the "truth" and therefore to "induce an error," or an inaction such as a failure to act or the withholding of the "truth" so as to "induce an error." ...

As the description of fraud in Art. 1953 suggests, the material element of fraud may consist in maneuvers, a scheme, a behavior, lies, withholding information or silence, such that a reasonable person would be led to make an error....

On the other hand, there may exist factual circumstances which are such that maneuvers [and] schemes ... ought not lead a reasonable person to make an error. Such circumstances would fall under the wording of LSA-C.C. Art. 1954-1, which provides that "the party against whom the fraud was directed could have ascertained the truth without difficulty, inconvenience, or special skill." ...

The error made by the first party must have been "substantially" induced by the fraud committed by the second party and the fraud must have been committed by that second party or someone else but with the knowledge of that second party.

In the words of LSA-C.C. Art. 1955: "Error induced by fraud need not concern the cause of the obligation to vitiate consent, but it must concern a circumstance that has substantially influenced that consent." ...

In other words, when "fraud" is established, the contract could be annulled for errors of consent other than when the "error concerns a cause without which the obligation would not have been incurred and that cause was known or should have been known to the other party." (LSA-C.C. Art. 1949.) More errors than an error as to "the cause" can become grounds for the relative nullity of the contract when those errors have been the outcome of fraud....

Since "fraud" may lead to error as a vice of consent if fraud itself meets the requirements above and if it induces an error "substantial" enough but lesser than an error as to the principal cause of the contract, it is logical to grant to the party victim of the fraud and error the right to seek the relative nullity of the contract for lack of free and informed consent. Under LSA-C.C. Art. 2031 "A contract is relatively null when it violates a rule intended for the protection of private parties, as when a party lacked capacity or did not give free consent at the time the contract was made. A contract that is only relatively null may be confirmed.

"Relative nullity may be invoked only by those persons for whose interest the ground for nullity was established, and may not be declared by the court on its own initiative." ...

In addition to, or in lieu of, the nullity of the contract, "The party against whom rescission is granted because of fraud is liable for damages and attorney fees." (LSA-C.C. Art. 1958)....

Duress

Duress is made up of two component elements: a psychological element, the fear felt by a party to a contract, hence the vice of consent; and a material anti-social element consisting in the duress itself or the threats directed by the perpetrator against a party to a contract. These two component elements of duress make up its nature as described by LSA-C.C. Art. 1959: "Consent is vitiated when it has been obtained by duress of such a nature as to cause a reasonable fear of unjust and considerable injury to a party's person, property, or reputation.

"Age, health, disposition, and other personal circumstances of a party must be taken into account in determining reasonableness of the fear." ...

LSA-C.C. Art. 1960 states that "Duress vitiates consent also when the threatened injury is directed against the spouse, an ascendant, or descendant of the contracting party.

If the threatened injury is directed against other persons, the granting of relief is left to the discretion of the court." ...

LSA-C.C. Art. 1961 provides that "Consent is vitiated even when duress has been exerted by a third person." Indeed, what is of greater concern to the law on formation of contracts is the integrity of a party's consent, that party's freedom to contract or not to contract....

However, not all contracts entered into under duress are automatically relatively null. Under the circumstances described in LSA-C.C. Art. 1963 "A contract made with a third person to secure the means of preventing threatened injury may not be rescinded for duress if that person is in good faith and not in collusion with the party exerting duress." ...

LSA-C.C. Art. 1964 states that When rescission is granted because of duress exerted or known by a party to the contract, the other party may recover damages and attorney fees.

When rescission is granted because of duress exerted by a third person, the parties to the contract who are innocent of the duress may recover damages and attorney fees from the third person." ...

Cases

1 **Mrs. Joyce DEUTSCHMANN, wife of/and Frank Deutschmann**

2 **v.**

3 **STANDARD FUR COMPANY, INC.**

4 Louisiana Court of Appeal

5 Fourth Circuit

6 April 13, 1976

7 331 So.2d 219

8 GULOTTA, Judge.

9 Plaintiffs appeal from a judgment dismissing their suit for return of a $400.00 deposit
10 on a $2,000.00 mink coat ordered by Mrs. Joyce Deutschmann from defendant. We reverse.

11 In November, 1974, Mrs. Deutschmann placed an order with Elza Abel, president of
12 Standard Fur Company, for a mink coat to be made by a New York furrier. Plaintiff-wife

deposited with defendant the sum of $400.00 to be credited against the price of the coat. Mrs. Deutschmann specified that the coat was to be made with the furs running horizontally; that quality female continuous, not pieced together, furs be used; and, that the furs be of the same width as the furs selected by her from a model coat at Standard Fur.[1]

Plaintiff testified that she refused to accept the coat for the reasons that 1) the skins of the coat were wider than the skins of the model coat at Standard Fur Company; 2) the horizontal skins were not continuous, but pieced together; and, 3) in 'letting out the skins', the pelts had been sliced and sewn back together, rather than stretched.

The coat was returned by defendant to the New York furrier in an attempt to make alterations to satisfy plaintiff's complaints. After the coat had been returned from the furrier a second time, plaintiff rejected the coat and requested return of the deposit. Defendant refused and this suit followed.

This case is a classic example of a misunderstanding between two parties to a purported agreement resulting in lack of consent on the part of the purchaser. LSA-C.C. arts. 1797[2] and 1798.[3] Consent on the part of Mrs. Deutschmann was lacking (LSA-C.C. art. 1812)[4] because of error of fact on the part of the purchaser which was a principal cause for making the agreement. See LSA-C.C. arts. 1821,[5] 1823[6] and 1825.[7]

Our jurisprudence is well settled that a contract may be invalidated for a unilateral error as to a fact which was the principal cause for making the contract, where the other party knew or should have known it was the principal cause. LSA-C.C. art. 1845: Savoie v. Bills, 317 So.2d 249 (La.App.3d Cir. 1975); West Esplanade Shell Service, Inc. v. Breithoff, 293 So.2d 595 (La.App.4th Cir. 1974). Error as to the nature or object of a contract may be with regard to either the substance or the object of the agreement, or substantial quality of the object, or some other quality of the object if such quality is the

---

1. Mrs. Deutschmann further specified that the coat be belted and have no buttons. The finished coat was made with four buttons and no belt, however, this problem was rectified to Mrs. Deutschmann's satisfaction by defendant and is not an issue in this case.

2. 'Art. 1797. Necessity for consent; proof. Art. 1797. When the parties have the legal capacity to form a contract, the next requisite to its validity is their consent. This being a mere operation of the mind, can have no effect, unless it be evinced in some manner that shall cause it to be understood by the other parties to the contract. To prevent error in this essential point, the law establishes, by certain rules adapted to the nature of the contract, what circumstances shall be evidence of such consent, and how those circumstances shall be proved; these come within the purview of the law of evidence.'

3. 'Art. 1798. Offer and acceptance. Art. 1798. As there must be two parties at least to every contract, so there must be something proposed by one and accepted and agreed to by another to form the matter of such contract; the will of both parties must unite on the same point.'

4. 'Art. 1812. Unequivocal language for express acceptance. Art. 1812. Express consent must be given in a language understood by the party who accepts, and the words by which it is conveyed must be in themselves unequivocal; if they may mean different things, they give rise to error, which, as is hereinafter provided, destroys the effect of a contract.'

5. 'Art. 1821. Error of fact. Art. 1821. That is called error of fact, which proceeds either from ignorance of that which really exists, or from a mistaken belief in the existence of that which has none.'

6. 'Art. 1823. Sufficiency of error to invalidate contract. Art. 1823. Errors may exist as to all the circumstances and facts which relate to a contract, but it is not every error that will invalidate it. To have that effect, the error must be in some point, which was a principal cause for making the contract, and it may be either as to the motive for making the contract, to the person with whom it is made, or to the subject matter of the contract itself.'

7. 'Art. 1825. Error as to motive. Art. 1825. The error in the cause of a contract to have the effect of invalidating it, must be on the principal cause, when there are several; this principal cause is called the Motive, and means that consideration without which the contract would not have been made.'

principal cause of making the contract. Jefferson Truck Equipment Co. v. Guarisco Motor Co., 250 So.2d 211 (La.App.1st Cir. 1971).

Applying the above articles and jurisprudence to the instant case, we conclude that consent was lacking and the purported agreement was vitiated because of error of fact which constituted a principal cause for making the agreement. Mrs. Deutschmann testified that she understood the coat would be made of continuous skins, i.e., horizontal pelts that were not 'pieced together' and which were 'let out' and would extend all around the coat. According to Mrs. Deutschmann, her definition of a continuous skin was, 'I mean a long continuous skin, not several short ones pieced together.' Her definition of a 'fully let out' fur was as follows: 'My understanding that they stretch the pelts instead of taking several small pieces and putting them together. If he could not have made it, I would have changed my plans.' Mrs. Deutschmann further indicated that the furs used in the purchased coat were wider than the ones used in the model coat selected by her.

On the other hand, Abel's (a furrier with 40 years experience) understanding, according to trade usage, of the meaning of the terms 'pieced together' and 'let out', graphically illustrates the lack of understanding between the parties. Abel admitted that plaintiff wanted a coat with continuous horizontal furs and without seams. However, he differentiated between a fur 'pieced together' with straight seams, which he defined as a pieced together coat, and furs pieced together with a 'V-type seam', which he defined as 'set up' and not 'pieced together'. According to Abel, use of a V-type seam is an acceptable method of joining skins, and, in trade jargon, is not considered piecing together. Significantly, Abel failed to communicate to plaintiff the trade usage difference between 'pieced together' and 'set up V-type seams'. Abel further testified that female skins are not long enough, i.e., 36 inches long, to be used continuously in a wrap-around horizontal fur coat, but must be pieced together.

Abel failed to communicate to plaintiff that the width of horizontal skins was different from the width of vertical skins. Significantly, although the model coat shown Mrs. Deutschmann was made of vertical skins, Abel did not communicate the difference in width to plaintiff.

Abel also stated that the term 'let out' means that the fur is sliced and sewn back together. A let out skin, according to Abel, is one that has been cut and then let out.

Abel is the expert. He was aware that Standard Fur was unable to deliver to plaintiff that which she thought she had ordered. It was his responsibility to communicate to Mrs. Deutschmann information which, clearly, would have avoided the confusion. For reasons best known to himself, he failed to do so. Abel's lack of communication caused the misunderstanding on the part of Mrs. Deutschmann, resulting in the error of fact on the part of the purchaser which was a principal cause for making the agreement. See LSA-C.C. arts. 1812, 1821 and 1825. We find that consent was lacking in the instant case and that no agreement existed. The parties revert to the same position which they occupied prior to the purported formation of the agreement. Plaintiff is entitled to the return of her deposit.

Accordingly, the judgment, of the trial court is reversed and set aside. Judgment is now rendered in favor of Mrs. Joyce Deutschmann and Frank Deutschmann, and against Standard Fur Company, Inc., in the sum of $400.00, together with legal interest thereon from date of judicial demand and for all costs.

REVERSED AND RENDERED.

Questions

1. Lines 9 *et seq.*: The court refers to Mrs. Deutschmann as having placed an "order", or "she refused to accept the coat …" or "consent on the part of Mrs. Deustchmann was

lacking...." Where is the offer, if any, and if one exists, who is the offeror? Note that the Court cites former Louisiana Civil Code articles 1797, 1798, 1812 etc.... *See* La. Civ. Code arts. 1927–1952. Was there a misunderstanding between an offeror and an offeree?

2. Lines 31 *et seq*.: Is the court correct to refer to the contract being invalidated for a unilateral error as to a fact? If error there was, would it make a difference if the error was about the "substance" of the thing, the coat, as opposed to the error being about a "substantial quality" of the thing, the coat? *See* La. Civ. Code arts. 1950 and 1967. Or was there an even more serious error as to the nature of contract?

3. Lines 51 *et seq*.: Should it matter that one party is a professional, a merchant? Is the court putting an undue burden on the furrier? If you answer in the affirmative, is there any acceptable justification? Should that justification be extended to all professionals? *See* lines 67 *et seq*. Where the court says that "Abel—the furrier—is the expert", is the court limiting its statement to this particular case of a furrier or should the court be understood to refer to all experts? Is there any impact on whether or not there was an offeror and an offeree? In lines 62/63–68, is the court suggesting that whoever speaks in a technical language is under a duty to make that language understandable to the average consumer? Could that duty, if any, fall under the principle of good faith under Louisiana Civil Code article 1759?

Mrs. Corinne Clohecy WISE, Widow of Daniel J. Wise,
v.
Vester PRESCOTT et al.
Supreme Court of Louisiana
March 25, 1963
151 So.2d 356

HAWTHORNE, Justice.

This suit arose out of an intersectional collision at St. Roch Avenue and North Miro Street in New Orleans, between a passenger bus owned by New Orleans Public Service, Inc., and operated by one of its employees, Harry J. Miller, Jr., and a car driven by Vester Prescott.

[....]

The plaintiff, Mrs. Corinne Clohecy Wise, a fare-paying passenger on the bus, who received injuries as a result of this collision, instituted suit for damages for physical injuries, claiming that the collision was caused by the concurring negligence of both Miller, the bus driver, and Prescott, the driver of the automobile. [**The trial court ruled in Mrs. Wise's favor against all defendants**]. [....]

All defendants appealed to the Court of Appeal, Fourth Circuit. That court concluded at [*sic*] to Prescott and his insurer Allstate that plaintiff had entered into a transaction or compromise with these two defendants under which they had paid plaintiff $105.00, and that this compromise barred her action against these two defendants [...] and [**the court**] dismissed plaintiff's suit against Prescott and Allstate Insurance Company. See 142 So.2d 613.

[....] The [**writ**] application of Mrs. Wise was granted to review the Court of Appeal's holding that the release signed by her was a compromise which barred her action against Prescott and Allstate. [....]

1
2
3
4
5
6
7
8
9
10
11
12
13
14
15
16
17
18
19
20
21
22
23
24
25
26

[....]

On the Question of Liability of Public Service

[....]

Insofar as Public Service and Miller are concerned, the law applicable to the case was correctly stated by the Court of Appeal thus:

'The mere showing of injury to a farepaying passenger on a public conveyance and his failure to reach his destination safely establishes a prima facie case of negligence and imposes the burden on the carrier of convincingly overcoming such case. Adams v. Great American Indemnity Company, La.App., 116 So.2d 307; Johnson v. Continental Southern Lines, Inc., La.App., 113 So.2d 114, 74 A.L.R.2d 1328; Coleman v. Continental Southern Lines, Inc., La.App., 107 So.2d 69; Peters v. City of Monroe, La.App., 91 So.2d 428.

'A public carrier of passengers while not an insurer is required to exercise the highest degree of vigilance, care and precaution for the safety of those it undertakes to transport and is liable for the slightest negligence. Gross v. Teche Lines, Inc., 207 La. 354, 21 So.2d 378. The carrier must do all that human sagacity and foresight can do under the circumstances, in view of the character and mode of conveyance adopted, to prevent injury to passengers, the carrier being held liable for the slightest negligence with reference to the exercise of such care. Mire v. Lafourche Parish School Board, La., 62 So.2d 541.'

[....]

In view of the high degree of care required of public carriers toward their fare-paying passengers, the vigilance and prudence that must be exercised in the face of a slow sign, and the fact that the burden is on the carrier to show its freedom from negligence, we cannot say that the jury and the Court of Appeal erred in holding Public Service and Miller liable. The bus driver's complete lack of awareness of the Prescott car's approach under the circumstances of this case appears to us to be sufficient to justify the conclusion that he and Public Service failed to prove that he was maintaining the proper lookout, vigilance, and caution required at this intersection. Consequently we conclude that Public Service and Miller have not sustained the burden required under the law of overcoming the prima facie case of negligence against them.

[....]

On the Validity of the Release by Mrs. Wise of Prescott and His Insurer Allstate

The release in this case is a printed form, bears the signature of Mrs. Wise, and recites a consideration of 105.00.[1] Its language is broad, general, and all-inclusive, and it contains such expressions as 'release and forever discharge', 'all claims' for 'damages' 'sustained', or 'may hereafter sustain', 'consequences not now anticipated', 'all unknown and unanticipated injuries and damages'.

The negligence of Prescott is conceded and is no longer an issue in the case. Prescott and his insurer, Allstate Insurance Company, seek to evade liability on the theory that no judgment can be rendered against them because all matters in dispute between them and plaintiff were settled by the release, which is a transaction or compromise and as between

---

1. Prior to instituting suit plaintiff tendered this amount of Allstate, but it was refused.

the parties has the force equal to the authority of the thing adjudged under Articles 3071 and 3078 of the Civil Code.

Plaintiff Mrs. Wise, who was over 70 years old when the accident occurred, gave the following version relating to the procuring of the release: As a result of the collision she was thrown to the floor of the bus. Immediately afterwards she was taken to Charity Hospital, where X-rays were made and medication given her for pain. She spent the night in her apartment but did not sleep because of the pain in her head, and the medication made her 'woozy'. The next morning she was bruised and sore all over, and her face and eyes were bruised and swollen. She did not feel well enough to get around, and a neighbor came to look after her while she reclined in an easy chair. That afternoon at about 3:30 an adjuster from Allstate, on his own solicitation, came to her apartment and was admitted by the neighbor. The adjuster did not report himself to be such, and no insurance company was mentioned. This young man, who was nice and friendly, told Mrs. Wise that he came in behalf of Mr. Prescott, who had been worrying about her and felt sorry for her because of her age and wanted to give her some money to help with the X-rays and medical bills. She asked him whether this would have anything to do with the case, and he answered, 'No.' She would not have signed the document presented to her if she had known it was a release. She signed the paper which he told her was to show her thanks to Prescott and to show his good faith in representing Prescott. She could not read what was on the paper she signed because her glasses had been broken in the accident and she could not read without them. She had an extra pair but did not know where they were, and in any event her face was so swollen that she could not have gotten them on. No copy of the paper she signed was left with her.

On the other hand, the adjuster's version was this: He told the plaintiff he was a claims agent for the insurance company and wanted to negotiate a settlement. Mrs. Wise accepted the $105.00 he offered her without hesitation or complaint, there was no discussion about the amount, and there was no discussion about liability or fault as the release taken denied any liability of Prescott and Allstate. He thought Mrs. Wise read the release because she held it in front of her long enough to do so. The entire negotiations were consummated in about 15 minutes.

It is obvious that the testimony of Mrs. Wise and that of the adjuster are in conflict. This case, as stated previously, was tried before a jury. The jury pursuant to a specific question of the court found that the release was invalid, and the trial judge refused to grant defendants a new trial. The jury was called upon to determine the credibility of the witnesses and the weight to be given to their testimony, and it is apparent from their finding that the release was invalid that they accepted Mrs. Wise's version of the procuring of the release.

According to Mrs. Wise's testimony, accepted by the jury, she took the money in the belief that it was a gift from Prescott and that the document she signed was a receipt for the money, and she signed the document under the assurance that it would not have anything to do with her case. The question is whether under these facts the jury's finding that the release was invalid was correct as a matter of law.

This kind of release is often called in personal injury cases a 'rush release', and is executed in a situation wherein there exists a high potential of error. Recognizing this great possibility for error inherent in rush releases, the legislatures of at least seven states have passed measures affecting their validity, and two of these have expressly labeled them as 'crimes against public policy'. Connecticut in 1959, and Vermont and Idaho in 1961, enacted statutes permitting persons receiving personal injuries in accidents to repudiate and

115 void any settlement or release entered into within 15 days of the injury.[2] Maryland enacted
116 a similar provision in 1955 with a five-day period from the injury,[3] and North Dakota
117 since 1943 has had a statute with a 30-day period.[4] In Massachusetts since 1950 any set-
118 tlement or release obtained from a hospital patient within 15 days of the injury is null
119 and void unless the injured party indicates his consent in writing at least five days prior
120 to the procuring of the release.[5] Maine's similar provision enacted in 1959 provides that
121 a settlement or release obtained within 10 days of the injury is null and void.[6]

122   Up to this time the Legislature of our state has not enacted any law to protect persons
123 suffering personal injuries from the possibility of error inherent in quick releases, com-
124 promises, or settlements, and this court would not be justified in law in declaring a 'rush
125 release' invalid simply because it was obtained within a very short time of the accident.
126 In such cases, however, we feel that we are justified in recognizing that high potential for
127 error in our consideration of all the facts and circumstances connected with the execu-
128 tion of this type of release.

129   The adjuster here sought out Mrs. Wise within 24 hours of the accident, after she
130 had spent a sleepless and painful night, while she needed someone to attend her, while
131 she was feeling sore and miserable from the injuries she had received in the accident, and
132 at a time when she, especially because of her age, could not reasonably have been ex-
133 pected to have recovered from the nervousness and upset which follow such an experi-
134 ence. According to the adjuster the whole conversation with Mrs. Wise lasted about 15
minutes.

135   The facts and circumstances of the execution of the release in the instant case, in our
136 opinion, clearly justify the finding of the jury, concurred in by the judge, that Mrs. Wise
137 executed the release through error, and that she signed it reasonably believing it to be a
138 receipt for a gift from Prescott and believing that it would not have anything to do with
139 her case. Her error is one recognized under the general articles of our Civil Code on
140 Obligations as 'Error as to the Nature of the contract' which will render it void, La.Civ.Code
141 Art. 1841. (Italics ours.)

142 The judgment of the Court of Appeal dismissing plaintiff's suit against Vester Prescott
143 and Allstate Insurance Company is annulled and set aside[.] [....]

Questions

1. After you have read this case carefully, can you identify the nature of the legal sources
    of the multiple legal relationships created? For example, was the source of one rela-
    tionship a contract? The source of another, a delict/tort? Or was it the law, a statute/

---

2. The Connecticut statute, C.G.S.A., s 52-572a, expressly forbids the negotiation of any contract
with the injured person by one having an adverse interest within 15 days of the 'tortious act'. No limitation is made as to time within which such a reprobated contract may be avoided. The Vermont
statute, 12 V.S.A. 1076, provides a three-year limitation for disavowal; Idaho's, 5 Idaho Code s 29-
113, provides a one-year period for disavowal.

3. 7 Annotated Code of Maryland (1957), Art. 79, s 11. A short 60-day period is allowed for void-
ing the release.

4. 1 North Dakota Century Code Annotated, ss 9-08-08, 9-08-09. The contract may be avoided
within six months.

5. M.G.L.A., c. 271, s 44. Massachusetts classifies it under the chapter heading 'crimes against
public policy'.

6. 4 Rev'd Stats of Maine (1954), c. 137, s 49-A. Maine classifies the matter also under the heading 'crimes against public policy'.

code articles? To be prepared to answer some questions, read some code articles on donations (La. Civ. Code arts. 1541–1551), on solidarity (La. Civ. Code arts. 1786–1806), and on compromise (La. Civ. Code arts. 3071–3083).

2. Lines 32 *et seq.*: What kind of obligation is identified in the legal expression of this statement: "the mere showing of injury to a fare paying passenger ... establishes a prima facie case of negligence...."?

3. Lines 69 *et seq.*: Consider very carefully the fact that the title of this paragraph and the court's legal analysis refer to "Prescott and His Insurer Allstate", two parties therefore. Under what kind(s) of obligation(s) could any two of the following parties be bound one vis-à-vis another: Mrs. Wise, Prescott, the insurance company, NOPSI? Would a release or discharge have the same or different effects on the kind(s) of obligations you have identified (joint v. solidary)? Look carefully at Louisiana Civil Code articles 1802 and 1803. Is a release or renunciation of solidarity the same thing as a remission of debt? What about a release of a joint obligor? A remission of debt to a joint obligor? Do you see now why you were asked, above, to read the Louisiana Civil Code articles on compromise?

4. Lines 104 *et seq.*: Was it possible that Mrs. Wise made an error? If you answer affirmatively, is it error as to: the nature of a legal document; the legal effects of that document; or the person of the other party to the document? What could be the impact of Louisiana Civil Code articles 3079, 3080, and 3082?

5. Lines 109 *et seq.*: There is no rush release law in Louisiana but can "facts and circumstances connected with the execution of this type of release" be indicative of error on the part of the party under pressure to grant a release? What kind of standard, *in abstracto* or in *concreto*, is the court applying here to Mrs. Wise? Could the Court have required, as it did in the *Deutschmann* case, the expert to explain to Mrs. Wise what the document actually was intended to be? Could the silence of the insurance agent amount to fraud? *See* La. Civ. Code arts. 1953–1958.

Daniel G. GRIFFIN, d/b/a Checkwriter Service Co.
v.
SEISMIC SERVICES, INC.
Louisiana Court of Appeal
First Circuit
Feb. 24, 1972
259 So.2d 923

LANDRY, Judge.

This appeal by plaintiff, Daniel G. Griffin (Appellant), is from the judgment of the trial court rejecting his demands against defendant, Seismic Services, Inc. (Appellee), for specific performance of a contract to sell a checkwriting machine[....] The trial court rejected Appellant's demand for specific performance upon finding that Appellee's agreement to purchase a checkwriter from Appellant was vitiated by errors of fact, namely, that Michot was mistaken with regard to the make of machine offered for sale by Appellant, and as to the manufacturer whom Appellant allegedly represented. We affirm.

Appellant maintains the lower court erred in the following respects [, **among others**] [....] believing the testimony of Appellee's witnesses rather than that of Appellant; [....]

18   admitting parol evidence to vary the terms of a written document, namely, a purchase order
19   signed by Michot[;] and (4) finding that any error of fact existed.

20   It is conceded that for several years prior to August 11, 1970, Appellant was selfemployed
21   as a salesman of several types of office machines, principally checkwriters. At one time,
22   Appellant represented Paymaster Corporation, manufacturer of a checkwriter bearing
23   the brand name Paymaster. Each time Appellant sold a checkwriter, he also sold or attempted
24   to sell the purchaser a policy of insurance against fraudulent use of the machine. Michot,
25   President of defendant corporation, also owned and controlled several other companies
26   which he operated out of a single office. In his businesses, Michot used a Paymaster check-
27   writer. Approximately one or two years prior to the sale in question, Appellant called on
28   Michot, ascertained that Michot's insurance contract on his Paymaster had another year
29   or two to run and made some minor adjustments on the Paymaster checkwriter. Appel-
30   lant did not attempt to sell Michot a new checkwriter at this time. On an undisclosed
31   date prior to August 11, 1970, Appellant's authority to represent Paymaster Corporation
32   was terminated. On August 11, 1970, Appellant sold Michot an F & E checkwriter for the
33   price of $95.00, and a new insurance policy on the machine. Later that same day, Michot
34   learned that Appellant no longer represented Paymaster, and that the machine he purchased
35   was not a Paymaster. Michot stopped payment on the check issued to Appellant, and
36   wrote the insurance company canceling the contract on the ground that Appellant falsely
37   represented himself to be the agent of Paymaster Corporation.

38   In essence, Appellant testified that approximately one week prior to the sale, he called
39   at Michot's office and introduced himself to Michot's secretary, Paula Van Ness, as 'Dan
40   Griffin, Checkwriter Service.' Michot was not in at the time. Approximately one week
41   later, on August 11, 1970, he returned, introduced himself in the same manner, and was
42   ushered into Michot's private office. He introduced himself to Michot as 'Dan Griffin,
43   Checkwriter Service', and began his sales routine. Michot produced his old checkwriter
44   and Appellant demonstrated certain defects in the machine, primarily, how numbers
45   printed by the old Paymaster could be altered. Appellant then took out a new F & E check-
46   writer, demonstrated the machine and explained its advantages over the old Paymaster model.
47   He answered Michot's numerous questions about the machine, and also pointed out that
48   the F & E machine was slightly more expensive than a Paymaster. He told Michot, how-
49   ever, that if Michot bought the new F & E machine and renewed his insurance, Appel-
50   lant would sell Michot the F & E checkwriter for $95.00 and pay the tax involved. Michot
51   then wrote a check for $95.00 payable to Dan Griffin, Checkwriter Service, and Appel-
52   lant requested Michot to sign a purchase order for the machine. At first, Michot declined
53   to sign the order stating that it was unnecessary since he had given a check in payment.
54   Appellant, however, insisted that a signed purchase order was required by the manufac-
55   turer of the machine, where-upon Michot signed the document which covered the sale
56   of an F & E checkwriter. Appellant denied that he represented himself to Miss Van Ness
57   and Michot as a representative of Paymaster Corporation. Appellant vigorously contended
58   he made it clear to Michot that the machine involved was an F & E checkwriter, not a
59   Paymaster.

60   Michot's testimony, in substance, is that he is an extremely busy executive. He had
61   used a Paymaster checkwriter in his several businesses for years and was satisfied with
62   the service it gave. On the day in question, his secretary informed him that a represen-
63   tative of Paymaster Corporation wished to see him. Plaintiff entered the office introduc-
64   ing himself as Daniel Griffin with Paymaster, and indicated it was time for renewal of
65   Michot's insurance on his checkwriter. Appellant explained the advantages of the new
66   machine, and Michot assumed it was a Paymaster. Michot did not examine the new ma-

chine. He was extremely busy at the time in that he answered several telephone and radio   67
calls within the 15 to 20 minutes interval Griffin was present. In essence Michot testified   68
he would not have dealt with Griffin knowing that Griffin did not represent Paymaster   69
Corporation, and would not have knowingly purchased any checkwriter other than a   70
Paymaster. By coincidence, the Paymaster representative called at Michot's office ap-   71
proximately two hours after Griffin left. Upon learning that he had not purchased a Pay-   72
master machine, Michot called his bank and stopped payment on the check given Appellant.   73
Michot explained that he made the check payable to Dan Griffin, Checkwriter Service, be-   74
cause Griffin requested it be made that way. He also stated he thought he was buying a   75
Paymaster checkwriter when he signed the purchase order which he did not read.   76

Miss Van Ness testified simply that when Appellant called at her employee's office, he   77
introduced himself as a representative of Paymaster Corporation, and she in turn intro-   78
duced plaintiff to Mr. Michot as a Paymaster representative.   79

[....]   80

[**After discussing the applicability of res ipsa loquitur, the court turned to the other**   81
asserted errors.] It is settled jurisprudence that the credibility of witnesses is a matter   82
within the sound discretion of the trier of fact who has the opportunity to personally ob-   83
serve the witnesses and judge their demeanor, reaction and responses. For these reasons,   84
the findings of the trier of fact will not be disturbed on appeal unless found to be man-   85
ifestly erroneous. Murphy v. Piro, La.App., 240 So.2d 111. In this instance, the trial court   86
accepted the testimony of defendant's witnesses.   87

In oral reasons dictated into the record, the trial court accepted the testimony of Miss   88
Van Ness and Michot to the effect that plaintiff represented himself to be the agent of   89
Paymaster Corporation. The trial court likewise concluded that Michot would not have   90
dealt with plaintiff knowing that plaintiff did not represent Paymaster Corporation and   91
neither would Michot have intentionally purchased a checkwriter which was not a Pay-   92
master product. In view of the record, we cannot say that the lower court erred in either   93
conclusion.   94

Neither, do we find any error in the trial court's admission of parol evidence to con-   95
tradict the purchase order which called for the sale of an F & E machine. Notwithstand-   96
ing LSA-C.C. art. 2275, which prohibits the admission of parol evidence to vary the terms   97
of a written document, parol evidence is admissible to contradict a written instrument   98
where fraud or error is alleged. Gulf States Finance Corporation v. Airline Auto Sales,   99
Inc., 248 La. 591, 181 So.2d 36. We find, as did the trial court that defendant has estab-   100
lished the error alleged.   101

Under our law and jurisprudence, a contract may be avoided for unilateral error as to   102
the substance of some substantial quality of the subject matter of the agreement where   103
the other party was apprised of the motive of the contract or where, from the nature and   104
circumstances of the transaction, it must be presumed the other party was aware of the   105
error. Jefferson Truck Equipment Co., Inc. v. Guarisco Motor Co., Inc., La.App., 250   106
So.2d 211, and authorities therein cited. The requisite consent to a contract is lacking   107
where an error of fact exists. LSA-C.C. arts. 1819 and 1820. To avoid a contract, an error   108
of fact must pertain to the principal cause for making the agreement, meaning the error   109
must exist either as to the motive for making the agreement or the person with whom the   110
agreement is made, or to the subject matter of the contract itself. LSA-C.C. art. 1823;   111
Jefferson Truck Equipment Co., Inc., above. Error as to the qualities of an object serves   112
to vitiate a contract if such qualities constitute the principal cause for making the agree-   113
ment. LSA-C.C. art. 1845.   114

115   We find, as did the trial court, that Michot was in error as to the person with whom
116   he was making the agreement, and also as to the nature of the object of the agreement.
117   We likewise agree with the implied finding of the trial court that plaintiff either knew of
118   the mistakes under which Michot was laboring or because of the circumstances, it must
119   be presumed plaintiff was aware of Michot's error. Under these circumstances, the error
120   on the purchaser's part vitiates the contract.

121   The judgment of the trial court is affirmed at appellant's cost.

122   Affirmed.

123   ON REHEARING

124   Rehearing denied.

125   BLANCHE, Judge (dissenting)

126   The majority correctly states the law concerning when a contract may be avoided for
127   unilateral error but is in error for failing to consider what plaintiff, Daniel G. Griffin,
128   knew or should have known. There is not even a suggestion by the evidence in the record
129   that Griffin either knew or should have known that defendant's president and general
130   manager, T. Warren Michot, wanted a Paymaster checkwriter and only a Paymaster check-
131   writer. Therefore, being unable to presume that Griffin was aware of Michot's error, I
132   think the contract should not be avoided.

133   While Michot may have been in error as to the person with whom he was dealing, he
134   should not have been in error as to the quality of the object of the contract. The pre-
135   ponderance of the evidence is that Michot should have known what he was purchasing.
136   It is uncontradicted that the qualities of both the F & E checkwriter which Michot pur-
137   chased and the Paymaster checkwriter were discussed. The two machines were side by
138   side on Michot's desk and bore distinguishable physical characteristics and lettering iden-
139   tifying the brand of each. Added to this is the fact that Michot signed an invoice show-
140   ing that he purchased an F & E checkwriter. The majority excuses Michot for being in
141   error as to the object of the contract by first finding that Griffin misrepresented himself
142   as an agent of Paymaster and then finding that Michot was a very busy man, talking on
143   the telephone and over the radio while Griffin was trying to sell him a checkwriter. If he
144   was too busy to hear what Griffin was telling him and if he did not bother to notice the
145   distinctly different machines placed before him and if he did not read the invoice show-
146   ing the type of checkwriter he was purchasing, he should be estopped from claiming that
147   he acted under an error because of the significant contribution he made thereto. There
148   is no reason to excuse Michot from not reading what he signed or not seeing what he
149   should have seen just because as an extremely busy executive he did not have sufficient
150   time for a ninety-five dollar checkwriter deal.

151   I am of the opinion that judgment should be rendered for the plaintiff for the pur-
152   chase price of the checkwriter, and to that extent I would reverse the judgment of the dis-
153   trict court.

Questions

1.   Lines 9 *et seq.*: Do you have any comment regarding the identity of the parties in-
     volved in this case? Should that identity have any bearing on the degree of knowl-
     edge expected from the parties when expressing their consent? The trial court
     ruled for the defendant on the ground of errors of fact. What errors of fact can you
     identify?

2. Lines 9 *et seq.*: Could the plaintiff have been guilty of fraud? *See* La. Civ. Code art. 1953–1958. Did Michot act reasonably in light of his status?

3. Lines 102 *et seq.*: Can a unilateral error lead to a contract being avoided? What does the word "unilateral" actually mean? Is it a misnomer?

4. Lines 115 *et seq.*: The Court of Appeal finds "that Michot was in error as to the person...." What do you think, keeping in mind the identity or status of the parties involved, was the particular feature of the "person" of the plaintiff salesman, Griffin, that was the ground of the error as to the person made by Michot? How much, if at all, did Michot contribute to his own error? In an onerous contract, such as a sale in this case, should error as to the person of the seller be as easily acceptable and be a ground for nullity of the contract as in a gratuitous contract such as a donation? Read Louisiana Civil Code article 1954 on fraud. Could Michot have ascertained the truth without difficulty? Even if Griffin committed no fraud but only knew that Michot was in error, should Griffin have the right to show that Michot would have had no difficulty in ascertaining the truth about the machine and, thus, about the company he now represented? What do you think now of the dissenting opinion on lines 125 *et seq.*?

Robert R. BOUCHER, A. C. Wilkinson, Jules R. Gueymard
v.
DIVISION OF EMPLOYMENT SECURITY, DEPARTMENT OF LABOR of the State of Louisiana

Louisiana Court of Appeal
First Circuit
Nov. 16, 1964
169 So.2d 674

ELLIS, Judge.

The three appellants, whose cases were consolidated for trial, have appealed from a ruling of the Commission affirming their discharge by J. Hadley Heard, Administrator of the Division of Employment Security, in accordance with letter of removal dated October 19, 1954 and we quote the material portion of this letter:

"You are hereby advised that a decision has been reached to terminate your services with this Department because evidence available to this Department discloses that you submitted *a false and fraudulent claim for travel expenses* during the period May 15, 1950–June 8, 1950. This termination will be effective at the close of business on June 24, 1953.

"In reaching this decision, careful consideration was given to your sworn statement of June 11, 1953, along with other information and evidence available to this Department. *It was recognized that you may have received commitments for the reimbursement of funds in the approximate amount for which you submitted a false and fraudulent claim and that coercion and intimidation may have been exercised in causing you to incur expenses for which you desired reimbursement,* but the conclusion that you had submitted a false and fraudulent expense claim was inescapable. Of necessity, consideration was given to the effect of this act on public opinion and employee morale. Accordingly, your removal is considered to be for such cause as to be in the best interest of this Department.

"As you have the right to appeal to the Civil Service Commission, there is attached for your information a copy of Chapter 13 of the Civil Service Rules.

s/ J. Hadley Heard

Administrator"

(Emphasis added)

The facts in the three cases under consideration are substantially and materially identical with those in the case of Colvin v. Division of Employment Security, La.App., 132 So.2d 909, which was decided by this court and in which the Supreme Court of the State of Louisiana denied certiorari. In that case, as in this, relator had appealed from a ruling of the Commission affirming his discharge, which grew out of one of the same incidents and the charge was the same, of filing a false and fraudulent expense account. Colvin obtained a severance or separate trial from the relators herein. The facts in the Colvin case show that in the year 1950 he and relator herein, A. C. Wilkinson, were selected to attend a convention in Omaha. Both said they could not afford to make the trip and upon the assurance and insistence of Mr. Marvin A. Thames, then Administrator of the Department, that they go and their expenses would be paid by the agency as he had cleared that question with the Regional Office of the United States Department of Labor, Bureau of Employment Security, as under the agency rules in effect at that time, advance written authority was required for such a trip to be made at agency expense, they proceeded to the convention in Omaha, Nebraska. Colvin and Wilkinson returned from the Omaha trip about May 1, 1950. Subsequent to their return, the facts as they affect the relators in the case now at bar on this appeal are practically identical with those in the Colvin case, supra. This court in the Colvin case held that while the findings of fact by the Commission, when based on evidence supporting the discharge of an employee for a valid cause, are not subject to review by this court, which we must do under the law, as appellate courts are restricted upon appeals from the Civil Service Commission to questions of law, nevertheless, taking the entire testimony and facts as found by the Commission, Colvin's 'dismissal' was without valid cause for the reasons therein stated, namely that he had filed a false and fraudulent claim for travel expenses during the period May 15, 1950–June 8, 1950.

While we feel that the judgment of this court in the Colvin case, supra, is controlling and decisive as the facts therein, and herein, are on all material questions of fact identical, we deem it necessary for a clear understanding of this decision that we proceed to a full discussion of these particular cases as they affect relators herein.

The facts of the case as found by the Civil Service Commission, as applicable to each of the relators herein, are as follows:

'FINDINGS OF FACT

'A. Boucher

'At the time of his dismissal, Boucher had attained permanent Civil Service status as an Employment Security Claims Investigator in the State Division of Employment Security. He had served the Division meritoriously since September 5, 1946, and he has an unblemished record for character and service during this period.

'In May, 1950, Marvin E. Thames, then Administrator of the Division, requested Boucher to attend an I.A.P.E.S. Convention in Long Beach, California. Boucher refused as he was unable to afford the expense of the trip. Thames advised Boucher that the trip could be made at agency expense. Under agency rules in effect at that time, advance written authority from the Dallas Regional Office of the United States Department of Labor, Bureau of Employment Security, was required for such a trip to be made at agency ex-

pense. Thames told Boucher that the Regional Office had authorized this trip, and Boucher 76
did not question the authority. There is no evidence that Boucher knew of the afore- 77
mentioned agency rules. Thames' testimony that the Regional Office granted its author- 78
ity by telephone prior to the departure of Boucher has not been contradicted. An advance 79
of $350 for expense was authorized by Thames and received by Boucher, who then attended 80
the Long Beach Convention. Upon their return from the convention, Thames advised 81
Boucher that the Regional Office had withdrawn its approval, and in Boucher's presence 82
Thames called the Dallas Office and spoke to one L. M. Crawford, who suggested that Boucher 83
execute an expense report for a Dallas trip, which would then be approved by the Re- 84
gional Office. This Boucher refused to do. Ultimately, at the suggestion of Thames, 85
Boucher prepared a travel expense report, showing certain trips in Louisiana which ac- 86
tually had never been made by Boucher. Annexed to this report were receipts with which 87
Boucher was not familiar. This report was apparently signed by Boucher, although Boucher 88
testified that he did not think he signed it. Boucher did endorse the check issued by the 89
Division on the strength of the report. Boucher actually spent, on the Long Beach trip, 90
the amount reported on the false travel expense report, which was the basis of his discharge. 91
He refunded a portion of this amount to the Division on or about December, 1950, and 92
the balance he refunded by certified check on or about May 22, 1953, and the Division 93
of Employment Security presently is holding this check, never having cashed same. 94

'B. Wilkinson 95

'At the time of his dismissal, Wilkinson had attained permanent Civil Service status as 96
an Employment Security District Supervisor in the State Division of Employment Secu- 97
rity. He had served the Division meritoriously since October 5, 1937, and he has an un- 98
blemished record for character and service during this period. 99

'In April, 1950, Marvin E. Thames, then Administrator of the Division, requested 100
Wilkinson to attend a Biannual Convention of the A.S.F.S. & M.E. being held in Omaha, 101
Nebraska. Wilkinson refused as he was unable to afford the expense of the trip. Thames 102
advised Wilkinson that the trip could be made at agency expense; whereupon Wilkinson 103
went on the trip to Omaha. Upon his return he was directed by Thames to render an ex- 104
pense account showing a trip to Dallas, Texas, not to Omaha, Nebraska, which Wilkin- 105
son did and was reimbursed by the agency for his expenses on the basis of a travel report 106
signed by him and approved by Marvin E. Thames, showing travel to Dallas from Lake 107
Charles covering the period 4-23-50 to 4-30-50. 108

'In May, 1950, Wilkinson was advised by Thames that he again wanted him to make 109
a trip at agency expense, this time to Long Beach, California, to attend the I.A.P.E.S. Con- 110
vention. Wilkinson made the trip and upon his return was again directed by Thames to 111
submit a travel report to Dallas, Texas, instead of to Long Beach, California. Wilkinson 112
submitted such a travel report showing a trip he did not take from Lake Charles to Dal- 113
las, Texas, and return covering the period 5-25-50 to 6-10-50 which report was approved 114
by Thames and paid by the agency. Prior to leaving for Long Beach, California, an advance 115
of $150 for expenses was authorized by Thames and received by Wilkinson and this 116
amount was deducted from his voucher when he received settlement of his purported 117
travel expense to Dallas, Texas. 118

'Wilkinson actually spent on his trip to Omaha the amount he claimed on the false 119
travel report he rendered showing a trip to Dallas, Texas, covering the period April 23, 1950, 120
to April 29, 1950, and actually spent on his trip to Long Beach California, the amount he 121
claimed on the second false travel report he rendered showing another trip to Dallas, 122
Texas, covering the period 5-25-50 to 6-10-50. On or about May 22, 1953, Wilkinson re- 123

funded to the agency by certified check the amount he had been paid for the purported trip to Dallas, Texas, which covered his actual expenses to Long Beach, California, and the agency is holding this check, never having cashed it. There is no evidence to show that he has made or attempted to make restitution of the amount he was paid for the first Dallas expense report.

'C. Gueymard

'At the time of his dismissal, Gueymard had attained permanent Civil Service status as an Employment Supervisor I in the State Division of Employment Security. He had served the Division meritoriously since March 16, 1936, and he has an unblemished record for character and service during this period.

'In May, 1950, Gueymard planned a trip to Long Beach, California, in his personal automobile to attend the I.A.P.E.S. Convention and, although not himself a delegate, was providing transportation for Mr. Macalusa, an official delegate and representative of the Division of Employment Security. They planned to travel from New Orleans to Long Beach by way of Houston, Texas. Gueymard did not contemplate, while first planning the trip with Macalusa, that he would be reimbursed by the agency any portion of his expense. However, at the request of Marvin E. Thames, then Administrator of the Division, he changed his plans and drove to California by way of Dallas, Texas, instead of Houston, so as to pick up a delegate to the convention who lived in Dallas. This change in plans was requested by Thames and with the approval of the Deputy Director of the Regional Office of the Bureau of Employment Security. Gueymard was told by Thames that he could claim reimbursement of expenses from New Orleans to Dallas and return. An advance of $250 for expenses was authorized by Thames and received by Gueymard before leaving Louisiana. Gueymard and his wife and Mr. Macalusa and his wife drove to Dallas where they were joined by the Texas delegate who accompanied them to California.

'Upon his return from the convention and other points on the West Coast which he visited, Gueymard was advised by Thames to execute an expense report showing a trip to Dallas, Texas and include thereon expenses for four or five days in Dallas, but to show dates different from the dates he was in Long Beach, California.

'He then filed a fraudulent expense report showing a trip on June 19, 1950, claiming reimbursement for use of his personal automobile at 7$ per mile plus meals and tips incurred while on the purported trip. While the evidence shows that he did travel to Dallas on his way to California, the evidence is equally clear that he did not remain in Dallas the number of days shown on his travel report and he did not make any trip at all to Dallas on the dates shown on his travel report.

'The expense report which he filed was approved by Thames and an agency check was written and delivered to Gueymard who endorsed it back to the agency. Gueymard also paid the agency the difference between the amount of this check and the amount of his travel advance. On or about May 22, 1953, Gueymard refunded to the agency the amount he had been paid for the Dallas trip and according to the record the certified check covering the refund is being held by the Division of Employment Security which has never cashed it.'

Under the above set of facts, the Commission found that the action of the employing authority in dismissing each of the relators from his employment on October 29, 1954 was for both a reasonable and legal cause.

There is no dispute as to the material facts in these cases which was also true in the Colvin case. The relators herein felt they were financially unable to make the trips involved in these expense accounts — Wilkinson to Omaha and California and the other relators to California and that they only went after being assured by the Administrator of the Division, Mr. Marvin E. Thames, that he had cleared the question of expenses with the federal agency in Dallas and that they could make the trip at agency expense. In accordance with this assurance, upon the insistence of Thames, they were advanced expense money and made this trip. Some time after their return, the question fo [*sic*] filing a detailed expense account came up, the Administrator informed them that the federal department in Dallas had in effect reversed itself and that expenses to California could not be approved, but he had discussed the matter with this agency, which in fact the record fully proves, and these parties were to file expense accounts as if they had gone to Dallas, Texas rather than Long Beach, California. All of them objected to this but Thames was so insistent that they felt to refuse would be probably fatal to their future as employees and as the record shows each had a long and meritorious service up to that time. They had reached an age of service and years that meant a great deal to their future security so they put Dallas on the expense account. Otherwise, the account was completely correct in that it contained nothing but the legitimate expenses that they had incurred in going to Long Beach, California and return. The record shows that the receipts attached to support Boucher's expense account were not even made up by him and he was not familiar with them. It is evident that Mr. J. Hadley Heard, the Administrator, who was appointed after a change in administrations, was quite familiar with the truth concerning the filing of the expense account by these relators which stated Dallas rather than Long Beach, California, for in his letter of dismissal he states '* * * that coercion and intimidation may have been exercised'. There is also positive testimony in the record that Heard was orally apologetic in talking to relators about their dismissal. He put it on the ground that he was on the hot seat and under great pressure. All in all, it doesn't appear from his testimony that he actually and really believed they were guilty of any fraud.

Furthermore, everybody in the Department knew about the whole thing, there was nothing hidden and the superiors who had to approve these accounts did so despite the fact that they were familiar with the situation, and these same employees continued in their employment without any question.

We believe that our discussion in the Colvin case is applicable and controlling in the cases under discussion and we quote therefrom:

'The basis of the decision of the Civil Service Commission in dismissing appellant was that he submitted 'a false and fraudulent claim for travel expenses.'

'(1) Upon our examination of the term 'fraud' or 'fraudulent' we find that two elements are essential to constitute legal fraud, the intention to defraud and loss or damage or a strong probability of loss or damage. Slocomb and others v. Real Estate Bank of Arkansas, 2 Rob. 92. A mere misrepresentation or in this instance, a false or incorrect account, is not synonymous with fraud as used in the legal sense. Buxton et al. v. McKendrick et al., 223 La. 62, 64 So.2d 844.

'The necessity for the combination of the two elements is emphasized in L.S.A.-Civil Code article 1847 in defining fraud as applied to contracts as:

'"Fraud, as applied to contracts, is the cause of an error bearing on a material part of the contract, created or continued by artifice, with design to obtain some unjust advantages to the one party, or to cause an inconvenience or loss to the other."

'(2) The uncontroverted facts present in the record and those findings of fact found by the Commission reveal that appellant had been selected to represent his agency at a meeting in Omaha, Nebraska, and that his travel expenses to attend said meeting would be paid by the agency. When he returned from the trip he filed the questioned account, including therein the actual expenses incurred by him in his trip to Omaha, but at the insistence and order of Marvin E. Thames, the then Administrator of the Division, he represented in the account the fact that the expenses were incurred in connection with a meeting in Dallas rather than in Omaha.

'Nowhere in the record is it shown that by the submission of the account did he acquire a profit or monies to which he was not entitled, nor is there any showing that by being reimbursed caused 'an inconvenience or loss' to the agency. There is not one iota of evidence in the record to even indicate that at the time he was selected for the trip to Omaha that such expenses incurred by him on said trip were not validly authorized and there is no evidence whatever that he had conspired with the Administrator of the agency to defraud, or that appellant alone intended or by artifice conceived a plan to gain an unjust advantage by the filing of the account. Though it is true that the account so filed, showing a trip to Dallas, Texas, is false in that respect, if the misrepresentation was made without the intention to defraud on the part of appellant and if the error did not gain appellant an advantage to which he was not due, it is evident that neither of the elements of fraud have been satisfied and thus the incorrect account is not fraudulent.

'Upon his severance from the Civil Service position the record reveals that there was deducted from his accrued earnings the $206.90 which was the total amount of the items expended by him on his trip to Omaha and itemized in the erroneous account filed representing that the items of expenses covered the trip to Dallas, Texas.

'We are of the opinion that upon appellant's reinstatement in his position, upon submission of a corrected travel account itemizing the expenses incurred by him on his trip to Omaha, he would be entitled to reimbursement of the amount of his expenses, which in itself is recognition by us that the questioned account was not fraudulent.'

[....]

In conclusion, we wish to add that the plan to substitute Dallas for Omaha and/or Long Beach, California, was agreed upon between Thames, the Louisiana Administrator who was indicted by the federal government for conspiring with William L. Crawford, Deputy Regional Director of the Federal Bureau of Employment Security at Dallas, Texas, to defraud the United States by means of the false reports in question[1] and the same William L. Crawford, both of whom continued in their jobs. Additionally, Ed McDonald, Regional Representative at the Federal Dallas office, whose written authorization for the fictitious travel to Dallas appears in the record, as late as December 1954 continued in his job as Director of the Federal Bureau of Employment Security at Dallas. Furthermore, the Boucher travel report was 'approved' by superior Jules L. Lamothe and Gueymard's by G. Messina, their immediate superiors who also knew that the trips were not made on the dates or to the places stated. They were still in service and testified. Also, Mr. L. M. Langford, Comptroller of the agency in charge of accounting for travel expenses, was still in office at the time of the hearing for dismissal, and he frankly admitted on the trial that he was fully and 'definitely' aware at all times that the travel was actually to Long Beach and to Omaha and not to Dallas and was aware of all the circumstances surrounding the trips, the expenses and the reports stating Dallas as the travel point. With this knowledge, he officially certified each travel report as 'Comptroller', certifying

'* * * that travel was authorized from and to the point stated; that it was on official business * * *.'

---

1. The federal indictment against Thames was dismissed by directed verdict.

He testified that he did this on the authority of Mr. Thames. In fact, there is no doubt   265
that all of these relators' superiors knew the facts and circumstances surrounding the re-   266
port and expense account which formed the basis for dismissal of relators. There was no   267
effort to conceal anything or to defraud anybody and the facts show that no one was de-   268
frauded and no artifice was practiced by relators.   269

Accepting the facts found by the Commission herein and additional facts which might   270
be stated in this report as proven by this record and which are not in conflict or contra-   271
diction of the facts found by the Commission, all of which is on all fours with the facts   272
in the Colvin case, and the reasons hereinabove given we do not believe that these rela-   273
tors were guilty of filing a false or fraudulent claim for travel expenses in the sense nec-   274
essary to constitute legal fraud as we emphasized in the Colvin case.   275

It is therefore ordered that the judgment appealed from is reversed, annulled, and set   276
aside, and judgment is hereby rendered reinstating Robert R. Boucher, appellant, in his   277
former position and there be judgment in his favor and against the Division of Employ-   278
ment Security for back pay from October 29, 1954 in accordance with law.   279

It is also ordered, adjudged and decreed that there be judgment rendered reinstating   280
A. C. Wilkinson, appellant, in his former position and awarding him judgment in his   281
favor and against the Division of Employment Security for back pay from October 29,   282
1954 in accordance with law.   283

It is also ordered, adjudged and decreed that the dismissal of Jules R. Gueymard, de-   284
ceased, is hereby decreed to have been illegal and that there now be judgment in favor of   285
Mrs. Ethel Dickinson, widow of Jules R. Gueymard, Testamentary Executrix of the Suc-   286
cession of Jules R. Gueymard, No. 411-161 of the Docket of the Civil District Court for   287
the Parish of Orleans, State of Louisiana, substituted party herein, and against the Divi-   288
sion of Employment Security for back pay from October 29, 1954 through January 23,   289
1963 in accordance with law.   290

REVERSED AND RENDERED.   291

Question

1.   Lines 197 *et seq.*: Notice how well the court coordinates former Louisiana Civil Code
     article 1847 and the two required elements of fraud with the holdings of some prior
     cases. Do you find the same two elements of fraud in Louisiana Civil Code article
     1953 today?

Curley WILSON   1

v.   2

AETNA CASUALTY & SURETY COMPANY   3

Louisiana Court of Appeal   4
Third Circuit   5
Oct. 30, 1969   6
228 So.2d 229   7

TATE, Judge.   8

The plaintiff Wilson sues for personal injuries. Made defendant is the liability insurer   9
of the motorist who struck him. The defendant appeals from adverse judgment awarding   10
$16,658.50 to Wilson, subject to a credit of $5,000 received by him on an earlier 'release'.   11

The substantial issue of this appeal is whether the trial court erred in overruling the defendant's exception pleading res judicata.[1] This plea is based upon Wilson's execution of this release on October 6, 1967 for $5,000, discharging the insurer from all claims arising out of the accident of May 22, 1967.

I.

The plaintiff contends, and the trial court held, that the release was invalid because there was no real consent of the plaintiff to the compromise, due to the intolerable physical and financial circumstances in which the plaintiff was situated and which destroyed his freedom of will. The defendant replies that this is not a cause recognized by our law for annulling a compromise. We find the defendant is correct.

A valid compromise has the 'authority of things adjudged'. Civil Code Article 3078. A compromise cannot be annulled for error of law or for lesion. Id. It may, however, be rescinded for fraud or violence, as well as for error of fact as to a principal cause (motive) for making the contract, as to the person with whom it is made, or as to the subject matter of the dispute. Civil Code Articles 3078, 3079; see also, Civil Code Articles 1824–1826, 1850–1853; Cole v. Lumbermens Mutual Cas. Co., 160 So.2d 785 (La.App.3d Cir. 1963); Note, Compromise in Louisiana, 14 Tul.L.Rev. 282 (1940).

The plaintiff apparently contends (a) that there was error as to the principal motive, in that he did not know his claim was worth far more than the $5,000 for which he settled it, and (b) that his will was vitiated by lack of consent through the violence or duress exercised upon him by external circumstances and by the misinformation from a third person that a lawyer could not help him. See Smith, A Refresher Course in Cause, 12 La.L.Rev. 2, 9–13 (1951). (No contention is made as to any fraud or deception by the insurer's adjuster, nor as to this adjuster's participation in or knowledge of any alleged misinformation causing the plaintiff to settle his claim.)

We accept the trial judge's findings of fact as to the circumstances surrounding the execution of the release:

'Plaintiff was 66 years old on the date of the accident and is classified as illiterate. He has no wife nor children and his only relatives consist of an aged and almost helpless mother and a sister who live in an adjoining parish. The only person that visited plaintiff with regularity during his 140 days in the hospital was Mrs. Lenad Enard with whom plaintiff boarded prior to the accident and who undertook to care for and nurse plaintiff when he was released from the hospital.

'On the Monday or Tuesday prior to the signing of the settlement on Friday, Mr. Wheeldon (defendant's adjuster) offered plaintiff $5,000.00 in settlement of the claim. Plaintiff turned this down and made a counter offer of $10,000.00. Mr. Wheeldon refused that but told plaintiff that if he changed his mind he could notify him and he would receive $5,000.00 less the amounts owed to the hospital and physicians.

'Prior to this time plaintiff had made an effort to get an attorney, but (for some reason or other) no attorney was consulted. Dr. Louis E. Shirley, Jr., plaintiff's physician, is of the impression that he talked to an attorney about the claim but cannot recall the attorney. Dr. Shirley did advise plaintiff that the only way he

---

1. We may say that the evidence supports the trial court's findings of the motorist's undoubted negligence, of Wilson's freedom from contributory negligence, and of the award for Wilson's serious permanent injuries—issues we need not discuss, in view of our holding that res judicata bars the suit.

could get prompt settlement was to take the amount offered; that if plaintiff employed an attorney it would take a year or more to have the suit tried; and, further, that he would have to pay a substantial fee for the attorney and might not get a great deal more than the $5,000.00 offered.

'Dr. Shirley also advised plaintiff that it was time for him to be discharged from the hospital; that Charity Hospital would not accept him as a patient; that if plaintiff was not discharged from the hospital his hospital bill would increase at the rate of approximately $30.00 per day; and that medicare benefits were exhausted.

'Plaintiff's bill at that time was already $3,268.00, and his doctor bill was approximately $900.00, of which medicare had paid approximately $2,200.00.

'Plaintiff had just recently been released from traction and was then casted from his hip to his toes on his left leg, and with another cast on his right hip down to his knee, which immobilized his hip. Plaintiff was immobilized during his entire hospital stay. It is obvious that plaintiff needed nursing attention and, furthermore, that he needed physical therapy. * * *'

Some additional facts of relevance include:

— The plaintiff's normal income is limited to his monthly social security payments plus whatever income he can derive from doing odd jobs around Jennings. Prior to his accident, this 66-year-old laborer received $92 monthly from social security and approximately $40 weekly from odd jobs. Since the accident he receives $97 monthly from social security, but he has been unable to accept employment.

— Signing the release and compromising his claim enabled plaintiff to pay Mrs. Enard $40 weekly — as long as the money from the settlement lasted — to care for him. Had he not been able to pay, she would have been unable to care for him, and he had no place else to stay or to be cared for in his helpless condition.

III.

Plaintiff's principal arguments for annulling the release arise from:

— The economic straits plaintiff faced once his discharge from the hospital became imminent. Dr. Shirley testified: 'He felt like he had no place to go.'

— The influence on plaintiff's decision to settle exerted by third persons who, plaintiff claims, had an overriding interest in an early settlement — particularly the attending physician, who said: 'I may have influenced him more than I should have. By this, I mean, I did emphasize to him that he could either get the lawyer and make the settlement in a year or two, or either he could settle and have his money to go on now.', and

— The fact that plaintiff, though he knew the advice of an attorney was desirable, did not consult one prior to making the settlement.

In annulling the release, our brother at trial was noticeably moved by the difficulties of plaintiff's situation:

'(S)ince we are dealing with an illiterate, aged plaintiff with no family, who was under serious financial pressure and in the intolerable position of having to leave the hospital; having to pay a hospital bill; having to pay for future nursing care, and having only one source to raise funds, and who was not advised by any attorney, this Court holds that the release was signed in error and must be annulled. * * * (T)he more thought given to the intolerable and untenable position

in which this plaintiff found himself, the more convinced this Court is that the
release must be set aside.'

IV.

Nevertheless—despite these reasons which indicate that the plaintiff Wilson had no
bargaining power to resist the defendant's offer and was instead under strong economic
duress to accept it—, we are unable to find that these constitute a ground recognized by
our law for the rescission of a compromise.

Louisiana Civil Code Articles 1851 through 1853 provide that a contract entered into
under duress that would cause fear of great injury to person, reputation, or fortune is
invalid, even if the person favored by the contract did not exercise the violence or make
the threats and was unaware of the duress. A compromise is subject to rescission when
executed under such duress. Civil Code Article 3079.

However, the contract—invalidating duress referred to is that which proceeds from a
fear of force or violence which wipes out freedom of consent; it connotes an actor performing an exterior act which gives rise to the duress, rather than the entire set of objective
circumstances causing the victim to act as he does. Planiol, Civil Law Treatise, Volume
1, Nos. 277, 278 (LSLI translation, 1959); Ibid, Volume 2, Nos. 1070, 1072; Aubry &
Rau, Obligations, Section 343a (1 Civil Law Translations 314, LSLI translation, 1959);
Holstein, Vices of Consent in the Law of Contracts, 13 Tul.L.Rev. 362 and 561 at 569–79
(1939). No doctrinal or jurisprudential authority to the contrary is cited.

The duress here relied upon does not constitute a Code-recognized ground to rescind
a compromise.

Nor did the advice of Dr. Shirley amount to duress. There was no element of threatening the plaintiff's person or property. The doctor simply counselled the patient that
settlement under the circumstances was in the latter's best interest. By itself, the bad advice of a stranger to the compromise is not ground for rescinding it. LeBlanc v. Brou,
205 So.2d 141 (La.App.1st Cir. 1967).

V.

The plaintiff-appellee cites numerous decisions. We find they concern situations differentiated from the present.

This is not a case of error as to the nature of the contract. Civil Code Article 1841;
Wise v. Prescott, 244 La. 157, 151 So.2d 356 (1963); Bergeron v. Port Allen Mortuary,
Inc., 178 So.2d 442 (La.App.1st Cir. 1965). The present plaintiff knew he was executing
a settlement of his claim for personal injuries, and that the document he signed was a release in full.

Nor was the plaintiff in error as to the person with whom he was contracting or as to
the matter in dispute. Civil Code Articles 3073, 3079; Moak v. American Auto. Ins. Co.,
242 La. 160, 134 So.2d 911 (1961); Harris v. Stockman, 197 So.2d 365 (La.App.2d Cir. 1967).
The plaintiff knew that Mr. Wheeldon was the defendant's adjuster, and that he himself
was compromising all claims arising out of the accident causing his injury. He did not think
the settlement merely for medical expenses, as in Harris, but knew that it included all
claims for damages for personal injury. He received a sum noticeably in excess of accrued
medical costs to him.

A release may also be rescinded for error as to the principal cause or motive, i.e., 'that
consideration without which the contract would not have been made.' Civil Code Article
1825; McKneely v. Turner, 193 So.2d 373 (La.App.2d Cir. 1966). The plaintiff knew that

he was releasing his claim against the defendant and granting a full discharge in return   147
for being paid $5,000 immediately. He was not acting under any error of fact as to prin-   148
cipal cause of the contract.   149

Error as to a material though not the principal cause may also be ground for annul-   150
ment of a contract, but only if the other party knew or, from the circumstances, should   151
have known, that the party acting in error regarded it as of the essence, as his motive.   152
Civil Code Article 1826; Cole v. Lumbermens Mut. Cas. Co., 160 So.2d 785 (La.App.3d   153
Cir. 1964). No evidence supports such a ground for rescission here.   154

Nor is there any evidence to support rescission for fraud, Carter v. Foreman, 219 So.2d   155
21 (La.App.4th Cir. 1969), or for coercion through illegal exaction, New Orleans & N.E.R.R.   156
Co. v. Louisiana Const. & Imp. Co., 109 La. 13, 33 So. 51.   157

It is unfortunate that the plaintiff did not receive the advice of an attorney before he   158
executed the release in question. However, in the absence of legal requirement that he   159
have done so, the compromise is not invalid on that account. Further, the plaintiff was   160
fully aware of his right to consult with an attorney, and he could have refused to sign the   161
release until he consulted with an attorney.   162

VI.   163

The plaintiff was fully aware of his situation, the nature and effect of the release, and   164
the extent of the claim compromised. His consent to the release was voluntary. We can-   165
not annul the transaction because it was a bad bargain for him or out of sympathy for the   166
plaintiff's desperate plight at the time he compromised his claim.   167

The release was valid. The exception of res judicata should have been sustained, bar-   168
ring trial on the merits and the subsequent award of damages.   169

The judgment of the trial court is reversed, and the plaintiff's suit is dismissed at his cost.   170

[....]

Questions

1. Lines 22 *et seq.*: Read carefully Louisiana Civil Code articles 3071–3083 on compro-
    mise and, particularly, for the purpose of this case Louisiana Civil Code article 3082.
    Read also the Louisiana Civil Code articles on error (La. Civ. Code arts. 1948–1952),
    fraud (La. Civ. Code arts. 1953–1958), and duress/violence (La. Civ. Code arts.
    1959–1964). Consider Louisiana Civil Code article 1963. Could Mr. Wilson fit under
    this article? Would it be of any help to him? Where the article reads "... not in col-
    lusion with the party exerting duress", could the hospital/doctors be that "party" ex-
    erting duress? *See* lines 59 *et seq.* What kind of duress does the civil code contemplate?
    Does it contemplate economic duress? *See* lines 71–80.

2. Lines 39 *et seq.*: What kind of standard of behavior is the court applying to the plain-
    tiff's behavior? Is this standard compatible with the plaintiff making a counteroffer?
    Were the doctors and/or hospital making a legitimate-lawful exercise of their rights
    in their dealings with the plaintiff? Could the doctors and/or hospital be said to have
    abused their rights or not acted in good faith? *See* La. Civ. Code art. 1759.

3. Lines 82–102: Can the plaintiff's arguments amount to grounds of error? What about
    duress?

4. Lines 104–127: Why did the Court of Appeal overrule the trial court? Although the
    Court acknowledges the existence of a form of duress, why did the Court never-

theless reject it as a basis for rescission? So, what kind of duress does the Code recognize?

5. Lines 129 *et seq.*: How would you explain the rejection by the Court of the ground of error as to the nature of the contract? Error as to the person? Error as to the motive/reason? Why was there no fraud?

John C. SKANNAL

v.

Dennis BAMBURG, Margie Dumas, Bamburg & Sligo Hills, L.L.C.

Louisiana Court of Appeal

Second Circuit

Jan. 27, 2010

33 So.3d 227

MOORE, J.

Dennis and Margie Bamburg appeal a judgment which nullified four contracts with their former business partner, the late John C. Skannal, and awarded damages and attorney fees. After a 16-day trial, the district court found that out of nine contested contracts entered between 1996 and 2004, four—exclusive right to sell agreement (10/9/03), act of sale of membership interest in Sligo Hills LLC (2/27/04), act of sale of common stock in Sligo Enterprises Inc. (3/2/04), and mineral deed with assignment of leases (3/2/04)— occurred when Skannal lacked mental capacity to enter business transactions owing to alcohol-induced dementia, Alzheimer's disease and prostate cancer. The court also found that Skannal was "under the influence of Dennis Bamburg." For these reasons the court declared the contracts null. By a supplemental opinion, the court further found that Dennis Bamburg's dealings with Skannal constituted fraud, entitling Skannal's succession to a penalty of 25% of the purchase prices and attorney fees. By a second supplemental opinion, the court set attorney fees and fixed costs.

The court rendered judgment which (1) nullified the four contracts, (2) ordered Skannal's succession to restore the purchase prices of $843,752, (3) ordered the Bamburgs to pay damages of $307,315 for fraud, attorney fees of $500,000, and costs, and (4) ordered incidental relief not contested on appeal.

The Bamburgs have appealed, raising [....] [**numerous**] assignments of error. [....]

Factual Background

Skannal owned a large tract of land called Sligo Plantation (said to have been in his family since the 1840s) in south Bossier Parish where he ran a livestock operation but primarily lived off his oil and gas royalties. He was retired from the state police and still was a notary public. A host of witnesses described him as reclusive, asocial, a chronic alcoholic and generally unpleasant person. Although many said he was miserly and loath to part with any of his assets, in the mid-1970s he was trying to sell a country lot on Skannal Road when he met the Bamburgs. Dennis was an Air Force vet working as a ticket agent for Delta Airlines when he called Skannal about buying the lot. The Bamburgs bought it and moved their mobile home there.

According to the Bamburgs, Skannal wanted more than just a neighbor; he wanted a business partner. At Dennis's suggestion, they formed a corporation to develop part of Skannal's land into a 148-unit mobile home park called Plantation Acres. A few years later they formed another corporation, Sligo Enterprises Inc., to develop a tract that Skannal's father had subdivided but never completed, Shadow Ridge. Dennis was president, Skannal vice-president, and Margie secretary-treasurer. In both these companies, Skannal contributed the land and the Bamburgs the "sweat equity," and each held 50% of the capital stock. For many years Skannal voiced no objection to this business model, and apparently both projects were financially successful.

In the early 1990s, Skannal's marriage ran aground; his wife moved out while he was at a ham radio convention in Texas, and at least two of his three children sided with their mother. This resulted in a long period of estrangement which, according to the succession, isolated Skannal and accelerated his drinking. Also, it meant that Skannal's immediate family were [sic] not able to provide any insight into his thoughts, motives and mental status from about 1992 on.

In the mid-1990s, Skannal and the Bamburgs entered into a series of contracts to develop a large tract of Skannal's land into a golf course with an adjacent subdivision called Olde Oaks. Several different agreements were involved. Initially, Skannal contributed the land, some 332 acres with a reservation of mineral rights, and the Bamburgs paid cash for the equivalent value, $154,750, and each received an equal number of additional shares in Sligo Enterprises Inc.

In February 1999, Skannal and Dennis formed another business, Sligo Hills LLC, to facilitate the project further. As before, Skannal put in a large amount of land (according to the petition, over 1,300 acres, virtually the last remnant of Sligo Plantation, but with a reservation of minerals) and the Bamburgs put in a promissory note for $533,000 (which they and Skannal agreed was an equivalent value), for a 50% interest each in the LLC.

Around this time, Skannal was diagnosed with inoperable prostate cancer. He enrolled in an experimental treatment program at the Feist-Weiller Center at LSU Health Sciences Center from January 2000 through February 2003, under the direction of Dr. Richard Mansour, who saw him regularly for these critical three years. Dr. Mansour found him to be a compliant patient who seemed to understand the nature of the experimental program.

Other witnesses, however, described a man in rapid decline, physically and mentally. His office in the old plantation store was unkempt and littered with mounds of beer cans and bourbon bottles. Another person with whom Skannal did business, a fertilizer salesman named Jimmy Pete Burks, testified that by 2003 Skannal's farm was a shambles. Burks began to assist him with the farming operation, and brought him liquor anytime he wanted it. One day in August 2003, Burks found him flat on his face in the flowerbed, seriously drunk and injured in the fall. Skannal had to be hospitalized, first at Highland Hospital, then at LifeCare, and then at the psychiatric ward of Promise Hospital, where a geriatric psychiatrist, Dr. Keith Kessel, described him as delusional and combative. Dr. Kessel testified that he phoned Skannal's daughter, Elizabeth, to advise that in his current state, Skannal could be interdicted. Elizabeth testified that she conveyed this information to Dennis, but she never took any action to interdict her father.

For several years, the Municipal Police Employees Retirement System ("MPERS") had been seeking to diversify its portfolio by acquiring real estate, particularly golf courses. According to MPERS's chairman, Bill Fields, Skannal (a retired state policeman) had always been eager to sell, and on two occasions had literally flagged down his red patrol car to press the issue, but Dennis was holding out. In 2000, MPERS bought a portion of the property for $6.5 million, but when the project foundered, MPERS escalated its requests in the belief that additional land for the surrounding subdivision would help the golf club. After long negotiations between Dennis and MPERS, Sligo Enterprises agreed to sell the remaining property for $4.544 million. Skannal and the Bamburgs both pocketed $2.1 million from the deal, making Sligo Enterprises even more lucrative than their prior ventures. At the closing on February 13, 2004, nobody from MPERS suspected that Skannal was an assisted living patient with multiple forms of dementia. The court did not rescind any of the MPERS contracts.

The Nullified Contracts

On October 9, 2003, while Skannal was still in the psychiatric ward at Promise Hospital, Dennis brought him a document, "Exclusive Right to Sell Agreement," whereby Sligo Enterprises granted Dennis the exclusive right to sell corporate property at a 10% commission. Skannal and Dennis both signed this. When Sligo Enterprises later sold its property to MPERS, Bamburg paid himself a commission of $449,400 pursuant to the exclusive right to sell agreement, the first transaction nullified by the court.

After Skannal was discharged from Promise Hospital on October 13, 2003, Burks resumed carrying him liquor. Burks testified that at Skannal's direction, he sold off the remainder of Skannal's cattle. He also testified that around this time, Skannal was earning $40,000 to $70,000 *a month* in mineral royalties. Burks admitted skimming off some of this money for his personal use, as did Elizabeth.

Skannal was again hospitalized from January 14 to February 10, 2004, after which Dennis moved him to The Arbor, an assisted living center. While he was living at The Arbor, he signed the three other contracts ultimately nullified by the court.

According to the Bamburgs, after the golf course deal was completed, Skannal wanted to convert his assets to cash. On February 27, 2004, Dennis drove him to the office of real estate attorney Jeff DeLaune, who had handled several of the parties' transactions. Using information supplied by Dennis, DeLaune drew up a two-page "Act of Sale of Membership Interest in Sligo Hills, LLC" whereby Skannal sold his remaining 50% interest in the LLC to the Bamburgs for $400,000, which Skannal received by check and deposited. DeLaune, his wife, and Janelle Ward, the notary, all testified that Skannal chatted with them about the business climate in Bossier, especially the riverboats, where Skannal had become a frequent patron, often losing thousands of dollars a night on the slots. These witnesses described a man perfectly aware of what the sale purported to do. They were not aware that he was in an assisted living center or diagnosed with dementia, and they agreed that no separate counsel was present to explain the deal to him. This was the second contract the court nullified.

Four days later, on March 2, 2004, Dennis again drove Skannal to DeLaune's office, where DeLaune had drawn up two documents based on information provided by Dennis. The first was a two-page "Act of Sale of Common Stock of Sligo Enterprises Inc." whereby Skannal sold his remaining 2400 shares of the company to the Bamburgs for $323,752, which Skannal received by check and deposited. Second was a two-page "Mineral Deed with Assignment of Leases" whereby Skannal sold the naked ownership of all his mineral interests to the Bamburgs for $120,000, which Skannal received by check and deposited. The mineral deed was subject to Skannal's lifetime usufruct. Ms. DeLaune notarized these acts; as on the prior occasion, she and the witnesses testified that Skannal appeared sober and sentient, but they were unaware of his medical condition, and there was no other attorney present to advise him separately. These were the other two contracts nullified by the court.

Subsequent Events and Procedural History

After these events, Skannal's health deteriorated rapidly. Jimmy Pete Burks was bringing him liquor all the time, and the staff at The Arbor reported that Skannal was usu-

ally drunk and ornery, fell down frequently, and could not control his bowels. Because   136
drinking was against The Arbor's regulations, Dennis moved him to Garden Court,   137
where the situation continued. In moments of apparent lucidity, however, he began   138
telling Burks that "they" had robbed him blind and that he had nothing left. By "they,"   139
he meant the Bamburgs. Burks relayed this information to Elizabeth, who contacted her   140
two brothers, A.C. and Barron. The children then revived a relationship with their mori-   141
bund father, and in March 2005 they took him to attorney John Odom's office and   142
painted the whole scenario.   143

On March 14, Skannal filed this suit to rescind his contracts with the Bamburgs, dat-   144
ing back to 1999, on grounds of incapacity, error, fraud and lesion. Skannal died in No-   145
vember 2005, and his son Barron (an undertaker in Texas), the succession representative,   146
was substituted as plaintiff.   147

By amended petitions, the succession added contracts dating back to January 1996   148
and demanded damages for fraud. A prodigious course of discovery and pretrial motions   149
ensued. [....]   150

Overview of Trial Testimony and Action of District Court   151

After a daylong *Daubert* hearing, the trial took 16 days from March to July 2007. The   152
succession presented several medical experts. Dr. Ronald Goebel, a clinical neuropsy-   153
chologist, and Dr. Keith Kessel, a geriatric psychiatrist, had examined Skannal at Life-   154
Care and Promise Hospital, respectively, in late 2003 through mid-2004. They diagnosed   155
neurological deficits, a reduced IQ of 80, and alcohol-related dementia. Dr. Kessel had   156
suggested interdicting Skannal. Dr. Marjorie Fowler, the pathologist who performed   157
Skannal's autopsy, confirmed that he had Alzheimer's disease and widespread prostatic   158
cancer.   159

The succession also presented the testimony of four medical experts, psychiatrist Dr.   160
Paul Ware, forensic psychiatrists Dr. Richard Williams and Dr. George Seiden, and gen-   161
eral practitioner Dr. David T. Henry, each of whom examined Skannal one time shortly   162
before his death. To compensate for the obvious lack of patient time, these doctors reviewed   163
two volumes of medical records, depositions and interviews that ran to nearly 8,000 pages.   164
A fifth medical expert, geriatric and forensic psychiatrist Dr. Bennett Blum, of Tucson,   165
Arizona, never saw Skannal but dilated on his teaching tool for gauging undue influence.   166
These experts held the unanimous view that from about 1997 on, Skannal was so afflicted   167
with alcohol-induced dementia, vascular dementia, Alzheimer's disease and prostate can-   168
cer that he could not possibly understand any complex business transaction. They fur-   169
ther expounded that even though Skannal might not have been drunk on a given day,   170
the dementia and incapacity were present at all times. They added that during sober in-   171
tervals, a patient like Skannal would not appear impaired to anyone but a highly skilled   172
forensic psychiatrist. They also concluded that because of his cancer and isolation from   173
his family, Skannal was particularly susceptible to influence from Dennis, who had been   174
his trusted business associate for over 20 years. They reviewed statements from many,   175
but by no means all, persons who dealt with Skannal in his fading years.   176

The Bamburgs called one expert psychiatrist, Dr. James Phillips, who never examined   177
Skannal but reviewed the medical records. He concluded that Skannal suffered from very   178
mild vascular dementia, mild alcoholic dementia, and no clinical symptoms of Alzheimer's   179
disease. He agreed that Skannal had borderline dementia and did poorly at LifeCare, and   180
was still in a diminished state when admitted to Promise Hospital, but improved dra-   181
matically by the end of his stay in October 2003. He felt that Skannal had complete men-   182
tal capacity in February and March 2004.   183

184   The Bamburgs also called Dr. Ted Warren, a family practitioner in Bossier City, and
185   Dr. Dennis Venable, a urologist at LSU Health Sciences Center, who testified that in their
186   treatment of Skannal, they never had any concerns about his competency. Dr. Venable added
187   that in July 2003, during the experimental treatment program at Feist-Weiller, Skannal
188   had elected intermittent self-catheterization, a process requiring a certain level of un-
189   derstanding and skill.

190   Another major portion of expert testimony came from appraisers, economists and
191   CPAs. Much of their testimony addressed the fiscal soundness of contracts Skannal exe-
192   cuted between 1996 and 2002, not nullified by the court and not issues on appeal. There
193   were diverse opinions of the value of Skannal's 50% interest in the closely held corpora-
194   tion and LLC; the succession's experts felt these were worth much more than the Bam-
195   burgs paid for them in 2004, while the Bamburgs' experts testified that both companies
196   did remarkably well (26% annual return over nearly 30 years), and that across the life of
197   the companies both sides received equivalent value.

198   These experts also disputed the value of the naked ownership of Skannal's mineral
199   rights. After years of depressed natural gas prices, in the early 2000s these wells began
200   paying him an average of $60,000 per month. The succession's petroleum engineer, Henry
201   Coutret, testified that the standard multiplier for selling interest in a producing well is
202   30–60 times its monthly income, but he had never heard of a sale in which the vendor
203   reserved all income for life. The Bamburgs' CPA, John Walter Dean, testified that Skan-
204   nal received this much in royalties between the date of the sale and his death.

205   The district court rendered a 19-page opinion restating and largely adopting the view
206   of the succession's medical experts but finding that Skannal's dementia did not render
207   him incapacitated until October 2003 and late February to early March 2004. The court
208   further found, "as a matter of law," that Skannal was "under the influence of Mr. Bam-
209   burg," but not Ms. Bamburg, and set aside the four contracts listed above. The court
210   specifically declined to nullify five other contested contracts.

211   On Odom's motion, the court issued a supplemental opinion stating that "the previ-
212   ous factual findings" also supported a finding that Dennis committed fraud with respect
213   to the four nullified contracts. The court assessed a penalty of 25% of the purchase price
214   of the stock in Sligo Enterprises Inc., the interest in Sligo Hills LLC and Skannal's min-
215   eral rights. [....]

216   [....]

217   The judgment nullified the four contracts, directed the succession to restore the pur-
218   chase price of $843,752, and ordered the Bamburgs, in solido, to pay a penalty of $307,315
219   (including 25% of the purchase price of the acts of sale and mineral deed, *and* one-half
220   of the real estate commission paid under the exclusive right to sell, an item not men-
221   tioned in the supplemental opinion), expert costs of $95,486, and attorney fees of $500,000.

222   As noted, the Bamburgs have appealed, contesting [**among other things**] (1) the find-
223   ing that Skannal lacked capacity to contract, (2) the finding that the Bamburgs commit-
224   ted fraud, (3) the finding that the Bamburgs exerted undue influence over Skannal [....]

225   [....]

Discussion: Lack of Capacity

227   By their first assignment of error, the Bamburgs urge the court was manifestly erro-
228   neous to find that Skannal lacked capacity to engage in routine business transactions.
229   They show that under La. C.C. art. 1918, only "persons deprived of reason" lack capac-
230   ity to contract; they contend that the court applied too high a standard, relying on the suc-

cession's suggestion that Skannal could sign a contract only if he had been sober for weeks, had independent counsel, and somebody first read the document to him. They urge the proper standard is clear and convincing evidence of lack of capacity. *Meadors v. Pacific Int'l Petr.*, 449 So.2d 26 (La.App. 1 Cir.), *writ denied*, 450 So.2d 964 (1984). They argue, contrary to the defense experts' view, that Skannal was able to do many things, and do them well, after 1997. Finally, they urge that under La. C.C. art. 1926, a contract made by a non-interdicted person may be attacked after his death, on grounds of incapacity, only when the contract is gratuitous, evidences lack of understanding, or was made within 30 days of death. They submit that the succession's claims were raised after Skannal's death and meet none of the criteria of art. 1926.

The succession responds that under the manifest error standard of review, considering the voluminous evidence in the entire record on which the court based its ruling, the finding should be affirmed. It contends the expert testimony overwhelmingly proved that Skannal suffered from alcohol dementia, vascular dementia and Alzheimer's disease, and these conditions deprived him of reason. It submits that the court carefully weighed the evidence, as it refused to nullify the contracts executed before 2001, and reasonably resolved the conflicting claims.

All persons have capacity to contract, except unemancipated minors, interdicts, and persons deprived of reason at the time of contracting. La. C.C. art. 1918. The presumption is that all persons have capacity to contract; lack of capacity must be shown by clear and convincing evidence. *Succession of Hollis*, 43,315 (La.App. 2 Cir. 6/18/08), 987 So.2d 387, *writ denied*, 2008-1632 (La.10/24/08), 992 So.2d 1035. A contract made by a person without legal capacity is relatively null and may be rescinded only at the request of that person or his legal representative. La. C.C. art. 1919. A noninterdicted person, who was deprived of reason at the time of contracting, may obtain rescission of an onerous contract upon the ground of incapacity only upon showing that the other party knew or should have known that person's incapacity. La. C.C. art. 1925. *Succession of Hollis, supra.*

The succession correctly shows that the expert evidence addressing Skannal's capacity was voluminous; this court cannot belabor the detailed, prolonged and often repetitive testimony of Drs. Ware, Williams, Seiden, Henry and Phillips. It is sufficient to say that the succession's experts felt that Skannal lacked capacity from about 1997 on, while the Bamburgs' expert felt he retained reasonable capacity until the summer of 2004. Burks became Skannal's gofer and booze runner sometime in 2002, carrying him copious amounts of alcohol that he quaffed daily, as confirmed by photos of Skannal's office and by numerous lay witnesses. Burks also testified that by this time, Skannal's farm was a shambles. We further note that for years, Skannal had kept a meticulous journal of temperature, rainfall, and financial matters, noting the sale of every calf and the outcome of every trip to the Bossier City casinos, but the journal appears to have ended in 2002. Skannal was a patient at Promise Hospital on October 9, 2003, when he signed the exclusive right to sell agreement, and a resident of The Arbor on March 2, 2004, when he signed the act of sale of common stock and the mineral deed with assignment of leases.

Admittedly, the record presents factual anomalies that are difficult to reconcile. Bill Fields testified that Skannal twice flagged down his patrol car to badger him about the MPERS deals; Dr. Venable testified that in mid-2003, Skannal showed sufficient understanding to elect self-catheterization; the notaries, attorneys and witnesses present when Skannal signed the nullified acts all felt that he appeared feeble and somewhat immobile, but was cogent and well informed. Robert Cockrell, the investment counselor at Morgan Stanley, where Skannal deposited nearly $3.5 million in proceeds from the deals with the Bamburgs in early 2004, understandably thought there was nothing wrong with his client's mind. All these facts show a man in reasonable possession of his faculties.

Moreover, we would almost agree with the Bamburgs that the succession set the standard unreasonably high for proving capacity. If any contract could be nullified because one party was drunk the previous day, or because no independent counsel was present to advise the party and read the document to him before signing, then virtually all real estate, auto and securities transactions would be vulnerable. Skannal, however, was amply shown to be a special case, diagnosed with multiple forms of dementia, prostate cancer, and falling-down drunk almost daily.

Even with the anomalies so ably urged by the Bamburgs, the record is sufficient to establish by clear and convincing evidence that Skannal suffered from multiple forms of dementia, prostate cancer and habitual drunkenness that deprived him of reason at certain times. On this immense and difficult record, we cannot say the district court was plainly wrong in finding that Skannal lacked contractual capacity on October 9, 2003, February 27, 2004, and March 2, 2004, when these transactions were executed.

Finally, we note that Skannal filed this suit before his death, so the limitations of La. C.C. art. 1926 do not apply. This assignment does not present reversible error.

Fraud

By their second assignment of error, the Bamburgs urge the court erred as a matter of law in finding that fraud was proved in any of the challenged transactions. They contend that under La. C.C. art. 1953, the first element of any action for fraud is a misrepresentation, suppression, or omission of true information, and that in this enormous record "plaintiff failed to articulate any instance of misrepresentation by Bamburg to Skannal." They argue that all contracts were reduced to writing, the Bamburgs paid every dollar and fulfilled every promise, and the succession produced no evidence that they ever lied to Skannal.

The succession responds that the proper standard for reviewing a finding of fraud is manifest error. *Chambers v. Kennington*, 35,079 (La.App. 2 Cir. 9/28/01), 796 So.2d 733. It contends that because of their relation of confidence, Skannal had no duty to ascertain the truth of any representations the Bamburgs may have made to him. La. C.C. art. 1954. It argues that even without evidence of specific statements, fraud may be proved by "highly suspicious facts and circumstances surrounding a transaction." *Bell v. Vickers*, 568 So.2d 160 (La.App. 2 Cir.1990). It concludes that on this record, the finding of fraud was not plainly wrong.

Fraud is a misrepresentation or a suppression of the truth made with the intention either to obtain an unjust advantage for one party or to cause a loss or inconvenience to the other. Fraud may also result from silence or inaction. La. C.C. art. 1953. The basic elements of an action for fraud against a party to a contract are (1) a misrepresentation, suppression or omission of true information, (2) the intent to obtain an unjust advantage or to cause damage or inconvenience to another, and (3) the error induced by a fraudulent act must relate to a circumstance substantially influencing the victim's consent to the contract. *Shelton v. Standard/700 Associates*, 2001-0587 (La.10/16/01), 798 So.2d 60. Fraud does not vitiate consent when the party against whom the fraud was directed could have ascertained the truth without difficulty, inconvenience, or special skill. However, this exception does not apply when a relation of confidence has reasonably induced a party to rely on the other's assertions or representations. La. C.C. art. 1954. When a claim of fraud is based on silence or suppression of the truth, the plaintiff must prove a duty to speak or to disclose information. *Greene v. Gulf Coast Bank*, 593 So.2d 630 (La.1992).

Fraud need only be proved by a preponderance of the evidence and may be established   327
by circumstantial evidence. La. C.C. art. 1957; *Succession of Hollis, supra*.   328

The succession correctly shows that the standard of review of a finding of fraud is   329
manifest error. *Mayfield v. Reed*, 43,226 (La.App. 2 Cir. 4/30/08), 981 So.2d 235; *Lafayette*   330
Ins. Co. v. Pennington, 42,434 (La.App. 2 Cir. 9/19/07), 966 So.2d 136. Also, the succes-   331
sion correctly shows that a duty of full disclosure arose from the parties' relation of con-   332
fidence, their work together in numerous business ventures over a 25-year period. Notably,   333
Skannal was usually the "silent" partner, providing the real estate and relying on information   334
from the Bamburgs, who performed the physical element of development and sales.   335

As with the lack of capacity, this record provides a long procession of facts for and against   336
the finding of fraud. The Bamburgs correctly show that for each of the annulled transac-   337
tions, they paid and performed precisely as stated in the contract; that not one shred of tes-   338
timony directly implicates them in a misrepresentation or suppression of the truth; and that   339
because of the parties' long and lucrative business association, Skannal may have intended   340
to treat them more favorably than an arm's-length buyer. On the other hand, the Bamburgs,   341
more than anyone, knew or should have known of Skannal's deepening cognitive deficits,   342
chronic alcoholism, and dependence on them. Moreover, the absence of direct proof of   343
fraud likely results more from Skannal's dementia than from the purity of the Bamburgs'   344
statements to him. The whole course of events in late 2003 and early 2004 can equally well   345
be viewed as an elaborate scheme to "clean the man out" before his death or interdiction.   346

Most impressive to this court is the gross inequity of the annulled contracts, particu-   347
larly the mineral deed with assignment of leases. Henry Coutret, the succession's expert   348
petroleum engineer, testified that mineral rights usually sell for 30 to 60 times their   349
monthly production, and the sale price of $120,000 was less than 10% of fair market   350
value. He had never heard of a sale of the naked interest only, reserving usufruct to the   351
seller. The Bamburgs' CPA and expert in business valuation, John Walter Dean, testified   352
that he would have used a multiple of 24, by which a fair market value was $1,133,000;   353
even though the Bamburgs paid only $120,000, Skannal received royalties of $1,391,987   354
between March 2003 and his death in 2005, meaning he ultimately got a fair market value.   355
Counting royalties from lessees as part of the purchase price is, in our view, a mislead-   356
ing inducement. The district court was entitled to find that this deal was so peculiar and   357
unfavorable to Skannal that it could not have occurred in the absence of fraud.   358

The district court was not plainly wrong to find that Dennis Bamburg committed   359
fraud to obtain an unfair advantage over Skannal. This assignment does not present re-   360
versible error.   361

Undue Influence   362

By their third assignment of error, the Bamburgs urge that the court's finding that Den-   363
nis Bamburg unduly influenced Skannal is legally flawed and manifestly erroneous. They   364
show that under La. C.C. art. 1479, "influence" is a ground for revoking a donation inter   365
vivos or mortis causa, and not for rescinding an onerous contract. This article also re-   366
quires proof that the influence "so impaired the volition of the donor as to substitute the   367
volition of the donee * * * for the volition of the donor." They contend that the evidence   368
shows only that Skannal relied on their advice, which had been sound and lucrative for over   369
20 years, but that the irascible and determined Skannal never allowed *anyone* to usurp his   370
own volition. They also show that the succession's own expert, Dr. Seiden, testified that   371
Skannal was "vulnerable" to coercion, but declined to state that he was actually coerced.   372

The succession does not directly address the Bamburgs' construction of Art. 1479, but   373
urges that the evidence was sufficient to support the finding of undue influence.   374

375   For the reasons already discussed, this court has affirmed the findings of lack of capacity
376 and fraud, both of which would result in the rescission of the affected transactions. La.
377 C.C. arts. 1919, 1958. With due respect to the Bamburgs' articulate argument, we con-
378 clude that even if the finding of undue influence were legally wrong, reversing it would
379 not result in reinstating the affected transactions. We therefore pretermit this issue. We
380 would only note that despite the literal language of Art. 1479, courts have applied the
381 concept of undue influence to a marriage contract, *Brumfield v. Brumfield,* 477 So.2d
382 1161 (La.App. 1 Cir.1985), *writ denied,* 479 So.2d 922 (1985), and stated in dictum that
383 it applied to "a deed or a contract," *Mitchell v. Bertolla,* 340 So.2d 287 (La.1976). This as-
384 signment does not present reversible error.

385   [....]

Questions

1. Lines 226 *et seq.*: This case is self-explanatory as regards fraud and undue influence
    as vices of consent. Do you disagree with the court? Is drunkenness on the part of
    one party a sufficient ground for nullity of a contract on the basis of error? *See* lines
    1–287. Does the court require a certain degree of error?

2. Lines 297 *et seq.*: The court rules that "Dennis Bamburg committed fraud to obtain an
    unfair advantage over Skannal". Do you agree that the requirements for fraud were met?

3. Lines 363–386: The court cites Louisiana Civil Code article 1479 in part (*see* lines
    365–369) and goes on to state that this article is about undue influence. Read Louisiana
    Civil Code article 1479 and you will see that it mentions the word "influence", but
    nowhere does it explicitly refer to the phrase "undue influence". So, did the court
    read and rely on the title of Louisiana Civil Code article 1479, which includes the
    adjective "undue"? If the court did this, then the court turned the title of the article
    into law in violation of La. R.S. 1: 13 which provides: "*A. Headings to sections, source
    notes, and cross references are given for the purpose of convenient reference and do not
    constitute part of the law.*" Or did the court give its own interpretation of the word "in-
    fluence" to mean undue influence, which the court could have done by interpreting
    the law? Why didn't the court look at the next article, Louisiana Civil Code article 1480,
    in the text of which the court would have found an express reference to undue influence?
    If undue influence is a vice of consent where donations are concerned, could undue
    influence also be a vice of consent in any contract, not just gratuitous contracts like
    donations? Can an *a pari ratione* reasoning be used to broaden the scope of applica-
    tion of undue influence?

See also *Millet v. Millet,* 888 So.2d 291 (La. 5th Cir. 2004)

Comparative Law Perspective

Alex Weill, Droit Civil: Les Obligations
n° 187, at 200 (1971)

187. Diverse sanctions. — 1° Insofar as fraud vitiates the consent of the victim, the
normal sanction is the *relative nullity* of the contract.

2° But the fraud is also a fault that can be sanctioned by *damages.* If, despite the nullity, the victim experiences a prejudice, he can demand damages from the author of the

fraud and from all those who, by their fault, have permitted or facilitated the fraud. Besides, nothing obliges the victim to demand the nullity of the contract, if he prefers to limit himself to recovering damages.

Moreover, damages constitute the sole sanction in the case of fraud caused by a third party. It is the same with the sanction for incidental [non-material] fraud.

3° One can conceive of still another sanction for fraud—the *refusal of nullity*. An incapable who has dissimulated his condition by means of fraudulent maneuvers will not be able to obtain the nullity of the contract on account of his incapacity.

Section IV—Object and Matter of Contracts

Louisiana Sources of Law

Louisiana Civil Code

Art. 1971. Freedom of parties.

Parties are free to contract for any object that is lawful, possible, and determined or determinable. (Acts 1984, No. 331, § 1, eff. Jan. 1, 1985.)

Art. 1972. Possible or impossible object.

A contractual object is possible or impossible according to its own nature and not according to the parties' ability to perform. (Acts 1984, No. 331, § 1, eff. Jan. 1, 1985.)

Art. 1973. Object determined as to kind.

The object of a contract must be determined at least as to its kind.

The quantity of a contractual object may be undetermined, provided it is determinable. (Acts 1984, No. 331, § 1, eff. Jan. 1, 1985.)

Art. 1974. Determination by third person.

If the determination of the quantity of the object has been left to the discretion of a third person, the quantity of an object is determinable.

If the parties fail to name a person, or if the person named is unable or unwilling to make the determination, the quantity may be determined by the court. (Acts 1984, No. 331, § 1, eff. Jan. 1, 1985.)

Art. 1976. Future things.

Future things may be the object of a contract.

The succession of a living person may not be the object of a contract other than an antenuptial agreement. Such a succession may not be renounced. (Acts 1984, No. 331, § 1, effective January 1, 1985.)

Art. 1977. Obligation or performance by a third person.

The object of a contract may be that a third person will incur an obligation or render a performance.

The party who promised that obligation or performance is liable for damages if the third person does not bind himself or does not perform. (Acts 1984, No. 331, § 1, eff. Jan. 1, 1985.)

Art. 1978. Stipulation for a third party.

A contracting party may stipulate a benefit for a third person called a third party beneficiary.

Once the third party has manifested his intention to avail himself of the benefit, the parties may not dissolve the contract by mutual consent without the beneficiary's agreement. (Acts 1984, No. 331, § 1, eff. Jan. 1, 1985.)

Art. 1979. Revocation.

The stipulation may be revoked only by the stipulator and only before the third party has manifested his intention of availing himself of the benefit.

If the promisor has an interest in performing, however, the stipulation may not be revoked without his consent. (Acts 1984, No. 331, § 1, eff. Jan. 1, 1985.)

Art. 1981. Rights of beneficiary and stipulator.

The stipulation gives the third party beneficiary the right to demand performance from the promisor.

Also the stipulator, for the benefit of the third party, may demand performance from the promisor. (Acts 1984, No. 331, § 1, eff. Jan. 1, 1985.)

Précis: Louisiana Law of Conventional Obligations— §§ 6.1.1 to 6.2.2 and §§ 7.1 to 7.3.3

LSA-C.C. Art. 1971 lists the three characteristics which must be met by an object to be the object of a contract: "Parties are free to contract for any object that is lawful, possible, and determined or determinable." ...

Laws for the preservation of public order prohibit parties from entering a contract which would have an unlawful object or an immoral object. In the words of **LSA-C.C. Art. 7**: **"Persons may not by their juridical acts derogate from laws enacted for the protection of the public interest. Any act in derogation of such laws is an absolute nullity."** ...

LSA-C.C. Art. 1973 makes the determination of the object of a contract conditional upon the parties agreeing on the "kind" of object and the "quantity" of that object. Nothing is said of the "quality" of the same contractual object. In this respect, one has to refer to LSA-C.C. Art. 1860 listed in the civil Code under "Extinction of Obligations" and "Performance."

What is a "kind"? In the absence of a definition in the Civil Code, we are told by **LSA-C.C. Art. 11** that **"The words of a law must be given their generally prevailing meaning. Words of art and technical terms must be given their technical meaning when the law involves a technical matter."** In this instance, the general meaning of the word "kind" can be found in a dictionary as referring to "a class that is defined by the common attribute or attributes possessed by all of its members <flowers of all kinds>, <the kind of person who gets angry easily> [sic]." ...

A second facet of the determination of an object can be its quantity. **"The quantity of a contractual object may be undetermined"** at the time the parties enter their contract **"provided it is determinable"** at the time performance is due ...

The determination of the quantity of an object can be left, as per the intent of the parties, to a third person. **"If the determination of the quantity of the object has been left to the discretion of a third person, the quantity of an object is determinable. . . .**

If the parties fail to name a person, or if the person named is unable or unwilling to make the determination, the quantity may be determined by the court." (LSA-C.C. Art. 1974)....

As far as the quality of an object or a thing might be important, even essential, to its determination, the civil Code includes a suppletive rule of law in Article 1860....

The law will feel the gap of "quality" of the thing when the parties fail to agree.

A third legal requirement that must be met by the object of a contract is that the object be "possible." ...

Only an object/thing that is absolutely impossible of ever existing or that existed at one time but no longer exists leads to the absolute nullity of the contract....

On the other hand, the impossibility could be "relative," in the sense that for personal reason(s) the obligor himself could not carry out his performance although somebody else could....

Such an obligor will be validly bound by the contract; he will be in breach of a "possible" object of an obligation and, thus, liable to pay compensatory damages for breach of an obligation to do something....

Promesse de Porte-Fort

[I]n a promesse de porte-fort the principal or third person is not bound to perform the contract entered into by the porte-fort with his co-contracting party. In a triangular porte-fort situation, the principal-third person is not aware that someone may be acting for his benefit since the porte-fort has received no instruction from "anyone" to act for a third person-principal....

Two effects flow from a ratification by the principal-third person of the juridical act or contract entered into between the porte-fort and the contracting party.

One first effect is that the third person-principal is now "bound to perform the contract that the porte-fort has made with his co-contracting party." ...

A second important effect of ratification is that it releases the porte-fort of any subsequent obligation; he is now out of the picture so much so that he is not liable for any breach, by the principal, of the obligations created by the ratified contract....

The principal is free not to ratify the contract entered into by the porte-fort with a third person. The principal cannot be compelled "to do" something, i.e. "ratify," against his will....

Third Party Beneficiary—Stipulation Pour Autrui

A stipulation pour autrui is a legal device bringing together three parties: one of them is called "stipulator", another "promisor", and the third "beneficiary". The interplay among these parties is such that the stipulator receives the commitment of the promisor that the latter will render a performance to the beneficiary. Thus, the beneficiary becomes an obligee, a creditor, as a consequence of the obligation created by the contract between the stipulator and the promisor. The beneficiary is, therefore, a "third party" to that contract. Yet, although a "non-party" to the contract and not represented in the contract, the beneficiary will receive "the benefit of the effects" of that contract. In a word, a stipulation for the benefit of another is "bilateral" in its creation but "triangular" in its effects....

The mechanism of a third party beneficiary stipulation is such that it creates a right of its own nature, the "benefit", in the sense that neither the stipulator nor the promisor ever had this right in their patrimonies to transfer it to the beneficiary. This right vested in the beneficiary is created, therefore, by a contract between the stipulator and the promisor out of their own bilateral legal relationship. Therefore, the actual vesting of this right into the patrimony of the beneficiary is contingent not only on the validity of the contract between stipulator and promisor but also on the performance of their obligations by these two parties....

A "stipulation" being a clause in a contract, that contract must meet all the requirements for a valid contract. The requirement of cause is the one of greater concern because the stipulator cannot use the device of a stipulation to transfer "indirectly" to the beneficiary and via the promisor a right which he, the stipulator, could not have transferred "directly" by a contract with the beneficiary himself....

The contract between the stipulator and the promisor must be binding between the parties as the "principal contract" which includes an accessory stipulation. Thus a stipulation pour autrui could not exist in the absence of a supporting-principal contract. This contract, whether onerous or gratuitous, must meet the requirements for the validity of any contract in addition to meeting the specific requirements of the nominate contract the parties may have intended to enter into, like a sale or a donation. This fundamental requirement of a valid principal contract explains why the subsequent enforcement by the "beneficiary" of the accessory stipulation for his benefit will depend on the performance of their obligations by the parties to the principal contract....

A stipulation being a juridical act, that act must meet the requirements for any valid juridical act....

A first set of effects is created by the principal contractual relationship between the stipulator and the promisor. These effects are those of the contract these parties entered into....

The second set of effects bears on the accessory clause, the stipulation created by the contract....

The relationship between the stipulator and the third party beneficiary is not a direct "effect" of the stipulation. It is only indirectly, through the promisor, that the stipulator is in a legal relationship with the third party. Thus the cause that prompted the creation of the stipulation is to be found in the interest or reason the stipulator has in having the promisor carry out a performance for the benefit of the third party....

Should the stipulation pour autrui be lawfully revoked, the principal contract between stipulator and promisor remains in existence....

A stipulation may be for a stipulator a means of performance of an obligation he owes the third party....

A stipulation pour autrui can also be "gratuitous" when the stipulator wishes to make a donation to the third party through the promisor's performance....

Once the third party has **"manifested his intention to avail himself of the benefit,"** (Art. 1978), she is vested with **"the right to demand performance from the promisor."** (Art. 1981)....

The stipulation being "accessory" to the principal contract to which the third party is not a "contractual party," the obligations created by that principal contract cannot take second rank to the stipulation. The promisor has a primary interest in the performance of the obligations created by the principal contract....

Cases

TAC AMUSEMENT COMPANY
v.
Kermit J. HENRY

Louisiana Court of Appeal
Fourth Circuit
Aug. 3, 1970
238 So.2d 398

REDMANN, Judge.

Plaintiff appeals from a judgment dismissing on the merits its suit for contractually-stipulated damages for breach of a contract.

Under the contract defendant agreed that during its ten-year term 'no coin operated music boxes or other commercial music system, nor other legal coin boxes or other commercial music systems, nor other legal coin operated amusement devices will be installed or operated at (defendant's) premises except such as are installed and operated by you (plaintiff) or by such other party designated by you.'

Plaintiff agreed to 'install, operate and maintain on said premises one or more coin operated music devices, and/or one or more legal coin operated amusement devices with the number and type of such being within your (plaintiff's) sole discretion and at your option.'

The contract stipulated a division of the proceeds from the machines, and further provided:

'In event of any breach of this agreement, in addition to any other remedy which you may have, your company may elect to terminate this agreement and remove all such equipment without interference from said location and shall be entitled to liquidated damages in a sum equal to your company's average weekly share of the coin boxes prior to said breach multiplied by the number of weeks remaining in the unexpired term of this agreement.'

There were other provisions unnecessary to recite here in our view of the case.

The evidence shows that defendant caused the removal of the machines seven weeks after the date of the contract (although defendant denies the contract date). Plaintiff sought the 'liquidated damages' of its average weekly proceeds-share of $38.85 for each week of the remainder of the ten-year contract, said to amount to $20,430.00. (By amending petition filed after trial plaintiff voluntarily reduced its demand to $6,060.20, although the evidence supports the $38.85 weekly figures.)

We note that the 'liquidated damages' may not be such. Plaintiff had costs of operation, such as providing phonograph records, maintenance and depreciation of its machines which presumably would not have been covered by the $10 weekly service charge. Furthermore, the proceeds from performance were receivable over a ten-year period and thus worth much less than the entire gross proceeds payable at once. If the service charge truly covered only service, the 'liquidated damages' clause is rather a provision for a penalty far in excess of conceivable actual damages.

More importantly, it seems altogether improbable that the performance promised by plaintiff was what defendant bargained for, the motive or cause of defendant's obligation, LSA-C.C. art. 1896. Presumably defendant either definitely wanted a music box; or he definitely wanted an amusement device; or he definitely wanted both. Plaintiff promised nothing definite, and defendant could not have exacted any definite machine nor even any definite kind of machine. C.C. art. 1886 requires an obligation to have 'for its object something determinate, at least as to its species.'

Planiol observes in his Civil Law Treatise (La.Law Inst. trans.), II s 1001,

'The obligatory relationship is not formed when the object of the obligation is not determined.

'If the indefiniteness bears on the nature of the object, one does not know what thing or what fact can be demanded of the debtor. He who promised 'an animal' in reality has not promised at all, since he can free himself by furnishing to his creditor an insignificant insect. If the indefiniteness relates to the quantity, the thing being specified in its kind, the debtor again can liberate himself by offering a derisive performance: if he has promised grain or wine, without further precision, his obligation can reduce itself to a sip of wine or a grain of wheat, and the credit would be a sham.'

Yet C.C. art. 2066 does authorize 'alternative' obligations, and it may be said that plaintiff obliged itself to provide one or more music boxes or, alternatively, one or more amusement devices or, further alternatively, one or more of both machines.

Still a derisive performance, as Planiol names it, arguably might fill defendant's bar with music boxes and pinball machines, at plaintiff's 'sole discretion and at (its) option.' Or it might consist of one 12-record 78 r.p.m. 1930 vintage juke-box, or some trifling 'amusement device'.

Thus although, as plaintiff argues, plaintiff may not have been free to perform or not perform under a potestative condition depending 'solely on the exercise of the obligor's will', C.C. art. 2035, nevertheless both the quality and the quantity of the object of plaintiff's obligation was, in our opinion, too indeterminate to meet the requirement of C.C. art. 1886, and therefore defendant's obligation was unenforceable because without cause, C.C. art. 1893.

We might add that, because of the absence of any obligation on plaintiff to supply the very machines that had produced $38.85 weekly, even if defendant could be said to have had as his motivating cause only to have some indefinite kind of machine (and plaintiff did oblige itself to that) the proper measure of damages would be loss of proceeds from a minimum performance (the least productive machine) plaintiff might have provided. The so-called liquidated damages, obviously far in excess of hoped-for profit from a voluntarily maximum performance, are so far out of proportion to the only real obligation of plaintiff as to invoke C.C. art. 2464's serious and proportionate consideration requirement, applicable generally to all contracts, Blanchard v. Haber, 166 La. 1014, 118 So. 117 (1928). The liquidated damages clause would be unenforceable even if the contract were otherwise valid.

We have not previously mentioned the circumstance that the contract recites a $500 loan by plaintiff to defendant, represented by a promissory note, as further consideration for the contract. In fact no note was executed. A $500 check was given to and cashed for defendant, but defendant disputes the purpose of the check. If it were a loan (a question not before us), even interest free, its value at maximum legal interest would have been $40 a year, which we consider insufficient as serious and proportionate consideration for an obligation to pay over $20,000 of 'liquidated damages.'

The judgment appealed from is affirmed at plaintiff's cost.

Affirmed.

Questions

1. Lines 14 *et seq.*: Please read the Code articles on Lease (La. Civil Code arts. 2668–2729) and Of the Letting Out of Labor or Industry (La. Civ. Code arts. 2745–2777). After you have the read the whole case, ask yourself the following question: Has the court given a proper legal identification of the nature of the contract for the breach of which the plaintiff is seeking contractually-stipulated damages?

2. Lines 16–18: Can you identify the kinds of obligations that fit in this description? For example, do you see any conjunctive obligation? Is/are the object(s) of these obligations sufficiently identified, determined so as to become objects of obligations? Do you see any condition? If you answered affirmatively, on whose part is the condition, the obligor or obligee? Does it matter?

3. Lines 41–47: Why is the court saying, in fact, that there is no object? How should the issue of object be dealt with in the event an obligation is alternative? *See* lines 58–60.

4. Lines 65–70: Why was defendant's obligation unenforceable? Should the court be concerned about the quality of the object to the same extent it is concerned with the quantity of that object?

5. Lines 65–80: The court refers to the concept of "out of proportion" and to "serious and proportionate consideration requirement" and cites Louisiana Civil Code article 2464 which is concerned with the price in a contract of sale. Is this case dealing with a contract of sale? Why do you think the court can still say that the concepts of "out of proportion" and "serious and proportionate consideration" found in Louisiana Civil Code article 2464 are "applicable generally to all contracts"? Isn't to "all" contracts somewhat too broad a statement, and if so, why?

The SPRINGS THUNDER AGENCY, INC.
v.
ODOM INSURANCE AGENCY, INC.
Louisiana Court of Appeal
First Circuit
April 13, 1970
237 So.2d 96

ELLIS, Judge.

Plaintiff, The Springs Thunder Agency, Inc., operated a fire and casualty insurance agency in Denham Springs, Louisiana. In early 1968, a representative of Odom Insurance Agency, Inc., the defendant, contacted Mr. Spring, plaintiff's president, relative to buying the business. After some negotiation, the sale took place, as of June 1, 1968. A written contract was entered into which contained the following pertinent language:

'Things Sold: Seller conveys all records and files of the agency sold to Buyer and the exclusive right to the renewals on existing active accounts of the agency. Seller further agrees, in consideration of the price and other provisions of this agreement not to engage in the fire and casualty insurance business in competition with Buyer in Livingston Parish or in any Parish adjoining Livingston Parish for a period of five (5) years from the effective date of this agreement. Nothing herein shall be construed as prohibiting Seller brokering such business through the Buyer.

'Price: The price for which the agency is sold is the sum of Nine Thousand Sixteen and 71/100 ($9,016.71) Dollars which is allocated between the things sold as follows:

"Renewals of existing active accounts	$4,016.71
"Covenant not to compete with Buyer	5,000.00
"Total	$9,016.71"

A promissory note for $9,573.36, including interest, was given for the purchase price. The note was payable in 24 installments of $398.89 each, called for 8% Interest on each installment from maturity until paid, and 10% Attorney's fee, and contained an acceleration clause.

Among the accounts transferred was the Livingston Parish School Board account, which accounted for over 40% of the premium income of the agency. The School Board business was let by bids, and had been awarded to plaintiff for several years.

Defendant bid on the School Board business shortly after the sale was completed, but was unsuccessful. It then demanded a reduction in the purchase price by the amount of the premiums lost. Plaintiff refused this, but did agree to an adjustment of $261.11 for eight policies on which it had requested cancellation because of nonpayment of the premium.

Defendant then stopped paying on the note, beginning with the payment due on November 1, 1968. Four payments had been made prior to that time. Plaintiff filed this suit for the balance of $7,977.80 due on the note, together with 8% Interest on the balance from maturity until paid, and 10% Attorney's fee.

Defendant answered, admitted the execution of the note, and the payments thereon, but denied the indebtedness. In its reconventional demand, defendant alleged that plaintiff had withheld from defendant certain facts of which it had knowledge which showed that the School Board business and other business would not be renewed, and that Odom would not have entered into the contract if full disclosure had been made. The answer further alleges an additional agreement between the parties that the price would be adjusted down pro rata to the extent that any of the then existing accounts failed to renew, but that this part of the agreement was inadvertently omitted from the agreement.

After trial on the merits, and without assigning reasons, the trial court rendered judgment for plaintiff for $7,725.60, with interest from October 4, 1968, until paid, and 10% Attorney's fee. From this judgment, defendant has appealed suspensively. Defendant has answered, asking that the judgment be increased to the full amount prayed for, and for damages for a frivolous appeal.

We find no evidence in the record to substantiate the allegation that there was any misrepresentation, or the withholding of any information by the plaintiff.

[....]

What plaintiff sold and what defendant bought was the present right to such future renewals as might occur. This is the sale of a hope under Article 2451 of the Civil Code, as opposed to the sale of a future thing or thing to come, under Articles 1887 and 2450 of the Civil Code. In the latter case, if the thing sold never comes into existence, the contract can have no effect. Had plaintiff sold the 'renewals' only, the sale would be governed by Article 2450. But plaintiff sold the 'right to renewals' and the failure of any or all of the accounts to renew can have no effect on the validity of the contract. See Losecco v. Gregory, 108 La. 648, 32 So. 985 (1901).

Since we are of the opinion that defendant got what he paid for, we need not consider his argument relative to failure of consideration.   62
63

Defendant claims, alternatively, that since interest is included in the note, the judgment appealed from is, in effect, forcing defendant to pay interest on interest. This contention is without merit under the express provisions of Article 2924 of the Civil Code. Williams v. Alphonse Mortgage Co., 144 So.2d 600 (La.App. 4 Cir. 1962).   64 65 66 67

Plaintiff asks for judgment on the full amount prayed for. He claims that the credit of $261.11 offered in plaintiff's letter of October 14, 1968, was a compromise offer and should not be considered by the court in rendering its judgment. However, as we understand the letter, as explained by the testimony of plaintiff's president, these accounts were cancelled because the premiums were never paid, and, therefore, should not have been included in the gross premium income figure used in computing the purchase price.   68 69 70 71 72 73

[....]

Questions

1. Lines 9–26: What kind of parties are involved in this case? Should it matter? Read carefully lines 14–20. How many objects are listed under "Things Sold"? How are those things related one to the other? Are all of the things of the same legal nature? *See* La. Civ. Code arts. 448–475 on "Things" and "Division of Things". Now read lines 21–23. Are the things listed under "Price" referred to in the same manner as they are listed above under "Things Sold"? Could there exist a problem of interpretation?

2. Lines 30–37: What did defendant buy: an existing thing (if so, what is it?) or a future thing (and if so, what is it?)?

3. Lines 54–63: Do you agree with the Court's analysis of "a future thing" (*see* La. Civ. Code arts. 1976, 1887, 2450), "a hope" (*see* La. Civ. Code art. 2451), and "an aleatory contract" (*see* La. Civ. Code art. 1912)? How would you distinguish between a hope and a future thing?

Nolton ANDREPONT   1

v.   2

ACADIA DRILLING CO., Inc., et al.   3

Supreme Court of Louisiana   4
Feb. 24, 1969   5
231 So.2d 347   6

SANDERS, Justice.   7

Nolton Andrepont, a tenant farmer, sued for damages to his soybean crop caused by defendants during the drilling of an oil well on the land. [....]   8 9

Andrepont entered into a verbal lease with the heirs of A. A. Bundick, whereby plaintiff acquired the right to farm a tract of land for a rental of twenty per cent of the crop harvested. Thereafter, the landowners executed an oil lease on the property, granting the lessee the right to use the land to explore for oil. The oil lease was duly recorded.   10 11 12 13

Paragraph 8 of the lease originally read, 'The lessee shall be responsible for all damages to timber and growing crops of lessor caused by lessee's operations.' However, the words   14 15 'to timber and growing crops of lessor' were struck out. Thus the lease provided: 'The lessee shall be responsible for all damages caused by lessee's operations.'

Under the lease, a drilling company drilled a well on the land in search of oil. Later, the defendants paid the landowners $125.00 for damages and received a release from them.

Defendants made no payment to Andrepont, the tenant, and he brought this action ex delicto, or in tort, for damages to his growing soybean crop. In this Court he also contends he is entitled to recover under the mineral lease provision obligating the lessee to pay for all damages, asserting that the provision is a stipulation Pour autrui.

When standing crops do not belong to the owner of the land, they are regarded as movables subject to separate ownership rather than as a part of the land. Such crops are treated as if they were harvested. LSA-C.C. Art. 465. See Fallin v. J. J. Stovall & Sons, 141 La. 220, 74 So. 911; Citizens' Bank v. Wiltz, 31 La.Ann. 244; Porche v. Bodin, 28 La.Ann. 761; Yiannopoulos, Civil Law Property, s 44, pp. 134–135 (1966). Such separate ownership may be derived from a variety of contractual relationships. When it is derived from a farm lease, the lease is of course subject to the law of registry insofar as third persons are concerned.

LSA-R.S. 9:2721 provides:

'No sale, contract, counter letter, lien, mortgage, judgment, surface lease, oil, gas or mineral lease or other instrument of writing relating to or affecting immovable property shall be binding on or affect third persons or third parties unless and until filed for registry in the office of the parish recorder of the parish where the land or immovable is situated; and neither secret claims or equities nor other matters outside the public records shall be binding on or affect such third parties.'

Under the foregoing statute, an unrecorded lease is ineffective against third persons to establish separate crop ownership. Separate ownership arising from a lease can be asserted against third persons only when the lease is recorded. LSA-R.S. 9:2721; LSA-C.C. Arts. 2264, 2266. See Minter v. Union Cent. Life Ins. Co., 180 La. 38, 156 So. 167; Summers & Brannins v. Clark, 30 La.Ann. 436; Yiannopoulos, Civil Law of Property, s 44, p. 135 (1966).

In the present case, plaintiff's farm lease is unrecorded. It is a verbal contract, foreign to the public records. He cannot assert his separate ownership of the standing crop against the defendants, since they are third persons. As to them, the standing crop is considered as part of the land. LSA-C.C. Art. 465. Hence, under neither theory, can plaintiff recover crop damages from defendants.

For the reasons assigned, the judgment of the Court of Appeal is affirmed.

ON REHEARING

SUMMERS, Justice

Nolton Andrepont brings this action for damage to his soybean crop. He is the share crop tenant or farm lessee of Estelle Berdick Murphy who owns the land upon which the crop was grown and a portion of the minerals which underlie the tract. [....]

[....] On original hearing in this Court, plaintiff's demands were rejected. Upon reconsideration we find that we erred. Plaintiff should recover.

During 1964 Andrepont was granted a verbal lease to farm soybeans on a 35-acre tract in Acadia Parish, a condition being that he pay the landowner twenty percent of the crop as rent. Thereafter, on September 15, 1964, the land and mineral owners of the tract executed an oil and gas lease granting to the lessees the right to go upon the land to explore for and produce oil, gas and other minerals. In the printed form used to confect the lease, it was provided as a condition of the contract that 'The Lessee shall be responsible for all damages to timber and growing crops of Lessor caused by Lessee's operations.' This clause was altered by deleting the words 'to timber and growing crops of Lessor' with the result that the clause then read: 'The Lessee shall be responsible for all damages caused by Lessee's operations.'

During the spring of 1965 Andrepont cultivated and planted the field in soybeans with early indications of a successful crop. Then, during July, the oil and gas lessee entered upon the land, built a board road across Andrepont's field, dug waste pits and proceeded to drill a well in search of minerals. Construction of the road, the drill site and pits destroyed part of the crop and impaired drainage in the remainder of the soybean field. The lack of adequate drainage left water standing in the field and made it impracticable to work the crop. As a result, the remainder of Andrepont's crop was damaged by 'scalding' and excessive weeds.

When the drilling operations resulted in a dry hole, defendants removed their equipment. In consideration of $125, they obtained a release from the landowner for 'her' damage as a result of their operations. In spite of Andrepont's repeated efforts to contact persons in authority at the well site to demand reparations, he was unable to do so. He received no payment from defendants, and on October 18, 1965 this suit was filed claiming damages to the crop caused by the oil and gas lessee's operations.

In our initial consideration of the case, we found that the verbal farm lease, which would establish ownership of the farm lessee's share of the crop in the farm lessee and permit the crop to be classified in law as a movable, could have no effect against third persons, for the farm lease was not recorded as required by Section 2721 of Title 9 of the Revised Statutes, providing:

No sale, contract, counter letter, lien, mortgage, judgment, surface lease, oil, gas or mineral lease or other instrument of writing relating to or affecting immovable property shall be binding on or affect third persons or third parties unless and until filed for registry in the office of the parish recorder of the parish where the land or immovable is situated; and neither secret claims or equities nor other matters outside the public records shall be binding on or affect such third parties.

Hence we decided Andrepont could not recover for damage to the crop, which was an immovable and part of the land insofar as third parties were concerned, and only the record owner of rights in the land could assert claims for damage to the crop against third persons. We gave no consideration to Andrepont's contention that he was entitled to recover under the mineral lease provision, which he contends is a stipulation Pour autrui in his favor, obligating the lessee to pay all damages caused by its operations.

We now feel that a proper disposition of this case requires a recognition that the quoted clause of the lease is a stipulation Pour autrui in favor of Andrepont. As the beneficiary of the stipulation, Andrepont has a direct right of action against the oil and gas lessee to recover for his damages, and the law of registry is inapplicable to his claim.

Andrepont is not asserting 'secret claims or equities' unknown to defendants. He is seeking to enforce a benefit stipulated in his favor by the landowner lessor as a condition of a commutative contract between the landowner lessor and the oil and gas lessee. Defendants, as assignees of the oil and gas lessee, are, therefore, parties to the contract in which the stipulation is a condition; defendants are not third persons protected by the laws of registry insofar as Andrepont's claim is concerned. In reaching this conclusion, we have, in effect, paraphrased the language of Mr. Justice McCaleb writing for the Court in

110 Mallet v. Thibault, 212 La. 79, 92, 31 So.2d 601 (1947) where a like contention was made
111 in a different factual context. However, the principle involved in the case at bar is the
112 same, and the Mallet decision is authority for the reasons we have expressed.

113   Stipulations in favor of third persons (stipulation Pour autrui) are favored in our law.
114 They are specifically authorized in broad terms in Articles 1890 and 1902 of the Civil Code.

115   Article 1890 provides:

116   A person may also, in his own name, make some advantage for a third person the con-
117 dition or consideration of a commutative contract, or onerous donation; and if such third
118 person consents to avail himself of the advantage stipulated in his favor, the contract can
119 not be revoked.

120   Article 1902 provides:

121   But a contract, in which anything is stipulated for the benefit of a third person, who
122 has signified his assent to accept it, can not be revoked as to the advantage stipulated in
123 his favor without his consent.

124   Professor J. Denson Smith, in a study of the history, legislation and jurisprudence
125 which have formed the doctrine of stipulations in favor of third persons in this State, has
126 enumerated the factors to be considered in deciding whether an advantage for a third
127 person has been provided by contract between others. They are:

128   (1) The existence of a legal relationship between the promisee and the third person
129 involving an obligation owed by the promisee to the beneficiary which performance of the
130 promise will discharge; (2) the existence of a factual relationship between the promisee
131 and the third person, where (a) there is a possibility of future liability either personal or
132 real on the part of the promisee to the beneficiary against which performance of the
133 promisee (sic) will protect the former; (b) securing an advantage for the third person
134 may beneficially affect the promisee in a material way; (c) there are ties of kinship or
135 other circumstances indicating that a benefit by way of gratuity was intended. See Smith,
136 Third Party Beneficiaries in Louisiana: The Stipulation Pour Autrui, 11 Tul.L.Rev. 18, 58
137 (1936).

138   The obligation created by the relationship of lessor and lessee which is pertinent to
139 this case is expressed in the following language of Civil Code Article 2692:

140   The lessor is bound from the very nature of the contract, and without any clause to
141 that effect:

142   3. To cause the lessee to be in peaceable possession of the thing during the
143   continuance of the lease.

144   Section 3203 of Title 9 of the Revised Statutes also imposes an obligation upon the
145 lessor in favor of the lessee in these words:

146   Any lessor of property to be cultivated who fails to permit the lessee to occupy or cul-
147 tivate the property leased, is liable to the lessee in an amount equal to the market value
148 of the average crop that could have been grown on the land or on like land located in the
149 immediate vicinity.

150   Viewed in the context of the facts of this case, and upon application of the formula ar-
151 ticulated by Smith, it is readily apparent that the legal relationship between the promisee
152 (landowner lessor) and the third person (the farm lessee Andrepont) involved an oblig-
153 ation ('to cause the lessee to be in peaceable possession') owed by the promisee (landowner
154 lessor) to the beneficiary (farm lessee) which performance of the promise (payment of all
155 damages caused by the oil and gas lessee's operation) would discharge.

Thus each requirement of the law is satisfied. The obligation imposed by the landowner lessor and undertaken by the oil and gas lessee as a condition of the lease—that is, to 'be responsible for all damages caused by Lessee's operations', constitutes a stipulation for the benefit of a third party, the farm lessee Andrepont, to pay for damage to his crop caused by the oil and gas lessee's operations.

Because the inference is clear that drilling operations in a cultivated field must damage the crop and bring about a disturbance in the peaceable possession of the farm lessee, the landowner lessor is obviously interested in requiring the oil and gas lessee to undertake her obligation to indemnify the farm lessee in the event the oil and gas lessee's operations should result in a failure to maintain the farm lessee in peaceable possession of the leased premises. Otherwise the farm lessee's forthcoming claim for damages must be satisfied by her. See La.Civil Code Art. 2692 and La.R.S. 9:3203.

In addition to her interest in having the oil and gas lessee discharge the obligation which she owed to the farm lessee, the relationship between the landowner and the farm lessee was sufficient to support the inference that there was a possibility of future liability either personal or real on the part of the landowner to the farm lessee against which performance of the promise would protect the landowner. This possibility of future liability stems from the very obligation the landowner was anxious to have the oil and gas lessee discharge. And the liability is the very crop damage involved here. In other words, the case at bar fits into two of the categories envisaged by Smith in formulating the rules applicable to stipulations Pour autrui.

Another factor which persuades us to conclude that there was an intention to require the oil and gas lessee to repair the farm lessee's damage is the deletion from the printed oil and gas lease of the words 'to timber and growing crops of Lessor' so that the clause would read: 'The Lessee shall be responsible for all damages caused by Lessee's operations.' This deletion results in a change from the particular to the general and means that damages caused by the oil and gas lessee's operations to parties other than the lessor were clearly contemplated. And since drilling operations on the cultivated field must result in damage to the farm lessee, the farm lessee was undoubtedly intended as a beneficiary of this stipulation.

Defendants' briefs suggest two principal defenses to the application of the doctrine of stipulation Pour autrui here. It is asserted that (1) the third party beneficiary in the case at bar was not named or determinable, and (2) there was no consent to or acceptance of the benefits by the third party beneficiary.

The contention that the third party was not named is without merit. Planiol gives the answer to this contention in his treatise 'Traite E le mentaire De Droit Civil', An English Translation by the Louisiana State Law Institute, Vol. 2-Part 1, No. 1236 (1959):

Can one stipulate for undetermined persons? Yes, on the condition that the beneficiaries of the stipulation, at present undetermined, are determinable on the day on which the agreement is to have effect for their benefit. The obstacle to the effectiveness of a stipulation for another, is not therefore strictly speaking the simple present undetermined character of its beneficiaries, provided there are means to ascertain who they are when it becomes necessary to do so, but their future undetermined character, which must remain undefined, in other words, their undeterminability. * * *

The principle has been recognized and has found application in the jurisprudence.

A materialman, though furnishers of materials were not named as obligees in the condition of a bond in favor of the owner in a building contract, was given a right of action against the surety on the bond in Lichtentag v. Feitel, 113 La. 931, 37 So. 880 (1905). This conclusion was reached on the theory that since the bond was conditioned on the contractor's fulfilling the terms of his contract with the owner, payment of such claims by the contractor was necessary in order to fulfill the condition of the bond, and it could not be satisfied if the latter had left outstanding claims of materialmen to be paid by the owner enforceable by lien against the property. In like manner the stipulation that the oil and gas lessee would be 'responsible for all damages caused by Lessee's operations' cannot be considered as fulfilled if a farm lessee's damage claim 'caused by Lessee's operations' remains unsatisfied. To the same effect see Minden Presbyterian Church v. Lambert, 167 La. 712, 120 So. 61 (1929).

A contractor removing dirt from a public road, who contracted with the public authority to maintain a nearby bridge during his operations, was deemed to have obligated himself in favor of the traveling public. Thus the Court held that a traveler whose wagon fell through the bridge could maintain a cause of action against the contractor for his damages. Lawson v. Shreveport Waterworks Co., 111 La. 73, 35 So. 390 (1903).

In Volquardsen v. Southern Amusement Company, 156 So. 678 (La.App.1934) a member of a union, though unnamed, was permitted to entertain suit on a contract between the union and the defendant as a beneficiary of a stipulation in his favor made by the union with the defendant.

Children in a parish, though unnamed and then undetermined, were recognized to have the right as third party beneficiaries to enforce a stipulation in their favor contained in a contract between a parish school board and superintendent of schools with the United States. Lemon v. Bossier Parish School Board, 240 F.Supp. 709 (D.C.1965).

The facts of this case readily fall within the rule of law established by these cases and expounded by Planiol. There is no problem in determining who the beneficiary of the stipulation Pour autrui is. He is the party suffering damages on the leased premises as a result of the oil and gas lessee's operations. He is in this case Andrepont, the farm lessee.

Equally without merit is the argument that the third party beneficiary cannot avail himself of the stipulation in his favor for he has not consented to or accepted the stipulation. A categorical answer to this contention is found in a recent decision of this Court. Mr. Justice LeBlanc, speaking for the Court in First State Bank v. Burton, 225 La. 537, 549, 73 So.2d 453, 457 (1954), said:

The law does not provide for an express acceptance of or consent to a stipulation pour autrui by the beneficiary nor does it prescribe and particular form of acceptance or consent. In some cases it was held that the appearance of the beneficiary as claimant in a suit before the Court is evidence of acceptance and certainly it would seem, under that jurisprudence that the claim now being asserted by Morris & Kendrick in this proceeding, regardless of any proof of their assent, is sufficient. See Muntz v. Algiers & Gretna Ry. Co., 114 La. 437, 38 So. 410; Vinet v. Bres, 48 La.Ann. 1254, 20 So. 693.

See also Twichel v. Andry, 6 Rob. 407 (La.1844); Smith, Third Party Beneficiaries in Louisiana: The Stipulation Pour Autrui, 11 Tul.L.Rev. 18, 55 (1936).

As beneficiary of the stipulation, therefore, Andrepont should recover for damage to his crop. After a careful review of the evidence, the trial court awarded $1,298.25. We find no cause to disturb this award.

In doing so we reject Andrepont's contention that the trial judge erroneously deducted twenty percent from the amount of the crop loss because the landowner had settled for 'her' damages. In a lease of land for part of the crop, that part which the lessor is to receive is considered at all times the property of lessor. La.R.S. 9:3204. It was, therefore, permissible for the landowner to accept a nominal amount for the damage to her share, and Andrepont cannot recover a second time for the same damage.

For the reasons assigned, the judgment of the Court of Appeal is reversed. There is judgment in favor of plaintiff and against defendants for $1,298.25, with interest from date of judicial demand until paid and for all costs.

HAMITER, J., dissents.

SANDERS, J., dissents, adhering to the views expressed on original hearing.

BARHAM, Justice (dissenting).

I dissent, being of the view that our original opinion is correct. I voted for the rehearing for clarification of the applicant's strongly urged contention that we had incorrectly made R.S. 9:2721 (registry of instruments affecting immovables) applicable to movables. The court on first hearing stated the proposition, and in its citation of cases and of Yiannopoulos, Civil Law of Property, appropriately disposed of the plaintiff's contention. R.S. 9:2721 states: 'No * * * surface lease * * * or other instrument of writing *relating to* or *affecting* immovable property shall be binding on or affect third persons or third parties unless and until filed for registry * * *.' (Emphasis supplied.) The separation of the ownership of the standing crop from the ownership of the land by lease is a surface lease 'relating to or Affecting immovable property' within the contemplation of R.S. 9:2721, for it changes the character of the property from immovable to movable, and therefore the provisions of the lease have no effect upon third parties except through the notice required under R.S. 9:2721.

I respectfully dissent, adhering to our conclusion on first hearing.

Questions

1. Lines 8–13: Notice that the lease between the farmer and the Bundicks was oral, whereas the lease with Acadia Drilling Co. was in writing and recorded. Now read the Louisiana Civil Code articles on Lease (La. Civ. Code art. 2668 *et seq.*). Must a lease be in writing? Is there any benefit in a lease being recorded? Notice how the farmer is to pay the rent: 20% of the crop harvested. Now read Louisiana Civil Code articles 474, 480, 490, 491. Do you have any comment?

2. Lines 14–23: Explain how the change in words could amount to a stipulation pour autrui (a stipulation for the benefit of another). How can the farmer take advantage of a contract between his landlord and Acadia Drilling, a contract to which that farmer is not a party?

3. Lines 24–31: Would Civil Code articles 463 and 474 have been relevant here and have been relied on by the Court?

4. Lines 53 *et seq.*: Do you think that in rewriting the contract, the landlord and the oil company did intend to involve the farmer, to stipulate in his favor so as to make him a party to the contract? What could have motivated the court to find a stipulation pour autrui in the rewriting of the contract?

5. Lines 82 *et seq.*: Read carefully the following paragraphs as they give a good explanation of the court's interpretation of the contract in favor of the farmer. Since a stipulation for the benefit of another vests a benefit (never can it create a detriment) in the farmer, his consent is not required for the benefit to be created in his favor (in

other words, one is always presumed to be willing to accept a benefit). Read Louisiana Civil Code article 1978. What is the consequence of the third party beneficiary manifesting his intent to avail himself of the benefit?

6. Lines 168–185: As the court is expanding on the rewriting of the contract, is the court giving any hint as to how the landlord and the oil company could be held liable to the farmer? What would be the source of the oil company's liability? What would be the source of the landlord's liability? Are those sources of liability different? What type of liability could exist between the landlord and the oil company?

Note: This case is a good illustration of a well-known principle at civil law according to which "no one can transfer to another a greater right than he has" (*Nemo potior jure ad alium transfere potest quam ipse habet*). *See* the following Louisiana Civil Code articles as an illustration: 2700–2702.

1 **Dr. Willie John JOSEPH, III, Dr. Michelle T. Brumfield, and**
2 **St. Mary Anesthesia Associates, Inc.**
3 **v.**
4 **HOSPITAL SERVICE DISTRICT NO. 2 OF the PARISH OF**
5 **ST. MARY, State of Louisiana, Our Lady of the Lake Hospital, Inc.,**
6 **Melvin Bourgeois, M.D., James Broussard, John Guarisco, Sharon**
7 **Howell, Y. George Ramirez, Clifford M. Broussard, National Union**
8 **Fire Insurance Company of Louisiana and Louisiana Hospital**
9 **Association Malpractice and General Liability Trust [....]**
10 Supreme Court of Louisiana
11 Oct. 15, 2006
12 939 So.2d 1206

13 WEIMER, Justice.

14 We are called upon to determine whether a contract between a hospital and a medical
15 corporation provides a stipulation for a third party (also referred to as a stipulation *pour*
16 *autrui*) in the form of benefits for individual doctors affiliated with the medical corpo-
17 ration. This matter is before the court on defendants' exceptions of no right of action,
18 which contend the doctors are not third party beneficiaries of the contract. The trial court
19 granted defendants' exceptions and dismissed the plaintiff doctors' claims with prejudice.
20 The court of appeal reversed and defendants filed an application for writ of certiorari.
21 For reasons that follow, we reinstate the judgment of the trial court finding the contract
22 at issue does not create a stipulation *pour autrui* in favor of the plaintiff doctors. Conse-
23 quently, the doctors have no right of action.

24 FACTS AND PROCEDURAL BACKGROUND

25 On December 13, 1990, Hospital Service District No. 2 of the Parish of St. Mary (Hos-
26 pital), operator of Lakewood Medical Center, entered into a contract with St. Mary Anes-
27 thesia Associates, Inc. (SMAA) for the purpose of obtaining general anesthesia services
28 for the hospital's patients. The contract was signed by Raymond J. Rowell, chief operat-
29 ing officer of the Hospital, and Willie J. Joseph, III, M.D., president of SMAA. The con-
30 tract provided for automatic annual renewal unless terminated by the Hospital for cause
31 as defined in the contract or by SMAA giving no less than 60 days notice prior to the end
32 of the original term or any renewal period.

In November 2000, then chief operating officer of the Hospital, Clifford M. Brous- 33
sard, advised SMAA that the contact would terminate within 30 days from the date of 34
the letter because the contract was not in the Hospital's best interest. 35

Dr. Willie John Joseph, III, Dr. Michelle T. Brumfield, and SMAA filed suit on August 36
19, 2003, naming as defendants the Hospital, Our Lady of the Lake Hospital, Inc., Melvin 37
Bourgeois, M.D., James Broussard, John Guarisco, Sharon Howell, Y. George Ramirez, Clif- 38
ford M. Broussard, National Union Fire Insurance Company of Louisiana, and Louisiana 39
Hospital Association Malpractice and General Liability Trust. 40

Alleging breach of contract, the petitioners sought damages, including, but not lim- 41
ited to, past and future loss of earnings, costs of relocation and "moral damages," men- 42
tal anguish, grief and anxiety on behalf of the doctors, and future loss of earnings on 43
behalf of SMAA. Pursuant to a provision contained in the contract, plaintiffs also sought 44
attorney fees in connection with this litigation.[1] 45

Defendants filed exceptions of no right of action regarding the claims asserted by the 46
doctors contending that SMAA was the only party with a real and actual interest in the 47
contract and the doctors had no individual right to sue for a corporate loss. The doctors 48
argued the contract expressed an intent to stipulate a benefit in favor of the doctors and 49
that this benefit was a material consideration for the contract. 50

[....] 51

[....] Thus, the question to be resolved is whether the contract clearly manifested an 52
intent to stipulate a benefit for a third person. The court of appeal rejected the hospital's 53
argument that the stipulation itself must be in writing to be valid and questioned the va- 54
lidity of the statement in *Fontenot v. Marquette Casualty Co.*, 258 La. 671, 247 So.2d 572 55
(1971), requiring a stipulation *pour autrui* to be in writing. The focus of the court's con- 56
cern involved the following statement in *Fontenot*: "In Louisiana contracts for the bene- 57
fit of others, or the stipulation pour autrui, must be in writing and clearly express that 58
intent." *Fontenot*, 247 So.2d at 579. The *Fontenot* court cited former Civil Code articles 59
1890 and 1902 as authority for the statement.[2] 60

[....] 61

DISCUSSION 62

[....] 63

Collectively, the defendants contend the claims set forth in this case belong to SMAA, 64
not the doctors/employees, thus the exception of no right of action is proper. Defendants 65
also argue the decision of the court of appeal conflicts with this court's decision in Fontenot, 66
as well as decisions from other appellate courts and should be overturned. They claim 67
the stipulation *pour autrui* must be in writing and, thus an oral stipulation *pour autrui* 68
is unenforceable. 69

It is plaintiffs' position that the court of appeal was correct in its interpretation of the 70
Fontenot decision. *Fontenot* involved a reinsuring agreement[3] which is statutorily required 71

---

1. A judgment granting the peremptory exception of prescription filed on behalf of defendants against plaintiffs and dismissing the cause of action in tort (including the intentional interference with contract and the denial of due process rights) asserted on behalf of plaintiffs was signed on July 7, 2004.
2. The substance of these articles was reproduced in LSA-C.C. art. 1978 when the Civil Code was amended in 1984. 1984 La. Acts No. 331 § 1, effective Jan. 1, 1985.
3. Reinsurance is a contract by which one insurance company agrees to indemnify another in whole or in part against loss or liability which the latter has incurred under a separate contract as insurer of a third party. *Fontenot*, 247 So.2d at 575. Reinsurance indemnifies the insurer for a loss which

to be in writing. Plaintiffs assert the statement in *Fontenot* requiring a stipulation *pour autrui* to be in writing is merely dicta. In this case, plaintiffs argue the benefits they were to receive were clearly contemplated by the parties to the contract and were not merely incidental. They assert the court of appeal decision is correct and should be affirmed.

At the hearing on the exceptions, defendants introduced a copy of the contract dated December 13, 1990. The contract, an anesthesia service agreement, was executed by and between the Hospital and SMAA. Dr. Joseph signed the contract on behalf of SMAA, but not in his individual capacity. Dr. Brumfield is not mentioned in the contract. In the contract, SMAA was referred to as the "Contractor." The Hospital agreed to retain the Contractor to exclusively provide anesthesia services. The Hospital agreed to provide facilities, equipment, and supplies necessary and proper for the administration of anesthesia to its patients. Additionally, the Hospital agreed to recognize Dr. Joseph as a "medical specialist" providing services on behalf of the Contractor. The Hospital also agreed to recognize any employee of the Contractor (any duly licensed and qualified physician trained in delivery of anesthesia services and licensed to practice in Louisiana) as a "medical specialist" on behalf of the Contractor, SMAA.

The contract further provided that the Contractor may from time to time retain the services of other physician specialists who were to comply with all of the terms and conditions of the agreement.

The contract specifically provided that the Contractor was an "independent contractor" and clearly stated there was no intent to create an employer/employee relationship, a joint venture relationship, or lease or landlord/tenant relationship. The agreement was to be binding on the Hospital and Contractors, their successors and assigns.

Because the plaintiff doctors were not parties to the contract, they can only avail themselves of the benefit of the Hospital/SMAA contract if they are third party beneficiaries. LSA-C.C. art. 1978 provides:

A contracting party may stipulate a benefit for a third person called a third party beneficiary.

Once the third party has manifested his intention to avail himself of the benefit, the parties may not dissolve the contract by mutual consent without the beneficiary's agreement.

The Revision Comments indicate this article reproduces the substance of LSA-C.C. arts. 1890 and 1902 and the law was not changed. Under Louisiana law, such a contract for the benefit of a third party is commonly referred to as a "stipulation *pour autrui*."[4] *Paul v. Louisiana State Employees' Group Benefit Program*, 99-0897, p. 5 (La.App. 1 Cir. 5/12/00), 762 So.2d 136, 140.

Under Roman law, a stipulation for a third party was unenforceable, despite the fact that the word "stipulation" comes from the Roman *stipulatio*. Nevertheless, the French and Louisiana Codes set to rest any contention that a third party could not recover on a contract merely because he was not a party to the contract. *See* discussion by Professor J. Denson Smith of the historical development of this doctrine in his article *Third Party*

---

is actually sustained. In *Fontenot*, an insured of one insurance company filed suit claiming the contract of reinsurance between his insurer and another company contained a stipulation *pour autrui* inuring to his benefit. The court held the contract was governed by the insurance code and the contract of reinsurance did not create any right of action in third parties directly against the reinsurer. *Fontenot*, 247 So.2d at 581.

4. BLACK'S LAW DICTIONARY 1427 (7th ed.1999), refers to stipulation *pour autrui* as a French civil law term meaning a stipulation "for other persons."

Beneficiaries in Louisiana: The Stipulation Pour Autrui at 11 Tul. L.Rev. 18, 18-28 (1936). Although the current Article 1978 had its underpinnings in the French Civil Code, the term "*stipulation pour autrui*" was not employed in the Louisiana Civil Code. Professor Smith, however, called the term a "well established part of our legal language." Smith, 11 Tul. L.Rev. at 23. The term remains a part of our legal language today.

There has been a codal provision in Louisiana recognizing a stipulation for a third party since 1808. *See* Article 21 of the Louisiana Civil Code of 1808; *see also* Art. 1890, La. C.C. Comp. Ed., in 16 West's LSA-C.C. pp. 1076–1077 (1972).

A true third party beneficiary is never a party to the contract in question; he is never a promisee. Smith, 11 Tul. L.Rev. at 33. The promisee is the stipulator and the promise runs to him and is merely in favor of the third party. *Id.*

The Louisiana Civil Code recognizes that a third party beneficiary contract can exist, but provides few governing rules. *See* LSA-C.C. arts. 1978–1982. The code provides no analytic framework for determining whether a third party beneficiary contract exists. Professor Smith acknowledges that a determination of the circumstances under which a stipulation *pour autrui* will exist is the "primary question" in any given case. Smith, 11 Tul. L.Rev. at 24. Thus, the code has left to the jurisprudence the obligation to develop the analysis to determine when a third party beneficiary contract exists on a case by case basis. Each contract must be evaluated on its own terms and conditions in order to determine if the contract stipulates a benefit for a third person.[5]

In a study of the history, legislation, and jurisprudence which formed the doctrine of stipulations in favor of third persons, Professor Smith enumerated the following factors as being important in deciding whether the contract provides a benefit for a third person:

(1) The existence of a legal relationship between the promisee and the third person involving an obligation owed by the promisee to the beneficiary which performance of the promise will discharge; (2) the existence of a factual relationship between the promisee and the third person, where (a) there is a possibility of future liability either personal or real on the part of the promisee to the beneficiary against which performance of the promisee [sic] will protect the former; (b) securing an advantage for the third person may beneficially affect the promisee in a material way; (c) there are ties of kinship or other circumstances indicating that a benefit by way of gratuity was intended. See Smith, Third Party Beneficiaries in Louisiana: The Stipulation Pour Autrui, 11 Tul.L.Rev. 18, 58 (1936).

Andrepont, 231 So.2d at 350–351.

Our study of the jurisprudence has revealed three criteria for determining whether contracting parties have provided a benefit for a third party: 1) the stipulation for a third party is manifestly clear; 2) there is certainty as to the benefit provided the third party; and 3) the benefit is not a mere incident of the contract between the promisor and the promisee. In applying these criteria, we ultimately rely on the words of Article 1978 that the contract must "stipulate a benefit for a third person."

The most basic requirement of a stipulation *pour autrui* is that the contract manifest a clear intention to benefit the third party; absent such a clear manifestation, a party

---

5. In *Andrepont v. Acadia Drilling Co.,* 255 La. 347, 231 So.2d 347 (1969), this court utilized the factors proposed by Professor J. Denson Smith to be considered in deciding whether an advantage for a third person has been provided by a contract between others. We recognize Professor Smith's test is an analytical tool to determine whether a stipulation *pour autrui* has been established — not a definitive analysis.

claiming to be a third party beneficiary cannot meet his burden of proof. *Paul*, 99-0897 at 7–8, 762 So.2d at 141–142; *see also, Doucet v. National Maintenance Corporation*, 01-1100, pp. 6–7 (La.App. 1 Cir. 6/21/02), 822 So.2d 60, 66. A stipulation *pour autrui* is never presumed. The party claiming the benefit bears the burden of proof. *See* LSA-C.C. art. 1831;[6] *see also Paul*, 99-0897 at 5, 762 So.2d at 140.

The second factor, certainty as to the benefit provided, is a corollary of the requirement of a manifestly clear stipulation. "To create a legal obligation enforceable by the beneficiary there must be certainty as to the benefit to accrue to the beneficiary." *Berry v. Berry*, 371 So.2d 1346, 1347 (La.App. 1 Cir.), *writ denied*, 373 So.2d 511 (1979).

In connection with the third requirement that the benefit cannot be a mere incident of the contract, we find pertinent the discussion of "incidental benefits" by Professor Smith, 11 Tul. L.Rev. at 28: "[N]ot every promise, performance of which may be advantageous to a third person, will create in him an actionable right. The problem is to separate the cases where an advantage has been stipulated from those where the advantage relied upon is merely an incident of the contract between the parties." Illustrative is *City of Shreveport v. Gulf Oil Corporation*, 431 F.Supp. 1 (W.D.La.1975), *aff'd*, 551 F.2d 93 (5th Cir.1977). The city brought an action against the oil company alleging that the oil company failed to provide over 670,000 gallons of gasoline to the city pursuant to a contract existing between the oil company and the State of Louisiana, thereby damaging the city. The court found the oil company/state contract provided "some benefit" to the city: in a time of serious inflation and energy shortage, Shreveport could purchase its fuel needs at a modest cost when compared to the market price. However, "[t]he contract was not made to obtain discharge of any legal obligation owed by the State to Shreveport.... Furthermore, the advantage which would accrue to the City would not beneficially affect the State." Thus, the advantage to the city was "an easily seen ... incidental benefit to the City" (*Id.* at 1210), which did not support a finding of third party beneficiary.

In *Allen & Currey Mfg. Co. v. Shreveport Waterworks Co.*, 113 La. 1091, 37 So. 980 (1905), a water company entered into a contract with the city to furnish water and maintain hydrants in good repair. The plaintiff sued the water company for damages sustained as a result of the loss of its building due to fire because of an alleged breach of the water company's obligation to maintain the hydrants. The supreme court held that the plaintiff had no right of action. The contract was between the city and the water company. The plaintiff, as an inhabitant of the city, was an incidental beneficiary[7] and as such had no right of action. *See* discussion in Smith, 11 Tul. L.Rev. at 50.

In this matter, the court of appeal found administration of anesthesia service to the hospital's patients was the object of the contract and concluded that SMAA, as a juridical person only,[8] was incapable of rendering such service. The court of appeal noted there was no allegation of breach of fiduciary trust and the damages alleged were personal to the doctors. The court of appeal found the contract clearly manifested an express intent to benefit Dr. Joseph and also manifested an intent to benefit Dr. Brumfield.

---

6. LSA-C.C. art. 1831 provides, in part:
    A party who demands performance of an obligation must prove the existence of the contract.
7. The Restatement of the Law of Contracts distinguishes intended beneficiaries who have legal rights from incidental beneficiaries who have no legal rights to enforce the contract. Restatement (Second) of Contracts, Introductory Note to Chapter 14 at 439 and § 302 (1979).
8. In a footnote the court noted the fact that SMAA was a corporation was not relevant to a decision in this matter.

We disagree. Following a thorough review of the provisions of the contract, we also conclude the contract is unambiguous. However, we find there are no provisions included in the contract which establish a stipulation for the doctors in a manifestly clear manner. We find no certainty as to the benefit provided the doctors. We find any benefit to the doctors a mere incident of the contract between the Hospital and SMAA.[9]

Ultimately, we find there is no benefit in the contract flowing directly to the doctors such that a benefit was stipulated in their favor. While the contract imposed certain obligations on the doctors regarding their qualifications, there was no benefit provided in the contract directly to the doctors that they could demand from the Hospital. The doctors were not to be paid by the Hospital. The doctors were not hired by the Hospital. The doctors had no right to demand employment by the Hospital. In fact, the contract specifically provided there was no intent to create an employer/employee relationship between the parties. Based on our review of the contract, there is no obligation owed by the Hospital to the individual doctors which will be discharged by performance of the contract because the contract provides no direct benefit to the doctors.

While the doctors can perform the services to satisfy the contractual obligations of the corporation, there are no direct benefits flowing to the plaintiff doctors. Simply stated, in the absence of a direct benefit conferred by the contract, the doctors cannot be third party beneficiaries pursuant to LSA-C.C. art. 1978.

A person may derive a benefit from a contract to which he is not a party without being a third party beneficiary. In this case, any benefit created by the contract in favor of the doctors was only incidental to their employment with SMAA.

The doctors contend that they benefitted from the contract because the Hospital granted them the exclusive right to provide anesthesiology services. However, a review of the contract establishes it is SMAA as the Contractor which is granted the exclusive right to provide anesthesia services. The contract provides: "HOSPITAL hereby EXCLUSIVELY retains CONTRACTOR, and CONTRACTOR hereby accepts such retention, to make available anesthesia services and to provide such other services in accordance with this agreement." Thus, SMAA is specifically and clearly granted the exclusive right to provide anesthesia services. Additionally, the contract provides SMAA can "from time to time retain the services of other physician SPECIALISTS," further indicating it is not the plaintiff doctors which have exclusivity, but rather SMAA. Based on this clause, physicians other than the plaintiff doctors could provide services on behalf of SMAA. As such, the contract does not provide the plaintiff doctors the exclusive right to provide anesthesia services at the hospital.

The contract goes on to recognize, not only Dr. Joseph, but any employee of SMAA as a medical specialist for the purpose of providing anesthesia services. However, that recognition merely establishes how the obligations of the contract are to be discharged by SMAA and does not, in a manifestly clear fashion, confer a benefit on the doctors as third parties. The doctors further contend they were afforded exclusivity because the contract would be terminated if, among other reasons, Dr. Joseph's license to practice medicine were sus-

194
195
196
197
198

199
200
201
202
203
204
205
206
207
208

209
210
211
212

213
214
215

216
217
218
219
220
221
222
223
224
225
226
227

228
229
230
231
232
233

---

9. We note one exception which is not at issue in this litigation. The contract does contain a stipulation *pour autrui* in the section of the contract addressing recruitment. The Hospital agreed to pay relocation costs incurred by a second physician specialist moving to Morgan City. Thus, although the contract did provide a stipulation *pour autrui* for the benefit of a doctor to be recruited by SMAA in the form of reimbursement of relocation costs, that benefit was manifestly clear, and outlined in the recruitment provision of the contract addressing relocation costs. The contract could have included additional benefits to inure to the doctors; however, it did not do so in a manifestly clear manner. Nevertheless, after a review of the record and as acknowledged at oral argument, that provision is not at issue.

234 pended, revoked, or terminated. However, the termination provision does not confer a
235 benefit. Rather, this provision merely recognizes conditions which serve to terminate the
236 contract. Regardless, the language from the contract, quoted above, establishes that the
237 exclusivity provision of the contract is in favor of SMAA and not the individual doctors.

238   Not every breach of a contract with a corporation provides a cause of action to the
239 employees or shareholders of that corporation. In essence, the court of appeal decision
240 created an implied right of action for employees of juridical entities to contest any con-
241 tract between the employing corporation and another entity if any benefit flowed to the
242 employee. In *Scaffidi and Chetta Entertainment v. University of New Orleans Foundation*,
243 04-1046 (La.App. 5 Cir. 2/15/05), 898 So.2d 491, *writ denied*, 05-0748 (La.5/6/05), 901
244 So.2d 1102, Scaffidi and Chetta established a corporation which entered into a contract
245 with the University of New Orleans Foundation. The court denied the personal claims of
246 shareholders Scaffidi and Chetta finding they were not third party beneficiaries of the
247 contract. The court further found the cause of action belonged solely to the corpora-
248 tion.[10] This decision reflects an appropriate reluctance to find a stipulation *pour autrui* in
249 favor of each shareholder or officer or employee of a juridical person. Once established,
250 the separate nature of the corporate existence must be respected.

251   The doctors urge us to ignore the corporate status of SMAA because a medical corporation
252 can only act through a physician. We refuse to do so. As a legal fiction, all corporations
253 act through individuals. Dr. Joseph chose to establish a medical corporation. This sepa-
254 rate juridical entity cannot be disregarded. *See* LSA-C.C. art. 24.[11] The breach of con-
255 tract claim is a claim to be asserted by the corporation, not the employees, officers or
256 shareholders of the corporation.

257   Finally, we agree that the court of appeal was correct to question the requirement of a writ-
258 ing to establish a stipulation *pour autrui*. The statement in *Fontenot* indicating that con-
259 tracts for the benefit of others must be in writing was dicta. The *Fontenot* court cited former
260 Civil Code articles 1890 and 1902 for that proposition. Review of the former articles, as well
261 as current articles related to a third party beneficiary contract (*See* Articles 1978–1982), in-
262 dicates there is no statutory requirement that the stipulation *pour autrui* be in writing.[12]

263   We note the statement in *Fontenot* that a stipulation *pour autrui* must be in writing
264 was criticized by Judge Covington in his dissent in *Berry*, 371 So.2d at 1352–1353, and
265 in Katherine Shaw Spaht & H. Alston Johnson, III, *The Work of the Appellate Courts for
266 the 1975–1976 Term-Obligations*, 37 La. L.Rev. 332, 346–347 (1977), which he cited.

267   Although the appellate court correctly found it unnecessary for a stipulation *pour
268 autrui* to be in writing, these parties contracted that their entire agreement must be in writ-

10. *See also Joe Conte Toyota, Inc. v. Toyota Motor Sales, U.S.A., Inc.*, 95-1630, (La.App. 4 Cir. 2/
12/97) 689 So.2d 650, *writ denied*, 97-0659 (La.4/25/97) 692 So.2d 1090, where the court affirmed
the trial court judgment granting an exception of no right of action ruling that shareholders and officers of a corporation and a guarantor of corporate obligations had no right to recover for acts committed against or causing damage to a corporation. Only the corporation can sue for breach of a
contract to which the corporation is a party.
11. LSA-C.C. art. 24 provides:
There are two kinds of persons: natural persons and juridical persons.
A natural person is a human being. A juridical person is an entity to which the law attributes personality, such as a corporation or a partnership. The personality of a juridical person is distinct from
that of its members.
12. There is no general requirement that stipulations *pour autrui* be in writing. However, if the
contract must be in writing (*See e.g.*, LSA-C.C. arts. 1536 and 2440. *See also* LSA-C.C. art.1832.),
then the stipulation *pour autrui* must also be in writing.

ing. The contract provides: "This Agreement contains the entire understanding of the   269
parties and shall be modified only by an instrument in writing signed on behalf of each   270
party hereto." Thus, these parties contractually limited themselves to a written contract.   271

CONCLUSION   272

For the foregoing reasons, the decision of the court of appeal is reversed and the judg-   273
ment rendered by the district court granting defendants exceptions of no right of action   274
is reinstated.   275

REVERSED. JUDGMENT GRANTING EXCEPTION REINSTATED.   276

JOHNSON, J., concurs in result.   277

Questions

1. In *Joseph,* the supreme court concludes that it was permissible for the court of ap-
    peal to reject and, in the end, to refuse to follow the rule of *Fontenot v. Marquette Ca-
    sualty Co.,* a prior supreme court case. *See,* lines 52–60, 257–266. Is that correct?
    Why? Imagine that *Joseph* had been decided in, say, Alabama. Do you suppose that
    the Alabama Supreme Court would have reacted in the same way had one of the
    state's intermediate appellate courts refused to follow one of its precedents? Why or
    why not? *See generally* La. Civ. Code. arts. 1 to 4.

2. What role did "doctrine" (what an Anglo-American lawyer would call "legal schol-
    arship") play in the *Joseph* court's interpretation of the legislation governing stipu-
    lations pour autrui?

3. One of the principal linchpins of the Joseph court's analysis involves the distinction
    between true third-party benefits, on the one hand, and "incidental" benefits, on the
    other. *See,* lines 163–227. What is the essence of this distinction? Does footnote 7
    help? In that footnote, the *Joseph* court acknowledges that the contract between the
    Hospital and SMAA did, at least on one point, create a stipulation pour autrui in
    favor of the plaintiffs. What was that point? How was the part of the contract that
    pertained to that point different from the part of the contract on the basis of which
    the plaintiffs had predicated their claims?

Charles Robert McKEE, IV   1
v.   2
SOUTHFIELD SCHOOL and the Board of Trustees   3
of Southfield School   4

Louisiana Court of Appeal   5
Second Circuit   6
Jan. 20, 1993   7
613 So.2d 659   8

NORRIS, Judge.   9

Defendant, Southfield School, appeals the trial court's order issuing a preliminary in-   10
junction requiring the school to deliver to Plaintiff, Charles Robert McKee IV, an official   11
transcript of his academic record.   12

At the time of trial, McKee was an 18-year-old high school junior at Trinity Heights   13
Christian Academy ("Trinity") in Shreveport. Prior to his enrolling at Trinity, McKee had   14

attended Southfield School ("Southfield") since 1987. Southfield is a private school, and McKee's attendance there was established by annual contracts executed between Southfield and McKee's father, Charles Robert McKee III. The plaintiff was not a party to these contracts.

In June 1990, the summer before McKee's sophomore year at Southfield, Jeff Stokes became the new headmaster for the school. Shortly after arriving at Southfield, Stokes discovered that McKee's tuition account was $5,000.00 delinquent, dating back several years. No payments at all were made during the preceding school year, 1989–90.

In August 1990, Stokes met with McKee's father to make arrangements to bring the account up to date. At that meeting, Stokes agreed to allow McKee to continue in school provided his father begin making monthly payments of $600.00, starting in September 1990. When the school failed to receive payment, Stokes sent McKee's father a letter dated October 3, 1990 advising him that he was behind on the account. A second letter dated October 8, 1990 was sent by Stokes to McKee's father, advising him that "unless a payment of at least $1,200.00 is received by the end of October, the school will no longer enroll your son." (Southfield ex. # 1). Although McKee's father denies ever receiving this letter,[1] the school's records show receipt of a $1,200.00 payment on October 31, 1990. (Southfield ex. # 4). No payments were made in November, December, or January.

In February 1991, Southfield's business manager sent a third letter to McKee's father requesting payment of $1,800.00 by the end of the month. In response to this letter, McKee's father made two $600.00 payments in February. No further payments were made. Nevertheless, McKee was permitted to complete the school year at Southfield because, as Stokes stated at trial, the Southfield Board of Trustees' policy, obviously unwritten, was to allow students with delinquent accounts to remain enrolled but to withhold all records. (R.p. 76). At the end of the school year, McKee's tuition account was more than $8,000.00 delinquent.

Whether Southfield would have prevented McKee from returning for his junior year, as Stokes testified, is not known because the Southfield Board of Trustees decided to close Southfield's upper school at the end of the 1990–91 school year. (R.p. 78). As a result of the upper school's closure, in August 1991 McKee enrolled for his junior year at Trinity, another private school. As a prerequisite to enrollment, Trinity required a transcript from McKee's previous school. When McKee's father requested a transcript from Southfield, he was informed that a transcript would not be released until the outstanding debt was satisfied.

Even without the transcript, McKee was allowed to attend Trinity because Trinity's principal, James Corley, believed "the kid need[ed] to be in school somewhere." (R.p. 42). However, Corley stated that the school would not be able to issue a diploma to McKee without the transcript unless he repeated the two years of courses he has already taken at the Southfield upper school. (R.p. 36). In the absence of a transcript, repetition of the courses would be the only way the school could be certain that state requirements had been met. According to Corley, a public school would have the same requirements. (R.p. 37).

As a further result of his inability to produce a transcript, McKee was not allowed to play basketball for Trinity due to the eight-semester rule. This rule prohibits a student from competing in high school sports beyond his eighth semester of high school. Since McKee could not produce a transcript, he could not prove that he had been in high school

---

1. Each of the three letters discussed herein was addressed to 35 Madonna Street. The McKees' correct address is 34 Madonna Street.

for fewer than eight semesters. Thus, McKee was not permitted to play even though he had been a starter for Southfield's team in both his freshman a sophomore years.

On January 29, 1992, after several failed attempts by McKee's father to settle the debt owed to Southfield and have the transcript released, McKee filed a Petition for Damages and Equitable Remedies against Southfield School and its Board of Trustees.[2] In his petition, McKee prayed for a temporary restraining order, preliminary and permanent injunctions, and damages for the interference in his participation in high school athletics. Judge C.J. Bolin, Jr. denied the temporary restraining order but on February 20, 1992 signed an order issuing a preliminary mandatory injunction requiring Southfield to deliver one official transcript to McKee. The trial court found that Southfield, by its actions and agreement to continue educating McKee, indicated that it would forego the harsh remedy of withholding the transcript. In essence, the court held that Southfield was estopped from withholding the transcript. Southfield filed a suspensive appeal. McKee did not file a response.

THE CONTRACT

At trial, McKee introduced the Contract for Enrollment executed between his father and Southfield School. (Plaintiff's ex. # 1). While this contract only applied to the 1989–90 school year, McKee's father testified to the best of his memory, and Southfield did not dispute, that each of the annual contracts were of the same form. (R.p. 61). We note from the outset that McKee, while not a party to the contract, is an intended beneficiary of the agreement and is, therefore, entitled to a direct action against Southfield. La.C.C. art. 1978; *Dartez v. Dixon*, 502 So.2d 1063 (La.1987); *Litton v. Ford Motor Co.*, 554 So.2d 99 (La.App.2d Cir.1989), writ denied 559 So.2d 1353 (1990). See also *Bossier Parish School Board v. Lemon*, 370 F.2d 847 (5th Cir.), cert. denied 388 U.S. 911, 87 S.Ct. 2116, 18 L.Ed.2d 1350 (1967) (holding children of Barksdale Air Force Base personnel to be third party beneficiaries of an agreement to educate executed by the United States and Bossier Parish school system).

The pertinent parts of the contract provide as follows:

Subject to the following provisions, I enroll my child in Southfield School for the 1989–1990 school year in the Ninth grade.

....

I understand that ... this contract covers the enrollment of my child in the school for the entire school year.

UPON ACCEPTANCE OF THIS CONTRACT BY THE SCHOOL THE PARENT SHALL BE OBLIGATED FOR THE FULL TUITION FOR THE YEAR IN THE AMOUNT OF $2,750.00.

....

I understand that the school reserves the right to ask for the withdrawal of a child at any time.

The contract is silent with regard to the academic transcript. It states neither that the school is obligated to provide a transcript nor that it is free from that obligation in the event that tuition is not paid. However, not all obligations arising out of contract need be explicitly stated. *National Safe Corp. v. Benedict and Myrick, Inc.*, 371 So.2d 792

---

2. The Southfield Board of Trustees was never served with citation or a copy of the petition. Consequently, the trial court's judgment was issued against Southfield School only.

(La.1979). When interpreting a contract, the court must look to the common intent of the parties. La.C.C. art. 2045. Article 2045 of the Civil Code further provides that:

When the parties made no provision for a particular situation, it must be assumed that they intended to bind themselves not only to the express provisions of the contract, but also to whatever the law, equity, or usage regards as implied in a contract of that kind or necessary for the contract to achieve its purpose.

In the context of the instant contract, we find that the parties intended not only that Southfield furnish McKee with an education in return for money, but also that it furnish documentation of that education. While it is conceivable that one might contract to be formally educated merely for education's sake, in this modern era, it is far more likely that one entering into such a contract intends the education to be a springboard into the job market or into higher education. Neither of these goals would be a likely result of formal education absent the ability to prove, via documentation, that one had indeed been educated. Certainly, McKee's father intended that Southfield furnish his son with documentation sufficient to show the world that he had indeed completed a course of study at Southfield. Similarly, Southfield surely contemplated the necessity of furnishing to McKee and its other students written proof of their academic accomplishments. Thus, under the agreement Southfield was obligated to provide McKee with an education and written verification of that education; McKee's father, in turn, was obligated to pay tuition to Southfield.

However, McKee's father, by his own admission, failed to perform his obligation under the contract, as written, or under the subsequent agreement to pay back arrearages and keep tuition current. He fell behind on the monthly tuition payments and eventually stopped making payments altogether, acquiring a delinquency of over $8,000.00. Under these circumstances, McKee's father, as a party to the contract, would be in no position to demand further performance from Southfield. See La.C.C. art. 2013. As a third party beneficiary, McKee's rights under the contract are subject to the terms and conditions of the contract entered into by his father and Southfield. *Pelican Well & Tool Supply Co. v. Johnson*, 194 La. 987, 195 So. 514 (1940); *A.F. Blair Co. v. Haydel*, 504 So.2d 1044 (La.App. 1st Cir.1987). Thus, McKee is in no better position than would be his father to demand that Southfield further perform under the contract. See La.C.C. art. 1982.

DETRIMENTAL RELIANCE

Although McKee cannot demand performance under the contract, he may do so on the basis of detrimental reliance. In this regard, article 1967 of the Civil Code provides, in pertinent part:

A party may be obligated by a promise when he knew or should have known that the promise would induce the other party to rely on it to his detriment and the other party was reasonable in so relying.

Under this article, the court may grant either specific performance or damages. C.C. art. 1967, comment (e); *Woodard v. Felts*, 573 So.2d 1312 (La.App. 2d Cir.1991).

In *A.F. Blair*, supra, the court held that a third party beneficiary may bring an action based on detrimental reliance against a principal party to a third party beneficiary contract. In that case, a bank entered into an agreement with a doctor whereby the bank would provide financing for the construction of the doctor's field house. Prior to construction, the bank furnished the construction company with a letter indicating that the bank had approved a loan sufficient to satisfy the construction contract between the doctor and the construction company. However, when the completion cost turned out to be more than originally expected, the bank refused to tender the difference. Although the court found the construction company to be a third party beneficiary of the financing agreement, it held that the company was not entitled to recovery in contract because the bank had fully performed under the contract. Nevertheless, the court remanded the case, stating that the construction company had alleged facts sufficient to state a claim in detrimental reliance.

This court, in *Kethley v. Draughon Business College, Inc.*, 535 So.2d 502 (La.App. 2d Cir.1988), held that a business college instructor was entitled to recovery from the college on the basis of detrimental reliance. The instructor contracted with the college to teach one paralegal course during the fall quarter in return for a $200 per month payment. Some time later, the instructor agreed to teach two paralegal courses during the winter quarter. Although the parties had not discussed compensation for the winter quarter, the instructor assumed he would be paid $400 per month. The college maintained that it intended to pay the instructor only $200 per month since the second course was taught in a combined format.

This court held that the instructor could not recover in contract because there had been no meeting of the minds. However, we permitted recovery under the theory of detrimental reliance. When the college agreed to employ the plaintiff to teach two courses, it implicitly promised that it would pay plaintiff more than he received for teaching one course. The plaintiff's reliance on this implied promise was reasonable, and he was therefore awarded damages. See also *Woodard,* supra; *Morris v. People's Bank & Trust Co.,* 580 So.2d 1029 (La.App. 3d Cir.), writs denied 588 So.2d 101, 102 (1991).

In the instant case, Southfield was well aware of the considerable delinquency on McKee's tuition account. Nevertheless, Stokes agreed to allow McKee to continue pursuing his education at Southfield provided his father met the revised payment schedule. The record clearly indicates that, when McKee's father failed to abide by the revised payment schedule, the school contacted him on several occasions in an attempt to collect the sum he owed. Indeed, in a letter to McKee's father, Stokes suggested that the school might ask for McKee's withdrawal; however, Southfield never did so. Rather, it permitted McKee to attend until the end of the 1990–91 school year.

When Southfield permitted McKee to continue his education, notwithstanding his father's clear failure to perform under the contract as written or as revised, it implicitly promised McKee's father that it would grant credit to McKee for the academic work he successfully completed. As the beneficiary of this promise, McKee relied upon it and continued to attend Southfield, performing the coursework required of him by Southfield teachers.

Indeed, by permitting McKee to continue as a student, Southfield implicitly promised to McKee, himself, that he would receive credit toward his high school diploma if he successfully met academic requirements. Also implicit in Southfield's continued performance was that it would supply documentation of McKee's academic accomplishments. McKee was certainly reasonable in expecting this performance as the school never indicated that it might withhold his academic transcript. See *Woodard,* supra; *Kethley,* supra.

McKee's reliance on Southfield's continued enrollment would undoubtedly have a detrimental effect upon him were Southfield now permitted to withhold documentation of his education at Southfield. Absent proof of his academic credits in the form of a transcript, McKee would be forced to repeat two years of high school before he could receive a diploma. It would be grossly unfair to allow a student to be lulled into thinking he would receive credit upon satisfactory completion of his coursework, and then to refuse him any evidence of ever having completed the coursework. Under these circumstances,

198 we agree with the trial court's result and find that McKee is entitled to a transcript evi-
199 dencing his academic accomplishments at Southfield.

200   Finally, we note that the out-of-state jurisprudence cited by Southfield is inapplicable to
201 the instant case. Of the cases cited, only one, *Fayman v. Trustees of Burlington College,* 103
202 N.J.Super. 476, 247 A.2d 688 (N.J.Ch.1968), has an analogous fact pattern. Yet, even *Fay-*
203 *man* is clearly inapposite; there, the contracting parents, not the student, sought to com-
204 pel the issuance of a transcript notwithstanding their breach of the enrollment contract.

205   In conclusion, the trial court judgment issuing a mandatory preliminary injunction re-
206 quiring Southfield School to issue a transcript to McKee is affirmed. Costs are assessed
207 to Southfield School.

208   AFFIRMED.

209   VICTORY, Judge, dissenting.

210   I agree with the part of the majority opinion that holds plaintiff cannot recover in
211 contract.

212   However, in my view, Southfield's decision to not disenroll plaintiff in February 1991
213 cannot be construed to imply it would certify his work in a transcript without the bill
214 being satisfied. If Southfield's actions amount to an implied promise at all, at best, they
215 merely imply plaintiff would not be disenrolled during the semester once it had begun.

216   Assuming, arguendo, that detrimental reliance can be applicable to a situation where
217 the third party beneficiary is the child of the party breaching a contract, the plaintiff
218 failed to prove (1) he relied on Southfield's actions to his detriment, and (2) he was rea-
219 sonable in so relying. Indeed, he did not even attempt to prove detrimental reliance,
220 which was not raised by the parties in the trial court or this court.

221   The detriment mentioned in the majority's opinion comes not from reliance on South-
222 field's "implied promise," but from its legal right to withhold the transcript. As the ma-
223 jority seems to acknowledge, if Southfield had chosen to disenroll plaintiff for breach of
224 contract when the spring semester began, it would not have been obligated to furnish
225 him a transcript. Plaintiff took no action relying on the school's forbearance that worked
226 to his detriment. In fact, he stayed in the school and finished the year, which was very much
227 to his advantage.

228   If Southfield had disenrolled plaintiff when his father stopped paying in February 1991,
229 he would now have no transcript and would not have completed the school year ending
230 in May 1991. Plaintiff has not even attempted to show he could have enrolled in another
231 school in mid-February 1991 without a certified transcript from Southfield. Because
232 Southfield allowed plaintiff to continue in school, he has actually completed the school
233 year, although he has no transcript. Upon payment of the outstanding bill, plaintiff will
234 receive a transcript showing he finished the school year and received the appropriate cred-
235 its for courses completed. Rather than relying on the school's actions to his detriment, the
236 plaintiff is in a much better position having completed the full year and earned credits in
237 the classes that he attended at Southfield, even if at this time he is unable to obtain a cer-
238 tified transcript due to the failure to pay the outstanding bill.

239   Plaintiff's father acknowledged that he owed the money to Southfield and took part
240 in discussions in early fall 1990 with Mr. Stokes, the headmaster, in an effort to reduce
241 his debt of over $5,000 through monthly payments of $600. Plaintiff testified that he was
242 aware of his father's financial problems and the problems with paying the school. The
243 plaintiff never testified that he thought, or was misled into believing, that the school
244 would furnish him a transcript just because it allowed him to finish the semester. The

plaintiff would be unreasonable to rely on the school not only to continue to educate him   245
without being paid, but to also certify his grades when they had no obligation under the   246
contract to do so unless they were paid.   247

In my view, this is a simple contract case in which the majority has erroneously applied   248
the doctrine of detrimental reliance to force the non-breaching party, Southfield, to *fully*   249
perform under the contract after repeated breaches of the contract by plaintiff's father,   250
in whose shoes he stands under the contract.   251

Because of this decision, schools, out of fear that they will lose the right to withhold   252
transcripts, will be more inclined to disenroll students immediately when they fall be-   253
hind on their debts to the school, a result that hurts the students and the schools.   254

For these reasons, I respectfully dissent.   255

Questions

1. Lines 10–73: Read these two pages and describe in legal terms the bonds, if any, between all the parties involved. Do all of the obligations created have the same legal
   sources? How different are the legal regimes of these obligations? Was young McKee
   a party to any contract?

2. Lines 75–86: On what legal ground can the court rule that McKee is "entitled to a direct action"? Should this ruling be restricted to the facts of this case or should it be
   given a broad range of application? What kind of public policy could justify expanding or restricting the application of this ruling?

3. Lines 109–133: In your opinion, did the "instant contract" (line 109) really create
   two obligations on Southfield, one, to furnish an education and, two, to furnish documentation of that education? Are these two obligations bound together, somehow?
   Could they be dissociated and still bind the school but on different grounds? Could
   the education received by McKee be returned to the school? What of the tuition paid
   by the father: could it be returned to the father? Is the documentation to serve as evidence that the father has paid the tuition? Or is the documentation meant to serve
   another purpose which would be for the school to raise a means of defense against
   the father when the latter fails to carry out his own obligation (*see* lines 123–133)?
   Do you agree with the Court's statement that "McKee is in no better position than
   would be his father to demand...." (lines 132–133)? Would you agree that such a
   statement is a proper and necessary application of the principle seen above: *nemo
   potior jure ad alium transfere potest quam ipse habet*? In other words, the father cannot transfer to his son greater rights than he, himself (the father), has.

4. Lines 135 *et seq.*: What do you think of this turnaround? Read Louisiana Civil Code
   article 1967.

5. Lines 150–208: Where is detrimental reliance located in the Louisiana Civil Code? Notice that detrimental reliance is tied to the concept of 'cause' (*see* below next chapter).
   'Cause' is a requirement for a contract. Was there a contract between the school and
   McKee? The contract was between the school and McKee's father. We saw also, above,
   that the Court ruled that the father had breached his obligation to the school by not
   paying his son's tuition. How can the Court now say that on the basis of the contract
   that his father breached, McKee nevertheless benefits from the right to make a claim
   because of that very contract? Doesn't that make McKee a third-party beneficiary? What
   did the court say about this above on lines 109–133? Wouldn't the court have been

wiser to give a remedy to McKee from the law of delicts/torts, Louisiana Civil Code articles 2315 and 2316 in particular?

6.   Lines 209–255: What do you think of Judge Victory's dissenting opinion?

See also *Hargroder, et al. v. Columbia Gulf Transmission Co.*, 290 So.2d 874 (La. 1974).

Comparative Law Perspective

Marcel Planiol, Treatise on the Civil Law
Vol. 2, pt. 1, nos 1020–1025, at 586–87
(Louisiana State Law Institute tr., 11th ed. 1939)

1020. Definition

A person undertakes to answer for another when he promises that the person whom he names will consent, as he has, to the agreement which he makes. It is generally said that the *porte-fort* or the person answering for another, obligates himself to obtain the signature of another. Just what is the object of the obligation? The *porte-fort* obligates himself to do what is necessary to obtain the signature promised; his obligation therefore has an object which is personal to him which consists of the effort, the steps, and the sacrifices of money which he must make to persuade the indicated person to give his consent. He is therefore bound by an obligation to do; if he succeeds in obtaining the consent of the other, he is liberated; if he does not succeed, he fails in his obligation and must pay damages. There is nothing in this contrary to principle.

1023–1025. Comparison of the Porte-fort with the Surety

The surety is like the *porte-fort*, a person who engages himself for another; there is, however, a characteristic difference between them. The *porte-fort* promises only that the third person, of whom he believes himself sure, will consent to engage himself, and take upon himself the contract which has been made, to "ratify it," or to "keep the engagement" ... The surety on the contrary, appears for someone who immediately consents to obligate himself, or has even already done so, and he guarantees to the creditor the execution of the debt. He undertakes to pay the debt of another, if the debtor does not carry out his own obligation. His obligation therefore commences when that of the *porte-fort* ends.

Section V — Cause or Consideration

Louisiana Sources of Law

Louisiana Civil Code

Art. 1966. No obligation without cause.

An obligation cannot exist without a lawful cause. (Acts 1984, No. 331, § 1, eff. Jan. 1, 1985.)

Art. 1967. Cause defined; detrimental reliance.

Cause is the reason why a party obligates himself.

A party may be obligated by a promise when he knew or should have known that the promise would induce the other party to rely on it to his detriment and the other party was reasonable in so relying. Recovery may be limited to the expenses incurred or the damages suffered as a result of the promisee's reliance on the promise. Reliance on a gratuitous promise made without required formalities is not reasonable. (Acts 1984, No. 331, § 1, eff. Jan. 1, 1985.)

Art. 1968. Unlawful cause.

The cause of an obligation is unlawful when the enforcement of the obligation would produce a result prohibited by law or against public policy. (Acts 1984, No. 331, § 1, eff. Jan. 1, 1985.)

Art. 1969. Cause not expressed.

An obligation may be valid even though its cause is not expressed. (Acts 1984, No. 331, § 1, eff. Jan. 1, 1985.)

Précis: Louisiana Law of Conventional Obligations — §§ 5.1.1 to 5.1.2

Much has been written on the concept of cause and debates have taken place on the usefulness or not of this concept....

The word "causa" appears in some Roman law texts but it is clothed with many different meanings....

The word "causa" was actually identified with a particular "form," such as "specific words and phrases" or "the actual transfer of a thing" or "particular types of writings." The closest connection between the Roman "causa" and our civil law concept of "cause" can be found in the Roman law "stipulatio," which was a "formal" contract but which could be annulled for lack of "causa" whenever the promisor, who had carried out his obligation, would not receive in return from the stipulator the performance the latter was committed to carry out....

The concept of cause was turned into a "theory of cause" when the canon law lawyers did away with the formalism of Roman law to substitute to it a mere agreement as an exchange of wills between parties based on the moral obligation to fulfill one's word. As a consequence, one would be at fault for not performing that moral duty....

The idea of a commutative justice became a justification for one's commitment but it was a "moral" concept of justice not a "material (economic) justice." The glossators and postglossators merged the canon law concept of cause with the Roman law exchange of wills to explain that the binding nature of an exchange of wills was due to the cause of the obligations created by the parties' wills. "Cause" was then the "end, goal, aim, purpose" (causa finalis) pursued by a party who binds herself to an obligation....

Thus "cause" is a component part of a contractual obligation as is clearly stated in LSA-C.C Art. 1966 according to which: "**An <u>obligation</u> cannot exist without a lawful <u>cause</u>**." One will have noticed, in this Article, the connection between the "obligation" and the necessary requirement of its "cause" The same can be said about LSA-C.C. **Art. 1969: "<u>An obligation</u> may be valid even though <u>the cause</u> is not expressed**." ...

The contemporary theory of cause provides a justification for the binding effect of a person's will and the duty to perform legally entered into obligations; it also sets the limits of the binding effect of the will by declaring invalid obligations which have an illegal or immoral cause; it further provides some sort of guarantee to parties who are told that "**Contracts have the effect of law for the parties and may be dissolved only through the** consent of the parties or on grounds provided by law. Contracts must be performed in good faith." (LSA-C.C. Art. 1983)....

For a *reason* to become *"the cause"* of an obligation which, in turn, will become *the cause* of the contract, it is necessary, as a first step, to identify one reason from all other reasons as being the "determinant-prevailing" reason so that it could become the cause of the contract if it is "common" and if it is lawful....

That a "cause" must exist does not mean that the cause must be expressly stated in the contract....

Even when a contract is in writing, it is not necessary that the cause be expressed as is stated in **LSA-C.C. Art. 1969: "An obligation may be valid even though its cause is not expressed."** As long as there is an exchange of consent between parties and an obligation created as a result, we must presume that the obligation was created for "a reason" common to the parties....

Good faith, "Offenses and Quasi-Offenses" as well as the binding nature of a will or intent lawfully communicated, either expressly or implicitly, provide legal justifications for the expanded, but questionable, definition of cause which appears in the second paragraph of **Art. 1967: "A party may be obligated by a promise when he knew or should have known that the promise would induce the other party to rely on it to his detriment and the other party was reasonable in so relying. Recovery may be limited to the expenses incurred or the damages suffered as a result of the promisee's reliance on the promise. Reliance on a gratuitous promise made without required formalities is not reasonable."** ...

If among the reasons that prompted the parties to enter into a contract there happens to be one reason of an immoral or unlawful nature, it is very likely that a court would "pick" that reason, from among many others, as the cause of the contract even though that reason may not have been the determinant or prevailing reason for the parties. It is the courts' duty to preserve and maintain public order and good morals in the performance of contracts in particular....

Whether shared, common or not, any unlawful or immoral reason should carry with it the absolute nullity of the act of which it meant to be the "cause." ...

Cases

W. T. WEST

v.

LOE PIPE YARD et al.

Louisiana Court of Appeal
Third Circuit
Dec. 19, 1960
125 So.2d 469

HOOD, Judge.

This is an action for a money judgment instituted by W. T. West against Loe Pipe Yard, a commercial partnership composed of Bert Loe and Glen D. Loe, and against the two partners individually. Plaintiff alleges that he cashed drafts issued by defendant, Bert Loe,

aggregating the sum of $5,000, and that the amount due on those drafts has never been   12
paid. As evidence of this indebtedness he alleges that he is the holder and owner of nine   13
drafts drawn on the account of Loe Pipe Yard in the Olla State Bank, Olla, Louisiana, by   14
defendant, Bert Loe, a member of the partnership.   15

Defendants admit the execution of the drafts, but they deny that they are liable to   16
plaintiff for the amounts represented by them. They allege that the drafts were issued to   17
obtain money or chips to be used by Bert Loe for gambling purposes, and that plaintiff   18
is not entitled to recover because the transaction was one which is contra bonos mores.   19

[....]   20

One of the drafts on which plaintiff bases his claim is for the sum of $1,000 and is   21
dated September 3, 1954. The eight remaining drafts are for the sum of $500 each, and   22
each such draft is dated September 4, 1954. All of the drafts are made payable to 'Cash,'   23
are signed by 'Loe Pipe Yard, by Bert Loe,' are drawn on the Olla State Bank, and bear   24
the endorsement of W. T. West.   25

At the time these drafts were issued, plaintiff West was the assistant manager of the Fa-   26
mous Corner, a gambling establishment located in Natchez, Mississippi. Some of the   27
owners of this Mississippi gambling house also owned a substantial interest in the Plaza   28
Club, in Concordia Parish, Louisiana, which club had been leased to one Ed Jones, and   29
in September, 1954, it was being operated by him as a bar, restaurant and night club. On   30
the second floor of the Plaza Club was a room, equipped with a table and chairs, which   31
was used by customers to engage in gambling games of their own choice. Jones, the op-   32
erator of the club, testified that the 'house' had no interest in the gambling activities which   33
were conducted in the upstairs room, and that all such activities were spontaneously en-   34
gaged in by customers without supervision or regulation by employees of the Plaza Club.   35
The purpose of maintaining the room, he stated, was to attract customers and thus stim-   36
ulate the sale of food and drinks.   37

Late in the afternoon on Sunday, September 4, 1954, which was the day preceding   38
Labor Day, plaintiff and Ike Cowan happened to be in plaintiff's automobile near a motel   39
in Concordia Parish when they saw defendant Loe leaving the motel. Plaintiff engaged Loe   40
in conversation and invited him to accompany plaintiff to the Plaza Club for a drink. Loe   41
got into plaintiff's automobile and accompanied him to the Plaza Club, and after they   42
arrived Loe began drinking.   43

Shortly after Loe arrived at the Plaza Club, someone mentioned that a poker game ei-   44
ther was in progress or was about to begin in the upstairs room. Loe then gave a barmaid   45
$10 with instructions that she try to win something in the poker game, and a short time   46
later Loe went upstairs and began to participate in the poker game himself.   47

Loe apparently had little or no money with him, so he obtained a substantial sum   48
from plaintiff in order to enable him to participate in the game. During the course of   49
the game Loe borrowed additional amounts from plaintiff until he had obtained the   50
total sum of $2,000 from him. Drafts were issued by Loe and handed to plaintiff for   51
amounts aggregating $2,000. Plaintiff testified that he had only $1,700 in cash on his   52
person at that time, all of which was handed to Loe in exchange for the drafts, but   53
that he borrowed $300 from one Hal Kaizer and also handed that to defendant. After   54
obtaining $2,000 from plaintiff, Loe then obtained $2,500 from Clifton Vetch, a par-   55
ticipant in the poker game, and $500 from an unknown salesman who also was par-   56
ticipating in the game. Drafts were issued by Loe each time these additional funds were   57
obtained, and plaintiff endorsed the drafts which were given to Vetch and the salesman,   58
guaranteeing the payment of such drafts. Plaintiff contends that he later paid Vetch   59

and the salesman the amounts which they had advanced to defendant, and that he is
entitled to recover judgment for these amounts as well as for the sum which plaintiff
advanced directly.

Shortly after plaintiff and defendant arrived at the Plaza Club, the owner of that establishment turned over his keys and the complete management of the club to plaintiff
West, authorizing him to sell drinks to customers and to close the business up at any time
he saw fit. Plaintiff then tended the bar and remained in complete charge of the Plaza
Club from the time Jones left, which was late Sunday afternoon, until the gambling game
broke up sometime after daylight the following morning.

Defendant contends that plaintiff was one of the promoters of the gambling game in
which defendant was engaged, that the drafts were given for the purpose of enabling Loe
to engage in illegal gambling activities, that plaintiff had full knowledge of the purpose
for which the checks were given, and accordingly that plaintiff is not able to enforce obligations evidenced by those checks.

The Louisiana Constitution of 1921, Article XIX, Section 8, LSA, provides:

'Gambling is a vice and the Legislature shall pass laws to suppress [*sic*] it.'

The Louisiana Civil Code of 1870, LSA, provides:

'Art. 1893 — An obligation without a cause, or with a false or unlawful cause, can have
no effect.'

'Art. 1895 — The cause is unlawful, when it is forbidden by law, when it is contra bonos
mores (contrary to moral conduct) or to public order.'

'Art. 2983 — The law grants no action for the payment of what has been won at gaming or by a bet, except for games tending to promote skill in the use of arms, such as the
exercise of the gun and foot, horse and chariot racing.

'And as to such games, the judge may reject the demand, when the sum appears to
him excessive.'

The above quoted provisions of the constitution and statutes of the State have received
frequent interpretation by the courts of Louisiana. It is now well settled that one who
lends money to another to pay a gambling debt incurred in a transaction With which the
lender was wholly unconnected may be classified as an innocent bystander to the illegal
activity, and he, therefore, may maintain an action to recover the amount which he has
lent. Brand v. Evans, 1927, 7 La.App. 205; Celmons v. Succession of Johnson, 1929, 10
La.App. 230, 120 So. 664; Wilson v. Sawyer, La.App.1958, 106 So.2d 831. However, one
who owns or operates a gambling establishment and who lends money for the purpose
of paying a gambling debt incurred in such establishment cannot recover the money lent,
Because he was not wholly unconnected with the illegal activity. Sampson v. Whitney,
1875, 27 La.Ann. 294; Bagneris v. Smoot, 1925, 159 La. 1049, 106 So. 561; Russo v. Russo,
1927, 5 La.App. 566; Keen v. Butterworth, La.App.1938, 185 So. 37; Russo v. Mula,
La.App.1950, 49 So.2d 622; Domino v. La Bord, La.App.1957, 99 So.2d 841.

In this case we have no difficulty at arriving at the conclusion that the Plaza Club was
a gambling establishment, and that the owner or operator and those who promoted and
participated in the gambling activities in that club were participating in an illegal activity
prohibited by the above quoted provisions of the constitution and statutes of this State. Plaintiff, however, was not the owner of that establishment and he did not participate in the poker
game in the sense that he did not sit at the table, have cards dealt to him, make bets, etc.
An important question presented in this case, therefore, is whether plaintiff was wholly un-

connected with the illegal activities in which Loe was engaged, and accordingly, whether he can be classified as an innocent bystander under the circumstances presented here.

The trial judge concluded that although plaintiff was not the owner of the gambling establishment, he was in charge of it and his conduct was such that he could not be classified as an innocent bystander. In his written reasons for judgment, the trial judge said:

'I therefore am of the opinion that though Mr. West neither ran the game nor was the owner of the building, that yet his conduct was such that he cannot be held to be that of an innocent bystander. It was he that loaned the defendant the money to engage in the game. He knew exactly what the defendant was to do with the money. He further assisted in the continuance of the poker game by arranging to furnish or supply money. Though he was not the owner of the building he certainly was in charge of it by taking his own testimony the building was kept open throughout the evening and on each instance when the defendant needed money with which to play he either furnished it or arranged it by endorsing checks. That the plaintiff did aid in the gambling game of poker by furnishing funds for the game.'

In our opinion, the evidence amply supports the conclusion reached by the trial court. Plaintiff invited and brought the defendant to the Plaza Club, advanced him a substantial sum of money for the purpose of engaging in the poker game, and guaranteed the repayment of additional amounts borrowed by Loe from other participants in the game. Also, plaintiff accommodated those engaged in the poker game by tending the bar and managing the Plaza Club from late Sunday afternoon until after daylight Monday morning. The loans were made and guaranteed by plaintiff with the understanding that it would be necessary for him to go to the trouble and expense of driving to Olla, a distance of 75 miles, the following Tuesday in order to get the drafts cashed. According to plaintiff's testimony, he had seen Loe on not more than two occasions prior to this and they were only casual acquaintances. We could understand plaintiff's actions in accommodating Loe to the extent shown here if plaintiff had an interest in or some connection with the poker game, but we cannot conceive of plaintiff loaning such large sums of money to a casual acquaintance, guaranteeing the payment of additional sums and otherwise accommodating defendant as he did if plaintiff, in fact, was wholly unconnected with the gambling activities which were being conducted in the Plaza Club on that occasion.

There are other facts which we think have some significance in determining whether plaintiff was or was not an innocent bystander. Plaintiff's employers owned a substantial interest in the Plaza Club, and the testimony of Dalton Gentry and Ed Jones indicated that West occasionally worked in and tended the bar in that club. Also, a number of the participants in the poker game apparently were intimate friends of plaintiff. During the early part of the game, for instance, Cowan, who was with plaintiff when Loe was invited and taken to the Plaza Club, was 'at the chip rack,' which we presume means that he was serving as banker for the game. Later Cowan was replaced at the chip rack by Wickson, who was intimate enough with plaintiff to accompany him to Thibodeaux the following Tuesday just for the ride. Clifton Vetch, who not only participated in the poker game but loaned defendant $2,500 to be used in that game, was an intimate friend of plaintiff, having hunted with him frequently. Plaintiff testified that he did not know the name of the salesman who participated in the game, yet he stated that he had been cashing checks for this salesman for the last four or five years, and that one or two days after these drafts were issued he made an appointment with and met this salesman in Natchez and obtained the draft from him to take to Olla to have cashed, and that some time thereafter he paid this salesman the $500 which the salesman had loaned to Loe. We find it difficult to believe that plaintiff is unable to identify this salesman. All of these circumstances in-

1 dicate to us that plaintiff had some interest in the gambling activities which took place
2 in the Plaza Club on that occasion.

3   In this case we conclude, as did the trial judge, that although plaintiff did not own the
4 Plaza Club he was operating it temporarily and was in complete control of it while the poker
5 game was being conducted there, that plaintiff was not wholly unconnected with that il-
6 legal activity, that he was not an innocent bystander, and that the trial judge correctly re-
7 jected his demands.

[....]

Questions

1. Lines 9–15: Can you identify an objective cause for the drafts? Is such an objective cause of any relevance? Is there any purpose in identifying such a cause in any contract? Is there any possible impact on the classification of contracts?

2. Lines 21 *et seq.*: Does a draft or a check point to its cause? Must the cause be mentioned, indicated, or written for a draft or a check to be valid? Should the circumstances surrounding the making of a draft or a check be taken into account to help identify the cause of that draft or check? With what kind of cause, objective or subjective, are we then dealing?

3. Lines 68 *et seq.*: What purpose, motive, or cause could be common to both parties, the defendant and the plaintiff? How does a cause become common to two parties to a juridical act? Can the parties, because of who they are, and the environment in which they operate, contribute to the type of cause on which a juridical act can be created? What kind of contract is a gambling contract? On lines 68–72, what kind of defense is the defendant raising?

4. Lines 85–97: What do you think of this statement: "it is now well settled ..." and the listing of cases that follow? On what ground or grounds do the courts create, or do not create, the connection on which they erect their policy on gambling? Is there any impact of the connection as created by the courts on the cause of the juridical acts of gambling? Could that impact be extended to other juridical acts than gambling contracts?

5. Where does the court find any evidence of an unlawful cause? On lines 156–160, isn't the outcome of the case at odds with the defense of good morals in that the plaintiff, who has lost money, will not be allowed to get his money back and, thereby, will have enriched the defendant who was himself a party to this unlawful, contra bonos mores, gambling contract?

DAVIS-DELCAMBRE MOTORS, INC.
v.
Martin SIMON
Court of Appeal of Louisiana
Third Circuit
June 18, 1963
154 So.2d 775

8 FRUGE, Judge.

9   The plaintiff, Davis-Delcambre Motors, Inc., sued the defendant, Martin Simon, on
10 his promissory note dated June 14, 1957 in the amount of $300.00. Defendant, by spe-

cial plea, raised the defense of illegal consideration as a bar to collection on the note. From a judgment in the lower court granting plaintiff the relief prayed for, defendant has appealed.

The record discloses that during the first week of June 1957, Wilmer Mitchel purchased a 1952 Chevrolet automobile from the plaintiff. The sale of the automobile was to be a cash transaction. Pursuant to this sale, Mitchel gave plaintiff two checks, in the amounts of $200 and $100, drawn on the State National Bank of New Iberia. Plaintiff attempted to cash these checks at the named bank but was informed that Wilmer Mitchel had no account. Accordingly, payment was refused. About one week later plaintiff contacted Wilmer Mitchel and threatened to have him arrested for issuing worthless checks. Subsequently Martin Simon, Mitchel's employer, issued a promissory note in the exact amount of the worthless checks.

In urging lack of valid consideration, defendant argues that the note was given for an illegal consideration in that the only reason the note was given was plaintiff's forbearance in the prosecution of Mitchel for issuing worthless checks. Plaintiff, on the other hand, argues that the note was given in payment of the debt owed by Mitchel to plaintiff, and that as such was supported by good and valid consideration. [....]

[....]

Counsel for defendant argues that the consideration for the note at issue was the debt of Wilmer Mitchel, and that the payment of a debt of a third person is valid consideration. In our opinion, counsel has correctly stated the law in this regard. Dauzat v. Bordelon, La.App., 145 So.2d 41; Foster & Glassell Co. v. Harrison, 168 La. 500, 122 So. 595. However, viewing the evidence and testimony as a whole we are convinced that the payment of the debt of Wilmer Mitchel was not the cause which motivated defendant to make the note. Thus, Mr. Earl J. Davis, President and General Manager of Davis-Delcambre Motors, when questioned about the circumstances surrounding the making of the note, testified as follows:

'He (Wilmer Mitchel) gave us two checks, one dated that day, and the other check dated for a week to follow. Monday, morning we go to the bank to cash his check, and the check was no good, no account. And we got a hold of Mitchel, and he promised to make the checks good. And it was sometimes, oh, possibly a week or two weeks later before we was [sic] able to contact him again. He was working for Martin Simon. And Simon came in one afternoon and said that he was going to sign that check for Mitchel, rather, sign the note to clear Mitchel, *because I was threatening to have him locked in jail for giving me bad checks.*' (Tr. 57) (Emphasis added.)

'Q. Well, if Martin Simon had not given you the note, as you say you would have had Red picked up and put in jail on criminal charges.

'A. That's right, Wilmer T. Mitchel, 'Red' Mitchel.

'Q. You would have had him picked up and put in jail?

'A. Yes, sir.

'Q. And you would have filed a criminal charge of bad checks, is that right?

'A. Yes, sir.' (Tr. 60)

The only realistic conclusion that can be drawn from the testimony of Mr. Davis is that defendant gave the note in question in consideration of plaintiff's forbearance to prosecute Wilmer Mitchel for issuing worthless checks. Accordingly, we so hold.

Having determined the cause or consideration for defendant's making the note, we now turn to the question of whether such consideration is legal and valid.

All contracts which have as their object that which is forbidden by law or contrary to good morals are void. LSA-C.C. Art. 1892. By the 'cause' of a contract is meant the motive or consideration for making it. LSA-C.C. Art. 1896. 'The cause is unlawful, when it is forbidden by law, when it is contra bonos mores (contrary to moral conduct) or to public order.' LSA-C.C. Art. 1895. Accordingly, it has been held that the promise of a father to pay the debt of his insolvent son in exchange for the creditor's promise not to prosecute for fraud is without a good consideration and void, as against public policy. Field v. Rogers, 26 La.Ann. 574; Perry v. Frilot, 6 Mart. (N.S.) 217; Leggett v. Pett, 1 La. 288, 297. Similarly, the courts have refused to enforce promises to pay gambling debts. Wilson v. Sawyer, La.App., 106 So.2d 831.

As previously stated, the obvious consideration for the note in question was the forbearance to prosecute Mitchel for issuing a worthless check. We need not enter into any detailed discussion that such an act is a crime. See LSA-R.S. 14:71. In our opinion, it is axiomatic that the promise to suppress the prosecution of this crime is Contra bonos mores and results in rendering the note sued upon void for lack of consideration. In reaching this conclusion, we are mindful of plaintiff's argument that R.S. 14:71 requires an intent to defraud and that such intent on the part of Mitchel was not established on the trial of this case. However, as stated by the court in Perry v. Frilot, supra, 6 Mart. (N.S.) at 219, concerning this same contention:

'The evidence does not show whether the conduct of the son was fraudulent or not. But the want of proof on this head cannot affect the conclusion to which our duty requires us to come. If it was not fraudulent, the plaintiff practiced a gross fraud and deception on the defendant. If it was fraudulent, he cannot make the promise to conceal that fraud the basis of an action in a court of justice.'

The above quotation adequately expresses the views of this court on the matter.

For the reasons assigned, the judgment of the lower court is reversed and plaintiff's suit is dismissed; plaintiff-appellee to pay all costs of this appeal and of these proceedings.

Reversed.

HOOD, Judge (dissenting).

I cannot agree with the conclusion reached by the majority that defendant Simon executed the note on which this suit is based 'in consideration of plaintiff's forbearance to prosecute Wilmer Mitchel for issuing worthless checks.' Simon, himself, testified at the trial that at the time he executed and delivered the note he did not know that Mitchel had signed any checks in favor of Davis and that he knew nothing about the possibility that Mitchel might have to go to jail. His testimony to that effect is as follows:

'Q. Now, was Mitchel in any sort of trouble with Mr. Davis, do you know, at that time?

'A. Not that I know, no, sir.

'Q. Do you know about any checks that Mitchel had signed to Mr. Davis?

'A. No, sir. Mr. Davis never tell me nothing about no [sic] checks.

'Q. Did Mitchel talk to you about his checks?

'A. No, sir.

'Q. Did he talk to you about he might have to go to jail?

'A. No, sir.

'Q. Did you know that he might have to go to jail and he wouldn't be able to work for you?

'A. No, sir, I didn't know that.'   103

So far as I can find in the record, the only grounds upon which the majority can base   104
its holding that there was an agreement to not prosecute are the statements volunteered   105
by plaintiff's general manager, Mr. Earl J. Davis, which are quoted in the majority opin-   106
ion. I find nothing in his testimony which indicates a Promise on his part to not prose-   107
cute Mitchel. The only logical interpretation which can be placed on the evidence, I think,   108
is that although Davis intended to prosecute Mitchel if the checks were not paid, and he   109
may have said that to Mitchel, defendant Simon was never informed of any such intent   110
or even of the possibility that charges could be filed and no promise was ever made by Davis   111
to Simon or to anyone else to not prosecute Mitchel.   112

The majority has held that the agreement between Mr. Davis and Mr. Simon is 'un-   113
lawful,' and is 'forbidden by law,' and 'is a crime.' Although the specific crime which the   114
majority thinks has been committed is not set out in the opinion, it is apparent that they   115
feel that both of these men, by conducting this very ordinary and common business trans-   116
action, have committed the serious crime of compounding a felony, as prohibited by LSA-   117
R.S. 14:131. I strongly disagree. In the first place, I think it must be shown that a felony   118
has been committed before an accused can be guilty of compounding it, and there is no   119
showing here that a felony was committed by Mitchel. One of the elements of the offense   120
of issuing a worthless check, as provided in LSA-R.S. 14:71, is an 'intent to defraud.' No   121
10-day written notice of non-payment was given to Mitchel, so there is no presumption   122
of an intent to defraud, and I think the majority is in error in assuming that Mitchel had   123
committed a felony which could be compounded.   124

I agree with the majority that if the Only consideration for a promissory note is a   125
promise of the payee not to prosecute, then the obligation evidenced by the note is un-   126
enforceable because of a failure of consideration, whether there was or was not a valid ground   127
for criminal prosecution. But, in a case such as the instant one, Where there was a valid   128
consideration for the note (a stipulation pour autri), then it seems to me that the note Is   129
enforceable although there may have been additional promises or considerations which   130
were invalid, such as a promise to not prosecute.   131

The majority apparently relies principally on the case of Perry v. Frilot, 6 Mart.(N.S.)   132
217, as authority for its holding. In my opinion that case does not support the views ex-   133
pressed by the majority in the instant suit, because there the son was an insolvent debtor,   134
and the plaintiff had agreed as a part of the consideration for the father's promise to pay   135
a portion of the debt that plaintiff would 'get the other creditors to sign; that is, that he   136
would deceive them,' and would assist the son in fraudulently making a surrender of his   137
effects. The Perry case was decided in 1827, and so far as I have been able to find it has   138
never been cited or followed by any other court since that time. If it can be interpreted   139
as supporting the views expressed by the majority in the instant suit, then I must re-   140
spectfully disagree with the holding in that case.   141

[....]

Questions

1.   Lines 14–27: Is the use of the word "consideration" proper here? Read the Code ar-
     ticles on cause. Do you read anywhere this word "consideration"? Do you see any
     equivalent between "objective cause" and consideration? What about "subjective
     cause" and consideration? Could an illegal consideration in the sense of objective
     cause be illegal? Read lines 23–27 in particular.

2. Lines 29–36: Notice that on line 29 the Court refers to consideration, whereas on line 34 we read the word "cause". Is the court using the two words interchangeably? If so, is that proper and good legal writing? Then on lines 52–56, the court again uses the two words interchangeably, although the Court seems to favor the use of the word "consideration" particularly when it states that the question is whether such consideration is legal or valid.

3. Lines 57 *et seq.*: Can forbearance to prosecute ever be consideration at common law? On line 58 the court states: "by the 'cause' of a contract is meant the motive *or consideration* for making it. LSA-C.C. Art. 1896." However, the Court added the words *"or consideration"* to the words of the Louisiana Civil Code which do not include "consideration". Did the court find it necessary or useful or without any legal consequence to equate cause to consideration? Would a common law court do likewise if the two concepts mean the same thing? On line 67, is the court giving to the word "consideration" its proper common law meaning when it is preceded by the word "obvious"? Isn't it more subjective cause that the Court had in mind? How does the Court presume the commonality of the unlawful cause or, rather, the lack of consideration (*see* line 71)?

4. Lines 86–141: What do you think of Judge Hood's dissenting opinion? What do you think of his distinguishing the *Perry v. Frilot* case on which the majority reasoned by analogy? Could Judge Hood's opinion be considered as a warning to the Courts that there must be a limit to their role and authority to intervene in contractual relationships so as to police/regulate private contracts?

DAVIS-DELCAMBRE MOTORS, INC.

v.

Martin SIMON

Supreme Court of Louisiana

May 4, 1964

163 So.2d 553

HAMLIN, Justice.

[....]

Plaintiff, alleging itself to be the holder and owner in due course of business of a ninety day promissory note made by the defendant, dated June 14, 1957, in the sum of $300.00, payable to the order of State National Bank of New Iberia, bearing interest at the rate of eight percent (8%) per annum from maturity until paid, and providing for attorney's fees, instituted the present proceeding against the defendant for the full amount of the note. Plaintiff further alleged that despite repeated amicable demand, defendant had failed and refused to liquidate the indebtedness.

The facts of record, deduced principally from the testimony given at the trial on March 19, 1962, are to the effect that Wilmer Mitchel, an employee of the defendant, purchased a 1952 Chevrolet from Davis-Delcambre Motors, Inc. on a Saturday during the first week of June, 1957. In payment Mitchel gave two checks dated June 7, 1957, in the amounts of $100.00 and $200.00, respectively, drawn on the State National Bank of New Iberia; the checks were dishonored by said Bank on the Monday following the date of purchase, and plaintiff was informed that Mitchel had no account with the bank. Defendant subsequently issued the instant note.

Earl Joseph Davis, President and General Manager of plaintiff company, testified that he knew Martin Simon, and that Martin Simon signed the note herein sued upon; the note is for the identical amount of the two checks issued by Mitchel. [....] [He also testified that (1) Martin Simon executed the note because he (Mr. Davis) was threatening to have Wilmer Mitchell, who worked from Mr. Simon, "locked in jail" for issuing "bad checks"; (2) Mr. Simon had never made any payments on the note; (3) he (Mr. Davis) never took any legal action against Mr. Mitchell but would have had filed criminal charges against Mr. Mitchell had Mr. Simon not executed the note.]

Our appreciation of Davis's testimony is that it is devoid of any statement to the effect that he influenced Simon to sign the note or that he pressured him into such action by the exercise of threats or violence on Simon. He said that he did not return the checks to Simon or Mitchel. (They are now a part of this record.)

[....]

[The two people who witnessed the note testified that they witnessed Mr. Simon's signature. The testimony of each was devoid of any statement to the effect that violence or threats were exercised upon Simon. One of them also testified that the note was given to prevent Mitchel from going to jail.]

The note sued upon bears the defendant's name on the signature line in addition to a cross mark. The defendant testified that he had never attended school and could not sign his name; he said he had to use an 'X' mark; he denied that he signed the note sued upon. He testified that Davis had never requested him to pay the instant note, and that he had never promised to pay it. He admitted that Mitchel worked for him but said Mitchel did not work for him at the time the instant Chevrolet was purchased. Defendant knew Davis and was familiar with the car bought by Mitchel. He admitted that he went to see Davis about taking the car back; when asked what Davis told him, Simon responded, 'He didn't told me anything.' [sic] Simon also testified that Mitchel had been in previous trouble, and that Mitchel had previously signed his (Simon's) name by placing a cross similar to that affixed to the present note. Insofar as the instant note, he testified that he did not know who signed his name. Simon's testimony with respect to the checks given by Mitchel is confusing; he said that he had seen them in a lawyer's office. No testimony was adduced from Simon with respect to any threats, violence or pressure exerted upon him by Davis. [He also testified that (1) he did not know that Mitchel was in trouble with Mr. Davis; (2) he did not know anything about the checks Mitchel gave to Mr. Davis; and (3) Mitchel did not tell him he might have to go to jail.]

[....]

In reversing the trial court, the Court of Appeal relied on the case of Perry v. Frilot, 6 Mart., N.S., 217, which we find inapposite to the present matter. We agree with the following distinction made by Judge Hood in his able dissent in the present matter:

'The majority apparently relies principally on the case of Perry v. Frilot, 6 Mart.(N.S.) 217, as authority for its holding. In my opinion that case does not support the views expressed by the majority in the instant suit, because there the son was an insolvent debtor, and the plaintiff had agreed as a part of the consideration for the father's promise to pay a portion of the debt that plaintiff would 'get the other creditors to sign; that is, that he would deceive them,' and would assist the son in fraudulently making a surrender of his effects. * * *'

Herein, the Court of Appeal found:

70 '* * * the obvious consideration for the note in question was the forbearance to pros-
71 ecute Mitchel for issuing a worthless check. We need not enter into any detailed discus-
72 sion that such an act is a crime. See LSA-R.S. 14:71. In our opinion, it is axiomatic that
73 the promise to suppress the prosecution of this crime is contra bonos mores and results
74 in rendering the note sued upon void for lack of consideration. * * *'

75 The intent to defraud is an essential ingredient of the offense of issuing worthless
76 checks, LSA-R.S. 14:71; such intent must be alleged and proved. State v. Clayton, 236 La.
77 1093, 110 So.2d 111; State v. McLean, 216 La. 670, 44 So.2d 698; State v. Alphonse, 154
78 La. 950, 98 So. 430. Herein, Wilmer Mitchel drew two checks on a bank in which he had
79 no account; they were dated June 7, 1957, and the note allegedly given to cover the checks
80 was executed on June 14, 1957, one week after the date of the checks. We do not find that
81 plaintiff has proved an intent to defraud on the part of Mitchel; neither was there a suf-
82 ficient lapse of time for there to be presumptive evidence of Mitchel's intent to defraud.
83 Likewise, no written demand was made upon Mitchel to pay the dishonored checks. 'The
84 offender's failure to pay such check, * * * within ten days after the receipt by him of writ-
85 ten notice of its nonpayment upon presentation, shall be presumptive evidence of his in-
86 tent to defraud.' LSA-R.S. 14:71. We cannot presume therefore that Wilmer Mitchel was
87 guilty of violating LSA-R.S. 14:71, without proof of his intent to defraud plaintiff. It fol-
88 lows that if Mitchel was not guilty of violating LSA-R.S. 14:71, Simon and Davis were
89 not guilty of compounding a felony prohibited by LSA-R.S. 14:131.

90 [....]

91 [....] We also conclude from a reading of the testimony, supra, that Davis did not
92 make a promise to suppress the prosecution of Mitchel, and that no threats, violence or
93 pressure were exerted upon Simon so as to vitiate his consent. See, LSA-R.C.C. Arts. 1819
94 and 1850.

95 Having found that under the facts of this case, Mitchel was not guilty of the offense of
96 issuing worthless checks with intent to defraud, that no promise to suppress the prosecu-
97 tion of Mitchel was made by Davis, that Simon and Davis were not guilty of compounding
98 a felony, that no threats, violence or pressure were exerted upon Simon so as to vitiate his
99 consent, and that Simon did affix his mark to the note involved, we approach a determination
100 as to whether there was a valid consideration for the note. We find that the debt due by
101 Mitchel to plaintiff for the price of the 1952 Chevrolet was sufficient consideration to sup-
102 port the promise of a third party, Simon, to pay. Paige v. Mesico, La.App., 144 So.2d 908;
103 Louisiana Store & Market Equipment Co. v. Moore, La.App., 167 So. 477. We do not find
104 that the agreement between plaintiff and the defendant was unlawful or forbidden by law.
105 We conclude that the consideration for the note is valid and that the note is enforceable.

106 Because of our findings, supra, it is not necessary that we consider relator's other con-
107 tentions with respect to alleged errors committed by the Court of Appeal.

108 For the reasons assigned, the judgment of the Court of Appeal, Third Circuit, is re-
109 versed and set aside. The judgment of the trial court is affirmed. All costs are to be paid
110 by defendant.

Question

1. Lines 9–110: Why do you think the Supreme Court includes so much of Mr. Davis'
   pertinent testimony in its opinion? On lines 95–105, is the Supreme Court making
   a proper use of the common law concept of consideration? Is that concept, as used
   here by the court, equivalent to the concept of objective cause at civil law?

AARON & TURNER, L.L.C.

v.

Melissa Michelle PERRET and Continental Financial Group, Inc.

Louisiana Court of Appeal
First Circuit
May 4, 2009
22 So.3d 910

ON REHEARING[1]

HUGHES, J.

In this action on a promissory note and mortgage, the defendant/borrower appeals a summary judgment dismissing her reconventional demand, which asserted a negligence claim against the law firm that performed the loan closing. On June 6, 2008, this court handed down an unpublished opinion in this appeal, reversing in part the decision of the trial court. The matter is now before this court on application for rehearing. Having decided the application for rehearing has merit, we grant the rehearing and render the following decision reversing the trial court judgment and remanding the matter.

FACTS AND PROCEDURAL HISTORY

In 2001, Melissa Michelle Perret refinanced the mortgage on her home by executing a promissory note in favor of ABN AMRO Mortgage Group, Inc. (ABN) and an act of mortgage on her home to secure payment of the promissory note. Aaron & Turner, L.L.C. (Aaron & Turner), the law firm that acted as the closing agent for the transaction, disbursed funds to and on behalf of Ms. Perret during the transaction, acting on the belief that ABN had

funded the loan.

When it was discovered several years later that Aaron & Turner had never received the funds to finance the transaction from ABN, Aaron & Turner obtained the February 28, 2001 note by ostensible assignment from ABN and demanded payment from Ms. Perret of the total accumulated amount due on the note, plus late fees and interest. When Ms. Perret refused to remit the sum demanded, Aaron & Turner filed a petition in the 19th Judicial District Court on February 17, 2006, seeking to enforce the mortgage and to recover the amounts outstanding on the note, or in the alternative, to recover the amount loaned under the theory of unjust enrichment. [....] By a supplemental petition, Aaron & Turner amended its petition to declare Ms. Perret to be in default on the note and sought to recover the total amount of the note, plus late fees, interest, attorney fees, and court costs. Aaron & Turner also subsequently filed a separate proceeding against Ms. Perret for executory process in a different division of the 19th Judicial District Court.[2]

---

1. Because the original opinion rendered in this appeal was not designated for publication, we repeat herein those portions of the original opinion not changed on this rehearing.

2. Ms. Perret attempted to enjoin the executory proceedings without success and appealed the trial court's denial of her petition for injunctive relief to this court; however, because Ms. Perret's home was sold at sheriff's sale before this court could act on her appeal, her appeal of that judgment was dismissed as moot. *Aaron & Turner, L.L.C. v. Perret*, 2006-2433 (La.App. 1 Cir. 9/14/07), 971 So.2d 1049. Another appeal has been filed in the executory proceeding and is currently before this court on issues related to the disbursement of the sheriff's sale proceeds, which we also decide this date in *Aaron & Turner, L.L.C. v. Perret*, 2007-1425 (La.App. 1 Cir.5/4/09), ___ So.3d ___, 2009 WL 2857974 (unpublished).

In response to the instant ordinary proceeding, Ms. Perret filed a motion for partial summary judgment seeking to have the trial court dismiss "all rights, claims and causes of action" premised on the February 28, 2001 mortgage and note, declare the mortgage and note null, and order cancellation of the mortgage and note. Ms. Perret subsequently filed a reconventional demand seeking compensation for mental, emotional, pecuniary damages, and losses that she allegedly sustained as result of negligence committed by Aaron & Turner in performing the February 28, 2001 loan closing.[3] Aaron & Turner, in turn, filed a motion for summary judgment seeking dismissal of the claims raised by Ms. Perret in her reconventional demand.

Following a hearing on the cross motions for summary judgment, held May 14, 2007, the trial court denied Ms. Perret's partial motion for summary judgment and granted the motion for summary judgment filed by Aaron & Turner, dismissing with prejudice the claims asserted by Ms. Perret in her reconventional demand. A judgment to that effect was signed on May 29, 2007, from which Ms. Perret appeals. In this appeal, Ms. Perret contends that the trial court erred in dismissing her reconventional demand based on a finding that the note and mortgage at issue in these proceedings were enforceable.

[....]

DISCUSSION

In granting Aaron & Turner's motion for summary judgment, and consequently denying Ms. Perret's partial motion for summary judgment, the trial court found that "consideration" was given for the note.[4] It further found that Aaron & Turner was entitled to judgment as a matter of law based on a judgment declaring the note to be valid that was rendered in the executory process suit filed by Aaron & Turner.

[....]

Thus, turning to the merits of the motion for summary judgment, as previously outlined, Aaron & Turner filed the motion for summary judgment to obtain dismissal of Ms. Perret's reconventional demand. The law firm "pointed out," as the basis for seeking dismissal of her reconventional demand, that Ms. Perret would not be able to establish that the note and mortgage were invalid. The trial court agreed, stating its finding in open court that "consideration" was given for the note and mortgage, and granting Aaron & Turner's motion for summary judgment.

Our review of the pertinent Louisiana Civil Code articles and the record presented herein leads us to conclude that the parties and the trial court were misguided in examining the validity of the promissory note and mortgage at issue herein from the perspective of "consideration."

---

3. The basis for the invalidity of the promissory note and mortgage as well as the negligence of Aaron & Turner asserted by Ms. Perret is the fact that ABN did not fund the loan and Aaron & Turner conducted the closing without ensuring that ABN had funded the loan.

4. In oral reasons the trial court stated: "I don't agree with Ms. Perret's position that there was a lack of consideration. 1 think the funds were paid and I do think that plaintiff can proceed under this note.... I think, primarily based on Judge Calloway's prior ruling, plaintiff is entitled to judgment as a matter of law." When the written judgment was submitted for Judge Morvant's signature, it contained the following language: "IT IS FURTHER ORDERED, ADJUDGED AND DECREED that the defendant and plaintiff-in-reconvention, Melissa Michelle Perret *received consideration* in exchange for her execution of the note and related mortgage attached to the Petition...." (Emphasis added.) However, Judge Morvant crossed out, by hand, that portion of the judgment and initialed the alteration. Nevertheless, we find it unnecessary to resolve this discrepancy in light of our disposition herein.

"An obligation cannot exist without a lawful *cause.*" LSA-C.C. art.1966 (emphasis added). "*Cause* is the reason why a party obligates himself." LSA-C.C. art.1967 (emphasis added).[5]

The comments to Article 1967 state, in pertinent part:

Under this Article, *"cause" is not "consideration."* The reason why a party binds himself need not be to obtain something in return or to secure an advantage for himself. An obligor may bind himself by a gratuitous contract, that is, he may obligate himself for the benefit of the other party without obtaining any advantage in return.

LSA-C.C. art.1967, Comment (c) (emphasis added).[6]

Louisiana does not follow the common law tradition that requires consideration to effect an enforceable contract. Rather, the mere will of the parties will bind them, without what a common law court would consider to be consideration to support a contract, so long as the parties have a lawful "cause." The cause need not have any economic value. *Sound/City Recording Corp. v. Solberg,* 443 F.Supp. 1374, 1380 (D.C.La.1978).

Unlike the common law analysis of a contract using consideration, which requires something in exchange, the civil law concept of "cause" can obligate a person by his will only. The difference has been analogized to a civilian contract-consent approach compared to a common law contract-bargain approach. Consideration is an objective element required to form a contract, whereas cause is a more subjective element that goes to the intentions of the parties. Therefore, in Louisiana law, a person can be obligated by both a gratuitous or onerous contract. *Bains v. Young Men's Christian Association of Greater New Orleans,* 2006-1423, p. 5 (La.App. 4 Cir. 10/3/07), 969 So.2d 646, 649, *writ denied,* 2007-2146 (La.1/7/08), 973 So.2d 727.

In this case, each party had "cause" to enter into this contract: ABN in furtherance of its business as a money lender, and Ms. Perret in order to accomplish refinancing of her home. Ms. Perret complains only of the fact that ABN did not advance the sums it allegedly agreed to under the terms of the contract between the parties.

Under Louisiana law, nonperformance of a promise constitutes a breach of an obligation, rather than a failure of cause. *See Sound/City Recording Corp. v. Solberg,* 443 F.Supp. at 1380. Louisiana Civil Code article 1986 provides the remedy for breach of an obligation to do:

Upon an obligor's failure to perform an obligation to deliver a thing, or not to do an act, or to execute an instrument, the court shall grant specific performance plus damages for delay if the obligee so demands. If specific performance is impracticable, the court may allow damages to the obligee.

Upon a failure to perform an obligation that has another object, such as an obligation to do, the granting of specific performance is at the discretion of the court.

---

5. Article 1967 further provides: "A party may be obligated by a promise when he knew or should have known that the promise would induce the other party to rely on it to his detriment and the other party was reasonable in so relying. Recovery may be limited to the expenses incurred or the damages suffered as a result of the promisee's reliance on the promise. Reliance on a gratuitous promise made without required formalities is not reasonable."

6. At common law, lack of consideration is a good reason to deny enforceability of a promise. In civilian systems derived from the French, such as the Louisiana system of private law, absence of cause, or unlawfulness or immorality of the cause, is a good reason to deprive an obligation of its legal effect. In the law of Louisiana a promise is enforceable when it gives rise to an obligation with a lawful cause and not because it is supported by a consideration. Moreover, in spite of some confusion created by imprecise language in the Louisiana Civil Code of 1870, it is now clearly explained that cause is not consideration. Saul Litvinoff, *Still Another Look At Cause,* 48 La. L.Rev. 3, 3, 19 (1987).

108   In the instant case, ABN failed to perform the obligation dictated under the contrac-
109   tual provisions to advance the loan funds. Putting aside for the moment the advance-
110   ment of funds by Aaron & Turner, ABN's failure to perform (which Ms. Perret has
111   denominated a "failure of consideration") did not nullify the contractual agreement as
112   asserted by Ms. Perret, but rather entitled her to the recovery of damages and/or specific
113   performance in accordance with LSA-C.C. art.1986. [....]

114   However, there *was* performance in this case, though it was made by third party Aaron
115   & Turner. "Performance may be rendered by a third person, even against the will of the
116   obligee, unless the obligor or the obligee has an interest in performance only by the
117   obligor." LSA-C.C. art. 1855.[7] On this point, the supreme court has stated the following:

118   In general, the creditor cannot refuse payment offered by a third person whether
119   or not interested in the extinction of the obligation ... A payment made by a
120   third person and accepted by the creditor extinguishes the obligation as defini-
121   tively as one effected by the debtor personally, except where the third person is
122   legally or contractually subrogated to the rights of the creditor. In the last case,
123   the debtor is discharged toward the original creditor, but the obligation contin-
124   ues to exist in favor of the third person who has been subrogated thereto.

125   *Cox v. W.M. Heroman & Co.*, 298 So.2d 848, 853 (La.1974) (quoting Aubry & Rau, *Oblig-
126   ations, 1 Civil Law Transactions*, §§ 315–316, pp. 156–158 (1965)).

127   Under these precepts, payment of the sums ABN was obligated to pay under the con-
128   tractual terms by third party Aaron & Turner would constitute performance satisfying
129   ABN's contractual obligation to Ms. Perret.

130   However, the more appropriate legal question in the instant suit concerns whether
131   there was a "meeting of the minds" or agreement to contract between ABN and Ms. Per-
132   ret. The Louisiana Civil Code provides: "A contract is formed by the consent of the par-
133   ties established through offer and acceptance." LSA-C.C. art.1927. Consent of the parties
134   is necessary to form a valid contract. Where there is no meeting of the minds between the
135   parties, a contract is void for lack of consent. *Stockstill v. C.F. Industries, Inc.*, 94-2072, p.
136   25 (La.App. 1 Cir. 12/15/95), 665 So.2d 802, 820, *writ denied*, 96-0149 (La.3/15/96), 669
137   So.2d 428.

138   "A contract is null when the requirements for its formation have not been met." LSA-
139   C.C. art.2029. A contract to which one party has not consented is a nullity. *See Ferguson
140   v. Dirks*, 95-560, p. 5 (La.App. 5 Cir. 11/28/95), 665 So.2d 585, 587.

141   In this case, whether lender ABN consented to this contract was not established. It is
142   undisputed that Ms. Perret signed the necessary legal documents signifying her consent,
143   while Aaron & Turner partner William Aaron signed on behalf of ABN. In his deposi-
144   tion, Mr. Aaron testified that his firm was "instructed" to sign on behalf of ABN, but he
145   was unable to recall the circumstances of that instruction. However, it appears that Aaron
146   & Turner's only contact with respect to this transaction was with the loan broker, CFG,
147   and that there was no direct contact with ABN. Moreover, the petition filed by Aaron &
148   Turner stated that loan broker CFG "failed to request or obtain the funding of the loan
149   from [ABN]." While not dispositive of the issue, the fact that ABN never funded the loan
150   also militates in favor of a conclusion that ABN did not consent to contract with Ms. Per-
151   ret. Further, the testimony presented in this case clearly indicates that Aaron & Turner did
152   not *intend* to advance the sums disbursed at closing from its own funds, but rather did

7. Article 1855 further provides: "Performance rendered by a third person effects subrogation only when so provided by law or by agreement."

so on the mistaken belief that ABN had forwarded funds for the closing. No other pleading, deposition, answer to interrogatory, admission on file, or affidavit appearing in the
record addresses the issue of whether ABN had, in fact, consented to contract with Ms.
Perret.

Ms. Perret's reconventional demand and subsequent motion for summary judgment
sought to have the note and mortgage declared null and void. Aaron & Turner's cross
motion for summary judgment sought the dismissal of Ms. Perret's reconventional demand, urging that she would be unable to prove at trial that the note and mortgage are
null and void. Aaron & Turner's right to proceed under the note and mortgage is derived
solely from the *assignment* thereof by ABN in its favor, which conveyed to Aaron & Turner
only the rights ABN actually had in these contract documents. In order to prevail on the
issue of the validity of the promissory note and mortgage and its right to executory process
thereunder, Aaron & Turner must establish ABN had rights to convey in these contractual documents, i.e. that ABN had actually consented to enter into the contract with Ms.
Perret. No evidence was presented to resolve this issue. Hence, we hold that the validity
and enforceability of the note and mortgage have not been conclusively established in the
record and that therefore Aaron & Turner was not entitled to foreclose, via summary
judgment, Ms. Perret's right to a trial on the merits of her reconventional demand. Accordingly we conclude Aaron & Turner failed to show that no genuine issue of material
fact remains and that it is entitled to judgment as a matter of law; summary judgment was
inappropriately granted in this case.[8]

[....]

Based on these considerations, we conclude that the trial court erred in granting summary judgment in favor of Aaron & Turner.

CONCLUSION

For the reasons stated herein, we grant Melissa Michelle Perret's application for rehearing, reverse the summary judgment granted by the trial court, and remand this matter for further proceedings consistent with the foregoing. All costs of this appeal are
assessed to the appellee, Aaron & Turner, L.L.C.

[....]

GUIDRY, J., concurring.

While I agree that summary judgment was improperly granted and that the summary
judgment should be reversed (as was provided in the original opinion rendered in this matter), I previously voted to deny the granting of the rehearing herein, which the majority
uses to question the validity of the mortgage and note and then uses that as a basis to reverse the trial court's judgment in *Aaron & Turner, L.L.C. v. Perret*, 2007-1425 (La.App.
1st Cir.5/4/09), ___ So.3d ___, 2009 WL 2857974 (unpublished).

In a very lengthy and strained construction, the majority reasons that the summary judgment should be reversed because "whether lender ABN consented to this contract was
not established." Interestingly, the majority ignores the fact that no dispute has ever been

---

8. Although Ms. Perret asserts the note and mortgage are void and unenforceable because she
contends that consideration was not given, clearly the validity of these contractual documents has
been raised and the fact that this court renders its decision citing a different possible defect (i.e. failure of consent) is of no moment, considering this court's duty to review the motion for summary
judgment *de novo* using the same criteria that govern the trial court's consideration of whether summary judgment is appropriate. *See R.G. Claitor's Realty v. Rigell*, 2006-1629 at p. 4, 961 So.2d at
471–72.

raised by any party, or even the non-party ABN, regarding whether ABN consented to the transactions wherein the contractual agreements in dispute were produced. There is evidence in the record to indicate that ABN did consent, but the majority discredits this evidence based on mere allegations from the petition.

Since a contract is an agreement by two or more parties creating, modifying, or extinguishing obligations, La. C.C. art.1906, it is implicitly understood that only parties to a contract may assert its relative nullity based on a defect in consent. *Dugas v. Modular Quarters, Inc.*, 561 So.2d 192, 201 (La.App. 3d Cir.1990). Further, a relative nullity may be invoked only by those persons in whose interest the ground for nullity was established, and may not be declared by the court on its own initiative. La. C.C. art.2031. The right of action to declare a relative nullity is available only to the incapable person or to one whose consent has been defective. With regard to all other persons, including the other party to the contract, the contract is valid. *Armour v. Shongaloo Lodge No. 352 Free and Accepted Masons*, 342 So.2d 600, 604 (La.1977) (Summers, J., concurring); *see also In re Quirk*, 119 B.R. 99 (W.D.La.1990).

Accordingly, I find the majority's action of questioning whether ABN consented to the loan transaction as a possible basis for declaring the note and mortgage null to be inappropriate. I therefore concur in the opinion to the extent that the summary judgment is reversed. By granting rehearing and raising on its own the issue of consent, the majority provides a path to reversing the trial court's judgment in *Aaron & Turner, L.L.C. v. Perret*, 2007-1425 (La.App. 1st Cir.5/4/09), ___ So.3d ___, 2009 WL 2857974 (unpublished).

Questions

1. Lines 72 *et seq.*: Do you see any implied meaning in "cause" and "cause is not consideration" being **emphasized** by the Court? On lines 81–94: Read and weigh carefully the statements made by the Court. Do you see any purpose/value in these statements? Could cause be identified as a distinct feature of the Louisiana civil law system and, beyond, of the civil law tradition in general? Do you see any legal problem in forcing the Louisiana legal concept of cause into the common law concept of consideration?

2. Lines 95 *et seq.*: Can you make the connection between the Court saying that "each party had cause to enter into this contract" and the legal nature or kind of contract involved in the case? For example, since each party had a cause, does it mean that the contract is bilateral? The Court identifies the cause of each party. Can each cause be the cause of the contract? In the negative, how should the court select "the" cause of the contract? Is each cause identified here by the court more an objective cause than a subjective cause, or vice-versa?

3. Lines 130–137: Shouldn't this issue the of meeting of the minds have been raised much earlier in its opinion by this Court? Why, or why not?

4. Lines 157–173: Behind the statement by the Court that "Aaron & Turner's right to proceed under the note ... assignment thereof by ABN ...", what kind of right would have to have been created for Aaron & Turner to be able to proceed on that right? Is it heritable or strictly personal? Does the statement of the Court on lines 165–167 help you where the Court states that "Aaron & Turner must establish ABN had rights to convey"?

Comparative Law Perspective

Alain Levasseur, COMPARATIVE LAW OF CONTRACTS
79–91 (2008)

Cause and Consideration

Besides offer and acceptance, among the other legal requirements which are necessary, in both the civil law and the common law traditions, to make a contract binding and create obligations, is the requirement of "cause" at civil law and the requirement of "consideration" at common law.

Civil law systems

See: La.Civ.C: Articles 1966, 1967, 1969

Fr. Civ.C.

Art. 1108 "Four requirements are essential for the validity of a convention:

— consent of the party who binds herself;

— capacity to contract;

— an object which is the matter of the commitment;

— a cause which justifies the commitment"

Art. 1131 "An obligation without a cause, or based on a false cause, or on an illicit cause, can have no effects."

Art. 1132 "The convention is valid although its cause is not expressly stated."

C.C.Q.

Art. 1410 "The cause of a contract is the reason that determines each of the parties to enter into the contract.

The cause need not be expressed."

Art. 1411 "A contract whose cause is prohibited by law or contrary to public order is null"....

Philippe Malaurie, Laurent Aynès, Philippe Stoffel-Munck, Les Obligations, Defrénois 2003

603. Justification, limitation and guarantee.— 'The cause' is, at the same time, the justification, the limitation and the guarantee of the autonomous power of the will. It is its justification by explaining why the will can bind: it is not enough to say that one is committed because one wants to be bound, it is also necessary to know 'why'. It is also its limitation: an obligation, albeit wanted, is not binding, if it is without a cause or is grounded on an illicit cause (art. 1133). It is, finally, its guarantee because to deprive a will of its effects a judge is not free to make up his mind as regards the motives which have enticed a person to bind herself....

Common Law Systems: Consideration

Blackstone; Commentaries: Book II the Rights of Things

Having thus shown the general nature of a contract, we are, secondly, to proceed to the *consideration* upon which it is founded; or the reason which moves the party contracting to enter into the contract. "It is an agreement, upon *sufficient consideration*." The civilians hold, that in all contracts, either express or implied there must be something given in exchange, something that is mutual or reciprocal. This thing, which is the price or motive of the contract, we call the consideration ...

A CONSIDERATION of some sort or other is so absolutely necessary to the forming of a contract, that a *nudum pactum* or agreement to do or pay any thing on one side, without any compensation on the other, is totally void in law; and a man cannot be compelled to perform ...

G.H. Treitel

In English law, a promise is not, as a general rule, binding as a contract unless it is either made under seal or supported by some "consideration." The purpose of the doctrine of consideration is to put some legal limits on the enforceability of agreements even where they are intended to be legally binding and are not vitiated by some factor such as mistake, misrepresentation, duress, or illegality. [...].

The basic feature of that doctrine is the idea of reciprocity: something of value in the eye of the law" must be given for a promise in order to make it enforceable as a contract. An informal gratuitous promise therefore does not amount to a contract. A person or body to whom a promise of a gift is made from purely charitable or sentimental motives gives nothing for the promise; and the claims of such a promise are obviously less compelling than those of a person who has given (or promised) some return for the promise....

Restatement, 2d

Chapter 4 Formation of Contracts — Consideration

Topic 1. The Requirement of Consideration

§ 71. Requirement of Exchange: Types of Exchange

(1) To constitute consideration, a performance or a return promise must be bargained for.

(2) A performance or return promise is bargained for if it is sought by the promisor in exchange for his promise and is given by the promisee in exchange for that promise.

(3) The performance may consist of (a) an act other than a promise, or (b) a forbearance, or (c) the creation, modification, or destruction of a legal relation.

(4) The performance or return promise may be given to the promisor or to some other person. It may be given by the promisee or by some other person.

§ 73 Performance of Legal Duty

Performance of a legal duty owed to a promisor which is neither doubtful nor the subject of honest dispute is not consideration; but a similar performance is consideration if it differs from what was required by the duty in a way which reflects more than a pretense of bargain.

§ 79 Adequacy of Consideration: Mutuality of Obligation

If the requirement of consideration is met, there is no additional requirement of (a) a gain, advantage, or benefit to the promisor or a loss, disadvantage, or detriment to the promisee; or (b) equivalence in the values exchanged; or (c) "mutuality of obligation." ...

Allan Farnsworth

§ 2.2. **The Bargain Test of Consideration.** Among the limitations on the enforcement of promises, the most fundamental is the requirement of consideration.... By the end of the nineteenth century, at least in the United States, the traditional requirement that the consideration be either a benefit to the promisor or a detriment to the promise had begun to be replaced by a requirement that the consideration be "bargained for". […].

§2.3. **What Can Constitute Consideration.** Virtually anything that anyone would bargain for in exchange for a promise can be consideration for that promise. The same consideration can support a number of promises.

§2.11. **Peppercorns and Pretense of Bargain**. […] To be practical, then, we must restate the example in this way: a donor promises to make a gift of a farm to a donee, and, in order to make the promise enforceable, the donee gives a dollar to the donor. Is the donor's promise supported by consideration? There is some authority, including the first Restatement, that it is, at least if the transaction is cast in the form of a bargain. The more modern view, however, mirrored in the Restatement Second, requires an actual bargain, not merely a pretense of bargain, and such extreme disparity in the exchange as here supposed would reveal the purported bargain to be a sham. Under this view the donor's promise is not supported by consideration.…

The Significance of "Cause"
Henri Capitant, DE LA CAUSE DES OBLIGATIONS
nos 6–7, at 15–18 (1923)

7.—It is not only at the moment of the accord of wills that the idea of cause intervenes. Its importance is felt for as long as the contract has not been entirely performed. Indeed, the obligation can live only as long as it remains supported by its cause. In this respect, the cause is distinguished from the two other prerequisites that must exist in connection with the obligor for the contract to be valid: consent and capacity. It is sufficient, in fact, that consent and capacity exist at the moment at which the contract is made. It matters little that one of the other should disappear later on. For example, if the obligor becomes insane or is stricken with [some other] incapacity, that does not stop a previously contracted obligation from remaining valid.

It is otherwise with the cause. For the obligatory relation, once it has been formed, to continue to bind the obligor, it is necessary for the result that he desired to be realized. If it is not, the obligatory line cannot subsist; it must be ruptured.

Two additional consequences result from this notion, which [should be] … added to the preceding.

First, in a synallagmatic contract, when one of the parties demands execution of the performance that has been promised to him, he must prove … either [i] that the end desired by his adversary has already been attained, because he himself has fulfilled his own obligation, or [ii] that it is going to be attained, because he is ready to fulfill it. As result, a seller, for example, can pursue the buyer for the payment of the price only if he has already delivered or if, at the same time at which he makes the demand, he offers to deliver the sold thing. And reciprocally, … the seller [need] not deliver the thing to the buyer if the latter has not paid the price and if a delay has not been accorded him for the payment. In other words, in synallagmatic contracts, the reciprocal obligations contracted by the parties must be performed simultaneously or, as the Germans say, one for one. The contracting party who still has not received the performance that has been promised him can, then, assert against the enforcement suit of his adversary a defense that is called the *exceptio non adimpleti contractus*.

Finally, if, as a result of an event posterior to the creation of the obligation (fortuious event, *force majeure*, fault of the other party), the end pursued by the obligor cannot be realized, then he ceases to be obligated and he is freed. The obligation, in fact, disappears necessarily with its cause.

Section VI—Conclusion on Formation of Contracts

Del CRYER

v.

M & M MANUFACTURING COMPANY, INC.

Supreme Court of Louisiana
Oct. 4, 1972
273 So.2d 818

SANDERS, Justice.

This case raises the question of whether a sale of manufacturing rights to a multipurpose heater should be rescinded upon the demand of the purchaser, because of a deficiency in the performance of the manufactured heater. [....]

The facts are largely undisputed. Del Cryer, a Shreveport oil operator, acquired from the inventor the manufacturing rights to the 'JET-Glo Multi Purpose Heater,' described in a pending patent application. He also acquired a small stock of parts and dies for the heater at a judicial sale. Subsequently, he retained the Greene Research Engineering Company, operated by George J. Greene, Jr., a mechanical engineer, to improve and test the heater for orchard heating purposes. After making improvements and testing, the Greene Research Engineering Company made a written report to Cryer that the maximum burning rate of the heater, using kerosene as fuel, was 275,000 BTUs per hour, suitable for use by outdoor laborers, for preventing fruit and vegetables from freezing, and for protecting newly poured concrete. The report stated that the tests extended over two 24-hour periods.[1]

After receiving the report, Cryer contacted Thayer T. May, president of M & M Manufacturing Company, Inc., concerning the manufacture of the heater. On July 3, 1965, Cryer delivered the model heater and the Greene report to May, suggesting that he satisfy himself about the performance of the heater and determine whether or not he desired to acquire the manufacturing rights.[2] May demonstrated the heater to numerous fruit and vegetable growers to determine its marketability.

[....]

On August 17, 1965, by written contract, M & M Manufacturing Company, Inc., purchased the manufacturing rights to the heater from Cryer. M & M paid Cryer $12,500 in

---

1. The report recited: 'Tests were performed on two identical, standard production heaters and extended over two 24-hour periods. All tests were performed in an unsheltered area with no provisions made for wind shielding. A standard recommended kerosene fuel (higher heating value of 19,900 Btu/lb.) was used for all tests.'

2. "Q. And you and Mr. May subsequently negotiated verbally and worked out the signed contract which was previously introduced in evidence, is that correct?" "A. Well, he told me he was very much interested in something, some product, and I told him to take the heater and take the engineer's report and if he found that it was something that he was interested in why I would be happy to make a deal with him and told him the conditions of the deal that I would accept, so he takes the heater and the engineer's report, and then I didn't have any other personal contact with Mr. May then for a couple of weeks."

cash and agreed to pay him a royalty of $1.25 for each unit manufactured. In the sale, M & M obligated itself to manufacture a minimum of 5000 units in the first year. The sale contained no express warranty as to the capacity of the heater or its suitability for orchard heating.[3]

M & M manufactured an initial group of some fifty heaters. In testing the fuel system on one of these units, M & M discovered that the heater accumulated soot so badly that in three to five hours it failed to produce sufficient heat to protect vegetation. Ultimately, the heater would go out completely.

M & M then made extensive efforts to correct the soot problem, but failed. Although possessing some utility, the heater fell short of the long-burning feature needed for a superior orchard heater. Thus, considering it unmarketable, M & M abandoned its plan to manufacture the heaters.

At the end of the initial contract year, Cryer brought the present suit for royalties and attorney's fees due him under the contract. M & M reconvened, seeking rescission of the sale on the grounds of error, failure of cause, and redhibitory vice.

After trial on the merits, the district judge found that the heater was unsuitable for orchard heating and so imperfect that it must be supposed that a buyer would not have purchased it had he known of the defect. He denied redhibition, however, because M & M could not return the parts and dies delivered in the sale. Under Louisiana Civil Code Article 2543, he reduced the purchase price $6,250.00, the amount of the first year's royalty. On appeal, the Court of Appeal denied the reconventional demand for rescission of the sale and granted judgment in favor of the plaintiff against M & M Manufacturing Company in the sum of $6,250.00, the royalty on the guaranteed minimum of 5000 heaters for the first year, with legal interest from judicial demand until paid, and all costs. It rejected plaintiff's demand for attorney's fees. 253 So.2d 69. On application of M & M Manufacturing Company, Inc., we granted certiorari to review the judgment of the Court of Appeal denying rescission of the sale. 259 La. 1053, 254 So.2d 463 (1971).

Redhibition is the avoidance of a sale because of a vice or defect in the thing sold. LSA-C.C. Art. 2520. It is based upon an implied-in-law warranty that the thing sold is free of hidden defects that render it useless or impair its use to such an extent that it must be supposed that the buyer would not have purchased it, had he known of the vice. LSA-C.C. Arts. 2475, 2476, 2520; 23 Tul.L.Rev. 120.

As correctly noted by the Court of Appeal, the contested contract is a sale of the right to manufacture and distribute a heater built according to a design protected by patent law. The thing sold was an incorporeal right. LSA-C.C. Art. 460; Messersmith v. Messersmith, 229 La. 495, 86 So.2d 169 (1956); Yiannopoulos, Louisiana Civil Law Treatise: Property s 13, pp. 33–34 (1967).

In the sale of an incorporeal right, the implied warranty includes existence of the right at the time of the transfer and peaceable possession of that right. LSA-C.C. Arts. 2501, 2646; Tomlinson v. Thurmon, 189 La. 959, 181 So. 458 (1938). It does not extend to a deficiency in a physical object to which the right may ultimately relate. The thing sold and warranted is the right, not the object. Ratcliff v. McIlhenny, 157 La. 708, 102 So. 878 (1925); 2 Planiol Civil Law Treatise (Translation by Louisiana State Law Institute) No.

---

3. The sale, captioned 'Sale of Manufacturing Rights,' conveyed the manufacturing and distributing rights with 'legal warranties,' that is, with such warranties as are imposed by law. It also conveyed the stock of parts and dies.

73 1629, p. 904. See also Losecco v. Gregory, 108 La. 648, 32 So. 985 (1901); Succession of
74 Mahoney, 167 La. 255, 119 So. 40 (1928); Benner v. Van Norden, 27 La.Ann. 473 (1875).

75 We conclude that redhibition is unavailable in the present case because of the absence
76 of warranty extending to the performance of the manufactured heater.

77 M & M advances two additional reasons for rescinding the sale: error and failure of cause.
78 Although the arguments are variously phrased, the pervasive issue is whether the sale
79 should be rescinded because of error.

80 As to error, the Louisiana Civil Code provides:

81 Article 1823:

82 'Errors may exist as to all the circumstances and facts which relate to a con-
83 tract, but it is not every error that will invalidate it. To have that effect, the error
84 must be in some point, which was a principal cause for making the contract,
85 and it may be either as to the motive for making the contract, to the person with
86 whom it is made, or to the subject matter of the contract itself.'

87 Article 1825:

88 'The error in the cause of a contract to have the effect of invalidating it, must
89 be on the principal cause, when there are several; this principal cause is called
90 the Motive, and means that consideration without which the contract would not
91 have been made.'

92 Article 1826:

93 'No error in the motive can invalidate a contract, unless the other party was
94 apprised that it was the principal cause of the agreement, or unless from the na-
95 ture of the transaction it must be presumed that he knew it.'

96 In these articles, cause is identified with motive. Litvinoff, Louisiana Civil Law Trea-
97 tise: Obligations s 290, pp. 522–523 (1969); Smith, A Refresher Course in Cause, 12
98 La.L.Rev. 2, 15 (1952). Error in the determining motive, or principal cause, of a contract
99 vitiates consent and invalidates the contract. Error as to a subsidiary motive has no effect
100 upon the validity of the contract. Stack v. Irwin, 246 La. 777, 167 So.2d 363 (1964); Car-
101 penter v. Skinner, 224 La. 848, 71 So.2d 133 (1954).

102 Some motives are readily discernible from the inherent nature of a sale. For example,
103 an immediate end of the buyer is to acquire ownership of the thing sold. That motive
104 characterizes the transaction. Other motives, not discernible from the inherent nature of
105 the sale, rise to the status of principal cause only when the parties contract on that basis.
106 Although the parties need not make the motive an express condition of the contract, it
107 must appear from all the circumstances that the existence of the sale has been subordi-
108 nated to the reality of the motive. The special motive must have been a constitutive ele-
109 ment of the accord of wills. The reality of the motive becomes a tacit condition of the
110 contract. LSA-C.C. Arts. 1825, 1826, 1827; Aubry & Rau, Droit Civil Francais: Obliga-
111 tions (An English Translation by the Louisiana State Law Institute) s 343a, p. 313; 3 Toul-
112 lier, Droit Civil Francais (6th ed.) Title 3, Art. 1, ss 40–42, pp. 26–28; Litvinoff, Louisiana
113 Civil Law Treatise: Obligations s 220, pp. 394–395 (1969); Smith, A Refresher Course in
114 Cause, 12 La.L.Rev. 2, 10–11 (1952).[4]

---

4. The condition has also been described as 'unvocalized' (8 Tul.L.Rev. 194), 'undeveloped' (13
Tul.L.Rev. 363), and 'implied' (Litvinoff, Louisiana Civil Law Treatise: Obligations s 212, p. 378 at
f.n. 21 (1969).

In his article on Cause, supra, Dr. J. Denson Smith, an eminent civil law authority, states:

> 'Considering the nature of the contract, realization of the principal cause or motive is understood to be the basis upon which consent is given and it therefore becomes a tacit condition of the contract. This is because the final and principal motive for assuming an obligation must lie in the obvious end being sought, for example, obtaining ownership, or use, or services, or conferring a benefit. If this cause fails, the will is vitiated and the contract falls. At the same time, if the particular motive is not discernible by the nature of the contract it is subsidiary and does not rise to the status of a tacit condition because the other party is not chargeable with knowledge that the contract is conditioned on its realization. To be effective as a condition, the parties must contract on that basis. An example of this may be found in the rule that error as to the value of the thing purchased and sold does not vitiate consent. Although a buyer may not have bought if he had known the true value of the thing, it should be presumed that he is taking his chance—and the seller is in like position—unless the agreement is conditioned on value. All that the seller is required to know is that the buyer wants the thing being bought and sold, or supposedly so; why the buyer may want it, whether because of its supposed value or for any other reason is not the seller's concern if the parties do not contract on such basis. As the French writers put it, error will serve to invalidate consent only when it enters the contractual field. It does so tacitly if it relates to the principal cause, that is, the final and determining motive.' (Footnotes omitted).

The treatise of Aubry & Rau, Droit Civil Francais, supra, sets forth the principle as follows:

> '... (T)he error relative to the occasional motives or to the circumstances which may have induced one or both of the parties to contract, is a cause of nullity only where, according to the common intention of the parties, the reality of these motifs constitutes a condition to which they intended to subordinate the formation or the performance of the agreement.' (Footnote omitted).

Finally, Toullier in Droit Civil Francais, supra, s 42, p. 28, states:

> 'It is by the manner in which the act is expressed, by the nature of the contract, by the object of the promise, finally by the circumstances, that one may determine what the determining motive has been, and whether the consent given has been subordinated to or conditioned on the reality of this motive as an implicit condition.' [....]

In the present case, the transfer of ownership was effective. The buyer became the owner of the right to manufacture and distribute. The right conveyed is without defect. Hence, the immediate end that characterizes a sale generally was achieved.

M & M asserts, however, that its motive was to secure the manufacturing rights to a long-burning, high-output heater to sell to orchardists for freeze protection. It postulates that this motive was the principal cause of the contract, and the heater's failure to fulfill these requirements is an invalidating error. Finally, conceding the seller's good faith, it asserts that the error was induced by the seller's misrepresentation that the heater possessed the essential features to protect orchards from freezing.

Innocent misrepresentations may induce error when a purchaser justifiably relies upon them. When an error results from such non-fraudulent misrepresentations, the error invalidates the contract only if it bears upon the principal cause of the contract. LSA-C.C. Arts. 1823, 1825, 1845, 1847(2), 2529; Ganucheau v. Greff, La.App., 181 So.2d 854 (1966); Kardis v. Barrere, 17 La.App. 433, 136 So. 135 (1931); 12 La.L.Rev. 509.[5]

Cryer was an oil operator, with no special competence in heat engineering. Both lower courts found that he was in good faith and made no misrepresentations to the buyer.[6] We adopt this factual finding.

It is true that he transmitted a copy of the engineering report to the buyer when he delivered the model heater for testing. Under the circumstances, however, the transmission of the report cannot be considered as a representation of the seller that the heater met all the performance requirements of marketable orchard heater. On the contrary, the record reflects that the seller intended that the manufacturer itself test the heater and rely upon its own skill and judgment as to the heater's performance. He gave the company ample opportunity to conduct its investigation by supplying it with a working model more than a month before the sale. Apparently, the manufacturer's tests consisted only of burning the heater for short periods for demonstration purposes. Under no sound legal theory, however, is the inadequacy of these tests chargeable to the seller. See Henderson v. United States Sheet & Window Glass Co., 168 La. 66, 121 So. 576 (1929); Rocchi v. Schwabacher & Hirsch, 33 La.App. 1364 (1881).

The manufacturer was aware that the heater was newly developed. The purchase of manufacturing rights to it was speculative in some degree. One who expresses an unqualified will tp [sic] purchase such right should be bound accordingly such rights should be bound accordingly that the purchaser's will is conditional. No basis for this knowledge appears in the record. Rather, it appears that, following the manufacturer's investigation and exercise of judgment, the seller reasonably contemplated an unconditional transaction. We find nothing in the contract or the circumstances under which it was formed to raise manufacturer's expectations for the heater to be contractual level of principal cause.

In its well-written brief, the defendant relies upon several decisions of this Court dealing with error in contracts, including Stack v. Irwin, 246 La. 777, 167 So.2d 363 (1964); Carpenter v. Skinner, 224 La. 848, 71 So.2d 133 (1954); Overby v. Beach, 220 La. 77, 55 So.2d 873 (1951); and Pan American Production Co. v. Robichaux, 200 La. 666, 8 So.2d 635 (1942). We find these cases to be factually and legally inapposite.

We conclude, as did the Court of Appeal, that the sale is valid and that plaintiff's demand should be sustained.

For the reasons assigned, the judgment of the Court of Appeal is affirmed at defendant's costs.

HAMLIN, J., dissents in part with written reasons.

SUMMERS, J., dissents.

TATE, J., dissents in part and assigns written reasons.

HAMLIN, Justice (dissenting in part).

I respectfully dissent from the majority opinion and decree insofar as it affirms that part of the Court of Appeal decree which awarded plaintiff, Del Cryer, $6,250.00 with legal interest from judicial demand and costs.

---

5. In contrast, when error is induced by fraud, it need relate only to a 'material part of the contract.' LSA-C.C. Art. 1847(2); 12 La.L.Rev. 509; 33 Tul.L.Rev. 270.

6. On original hearing, the Court of Appeal stated: 'In this case there was no misrepresentation present.' This finding remained mained undistubed on rehearing.

As stated in the majority opinion, this suit was instituted by Del Cryer for the collection of royalties and attorneys' fees allegedly due under contract. Defendant answered and reconvened; averring redhibition, it prayed for rescission of the contract involved with reimbursement of $12,500.00 and payment of alleged expenses in the sum of $27,158.82.

The District Judge, the Court of Appeal, and the dissenting opinion of Judge Ayres accept the evidence of record to the effect that the accumulation of soot made the instant heater incapable of protecting orchards and tender vegetation. It, the heater, never performed as the Greene report, mentioned in the majority opinion, stated that it would. Mr. Greene himself testified that the heater would be of little use unless it was able to burn eight to ten hours at a sustained heat output.

In my opinion, the evidence of record conclusively reflects that the experimental heater could not do the intended job, and the instant parties were unable to make corrections to eliminate the soot buildup. A non-descript heater was the result of continued efforts; defendant proceeded no further with production.[7]

The trial judge in his reasons for judgment, rejecting the parties' demands, stated in part: 'The facts established leave no doubt that the heater would not perform completely up to the standards set forth in the engineering report made by Mr. Greene. This report is in evidence as plaintiff's exhibit 8. The engineer's report was relied on by plaintiff and defendant as to the performance capabilities of the heater. Both plaintiff and defendant were in good faith in expecting the heater to live up to its representations in the Greene report. Both plaintiff and defendant were entirely in good faith in the entire matter because the heater operated perfectly in the short test that each made.

'A fair construction of the report is to state that it represents that the heaters will operate for 24 continuous hours, while producing 275,000 BTU's per hour, while, in fact, they will only operate satisfactorily three to five hours with the use of an additional tank, and then would accumulate soot up to the point to be unsatisfactory. * * *

'This defect made the heater so inconvenient and imperfect that it must be supposed that a buyer would not have purchased it had he known of the defect, although it would apparently still be competitive with or even outperform the competitive heater on the market called a 'Salamander' heater, which produced 140,000 BTU's per hour for four or five hours and then had to be put out and re-lit. * * * When the two makes of heaters are compared, the instant heater does have some utility.

'Defendant has re-worked the dies and made extensive changes in the inventory received from the plaintiff and made new dies. * * * Defendant is not in position to return the same to the plaintiff for which reason the sale cannot be rescinded.'

In my opinion, under the facts and circumstances of this case, justice does not demand the rescission of the instant contract and the return to M & M of the $12,500.00 it paid Del Cryer. Likewise, I do not believe that M & M is entitled to the return from Del Cryer of expenses it incurred after the negotiation of the instant contract on August 17, 1965. As I analyze the record, M & M was not as vigilant as it should have been. Equity aids the vigilant, not those who slumber on their rights. 30A C.J.S. Equity s 113, p. 32.

---

7. In answer, defendant averred: 'Defendant admits that it has not manufactured 5,000 units of the Jet-Glo Multi-Purpose Heater, hereinafter referred to as the heater, but shows that it has manufactured 50 complete units and has on hand parts for approximately 500 additional units which have not been completed * * *.'

Article 1883 of the Civil Code recites that every contract has for its object something which one or both of the parties oblige themselves to give, or to do, or not to do. Herein, M & M obligated itself to manufacture heaters and pay royalties. The contract states, 'As further consideration the said M & M Manufacturing Company, Inc., is to pay unto the said Del Cryer a royalty upon each and every unit manufactured or caused to be manufactured by the said M & M Manufacturing Company, Inc., the sum of $1.25 per unit.' It further recites that M & M binds itself to manufacture and produce a minimum of 5,000 units during the first year of production.

Article 1891 of the Civil Code recites: 'The object of a contract must be possible, by which is meant physically or morally possible. The possibility must be determined, not by the means or ability of the party to fulfill his agreement, but by the nature of the thing which forms the object of it.' Herein, the object of the instant contract became physically impossible. M & M could not manufacture the 5,000 units. Under the articles of the Civil Code, reason dictates and justice demands that M & M not be assessed for the royalties prayed for by Del Cryer. I conclude that Del Cryer is not entitled to his demands.

Each case has a separate life of its own. The facts and circumstances of one case are not the facts and circumstances of another; each case must be decided on its own particular facts. Cf. 30 C.J.S. Equity s 89, p. 976. A court of equity is a court of conscience; it seeks to do justice and equity between all parties; it seeks to strike a balance of convenience as between litigants; and looks at the whole situation. It does not act unless justice and good conscience demand that relief should be granted, and acts only in accordance with conscience and good faith. 30 C.J.A. Equity s 89, pp. 978–979.

There is no case in the annals of Louisiana jurisprudence the facts of which are similar to those of the instant case. While both sides have cited numerous authorities, it is my view that they are not decisive of the instant case. I therefore look to Article 21 of the Revised Civil Code, the equity article in Louisiana. In addition to applying written law and jurisprudence to this matter, I would likewise apply equity.

My reasons are not the same as the trial court's reasons for its judgment; however, I reach the same conclusion as the trial judge.

I respectfully dissent in part.

TATE, Justice (dissenting in part).

The writer agrees with most of the analysis of the scholarly majority opinion. My main disagreement with the majority is in its implied holding that the ability to manufacture a Workable orchard heater was not the principal cause or motive of the Obligation to pay royalty. I find the royalty agreement to have a separate and distinct principal cause from the sales agreement.

The majority analyzed the contract as being solely a sale. Under my analysis, the contract between the seller Cryer and the buyer-manufacturer ('M&M') included at least two separate obligations: (a) the sale by Cryer to M&M for $12,500 of manufacturing rights and parts on hand pertaining to an orchard-heater; and (b) the agreement to pay $1.25 per unit royalty for each unit manufactured and to manufacture or produce at least five thousand units during the first year of production.

This contract thus produced a conjunctive obligation as defined by Civil Code Article 2063, with several connected objects contained in a single writing. As stated by the Article, 'This contract creates as many different obligations as there are different objects.' See also Civil Law Translations, Aubry & Rau, Obligations, Section 300 (LSLI translation,

1965). In my view, the 'principal cause or Motive.' Articles 1824, 1825,[8] is different as to obligations (a) and (b), as set forth above.

As to (a), the sale of the manufacturing rights, I agree with the majority's determination that it should not be rescinded because of any error as to principal cause. Both parties realized that this portion of the transaction was in some respects speculative and that the refined development necessary for future exploitation depended to some extent upon the manufacturer's skill. The manufacturer here took his chances that he would not be able to perfect a workable product.

The sale of the right to manufacture the orchard-heater was therefore unconditional, with the buyer-manufacturer bound for the purchase price despite his inability, despite due diligence, to develop the orchard-heater into a merchantable product. The seller Cryer is thus entitled to retain the $12,500 purchase price, and the buyer M&M is not entitled to recoup his expenses incurred in attempting to perfect the product.

However, as to (b) — the obligation to pay royalties of $1.25 per unit and to manufacture 5000 units during the first year of production —, I believe there was an independent principal cause or Motive: the underlying assumption that, in fact, the manufacturer could perfect a merchantable unit, using due diligence (as, in fact, he could not).

Although there was no misrepresentation by the buyer, the engineering report furnished by him indicated that the orchard-heater was a workable product. Certainly, the seller believed that this was so.

In agreeing to manufacture 5000 units the first year, the principal cause or motive must have included the mutual belief that the manufacturer could produce a unit that would work and be merchantable. The parties, could not have contemplated, in my opinion, that the buyer M&M would have to produce 5000 unworkable units or to pay royalty for the manufacture of an unusable product.

Therefore, I am unable to agree that the buyer unconditionally agreed to pay a royalty of $1.25 for 5000 units in the first year of production, whether or not it was possible to manufacture a merchantable orchard heater.

Under the agreement, the buyer paid $12,500 cash for the manufacturing rights and further agreed to pay 'a royalty upon each and every unit manufactured (in) ... the sum of $1.25 per unit.' The agreement concluded: 'It is further agreed and stipulated between the parties that the said M&M Manufacturing Company, Inc., (the buyer) shall use due diligence and good business practices in expanding the manufacture and distribution of said heater, and the said M&M Manufacturing Company, Inc., binds itself to manufacture and produce a minimum of 5000 units during the first year of production.'

While the buyer unconditionally agreed (a) to pay $1.25 for each unit manufactured, (b) to use due diligence in expanding the manufacture and distribution, and (c) to manufacture and produce a minimum of 5000 units during the first year of production, it seems to me that the understood principal cause or Motive for the obligation to pay royalty was that, using due diligence, it would be possible for the buyer-manufacturer to produce a merchantable orchard-heater. If it was able to perfect the orchard-heater, then the manufacturer was unconditionally bound to produce the minimum 5000 units during the first year and to pay the royalty of $1.25 per unit.

---

8. Civil Code Article 1825: 'The error in the cause of a contract to have the effect of invalidating it, must be on the principal cause, when there are several; this principal cause is called the Motive, and means that consideration without which the contract would not have been made.'

However, I am unable, in the absence of an express agreement to such effect, to hold as a matter of law that the motive or principal cause for an agreement to pay royalty for each unit manufactured does not include the ability of the manufacturer, using due diligence, to manufacture a workable and merchantable product. Since despite due diligence the manufacturer in the present case was unable to do so, this was an error as to a principal cause which invalidates the obligation to manufacture 5000 units during the first year and to pay royalties upon them. Civil Code Articles 1823, 1825.

Applicable here is Civil Code Article 1827: '… wherever the motive is apparent, although not made an express condition, if the error bears on the motive, the contract is void. A promise to give a certain sum to bear the expenses of a marriage, which the party supposes to have taken place, is not obligatory, if there be no marriage.'

Although I differ with the majority opinion in this respect, I must admit the force of its reasoning that, since the principal cause for the Sale agreement did not include the belief that in fact a workable orchard-heater could be manufactured, likewise the validity of the royalty agreement was not dependent upon such as a principal cause. Nevertheless, because of the difference between the obligations included in the sale of the right to manufacture the product, If perfectable, and the obligation to manufacture it and to pay royalty upon units manufactured (which Must assume that the product Was perfectable), I personally find no intellectual incongruity in an analysis contrary to the majority's.

In short, although there was an unconditional obligation to pay the purchase price for the right to manufacture the orchard-heater and to use due diligence in developing and merchandising same, nevertheless the conjunctive obligation to manufacture 5000 units and to pay royalty upon these units manufactured during the year was conditioned upon the existence (or not) of the principal cause of That obligation—that the manufacturer, using due diligence, Could produce a workable and merchantable product. Since this principal cause is shown not to exist, the royalty obligation should be held invalid because of error as to it.

I therefore respectfully dissent.

ON REHEARING

PER CURIAM.

Upon reconsideration of the issues, a majority of this court reaches the same conclusion as reached on our first hearing. We therefore adopt all the factual and legal conclusions of our original opinion and reinstate it and our original decree.

Original opinion and decree reinstated.

HAMLIN, C.J., dissents, adhering to the views expressed in his dissent to original opinion.

TATE, J., dissents and assigns additional written reasons.

BARHAM, J., dissents for reasons assigned by TATE, J.

TATE, Justice (dissenting).

The writer dissents in part and concurs in part. I adhere fully to the findings, legal analysis and statements of law of our original opinion in refusing to rescind the sale and in dismissing the reconventional demand praying for recission. I have reservations (as expressed in my dissent to the original opinion) to the majority holding that the ancillary minimum royalty agreement contained in the sales contract should not be rescinded on grounds of error in the Cause. Nevertheless, I find it unnecessary to rest my present dissent upon a contrary view: because, for reasons to be stated, such minimum royalty agreement is unenforceable because its Performance (unlike the validity of the sale itself) depended upon an implied condition which contemplated that it was possible to develop a merchantable heater.

The pertinent clauses of the 'Sale of Manufacturing Rights' agreement executed between the parties are set forth in the footnote below.[9] As there set forth, for the purchase of the manufacturing rights, the manufacturer-buyer M & M unconditionally agreed to pay the seller Cryer the sum of $12,500 (Clause a) plus royalty of $1.25 for each unit manufacturer (Clause b). Additionally, by Clause c M & M agreed to use due diligence in expanding the manufacture and distribution of the heater and—in order to effectuate This ancillary agreement of Clause c, it is important to note—bound itself to manufacture a minimum of 5000 units during the first year of production.

This sales agreement thus produced conjunctive obligations as defined by Civil Code Article 2063, with several connected objects contained in a single writing. As stated by the Article, 'This contract creates as many different obligations as there are different objects.' See also Civil Law Translations, Aubry & Rau, Obligations, Section 300 (LSLI translation, 1965). The minimum royalty agreement (Clause c) constituted an obligation separable in performance and enforceability from obligations of the buyer represented by Clauses a and b.

I disagree with the majority view that the $6,250 minimum royalties guaranteed by Clause c should be considered as part of the price to be paid by the buyer—as if the sales price were $12,500 plus $6,250 minimum royalties. Instead, in my view, the agreement to pay such minimum royalties was, by terms of the contract, intended as a means of enforcing the ancillary agreement of the contract that the buyer use 'due diligence and good business practices in expanding the manufacture and distribution of the heater.' Clause c.

The thrust of Clause c is that the buyer must manufacture and market the heater as quickly as possible, consistent with good business practices (but to produce at least 500 units the first year). However, the ability to manufacture a merchantable product was assumed to have existed. The agreement cannot have intended that the buyer manufacture at least 5000 heaters, whether or not it was possible to develop a heater that was economically competitive with other heaters on the market.

I should note that the record reflects that the buyer M & M used due diligence and did all possible to develop a heater as described in the patent and in the sale of manufacturing right to it. Nevertheless, despite these efforts, it proved impossible to develop a merchantable heater—one that was economically competitive with preexisting products designed to fill the same function as the present heater.

The obligation to pay minimum royalties depended upon, as an implied condition, an uncertain event: the ability to develop a merchantable heater. This condition is implied from the nature of the contract and from the presumed intent of the parties. Civil Code

9. (a) '* * * The consideration for this sale is as follows: $12,500.00 cash paid to the said Del Cryer this date, who acknowledges the receipt thereof and grants acquittance and discharge therefor. (b) As further consideration the said M & M Manufacturing Company, Inc., is to pay unto the said Del Cryer a. royalty upon each and every unit manufactured or caused to be manufactured by the said M & M Manufacturing Company, Inc., the sum of $1.25 per unit. * * *(c) It is further agreed and stipulated between the parties that the said M & M Manufacturing Company, Inc., shall use due diligence and good business practices in expanding the manufacture and distribution of said heater, and the said M & M Manufacturing Company, Inc., binds itself to manufacture and produce a minimum of 5000 units during the first year of production. * * *'

Article 2026.[10] (This, incidentally, is undoubtedly also an implied condition for the basis obligation of the contract to pay $1.25 royalty for each unit produced (Clause b); no obligation to pay royalties under this clause existed unless, in fact, the manufacture of heaters was commercially possible.)

The minimum royalty agreement is therefore what is known in our law as a conditional obligation—one which depended on an uncertain event, namely, the ability to manufacture a merchantable heater. Article 2021.[11] The obligation to pay the minimum royalties never came into effect because the event upon which it depended never happened: by the exercise of all reasonable efforts, it was impossible for the obligor to develop to manufacture. economically feasible to manufacture. [*Sic*]

Civil Code Article 1891 provides: 'The object of a contract must be possible, by which is meant physically or morally possible. The possibility must be determined, not by the means or ability of the party to fulfill his agreement, but by the nature of the thing which forms the object of it.' See Planiol, Civil Law Treatise, Volume 2, Sections 1006, 1007 (LSLI translation, 1959).

Thus, under traditional civilian principles, the unenforceability of the minimum royalty agreement can be ascribed not only to its dependence upon a suspensive condition which never came to happen, but also as resulting from the failure due to impossibility of the initial responsibility for performance. The Roman maxim, 'Impossibilium nulla obligatio est (There is no obligation to do impossible things)', Broom's Legal Maxims 248 (1974), expresses the principle which Gaius stated as 'If we stipulate for something to be given to us, which is of such a nature that this cannot be done, it is evident that such a stipulation is void by natural law * * *.' Gaius, Digest 44.7.1.9 (Scott translation, 1932). See also 2 Ripert & Boulanger, Traite de Droit Civil 182 (1952). Some reliance might also be placed upon the modern civilian *Théorie de l'imprévision* the power of the courts to hold negated an obligation when change of circumstance or impossibility voids the presuppositions or reasonable expectations of the parties, although not expressed, which formed an underlying basis for the agreement. Cf., Litvinoff, 1 Obligations, Sections 250, 297 (p. 538) (LISI Civil Law Treatise, V 1. 6, 1969).[12]

---

10. Article 2026: 'Conditions are either express or implied. They are express, when they appear in the contract; they are implied, whenever they result from the operation of law, from the nature of the contract, or from the presumed intent of the parties.'

11. Article 2021: 'Conditional obligations are such as are made to depend on an uncertain event. If the obligation is not to take effect until the event happen, it is a suspensive condition; if the obligation takes effect immediately, but is liable to be defeated when the event happens, it is then a resolutory condition.' Compare with Article 2020: 'Simple obligations are such as are not dependent for their execution on any event provided for by the parties, and which are not agreed to become void, on the happening of any such event.' See also Article 2043: 'The obligation contracted on a suspensive condition, is that which depends, either on a future and uncertain event, or on an event which has actually taken place, without its being yet known to the parties.' In the former case, the obligation cannot be executed till after the event; in the latter, the obligation has its effect from the day on which it was contracted. but it can not be enforced until the event be known.' And see also Article 2045: 'The dissolving condition is that which, when accomplished, operates the revocation of the obligation, placing matters in the same state as though the obligation had not existed.' It does not suspend the execution of the obligation; it only obliges the creditor to restore what he has received, in case the event provided for in the condition takes place.'

12. Also, in modern French law, a contract such as the present is termed a Contrat de licence. 2 Roubier, Le Droit de la propriete industrielle 260 (1954); Allart, Traite the orique et pratique des brevet d'invention 217 (3rd ed. 1911). According to French jurisprudence the licensor (brevete) warrants to the licensee (licencie): (a) the existence of the patent, and (b) the industrial feasibility, that is, that the thing can be manufactured. But the Brevete does not warrant the commercial success.

In summary, the consideration for the sale itself contemplated that the development   450
of a workable heater was somewhat speculative; the sale therefore is not invalidated by the   451
impossibility to do so, since there was no error in the cause of the sale. On the other   452
hand, the ancillary agreement within the sale—to use due diligence in producing and   453
marketing the product and to produce and pay royalties upon at least 5000 units the first   454
year—was entered into with the expectation that a merchantable heater Could be de-   455
veloped; when this event proved impossible of fulfillment, the obligation to pay the min-   456
imum royalties upon 5000 units the first year—which depended upon this event which   457
did not occur—never came into existence.   458

I agree with the district court conclusion that the plaintiff's demand for $6,250 min-   459
imum royalties should be dismissed.   460

For these reasons, I respectfully dissent from the award to Cryer of $6,250 minimum   461
royalties, although I concur with the dismissal of M &M's reconventional demand seek-   462
ing recovery of the $12,500 price paid for the manufacturing rights.   463

Questions

1. Lines 8–10: The court opens its opinion with the statement that "this case raises the
    question of whether a sale of manufacturing rights to a multipurpose heater. . . ." What
    kind of contract is a contract of sale? What kind of obligation does a contract of sale
    impose on the seller? In this particular sale, what kind of object is the Court saying
    is the object of the sale? If a sale is a contract of the kind you have identified, does
    that contract create one obligation only? Two obligations? In the latter case, what
    kind of second obligation has been created? Since that obligation must have an ob-
    ject (to give something, to do something or not to do something), what then is the
    object of this second obligation?

2. Lines 21–26: Can you better and more definitely identify the object of Cryer's offer
    to Thayer T. May? How would you qualify or describe Cryer's behavior against the
    background of Louisiana Civil Code article 1759? How many obligations, if more
    than one, did M & M owe to Cryer? If one, what kind is it? If more than one, are they
    connected somehow?

3. Lines 28–33: Is there one price or are there two or more prices for M & M to pay?
    How would you describe M & M's obligation to pay the price (or the prices): divis-
    ible or indivisible? Conjunctive or alternative?

4. Lines 34–44: When M & M abandons its plan to manufacture the heaters, is it be-
    cause M & M believes that the object of its obligation is to manufacture "workable
    and marketable heaters"? Was that object the object they bought from Cryer? Error?
    What kind of error and by whom is M & M talking about? About what cause is M &
    M talking?

5. Lines 75–76: According to the majority, what is (or what are) the object(s) sold by
    Cryer to M & M? Do you see any good/important reason (or reasons) in properly iden-

---

This means that, if the patent is real and it is possible to manufacture the thing, the commercial failure does not entitle the Licencie to resolution of the Contrat de licence. However, the Licencie who
does not exploit the patent because it is a commercial failure does not breach the contract and is regarded as having done as much as he could under the contract. Paris. Feb. 4, 1958, Ann.Prop.ind.1959,
224; Trib.gr.inst.Seine, Feb. 9, 1963, Ann.prop.ind.1963, 385, both cited in Burst, Brevete et Licencie, leur rapports juridiques dans le contrat de licence 112–113 (1970).

tifying the object of an obligation as the Supreme Court did here? Do you agree with the Court's conclusion?

6. Lines 151–159: If error there is, for that error to be a ground for nullity of a contract it must bear on the cause of the contract. Which cause did the Court identify as being the principal cause of the contract (*see* line 156)?

7. Lines 328–342: Is Justice Tate alluding to the manufacturing of a future object or "future thing"? If that is the case, isn't Justice Tate saying that M & M must both pay "a price or royalty per unit" and also "manufacture the object"? But isn't the object bought for a price by a buyer, M & M in this case, to be sold and delivered by a seller, therefore someone else than M & M? Isn't there something in these statements that does not fit with the law of the Louisiana Civil Code?

NOTE: On lines 444–449, Justice Tate brings into his analysis the "*théorie de l'imprévision*" which he finds, indirectly, in French law. There would be too much to explain in a few lines about this theory. Suffice it to say that this *théorie de l'imprévision* was created by the French administrative courts (Conseil d'Etat) to provide some protection to the State and its Agencies against financial disaster following some unforeseeable event, such as a war. This theory created by the administrative courts has never been used by the private-commercial law courts under the overall jurisdiction of the Cour de Cassation.

FIRST LOUISIANA BANK

v.

MORRIS & DICKSON, CO., LLC

Louisiana Court of Appeal
Second Circuit
Nov. 3, 2010
55 So.3d 815

GASKINS, J.

The plaintiff, First Louisiana Bank ("First Louisiana"), and the plaintiff in intervention, Ronald Tuminello, appeal from a trial court judgment finding that the defendant, Morris & Dickson Company, LLC ("Morris & Dickson"), was not liable for losses resulting from the default on loans by Material Management Systems, Inc. ("MMS"), a company with whom Morris & Dickson did business. For the following reasons, we affirm the trial court judgment.

FACTS

Morris & Dickson needed a package handling system for its warehouse. MMS was the low bidder and was chosen to install an Intertake Pallet Pick system. To facilitate the process, Morris & Dickson issued three purchase orders to MMS. One purchase order, # 031223-01, was for $249,853.47. A second purchase order, # 031223-02, the order at issue here, was for $196,450.50. The amount of the third purchase order was not specified.

MMS was operated by Robert Eizel. MMS did not have the funds to purchase the system. Mr. Eizel approached Bank One, Bancorp South, and First Louisiana about obtaining financing. First Louisiana requested, as additional security, that the bank be included as additional payee on all payments made by Morris & Dickson to MMS.

On January 15, 2004, Paul M. Dickson, vice-president of Morris & Dickson, wrote a "To Whom it May Concern" letter stating that:

Payment for the above referenced purchase order issued to Material Man-   27
agement Systems will be made payable to Material Management Systems and   28
First Louisiana Bank Attn: Ron Boudreaux.   29

The purchase order referenced in the letter was # 031223-02, for $196,450.50. The   30
letter does not specify an addressee. Morris & Dickson wrote similar letters to Bank One   31
for purchase orders # 031223-01, # 031223-02, and # 031223-03 and to Bancorp South   32
for # 031223-01 and # 031223-03. Bank One did not lend money to MMS; Bancorp   33
South and First Louisiana did. The two loans from First Louisiana are at issue in this   34
case. [....]

The loans from First Louisiana were evidenced by promissory notes from MMS and   35
Mr. Eizel to First Louisiana in the amounts of $50,070 and $65,072. Mr. Eizel signed as   36
a guarantor on the loans. In order to secure the two loans, MMS also made assignments   37
to First Louisiana of the contract purchase order from Morris & Dickson for $196,450.50.   38
The assignments were filed in the Uniform Commercial Code Registry with the Louisiana   39
Secretary of State.   40

The intervenor, Ronald Tuminello, partnered with Mr. Eizel on previous business ven-   41
tures. Mr. Tuminello signed as a guarantor on the loans from First Louisiana for this pro-   42
ject. Mr. Eizel gave Mr. Tuminello a promissory note for $100,000 to secure his signature   43
as guarantor.   44

MMS failed to complete the work on the warehouse and Morris & Dickson took over   45
the project. MMS also defaulted on its loan to First Louisiana. In August 2004, First   46
Louisiana sent a demand letter to Mr. Eizel to pay both notes. In June 2005, First Louisiana   47
obtained a default judgment against MMS and Mr. Eizel in the amounts of $51,160.57 and   48
$64,724.16, the sums due on the notes. MMS went out of business and Mr. Eizel filed   49
for bankruptcy. However, his debt to First Louisiana on these notes was not discharged   50
in bankruptcy.   51

Mr. Tuminello, as guarantor of the loans, paid interest on the notes. In September   52
2005, First Louisiana sent a letter to Morris & Dickson inquiring about checks issued   53
to MMS that did not include First Louisiana as an additional payee. The record contains   54
a copy of a check issued on April 28, 2004, payable to MMS only, in the amount of   55
$161,500.00. Another check issued on June 16, 2004 was for $50,000 and was payable   56
to MMS and Bancorp South. A third check for $50,000 was issued on April 12, 2004,   57
payable only to MMS. The checks do not specify which purchase orders they were in-   58
tended to pay.

On September 8, 2006, First Louisiana filed suit against Morris & Dickson seeking to   59
enforce the terms of the "To Whom it May Concern" letter. First Louisiana sought to re-   60
cover "sums proven to be due for payments made toward purchase order # 031223-02, which   61
were not made payable jointly" to First Louisiana and MMS.   62

In May 2007, Mr. Tuminello filed a petition of intervention to recover payments made   63
by Morris & Dickson for purchase order # 031223-02. In January 2008, Morris & Dick-   64
son filed a peremptory exception of prescription, arguing that First Louisiana and Mr.   65
Tuminello were seeking to recover under the theory of detrimental reliance. First Louisiana   66
and Mr. Tuminello contended that the loans and guaranty made to MMS were done in   67
reliance on Morris & Dickson's agreement to include First Louisiana as an additional   68
payee on all checks to MMS. According to Morris & Dickson, First Louisiana was aware   69
by 2004 that it was not included as an additional payee. Morris & Dickson contended   70
that detrimental reliance is a tort and is subject to a one-year prescriptive period.   71

In January 2008, the trial court held a hearing and concluded that the claims against Morris & Dickson had prescribed. First Louisiana and Mr. Tuminello appealed. In *First Louisiana Bank v. Morris & Dickson Company, LLC,* 44,187 (La.App.2d Cir.4/8/09), 6 So.3d 1047, this court reversed the trial court, finding that the claim against Morris & Dickson was based on contract and not tort and was subject to the 10-year prescriptive period for contracts. The matter was remanded to the trial court for further proceedings.

On remand, the trial court considered testimony and evidence adduced at the original hearing. Ron C. Boudreaux, president of First Louisiana, testified that there were two conditions for the loan to MMS. First, that the bank receive assignments of the purchase orders and second, that checks from Morris & Dickson for purchase order # 031223-02 be made payable to both MMS and First Louisiana.

Paul Dickson of Morris & Dickson testified that he wrote the letter at issue here so that Mr. Eizel could get a loan from some financial institution. Similar letters were written to other banks. Mr. Dickson said that Mr. Eizel came to his office and they discussed the wording of the letters. Mr. Dickson said his expectation was that, if and when MMS got a loan, Morris & Dickson would be notified. Mr. Dickson stated that he specifically asked Mr. Eizel to inform him whom to include on the payments if he got a loan. Further, Mr. Dickson said he expected that "if a bank extended these types of terms that I would get a phone call from the bank."

MMS obtained a loan from Bancorp South in addition to First Louisiana. Mr. Dickson said that Bancorp South contacted him and told him that it had loaned money to MMS and that Bancorp South should be included as a payee on checks to MMS. Mr. Dickson complied with that request. However, he stated that First Louisiana did not contact him and he did not know which banks lent money to MMS.

On remand, a hearing was held in the trial court in September 2009. First Louisiana argued that the "To Whom it May Concern" letter was an accessory contract and a stipulation for a third party (*stipulation pour autrui*). According to First Louisiana, it acted upon Morris & Dickson's representations in the letter. First Louisiana argued that there was no need for notice of the loan or formal acceptance of the terms of the letter.

Mr. Tuminello contended that, by virtue of the letter at issue here, Morris & Dickson contracted to put First Louisiana on its checks to MMS as a payee. He argued that notice of a loan made to MMS by First Louisiana was not necessary. Mr. Tuminello maintained that Morris & Dickson breached its contract with First Louisiana. As guarantor of the loans made to MMS, Mr. Tuminello claimed that he was damaged by having to pay $17,331.58 in interest on one loan and $21,786.28 in interest on the other loan.

Morris & Dickson argued that it had no notice that First Louisiana had actually loaned money to MMS and had no obligation to include First Louisiana as a payee on the checks.

The trial court found that Morris & Dickson authored the letter at issue here in an effort to help MMS obtain financing. Morris & Dickson was never notified that First Louisiana had issued credit based upon the letter. According to the trial court, notification to Morris & Dickson of the acceptance of the terms of the letter was essential to the formation of a binding agreement. The trial court determined that it could not hold Morris & Dickson liable. A judgment in favor of Morris & Dickson, rejecting the demands of First Louisiana and Mr. Tuminello, was signed by the trial court in December 2009. First Louisiana and Mr. Tuminello appealed.

First Louisiana argues that the trial court erred in failing to find that an obligation existed on the part of Morris & Dickson to pay First Louisiana monies toward purchase order # 031223-02, pursuant to the letter issued by Morris & Dickson dated January 15, 2004. First Louisiana also claims that the trial court erred in finding that the bank and/or MMS were required to give notice to Morris & Dickson before the company was obligated to pay pursuant to its letter.

The plaintiff in intervention, Mr. Tuminello, argues on appeal that the trial court erred by not applying the detrimental reliance provisions of La. C.C. art. 1967. He also argues that the trial court erred in finding that notice was required and/or was not given.

CONTRACT AND NOTICE

First Louisiana urges that the letter at issue here created a conventional obligation or contract between Morris & Dickson and First Louisiana once the bank accepted Morris & Dickson's offer by making a loan to MMS. First Louisiana argues that the trial court erred in finding that express acceptance of the terms of the letter was required to form a contract between Morris & Dickson and the bank. First Louisiana contends that the "To Whom it May Concern" letter to the bank became an accessory contract to the principal contract between Morris & Dickson and MMS.

First Louisiana also claims that the letter was a *stipulation pour autrui.* According to First Louisiana, the law does not provide for a particular form of acceptance or require an express acceptance of or consent to a *stipulation pour autrui.*

Closely tied with the arguments concerning whether there was a binding agreement in this matter, First Louisiana maintains that the trial court erred in finding that either the bank or MMS was required to give notice to Morris & Dickson to create an obligation on the part of the company to include the bank as a payee on checks to MMS. First Louisiana contends that Morris & Dickson knew that MMS was seeking financing for the project and Morris & Dickson had actual knowledge that MMS was dealing with First Louisiana and Bancorp South. According to First Louisiana, the letter by Morris & Dickson did not require the bank to contact the company to trigger the obligation of including First Louisiana as an additional payee on checks to MMS. These arguments are without merit.

Legal Principles

A contract is an agreement by two or more persons whereby obligations are created, modified, or extinguished. La. C.C. art. 1906. A contract is formed by the consent of the parties established through offer and acceptance. Unless the law prescribes a certain formality for the intended contract, offer and acceptance may be made orally, in writing, or by action or inaction that under the circumstances is clearly indicative of consent. Unless otherwise specified in the offer, there need not be conformity between the manner in which the offer is made and the manner in which the acceptance is made. La. C.C. art. 1927.

Unless otherwise specified by the offer or the law, an acceptance of a revocable offer, made in a manner and by a medium suggested by the offer or in a reasonable manner and by a reasonable medium, is effective when transmitted by the offeree. La. C.C. art. 1935. A medium or manner of acceptance is reasonable if it is the one used in making the offer or one customary in similar transactions at the time and place the offer is received, unless circumstances known to the offeree indicate otherwise. La. C.C. art. 1936.

When an offeror invites an offeree to accept by performance and, according to usage or the nature or the terms of the contract, it is contemplated that the performance will be completed if commenced, a contract is formed when the offeree begins the requested performance. La. C.C. art. 1939.

When commencement of the performance either constitutes acceptance or makes the offer irrevocable, the offeree must give prompt notice of that commencement unless the offeror knows or should know that the offeree has begun to perform. An offeree who fails to give the notice is liable for damages. La. C.C. art. 1941.

When, because of special circumstances, the offeree's silence leads the offeror reasonably to believe that a contract has been formed, the offer is deemed accepted. La. C.C. art. 1942.

The court must find that there was a meeting of the minds of the parties to constitute consent. The existence or nonexistence of a contract is a question of fact not to be disturbed unless clearly wrong. *Belin v. Dugdale*, 45,405 (La.App.2d Cir.6/30/10), 43 So.3d 272.

On appeal, the reviewing court may not set aside a trial court's findings in the absence of manifest error or unless they are clearly wrong. Where two permissible views of the evidence exist, the factfinder's choice between them cannot be manifestly erroneous or clearly wrong. Even though the appellate court may feel that its own evaluations and inferences are more reasonable than those made by the trial court, reasonable evaluations of credibility and reasonable inferences of fact are not disturbed on appeal where conflicting testimony exists. To reverse a trial court's factual determinations, the appellate court must find that a reasonable factual basis does not exist for the finding of the trial court and that the record establishes that the finding is clearly wrong. When findings are based on determinations regarding credibility of a witness, the manifest error-clearly wrong standard demands great deference to the trier of facts' findings. *Belin v. Dugdale, supra.*

Discussion

The trial court did not err in finding that the letter at issue here does not give rise to a binding contract between Morris & Dickson and First Louisiana. The letter was not addressed to First Louisiana or any other entity. It is a "To Whom it May Concern" letter agreeing to include First Louisiana as a payee on payments to MMS for purchase order # 031223-02. Another letter, covering this same purchase order as well as two other purchase orders, was also written concerning Bank One. A third letter was written concerning Bancorp South and purchase orders # 031223-01 and # 031223-03. If these letters, without notice of acceptance of the terms, created a contract, then Morris & Dickson would have been required to include not only First Louisiana, but also Bank One on any checks issued to MMS for purchase order # 031223-02. We find that this is not the case. The letter was an offer that required acceptance and communication of that fact to Morris & Dickson in order to form a contract.

Under La. C.C. art. 1927, unless the law prescribes a certain formality for a contract, offer and acceptance may be made orally, in writing, or by action or inaction that under the circumstances is clearly indicative of consent. While no formality was required by law for the alleged agreement at issue here, there was no communication of acceptance by First Louisiana orally, in writing, or by action or inaction which, under the circumstances was clearly indicative of consent.

La. C.C. arts. 1935 and 1936 provide that acceptance must be made in a manner and by a medium suggested by the offer or in a reasonable manner and by a reasonable medium. A medium or manner of acceptance is reasonable if it is the one used in making the offer or one customary in similar transactions at the time and place the offer is received. First Louisiana argued that the mere fact that it made a loan to MMS was sufficient to convey acceptance of the offer made by Morris & Dickson to include the bank as an additional payee on checks to MMS for purchase order # 031223-02. The offer was made in writing and First Louisiana did not provide written acceptance to Morris & Dickson. There is also no showing that simply making a loan to MMS would have constituted customary acceptance in such transactions.

First Louisiana argues that it conveyed its acceptance by performance in making the loan or by its silence. The facts of this case, measured against the Louisiana Civil Code provisions, do not support this argument. La. C.C. art. 1939 specifies that a contract is formed when an offeree begins the requested performance if the offeror invites acceptance by performance and it is contemplated that performance will be completed if commenced. However, La. C.C. art. 1941 states that when commencement of performance constitutes acceptance, the offeree must give prompt notice of the commencement unless the offeror knows or should have known that the offeree has begun performance.

In this case, the letter at issue does not show that Morris & Dickson invited acceptance by performance and First Louisiana did not give prompt notice to Morris & Dickson of the loan to MMS. Paul Dickson testified that Morris & Dickson did not know which financial institutions, if any, gave loans to MMS. Under these facts, MMS could have gotten financing from Bank One or First Louisiana, or could have secured financing from some other source unknown to Morris & Dickson. These circumstances do not show that Morris & Dickson knew or should have known that First Louisiana had begun to perform by making loans to MMS.

Further, First Louisiana's silence did not constitute acceptance of an alleged offer by Morris & Dickson. La. C.C. art. 1942 provides that an offer is deemed accepted when, because of special circumstances the offeree's silence leads the offeror reasonably to believe that a contract has been formed. In this matter, there is no showing of special circumstances that would have caused silence by First Louisiana to lead Morris & Dickson to reasonably believe that a binding agreement had been formed. As stated above, several letters were issued concerning different lenders. Only Bancorp South gave notice to Morris & Dickson that a loan had been made to MMS. Once Morris & Dickson was informed of Bancorp South's acceptance of the offer, the company included Bancorp South as an additional payee on checks concerning the purchase orders financed by that bank.

First Louisiana contends that the "To Whom it May Concern" letter was an accessory contract to the loan agreement. La. C.C. art. 1913 provides:

> A contract is accessory when it is made to provide security for the performance of an obligation. Suretyship, mortgage, pledge, and other types of security agreements are examples of such a contract.
>
> When the secured obligation arises from a contract, either between the same or other parties, that contract is the principal contract.

Had there been an enforceable agreement between First Louisiana and Morris & Dickson, it would have been an accessory contract. As discussed above, because First Louisiana failed to communicate acceptance to Morris & Dickson, there was no contract, accessory or otherwise.

The facts of this case fail to establish the existence of a *stipulation pour autrui*. La. C.C. art. 1978 provides:

> A contracting party may stipulate a benefit for a third person called a third party beneficiary.
>
> Once the third party has manifested his intention to avail himself of the benefit, the parties may not dissolve the contract by mutual consent without the beneficiary's agreement.

A *stipulation pour autrui* is never presumed. Rather, the intent of the contracting parties to stipulate a benefit in favor of a third party must be made manifestly clear. Additionally, to establish a *stipulation pour autrui,* the third party relationship must form the consideration for a condition of the contract and the benefit may not be merely incidental to the contract. The party demanding performance of an obligation pursuant to a *stipulation pour autrui* bears the burden of proving the existence of this obligation. Third parties can be the beneficiaries of the stipulation as long as they are determinable on the day on which the agreement is to have effect for their benefit. *Hudson v. Progressive Security Insurance Company,* 43,857 (La.App.2d Cir.12/10/08), 1 So.3d 627, *writ denied,* 2009-0235 (La.3/27/09), 5 So.3d 148. See also *Boyte v. Louisiana Ag Credit PCA,* 39,569 (La.App.2d Cir.4/6/05), 899 So.2d 765.

The trial court did not err in finding that notice of acceptance of the offer contained in the letter at issue here was necessary for the formation of a binding agreement between Morris & Dickson and First Louisiana. Because there was no showing that First Louisiana ever communicated acceptance of the offer, the trial court did not err in finding that no contract was formed between these parties. Further, if a *stipulation pour autrui* in favor of First Louisiana was intended by Morris & Dickson and MMS, there is no showing that First Louisiana manifested its intent to avail itself of the benefit.

Also, regarding the issue of notice, the record shows that MMS made assignments of purchase order # 031223-02 to secure the two loans made by First Louisiana. The bank made the necessary UCC registration of the assignments with the Louisiana Secretary of State's office. However, there was no showing of notice for Morris & Dickson to make payments to First Louisiana as the assignee. La. R.S. 10:9-406 provides in pertinent part:

(a) Discharge of account debtor; effect of notification. Subject to subsections (b) through (i) and R.S. 10:9-411, an account debtor on an account, chattel paper, or a payment intangible may discharge its obligation by paying the assignor until, but not after, the account debtor receives a notification, authenticated by the assignor or the assignee, that the amount due or to become due has been assigned and that payment is to be made to the assignee. **After receipt of the notification**, the account debtor may discharge its obligation by paying the assignee and may not discharge the obligation by paying the assignor. [Emphasis supplied.]

The result in this case is determined solely by the distinct facts presented here. The circumstances and timing of the Morris & Dickson letter are significant in the outcome of this matter. The letter was clearly written at a time when MMS and Mr. Eizel were attempting to obtain financing from various banks. Under these facts, First Louisiana should have communicated to Morris & Dickson its acceptance of the offer in the letter and First Louisiana's performance by loaning money to MMS. The result in this case may have been different if the letter had been written at a different time in the loan process.

DETRIMENTAL RELIANCE

Mr. Tuminello argues on appeal that the trial court erred in not applying the detrimental reliance provisions of La. C.C. art. 1967. He contends that Morris & Dickson knew that First Louisiana would not loan money to MMS without assurance from Morris & Dickson that it would make payments jointly to MMS and the bank. Mr. Tuminello claims that he would not have entered into the continuing guaranty agreement without the assurances of Morris & Dickson contained in the letter at issue here. He urges that notice is not required for detrimental reliance. He asserts that Morris & Dickson made a representation that he was justified in relying upon and that he changed his position to his detriment because of that reliance. This argument is without merit.

Legal Principles

La. C.C. art. 1967 provides:

Cause is the reason why a party obligates himself.

A party may be obligated by a promise when he knew or should have known that the promise would induce the other party to rely on it to his detriment and the other party was reasonable in so relying. Recovery may be limited to the expenses incurred or the damages suffered as a result of the promisee's reliance on the promise. Reliance on a gratuitous promise made without required formalities is not reasonable.

The doctrine of detrimental reliance is designed to prevent injustice by barring a party from taking a position contrary to his prior acts, admissions, representation, or silence. *Suire v. Lafayette City-Parish Consolidated Government*, 2004-1459 (La.4/12/05), 907 So.2d 37; *Belin v. Dugdale, supra.*

The focus of analysis of a detrimental reliance claim is not whether the parties intended to perform, but, instead, whether a representation was made in such a manner that the promisor should have expected the promisee to rely upon it, and whether the promisee so relies to his detriment. *Suire v. Lafayette City-Parish Consolidated Government, supra.*

To recover under the theory of detrimental reliance, a plaintiff must prove the following three elements by a preponderance of the evidence: (1) a representation by conduct or work; (2) justifiable reliance thereon; (3) a change in position to one's detriment because of the reliance. *Belin v. Dugdale, supra.*

It is difficult to recover under the theory of detrimental reliance because estoppel is not favored in Louisiana law. Claims of detrimental reliance must be examined strictly and carefully. *Northside Furniture of Ruston, Inc. v. First Tower Loan, Inc.*, 43,736 (La.App.2d Cir.12/3/08), 999 So.2d 151; *Belin v. Dugdale, supra.*

Discussion

We must first address the question of whether Mr. Tuminello's claim for detrimental reliance is properly before this court on appeal. In the trial court, Mr. Tuminello argued that he was damaged by the breach of an alleged contract between Morris & Dickson and First Louisiana to include the bank as an additional payee on checks to MMS. On remand, the trial court stated that the previous opinion of this court, denying the exception of prescription, held that any claims of detrimental reliance would have been prescribed. Therefore, the trial court's reasons for judgment on remand do not consider the merits of detrimental reliance.

Morris & Dickson contends that detrimental reliance is based in tort and that the prior decision of this court found that any detrimental reliance claims in this case had prescribed. To the contrary, this court's prior opinion held that any tort claims which might be involved in the case had prescribed but that the claims presented were based in contract. Delictual actions are subject to a liberative prescription of one year. La. C.C. art. 3492. An action on a contract is governed by the prescriptive period of 10 years for personal actions. La. C.C. art. 3499; *Trinity Universal Insurance Company v. Horton*, 33,157 (La.App.2d Cir.4/5/00), 756 So.2d 637. The correct prescriptive period to be applied in any action depends upon the nature of the action; it is the nature of the duty breached that should determine whether an action is in tort or in contract. *Trinity Universal Insurance Company v. Horton, supra.* The classical distinction between "damages ex contractu" and "damages ex delicto" is that the former flow from the breach of a special obligation contractually assumed by the obligor, whereas the latter flow from the violation of a general

354 duty to all persons. *Harrison v. Gore,* 27,254 (La.App.2d Cir.8/23/95), 660 So.2d 563, *writ*
355 *denied,* 95-2347 (La.12/8/95), 664 So.2d 426.

356   In the Louisiana Civil Code revision of 1984, La. C.C. art. 1967, which concerns cause
357 and detrimental reliance, was enacted. This article is contained in that portion of the
358 Louisiana Civil Code dealing with contracts. In Saul Litvinoff, *Still Another Look at Cause,*
359 48 La. L.Rev. 3 (1987), construing La. C.C. art. 1967, the author states that "the new ar-
360 ticle of the Louisiana Civil Code subtracts induced reliance from the quasi-delictual field
361 and places it where it belongs, in contract."

362   We also note that the jurisprudence holds that claims for detrimental reliance arising
363 out of contracts are not subject to the one-year prescriptive period for torts. See *Babkow v.*
364 *Morris Bart, P.L.C.,* 1998-0256 (La.App. 4th Cir.12/16/98), 726 So.2d 423. Therefore, Mr.
365 Tuminello's detrimental reliance claim, based upon an alleged contract, has not prescribed.

366   However, we find that Mr. Tuminello failed to carry his burden of proving a claim for
367 detrimental reliance in this matter. In the present case, Mr. Tuminello argues that he
368 would not have signed as a guarantor on the loan from First Louisiana to MMS without
369 the assurance that Morris & Dickson would include the bank as a payee on all checks is-
370 sued to MMS for payment of the purchase order at issue here. Under the facts presented,
371 we do not find that Mr. Tuminello was justified in his reliance on the "To Whom it May
372 Concern" letter. No promises were made to Mr. Tuminello and no representation was
373 made by Morris & Dickson in such a manner that the company should have expected
374 Mr. Tuminello to rely upon it. The facts simply do not support the argument that the
375 letter at issue here induced Mr. Tuminello to sign as a guarantor. Therefore, no claim for
376 detrimental reliance has been proved in this case.

377   CONCLUSION

378   For the reasons stated above, we affirm the decision of the trial court rejecting the
379 claims of First Louisiana Bank and Ronald Tuminello against the defendant, Morris &
380 Dickson Company, LLC. [....]

Questions

1. Lines 16–24: How would you describe the legal nature of a purchase order: a con-
    tract? A preliminary contract? An offer—an acceptance to purchase? Read the Code
    articles on offer and acceptance in Consent as you will need them later on in the legal
    analysis of this case. On lines 35–40: Mr. Eizel signed the loans as guarantor. How
    is Mr. Eizel bound, if at all, with MMS? On lines 41–71: As guarantor on the loans
    from First Louisiana, how is Tuminello bound? Is he bound with anyone else? On what
    ground(s) can First Louisiana seek to enforce the provisions of "To Whom ..."? What
    about Tuminello? What does detrimental reliance have to do here? Can you find it
    in the Louisiana Civil Code?

2. Lines 69 *et seq.*: Instead of looking at detrimental reliance as being a tort, couldn't detri-
    mental reliance be considered and identified as the cause of a pre-contract (like a
    contract to sell, *see* La. Civ. Code arts. 2623 *et seq.*, which precedes the sale) entered
    into by the parties before they actually enter into the contract itself, such as a loan?
    Since a pre-contract is a contract, breach of that contract would be ground for pay-
    ment of contractual damages (*see* lines 187 *et seq.*).

3. Lines 78–125: Can you find an implicit stipulation pour autrui, stipulation for the
    benefit of a third party, in the facts or circumstances of this case?

4.   Lines 127–145: How can an acceptance by M & D making a loan to MMS be tantamount to forming a contract between M & D and First Louisiana? To what kind of accessory contract to the principal contract is First Louisiana referring? What are the different possible forms of acceptance? According to First Louisiana, what was its form of acceptance forming the accessory contract? Read lines 134–136 and the Louisiana Civil Code articles on Third Party Beneficiary (La. Civ. Code arts. 1978–1982) and evaluate this statement by First Louisiana: "… the law does not provide for a particular form of acceptance or require an express acceptance of or consent to a *stipulation pour autrui*." Compare your answer with the Court's statement on lines 259–269. What do you think? Focus on lines 143–145. Do you agree with the Court that "these arguments are without merit"? Go back now to questions 1 and 2. Do you have any different view?

5.   Lines 243–296: After you have read Louisiana Civil Code article 1978 included here, can you explain where the Court finds this requirement that a *stipulation pour autrui* is never presumed? Return to the leading case of *Andrepont v. Acadiana Drilling* above. What was the *Andrepont* Court's understanding of the requirements for the existence of a *stipulation pour autrui*? Didn't First Louisiana manifest some form of intent to be included, in some way, in the contract between M & D and MMS? Didn't M & D know that MMS would have to borrow money and thus obtain a loan? Is First Louisiana a total stranger to the contract between M & D and MMS?

6.   Lines 333–355: Is the Court suggesting that detrimental reliance can be relied on only in matters of contracts? The Court makes an important point here: at civil law there are two kinds of damages, damages ex contractu (literally "out of a contract") or ex delicto (out of a delict/tort).

Chapter Three

Effects of Obligations

Louisiana Sources of Law

Louisiana Civil Code

Art. 1983. Law for the parties; performance in good faith.

Contracts have the effect of law for the parties and may be dissolved only through the consent of the parties or on grounds provided by law. Contracts must be performed in good faith. (Acts 1984, No. 331, § 1, eff. Jan. 1, 1985.)

Art. 1984. Rights and obligations will pass to successors.

Rights and obligations arising from a contract are heritable and assignable unless the law, the terms of the contract or its nature preclude such effects. (Acts 1984, No. 331, § 1, eff. Jan. 1, 1985.)

Art. 1985. Effects for third parties.

Contracts may produce effects for third parties only when provided by law. (Acts 1984, No. 331, § 1, eff. Jan. 1, 1985.)

Art. 2025. Definition; simulation and counterletter.

A contract is a simulation when, by mutual agreement, it does not express the true intent of the parties.

If the true intent of the parties is expressed in a separate writing, that writing is a counterletter. (Acts 1984, No. 331, § 1, effective January 1, 1985.)

Art. 2026. Absolute simulation.

A simulation is absolute when the parties intend that their contract shall produce no effects between them. That simulation, therefore, can have no effects between the parties. (Acts 1984, No. 331, § 1, eff. Jan. 1, 1985.)

Art. 2027. Relative simulation.

A simulation is relative when the parties intend that their contract shall produce effects between them though different from those recited in their contract. A relative simulation produces between the parties the effects they intended if all requirements for those effects have been met. (Acts 1984, No. 331, § 1, effective January 1, 1985.)

Art. 2028. Effects as to third persons. [*Amended*]

A. Any simulation, either absolute or relative, may have effects as to third persons.

B. Counterletters can have no effects against third persons in good faith. Nevertheless, if the counterletter involves immovable property, the principles of recordation apply with respect to third persons. (Acts 1984, No. 331, § 1, eff. Jan. 1, 1985; Acts 2012, No. 277, § 1.)

Précis: Louisiana Law of Conventional Obligations—
§§ 8.1.1 to 8.1.2

[A]ll contracts, regardless of their specific nature (unilateral or bilateral, onerous or gratuitous, for example), are subject to the control of two fundamental principles which are laid down in **LSA-C.C. Art. 1983**: "**Contracts have the effect of law for the parties and may be dissolved only through the consent of the parties or on grounds provided by law. Contracts must be performed in good faith.**" These two principles are, first, the 'effect of law' of any contract and, second, the 'performance in good faith' of the obligations created by the contract.

The second set of effects triggered by a contract will depend on the kind or kinds of obligations which bind the parties. These obligations may bind one or both parties to "**render a performance ... [which] ... may consist of giving, doing, or not doing something.**" **Art. 1756.** This second set of effects of a contract will be determined, therefore, by the 'giving' something, the 'doing' something or the 'not doing' something....

First, only the parties themselves are bound by their contract; their contract is their "law". A contract, being the *expression of the wills* of two parties, is as binding between them as "legislation", which is itself the "*expression of the legislative will*," is binding on and between the citizens....

Second, ... it is easy to understand why **Art. 1985** states that "**Contracts may produce effects for third parties only when provided by law.**" In other words, a contract between parties A and B cannot have effects "*against*" a third person C who is not a "party" to that contract....

Third parties, heirs in particular, can be brought into the contract between A and B and incur obligations if they agree and if the obligations are transferable ...

Third, a corollary of the principle that a contract is the law of the parties is stated in **Art. 1983** in these words: "**Contracts ... may be dissolved only through the consent of the parties ... or on grounds provided by law.**" ...

[I]f one party fails to perform her obligations in violation of either the trust placed in her by the other party or the duty of good faith in the performance of obligations, then the "aggrieved" party "**has a right to the judicial dissolution of the contract or, according to the circumstances, to regard the contract as dissolved ...**"**Art. 2013 (1).**...

Parties to a contract can, for lawful reasons, hide their true intent in a hidden contract, called **counterletter** because the letter and the intent of that hidden contract go against or counter to the intent of the open contract which is called a *simulated contract*. **LSA-C.C. Art. 2025** states that "**A contract is a simulation when, by mutual agreement, it does not express the true intent of the parties. If the true intent of the parties is expressed in a separate writing, that writing is a counterletter.**"

The existence of such an Article in the civil Code emphasizes the freedom to enter into any lawful contract and the role given to the intent or will of parties to a contract. They are free, within the boundaries of the law, to contract as they wish....

"**A simulation is absolute when the parties intend that their contract shall produce no effects between them. That simulation, therefore, can have no effects between the parties.**" **Art. 2026.**...

"**A simulation is relative when the parties intend that their contract shall produce effects between them though different from those recited in their contract. A relative sim-**

ulation produces between the parties the effects they intended if all requirements for those effects have not been met." Art. 2027....

Art. 1983 states, in part, that "contracts must be performed in good faith." This Article is to the Effects of Contracts or Conventional Obligations what Art. 1759 is to the whole subject matter of Obligations....

It is the embodiment of the general duty of honest and fair behavior....

Comparative Law Perspective

Alain Levasseur, COMPARATIVE LAW OF CONTRACTS
99–111 (2008)

Contracts: Good Faith, Estoppel ...

We find in the Institutes that "the precepts of the law are, to live honestly, to hurt no one, to give every one his due". [The Institutes of Justinian, Title I, D.1. T.1 § 1 and § 3]....

Such, among others are these principles: that we should live honestly, should hurt nobody, and should render to every one his due; to which three general principles Justinian has reduced the whole doctrine of law" [W. Blackstone, Commentaries on the Laws of England in Four Books, Introduction]....

[T]he common law and the civil law have, in the field of contract (in civil law) or contracts (in common law), somewhat different approaches to those precepts of the law as Justinian and, centuries later, Blackstone expressed them. At civil law, the concept of "good faith" has played, for centuries, and still play, today, a major role in the *theory* of the law of contract. Most civil law systems, because of their inherent ability at elaborating theories, are referring to this single and comprehensive concept of "good faith" to cover, but not to its full civil law extent, a variety of concepts used by the common law in different contexts. Despite their variety, such concepts have nevertheless a common foundation which is to bring some 'fairness', 'equity', 'balance' to contractual transactions....

"Good Faith" in the Civil Law

See: La.Civ.C.: Articles: 1759, 1770, 1975, 1983, 2028, 2035

Fr. Civ.C.

Article 1134: Conventions legally entered into have the effect of law for the parties.

They may be revoked only by their mutual consent or on grounds provided by legislation.

They must be performed in good faith.

Article 1135: Conventions are binding not only as to what they expressly state, but also as to all that equity, usage or statute relate to an obligation according to its nature.

C. C. Q.

Article 1375: The parties shall conduct themselves in good faith both at the time the obligation is created and at the time it is performed or extinguished.

Article 1397: A contract made in violation of a promise to contract may be set up against the beneficiary of the promise, but without affecting his remedy for damages against the promisor and the person having contracted in bad faith with the promisor.

The same rule applies to a contract made in violation of a first refusal agreement.

Article 1426: In interpreting a contract, the nature of the contract, the circumstances in which it was formed, the interpretation which has already been given to it by the parties or which it may have received, and usage, are all taken into account.

Article 1434: A contract validly formed binds the parties who have entered into it not only as to what they have expressed in it but also as to what is incident to it according to its nature and in conformity with usage, equity or law.

Article 1452: Third persons in good faith may, according to their interest, avail themselves of the apparent contract or the counter letter; however, where conflicts of interest arise between them, preference is given to the person who avails himself of the apparent contract.

Planiol et Ripert Vol. VI Obligations LGDJ, 1952

§ 379 quater. Good faith. Conventions must be performed in good faith, states Article 1134. Inherited from Roman law wherein, besides the other meanings it still has today, good faith had a precise meaning only in the actions in good faith as opposed to actions based on law in the narrow sense of the word, today the concept of good faith in Article 1134 has only a more ambiguous scope of application. It means that any contracting party must act as an honest person in whatever relates to the performance of the contract. Not to act as an honest person amounts to being at fault.... In any case, it is useful to resort to an expression to refer to a breach of the duty of honesty which arises from the fact that one has bound himself by a contract.

Malaurie, Aynès et Stoffel-Munck, Les Obligations, Defrénois 2003.

764. An expanding principle ... Good faith, in the execution as well as in the formation of a contract, amounts to each party not betraying the confidence created by the willingness to enter into a contract; such an expectation is at the heart of the contract particularly when the contractual relationship is to last over a period of time. It is the embodiment of the general duty of honest and fair behavior, which does exist in many other branches of the law: criminal and civil procedure, ... competition ...; the opposite of fairness and honesty is duplicity ... which undermines the long term expectations ... Good faith is the mere extension of the binding force of a contract, rather than a limitation imposed on the creditor; the latter is not required to waive his right or interest in the name of some vague juridical solidarity but, instead, to give the contract its full force to an extent compatible with his own personal interest ...

"Good faith" in the Common Law: consideration, estoppel, reliance, good faith ...
Butterworths

1.87 [...], the case against the adoption of a general principle of good faith is that English contract law is premised on adversarial self-interested dealing (rather than other—regarding good faith dealing); that good faith is a vague idea, threatening to import an uncertain discretion into English law; that the implementation of a good faith doctrine would call for difficult inquiries into contracting parties' reasons in particular cases; that good faith represents a challenge to the autonomy of contracting parties; and, that a general doctrine cannot be appropriate when contracting contexts vary so much—in particular, harking back to the first objection, a general doctrine of good faith would make little sense in those contracting contexts in which the participants regulate their dealings in a way that openly tolerates opportunism.

1.89 The paradigm of neutrality holds: (i) that there is a strict equivalence between a general doctrine of good faith and the piecemeal provisions of English law that regulate fair dealing (we can call this 'the equivalence thesis'); and (ii) that it makes no difference whether English law operates with a general doctrine or with piecemeal provisions (we can call this 'the indifference thesis').

Restatement, 2d

§ 205. Duty of Good Faith and Fair Dealing

Every contract imposes upon each party a duty of good faith and fair dealing in its performance and its enforcement.

Comment: *a. Meaning of "good faith"*.... The phrase "good faith" is used in a variety of contexts, and its meaning varies somewhat with the context. Good faith performance or enforcement of a contract emphasizes faithfulness to an agreed common purpose and consistency with the justified expectations of the other party; it excludes a variety of types of conduct characterized as involving "bad faith" because they violate community standards of decency, fairness or reasonableness ...

c. Good faith in negotiation

Particular forms of bad faith in bargaining are the subjects of rules as to capacity to contract, mutual assent and consideration and of rules as to invalidating causes such as fraud and duress.

UCC

§ 1-201. General Definitions.

(20) "Good faith", except as otherwise provided in Article 5, means honesty in fact and the observance of reasonable commercial standards of fair dealing.

§ 1-304. Obligation of Good Faith.

Every contract or duty within [the Uniform Commercial Code] imposes an obligation of good faith in its performance and enforcement.

POSNER, Circuit Judge, 7th Circuit, United States Court of Appeals.

... The duty of honesty, of good faith even expansively conceived, is not a duty of candor ... Before the contract is signed, the parties confront each other with a natural wariness. Neither expects the other to be particularly forthcoming, and therefore there is no deception when one is not. Afterwards the situation is different. The parties are now in a cooperative relationship the costs of which will be considerably reduced by a measure of trust. So each lowers his guard a bit, and now silence is more apt to be deceptive ... The concept of duty of good faith like the concept of fiduciary duty is a stab at approximating the terms the parties would have negotiated had they foreseen the circumstances that have given rise to their dispute. The parties want to minimize the costs of performance.... The office of the doctrine of good faith is to forbid the kinds of opportunistic behavior that a mutually dependent, cooperative relationship might enable in the absence of rule. "Good faith" is a compact reference to an implied undertaking not to take opportunistic advantage in a way that could have been contemplated at the time of drafting, and which therefore was not resolved explicitly by the parties".... The formation or negotiation state is precontractual, and here the duty is minimized. It is greater not only at the performance but also at the enforcement stage, which is also postcontractual ... At the formation of the contract the parties are dealing in present realities; performance still lies in the future.... [W]hether we say that a contract shall be deemed to contain such implied conditions as are necessary to make sense of the contract, or that a contract obligates the parties to cooperate in its performance in "good faith" to the extent necessary to carry out the purposes of the contract, comes to much the same thing. They are different ways of formulating the overriding purpose of contract law, which is to give the parties what they would have stipulated for expressly if at the time of making the contract they had had complete knowledge of the future and the costs of negotiating and adding provisions to the contract had been zero.... [Market Street Associates Limited Partnership v. Dale Frey, et al., 941 F.2d 588, 1991]

Section I — Obligation to Give — Putting in Default

Louisiana Sources of Law

Louisiana Civil Code

Art. 1854. Extinction by performance.

Performance by the obligor extinguishes the obligation. (Acts 1984, No. 331, § 1, eff. Jan. 1, 1985.)

Art. 1855. Performance by a third person.

Performance may be rendered by a third person, even against the will of the obligee, unless the obligor or the obligee has an interest in performance only by the obligor. Performance rendered by a third person effects subrogation only when so provided by law or by agreement. (Acts 1984, No. 331, § 1, eff. Jan. 1, 1985.)

Art. 1860. Quality of thing to be given.

When the performance consists of giving a thing that is determined as to its kind only, the obligor need not give one of the best quality but he may not tender one of the worst. (Acts 1984, No. 331, § 1, eff. Jan. 1, 1985.)

Art. 1861. Partial performance.

An obligee may refuse to accept a partial performance.

Nevertheless, if the amount of an obligation to pay money is disputed in part and the obligor is willing to pay the undisputed part, the obligee may not refuse to accept that part. If the obligee is willing to accept the undisputed part, the obligor must pay it. In either case, the obligee preserves his right to claim the disputed part. (Acts 1984, No. 331, § 1, eff. Jan. 1, 1985.)

Art. 1862. Place of performance.

Performance shall be rendered in the place either stipulated in the agreement or intended by the parties according to usage, the nature of the performance, or other circumstances.

In the absence of agreement or other indication of the parties' intent, performance of an obligation to give an individually determined thing shall be rendered at the place the thing was when the obligation arose. If the obligation is of any other kind, the performance shall be rendered at the domicile of the obligor. (Acts 1984, No. 331, § 1, eff. Jan. 1, 1985.)

Art. 1863. Expenses.

Expenses that may be required to render performance shall be borne by the obligor. (Acts 1984, No. 331, § 1, eff. Jan. 1, 1985.)

Art. 1989. Damages for delay.

Damages for delay in the performance of an obligation are owed from the time the obligor is put in default.

Other damages are owed from the time the obligor has failed to perform. (Acts 1984, No. 331, §1, eff. Jan. 1, 1985.)

Art. 1990. Obligor put in default by arrival of term.

When a term for the performance of an obligation is either fixed, or is clearly determinable by the circumstances, the obligor is put in default by the mere arrival of that term. In other cases, the obligor must be put in default by the obligee, but not before performance is due. (Acts 1984, No. 331 §1, eff. Jan. 1, 1985.)

Art. 1991. Manners of putting in default.

An obligee may put the obligor in default by a written request of performance, or by an oral request of performance made before two witnesses, or by filing suit for performance, or by a specific provision of the contract. (Acts 1984, No. 331, §1, eff. Jan. 1, 1985.)

Art. 1993. Reciprocal obligations.

In case of reciprocal obligations, the obligor of one may not be put in default unless the obligor of the other has performed or is ready to perform his own obligation. (Acts 1984, No. 331, §1, eff. Jan. 1, 1985.)

Précis: Louisiana Law of Conventional Obligations — §8.2.2

An obligor is not bound merely to carry out his performance of the principal object of his obligation. That principal performance must also be carried out on time....

There exists, therefore, in every obligation an element of "time", actually an obligation to perform "on time"....

This obligation to perform on time by one party, obligor, gives the other party, obligee, the right to **"put the obligor in default" (Art. 1991)** so that **"damages for delay in the performance** [will be] **owed"** by the obligor to the obligee **"from the time the obligor is put in default"** Art. 1989....

[T]he purpose of putting an obligor in default is to inform him that the obligee cannot wait any longer for the obligor to perform his obligation....

The fault of the obligor is in not performing on time and, as a consequence, in causing a damage to the obligee. The damage caused to the obligee will entitle him to receive *"moratory damages"*, that is to say **"damages for delay in perform[ing] ..."** Art. 1989....

The requirement of putting an obligor in default is justified as long as the obligor could still perform and the performance would still be of benefit to the obligee....

[W]henever a term is fixed or clearly determinable, the mere arrival of the term will automatically put the obligor in default: **"When a term for the performance of an obligation is either fixed or clearly determinable by the circumstances, the obligor is put in default by the mere arrival of that term. In other cases, the obligor must be put in default by the obligee, but not before performance is due."** Art. 1990....

Where there is no term, fixed or determinable, attached to the timing of performance of his obligation by an obligor, the obligee, if he has the right to demand performance from his obligor, will have to " ... **put the obligor in default by written** request of performance, or by an oral request of performance made before two witnesses, or by filing suit for performance, or by a specific provision of the contract." Art. 1991....

According to Art. 1993, "In case of reciprocal obligations, the obligor of one may not be put in default unless the obligor of the other has performed or is ready to perform his own obligation." ...

Précis: Louisiana Law of Obligations in General § 7.1.1

Performance of an obligation is the normal mode of extinction of an obligation by an obligor. As **LSA-C.C. Art. 1854** states: **"Performance by the obligor extinguishes the obligation."** Performance is, thus, the fulfillment of the juridical act or fact undertaken by the obligor with the intent to discharge his obligation *vis-à-vis* the obligee as is called for by the nature of their legal relationship....

Therefore, performance can, or should, always be rendered by the obligor *[solvens]* although, in proper circumstances, that same performance can be rendered by a representative of the obligor, or a person concerned, such as a surety or a co-obligor, or, even, a third person, a gestor, for example....

A voluntary performance of his obligation by the obligor being a juridical act meant to extinguish that obligation, it is necessary that the obligor be capable of performing....

In the words of **LSA-C.C. Art. 1857:**

"Performance must be rendered to the obligee or to a person authorized by him." ...

Therefore, a performance may be validly rendered to the obligee himself or to a third person empowered to receive the performance in the place and in the name of the obligee....

The object of the obligor's performance must be the very same object of the obligation entered into. There must be identity between the object of the obligation and the object or item of the performance carried out to extinguish the obligation whether that object or item be a service to be performed or a thing to be delivered....

A fundamental principle which governs an obligor's performance is the principle of indivisibility of that performance. In a few specific instances this principle will suffer some exceptions....

The indivisibility of an obligor's performance simply means that the obligor owes the entirety of the thing or item in one single performance. Unless the parties to a juridical act have provided otherwise, or unless the law states differently, an obligee-creditor cannot be compelled to receive a partial performance from his obligor....

The indivisibility of the performance is controlling whether the object of that performance is indivisible by nature or susceptible of division....

Cases

Roger LEON, Sr.

v.

Aubin DUPRE and Mrs. Aubin Dupre

Louisiana Court of Appeal
Fourth Circuit
Sept. 4, 1962
144 So.2d 667

McBRIDE, Judge.

On November 1, 1956, plaintiff placed a music box in the Three Leaf Bar operated by defendants in St. Bernard Parish under a written agreement reading thus:

> 'I, Mr. Aubin Dupre and Mrs. Dupre, give Roger Leon permission to place his music box in my place of business 'The Three Leaf Bar'. If at any time I should have him remove it, I agree to pay him $190.00.'

We gather that the music box is the usual coin-operated device placed in some types of business establishments for the amusement and entertainment of the patrons thereof. On what basis it was installed in defendants' bar we do not know.

On November 10, 1956, Mrs. Dupre in writing ordered plaintiff to remove the box, which he did, whereupon he sued the defendants for the sum of $190 mentioned in the agreement. [....]

After a trial on the merits, the judge rendered judgment in plaintiff's favor for $50. [....]

Defendants agreed to pay plaintiff $190 in the event they should have plaintiff remove the music box. They had the box in their establishment but ten days, and it seems harsh that they should pay plaintiff $190. Perhaps that is why the trial judge rendered judgment in favor of plaintiff for only $50. The contract, so far as the record shows, was not entered into for any immoral purposes nor was it contrary to law, and defendants must be held to their agreement.

LSA-C.C. art. 1901 recites:

> 'Agreements legally entered into have the effect of laws on those who have formed them.

> 'They can not be revoked, unless by mutual consent of the parties, or for causes acknowledged by law.

> 'They must be performed with good faith.'

The parties may make their own contracts, and however unusual they may be or what drastic or unreasonable features there may be therein, they form the law between them and should be enforced so long as they do not contravene good morals or public policy. Salles v. Stafford, Derbes & Roy, Inc., 173 La. 361, 137 So. 62; Blakesley v. Ransonet, 159 La. 310, 105 So. 354; Stewart, Hyde & Co. v. Buard & Dranguet, 23 La.Ann. 201; Arkansas Fuel Oil Corporation v. Maggio, La.App., 141 So.2d 516; Oil Field Supply & Scrap Material Co. v. Gifford-Hill & Co., Inc., La.App., 16 So.2d 77 (annulled on other grounds—

204 La. 929, 16 So.2d 483); Yates v. Batteford, 19 La.App. 374, 139 So. 37, rehearing de- 41
nied and amended 19 La.App. 374, 139 So. 746. 42

For the reasons assigned, the judgment appealed from is affirmed. 43

Affirmed. 44

Questions

1. Lines 11–16: what types/kinds of obligations are created in this written agreement? Can you give a name to this contract? Are you surprised by the Court's statement on line 16? Yet, are the requirements for a contract met? Are the objects and the causes/motives lawful? What kind of cause are you referring to? If this is a contract, does it have a name?

2. Lines 22–27: What purpose or cause is the Court considering as "not immoral"?

3. Lines 28–44: What does the Court mean by "they form the law between them and should be enforced...." (*see* lines 34–36)? Does the "performance in good faith" by a party (for example, Louisiana Civil Code article 1901, now Louisiana Civil Code article 1983) add anything to the statement that an agreement/a contract has the effect of law for the parties? Have you encountered this requirement of good faith somewhere else in the Louisiana Civil Code? What is the bottom line of this unusually short case?

AMERICAN CREOSOTE WORKS   1
v.   2
BOLAND MACHINE & MFG. CO.   3
Supreme Court of Louisiana   4
April 26, 1948   5
35 So.2d 749   6

FOURNET, Justice.   7

The plaintiff instituted this suit to recover the sum of $1,924.81, the price of certain cre- 8
osoted fir pilings allegedly sold and delivered to the defendant, and the matter is now be- 9
fore us for a review of the judgment of the Court of Appeal for the Parish of Orleans affirming 10
the judgment of the district court in favor of the plaintiff, as prayed for. (28 So.2d 342.) 11

On August 4, 1943, the plaintiff, the American Creosote Works, entered into a contract 13
with the defendant, Boland Machine & Manufacturing Company, a copartnership. This 14
contract is incorporated in one of the plaintiff's order forms. According to its terms the 15
plaintiff agreed to supply the defendant with 24 creosoted fir pilings treated by what is known 16
as the Full Cell Bethel Process and conforming to Navy specifications No. 39P14a (mean- 17
ing 13 inches in diameter 3 feet from the butt or bottom end of the tree) in four lots of 18
six units each, i. e., six 75' long, six 80' long, six 85' long, and six 90' long, at a price of 19
95¢ per lineal foot, f. o. b. the plaintiff's plant at Southport in New Orleans, at which 20
place they were to be loaded on the defendant's truck, subject to inspection and accep- 21
tance by the defendant. Subsequently, according to a letter of August 17 confirming a 22
telephone conversation had with the defendant, the contract was amended to provide for 23
the loading of these pilings on the defendant's barge at the plaintiff's Southport plant 24
wharf on Saturday, August 21, 1943. An extra charge of $25 was to be included in the 25
purchase price under this new agreement for the barge loading. 26

27 Since the plaintiff did not have these fir pilings in stock, they had to be specially or-
28 dered for treatment according to the detailed specifications and after they were processed
29 the plaintiff, on August 20, under the provision in the contract calling for one day ad-
30 vance notice, notified the defendant by telephone to have a barge at its wharf so that
31 loading might begin at seven the next morning, for delivery around noon. Accordingly,
32 the defendant, on Friday afternoon, ordered a barge from the Bisso Coal and Towboat
33 Company and it was tied up at the wharf ready for loading at the specified time. The
34 actual loading was completed about eleven. The defendant, upon advice from the plain-
35 tiff, likewise asked the Bisso people to have a tug pick the barge up about noon, but be-
36 fore that time a fire started on the wharf of the plaintiff company and spread to the
37 barge. When the tug did approach the wharf as instructed, the barge had been cut away
38 from the wharf in an effort to save it and was drifting down the river enveloped in
    flames.

39 The defendant denied liability, contending that under the contract title did not pass
40 to them until the property was loaded on the barge and tendered to them or their agent
41 for inspection and acceptance.

42 The plaintiff, relying on Articles 1909, 2456, 2458, 2467, and 2468 of the Revised Civil
43 Code, contends that title to these pilings passed to the defendant the moment they were
44 treated and removed from the processing shed; in any event, that title passed when the
45 pilings were measured, counted, and loaded on the barge.

46 In passing on these issues, the Court of Appeal found that neither these codal arti-
47 cles nor the cases relied on by the defendant were applicable under the facts of this
48 case, but concluded that title to the pilings had passed to the defendant prior to the
49 fire inasmuch as they were, at that time, loaded on the barge furnished by the defen-
50 dant in accordance with the court's construction of the contract, the fact that the de-
51 fendant was not to take possession of them nutil [*sic*] a later time, i. e., around noon,
    being immaterial.

52 We think the court's conclusion with respect to the inapplicability of the codal articles
53 is correct. A mere reference to these articles will show their general tenor to be that the
54 sale of an object is perfect and complete and the article is at the risk of the buyer as soon
55 as there exists an agreement as to the object and price, although actual delivery has not
56 been made and the price has not been paid, and that once the sale is perfected and com-
57 pleted, the only responsibility then resting on the seller is that of guarding the goods as
58 a faithful administrator. But this rule applies only '*if the contract is one of those that pur-
59 port a transfer.*' Article 1909. The contract in this case does not purport to be a transfer
60 of the pilings to the defendant. On the contrary, its terms show very plainly that the pil-
61 ings are to be transferred to the defendant only after they have been tendered for inspec-
62 tion and have actually been accepted. (Italics ours.)

63 Under this contract the plaintiff agreed to furnish the defendant with goods that had
64 to meet certain specifications, that is, the pilings had to be of definite lengths and size
65 and they had to be treated with creosote under a special process. While on the reverse
66 side of this contract there is to be found, along with other printed provisions, the gen-
67 eral stipulation that the 'Buyer agrees to receive material when and as delivered on cars
68 at Seller's plant. It is specifically agreed that there shall be no claims of any kind after ma-
69 terial is delivered as above,' this general stipulation is not controlling in this case for it has
70 been abrogated by the very positive provision on the face of the contract, where all of the
71 detailed specifications and conditions are clearly set out, that the pilings were to be sub-
72 ject to final inspection and acceptance by the defendant at the plaintiff's plant.

The intention of the parties as to when the pilings would be transferred to the defen- 73
dant is not only thus clearly shown on the face of the contract itself, but is further demon- 74
strated by the oral and documentary evidence in the record unmistakably showing the 75
property belonged to the plaintiff until delivery was completed and that delivery could 76
not be completed until the defendant, who was given the right to inspect and check it, 77
had actually inspected it and accepted it, such acceptance being evidenced by the defen- 78
dant's signature on the delivery slip prepared for that purpose which constituted the de- 79
fendant's acknowledgment that the goods had been received in good condition and 80
accepted.

We think our conclusion that the plaintiff did not consider ownership of the prop- 81
erty passed to the defendant until after delivery had been completed is evidenced by its 82
own construction of the contract as expressed in its letter to the defendant on August 83
27, 1943, a few days after the fire, wherein it is said: 'Under the terms of our insurance 84
policies *our liability ends with completed delivery*, and both the insurance adjustors and 85
our attorneys have advised me that our policies will not cover this damage. *After de-* 86
livery is completed, it is customary for the then owner of the pilings to have them in- 87
sured * * *.' And the plaintiff's understanding of the time when the delivery could be 88
considered as completed is emphasized by the testimony of Mr. Theester A. Hamby, 89
the plaintiff's secretary-comptroller, to the effect that it was not necessary for the de- 90
fendant to have the pilings insured until 'the time he (defendant) takes possession of 91
them, or when they come under this control—when they leave our control.' (Italics 92
and brackets ours.)

And there can be no question but that the defendant had the right to check and in- 93
spect the pilings before accepting them, as stipulated in the contract and also in ac- 94
cordance with the custom of the plant. According to the testimony of the plaintiff's 95
employees, the pilings ordered were stored in a pile on the yard after they had been 96
creosoted, pending delivery. After the barge ordered by the defendant was tied up to the 97
wharf the office furnished the yard checker with a card containing pertinent informa- 98
tion relative to the specifications of the order being supplied the defendant. The checker 99
measured and counted the pilings against this card to see that they met specifications 100
before they were loaded on flat cars that took them from the yard, across the levee, and 101
down to the wharf where they were turned over to another checker. This checker was 102
also furnished with a card containing the specifications covering the order and he 103
rechecked the pilings as they were loaded on the barge. After the last piling was loaded, 104
this checker went back to the office and there filled out a slip listing the material that 105
had been loaded under his supervision. This slip was left with the office force to be 106
presented to the defendant customer or representative for signature at the time they 107
were taken possession of, signifying the defendant's acceptance and receipt of the goods 108
in good condition.

We therefore conclude that delivery was never completed under the terms of this con- 109
tract and under the facts of this case and that title had not passed to the defendant at the 110
time the pilings were destroyed by fire; consequently, their loss was at the risk of the plain- 111
tiff and not that of the defendant. 112

For the reasons assigned, the judgment of the district court in favor of the American 113
Creosote Works, as prayed for, and that of the Court of Appeal for the Parish of Orleans 114
affirming the same, are reversed, and it is now ordered, adjudged, and decreed that the 115
plaintiff's suit be dismissed at its cost. 116

McCALEB, J., recused. 117

Questions

1. Lines 8–26: What adjectives would you use to describe the parties involved here? Should the types of parties involved here have an impact on one or some of the requirements for the formation of a contract between them? What requirements must be met for the object of the plaintiff's obligation to become "the" object of the contract? Can you identify the cause of this contract? Are there any modalities in this contract (i.e. condition, term …)? What legal identification(s) can you give to the contractual requirement "subject to inspection and acceptance"? Are "inspection" "acceptance" conditions or are they essential elements of the formation of the contract?

2. Lines 27–38: What kinds of obligations were those of the plaintiff/seller? Are delivery by the seller (*see* Louisiana Civil Code articles 2475, 2477, 2484, and 2489) and taking delivery (*see* Louisiana Civil Code article 2549) by the buyer the same thing? Are delivery and possession the same thing?

3. Lines 42–62: Read the new Louisiana Civil Code articles 2456, 2457, 2458, and 2467. On what ground does the Court rely to hold that ownership of the pilings had not passed? What do you think of this language used by the Court: "[T]his rule applies only 'if the contract is one of those that purport a transfer'" (*see* lines 58–59)? Didn't the contract here intend to transfer the pilings from one party to the other?

4. Lines 63–116: Comment, first, on the Court's analysis of the existence of a suspensive condition and its effects and, second, on the connection between the suspensive condition and the delivery of the pilings.

Section II — Obligations to Do or Not to Do; Specific Performance

Louisiana Sources of Law

Louisiana Civil Code

Art. 1986. Right of the obligee.

Upon an obligor's failure to perform an obligation to deliver a thing, or not to do an act, or to execute an instrument, the court shall grant specific performance plus damages for delay if the obligee so demands. If specific performance is impracticable, the court may allow damages to the obligee.

Upon a failure to perform an obligation that has another object, such as an obligation to do, the granting of specific performance is at the discretion of the court. (Acts 1984, No. 331, § 1, eff. Jan. 1, 1985.)

Art. 1987. Right to restrain obligor.

The obligor may be restrained from doing anything in violation of an obligation not to do. (Acts 1984, No. 331, § 1, eff. Jan. 1, 1985.)

Art. 1988. Judgment may stand for act.

A failure to perform an obligation to execute an instrument gives the obligee the right to a judgment that shall stand for the act. (Acts 1984, No. 331, § 1, eff. Jan. 1, 1985.)

Précis: Louisiana Law of Conventional Obligations — § 8.2.1

With respect to obligations to give and obligations to do, Article 1986 of the civil Code is clear in the distinction therein made between these two kinds of obligations.

With respect to an obligation to give, i.e. the transfer of a real right over a thing, such as the ownership of a thing to someone, specific performance may be obtained by constraint. The Code of civil procedure provides for some remedies ...

In addition, **Article 1988** of the civil Code gives an **"obligee the right to a judgment that shall stand for the act"** or instrument that the obligor failed to execute. So, in general, under the civil Code and the Code of civil procedure, obligations to give are susceptible of being specifically enforced.

The specific enforcement of an obligation to do is quite another matter. As **Art. 1986** states in fine, **"the granting of specific performance is at the discretion of the court."** In reality it is impossible to have an obligation to do specifically enforced for fear of infringing, a little or excessively, upon the individual freedom of the obligor....

One can state that if the element of *"intuitu personae"* is dominant in the kind of obligation to do under consideration, then specific performance will not be available.

On the other hand there are obligations to do which ought to be specifically enforceable....

Article 2501 of the Code of civil procedure which allows the use of force against someone who refuses to vacate an immovable property. Thus, as **Art. 1986** of the civil Code expresses in a wise statement, the use of force amounting to specific performance of an obligation to do **"is at the discretion of the court."** ...

Cases

Lee R. CENTANNI, M.D.   1
v.   2
A. K. ROY, INC.   3
Louisiana Court of Appeal   4
Fourth Circuit   5
Feb. 7, 1972   6
258 So.2d 219   7

CHASEZ, Judge.   8

Plaintiff, Dr. Lee R. Centanni, instituted this suit against the defendant, A. K. Roy, 9
Inc., a real estate agency or brokerage company, for a return of $850.00, attorney's fees 10
and costs. The sum of $850.00 represents the amount allegedly due as a penalty for the 11
alleged non-performance of an agreement to sell and convey certain real estate. Plain- 12
tiff's petition was later supplemented and amended to include J. Folse Roy personally as 13
a defendant.   14

[....]   15

On March 30, 1967 plaintiff signed a written agreement to purchase a lot in Jefferson 16
Parish for $8,500.00 and made a deposit of $850.00. The agreement was accepted[....]   17
The sale was to pass before Roy Price, as notary named in the agreement, on April 25, 1967. 18

19   [....] On the day set for the sale, plaintiff appeared at the Notary's office but the seller
20 did not. Plaintiff then prepared and signed a document to allow an extension of time for
21 the passage of the act of sale but the vendor did not sign it and denies any knowledge of
22 the extension. Suffice it to say that at no time has the vendor appeared before a notary with
23 plaintiff to transfer the lot in question to plaintiff. However, the evidence shows that al-
24 though Jeff, Inc. claimed it could not sell the property in April of May of 1967 it was sub-
25 sequently sold by Jeff, Inc. under an agreement arranged in September of 1967.

26   A return of plaintiff's deposit, held by Price, was made. Plaintiff then made demand
27 on J. F. Roy for an additional $850.00 which constitutes double the deposit as contained
28 within the agreement to sell. Defendant has denied liability.

29   [....]

30   **[After ruling on plaintiff's argument regarding Louisiana mandate law, the court turned
31 to defendant's argument that plaintiff is not entitled to damages because he failed to put
32 defendants in formal default through process verbal.]** [....] Defendants also contend that
33 under the terms of the contract, if seller cannot deliver a merchantable title, then pur-
34 chaser is only entitled to the return of his deposit which the defendants have returned.

35   A demand in writing for the delivery of title and the placing in formal default is a pre-
36 requisite to the recovery of damages or to the rescission of the contract. LSA-C.C. Arti-
37 cle 1911 and Article 1912. However, putting in default is not required when such action
38 would be a vain, futile and useless gesture. Poche v. Ruiz, 239 La. 573, 119 So.2d 469
39 (1960); Fox v. Doll, 221 La. 427, 59 So.2d 443 (1952).

40   Defendant was sent a letter of damand [*sic*] on June 20, 1967 by Roy Price who was
41 acting as attorney for plaintiff at that time. A subsequent demand for double return of
42 deposit was again made on November 10, 1967 to which defendant denied liability.

43   The defendant asserts that the property in question had an outstanding mortgage on
44 it and the mortgagee refused to release the property and therefore he felt there was no
45 reason for him to be present for the transfer of title to the plaintiff on April 25, 1967. J.
46 F. Roy also testified that he had told Price of the mortgage and possible difficulties with
47 same. This testimony is corroborated by his letter of March 31, 1967 which disclosed the
48 true owner.

49   Accepting for purposes of this case that the letters of demand previously herein dis-
50 cussed are not a formal putting in default we are convinced that no formal placing in de-
51 fault is required.

52   In Poche v. Ruiz, supra, the Supreme Court held that where a title is known to be liti-
53 gious a demand by purchasers for vendor to convey title is vain; futile and a useless ges-
54 ture and therefore unnecessary.

55   There is no necessity to formally put one in default when he refuses to perform or ac-
56 knowledges an inability to perform. Fox v. Doll, supra.

57   Pierre v. Chevalier, 233 So.2d 61 (La.App., 4th Cir., 1970); writ refused, 256 La. 253,
58 236 So.2d 31 (1970), contains certain similarities with the facts of the present case. In
59 the case there was a cloud on the title because of an outstanding adverse tax title. In that
60 case Chevalier assumed that title to land he was selling was not defective and maintained
61 that position throughout the negotiations, however, the title was in reality unmerchantable.
62 The owner made no attempt to determine and remove the cloud on his title. In the pre-
63 sent case defendants show no evidence that they made a serious effort to remove the out-
64 standing mortgage on the lot but preferred instead to simply not show at the time for
65 passing of the sale.

'[S]ince Chevalier assumed the attitude that the title was not defective and took no   66
steps to determine and correct them and was in no position to offer a merchantable title,   67
a demand by Pierre for performance would have been vain and useless. No formal putting   68
in default was necessary under the circumstances.'   69

In the present case where the vendor refused to pass the act of sale because of an out-   70
standing mortgage and did not offer a merchantable title, demand by Centanni for per-   71
formance is not necessary; any such attempt being vain and useless.   72

The contractual agreement entered into contains the following specific conditions: 73

'The seller shall deliver to purchaser a merchantable title. Should the purchaser   74
refuse to take the title because same is not merchantable, or for any defects   75
therein, then in that event the seller is only liable for the return of the deposit   76
made by the purchaser, anything to the contrary notwithstanding.   77

'In the event the seller does not comply with this agreement within the time   78
specified, the purchaser shall have the right either to demand the return of his   79
deposit in full plus an equal amount to be paid as penalty by the seller; or the   80
purchaser may demand specific performance at his option.'   81

Centanni has not refused to take title, rather defendants [....] have refused to offer the   82
title. By the very terms of the agreement plaintiff is entitled to double the deposit as dam-   83
ages.   84

Plaintiff, in his petition, has requested reasonable attorney's fees. However, the agree-   85
ment contains no stipulation that fees for attorneys are intended other than fees allowed   86
for enforcing collection of the agent's commission. In such a situation as this case we have   87
maintained that attorney's fees are not provided for, nor recoverable. See Scurria v. Russo,   88
134 So.2d 679 (La.App., 4th Cir., 1961). Where not specifically allowed for by law or by   89
contract, attorney fees are not recoverable.   90

For the reasons hereinabove set forth judgment of the lower court is affirmed in part   91
and reversed in part and it is now ordered, adjudged and decreed that there be judgment   92
in favor of the plaintiff, Dr. Lee R. Centanni and against the defendant, A. K. Roy, Inc.,   93
in the sum of $850.00, all with legal interest thereon from date of judicial demand, with   94
all costs of court.   95

Affirmed in part, reversed in part, and rendered.   96

Questions

1. Lines 9 *et seq.*: How many parties are involved in this case? How many bilateral con-
    tracts have been entered into? Is there any issue of capacity? *See* the Louisiana Civil
    Code articles on "Representation and/or Mandate" (La. Civ. Code arts. 2985–3032).
    What kind of obligation(s) does a contract of "agency" create?

2. Lines 57–72: What is the purpose of a "putting in default"? Can this "purpose" ex-
    plain why and when a putting in default may either be unnecessary or useless? Is the
    possibility of putting an obligor in default contingent upon the nature of the oblig-
    ation owed by that obligor? Could it be relevant, not to say important, to keep this
    in mind when negotiating a contract?

3. Lines 40–96: What kind of obligation(s) (the Court refers to them as "conditions")
    was/were created in the contract? Is there any benefit for a party to include such an
    obligation in a contract? If you answered affirmatively, which party benefits?

H. B. 'Bud' FLETCHER

v.

Carol RACHOU, d/b/a La Louisianne Records and Recording Studio

Louisiana Court of Appeal
Third Circuit
Nov. 20, 1975
323 So.2d 163

WATSON, Judge.

This suit involves disputes between a recording artist and the owner of a recording studio. H. B. 'Bud' Fletcher, the plaintiff and defendant-in-reconvention is an entertainer specializing in the telling of jokes and stories in 'Cajun'[1] dialect. The defendant and plaintiff-in-reconvention is Carol Rachou who does business as La Louisianne Records and Recording Studio. At issue was Rachau's failure to make payment of royalties and Fletcher's failure to make additional recordings. The trial judge held that Rachou owed Fletcher $2,286.50 and Rachou had no valid claims against Fletcher.

Fletcher has appealed, claiming that the amount due is considerably in excess of the award; and Rachou has appealed, contending that the trial court erred in rendering a money judgment in favor of Fletcher and in failing to award damages to Rachou.

Prior to December 9, 1967, Fletcher made several recordings for Rachou which the latter sold successfully. The exact financial arrangement concerning these recordings is unclear from the record. On December 9, 1967, the parties entered into a written contract[2] for a five-year term which provided basically: that Fletcher would record exclusively for Rachou; that recordings would be made at 'mutually agreeable times'; that a royalty of 5% Of the retail price (which amounted to 25 cents per album) would be paid; and that payment would be made semi-annually within 45 days after June 30 and within 45 days after December 31 of each year, subject to a deduction for all advances against royalties.

'For the rights herein granted and for the services to be rendered hereunder by you, we shall pay you a royalty of 5% Of the retail price of all LP albums and tape cartridges (25¢ per album for albums that retail for $4.79), manufactured and sold by us and paid for by purchaser. '4. Payment of accrued royalties accompanied by statements shall be made semiannually, within 45 days after June 30, and within 45 days after December 31, in each year. However, we shall have the right to deduct from the amount of royalties due all advances against royalties.' (TR. 48)

---

1. 'Cajun' is a contraction of the word 'Acadian' used in reference to persons of Acadian descent, many of whom live in the southern part of the State of Louisiana.

2. While the wording of the contract is not at issue, for ease of reference we will quote the first four paragraphs: '1. This contract for your personal services is made between Carol J. Rachou D/B/A La Louisianne Records as the employer and you. We hereby employ to you render personal services and you agree to render such personal services exclusively for us for the purpose of recording and making records for phonograph records and/or tape recordings and other similar devices for home use. 2. Recordings will be made at recording sessions in the studios we designate at mutually agreeable times. Compositions to be recorded shall be designated by La Louisianne Records and each recording shall be subject to our approval as satisfactory for manufacture and sale. We shall at all times have complete control of the services to be rendered by you under the specifications of this contract and you agree that your services are unique, exceptional, and extra-ordinary.'

Significantly the recording contract did not call for the recordation of any particular number of records per year or during the term of the contract. There is no reference in the contract to royalties payable for prior recordings. The contract provides that, in the event of Fletcher's death, the royalties will thereafter be payable to his wife.

Pursuant to this contract, Fletcher made only one record despite attempts by Rachou and his employees to encourage additional recording. Certain recording dates were set up, but Fletcher contacted the studio on each occasion and indicated that, for some reason, usually sore throat, he would be unable to record. In an effort to encourage Fletcher to make additional records, Rachou withheld payment of royalties earned by Fletcher, but on one or two occasions gave him a check for royalties with an understanding that a new record would be made shortly thereafter.

It is undisputed that, during the contract period, Fletcher did not make recordings for anyone else and that, as of the date of trial he had, to a large extent, retired from his activities as a 'Cajun' humorist.

The contract between the parties expired on December 2, 1972, and, on December 6, 1973, Fletcher filed a petition alleging the existence of the contract, contending that no royalties had been paid since September 9, 1970 and that he was due an accounting and payment of all royalties. The petition was thereafter amended to claim the precise sum of $4,132.25. At no point in his petition or his amended petition did plaintiff assert a precise claim for royalties due under any prior contract on the several other records which he had made for Rachou prior to the December 9, 1967, contract.

Defendant Rachou answered, denying plaintiff's claims and asserting a reconventional demand for $10,000. He claimed loss of expenses and profits from Fletcher's failure to make recordings during the contract period, as the result of which Rachou lost the sale of those records and enhancement of the value of Fletcher's other records.

There is a certain lack of collision on the issues by the parties to this lawsuit, one side arguing certain issues and the other side arguing different and sometimes unrelated issues. However, following the propounding and answering of extensive written interrogatories, as well as other pre-trial activities, the matter was tried on the merits and the trial court found essentially that:

1. the parties did not contract to make any particular number of records;

2. defendant failed to make timely payment of royalties;

3. defendant admitted that he owed plaintiff $2,286.50 and such sum was due and owing;

4. defendant was not entitled to recover on the reconventional demand for alleged loss of profits, and even if he were so entitled, the proof was not sufficiently clear to arrive at any amount due; and

5. the claim for out of pocket expenses was not corroborated in the evidence and could not be allowed.

[....]

On appeal, Fletcher emphasizes the alleged error of the trial court in failing to hold that the royalties were continuing rather than limited to the five-year term of the contract. Rachou contends that the court erred in ordering payment of royalties to Fletcher, who, according to Rachou, either breached the contract or failed to perform under it, thereby entitling Rachou to have the contract dissolved and also entitling him to recover damages.

80   The issues to be decided on appeal are:

81   1. whether the trial court erred in awarding Fletcher $2,286.50 as past due
82   royalties;

83   2. whether the trial court erred in failing to recognize that the payment of
84   royalties is a continuing obligation; and

85   3. whether Rachou is entitled to:

86   (a) release from his obligation to pay royalties because of breach or non-
87   performance of the contract by Fletcher, and

88   (b) payment of damages.

89   I. Royalties

90   The trial court was correct in awarding the amount of $2,286.50 as past due royalties.
91   Rachou concedes that this was the royalty only on the one record made under the con-
92   tract. Fletcher persists in claiming royalties on all recordings made for Rachou, but this
93   suit, as delineated by the petition and amending petition, is basically a demand for roy-
94   alties due under the five-year contract of December 9, 1967, under which only one record
95   was made. As to the prior records made by Fletcher for Rachou, the sale of which was al-
96   luded to in various interrogatories and answers to interrogatories, the trial court was not
97   furnished any evidence concerning the agreement between the parties as to the amount
98   of royalty, if any, payable on these records. The contract of December 9, 1967, did not
99   relate to or refer to previous sales of records.

100   In his testimony, Rachou admitted owing Fletcher the amount awarded by the trial
101   court, and under the circumstances, we find no error in this award.

102   We do not agree with the trial court, however, that the obligation to pay royalties ter-
103   minated at the conclusion of the five-year contract. Certainly, since the contract did not
104   relate to the several other records made by Fletcher for Rachou, it could have no effect on
105   any obligation for payment of royalty under other agreements.

106   As to the single record made under the contract, Rachou contends apparently that the
107   five-year contract itself provides that royalties would be payable only for five years. How-
108   ever, there is no such provision in the contract and no legal authority has been cited for
109   Rachou's contention. The five-year term relates to Fletcher's obligation to make records
110   exclusively for Rachou. Fletcher contracted only that any records he made during the five
111   years would be made for Rachou. The obligation to pay royalties on any record made
112   under the contract continues. The contract even provides for payment of royalties to
113   Fletcher's wife after his death.

114   Breach of Contract

115   This brings us to Rachou's contention that Fletcher breached the contract and deprived
116   him of profits. There is no evidence that Fletcher made recordings for any other person
117   or firm during the contract period; the only indication of other professional activity by
118   Fletcher was the testimony by the witnesses, Faulk, Fontenot, Stoma and Oliver, that
119   Fletcher had made personal appearances at a bowling conference and Evangeline Downs
120   Race Track and had made commercials for a dairy. (The contract related only to making
121   records; see footnote 2). There was evidence by other witnesses, Leroy LeBlanc (profes-
122   sionally known as 'Happy Fats') and B. C. Fletcher (Fletcher's brother), that, during the
123   contract period, Fletcher suffered considerable difficulties with his throat.

124   Rachou's contention is that Fletcher breached the contract to record by only making
125   one record in five years and that this relieved Rachou of the obligation of paying royal-

ties and also entitled him to payment of damages. This argument presupposes the validity and enforceability of the contract between Fletcher and Rachou. It assumes that Rachou could have affirmatively required Fletcher to make recordings. The argument fails for two reasons: first, under its terms the contract calls for no particular number of records to be made; and second, a contract for personal services is not affirmatively enforceable.

As to the first reason, the contract is clear; no particular number of records was required. As to the second reason, some consideration must be given to the basic nature of the contract. It was an agreement by an artist or performer to render personal services, akin to the contract of a singer to sing or a musician to play.

Under the law of contracts in our sister states, a contract for personal services by an artist or a performer will not be specifically enforced by an affirmative decree.[3] Reinstatement of the Law of Contracts, s 379. According to the recognized authority in the field of contracts, Professor A. L. Corbin, there are three reasons usually given for this rule of law:

(1) difficulty of enforcing the decree and gauging the quality of the performance;

(2) strength of the American prejudice against any kind of involuntary personal servitude; and

(3) frequent close association between employer and employee and the consequent undesirability of enforcement where confidence and loyalty have been disrupted by dispute.

See Corbin on Contracts, s 1204, pp. 400–401.

In Louisiana, the courts have recognized the abrogation of personal contracts by inability to perform. Most notable are the cases in which persons have contracted for a prolonged series of dancing lessons and later have become physically incapacitated to dance. Louisiana courts have held that, under these circumstances, particularly relying on LSA-C.C. art. 2003,[4] such contracts are unenforceable. Acosta v. Cole, 178 So.2d 456 (La.App. 1 Cir. 1965), writ refused, 248 La. 432, 433, 179 So.2d 273, 274; Richardson v. Cole, 173 So.2d 336 (La.App. 2 Cir. 1965).

We think the reasoning expressed in Richardson and Acosta, as well as the considerations mentioned by Professor Corbin (which we find equally persuasive in Louisiana) justify our adopting and following the rule of law that a contract for personal services is not specifically enforceable by affirmative decree.

Also, the inability to perform as found in Richardson and Acosta, would, in our opinion, be an adequate basis on which the trial court could have found that Fletcher was not physically able to make additional recordings during the record period.

It does not follow, however, that, becasue [sic] Fletcher could not be required to perform or make additional records, royalties for records recorded during the contract period were not payable. The royalties are payment for services already performed, not, as Rachou seemingly believed, dependent on future recordings.

---

3. A clear distinction should be made between the enforcement of a contract by an affirmative order to perform and the negative enforcement by preventing performance of similar services for another. Other considerations are involved in negative enforcement and that is not the question here because there is no assertion of recordings made by Fletcher for anyone else.

4. The portion of art. 2003 relied on is as follows: '* * * if the obligation be purely personal as to the obligee who dies before performance, his heirs may recover from the obligor the value of any equivalent he may have received.' Total disability has been analogized to death in the dancing cases and the disabled dancing student has been held to be entitled to recover the unearned portion of payment for lessons.

Therefore, we find that the trial court was correct in its conclusion that there was no breach of the contract on the part of Fletcher and, accordingly, Rachou was not entitled to any damages. Likewise, the trial court was correct in holding that there was not sufficient evidence to award Rachou out of pocket expenses resulting from the cancellation of recording dates by Fletcher.

For the reasons assigned, the judgment of the trial court is affirmed, but it is amended to reserve to Fletcher the right to claim any additional royalties due: (1) on the one record made under the contract of December 9, 1967, but accruing subsequent to the five-year term of the contract, and (2) on recordings made under any agreement other than the contract of December 9, 1967.

[....]

Questions

1. Lines 10–173: Read the whole case while attempting to identify with the two main parties to the contract. Then read footnote 2. Can you identify some of the many legal features of this excerpt of the contract, for example, kinds of obligations, modalities ...?

2. Lines 35–64: What legal qualification would you give to Fletcher's obligation? What legal qualification would you give to Rachou's obligation to pay the royalties to Fletcher's wife? Were these two obligations dependent on one another? Could one continue to exist without the other? Why or why not? What did Rachou contract for: a hope or a future thing? *See* La. Civ. Code arts. 1976 and 2450–2451. Would it make a difference as to Rachou's rights against Fletcher?

3. Lines 89–113: What is the ground of the disagreement between the lower court and the Court of Appeal? Are an extinctive term and a continuous obligation compatible? Can a continuous obligation be compatible with an obligation to do? What about with an obligation to give?

4. Lines 115–173: Is there a relationship between the legal nature/kind of obligation and the right to demand specific performance? Can you illustrate with the case at hand?

J. WEINGARTEN, INC.
v.
NORTHGATE MALL, INC. and Pickens Bond
Construction Company

Supreme Court of Louisiana
Sept. 8, 1981
404 So.2d 896

DENNIS, Justice.

We are called upon to decide whether, under the circumstances of this case, a court should specifically enforce a lease by ordering the destruction of the major part of a $4 million building which a shopping center developer erected in an area reserved to its tenant for customer parking. The trial court refused to order the building razed, but the court of appeal reversed, requiring that approximately 60% of the building be torn down and removed within six months of the effective date of its judgment. We reserve the judgment of the court of appeal. Although specific performance is the preferred remedy for breach of a contract it may be withheld by the court when specific relief is impossible, when the inconvenience or cost of performing is greatly disproportionate to the damages caused, when the obligee has no real interest in receiving performance, or when the latter would have a substantial negative effect on the interests of third parties. In view of the great disparity between the cost of specific relief and the damages caused by the contractual breach, the magnitude of the economic and energy waste that would result from the building's destruction, the substantial hardship which would be imposed on individuals who are not parties to the contract or to this litigation, and the potential negative effect upon the community, the circumstances and nature of this case do not permit specific performance. Accordingly, the case will be remanded to the trial court for proceedings necessary to the assessment and award of any damages to which the plaintiff may be entitled.

The defendant, Northgate Mall, Inc., in 1967 and subsequently, developed an enclosed shopping mall on approximately 35 acres of land in Lafayette, Louisiana. In 1968, the defendant subleased space in the mall to the plaintiff, J. Weingarten, Inc., for the operation of a grocery store.

In early 1978, the defendant began planning to renovate and expand the mall to counter expected competition from a new mall to be built in Lafayette. The plaintiff, upon learning of the expansion plans, informed the defendant that it wished to remodel or enlarge its own store in conjunction with the defendant's activities. Later the plaintiff sent rough plans of its enlargement to the defendant for approval. The plans would have allowed the plaintiff to extend its store front fifty feet into the parking lot adding roughly 7400 additional square feet of building area. Under the lease, the plaintiff had no contractual right to expand. The defendant's right to expand was limited to roughly 40,000 square feet, but it proposed to add slightly over 100,000 square feet. Therefore, consent of both parties was necessary under the lease to permit either party's proposed expansion. However, no written modification ever resulted from their preliminary negotiations.

In February, 1979, the defendant erected a construction fence and began moving construction equipment and material onto the job site. The plaintiff alerted the defendant that it considered the defendant's activities a breach of contract and that injunctive relief would be sought if such activities did not cease. Last minute negotiations between the parties were unsuccessful, and the plaintiff filed suit on March 1, 1979 seeking preliminary and permanent injunctive relief.

Pursuant to plaintiff's petition, the trial court issued a temporary restraining order prohibiting further construction activities and continued the order until March 19, 1979 when a hearing was held on plaintiff's motion to dissolve the restraining order. The trial court denied the preliminary injunction and dissolved the temporary restraining order based on its finding that Weingarten failed to show that it would sustain irreparable damage without injunctive relief. Realizing the great costs attendant to the delay of a multi-million dollar construction project, the trial court pledged itself to speedy action in the case and encouraged the plaintiff to appeal the correctness of its ruling. The plaintiff did not take an appeal as a matter of right, see La. C.C.P. art. 3612, or apply for supervisory writs. See La. C.C.P. art. 2201. The trial on the merits of the petition for a permanent injunction was not held until October 25 and 26, 1979. By this time the $4 million expansion project was virtually complete and the new stores therein were open for business.

After the trial on the permanent injunction, the trial court reaffirmed its earlier finding that the plaintiff had not demonstrated that it would be irreparably harmed and could be adequately compensated monetarily. The court refused to enforce specifically a provision in the lease stipulating that an injunction to enforce Weingarten's rights to egress and

64 passage over the parking area occupied by the new building could be obtained without the
65 necessity of showing irreparable harm or the inadequacy of damages. The trial court con-
66 cluded the agreed remedy provision was against public policy relying on Termplan Arabi,
67 Inc. v. Carollo, 299 So.2d 831 (La.App. 4th Cir.), writ denied 302 So.2d 29 (La. 1974).

68 The court of appeal reversed the trial court, holding that the plaintiff was entitled to
69 permanent injunctive relief because the agreed remedy provision was valid and because
70 the plaintiff was irreparably harmed. J. Weingarten, Inc. v. Northgate Mall, Inc., 390
71 So.2d 527 (La.App.3d Cir. 1980). We granted defendant's application to consider the ap-
72 propriateness of specific performance in this case. 396 So.2d 1326 (La. 1981).

73 Northgate agreed not to erect any additional buildings in the parking area of the shop-
74 ping center except within the space shown on a plat attached to the lease designated as
75 sites for future department store and a proposed theater. The defendant also promised to
76 maintain a ratio of six car parking spaces for each 1,000 feet of floor space in the shop-
77 ping center. It further agreed that its tenant, Weingarten, would have the right to an "ir-
78 revocable non-exclusive easement" over all parking areas shown on the plat attached to
79 the lease. In connection with the "easement," the lease provided that Weingarten "shall
80 have the right to obtain an injunction specifically enforcing such rights and interests with-
81 out the necessity of proving inadequacy of legal remedies or irreparable harm."

82 We concur in the court of appeal's findings that Northgate breached each of the con-
83 tractual provisions. Whereas the lease reserved a 39,375 square foot area for future expansion,
84 Northgate's new building consumed over 100,000 square feet, covering part of the area
85 reserved for customer parking and reducing the parking ratio from 5.7 spaces per 1000
86 square feet, in which Weingarten had acquiesced, to 5.0 spaces per 1000 square feet. How-
87 ever, we disagree with the court of appeal finding that the plaintiff had shown that it
88 would be irreparably injured by the breaches of contract. The evidence fully supports the
89 trial judge's determination that plaintiff failed to demonstrate that its injury would be ir-
90 reparable or insusceptible to adequate compensation.

91 The decisive issue presented by the breaches of contract is whether Weingarten is en-
92 titled to the substantive right of specific performance under the circumstances of this
93 case. Specific performance may be enforced by the extraordinary remedy of injunction,
94 among other procedural methods.[1] It is self-evident, however, that unless Weingarten has
95 a substantive right to specifically enforce the obligation, neither an injunction nor any
96 other procedural remedy may be used.[2]

---

1. A judgment may also be issued directing a party to perform a specific act. When the party so adjudged fails to perform, the judgment may be enforced by various procedural methods including the use of distringas, an assessment for damages, and punishment for contempt all as authorized by La.C.C.P. art. 2502. In addition, La.C.C.P. art. 2504 authorizes the court to direct performance by the sheriff or another person appointed by the court, at the cost of the disobedient party. See Comment, 40 Tul.L.Rev. 340, 352 (1966).

2. A party seeking an injunction has no standing to sue unless he has a substantive right, which the law will recognize, assertable against a defendant having a substantial adverse interest. Terrebonne Parish Police Jury v. Mathrene, 405 So.2d 314 (La. 1981); La. Hotel-Motel Ass'n Inc. v. Parish of East Baton Rouge, 385 So.2d 1193 (La. 1980); League of Women Voters of N.O. v. City of New Orleans, 381 So.2d 441 (La. 1980); Abbott v. Parker, 259 La. 279, 249 So.2d 908 (1977); Stoddard v. City of New Orleans, 246 La. 417, 165 So.2d 9 (1964). Cf., Moore, Federal Practice, s 65.17. Moreover, the injunction question appears entirely academic. If Weingarten is entitled to specific performance, its right may be enforced by other procedural methods even if an injunction is unavailable. See footnote 1, supra. Nevertheless, it should be noted that the court of appeal's conclusion that parties contractually may dispense with procedural requisites for an injunction is subject to serious question because of the effects it may have on court dockets and litigants in other cases. If Civil Code article 11 applies

Plaintiff Weingarten has asked specific performance of defendant Northgate's obliga- 97
tion not to do something namely, not to infringe on plaintiff's contractual rights over 98
areas reserved for parking by the lease.[3] Civil Code articles 1926 through 1929 govern the 99
enforcement of obligations to do, or not to do. 100

Articles 1926 and 1929 provide: 101

Art. 1926. On the breach of any obligation to do, or not to do, the obligee is 102
entitled either to damages, or, in cases which permit it, to a specific performance 103
of the contract, at his option, or he may require the dissolution of the contract, 104
and in all these cases damages may be given where they have accrued, according 105
to the rules established in the following section. 106

Art. 1927. In ordinary cases, the breach of such a contract entitles the party 107
aggrieved only to damages, but where this would be an inadequate compensa- 108
tion, and the party has the power of performing the contract, he may be constrained 109
to a specific performance by means prescribed in the laws which regulate the 110
practice of the courts. 111

Art. 1928. The obligee may require that any thing which has been done in vi- 112
olation of a contract, may be undone, if the nature of the cause will permit, and 113
that things be restored to the situation in which they were before the act com- 114
plained of was done, and the court may order this to be effected by its officers, 115
or authorize the injured party to do it himself at the expense of the other, and 116
may also add damages, if the justice of the case require it. 117

Art. 1929. If the obligation be not to do, the obligee may also demand that 118
the obligor be restrained from doing any thing in contravention of it, in cases where 119
he proves an attempt to do the act covenanted against. 120

Since they are not models of clarity, the articles are susceptible to more than one rea- 121
sonable interpretation. 122

A literal reading of the codal language may lead one to conclude that the general rule, 123
i.e., the one to be applied in ordinary cases, is that the breach of a contract entitles the 124
party aggrieved only to damages; and specific performance may only be obtained where 125
damages would be an inadequate compensation. Under this view, an obligee could only 126
require a thing done in violation of the contract to be undone if the nature of the cause 127
would permit, viz., in the exceptional case in which damages are an inadequate remedy. 128
Such an interpretation is suspect, however, because of its common law overtones. 129

Eminent Louisiana civilian commentators have argued persuasively to the contrary 130
that these articles of the code where designed to enhance the rank of specific performance 131
over damages as a remedy for the nonperformance of obligations to do or not to do in a 132
manner not expressed in the comparable French articles. 2 S. Litvinoff, Obligations, s 133
168 in 7 Louisiana Civil Law Treatise (1975); Comment, Louisiana Law of Specific Per- 134
formance: Codal Provisions and Methods of Enforcement, 40 Tul.L.Rev. 340 (1966). In 135
their view, several circumstances support such an interpretation of the code: Article 1926 136
was mistranslated from the French; it should read: "On the breach of any obligation to 137

---

to public law with the same force as it does to private law, renunciation of an important rule of court,
procedure may in fact be contrary to the public good. See Garro, Codification Technique and the
Problem of Imperative and Suppletive Laws, 41 La.L.Rev. 1007, 1012–1015 (1981).

3. We agree with the trial court that the lease does not confer a servitude to plaintiff since defendant-
lessor is not the owner of the property. See La. C.C. arts. 697, 710–14; Hawthorne Oil & Gas Corp.
v. Continental Oil Co., 368 So.2d 726, 737 (La.App. 3d Cir., rev'd on other grounds, 377 So.2d 285
(La. 1979).

138 do, or not to do, the obligee is entitled either to damages, or, if the execution is possible,
139 (rather than in cases which permit it) to specific performance of the contract....'" (em-
140 phasis added) S. Litvinoff, Obligations, s 168 in 7 Louisiana Civil Law Treatise 310–315
141 (1975); Comment, Louisiana Law of Specific Performance: Codal Provisions and Meth-
142 ods of Enforcement, 40 Tul.L.Rev. 340, 343–345 (1966). Article 1927's restriction of spe-
143 cific performance to cases where damages would be "inadequate compensation" is consistent
144 with the idea that recovery of damages is never an adequate remedy when specific per-
145 formance is possible. S. Litvinoff p. 312; Comment, 40 Tul.L.Rev. p. 344. Article 1927's
146 provision that, in "ordinary cases," a breach of contract entitles the creditor "only to dam-
147 ages," only implies a reference to nemo praecise cogit ad factum, that is, only damages should
148 be granted when specific performance would require a violation of the obligor's freedom.
149 S. Litvinoff, p. 313. Article 1928, which allows the obligee to require that anything which
150 has been done in violation of a contract, "may be undone, if the nature of the cause will
151 permit," shows greater care for the procedural aspects of the remedy of specific performance
152 than does its French equivalent. S. Litvinoff, p. 313.

153   We agree with the distinguished doctrinal writers that Articles 1926 through 1929 were
154 intended to give first rank to the obligee's right to performance in specific form, consis-
155 tently with other provisions of the Code. See 2 S. Litvinoff, Obligations, s 168, n. 77.
156 Therefore, we reject the common law view that the obligee must first clear the inade-
157 quacy of damage-irreparable injury hurdle before invoking the remedy.[4]

158   A reading of the articles as a whole, however, implies that courts are empowered to with-
159 hold specific performance in some exceptional cases even when specific performance is
160 possible. The phrases, "if the nature of the cause will permit" and "in ordinary cases,"
161 suggest a reference to a traditional civilian concept. The civil law systems, i.e., those de-
162 scended from Roman law, have by and large proceeded on the premise that specific re-
163 dress should be ordered whenever possible, unless disadvantages of the remedy outweigh
164 its advantages. Farnsworth, Legal Remedies for Breach of Contract, 70 Columbia L.Rev.
165 1145 (1970). The main reservations have been for cases where specific relief is impossi-
166 ble, would involve disproportionate cost, would introduce compulsion into close per-
167 sonal relationships or compel the expression of special forms of artistic or intellectual
168 creativity. Dawson, Specific Performance in France and Germany, 57 Mich.L.Rev. 495,
169 520 (1959). Professor Litvinoff has described the French jurisprudence as allowing courts
170 to deny specific performance whenever the inconvenience of such forced execution would
171 exceed the advantage, as when the cost of performing in kind is disproportionate to the
172 actual damage caused, or when it is no longer in the creditor's interest, or when it would
173 have a negative effect upon the interest of third parties. 2 Litvinoff, Obligations, s 166;
174 See also, 2 M. Planiol, Civil Law Treatise pt. 1, no. 171A at 103 (11th ed. La. St. L. Inst.
175 trans. 1959); Szladits, The Concept of Specific Performance in Civil Law, 4 Am.J.Comp.L.
176 208, 217 (1955).[5]

---

4. For discussions distinguishing the civil and common law approaches to specific performance and critiques of Louisiana jurisprudence see: 2 S. Litvinoff, Obligations, ss 162–171 in 7 Louisiana Civil Law Treatise (1975); Jackson, Specific Performance in Louisiana, Past and Future, in Essays in the Civil Law of Obligations 195 (J. Dainow ed. 1969); Jackson, Specific Performance of Contracts in Louisiana, 24 Tul.L.Rev. 401 (1950); Krassa, Interaction of Common Law and Latin Law: Enforcement of Specific Performance in Louisiana and Quebec, 21 Can. Bar Rev. 337 (1943); Comment, Louisiana Law of Specific Performance: Codal Provisions and Methods of Enforcement, 40 Tul.L.Rev. 340 (1966).

5. Twentieth century French commentators argue that courts are justified in not granting specific performance only when it is materially or morally impossible. "Moral impossibility refers to a case 'when satisfaction in nature can by the hardest be procured from the defendant, but at the price of an act

For the foregoing reasons, we conclude that the legislative aim of the redactors of the code was to institute the right to specific performance as an obligee's remedy for breach of contract except when it is impossible, greatly disproportionate in cost to the actual damage caused, no longer in the creditor's interest, or of substantial negative effect upon the interests of third parties.[6] Applying this interpretation to the present case, we conclude that its nature will not permit specific performance.

The evidence clearly reflects that that the cost of tearing down most of the $4 million building and doing incalculable damage to the remainder of the shopping center greatly outweighs any actual damage caused to the plaintiff. It is dubious that the devastation of such a building in a shopping center built with the hope of competing with a neighboring market complex is in Weingarten's real interest. It is evident that the third persons not party to the contract or to this lawsuit would be negatively affected. Shopping center tenants in the new building would lose their store space and risk losing their investments. H.J. Wilson Company, which occupies over 63,000 square feet of the building, would be particularly disadvantaged. The owners of the land and John Hancock Mutual Life Insurance Company, whose long term loan is secured by a mortgage on the shopping center and pledges of the leases of the five major tenants, would suffer a substantial negative effect. Although perhaps not controlling, additional considerations weighing against specific performance and its consequent destruction of a major commercial building are the potential negative effects upon the community in the form of economic waste, energy dissipation, and possible urban blight.

Although the contractual provisions involved here cannot be specifically enforced under the circumstances of this case, we hold that they could have been under different conditions. Indeed, unless exceptional conditions prevail as in this case anything which has been done in violation of the contract may be undone, including the destruction of a building. Moreover, plaintiff is not without a remedy because it is entitled to be compensated fully in damages for any loss it sustains as a result of the breach of contract. Because the record presently does not provide an adequate basis for the assessment of damages, however, the case will be remanded to the trial court for that purpose.

REVERSED AND REMANDED.

WATSON and MARCUS, JJ., concur.

LEMMON, J., concurs and assigns reasons.

LEMMON, Justice, concurring.

When construction began, Weingarten sought to enjoin Northgate's blatant violation of the contract, and injunctive relief should have been granted. When preliminary injunctive relief was denied, Weingarten did not seek review of that ruling.

After construction was completed, the permanent injunction was tried on the merits. Of course, it was impossible at that point to prevent construction, and Weingarten's only relief was to undo the contractual violation by requiring removal of the building. By this

---

of violence which would be scandalous. Colin & Capitant, Cours EelEementaire de droit civil fran cais II (3 e ed. 1921) p. 17ff.; Planiol & Ripert, TraitEe Pratique de droit civil fran cais VII (1931) 69 f. f." Jackson, Specific Performance of Contracts in Louisiana, 24 Tul.L.Rev. 401, 415 (1950).

6. Even when a valid agreed remedy provision such as stipulated damages is included in the parties' contract, the court retains some discretion to modify that provision when circumstances such as partial performance make the agreed remedy inappropriate or unjust. See, La.C.C. arts. 1934 (5), 2120, 2127; La.C.C.P. art. 2164; Comment, Judicial Modification of Penal Clauses A Survey of Recent Developments, 53 Tul.L.Rev. 523 (1979).

216 time, however, the rights of third parties had become involved, such as the landowners
217 and the mortgage holders (as well as new lessees, by the time the matter reached this
218 court). Although Northgate's breach was no less culpable, the court's weighing process in
219 determining the appropriate remedy was complicated by the involvement of the rights of
220 innocent third parties.

221 At this point in the litigation I agree with the majority's analysis. Northgate's tram-
222 pling on other parties' rights should have been halted earlier, when all of the equities fa-
223 vored Weingarten. Because of inherent flaws in the judicial process Weingarten must now
224 obtain its relief through an award of damages.

Questions

1. After you have read the case in its entirety, ponder over the nature, purpose and usefulness of specific performance as the preferred remedy at civil law.

2. Lines 9–26: Was the court of appeal wrong in requiring that "approximately 60% of
   the building be torn down and removed within six months of the effective date" of
   the judgment? Do you see any benefit, not necessarily in this case only, in a court
   ordering specific performance? What kind of obligation (give, do, not do) was the court
   of appeal requiring the defendant to carry out? Would it have been impossible for the
   defendant to specifically carry out that obligation? Does the law require the courts
   to consider the cost of performing in relation to the "damages caused"? Why should
   the interests of third parties interfere with the rights and obligations of the parties to
   a contract? What could become of the civil law principle according to which "a contract is the law for the parties" just as much legislation is the law for all? Isn't the
   Supreme Court kind of rewriting the contract (against the will of one party at least)
   on the basis of grounds or circumstances that were foreign to the parties at the time
   they entered into their contracts with their own economic/business grounds? Was
   their contract at all against the law? How reliable and predictable are the grounds on
   which the Supreme Court is to justify its ultimate decision? Under these circumstances, what legal advice would you give to business parties to a contract? What
   about private parties to a contract? Is there any difference in your advice? Shouldn't
   the law of contract be the same for all?

3. Lines 101–157: Note the Court's learned and effective integration of doctrine into
   the code articles as the primary sources of law. What is the Court's conclusion as regards the remedy of specific performance? What do you think of the Court's statement on lines 128–129? Is it a judgment of value or one of principle? Read now lines
   153–157. What do you think? Could this difference in remedies between the civil law
   and the common law be indicative and illustrative of more fundamental differences
   between the civil law and the common law?

4. Lines 158–182: What do you think of the Court's reading of the Louisiana Civil Code
   articles and particularly of the Court writing that "a reading of the articles as a *whole*,
   however, *implies* that courts are *empowered* to withhold specific performance...."?
   (emphasis ours). On lines 177–182, what is the *ratio legis* (reason for the legislation)
   that the court singles out? Is there any reason why the Court identifies such a reason?
   Is the answer in lines 181–182 and aren't the coming holdings or grounds of the opinion summarized in this one sentence? (Note that on lines 132–135, the three co-
   authors of this casebook do not share the statements attributed to the French
   jurisprudence, particularly in case Cass. 5-22-1997, J C P ed. G. 1997. 1. 4070 # 26.)

5. Lines 183–197: Of what nature are all of the grounds or reasons advanced by the Court to deny specific performance? Are any of them legal grounds/reasons? Are any of them contractual grounds/reasons?

Glenn Edward GREZAFFI

v.

R. Craig SMITH

Louisiana Court of Appeal
First Circuit
June 24, 1994
641 So.2d 210

CARTER, Judge.

This is an appeal from a trial court judgment granting a motion for summary judgment in a suit for specific performance.

FACTS

On June 16, 1988, plaintiff, Glenn Edward Grezaffi, entered into a purchase agreement with defendant, R. Craig Smith, for the sale of a 2.536-acre tract of land located in Pointe Coupee Parish for $60,864.00.[1] The sale was to take place on September 1, 1988. Among other things, the purchase agreement was contingent upon the rezoning of the property as "R-4" and the release of the existing mortgage upon the execution of the act of sale. On August 9, 1988, the 2.536-acre tract of property was rezoned as "R-4." Thereafter, Smith failed to execute the act of sale for the purchase of the property.

[....]

[....] Smith filed an answer to Grezaffi's petition and alleged that Grezaffi had intentionally interfered with his rights to obtain zoning on other projects.[2]

On July 22, 1992, Grezaffi filed a motion for summary judgment. [....]

In opposition to Grezaffi's motion for summary judgment, Smith alleged that the purchase agreement was null and void because of lack of consent in that his consent had been induced by duress. [....]

On September 18, 1992, the hearing on the motion for summary judgment was held. After considering the evidence and argument of counsel, the trial court rendered judgment on October 15, 1992, granting Grezaffi's motion for summary judgment and ordering Smith to pay Grezaffi $64,864.00 plus legal interest from September 1, 1988, until paid. The judgment also ordered Smith to appear at a specific time and place to execute the appropriate documents transferring title of the 2.536-acre tract from Grezaffi to Smith. The trial judge also cast Smith for all costs.

Thereafter, Smith filed a motion for new trial, alleging that the judgment granted Grezaffi more rights than he had under the purchase agreement. The new trial was granted, and, on April 14, 1993, the trial court rendered judgment in favor of Grezaffi and against Smith as follows:

---

1. The agreement provided that Smith would pay $15,000.00 cash at the time of the execution of the act of sale and that Grezaffi would finance $45,864.00 at 12% interest for eighteen months.
2. In his answer, Smith alleges, by appellation, the defenses of failure of consideration, estoppel, and set-off. However, his answer also alleges specific facts which give rise to the defense of duress.

1. Smith was ordered to pay Grezaffi the sum of $15,000.00 on or before April 15, 1993, and $45,864.00 at 12% interest in eighteen months from April 15, 1993.

2. Smith was also ordered to appear on or before April 15, 1993, to execute an act of sale to effectuate a transfer of the property from Grezaffi to Smith.

3. Smith was ordered to pay Grezaffi legal interest on the $15,000.00 from October 26, 1988, until paid.

4. Smith was ordered to pay Grezaffi legal interest on the $45,864.00 from April 26, 1990 through April 15, 1993.

From this adverse judgment, Smith appeals, assigning the following errors:

1. The trial court erred in granting plaintiff's Motion for Summary Judgment and finding that there existed no genuine issues of material fact.

2. The trial court erred in ordering specific performance of a contract which was invalid.

[....]

DISCUSSION

Two Civil Code articles expressly address sales and promises to sell.

LSA-C.C. art. 2456 provides as follows:

The sale is considered to be perfect between the parties, and the property is of right acquired to the purchaser with regard to the seller, as soon as there exists an agreement for the object and for the price thereof, although the object has not yet been delivered, nor the price paid.

LSA-C.C. art. 2462 provides, in pertinent part, as follows:

A promise to sell, when there exists a reciprocal consent of both parties as to the thing, the price and terms, and which, if it relates to immovables, is in writing, so far amounts to a sale, as to give either party the right to enforce specific performance of same.

These articles clearly establish that a sale exists as between the parties when there is agreement as to the object and the price and that, even if there is only a promise to sell, it may be specifically enforced by either party. *Succession of Dunham*, 393 So.2d 438, 445 (La.App. 1st Cir.1980), *affirmed in part, reversed in part on other grounds*, 408 So.2d 888 (La.1981). The inquiry must always be whether or not there existed a reciprocal consent as to the thing, the terms, and the price. *Dunaway v. Woods*, 470 So.2d 574, 577 (La.App. 1st Cir.1985); *Wallace v. Lafourche Parish School Board*, 394 So.2d 1329, 1330 (La.App. 1st Cir.1981).

A major requirement of one who seeks specific performance is proper performance of his part of the contract. *Thompson v. Johnson*, 602 So.2d 272, 274 (La.App. 2nd Cir.1992). In the absence of proper performance, plaintiffs must prove that they are and were ready to comply with whatever obligations devolved upon them to perform. *Thompson v. Johnson*, 602 So.2d at 274. The courts are bound to enforce the contract as written. *Cooper v. Olinde*, 565 So.2d 978, 983 (La.App. 1st Cir.), *writ denied*, 569 So.2d 966 (La.1990). The burden of proof in an action for breach of contract is on the party claiming rights under the contract. The existence of the contract and its terms must be proven by a preponderance of the evidence. *See Baxter v. Zeringue*, 501 So.2d 327, 329 (La.App. 5th Cir.), *writ denied*, 504 So.2d 879 (La.1987); *Phillips v. Insilco Sports Network, Inc.*, 429 So.2d 447, 449 (La.App. 4th Cir.1983); *North American Contracting Corporation v. Gibson*, 327 So.2d 444, 449 (La.App. 3rd Cir.1975), *writ denied*, 332 So.2d 280 (La.1976); *New Or-*

leans Silversmiths, Inc. v. Wormser, 258 So.2d 592, 593 (La.App. 4th Cir.1972); *Walters v. Edwards,* 212 So.2d 749, 754 (La.App. 1st Cir.1968).

In the instant case, the record clearly reveals that Grezaffi and Smith entered into a written agreement for the purchase of the 2.536-acre tract in Pointe Coupee Parish. The agreement set forth the thing and the price. However, Smith contends that there was no mutual consent because his consent was vitiated by duress.

Consent is vitiated when it has been obtained by duress of such a nature as to cause a reasonable fear of unjust and considerable injury to a party's person, property, or reputation. LSA-C.C. art. 1959; *Wolf v. Louisiana State Racing Commission,* 545 So.2d 976, 980 (La.1989); *Cagle v. Loyd,* 617 So.2d 592, 598 (La.App. 3rd Cir.), *writs denied,* 620 So.2d 877 (La.1993); *Adams v. Adams,* 503 So.2d 1052, 1057 (La.App. 2nd Cir.1987). Age, health, disposition, and other personal circumstances of a party must be taken into account in determining the reasonableness of the fear. LSA-C.C. art. 1959; *Adams v. Adams,* 503 So.2d at 1057.

Duress results when "a person makes an improper threat that induces a party who has no reasonable alternative to manifest his assent. The result of this type of duress is that the contract that is created is voidable by the victim." LSA-C.C. art. 1959, official comment (b); *Wolf v. Louisiana State Racing Commission,* 545 So.2d at 980. The threat of doing a lawful act or a threat of exercising a right does not constitute duress. LSA-C.C. art. 1962; *Adams v. Adams,* 503 So.2d at 1057. However, a threat of doing an act that is lawful in appearance only may constitute duress. *Wolf v. Louisiana State Racing Commission,* 545 So.2d at 980.

In the instant case, in support of his motion for summary judgment, Grezaffi presented his own affidavit, a copy of the purchase agreement, a copy of a plat of the Grezaffi property, an affidavit by Joseph B. Laurent, the minutes of the city council meeting, an affidavit by John Donald LeBlanc, a copy of the demand letter, and a title opinion by James C. Dewey.

The affidavit of Grezaffi reveals that he is the owner of the 2.536-acre tract of land in Pointe Coupee Parish. On June 16, 1988, he entered into a purchase agreement with Smith for the sale of the 2.536-acre tract of land. A copy of the purchase agreement was attached to Grezaffi's affidavit. Grezaffi further stated that the property was rezoned as "R-4" by the City Council and that the Bank of New Roads agreed to release the mortgage on the property upon execution of the act of sale. According to Grezaffi, prior to the date on which the act of sale was to be consummated, he informed Smith of these facts and advised Smith that he stood ready, willing, and able to fulfill his obligations under the terms of the purchase agreement. Grezaffi further stated that, to date, Smith has refused to comply with the purchase agreement.

In his affidavit, Joseph B. Laurent, secretary/treasurer of the City of New Roads, stated that, at the regularly scheduled meeting of the City Council of the City of New Roads on August 9, 1988, the Grezaffi property was rezoned "R-4." Attached to Laurent's affidavit was a copy of the minutes of the council meeting.

The affidavit of John Donald LeBlanc, loan officer at the Bank of New Roads, revealed that the bank held a mortgage on the Grezaffi property sought to be transferred to Smith. According to LeBlanc, prior to September 1, 1988, Grezaffi informed him that the mortgaged property was to be sold to Smith and requested that the mortgage on the property be released. LeBlanc stated that, upon the closing of the sale and application of the proceeds to the debt owed to the Bank of New Roads, the mortgage would be released.

129   Smith's affidavit revealed that, in the fall of 1987, he entered into a purchase agree-
130 ment with Luke J. Grezaffi for property in close proximity to the property which is the
131 subject of the instant suit. Smith stated that he signed the purchase agreement with
132 Luke Grezaffi to build a Farmers Home rental-assisted elderly housing complex. Smith
133 further stated that he subsequently engaged numerous professionals to complete the
134 necessary financing to acquire the property and fund the construction. Smith also stated
135 that he filed an application with the Farmers Home Administration for financing and
136 obtained approval to begin the project. Subsequent thereto, Luke Grezaffi filed an ap-
137 plication for rezoning of the property with the City of New Roads. According to Smith,
138 he was then contacted by Glenn Grezaffi, plaintiff in the instant suit, and Grezaffi's
139 sister regarding their opposition to the rezoning application, which Smith stated was
140 based upon internal strife within the Grezaffi family. Smith stated that Grezaffi and
141 Grezaffi's sister threatened him in that "if Luke Grezaffi did not purchase the land
142 owned by Glenn Grezaffi which was contiguous to the property ... [Smith] had previ-
143 ously agreed to purchase from Luke J. Grezaffi, then Glenn Grezaffi and his sister would
144 use their influence with the New Roads Planning and Zoning Commission and City
145 Council to oppose the rezoning requests filed" by Luke Grezaffi. Smith further stated
146 that it was made clear to him that his application for rezoning would be denied if
147 Grezaffi and Grezaffi's sister opposed the application for rezoning. Smith also stated that,
148 faced with the prospect of losing his ability to build and complete the development
149 and the associated monetary losses caused by Grezaffi's threats, he executed the purchase agreement with Grezaffi.

150   After reviewing the record and the evidence submitted, we find that no genuine issues
151 of material fact exist and that reasonable minds must inevitably conclude that Grezaffi is
152 entitled to judgment as a matter of law. The record reveals that Grezaffi showed that he
153 is and was ready to comply with the obligations devolved upon him to perform. The
154 property had been rezoned as "R-4," and the existing mortgage would be released upon
155 the execution of the act of sale. Although Smith alleged that his consent to the agreement
156 was vitiated because of duress, the record unequivocally established that the alleged eco-
157 nomic duress was not of the type sufficient to vitiate his consent. As a landowner in the
158 area, Grezaffi had a legal right to oppose the rezoning of the property. Informing Smith
159 that he would oppose the rezoning was not a threat. Accordingly, we find that the trial judge
160 properly granted the motion for summary judgment.

161   *CONCLUSION*

162   For the above reasons, the judgment of the trial court, granting Grezaffi's motion for
163 summary judgment is affirmed. Smith is cast for all costs of this appeal.

[....]

Questions

1.   What kinds and how many obligations are created by a purchase agreement or an
act of sale for the purchase of the property? Is it important, from the point of view
of benefiting from the right of specific performance, to properly identify the kind of
obligation created by a contract? Would you say that when a party enters into a contract, it should ask itself whether or not it definitely wants specific performance of
its obligation by the other party to the contract or whether it would be satisfied by
receiving damages instead? How is this decision having an impact on whether an
obligation is to do, to give, or not to do?

2.   Lines 52 *et seq.*: Note how the court is approaching its discussion of the issues. It refers, first of all, to the law, i.e. the controlling Louisiana Civil Code articles. Then the Court applies the articles to the facts. This is the proper approach to take in a jurisdiction governed by a civil code. How should the court have identified the nature or kind of obligation therein created by the parties (to give, to do, or to not do)?

3.   Lines 70 *et seq.*: Is a promise to sell a unilateral contract or a bilateral contract? What about a contract of sale? In these lines, is the Court making any kind of implicit reference to some means of defense or exception that can be raised by one first party against another second party who is seeking performance from the first party?

4.   Lines 84 *et seq.*: Explain the difference(s) between duress, on the one hand, and the threat of exercising a lawful right, on the other. What is the outcome of the "trial judge properly [having properly granted] the motion for summary judgment"? The price of the sale was $60.864.00 in 1988. In the trial court's summary judgment, the price was set at $64,864.00 (*see* line 29). From where does the difference in price come? A year later, in 1994, in affirming the trial court's summary judgment, is the Court of Appeal also affirming the price of $64,864.00? Shouldn't that price have been raised as the trial court did to take into account a five-year span between 1988 and 1993?

Section III — Damages Resulting from the Inexecution of Conventional Obligations

Louisiana Sources of Law

Louisiana Civil Code

Art. 1994. Obligor liable for failure to perform.

An obligor is liable for the damages caused by his failure to perform a conventional obligation.

A failure to perform results from nonperformance, defective performance, or delay in performance. (Acts 1984, No. 331, § 1, eff. Jan. 1, 1985.)

Art. 1995. Measure of damages.

Damages are measured by the loss sustained by the obligee and the profit of which he has been deprived. (Acts 1984, No. 331, § 1, eff. Jan. 1, 1985.)

Art. 1996. Obligor in good faith.

An obligor in good faith is liable only for the damages that were foreseeable at the time the contract was made. (Acts 1984, No. 331, § 1, eff. Jan. 1, 1985.)

Art. 1997. Obligor in bad faith.

An obligor in bad faith is liable for all the damages, foreseeable or not, that are a direct consequence of his failure to perform. (Acts 1984, No. 331, § 1, eff. Jan. 1, 1985.)

Art. 1998. Damages for nonpecuniary loss.

Damages for nonpecuniary loss may be recovered when the contract, because of its nature, is intended to gratify a nonpecuniary interest and, because of the circumstances surrounding the formation or the nonperformance of the contract, the obligor knew, or should have known, that his failure to perform would cause that kind of loss.

Regardless of the nature of the contract, these damages may be recovered also when the obligor intended, through his failure, to aggrieve the feelings of the obligee. (Acts 1984, No. 331, § 1, eff. Jan. 1, 1985.)

Art. 1999. Assessment of damages left to the court.

When damages are insusceptible of precise measurement, much discretion shall be left to the court for the reasonable assessment of these damages. (Acts 1984, No. 331, § 1, eff. Jan. 1, 1985.)

Art. 2000. Damages for delay measured by interest; no need of proof; attorney fees.

When the object of the performance is a sum of money, damages for delay in performance are measured by the interest on that sum from the time it is due, at the rate agreed by the parties or, in the absence of agreement, at the rate of legal interest as fixed by Article 2924. The obligee may recover these damages without having to prove any loss, and whatever loss he may have suffered he can recover no more. If the parties, by written contract, have expressly agreed that the obligor shall also be liable for the obligee's attorney fees in a fixed or determinable amount, the obligee is entitled to that amount as well. (Acts 1984, No. 331, § 1, eff. Jan. 1, 1985; Acts 1985, No. 137, § 1, eff. July 3, 1985; Acts 1987, No. 883, § 1.)

Art. 2002. Reasonable efforts to mitigate damages.

An obligee must make reasonable efforts to mitigate the damage caused by the obligor's failure to perform. When an obligee fails to make these efforts, the obligor may demand that the damages be accordingly reduced. (Acts 1984, No. 331, § 1, eff. Jan. 1, 1985.)

Art. 2003. Obligee in bad faith.

An obligee may not recover damages when his own bad faith has caused the obligor's failure to perform or when, at the time of the contract, he has concealed from the obligor facts that he knew or should have known would cause a failure.

If the obligee's negligence contributes to the obligor's failure to perform, the damages are reduced in proportion to that negligence. (Acts 1984, No. 331, § 1, eff. Jan. 1, 1985.)

Art. 2004. Clause that excludes or limits liability.

Any clause is null that, in advance, excludes or limits the liability of one party for intentional or gross fault that causes damage to the other party.

Any clause is null that, in advance, excludes or limits the liability of one party for causing physical injury to the other party. (Acts 1984, No. 331, § 1, eff. Jan. 1, 1985.)

Art. 2005. Secondary obligation.

Parties may stipulate the damages to be recovered in case of nonperformance, defective performance, or delay in performance of an obligation.

That stipulation gives rise to a secondary obligation for the purpose of enforcing the principal one. (Acts 1984, No. 331, § 1, eff. Jan. 1, 1985.)

Art. 2006. Nullity of the principal obligation.

Nullity of the principal obligation renders the stipulated damages clause null.

Nullity of the stipulated damages clause does not render the principal obligation null. (Acts 1984, No. 331, § 1, eff. Jan. 1, 1985.)

Art. 2007. Stipulated damages or performance.

An obligee may demand either the stipulated damages or performance of the principal obligation, but he may not demand both unless the damages have been stipulated for mere delay. (Acts 1984, No. 331, § 1, eff. Jan. 1, 1985.)

Art. 2008. Failure to perform justified.

An obligor whose failure to perform the principal obligation is justified by a valid excuse is also relieved of liability for stipulated damages. (Acts 1984, No. 331, § 1, eff. Jan. 1, 1985.)

Art. 2009. Obligee not bound to prove damage.

An obligee who avails himself of a stipulated damages clause need not prove the actual damage caused by the obligor's nonperformance, defective performance, or delay in performance. (Acts 1984, No. 331, § 1, eff. Jan. 1, 1985.)

Art. 2011. Benefit from partial performance.

Stipulated damages for nonperformance may be reduced in proportion to the benefit derived by the obligee from any partial performance rendered by the obligor. (Acts 1984, No. 331, § 1, effective January 1, 1985.)

Art. 2012. Stipulated damages may not be modified.

Stipulated damages may not be modified by the court unless they are so manifestly unreasonable as to be contrary to public policy. (Acts 1984, No. 331, § 1, eff. Jan. 1, 1985.)

Précis: Louisiana Law of Conventional Obligations — § 8.3.2

The word "damages", without any adjective in front of the word, refers usually to "compensatory damages" i.e. damages meant to compensate an obligee for the loss he suffered from the non performance of his obligation by the obligor....

The parties know that, under the law of the civil Code, failure to perform an obligation will result in the **"obligor [being] liable for the damages caused by his failure to perform a conventional obligation."** Art. 1994(1). That obligation to pay damages comes into existence if the obligor fails to perform without any lawful excuse, or if there is defective performance or delay in performance. **Art. 1994(2)....**

We can refer to these compensatory damages as conventional or contractual damages to distinguish them from "delictual" damages. Such delictual damages find their source of law in **Arts. 2315 et seq....**

By contrast with "delictual damages" which are due as a consequence of a juridical fact, conventional damages find their justification in a juridical act, a contract....

Since we are focusing, here, on conventional obligations or contract, the parties to a contract may, at the time of formation of the contract and in anticipation of a party not performing, **"stipulate the damages to be recovered in case of nonperformance ..."** Art. 2005....

Art. 1995 gives this instruction to the court that the **"Damages are measured by the loss sustained by the obligee and the profit of which he has been deprived."** ...

The contractual clause stipulating for damages creates an *accessory* or *secondary* obligation which will come into existence only in case of non performance by an obligor of his principal obligation....

Since a stipulated damages clause is included in a contract, the obligor knows in advance that his failure to perform will vest in the obligee the right to demand the payment of the stipulated damages. When "An obligee ... avail[s] himself of a stipulated damages clause [he] need not prove the actual damage caused by the obligor's nonperformance, defective performance, or delay in performance." Art. 2009....

As **Art. 2012** states: "**Stipulated damages may not be modified by the court unless they are so manifestly unreasonable as to be contrary to public policy.**" Furthermore, "**Stipulated damages for nonperformance may be reduced in proportion to the benefit derived by the obligee from any partial performance rendered by the obligor.**" Art. 2011....

The contractual obligation of the obligor to perform the principal obligation, first and foremost, and his accessory obligation to pay damages as a "back up" obligation are of such a paramount importance that the law issues, in **Art. 2004**, a stern warning to both parties to a contract: "**Any clause is null that, in advance, excludes or limits the liability of one party for intentional or gross fault that causes damage to the other party.**

Any clause is null that, in advance, excludes or limits the liability of one party for causing physical injury to the other party." ...

The principle stated in **Art. 1995** applies, as a general proposition, to obligations to give, to do and not to do: "**Damages are measured by the loss sustained by the obligee and the profit of which he has been deprived.**" Since these concepts of loss sustained (*damnum emergens*) and deprivation of profit (*lucrum cessans*) which are the two component parts of the damages owed by the obligor are often not susceptible of precise measurement in advance ...

One important first qualification is dictated by the obligor's good or bad faith....

It follows that "**An obligor in good faith is liable only for the damages that were foreseeable at the time the contract was made.**" Art. 1996. *A contrario*, "**An obligor in bad faith is liable for all the damages, foreseeable or not, that are a direct consequence of his failure to perform.**" Art. 1997. What damages are "foreseeable or not" and what damages "are a direct consequence" of the obligor's failure to perform will be for a court to determine following a "**reasonable assessment of these damages.**" Art. 1999....

A second qualification attached to the principle takes into consideration the behavior of the other party to the contract, the obligee. Good faith is required of both parties. Art. 2003....

Good faith and a corollary duty of loyalty explain also why "**An obligee must make reasonable efforts to mitigate the damage caused by the obligor's failure to perform. When an obligee fails to make these efforts, the obligor may demand that the damages be accordingly reduced.**" Art. 2002....

Art. 1998 applies to "non-pecuniary loss" or "*dommage/préjudice moral*" as are the legal expressions in French and Québec civil law. As a non-pecuniary loss, it affects a "value, a feeling, a belief" which has no patrimonial content or monetary value and which, therefore, is very personal to the party affected by the loss....

It is to this kind of loss, a non pecuniary loss, that Art. 1999 will be applied in most instances since such a loss will be difficult to evaluate. Therefore, the damages themselves will be difficult to measure precisely. That measurement will have to be given a **reasonable assessment** by a court exercising **much discretion**. (Art. 1999)....

Cases

Dr. Frank H. MAREK

v.

Dr. G. Gordon McHARDY et al.

Supreme Court of Louisiana
March 17, 1958
101 So.2d 689

McCALEB, Justice.

Plaintiff, a physician specializing in roentgenology, brought this suit to recover damages in the sum of $124,585.35, allegedly sustained as a consequence of defendants' breach of contract to give him a 10% Interest in a partnership to be formed for the practice of medicine. Primarily, he prays for a specific performance of the partnership agreement which, for reasons hereinafter pointed out, could not be granted but the principal demand stated in the petition is for damages in the amount claimed and, as a second alternative, for recompense on a quantum meruit.

[....]

[....] Sometime prior to February 19, 1948, Doctors McHardy and Browne, who were engaged in the practice of medicine as partners, contemplated expansion of their organization by forming a medical group to operate a clinic for the general practice of medicine. To this end, defendants acquired real estate to be used for the clinic and sought to obtain the services of various specialists to join them in their practice of internal medicine, the combined operation to be known as the 'Browne-McHardy Medical Group'.

During this time, plaintiff was practicing his specialty of radiology at the Mayo Clinic in Rochester, Minnesota. He was contacted by telephone by Dr. McHardy, who sought to enlist his services and have him join the planned group of physicians. Following this solicitation, Dr. McHardy wrote plaintiff a letter on February 19, 1948 in which he stated that he and Dr. Browne were forming a medical diagnostic group which was to include two other internists, a neuro-psychiatrist and a radiologist, who would have charge of the X-ray Department; that they were renovating the ground floor of the old Carol Hotel in New Orleans and would have a full complement of general X-ray equipment on hand; that they were desirous of having plaintiff take charge of this department and would pay him $8,000 per year for the first three years with a percentage interest at the beginning of the fourth year 'which percentage in the business and equipment will have been purchased by the three years of service the individual has dedicated to the group'. Plaintiff was requested by Dr. McHardy to give his reaction to this offer as early as possible. Following receipt of this letter, further telephonic conversations were had between plaintiff and Dr. McHardy, culminating in a letter written by the latter to plaintiff on March 23, 1948, stated to be a confirmatory letter 'which we will each consider equivalent to a contract'. The terms of this contract were that plaintiff was to join the Browne-McHardy Medical Group as a roentgenologist on October 1, 1948 and as a salaried member of the organization for 36 months, the yearly salary being $8,000 with the understanding that, at the end of each year, an evaluation of the financial structure of the organization would be reviewed to consider the possibility of an increase of the salary. It was further provided in the letter that 'Beginning October 1, 1951, having completed thirty-six months of your contract with us as specified, it is agreed that thereafter you will be a participating part-

45 ner to the extent of ten percent in all income, equipment and accounts payable to the
46 Browne-McHardy Medical Group. This partnership agreement drawn up in the proper
47 form will be completed on October 1, 1951 at which time it goes into effect'. On March
48 27, 1948 plaintiff accepted the proposition in writing and stated in his letter that 'My wife
49 and I are looking forward to October when we will come home to New Orleans to live.'

50 On October 1, 1948, plaintiff joined the group and remained in its service for some
51 34 months when, according to his allegations, he was informed by Dr. McHardy that the
52 defendants had no intention of granting him a one-tenth interest in the medical enter-
53 prise on October 1, 1951 but that, instead, he would have to buy this interest from them.
54 Plaintiff asserts that his expectancy of being made a partner constituted a material part
55 of the consideration for the three years employment and that, except for this promise,
56 he would not have worked at the salary paid by defendants.

57   [....]

58 [**After deciding that plaintiff's claim was not prescribed, the court turned to the issue**
59 **of appropriate remedies.**]

60 At the outset, it is appropriate to point out that, although plaintiff initially prays for
61 a specific performance of the partnership feature of the contract, it is plain from a con-
62 sideration of the alleged facts and the nature of the obligation that the case is not one in
63 which a specific performance could or should be ordered. Whereas, Article 1926 of the
64 Civil Code provides that, on the breach of any obligation to do or not to do, the obligee
65 is entitled to damages or, at his option, to a specific performance of the contract in cases
66 which permit it, the following Article 1927 limits the remedy in ordinary cases of breach
67 of contract, declaring that the party aggrieved is entitled only to damages unless this
68 would be inadequate, in which instance specific performance may be granted if the de-
69 faulting party has the power of performing the contract. Manifestly, in a case like this in-
70 volving personal services coupled with a promise of the obligees to make the plaintiff
71 their business partner, the court would not order the exceptional relief of a specific per-
72 formance. See Snyder v. Wilder, 146 La. 811, 84 So. 104. Hence, plaintiff's remedy is for
73 dissolution of the contract (see Articles 2046 and 2047 of the Civil Code) and for the
74 damages (Articles 1926 and 1927) he has occasioned by defendants' breach. This relief
75 he has prayed for and we think he would be entitled to it if he is able to sustain the well-
76 pleaded allegations of his petitions.

77 Plaintiff has also demanded, as a second alternative, recovery on a quantum meruit.
78 This claim is not tenable because plaintiff received compensation for the services he ren-
79 dered prior to the time he severed his connection with defendants. Hence, unless he is
80 able to sustain his claim for damages under the contract as a consequence of defendants'
81 breach of their promise to give him a 10% Interest in the partnership, which was to be
82 formed following the completion of 36 months service at the clinic, he is without a cause
83 of action.

84 Defendants contend that plaintiff states no cause of action for these alleged damages
85 for a number of reasons. They specify, first, that the alleged promise for the formation
86 of a partnership was too vague and indefinite to support its enforcement in that, among
87 other things, no provision was made for the duration of the partnership.

88 We find no merit in this postulation. The contract evidenced by McHardy's letter of
89 March 23, 1948 is clear and concise, constituting a valid working agreement supported
90 by adequate consideration. The omitted details, which defendants assert were essential,
91 were such matters as hours, days off, vacations, sick leave, retirement and plans depend-
92 ing on contingencies such as death or retirement of partners, all of which were suscepti-

ble of agreement or controlled by law without need for stipulation. In any case, subsequent failure to reach an agreement as to these details would not be destructive of the legal effectiveness of defendants' promise and bar an action by plaintiff for the damages he is able to prove he suffered as a consequence of the breach.

The next contention of defendants that their offer was never accepted by plaintiff is without basis in view of the letter of March 23, 1948 which denominates it as a contract. This letter contains succinct statements of a prior verbal understanding reached by the parties and the agreement was later placed in execution, apparently in good faith, when plaintiff came to New Orleans and took charge of defendants' radiology department.

We also find untenable defendants' next argument that the latter of March 23, 1948 was intended to be a contract only insofar as the three years employment was concerned and that the mention of the partnership was only by way of a proposal which would be negotiated after three years if both parties were still interested. The letter itself refutes this proposition as it states that '* * * having completed thirty-six months of your contract with us as specified, it is agreed that thereafter you will be a participating partner to the extent of ten percent * * *'.

Defendants further contend that plaintiff is not entitled to damages because the petitions show that he is admittedly in default. They say that plaintiff was bound under the contract to complete his three years of employment in order to entitle him to a 10% Interest in the partnership and yet, according to his own allegations, he left his employment on August 10, 1951, or before the end of the 36-month period. Closely connected with this contention is defendants' claim that they have not been put in default and their breach, if any, was merely passive.

Plaintiff alleges that the reason why he did not continue his performance for the full thirty-six months is that defendants informed him that they were not going to make him a partner in accordance with their promise and, therefore, it would have been vain and useless for him to continue to perform as the expectancy of being made a partner constituted a material part of the consideration for his three years employment and that, except for this expectancy, he would not have agreed to work for the salary paid by defendants.

Thus, the allegations of plaintiff's petition present the question of whether or not a party to a commutative contract in Louisiana may discontinue his performance when the other party notifies him that the contract will be repudiated. In other words, is the doctrine of anticipatory repudiation entitled to recognition in this State? If so, then defendants' claim that they have not been placed in default has no substance as the alleged unjustified repudiation by defendants of their promise is to be regarded as an active violation, of their obligation rendering them amenable to damages from that moment without the necessity of being placed in default. See Articles 1931 and 1932 of the Civil Code.

Under the common law, a breach of a contract before the time of performance allows the injured party to sue for damages immediately. 12 Am.Jur. Verbo Contracts, Sections 391, 401; Williston on Contracts, Revised Edition, Section 1296, et seq., especially Section 1314; Restatement of the Law of Contracts, Section 318 and Corbin on Contracts, Section 959, et seq. It is generally recognized, however, that the repudiator may retract his repudiation unless the promisee, in relying on the repudiation, has changed his position to such an extent that subsequent performance is impractical, in which case the injured party may, nevertheless, recover damages. Corbin, op. cit. Sections 977, 978.

In Section 1337A of Williston on Contracts, Rev.Ed., it is said that 'There seems no recognition of any doctrine of anticipatory breach in the civil law until within comparatively recent times.' A reference is made to the views obtaining in France and also in Germany where there are certain variations. The conclusions of Mr. Williston are founded on the difference in the civil law system's first choice of remedy in actions ex contractu, it being observed that damages are the rule at common law and specific performance the exception, whereas the reverse is true of the civil law. See also comment 'Anticipatory Repudiation in Louisiana', 7 Tulane L.Rev. 586.

While Mr. Williston may be correct that the civil law, as obtaining in France, accords a specific performance as its first choice of remedy, this is not the rule in Louisiana—for, as we have above pointed out, Article 1927 of the Civil Code plainly declares that the breach of an obligation to do or not to do entitles the party aggrieved in ordinary cases only to damages. See Article 'The Implied Resolutory Condition for Non Performance of a Contract', 12 Tulane L.Rev. 376–400 and 509–533. It is only where damages would not furnish adequate compensation and the defaulting party has the power of performing the contract, that specific performance will be allowed in the absence of a special statute authorizing this relief, such as Article 2462 of the Civil Code, as amended, dealing with an agreement to sell.[1]

On the other hand, Articles 2046 and 2047 of the Civil Code provide that in every commutative contract there is a resolutory condition to take effect if either party does not perform and, in cases where there is a willful breach, the contract is resolved only by suit in which the court may, in its discretion, allow a further time for performance. These Articles, we think, have no effect on Article 1927, declaring that damages are the rule and specific performance the exception, as this Article establishes the ordinary remedy accorded by law, whereas Articles 2046 and 2047 refer to the judicial discretion which may be exercised after a hearing where the defendant is pleading for a chance to perform.

From all of this we deduce that an anticipatory breach of contract is actionable in Louisiana. Whether the contract will be resolved depends upon the facts and circumstances of each particular case. Accepting as true the allegations of fact in the case at bar, we are of the opinion that plaintiff was legally justified in treating the contract breached when he was informed by defendants in August of 1951 that they would repudiate their promise to include him as a partner on October 1, 1951 and, therefore, he was not required to continue in their service until October 1st as a condition precedent to the assertion of a claim for damages.[2] The question of whether plaintiff's discontinuance of

---

1. It is to be noted that Article 1927 is not contained in the Code Napoleon and the jurisprudence construing the Article is that specific performance has never been favored in our law. See Pratt v. McCoy, 128 La. 570, 54 So. 1012 and the many authorities cited therein.

2. The authorities cited by defense counsel do not sustain their contention to the contrary. In Mortmain v. Lefaux, 6 Mart.,O.S., 654, the plaintiff was the manager and editor of defendant's newspaper. Defendant insisted that plaintiff print a controversial editorial and plaintiff, rather than merely refusing to print an article, left his position. The Court held that the plaintiff had a right to reject the article and the defendant's insistence did not warrant plaintiff's leaving his position. In Payne v. James and Louis Trager, 42 La.Ann. 230, 7 So. 457, defendant lessees had allowed the premises to fall into disrepair contrary to the terms of the lease. Since the lease had expired, the lessees no longer had possession and were no longer in a position to perform. The Court held that the plaintiff need not have alleged a putting in default in order to state a cause of action. In Braun v. Weill, 111 La. 973, 36 So. 87, the Court found that, because of the strained relations between employer and employee, these parties had mutually rescinded their agreement. In Jones v. Smalley, 5 La. 28, plaintiff agreed to haul some horses down the Mississippi River and sued for damages when defendant shipped them by other means. The Court ruled against plaintiff on the grounds that he had not been ready and willing to perform up to the last moment. The Court so held, despite the fact that defendant had made the other arrangements well before the time for performance. Referring to the defendant's making the

performance in August of 1951 deprived defendants of the right to retract their repudi-   171
ation and perform the contract is a matter of defense and does not affect the cause of ac-   172
tion stated by plaintiff. Obviously, this would be a matter of importance only if it is shown   173
on the trial that defendants were willing to perform their promise on the due date.   174

Finally, defendants' argument that no contract came into being until the writing of a   175
partnership agreement, is without merit for the reasons stated above. The letter of March   176
23, 1948 is a complete contract containing an executory promise of a 10% Interest in the   177
partnership. No new written agreements were absolutely essential to carry into effect the   178
covenants contained therein.   179

The exception of no cause of action is not well taken and should have been overruled.   180

The judgment appealed from is reversed and the case remanded for further proceed-   181
ings consistent with the views herein expressed.   182

Questions

1.   After you have read the case, identify the nature or kind of obligation(s) created by
     the contract. Do you see any connection between the kind of obligation created and
     the type of remedy to which it may give rise? What advice would you give to parties
     when negotiating a contract as far as the performance of their reciprocal-bilateral
     obligations is concerned?

2.   Lines 50–56: On what requirement or component part of the contract is the plain-
     tiff basing his argument? Was the defendant aware or apprised of such? Did the de-
     fendant breach the contract by anticipation?

3.   Lines 60–76: What is your analysis of the type of relationship created by a contract
     of partnership: commercial, financial, personal, or a mixture? What is the Court's po-
     sition and how much is it based on the Court classifying the obligation as one to do,
     not to do, personal, heritable, etc . . . ?

4.   Lines 84–96: Are the defendants making the argument that the contract did not have
     for its purpose to create a bilateral-commutative contract because of vagueness and
     indefiniteness? What is the opposite form of a commutative contract? Are the de-
     fendants making the argument that the plaintiff was taking a chance? (*See* lines
     122–44.)

5.   Lines 122–154: What do you think of the Court's review and analysis of the notion
     of anticipatory breach of contract? Hasn't the Court forgotten about a defense avail-
     able to a party to a bilateral commutative contract when the other party does not
     perform on time or when that party shows signs of its future inability to perform?

---

other contract of carriage, the Court said: 'It shows an unwillingness merely on the part of the defendant
to carry his contract into effect, not an impossibility for him to do so; and it is the latter which alone
excuses the plaintiff from the nonperformance of his part.' If the Court meant by this that a clear repudiation before the time of performance does not constitute a breach, it was mistaken. This, because the Court, in rejecting plaintiff's demands, acceded to his request and purportedly decided the
case under the common law, since the contract had been confected in Ohio. Finally, defendants cite
Shaughnessy v. D'Antoni, 5 Cir., 100 F.2d 422, 425. The opinion in this case is actually contrary to
defendants' contentions. Shaughnessy had been employed by D'Antoni, who had not paid as agreed,
whereupon Shaughnessy left and obtained employment elsewhere. The Court, in holding that plaintiff could only recover for time in actual employ, said: 'If Shaughnessy had offered to serve and D'Antoni had refused to let him, or had otherwise expressed a repudiation of his obligation, there would
have been an anticipatory breach of the obligation, but such a breach is not shown by silence.'

See La. Civ. Code arts. 1908–1911 and *supra* p. 133. What do you think of the Court's (superficial) comparison of the notion of specific performance in the common law and the civil law (of France and of Louisiana)? Shouldn't the Court have given some first-hand references to French law instead of making the statement, in passing, about the law of specific performance in France? Wouldn't the Court have been better inspired had it made a difference between obligations to do something (strictly) personal to the obligor as opposed to something to do that other obligors could do just as well? (*See* Obligations to do, *supra*, p. 307).

Bruce MEADOR and Gretchen Meador
v.
TOYOTA OF JEFFERSON, INC., et al.
Supreme Court of Louisiana
May 17, 1976
332 So.2d 433

CALOGERO, Justice.

May an automobile owner recover damages for aggravation, distress, and inconvenience from a repairman who has unnecessarily and excessively delayed completion of the vehicle's repair? This is the principal question presented in this case. It is to be answered by the construction to be given that portion of Civil Code article 1934(3) which allows the recovery of nonpecuniary loss '(w)here the contract has for its object the gratification of some intellectual enjoyment, whether in religion, morality or taste, or some convenience or other legal gratification....'[1]

Following a collision, an eighteen-year-old girl brought her first acquired automobile, a 1971 model Toyota, to defendant, Toyota of Jefferson, Inc., for repair late in February of 1972. It was returned to her on September 20, 1972, some seven months later. In her suit for damages (she was joined in the suit by her father), the trial court awarded her $1554.77, which included $602.77 as reimbursement for seven of her monthly car notes, $252 for seven monthly insurance payments, and $700 for aggravation, distress, and inconvenience. The Court of Appeal agreed that defendant had breached its contract, but concluded that the undue delay consisted of only five of the seven months' repair period. Accordingly, it reduced the $602.77 and the $252 portions of the award by two-sevenths, allowing, respectively, $430.55 and $180, for a total of $610.55. The Court of Appeal disallowed the $700 awarded by the trial court for aggravation, distress, and inconvenience, and in these particulars amended the judgment in favor of plaintiffs. Meador v. Toyota of Jefferson, Inc., 322 So.2d 802 (La.App.4th Cir. 1975).

We granted writs upon plaintiff's complaint that the Court of Appeal erred in disallowing the $700 portion of the award for aggravation, distress and inconvenience. Meador

---

1. L.C.C. art. 1934(3) provides:

'Although the general rule is, that damages are the amount of the loss the creditor has sustained, or of the gain of which he has been deprived, yet there are cases in which damages may be assessed without calculating altogether on the pecuniary loss, or the privation of pecuniary gain to the party. Where the contract has for its object the gratification of some intellectual enjoyment, whether in religion, morality or taste, or some convenience or other legal gratification, although these are not appreciated in money by the parties, yet damages are due for their breach; a contract for a religious or charitable foundation, a promise of marriage, or an engagement for a work of some of the fine arts, are objects and examples of this rule.'

v. Toyota of Jefferson, Inc., 323 So.2d 804 (La.1976). Defendant did not seek writs.[2] Accordingly, and because of the result we reach hereinafter on the only remaining issue in the litigation, the part of the Court of Appeal judgment awarding plaintiff $610.55 is not before us. C.C.P. art. 2167; Madison v. American Sugar Refining Co., 243 La. 408, 144 So.2d 377 (1962); Blades v. Southern Farm Bureau Casualty Ins. Co., 237 La. 1, 110 So.2d 116 (1959); May Finance Co. v. Nagy, 223 La. 816, 66 So.2d 860 (1953).

We have reviewed the transcript and agree with the factual findings of the Court of Appeal. Defendant did indeed breach the implied obligation to repair within a reasonable time; the undue delay amounted to five months; $610.55 is a fair assessment of plaintiff's recoverable pecuniary loss. (As noted earlier, this element is no longer before us). Furthermore, if recoverable, $700 would be a reasonable and proper award for plaintiff's nonpecuniary damages, i.e., her aggravation, distress, and inconvenience. Accordingly, we direct our attention to the principal question posed at the outset of this opinion.

Generally, recovery for damages upon the breach of a contract is limited to the loss a person has sustained or the profit of which he has been deprived.[3] However, in certain limited circumstances a person may, upon the breach of a contract, recover damages for nonpecuniary loss. It is this sort of damage which plaintiff herein seeks to recover. Plaintiff argues that she is due recovery for aggravation, distress, and inconvenience which resulted from her inability to use her automobile for the period during which defendant unreasonably delayed its repair. She argues that this damage is recoverable under Civil Code Article 1934(3) which, as we indicated earlier, allows recovery for nonpecuniary loss '(w)here the contract has for its object the gratification of some intellectual enjoyment, whether in religion, morality or taste, or some convenience or other legal gratification....' 'She argues specifically that the disjunctive 'or' in the article means that nonpecuniary damages are allowed where the contract has for its object the gratification either of 'some intellectual enjoyment' Or of 'some convenience.' Thus she contends that to gain recovery under the article, one need not show that the contract contained any intellectual element whatsoever; one may recover even when the object of the contract is purely physical gratification. This liberal position is supported by language, at least, in the First Circuit Court of Appeal opinion in Jack v. Henry, 128 So.2d 62 (La.App.1st Cir. 1961).[4] An alternative, broader position which also supports plaintiff's recovery is that it suffices, to permit nonpecuniary damages, that the object or objects of the contract include elements of both intellectual and physical gratification. See Holland v. St. Paul Mercury Ins. Co., 135 So.2d 145 (La.App.1st Cir. 1961), Meyer v. Succession of McClellan, 30 So.2d 788 (La.App.Orl.1947), Melson v. Woodruff, 23 So.2d 364 (La.App.1st Cir. 1945).

On the other hand, defendant contends that in order for plaintiff to recover nonpecuniary damages, the object of the contract must be exclusively intellectual enjoyment, as opposed to partially intellectual — partially physical, and as opposed to exclusively physi-

---

2. Originally sued by plaintiffs were Toyota of Jefferson, Inc., Toyota Motor Sales, U.S.A. Inc., Gulf States Toyota, Inc., and State Farm Mutual Automobile Ins. Co. Only respondent Toyota of Jefferson, Inc., was cast in damages by the trial court; the other defendants were dismissed.

3. L.C.C. art. 1934 provides:

'Where the object of the contract is any thing but the payment of money, the damages due to the creditor for its breach are the amount of the loss he has sustained, and the profit of which he has been deprived, under the following exceptions and modifications.'

4. In the Jack case, the court stated:

'(W)e believe that a contract for the construction of a home ... has as its object the convenience of the owner within the meaning and intendment of the phrase "or some convenience" as used in Paragraph 3, Article 1934, LSA-R.C.C. entitling the owner of a residence to damages for inconvenience resulting from a contractor's breach of the obligation....' 128 So.2d at 72.

68 cal enjoyment. This strict interpretation is given support in the jurisprudence by such cases
69 as Rigaud v. Orkin Exterminating Co., 236 So.2d 916 (La.App.3d Cir. 1970), Baker v.
70 Stamps, 82 So.2d 858 (La.App.Orl.1955), Lillis v. Anderson, 21 So.2d 389 (La.App.Orl.1945),
71 and Sahuc v. United States Fidelity & Guar. Co., 320 F.2d 18 (5th Cir. 1963).

72   This Court has never adopted a strict view but has reached results favoring the broader
73 interpretation of Art. 1934(3).[5] In Lewis v. Holmes, 109 La. 1030, 34 So. 66 (1903) a
74 bride had contracted with the defendant store for the manufacture, or sewing, of five
75 dresses, one for her wedding and the others for her trousseau. She was allowed recovery
76 for deprivation of intellectual enjoyment and for mental suffering in connection with de-
77 fendant's non-delivery of the four dresses for her trousseau. The contract's object was
78 not purely intellectual, but rather entailed features both physical (her need for comfort-
79 able clothing), and intellectual (her preference for style, or 'taste,' and concern with her
80 appearance on her wedding day and on her honeymoon).

81   Two other cases where the Court allowed recovery and where there existed elments
82 [sic] of both intellectual and physical gratification were O'Meallie v. Moreau, 116 La.
83 1020, 41 So. 243 (1906) and Jiles v. Venus Community Center Benevolent Mutual Aid
84 Assn., 191 La. 803, 186 So. 342 (1939). In O'Meallie, the Court awarded damages for an-
85 noyance and vexation to a social club for breach of a contract to lease a picnic area, and
86 in Jiles the Court awarded plaintiff damages for mental anguish from watching her child
87 die without proper medical attention because of defendant Association's breach of a con-
88 tract to supply doctors' services and medicine.

89   In none of the foregoing cases, however, has the Court historically viewed the source
90 of Article 1934(3) and the origin thereof.

91   The third paragraph of Article 1934 had no counterpart in the Code Napoleon or the
92 Louisiana Civil Code of 1808. The paragraph first appeared in the Louisiana Civil Code
93 of 1825.[6] That Code was drafted in French, translated into English. Both French and Eng-
94 lish versions are official texts of the Code.[7] To interpret the Article, then, where as here
95 the articles of the 1870 Code is not entirely clear,[8] we deem it helpful to examine the
96 French and English versions of the article in the Code of 1825.

97   In the French version of the 1825 Louisiana Civil Code, the pertinent clause of Art.
98 1928 read:

99   'Lorsque le contract a pour but de procurer a quelqu'un une jouissance pure-
100   ment intellectuelle, telle que celles qui tiennent a la religion, a la morale, au-
101   gout, a la commodite ou a toute autre espece de satisfaction de ce genre,....'

102 Translated into English this passage reads:

---

5. For an excellent comment on this subject, including the 'liberal,' 'broad,' and 'strict' interpretation in the jurisprudence see 'Damages Ex contractu: Recovery of Nonpecuniary Damages For Breach
of Contract Under Louisiana Civil Code Article 1934,' by Henri Wolbrette, III, 48 Tul.L.Rev. 1160
(1974).
6. It has been suggested that the source of this paragraph was Toullier, 6 Droit Civil, Liv. III, Tit.
III, Chap. III, Sec. IV, s III, n. 293 (305 seq.) and Domat, I Loix Civiles, Part. I, Liv. III, Tit. V, Sec.
II, ns. XI, XII (270). Batiza, The Actual Sources of the Louisiana Project of 1823: A General Analytical Survey, 47 Tul.L.Rev. 1, 80 (1972). Neither of these sources, however, contained the precise idea
contained in 1934(3), although Domat does include a passage suggestive of the principle incorporated in 1934(3). See 48 Tul.L.Rev., Supra at 1173.
7. I A General Digest of the Acts of the Legislature of Louisiana passed from the year 1804, to
1827, Inclusive 223 (1928); See generally Dainow, The Louisiana Civil Law, in Civil Code of Louisiana
(Dainow ed., 1961).
8. 48 Tul.L.Rev., supra at 1174.

'When the contract has for its object to confer to someone a purely intellectual   103
enjoyment, such as those pertaining to religion, morality, taste, convenience or   104
other gratifications of this sort,....'[9]   105

The foregoing French article was mistranslated to read in the English version of Arti-   106
cle 1928 of the Louisiana Civil Code of 1825, as follows: 107

'Where the contract has for its object the gratification of some intellectual   108
enjoyment, whether in religion, morality, or taste, or some convenience or other   109
legal gratification,....'   110

The English passage was copied verbatim into the Code of 1870.[10] Thus we conclude 111
that the clause should, as it may, logically, be read as follows: Where the contract has for   112
its object the gratification of intellectual enjoyment, such as that pertaining to religion,   113
or morality, or taste, or convenience,....   114

It is evident that the proper interpretation of Article 1934(3), is not, as plaintiff con-   115
tends, that nonpecuniary damages are allowable where the object is exclusively physical   116
gratification. On the contrary, 'convenience' in the source provision was not a contract   117
object triggering the availability of nonpecuniary damages, but was, rather, along with re-   118
ligion, morality, and taste, one example of 'purely intellectual enjoyment,' the intellec-   119
tual enjoyment being necessary as a contract's object before nonpecuniary damages became   120
available.   121

We find the French source provision of 1934(3) in the 1825 Louisiana Civil Code, if   122
not controlling, at least persuasive in our present interpretation of the article's ambigu-   123
ous counterpart in our 1870 Civil Code. While the foregoing interpretation does not allow   124
nonpecuniary damages where the sole object is physical gratification, a proper interpre-   125
tation of the entirety of Article 1934(3) does not in our view bar such damages in all in-   126
stances where there exists as An object physical gratification. We believe that a contract   127
can have 'for its object' intellectual enjoyment, assuming that intellectual enjoyment is a   128
Principal object of the contract, notwithstanding that a peripheral, or incidental, or even   129
perhaps concurrent object of the contract may be physical gratification.   130

Thus, we would interpret Article 1934(3) as follows: Where an object, or the exclu-   131
sive object, of a contract, is physical gratification (or anything other than intellectual grat-   132
ification) nonpecuniary damages as a consequence of nonfulfillment of that object are   133
not recoverable.   134

On the other hand, where a principal or exclusive object of a contract is intellectual   135
enjoyment, nonpecuniary damages resulting from the nonfulfillment of that intellectual   136

---

9. While the disjunctive 'or' prefacing 'some convenience' or other legal gratification might arguably suggest that nonpecuniary damages are allowed 'where the contract has for its object the gratification' of 'some convenience,' the ambiguity in the language of the paragraph becomes apparent
when article 1934 is read in its entirety and in conjunction with article 1926. Article 1926 provides
that in breach of contract cases damages may be given 'according to the rules established in the following section.' Article 1934 appears in the following section of the Code. It provides at the outset that
with an exception not here relevant damages due for breach of contract are the amounts of loss and
deprived profits, except for exceptions and modifications related thereafter in three numbered paragraphs. The third numbered paragraph recites the general rule, and then there appears the exception
which employs the language here at issue. See Footnote 1, second sentence of the quoted article
1934(3). If that sentence were intended to allow nonpecuniary damages where a contract has for its
object 'some' (virtually every contract of which we can conceive) convenience there would be no sense
to the outset language of article 1934 limiting damage to losses sustained and profits of which deprived as a general proposition.

10. Only the comma after 'morality' was deleted in the version of the passage in the 1870 Code.

object Are recoverable. Damages in this event are recoverable for the loss of such intellectual enjoyment as well as for mental distress, aggravation, and inconvenience resulting from such loss, or denial of intellectual enjoyment.

The foregoing principles are not at variance with the results obtained in the cases of Lewis v. Holmes, supra, O'Meallie v. Moreau, supra, and Jiles v. Venus Community Center Benevolent Mutual Aid Assn., supra.

Applying these principles to the case at hand, we conclude that plaintiff is not entitled to recover damages for aggravation, distress, and inconvenience caused by the five month loss of use of her automobile, because the procuring of intellectual enjoyment, while perhaps an incidental or inferred contemplation of the contracting parties, was not a principal object of the contract to have the car repaired. The principal object of the contract, the overriding concern of plaintiff, evident to defendant at the time the contract was entered into, was the repair of plaintiff's automobile with its consequent utility or physical gratification.

As noted, we clearly do not hold that the object of a contract must be exclusively intellectual enjoyment in order to trigger article 1934(3)'s nonpecuniary damages. We do hold, however, that such intellectual enjoyment must be a principal object of the contract, and that nonpecuniary damages, when allowed, are limited to those which compensate for, or are directly related to, nonfulfillment of the intellectual object.

We also deem it worth noting, however fundamental, that unlike the rule which we are required by the Civil Code to apply in this action for breach of contract, damages for mental anguish, aggravation, distress and inconvenience, are recoverable in an action sounding in tort. La.Civil Code art. 2315; 2 M. Planiol, Traite elementaire de droit civil, no. 252 at 152 (11th ed., La.State L.Inst.tranl.1959); 48 Tul.L.Rev., Supra at 1171.

Perhaps it would be better if damages for mental anguish in breach of contract cases were allowable just as in tort actions. However, such a matter directs itself to the law maker. Our responsibility is to interpret and apply the law, not to enact it.

For the foregoing reasons, the judgment of the Court of Appeal is affirmed. All costs of this appeal are chargeable to the plaintiff.

MARCUS, J., assigns additional concurring reasons.

DIXON, J., dissents with reasons.

MARCUS, Justice (assigning additional concurring reasons).

While I join in the majority opinion, in my view, damages are not awardable for annoyance and emotional distress in breach of contract cases unless the gratification of purely intellectual enjoyment is The principal object of the contract. Where only an incidental or concurrent object of the contract is the gratification of purely intellectual enjoyment, damages for annoyance and emotional distress are not recoverable.

DIXON, Justice (dissenting).

I respectfully dissent. We should not deny recovery for damages which are suffered, for which justice requires compensation, for the rather superficial reason that plaintiff's action is in contract, not tort. Nevertheless, even considering this a contract action, these damages are recoverable under the plain terms of C.C. 1934(1).

When plaintiff brought her vehicle to defendant for repairs, she had the right to expect that the repairs be completed within a reasonable time. They were not. As a result, not only did she suffer pecuniary loss, but also the aggravation of not having her car, the distress of not knowing when she would get it back, and finally the inconvenience of hav-

ing to find other methods of getting around. In a society as dependent on the automo-   183
bile as ours, where a car is not only a convenience but often a necessity, a plaintiff should   184
be able to recover damages representing the aggravation, distress and inconvenience suf-   185
fered when the repairman breaches his duty to fix the car within a reasonable time. Such   186
damages are reasonably within the contemplation of the parties at the time the contract   187
was entered into, and are therefore compensable. C.C. 1934(1).   188

This court has consistently awarded damages for mental anguish and inconvenience in   189
tort suits where property damage is sustained. In Dodd v. Glen Rose Gasoline Co., 194   190
La. 1, 193 So. 349 (1939), in which defendant's plant operated in a manner that prevented   191
plaintiff from getting a good night's sleep, this court awarded damages for inconvenience   192
and discomfort. In McGee v. Yazoo & M.V.R. Co., 206 La. 121, 19 So.2d 21 (1944), this   193
court awarded damages for mental anguish, worry and inconvenience caused by the de-   194
positing of soot, smoke and cinders into plaintiffs' houses by defendant's roundhouse   195
operation. In Fontenot v. Magnolia Petroleum Co., 227 La. 866, 80 So.2d 845 (1955), we   196
awarded damages for inconvenience and mental anguish suffered by plaintiff as a result   197
of defendant's blasting operations.   198

There is no logical reason to allow recovery of such damages when property is in-   199
volved in cases delineated as 'tort,' and yet deny recovery of similar damages when   200
property is involved (as in this case), simply because the cause of action is delineated   201
as 'contract.' Both involve a duty and a breach. Louisiana employs fact pleading. A   202
plaintiff need only state facts, which, if true, authorize recovery. Cox v. W. M. Hero-   203
man & Co., 298 So.2d 848 (La.1974). In the instant case, plaintiff has proved, to the   204
satisfaction of the trier of fact, that she suffered inconvenience, distress and aggrava-   205
tion because of defendant's breach of duty. She should recover therefor. As Planiol   206
states:

'... The big objection is that mental suffering can not be compensated with money.   207
But that is done every day in the case of torts; why act differently in contract cases? There   208
is no reason for not doing so, and as M. Boistel has well said, just because one can not   209
do so better, is no reason for doing nothing at all.'[11]   210

Questions

1. After you have read the whole case, can you draw a (mental) picture of the two
    parties involved in the case? Are they alike? Do they have the same capacity? Do they
    have the same technical knowledge? Do they have the same negotiating ability? Do
    any of these questions matter as regards the formation of a contract, the nature of the
    obligations created, and their performance? What about with regard to the remedies
    in case of breach of contract by one party or the other?

2. Lines 43–142: What is the major issue discussed by the Court? In this respect, read
    carefully the Court's analysis of former Louisiana Civil Code article 1934. What les-
    son should you learn about the translation of legal documents on the one hand,
    and the role of history on the other hand? Can comparative law be of any help?
    What role did the cases play in giving a meaning to former Louisiana Civil Code ar-
    ticle 1934? Which one of the three possible interpretations of Louisiana Civil Code
    article 1934 does the Court adopt as its interpretation? (*See* lines 131–134.) Is it
    clear to you?

---

11. 2 M. Planiol, Traité Elémentaire de Droit Civil No. 252 (11th ed. La.State L.Inst.Trans. (1959)).

3. Lines 143 *et seq.*: Can you restate the principles to which the Court is referring? In the Court's statement starting with "Applying these principles ... [to] ... physical gratification" is there any suggestion that the Court might use an objective standard or a subjective standard of this notion of intellectual enjoyment? In the next paragraph starting with "As noted ..." is the Court giving any indication as to the process that should be used by a Court to ascertain whether and how "such an intellectual enjoyment must be a principal object of the contract...."? In light of Question 1, could the kinds of persons involved in a contract, the age and ability of one party or the other, the type of transaction entered into (a sale rather than a lease), the particular cause of the obligation of one party, have some impact on the principal object of the contract, rending it more intellectual enjoyment for one party than for the other?

4. Lines 161 *et seq.*: What do you think of the distinction the Court makes between mental anguish in tort as opposed to contract? Is the notion of mental anguish a purely legal question confined to the type of action brought (tort v. contract)? Or is it rather a human element that becomes a part of any legal transaction in which a person is involved? Why should Ms. Meador (young and buying her first car to go to work) be granted moral damages in a tort action and not in a contract action? Wasn't Ms. Meador in good faith all through her ordeal? Can you say the same thing about the Toyota Dealership? Shouldn't the Court have made an issue of "good faith" (*see* La. Civ. Code art. 1759)? What do you think of Justice Dixon's dissenting opinion?

Brenda BOURNE

v.

REIN CHRYSLER-PLYMOUTH, INC. and Chrysler Corporation

Louisiana Court of Appeal

First Circuit

Dec. 28, 1984

463 So.2d 1356

JOHN S. COVINGTON, Judge pro tempore:

This is a suit for reduction of the purchase price of an automobile. Judgment was rendered against Chrysler Corporation, the manufacturer, and it appealed[.] [....]

[....]

ASSIGNMENTS OF ERROR

Defendant-appellant, Chrysler Corporation (Chrysler), assigns as error [...] by the District Court [**among others**] [...] the awarding of damages for inconvenience and mental anguish "which is clearly not recoverable in this type of action" [....]

ISSUES

The issue [...] presented for our resolution [is] [...] whether damages for inconvenience and mental anguish were properly awarded under the facts peculiar to the instant case [....]

FACTS

Brenda Bourne purchased a new 1981 Chrysler Cordoba automobile on February 27, 1981 from defendant Rein Chrysler-Plymouth, Inc. (Rein), for a total deferred sales price of $14,641.85. Rein's salesman did not disclose to Ms. Bourne that the automobile had

any mechanical defects which would render it "either absolutely useless, or its use so in- 24
convenient and imperfect" to give rise to the legal presumption that she "would not have 25
purchased it" if she had "known of the vice." C.C. art. 2520. Ms. Bourne accepted de- 26
livery of the car on Friday, February 27, 1981 after Rein's service department had closed 27
for the weekend. While enroute to her home, immediately after accepting delivery, Ms. 28
Bourne noticed the sluggish performance of the motor. During the weekend the engine 29
"died" several times while Ms. Bourne was driving so she took the vehicle to the service 30
department on Monday morning so that Rein's service technicians could resolve the en- 31
gine stalling problem but they did not attempt any repairs that day. She returned the 32
next day and was informed to bring the car back on Thursday because that would be the 33
earliest time the repairs could be made. Between Tuesday morning and Thursday morn- 34
ing, when she returned the car to the service department as instructed, the horn was ac- 35
tivated spontaneously and had to be disconnected to silence it. The technicians set the 36
timing so high the car "would get away from" Ms. Bourne and she was frightened by its 37
engine racing tendencies. After the horn was "fixed" on Thursday it did not function at 38
all. The malfunctioning headlights were also repaired at that time. Within a few days 39
after Ms. Bourne bought the car a part of the console and the door panel fell off and 40
had to be reglued. During the second week following the date of the purchase the vinyl 41
roof "was starting to bubble" so Ms. Bourne returned the car to the service department 42
where it remained two days because of the many problems to be dealt with. During that 43
two day stay at Rein's the timing was reset but after the resetting the car began stalling 44
out again.

From the very outset the cruise control never functioned. Early in April, 1981 the air 45
pollution pump became partially disconnected and it drilled a hole through the sheet 46
metal of the hood. About one month later the air pollution pump and pulley assembly 47
were replaced but the hole in the hood was not repaired. Late in June, 1981 the air con- 48
ditioner malfunctioned while Ms. Bourne was driving to New Orleans from Ponchatoula 49
and "all of a sudden the water came pouring in over" her feet; the water was coming from 50
"in the front under the dash" and even after she turned off the air conditioner "it still 51
kept coming"; the water flooded the interior of the car to a depth "up past the shoe". The 52
flooding ruined the carpet and resulted in an offensive odor which did not dissipate dur- 53
ing the two months Ms. Bourne ceased driving the car because Rein refused to replace the 54
carpet and because she was "already terrified of the car because of the pump" disengag- 55
ing and drilling a hole in the hood. 56

Chrysler issued three recall notices requesting owners of 1981 Chrysler Cordobas to take 57
their autos to the dealers to correct specified mechanical problems, including engine slug- 58
gishness and the pump. 59

The increasing frequency of taking the automobile to Rein for mechanical corrections 60
made her the butt of much laughter and unkind jokes by Rein's service personnel and 61
some other personnel. The many returns for repairs, with repeated failures in her endeavor 62
to have the vehicle so it would provide her safe and reliable transportation, caused Ms. 63
Bourne to suffer great embarrassment, humiliation, and inconvenience from the day she 64
bought the car and accepted its delivery up to the time she stopped driving the car in early 65
July, 1981. She was afraid to drive the car because of its shabby and unsafe condition. 66

Although Ms. Bourne continued to pay the monthly installments to Chrysler Credit 67
Corporation (Chrysler Credit) and was not delinquent with them, Chrysler Credit filed 68
suit to seize and sell the car under executory process. Upon receipt of petition for the 69
writ of seizure and sale, Ms. Bourne retained counsel to enjoin both the seizure and sale 70
in order to preserve her credit reputation and undo some of the embarrassment and hu- 71

miliation she suffered when the car was seized at her work place. The executory proceedings damaged Ms. Bourne's credit and she paid cash for a used car.

[....] DAMAGES

[....]

Chrysler simply argues in its brief that the lower court committed reversible error by awarding plaintiff damages for mental anguish and inconvenience. Chrysler relies on *Meador v. Toyota of Jefferson, Inc.,* 332 So.2d 433 (La.1976) as authority for its premise that because the record is devoid of any suggestion that Ms. Bourne "purchased the vehicle for any type of intellectual enjoyment" the lower court improperly awarded her non-pecuniary damages in her quanti minoris action based on C.C. art. 2520 et seq.

Meador, supra, was not a suit for redhibition or quanti minoris. The litigation in *Meador* had its origin in defendant's alleged excessive delay in completing repairs to an automobile brought to defendant to repair collision damage. The contractual obligation undertaken by defendant in *Meador* was the obligation to repair the automobile in a workmanlike manner in as short a period as possible under the total facts and circumstances. The Supreme Court held that C.C. art. 1934(3), dealing with damages generally, precludes awarding non-pecuniary damages in a breach of contract context unless intellectual enjoyment is a principal object of the contract, and that non-pecuniary damages, when allowed, are limited to those which compensate for, or are directly related to, non-fulfillment of the intellectual object.

The *Meador* rule is no longer applied inflexibly in contract actions. *Gele v. Markey,* 387 So.2d 1162 (La.1980); *Pike v. Stephens Imports, Inc.,* 448 So.2d 738, 743 (La.App. 4th Cir.1984).

Philippe v. Browning Arms Co., 395 So.2d 310, 318 (La.1981), on rehearing, stated the duty of a manufacturer as being "the obligation to produce a product which is reasonably safe for its intended use" and that "[b]reach of this obligation gives rise to a cause of action in favor of the purchaser of the product not only to demand the return of the purchase price, but also, because the manufacturer is presumed to know of defects in its products, to demand all damages caused by the defect and reasonable attorney's fees."

The court, in *Philippe,* supra, reasoned that "[t]here is no compelling reason to require a person injured by a defective product he has purchased to proceed either in contract or in tort. The seller's (manufacturer's) act of delivering a defective thing, when he knows of the defect, gives rise to delictual, as well as contractual, liability. (citations omitted)." The Supreme Court, per Lemmon, J., held "that the right and the extent of recovery by the purchaser of a thing against the seller or manufacturer is governed by the codal articles providing for responsibility in the seller-purchaser relationship, as applied through C.C. art. 2315. Since C.C. art. 2545 clearly provides for recovery of damages caused by a defective product and for reasonable attorney's fees, we conclude the court of appeal correctly made such award."

In reaching the conclusion stated above, the court in *Philippe* reasoned that: "The appropriate standard of conduct in this case is derived from the codal articles on sales, since the cause of action of the purchaser of a defective thing may be enforced against both the seller and the manufacturer of a thing"; "[o]ne of the obligations imposed on the seller (manufacturer) is the warranty against hidden defects of the thing sold"; and the manufacturer, imputed with knowledge of defects in his products, is liable not only for the return of the price and the expenses of the sale, but "also (is) answerable for damages and reasonable attorney's fees." *Philippe,* supra, at 318.

Philippe v. Browning Arms Co., supra, in our opinion, is authority for the proposition   119
that the purchaser who sustains damages because he or she purchased a redhibitorily de-   120
fective product is entitled to be compensated for all provable damages, including incon-   121
venience and mental anguish, if the causation link is established. *Philippe,* supra, mandates   122
judicial repudiation of the blanket exclusion of damages for inconvenience and mental an-   123
guish in redhibition and quanti minoris actions. To knowingly sell a redhibitorily defec-   124
tive product, such knowledge being imputed to a manufacturer, is to do a tortious act. It   125
is well settled that a tortfeasor's victim who sustains mental anguish as a result of the ac-   126
tion or inaction of the tortfeasor is entitled to be compensated for it.   127

While the Trial Judge did not assign detailed written reasons, he obviously believed   128
that plaintiff's uncontradicted evidence established that plaintiff in fact suffered mental   129
anguish, in addition to considerable inconvenience, because of the multiplicity of vices   130
or defects cumulatively constituting grounds for redhibition, which were never resolved   131
satisfactorily enough to defeat plaintiff's suit for quanti minoris. Factual conclusions of   132
a trier of fact are entitled to great weight and should not be disturbed on review absent   133
manifest error, especially when based on evaluation of credibility of live testimony. *Arce-*   134
neaux v. Domingue, 365 So.2d 1330 (La.1978). We have concluded that the obvious find-   135
ings of fact made by the lower court are supported by the record; his findings therefore   136
are not clearly wrong.   137

[....]

Questions

1. Lines 9–73: Do you think that there was any purpose in the Court giving such a de-
    tailed presentation of the facts of this case? Remember the *Meador* case? Do you see
    any difference with this case and the Court's focus here on one party, Ms. Bourne as
    buyer, as Ms. Meador was the buyer of the Toyota? Is the fact that Ms. Bourne was
    buying a new car of any significance? How would you describe the seller's behavior?
    Would you make any reference to good faith or bad faith? Could it be relevant in
    computing the amount of damages? Could there be fraud on the part of the dealer-
    ship? Read Louisiana Civil Code articles 2520, 2524 and 2545.

2. Lines 67–73: Would you say that Chrysler Credit Corporation made a lawful use of
    its rights under Louisiana Civil Code article 1962 or that it abused its rights?

3. Lines 76–137: In what respects is this Court distancing itself from the *Meador* Court?
    Is a difference between a delay in performing services resulting in mental anguish
    and inconvenience and the occurrence of defects in a thing sold resulting in men-
    tal anguish and inconvenience sufficient to justify a difference in the outcome of
    the respective legal actions? Aren't both actions concerned with non-performance
    or bad performance of obligations? *See* La. Civ. Code arts. 1994–1998. What do
    you think of the *Philippe v. Browning Arms* case particularly where it states: "There
    is no compelling reason...."? What do you think of this Court saying: "Philippe
    mandates judicial repudiation of the blanket exclusion of damages for inconve-
    nience ... actions"? (*See* lines 122–127.) Is the Court saying that whatever the cause
    or source of the damage, it is all a matter of tort? Could that classification of the
    cause of action have an impact on the length of the prescriptive period applicable
    to one action and not to the other? (*See* La. Civ. Code arts. 3492 and 3499.) Did the
    Philippe Court create law or did it merely interpret the law as written in the Louisiana
    Civil Code articles?

The KROGER COMPANY

v.

L.G. BARCUS & SONS, INC., et al.

Louisiana Court of Appeal
Second Circuit
June 17, 2009
13 So.3d 1232

WILLIAMS, J.

The plaintiff, The Kroger Company ("Kroger"), appeals a judgment in favor of the defendant, SCA Consulting Engineers, Inc. ("SCA"). The district court found that plaintiff's claim against defendant arising from the attempted repair of the building was based in tort and had prescribed. For the following reasons, we affirm.

FACTS

This matter arises out of a lawsuit filed by Kroger against numerous defendants, seeking damages caused by settlement of the foundation and floor of the Kroger store located on Youree Drive in Shreveport, Louisiana. The defendants included L.G. Barcus & Sons, Inc. ("Barcus"), which drilled and poured the auger cast piles, Professional Services, Inc. ("PSI"), the project geotechnical engineer, Travelers Casualty and Surety Company and St. Paul Fire & Marine Insurance Company, the insurers of the bankrupt contractor, Whitaker Construction Company, and SCA.

In its original petition filed in October 2002, Kroger alleged that the store's foundation was designed and constructed in 1996 and 1997 and that the store opened for business in 1997. Kroger further alleged that SCA's foundation design and specifications were substandard and inadequate, resulting in the cast piles not being installed to the correct depth. This allegation is referred to as the "design phase" claim. The petition also asserted that after the initial settling of the store, Kroger requested that SCA make recommendations to remedy the settlement problem, but the attempts at remediation had not been successful.

More than three years later, in March 2006, Kroger filed an amended petition reiterating the design phase allegations of the original petition and asserting a "repair phase" claim against SCA and another defendant, Hayward Baker, Inc. Specifically, in paragraphs 25, 26 and 27 of the amended petition, Kroger alleged that following completion of the original construction, Kroger retained the services of SCA to remedy the settlement problem, but that the engineering services provided by SCA were "ineffective, performed negligently, and their implementation caused additional damages to the Kroger Store."

Subsequently, SCA filed a motion for summary judgment on the grounds that the plaintiff's claims had prescribed. The district court rendered judgment granting in part the motion for summary judgment, dismissing plaintiff's design phase claims against SCA as prescribed, but denying summary judgment as to plaintiff's repair phase claims. Kroger appealed the judgment, which was affirmed by this court in *The Kroger Company v. L.G. Barcus & Sons, Inc.*, 43,804 (La.App. 2d Cir.1/14/09), 2 So.3d 1163, *writ denied*, 09-0382 (La.5/15/09), 8 So.3d 571.

In April 2008, while the appeal was pending, SCA filed an exception of prescription seeking dismissal of Kroger's repair phase claim. In response, Kroger asserted that its claim did not sound in tort, but in contract, and was thus subject to a ten-year prescriptive period. SCA argued that Kroger's claim was delictual and had prescribed, since the claim was not filed within the applicable one-year prescriptive period. After a hearing, the district court found that Kroger's claim was based on negligence and subject to the one-year prescriptive period. The court rendered judgment sustaining SCA's exception and dismissing Kroger's claims. Kroger appeals the judgment.

DISCUSSION

Kroger contends the district court erred in sustaining the exception of prescription. Kroger argues that the applicable prescriptive period is ten years because the dispute with SCA is based on the parties' contract.

Delictual actions are subject to a liberative prescription of one year, running from the day injury or damage is sustained. LSA-C.C. art. 3492. An action on a contract is governed by the prescriptive period of ten years for personal actions. LSA-C.C. art. 3499. The nature of the duty breached determines whether an action is in tort or contract. *Roger v. Dufrene*, 613 So.2d 947 (La.1993); *Trinity Universal Insurance Co. v. Horton*, 33,157 (La.App. 2d Cir.4/5/00), 756 So.2d 637. The distinction between damages *ex contractu* and damages *ex delicto* is that the former flow from the breach of a special obligation contractually assumed by the obligor, whereas the latter flow from the violation of a general duty owed to all persons. Even when a tortfeasor and victim are bound by a contract, courts usually apply the delictual prescription to actions that are actually grounded in tort. *Trinity, supra; Harrison v. Gore*, 27,254 (La.App. 2d Cir.8/23/95), 660 So.2d 563, *writ denied*, 95-2347 (La.12/8/95), 664 So.2d 426.

The mere fact that the circumstances arose in the context of a contractual relationship does not make the cause of action contractual. The courts are not bound to accept a plaintiff's characterization of the nature of his cause of action if unsupported by factual allegations. *Thomas v. State Employees Group Benefits Program*, 05-0392 (La.App. 1st Cir.3/24/06), 934 So.2d 753.

In this case, the alleged repair contract includes a writing drafted by SCA, dated October 10, 2001, stating in part: "SCOPE OF WORK: Field observation to observe possible foundation movements and negative drainage on an existing Kroger Food Store." Kroger also points to an outline prepared by SCA that proposed measures to strengthen the cast piles as forming part of the contract for services. We will assume the existence of a repair contract as alleged for the purpose of reviewing whether Kroger's claim has prescribed.

In its amended petition, Kroger does not allege that a specific contract provision was breached, but that SCA's services were ineffective and negligently performed. Thus, Kroger's petition states a cause of action for breach of a person's general duty to perform repair work in a non-negligent, prudent and skillful manner. *See* LSA-C.C. art. 2316. Liability for breach of this duty arises *ex delicto*. *Trinity, supra; K & M Enterprises of Slaughter, Inc. v. Richland Equipment Company, Inc.*, 96-2292 (La.App. 1st Cir.9/19/97), 700 So.2d 921. Accordingly, the district court was correct in finding that Kroger's cause of action was in tort and subject to the one-year liberative prescriptive period of Article 3492.

[....]

CONCLUSION

For the foregoing reasons, the district court's judgment sustaining SCA's exception of prescription is affirmed. The costs of this appeal are assessed to the appellant, The Kroger Company.

AFFIRMED.

BROWN, Chief Judge, dissents with written reasons.

93   BROWN, Chief Judge, Dissenting.

94   All personal actions, including actions to enforce contractual obligations, are subject
95   to a liberative prescription of ten years unless otherwise provided by legislation. La. C.C.
96   art. 3499. La. R.S. 9:5607 now provides for a five-year liberative prescriptive/peremptive
97   period in all actions, tort or contract, against, *inter alia*, professional engineers. This pro-
98   vision, however, was added by Acts 2003, No. 854, 51, and is therefore inapplicable to
99   the instant case. Delictual actions are subject to a liberative prescription of one year, run-
100   ning from the day injury or damage is sustained. La. C.C. art. 3492. Proper characteri-
101   zation of the nature of Kroger's cause of action is crucial to determination of the issue before
102   this court.

103   *In re St. Louis Encephalitis Outbreak in Ouachita Parish,* 41,250 (La.App. 2d Cir.09/01/
104   06), 939 So.2d 563, this court observed that it is well settled that the same acts or omis-
105   sions may constitute breaches of both general duties and contractual duties and may give
106   rise to both actions in tort and actions in contract. A plaintiff may assert both actions
107   and is not required to plead the theory of his case. *Dubin v. Dubin,* 25,996 (La.App. 2d
108   Cir.08/17/94), 641 So.2d 1036. When a person negligently performs a contractual oblig-
109   ation, he has committed an active breach of contract which may also support an action
110   in tort. *Id.*

111   In *Cameron v. Bruce,* 42,873 (La.App. 2d Cir.04/23/08), 981 So.2d 204, 207, *writ de-*
112   *nied,* 2008-1127 (La.09/19/08), 992 So.2d 940, we stated:

113   A home inspector has a duty to exercise reasonable care and skill in his under-
114   taking. A breach of that duty constitutes a tort as well as a breach of contract. One
115   has a prescriptive period of one year from date of injury and the other is subject
116   to a liberative prescriptive period of ten years. In medical and legal malpractice
117   as well as in products liability cases, the legislature has acted to reclassify the
118   wrongful act to impose the shorter prescriptive period. The amendment to the
119   petition adding Con-Claire as a defendant was within the ten-year prescriptive
120   period applicable to contract claims.

121   Kroger retained the professional engineering services of SCA in October 2001 to ad-
122   dress the settlement problem its Bayou Walk store was experiencing. The parties entered
123   into a three-page contract agreement drafted by SCA dated October 10, 2001, which out-
124   lined SCA's scope of work, fee, additional services, as well as additional general terms and
125   conditions such as provisions for site access, indemnification, risk allocation, and termi-
126   nation of services. The record also contains evidence of a verbal agreement for changes
127   in scope of work and/or revisions to drawings and specifications, as well as an outline/
128   proposal prepared by SCA regarding additional work.

129   Kroger alleged that SCA's services were ineffective, performed negligently, and that
130   their implementation caused additional damage to Kroger's store. This is an allegation
131   of a breach of a contractual duty. As such the ten-year prescriptive period applies.

132   As to the *ex delicto* claim, an amending petition relates back to an original petition
133   when the action asserted in the amending petition arises out of the conduct, transaction
134   or occurrence set forth or attempted to be set forth in the original petition. La. C.C.P.
135   art. 1153; *Reese v. State, Dept. of Public Safety and Corrections,* 03-1615 (La.02/20/04),
136   866 So.2d 244. Kroger's "design phase" claim, filed on October 18, 2002, provided alle-
137   gations that gave SCA fair notice of Kroger's cause of action for negligence arising out of
138   professional services performed by SCA during the "repair phase." In that 2002 petition,
139   Kroger asserted that, upon discovery of the initial settlement, requests were made in 2001
140   and 2002 upon the general contractor and SCA to address, remedy, and make recom-

mendations concerning the problem. Kroger sought damages in this 2002 petition for, among other things, the costs of repairs and remediation occurring in 2001 and 2002 of approximately $1,895,000.

In its original petition, filed on October 18, 2002, Kroger did more than, as defendant has argued, "indicate its awareness" that SCA's repair attempts in 2001 and 2002 had been unsuccessful. As this claim was asserted within the applicable one-year prescriptive period, it is deemed to have been filed timely. The amending petition filed by plaintiff on March 30, 2006, stated in greater detail allegations related to Kroger's "repair phase" claim against SCA, and therefore relates back to the filing date of the original petition inasmuch as it arises out of the same factual situation as that set forth in the original petition, i.e., that plaintiff has sustained damage as a result of negligence on the part of SCA during the "repair phase."

[....]

Questions

1. This case is particularly interesting in that it makes a very clear and well justified distinction between two types of action which have in common a breach of an obligation (*see* statements on lines 55–66). Considering that obligations can arise from different sources of law, do you see any major legal reason(s) in making the distinction that the court makes? Is there any reason based on prescription? See, in this respect, the sentence on lines 76–77 and La. Civ. Code arts. 3492 and 3499. What about the burden of proof? What about the types of damages?

2. Lines 67–71: How do you read these two statements in light of the rule of law which states that a contract has the force of law for the parties (*see* La. Civ. Code art. 1983)?

3. Lines 78–85: How logical/well-grounded legally are these statements? How can the court refer to services and the duty to perform repair work in a non-negligent, prudent and skillful manner and quote only a Louisiana Civil Code article from the law of torts (La. Civ. Code art. 2316) when Louisiana Civil Code articles 2762 and 2769 could have applied just as well, if not better, because of the court assuming the existence of a repair contract?

4. Lines 84–85: Would prescription have run had the court found the cause of action for the failure to repair in a contract for repair or "other works by the Job" (*see* La. Civ. Code arts. 2756–2777)? What about Louisiana Civil Code article 1994?

5. Contrast the majority opinion with chief judge Brown's dissenting opinion. Do you see any substantial difference? Which opinion appears to you to be more logical and better grounded in law?

See also *Chaudoir v. Porsche Cars of North America, et al.*, 667 So.2d 1995 (La. 3rd Cir. 1995).

Comparative Law Perspective

Alain Levasseur, COMPARATIVE LAW OF CONTRACTS
125–45 (2008)

Performance—Damages

"[...] [C]ourts in civilian legal systems, routinely grant specific performance by ordering parties to perform their contracts. But courts in common law systems, for reasons that are largely historical, regard specific performance as an "extraordinary" remedy, to be granted only when an award of damages would not be "adequate". (I might add here that we Americans sometimes rationalize the denial of specific performance on the ground that this permits a party to a contract to commit an 'efficient breach', but that concept of law and economics is one that not only does not travel well, but that struck most of my civilian colleagues as bordering on the immoral.) [E. Allan Farnsworth, A common lawyer's view of his civilian colleagues, 57 La.L.Rev.227, at 235.]

"[...] The consequences of a binding promise at common law are not affected by the degree of power which the promisor possesses over the promised event. If the promised event does not come to pass, the plaintiff's property is sold to satisfy the damages, with certain limits, which the promisee has suffered by the failure. The consequences are the same in kind whether the promise is that it shall rain, or that another man shall paint a picture, or that the promisor will deliver a bale of cotton. If the legal consequence is the same in all cases, it seems proper that all contracts should be considered from the same legal point of view.... If it be proper to state the common law meaning of promise and contract in this way, it has the advantage of freeing the subject from the superfluous theory that contract is a qualified subjection of one will to another, a kind of limited slavery. It might so regarded if the law compelled men to perform their contracts, of if it allowed promisees to exercise such compulsion ... It is true that in some instances equity does what is called compelling specific performance. But, in the first place, I am speaking of the common law, and, in the next, this only means that equity compels the performance of certain elements of the total promise which are still capable of performance ... The only universal consequence of a legally binding promise is, that the law makes the promisor pay damages if the promised event does not come to pass. In every case it leaves him free from interference until the time for fulfillment has gone by, and therefore free to break his contract if he chooses ... [O.W. Holmes, Jr., The Common Law, 1881 at 299 et seq.] ...

"[In an American law school ...]. We are trained to find ways of getting around or out of contracts, and, as lawyers, we occasionally even counsel clients to breach them. Civil lawyers, on the other hand, are much more committed to elaborating a legal mechanism to enforce as precisely as possible those promises that are actually made and intended. This part of their law is more systematized and coherent than is ours. These differences suggest that more is at stake than simply deciding where a particular loss should fall.

"Civilians justify their system by reference to the maxim *pacta sunt servanda*. This "basic and it seems universally accepted principle of contract law" means, in the civil law, that promises are binding ... As René David has explained, "the principle satisfies our philosophical and moral views; it is proper for individuals to be bound by their promises."... To the civilian mind, the maxim is entirely self-evident ... René David believed the proper translation to be this: "commitments that have been made must be performed."... American courts, however, generally adopt a translation that applies the maxim only to agreements: "agreements must be obeyed" ... ; "agreements must be respected" ... ; "agreements must be observed" ... [Richard Hyland, *Pacta Sunt Servanda*: A Meditation, 34 Va. J. Int. L. 405 et seq.]

"[...] The binding nature of a promise is of utmost importance to the civil law, and the courts accordingly bind individuals to their promises ... As Professors Flour and Aubert write ...'morality dominates civilian contract law. They state unequivocally that "the legal obligation incumbent on the contracting party to perform is none other than the moral duty to honor one's word, once given. The civilian focus on morality contrasts with the common law's concern for efficiency as the primary priority....

"This moral conception was translated into the civil codes of Europe by making specific performance the normal remedy for breach of contract, and monetary damages the exception, in contradistinction to the common law system of monetary remedies as the norm and specific performance as the exception...." [Comparative Law, An Introduction, Vivian Grosswald Curran, Carolina Academic Press 2002 p. 25-26].

Performance—Damages in civil law

See La. Civ. C. Aricles: 1756, 1983, 1986, 1989, 1994–1998, 2002

Fr.Civ.C.

Art.1134: Conventions legally formed.... must be performed in good faith.

Art. 1136: The obligation to give carries with it the obligation to deliver the thing and to preserve it until delivery, under the penalty to have to pay damages to the creditor.

Art.1138: The obligation to deliver is perfected by the mere exchange of consent between the contracting parties. The creditor becomes the owner of the thing ...

Art.1142: Any obligation to do or not to do, in case of non-performance by the obligor, is transformed into an obligation to pay damages.

Art. 1144: The creditor may also, in case of non-performance, be authorized to have the obligation performed on his own at the expense of the obligor.

Art. 1146: Damages are due only after the obligor has been put in default to perform his obligation, except when the thing the obligor was bound to give or do could only be carried out within a certain time that has expired.

Art. 1149: Damages owed the obligee are, in general, in an amount equal to the loss incurred and the gain of which he has been deprived, unless one of the following exceptions apply.

BGB

Section 242. The obligor must perform in a manner consistent with good faith taking into account common usage.

Section 241. (1) By virtue of the obligation the obligee is entitled to demand performance from the obligor. The performance may also consist of an omission.

Section 249. (1) Anyone liable in damages must restore the condition that would exist if the circumstance obliging him to pay damages had not occurred.

Section 252. The damage to be compensated also comprises the lost profits. Those profits are considered lost that in the normal course of events ... could in all probability be expected.

C. C. Q.

Art. 1590: An obligation confers on the creditor the right to demand that the obligation be performed in full, properly and without delay.

Where the debtor fails to perform his obligation without justification on his part and he is in default, the creditor may, without prejudice to his right to the performance of the obligation in whole or in part by equivalence, (1) force specific performance of the obligation; (2) obtain, ... (3) take any other measure provided by law to enforce his right to the performance of the obligation.

Art. 1601: A creditor may, in cases which admit of it, demand that the debtor be forced to make specific performance of the obligation.

Art. 1602: In case of default, the creditor may perform the obligation or cause it to be performed at the expense of the debtor....

Art. 1607: The creditor is entitled to damages for bodily, moral or material injury which is an immediate and direct consequence of the debtor's default.

Art. 1611: The damages due to the creditor compensate for the amount of the loss he has sustained and the profit of which he has been deprived. Future injury which is certain and able to be assessed is taken into account in awarding damages.

Art. 1613: In contractual matters, the debtor is liable only for damages that were foreseen or foreseeable at the time the obligation was contracted, where the failure to perform the obligation does not proceed from intentional or gross fault on his part; even then, the damages include only what is an immediate and direct consequence of the nonperformance.

Philippe Malaurie, Laurent Aynès, Philippe Stoffel-Munck, Les Obligations, Defrénois 2003

§ 1. Specific performance of Obligations in kind

1. — Direct constraint

[...] English law does grant specific performance only in exceptional cases, because, in general, it infringes upon individual freedom.

On account of the difficulties raised by specific performance by means of direct constraint, French law devised different measures of indirect constraint, the only surviving one being 'astreinte' (a daily penalty for delay in performing).

1129 [...], In reality, it is impossible to have an obligation to do specifically enforced by public authorities, for fear of satisfying the private interest of the creditor at the expense of the debtor's freedom. It is only in the case of the transfer of ownership of a thing that the creditor may obtain specific performance by constraint: seize a movable, expulsion from a building ... In other cases, the creditor may be allowed to perform himself at the expense of the debtor ... (see Civ. C. art 1144) ... which suggests that the obligation is not *intuitus personae.*

1130 [Civ. C. Art.1142], this text is an application of the rule *nemo precise cogi ad factum* (which) protects one's individual freedom.... Specific performance in kind is denied today when it would offend a moral, material or legal impossibility. Either because of the personal nature of the obligation; thus, one could not specifically and forcefully compel an artist to carry out his obligation (a painting, for instance); or because one would face too many and major material obstacles; or because of a legal impossibility to enforce the obligation which would not otherwise prevent an 'equivalent' performance (damages, for example).

1131 [...] Anytime an obligation to do can be enforced by constraint, performance in kind must be ordered. Thus, a buyer should be compelled to take delivery of the thing sold to him and delivered by the seller; ... a tenant who refuses to leave the premises at the end of the lease can be expelled; ...

2. — Astreinte

1132. **Indirect but effective.** — Astreinte ... targets the debtor's wallet to compel him to perform. Astreinte has for its purpose the execution of a judicial decision of which it is the accessory; the judge can, even of his own motion, sentence the debtor to pay a sum of money, for each day of delay in general; it is, therefore, in the interest of the debtor to perform as soon as possible.... Astreinte is 'personal' to the debtor in the sense that the debtor cannot pass it on to his sureties.

1134. Scope of application. Almost any court decision can have an astreinte attached to it, even when the object of the obligation is tainted with *intuitus personae* ... However very strictly personal obligations, such as an artist's obligation, cannot be enforced by way of an astreinte. (a capricious artist would act poorly under any constraint ...; damages are a better remedy ...)

1135.[...] Astreinte is different from damages and has for its main purpose to 'crush' the obligor's resistance to the court's decision; it is a kind of *contempt of Court*.

C. Performance—Damages in common Law

Restatement, 2d

§ 235. Effect of Performance as Discharge and of Non-Performance as Breach

(1) Full performance of a duty under a contract discharges the duty.

(2) When performance of a duty under a contract is due any non-performance is a breach.

§ 236. Claims for Damages for Total and for Partial Breach

(1) A claim for damages for total breach is one for damages based on all of the injured party's remaining rights to performance.

(2) A claim for damages for partial breach is one for damages based on only part of the injured party's remaining rights to performance.

§ 243. Effect of a Breach by Non-Performance as Giving Rise to a Claim for Damages for Total Breach

(1) With respect to performances to be exchanged under an exchange of promises, a breach by non-performance gives rise to a claim for damages for total breach only if it discharges the injured party's remaining duties to render such performance, other than a duty to render an agreed equivalent under § 240.

(2) Except as stated in Subsection (3), a breach by non-performance accompanied or followed by a repudiation gives rise to a claim for damages for total breach.

(3) Where at the time of the breach the only remaining duties of performance are those of the party in breach and are for the payment of money in installments not related to one another, his breach by non-performance as to less than the whole, whether or not accompanied or followed by a repudiation, does not give rise to a claim for damages for total breach.

(4) In any case other than those stated in the preceding subsections, a breach by non-performance gives rise to a claim for total breach only if it so substantially impairs the value of the contract to the injured party at the time of the breach that it is just in the circumstances to allow him to recover damages based on all his remaining rights to performance.

UCC

§ 2-703. Seller's Remedies in General.

... (2) If the buyer is in breach of contract the seller, to the extent provided for by this Act or other law, may:

(a) withhold delivery of such goods;

(h) recover damages for nonacceptance or repudiation under Section 2-708(1);

(i) recover lost profits ...

(k) obtain specific performance under Section 2-716;

(m) in other cases, recover damages in any manner that is reasonable under the circumstances.

§2-714. Buyer's Damages For Breach in Regard to Accepted Goods.

(1)The measure of damages for breach of warranty is the difference at the time an place of acceptance between the value of the goods accepted and the value they would have had if they had been as warranted, ...

§2-716 Specific Performance; Buyer's Right of Replevin.

(1) Specific performance may be decreed if the goods are unique or in other proper circumstances. In a contract other than a consumer contract, specific performance may be decreed if the parties have agreed to that remedy. However, even if the parties agree to specific performance, specific performance may not be decreed if the breaching party's sole remaining contractual obligation is the payment of money.

(2) The decree for specific performance may include such terms and conditions as to payment of the price, damages, or other relief as the court may deem just.

(3) The buyer has a right of replevin or similar remedy for goods identified to the contract if after reasonable effort the buyer is unable to effect cover for such goods or the circumstances reasonably indicate that such effort will be unavailing or if the goods have been shipped under reservation and satisfaction of the security interest in them has been made or tendered.

G.H. Treitel, Q.C.

SECTION 2. EFFECTS OF BREACH

A breach of contract may entitle the injured party to claim damages, the agreed sum, specific performance or an injunction, in accordance with the principles discussed ... In appropriate circumstances he may be entitled to more than one of these remedies: e.g. to an injunction and damages....

CHAPTER 21 **REMEDIES** (p. 717)

A breach of contract is a civil wrong. To break a contract can also occasionally be a criminal offence; ... In most cases, however, a breach of contract will involve only civil liability;.... A claim for specific relief is one for the actual performance of the defaulting party's undertaking. Where that undertaking is one to do, or to forbear from doing, some act, a claim for specific relief is made by the equitable remedies of specific performance or injunction; where the undertaking is one to pay a sum of money, a claim for specific relief is made by the common law action for an agreed sum. In an action for damages, the injured party claims compensation in money for the fact that he has not received the performance for which he bargained ... A person who has performed his part of the contract but has not received the agreed counter-performance may, finally, claim back his performance or its reasonable value ...

SECTION 1. DAMAGES

The action for damages is always available, as of right, when a contract has been broken. It should, from this point of view, be contrasted with claims for specific relief and for restitution, which are either subject to the discretion of the court or only available if certain conditions are satisfied. An action for damages can succeed even though the victim has not suffered any loss: in that event, it will result in an award of nominal damages. In such a case, the purpose of the action may simply be to establish what the rights and liabilities of the parties under a contract are ... Generally the victim will claim damages for a substantial loss; ...

SECTION 3. EQUITABLE REMEDIES

1. Specific Performance

The common law did not specifically enforce contractual obligations except those to pay money. Specific enforcement of other contractual obligations was available only in equity. It was (and is) subject to many restrictions. These are based partly on the drastic character of the remedy, which leads (more readily than an award of damages or of the agreed sum) to attachment of the defendant's person. But this is an important factor only where the contract calls for "personal" performance, *i.e.* for acts to be done by the defendant himself. Where the contract is not of this kind, it can be specifically enforced without personal constraint: for example, by sequestration, by execution of a formal document by an officer of the court, or by a writ of delivery ... The more recent authorities ... support some expansion in the scope of the remedy.

(1) Granted where damages not "adequate"

The traditional view is that specific performance will not be ordered where damages are an "adequate" remedy....

(2) Discretionary

Specific performance is a discretionary remedy: the court is not bound to grant it merely because the contract is valid at law and cannot be impeached on some specific equitable ground such as misrepresentation or undue influence ... The discretion is, however, "not an arbitrary ... discretion, but one to be governed as far as possible by fixed rules and principles."

Allan Farnsworth

B. ENFORCEMENT BY SPECIFIC PERFORMANCE AND INJUNCTION [p. 739 et seq.]

§ 12.4. **Historical Development of Equitable Relief.** [...] The common law courts did not generally grant specific relief for breach of contract. The usual form of relief at common law was substitutional, and the typical judgment declared that the plaintiff recover from the defendant a sum of money ...

§ 12.5. **Forms: Specific Performance and Injunction.** The most direct form of equitable relief for breach of contract is specific performance ... A court will not order a performance that has become impossible, unreasonably burdensome, or unlawful, nor will is issue an order that can be frustrated by the defendant through exercise of a power of termination or otherwise. Specific performance may be granted after there has been a breach of contract by either nonperformance or repudiation....

C. ENFORCEMENT BY AWARD OF DAMAGES

§ 12.8. **Basic Principles of Damages.** The award of damages is the common form of relief for breach of contract. Virtually any breach gives the injured party a claim for damages for at least nominal damages, "to which", as a distinguished federal judge put it "for reasons we do not understand every victim of a breach of contract, unlike a tort victim, is entitled." Thus, even if the breach caused no loss.... the injured party can recover as damages a nominal sum, commonly six cents or a dollar, fixed without regard to loss ...

In most successful actions for breach of contract, however, substantial damages are awarded.

The basic principle for the measurement of those damages is that of compensation based on the injured party's expectation ... At least in principle, a party's expectation is measured by the actual worth that performance of the contract would have had to that party, not the worth that it might have had to some hypothetical person ...

[...] [a] court will not ordinarily award damages that are described as "punitive", intended to punish the party in breach, or sometimes as "exemplary", intended to make an example of that party ... Punitive damages may, however, be awarded in tort actions, and a number of courts have awarded them for a breach of contract that is in some respect tortious ...

Performance—Damages in International Law

UNIDROIT

Article 5.1.4 (Duty to achieve a specific result, Duty of best efforts)

(1) To the extent that an obligation of a party involves a duty to achieve a specific result, that party is bound to achieve that result.

(2) To the extent that an obligation of a party involves a duty of best efforts in the performance of an activity, that party is bound to make such efforts as would be made by a reasonable person of the same kind in the same circumstances.

Article 7.2.1 (Performance of monetary obligations)

Where a party who is obliged to pay money does not do so, the other party may require payment.

Article 7.2.2 (Performance of non-monetary obligation)

Where a party who owes an obligation other than one to pay money does not perform, the other party may require performance, unless

(a) to (e)

Article 7.2.4 (Judicial penalty)

(1) Where the court orders a party to perform, it may also direct that this party pay a penalty if it does not comply with the order.

(2) The penalty shall be paid to the aggrieved party unless mandatory provisions of the law of the forum provide otherwise. Payment of the penalty to the aggrieved party does not exclude any claim for damages.

Article 7.4.2 (Full compensation)

(1) The aggrieved party is entitled to full compensation for harm sustained as a result of the non-performance. Such harm includes both any loss which it suffered and any gain of which it was deprived, taking into account any gain to the aggrieved party resulting from its avoidance of cost or harm.

(2) Such harm may be non-pecuniary and includes, for instance, physical suffering or emotional distress.

Article 7.4.4 (Foreseeability of harm)

The non-performing party is liable only for harm which it foresaw or could reasonably have foreseen at the time of the conclusion of the contract as being likely to result from its non-performance.

Damages for Fraud

Alex Weill, Droit Civil: Les Obligations

n° 187, at 200 (1971)

187. Diverse sanctions.— 1° Insofar as fraud vitiates the consent of the victim, the normal sanction is the *relative nullity* of the contract.

2o But the fraud is also a fault that can be sanctioned by *damages*. If, despite the nullity, the victim experiences a prejudice, he can demand damages from the author of the fraud and from all those who, by their fault, have permitted or facilitated the fraud. Besides, nothing obliges the victim to demand the nullity of the contract, if he prefers to limit himself to recovering damages.

Moreover, damages constitute the sole sanction in the case of fraud caused by a third party. It is the same with the sanction for incidental [non-material] fraud.

3o One can conceive of still another sanction for fraud—the *refusal of nullity*. An incapable who has dissimulated his condition by means of fraudulent maneuvers will not be able to obtain the nullity of the contract on account of his incapacity.

Section IV — What Contracts Shall Be Avoided by Persons Not Parties to Them; Simulation, Revocatory (Pauliana) Action, Oblique Action

Louisiana Sources of Law

Louisiana Civil Code

Art. 2025. Definition; simulation and counterletter.

A contract is a simulation when, by mutual agreement, it does not express the true intent of the parties.

If the true intent of the parties is expressed in a separate writing, that writing is a counterletter. (Acts 1984, No. 331, § 1, effective January 1, 1985.)

Art. 2026. Absolute simulation.

A simulation is absolute when the parties intend that their contract shall produce no effects between them. That simulation, therefore, can have no effects between the parties. (Acts 1984, No. 331, § 1, eff. Jan. 1, 1985.)

Art. 2027. Relative simulation.

A simulation is relative when the parties intend that their contract shall produce effects between them though different from those recited in their contract. A relative simulation produces between the parties the effects they intended if all requirements for those effects have been met. (Acts 1984, No. 331, § 1, effective January 1, 1985.)

Art. 2028. Effects as to third persons. [*Amended*]

A. Any simulation, either absolute or relative, may have effects as to third persons.

B. Counterletters can have no effects against third persons in good faith. Nevertheless, if the counterletter involves immovable property, the principles of recordation apply with respect to third persons. (Acts 1984, No. 331, § 1, eff. Jan. 1, 1985; Acts 2012, No. 277, § 1.)

Art. 2036. Act of the obligor that causes or increases his insolvency.

An obligee has a right to annul an act of the obligor, or the result of a failure to act of the obligor, made or effected after the right of the obligee arose, that causes or increases the obligor's insolvency. (Acts 1984, No. 331, § 1, eff. Jan. 1, 1985; Acts 2003, No. 552, § 1; Acts 2004, No. 447, § 1, eff. Aug. 15, 2004.)

Art. 2037. Insolvency.

An obligor is insolvent when the total of his liabilities exceeds the total of his fairly appraised assets. (Acts 1984, No. 331, § 1, eff. Jan. 1, 1985; Acts 2003, No. 552, § 1; Acts 2004, No. 447, § 1, eff. Aug. 15, 2004.)

Art. 2038. Onerous contract made by the obligor.

An obligee may annul an onerous contract made by the obligor with a person who knew or should have known that the contract would cause or increase the obligor's insolvency. In that case, the person is entitled to recover what he gave in return only to the extent that it has inured to the benefit of the obligor's creditors.

An obligee may annul an onerous contract made by the obligor with a person who did not know that the contract would cause or increase the obligor's insolvency, but in that case that person is entitled to recover as much as he gave to the obligor. That lack of knowledge is presumed when that person has given at least four-fifths of the value of the thing obtained in return from the obligor. (Acts 1984, No. 331, § 1, eff. Jan. 1, 1985.)

Art. 2039. Gratuitous contract made by the obligor.

An obligee may attack a gratuitous contract made by the obligor whether or not the other party knew that the contract would cause or increase the obligor's insolvency. (Acts 1984, No. 331, § 1, eff. Jan. 1, 1985.)

Art. 2040. Contract made in course of business.

An obligee may not annul a contract made by the obligor in the regular course of his business. (Acts 1984, No. 331, § 1, eff. Jan. 1, 1985.)

Art. 2041. Action must be brought within one year.

The action of the obligee must be brought within one year from the time he learned or should have learned of the act, or the result of the failure to act, of the obligor that the obligee seeks to annul, but never after three years from the date of that act or result. (Acts 1984, No. 331, § 1, eff. Jan. 1, 1985.)

Art. 2042. Obligee must join obligor and third persons.

In an action to annul either his obligor's act, or the result of his obligor's failure to act, the obligee must join the obligor and the third persons involved in that act or failure to act.

A third person joined in the action may plead discussion of the obligor's assets. (Acts 1984, No. 331, § 1, eff. Jan. 1, 1985.)

Art. 2043. Assets transferred must be returned.

If an obligee establishes his right to annul his obligor's act, or the result of his obligor's failure to act, that act or result shall be annulled only to the extent that it affects the obligee's right. (Acts 1984, No. 331, § 1, effective January 1, 1985.)

Art. 2044. Insolvency by failure to exercise right.

If an obligor causes or increases his insolvency by failing to exercise a right, the obligee may exercise it himself, unless the right is strictly personal to the obligor.

For that purpose, the obligee must join in the suit his obligor and the third person against whom that right is asserted. (Acts 1984, No. 331, § 1, eff. Jan. 1, 1985.)

Précis: Louisiana Law of Conventional Obligations— §§ 11.1.1 to 11.1.6

An obligee who watches over his own interest has two actions available to him to protect "indirectly" his right to obtain some form performance from his obligor. One action is known as the "Revocatory Action" and the other is the "Oblique Action"....

THE REVOCATORY ACTION

The action, named *revocatory* in the Louisiana civil Code, is also known in civil law jurisdictions as the "paulian action" or "pauliana action". It is described in LSA-CC. Art. 2036 in the following terms: **"An obligee has a right to annul an act of the obligor, or the result of a failure to act of the obligor, made or effected after the right of the obligee arose, that causes or increases the obligor's insolvency."** ...

Art. 2036 suggests that two sets of conditions must be met: one set of conditions concerns the obligee's right against his obligor and the second set focuses on the obligor's act or failure to act.

As regards the obligee's right, it is necessary that this right be either in existence and vested in the obligee or that this right be at least 'potential' before the obligor, by his act or failure to act, causes or increases his insolvency....

As regards the obligor's act or result of a failure to act it must have caused or increased the insolvency of the obligor. **Art. 2037** provides an explanation of the meaning of insolvency for the purpose of the revocatory action: **"An obligor is insolvent when the total of his liabilities exceeds the total of his fairly appraised assets."**

Furthermore, the act or result of a failure to act on the part of the obligor must not be or have been *strictly personal* to that obligor....

A reading of Articles 2036, 2038, 2040 leads one to state that the effect of a revocatory action is to have a juridical act or contract *annulled*. Therefore the rules governing nullity or dissolution of contracts should apply.

Actually, the outcome of a revocatory action is not to "annul" an act or contract between the obligor and a third person but, rather, to declare that the act or contract cannot be "opposed" to the obligee who brings the revocatory action....

Art. 2038 provides as follows: **"An obligee may annul an onerous contract made by the obligor with a person who knew or should have known that the contract would cause or increase the obligor's insolvency. In that case, the person is entitled to recover what he gave in return only to the extent that it has inured to the benefit of the obligor's creditors.**

An obligee may annul an onerous contract made by the obligor with a person who did not know that the contract would cause or increase the obligor's insolvency, but in that case that person is entitled to recover as much as he gave to the obligor. That lack of knowledge is presumed when that person has given at least four-fifths of the value of the thing obtained in return from the obligor." ...

As regards "gratuitous contracts", **Art. 2039** states very clearly, in a few words, that **"An obligee may attack a gratuitous contract made by the obligor whether or not the other party knew that the contract would cause or increase the obligor's insolvency."** ...

[A]n obligee could not bring a revocatory action whenever he would interfere with his obligor's strictly personal rights vis-à-vis a third person.

Art. 2040 adds explicitly the following exception: **"An obligee may not annul a contract made by the obligor in the regular course of his business."** ...

One additional requirement is the proper timing of the exercise of his right by the obligee. Under **Art. 2041** **"The action of the obligee must be brought within one year from the time he learned of the act, or the result of the failure to act, of the obligor that the obligee seeks to annul, but never after three years from the date of that act or result."** ...

In addition, **"In an action to annul either his obligor's act, or the result of his obligor's failure to act, the obligee must join the obligor and the third persons involved in that act or failure to act." Art. 2042(1).** As such, the third person will be allowed to raise the defense of the benefit of discussion as stated in **Art. 2042(2)** **"A third person joined in the action may plead discussion of the obligor's assets."**

As regards an important additional effect of a revocatory action, it is stated in **Art. 2043: "If an obligee establishes his right to annul his obligor's act, or the result of his obligor's failure to act, that act or result shall be annulled only to the extent that it affects the obligee's right."** ...

A single Article, **Art. 2044**, provides an obligee with an additional remedy against his obligor in the event the **"obligor causes or increases his insolvency by failing to exercise a right...."** In that case **"the obligee may exercise it himself, unless the right is strictly personal to the obligor. For that purpose, the obligee must join in the suit his obligor and the third person against whom that right is asserted."** This right of action of the obligee is known as the "oblique action"....

Once an obligee can ascertain that his obligor has caused or increased his insolvency, that obligee will have to select that right or those rights of his obligor that the latter "fails to exercise". Not every right of an obligor can be exercised by his obligee because the obligor is still in charge of his patrimony and no "stranger" should be allowed, without limitations, to interfere with the obligor's management of his patrimony....

Thus, rights which are "personal" to the obligor cannot fall in the hands of the obligee....

As to the outcome of the oblique action, it is the opposite of the outcome of the revocatory action. Should an obligee be successful in bringing an oblique action, the benefit of the action will be shared by _all_ the obligees....

Cases

The NATIONAL BANK OF BOSSIER CITY et al.
v.
Kenneth R. HARDCASTLE et al.

Louisiana Court of Appeal
Second Circuit
Oct. 30, 1967
204 So.2d 142

BARHAM, Judge.

This is a revocatory action by two creditors of Willis H. Hardcastle, deceased. The defendants are the surviving widow of the deceased, Mrs. Ora Hopkins Hardcastle, the two sons of the deceased, Kenneth R. Hardcastle and Willis S. Hardcastle, and the Succession of Willis H. Hardcastle.

Plaintiffs allege that on October 30, 1964, the deceased transferred the only real estate he owned to his two sons; that one of the sons was a creditor of the deceased; that deceased was insolvent at the time of transfer; that the transfers were for the purpose of defrauding the creditors; and that the creditors were injured by the transfers. Plaintiffs urged that the transfers were simulations, and, in the alternative, that they were subject to a revocatory action. They have abandoned their claim of simulation and appeal from the lower court judgment denying their right to revocation. Their suit for revocation is joined with an action to liquidate their debts as provided by LSA-C.C. art. 1975.

The two pieces of property involved in this action are the home of the deceased and a business lot upon which was situated a small office building and which was used in deceased's used car business. The stated consideration in the deeds was the assumption of mortgages. However, the sons delivered to their father approximately $1,600.00 as a part of the overall transaction. It is not disputed that the actual value received by the two sons exceeds the consideration which was paid for the properties. At the time of the transfer the deceased was recovering from a severe stroke, was, in fact, insolvent, was overdrawn approximately $800.00 at the plaintiff bank, and was unable to meet the monthly payment on the obligations assumed by the two sons.

It is the testimony of Kenneth Hardcastle that he and his brother had no knowledge of their father's business affairs and did not know that he was insolvent at the time of the transfer. They did know he was hard pressed temporarily for ready cash. Kenneth further testified that the motive for the transfer was to relieve their father of the monthly obligations attendant upon the mortgages they assumed, and to provide for his immediate need of cash. Mrs. Hardcastle attests to the fact that the family had no knowledge of the business situation of the deceased. None of the defendants participated in the operation of deceased's business at any time.

The claim of the plaintiff, The National Bank of Bossier City, is predicated upon an unsecured promissory note for $2,500.00 dated May 11, 1964. The claim of the plaintiff, Shreveport Auto Finance Corporation, is founded upon several notes secured by chattel mortgages representing a total debt of $12,733.03 after applying credits to the original indebtedness of $25,077.50.

The revocatory action in Louisiana is established by LSA-C.C. art. 1970 et seq.

LSA-C.C. art. 1971:

'This action can only be exercised when the debtor has not property sufficient
to pay the debt of the complaining creditor, or of all his creditors where there has
been a cession, or any proceeding analogous thereto.'

LSA-C.C. art. 1978:

'No contract shall be avoided by this action but such as are made in fraud of
creditors, and such as, if carried into execution, would have the effect of defrauding them. If made in good faith, it can not be annulled, although it prove
injurious to the creditors; and although made in bad faith, it can not be rescinded, unless it operate to their injury.'

LSA-C.C. art. 1993:

'No creditor can, by the action given by this section, sue individually to annul
any contract made before the time his debt accrued.'

The prerequisites for the revocatory action are: (1) insolvency of the debtor; (2) injury
to the creditor; (3) intent to defraud the creditors; (4) pre-existing and accrued indebtedness. See the discussion of the revocatory action in Louisiana in 9 Tul.L.Rev. 422.

The defendants contend that the Shreveport Auto Finance Corporation debt was not
pre-existing because of a refinancing maneuver which occurred after the transfer. Without a lengthy discussion as to the merits of this argument, we simply conclude that the
debt was such as was 'accrued' and which would give rise to an action for revocation when
liquidated.

Appellants strongly urge that Kenneth Hardcastle, one of the defendants, is a creditor
and that the presumption of fraud contained in LSA-C.C. art. 1984 should apply.

LSA-C.C. art. 1983:

'But if such fraud consisted merely in the endeavor to obtain a preference over other
creditors, for the securing of payment of a just debt, under circumstances in which
by law the endeavor to obtain such preference is declared to be a constructive fraud
in such case the party shall only lose the advantage endeavored to be secured by
such contract, and shall be reimbursed what he may have given or paid, but without interest; and he shall restore all advantages he has received from the transaction.'

LSA-C.C. art. 1984:

'Every contract shall be deemed to have been made in fraud of creditors, when
the obligee knew that the obligor was in insolvent circumstances, and when such
contract gives to the obligee, if he be a creditor, any advantage over other creditors of the obligor.'

Plaintiffs contend that a previous loan of $800.00 from Kenneth Hardcastle to his fa-
ther should categorize him as a 'creditor' under the above articles. However, the deeds
do not in any way attempt to satisfy or cancel this obligation, and it is the positive evidence in the case that the transfers were not motivated by or made with any consideration for that obligation. We also conclude that the transferees did not, at that time, have
knowledge of deceased's insolvency. Construing Articles 1983 and 1984 together, we are
constrained to hold that Kenneth Hardcastle is not such a 'creditor' as would give rise to
the presumption of fraud. We hold that plaintiff is not relieved from the burden of proof
in relation to all of the elements necessary to maintain a revocatory action.

That deceased was in fact insolvent is admitted. However, neither the creditors who complain nor the sons who purchased the property had real, factual and actual knowledge of

the insolvency until after his death. Mr. Ashworth, Secretary-Treasurer for the largest   90
creditor in this action, testified that his company did not consider the collection of de-   91
ceased's indebtedness to be in 'jeopardy' until several days after his death. He further tes-   92
tified that Mr. Hardcastle's financial reverses had existed for several months before the   93
transfer; that other used car dealers were in similar financial straits; and that the loan to   94
Mr. Hardcastle was secured as much by his 'integrity' as it was by legal security devices.   95
Upon the occasion of the renegotiation of Hardcastle's loan, which occurred after the   96
transfers which are sought to be revoked, Ashworth was of the opinion that Mr. Hard-   97
castle could solve his financial problems.   98

All of the testimony supports a finding by this Court that Mr. Hardcastle was a man   99
of great integrity and that he would not and did not, in fact, act to defraud his creditors.   100
The Court just as easily concludes that the sons of the decedent had no intent to defraud   101
the creditors of their father by their purchase of these properties. Contrarily, it was their   102
intent to assist their father in finding a solution to his financial problem. This was the   103
single and only motivation for their acceptance of the transfers.   104

We could belabor this opinion with great detail as to testimony and in a comparison   105
of cases involving the revocatory action. We simply cite cases and conclude that the fac-   106
tual situation in the instant case is far stronger for denial of the remedy than that which   107
exists in any of the following: J. Grossman's Sons v. Chachere, 136 La. 666, 67 So. 545 (1915);   108
Price v. Florsheim, 174 La. 945, 142 So. 135 (1932); Standard Plumbing, Heating & Sup-   109
ply Co. v. Dupree, La.App., 157 So. 759 (1934); Hendricks v. Phelps, La.App., 62 So.2d   110
185 (2d Cir., 1952).   111

We conclude herein that although the deceased was insolvent in fact, and although the   112
transfer did injure creditors who had pre-existing and accrued debts, that neither the   113
transferor nor the transferees had any intent to defraud the creditors of the deceased,   114
Willis H. Hardcastle. Under our conclusion the denial of the presumption provided by   115
LSA-C.C. arts. 1983 and 1984 is of no consequence since we believe the defendants have   116
so affirmatively countered the allegation of fraud.   117

The judgment of the district court is affirmed and appellant is taxed with the cost of   118
this appeal.   119

Questions

1. After you have read the case, please identify the many different legal relationships that exist in this case. Why could it be important to properly identify each one of these relationships?

2. Lines 43 *et seq.*: Compare the articles from the Louisiana Civil Code of 1870 with the new Louisiana Code articles 2036–2043. Have the prerequisites for a revocatory action changed? Are they more or less strict today? What could be a reason for the change and what consequence could it carry with it?

3. Lines 79–87: On which ground for the formation of contracts is the "loan" to be distinguished from the "deeds"? Is good faith somewhat relevant here?

4. Lines 88–98: According to the court, what was the principal cause that motivated the sons?

5. What would be or should be the ruling of a court under the Louisiana Civil Code articles of today? Under these new articles, would the 4/5th rule of Louisiana Civil Code article 2038 have found room for application?

Succession of Mrs. Alice BONING, Widow of Joseph P. HENICAN

Louisiana Court of Appeal
Fourth Circuit
May 10, 1971
248 So.2d 385

CHASEZ, Judge.

On August 12, 1968 Mrs. Alice Boning Henican departed this life, leaving an olographic testament. During the term of her marriage with her husband, Joseph P. Henican, the testator gave birth to two sons who are by virtue of law her forced heirs. One son, Joseph, Jr., predeceased his mother while the other son, C. Ellis Henican, is still alive, although not mentioned in the will of the deceased. Rather the testator bypassed C. Ellis Henican entirely in favor of his five children, her grandchildren. Pursuant to the terms of her will, one half of the property of the deceased was bequeathed to the children of Mrs. Henican's son, Joseph, Jr. The other one half was bequeathed to the children of her other son, C. Ellis Henican.

C. Ellis Henican is not contesting any portion of his mother's will. Although the testament deprives him of his forced portion, i.e., one quarter of his deceased mother's estate, he is making no attempt to have his reserved portion recognized. To the contrary, it is the National American Bank, hereinafter referred to as the Bank, that has so petitioned the court.

The Bank has alleged that it is the creditor of C. Ellis Henican and that its rights as a creditor are being prejudiced 'by an obvious attempt to avoid the payment to C. Ellis Henican of the legitime due to him in said succession' and 'by (the) failure of said C. Ellis Henican to assert his claim to the legitime due to him with reference to said succession.' The Bank therefore prays that it be authorized as a creditor of C. Ellis Henican to accept the succession of Mrs. Alice Boning Henican in the name of her son and forced heir, C. Ellis Henican, and that it be placed in possession of the legitime due C. Ellis Henican to the extent of his indebtedness.

Exceptions of no cause of action and/or no right of action were filed by C. Ellis Henican and C. Ellis Henican, Jr. executor of the estate of Mrs. Alice Boning Henican. The exceptions were maintained by the lower court and the suit of the National American Bank was dismissed at its costs. From this adverse judgment the Bank has appealed to this court.

The question thus squarely presented for our determination is whether or not a creditor of a forced heir may exercise the right of the forced heir to reduce a legacy which infringes on the forced portion of the debtor. We are of the opinion that the creditor has no such right.

LSA-C.C. art. 1504 enunciates the right of reduction and provides as follows:

'On the death of the donor or testator, the reduction of the donation, whether *inter vivos* or *mortis causa*, can be sued for *only by forced heirs, or by their heirs or assigns*; neither the donees, legatees, nor creditors of the deceased can require that reduction nor avail themselves of it.' (Emphasis added)

As may be seen from the literal terms of the article the right to compel a reduction does not extend to the creditor of the forced heir. Furthermore, the Supreme Court has refused to interpret the article so as to bring creditors of the forced heir within its terms and scope.

In Tompkins v. Prentice, 12 La.Ann. 465 (1857), one Joseph Prentice died testate, survived by his mother and father, one brother and one sister. In his will, Joseph Prentice con-

veyed his entire estate to his mother, brother and sister to the complete exclusion of his
father. Moreover, the father of the deceased executed a notarial act of renunciation of any
interest which he might have had in his son's succession. The creditors of the father and
forced heir of the deceased instituted suit to set aside the renunciation on the ground that
it was in defraud of their rights and to have their debtor's share of the succession determined and pro rated among them to satisfy the indebtedness. In that case the court specifically held that the wording of codal article 1504 did not create a right in the creditor of
the forced heir to assert the action to reduce a legacy. The court concluded that the term
'assign' used in the article did not include creditors but only 'those to whom rights have
been transferred by particular title: such as sale, donation, legacy, transfer or cession.'
LSA-C.C. art. 3556.

The result of the Tompkins case is further substantiated by the wording of LSA-C.C.
art. 1991 which provides:

> 'There are rights of the debtor, however, which the creditor (creditors) can not
> exercise, even should he refuse to avail himself of them.
>
> 'They can not require the separation of property between husband and wife; nor
> can they oblige their debtor to accept a donation Inter vivos made to him, nor
> can they accept it in his stead. Neither can they call on a coheir of the debtor to
> collate, when such debtor has not exercised that right.'

The rights of the debtor enumerated in paragraph two of the above quoted article are
illustrative in nature rather than exclusive. Therefore when Article 1991 is read in pari
materia with Article 1504, the result is to recognize the right to reduce a legacy as right,
personal in nature, which may not be exercised by a creditor of the forced heir-debtor. In
fact, the right to bring an action for reduction is closely analogous to the right to call on
a coheir to collate which article 1991 treats as a right personal to the debtor. Moreover,
LSA-C.C. art. 1991 must be considered as a modification of the terms of LSA-C.C. art.
1990, which provides as follows:

> 'In case the debtor refuse or neglect to accept an inheritance to the prejudice of
> his creditors, they may accept the same, and exercise all his rights in the man-
> ner provided for in the title of successions, and they are authorized, by virtue of
> the action given by this section, to exercise all the rights existing in favor of the
> debtor for recovering possession of the property to which he is entitled, in order
> to make the same available to the payment of their debts.'

When the two articles are read in conjunction, it is apparent that a creditor may exercise all rights of the debtor to obtain possession of property to which the debtor is entitled, except those rights which are personal to the debtor. The right to bring an action
to reduce a legacy like the right to force a co-heir to collate is a personal right which a creditor may not assert. As was stated in the Tompkins case:

> 'Possibly the law-giver may have preferred to give effect to the wishes of the tes-
> tator and allow his estate to take the direction he had indicated, rather than sub-
> ject it to the seizure of creditors of an heir who did not feel himself aggrieved by
> the universal legacy to another.'

After a careful review of the jurisprudence of the state, we find that the Tompkins case
has not been modified by subsequent legislation or jurisprudence and that the principle
of law enunciated therein is dispositive of the case at bar. This court is aware of the fact
that under the French Code Napoleon the result of this matter would be different — that
a creditor would have the right to assert the action to reduce a legacy if his debtor refused

93   to do so. However, the law of the state of Louisiana on this matter differs from the French.
94   As was stated in Cox v. Von Ahlefeldt, 105 La. 543, 30 So. 175 (1900):

95   '(The legislature) framed the law by which we are governed in language which ex-
96   pressly authorizes the bringing of the action to reduce the donations of the testa-
97   tor within the disposable quantum 'by forced heirs, or by their heirs or assigns.'
98   Rev.Civ.Code, art. 1504. And in this respect the Civil Code differs also from the
99   Code Napoleon, which authorizes the bringing of such action by the forced heirs,
100   or 'par leurs heritiers ou ayants cause'; the term 'ayants cause' including creditors,
101   a class not necessarily included in the term 'assigns.' Code Nap. art. 921; Fuzier-
102   Hermann, vol. 11, p. 526, No. 11; Rev.Civ.Code, art. 3556, verbo 'Assigns'; Tomp-
103   kins v. Prentice, 12 La.Ann. 465. We have no authority, then, to exclude collateral
104   heirs from the right here claimed because they were excluded by the Spanish law,
105   nor to include creditors because they are included under the French law.'

106   Accordingly, unless and until the legislature sees fit to make the appropriate changes,
107   the creditor of a forced heir has no right to assert the right of reduction of a legacy ab-
108   sent a specific assignment from the debtor.

109   For the foregoing reasons the judgment of the lower court is affirmed. Costs of this pro-
110   ceedings to be borne by plaintiff-appellant.

Questions

1.   You must read and understand this case in the legal context that prevailed in the 1970s, particularly the matters of succession and forced heirship.

2.   Lines 16–35: What legal adjectives would you use to describe the son Ellis' right to his mother's succession? Do you see any reason or, rather, any necessity to accurately legally describe this right before addressing the issue of the Bank's right of action? *See*, in this respect, the question the Court is asking in lines 33–35. Is the answer the Court gives, i.e. "We are of the opinion that the creditor has no such right", the logical outcome of your legal description of Ellis' right?

3.   Lines 36–110: What method or methods of reasoning is the Court using where it refers to Louisiana Civil Code articles 1504 and 1991 and the *Tompkins* case?

4.   Lines 79–83 & 88 *et seq.*: Is the Court making a purely legal statement derived from the legal analysis that precedes, or is the Court engaging in something more, a policy statement? Is the fact that French law would be different of some relevance to the nature of the Court's statement?

5.   What was the proper Louisiana Civil Code name of the action the Banks attempted to exercise: oblique or revocatory? Explain. What would be the outcome of this case under the Civil Code of today?

1   ## Succession of Elizabeth E. TERRAL and J. R. Terral

2   Supreme Court of Louisiana
3   April 24, 1975
4   312 So.2d 296

5   SUMMERS, Justice.

6   Although other issues were presented in the trial and appellate courts, on this review
7   we are solely concerned with an action in declaration of simulation involving one sale by

James R. Terral dated December 2, 1943, purporting to convey 83 acres of land in Winn   8
Parish to his son George Terral.   9

According to the record, a rule was filed in this succession proceeding on February 2,   10
1972 by four of the eleven forced heirs, children and grandchildren, of decedents James   11
R. Terral and his wife Elizabeth Eldridge. The object of the rule was to compel George Ter-   12
ral, who was then the administrator of the succession, to amend the descriptive list of   13
property composing the succession assets by including the 83 acres purportedly conveyed   14
to him by the deed of December 2, 1943.   15

The rule is based upon the contention of the petitioning heirs that the sale of 83 acres   16
by James R. Terral to George Terral was a simulation. The simulation took place, it is al-   17
leged, because the consideration was never paid. The deed, a cash sale in authentic form,   18
executed before a notary public and two witnesses, is signed by James R. Terral as ven-   19
dor and George Terral as vendee. It recites that the consideration was $581 'cash in hand   20
paid, the receipt of which is hereby acknowledged.'   21

In addition, the deed contains the following stipulation: 22

'It is understood and agreed that the said James R. Terral shall have the right to   23
remain on said property as long as he lives and have the management of said   24
lands sold herein and the said George Terral binds himself to (sic) not to sell   25
said land as long as the said James R. Terral lives.'   26

At a hearing on the rule, the depositions of Martha Anderson, a daughter of dece-   27
dents, and George Terral were introduced into evidence. Only Clifford Malon Moffett,   28
husband of one of the petitioning heirs, and George Terral testified in person at the   29
hearing.   30

Evidence to support the charge of simulation was entirely inadequate. Only the testi-   31
mony of Martha Anderson and Moffett was tendered. That testimony consisted princi-   32
pally of vague and uncorroborated statements purportedly made to them many years ago   33
by the deceased James R. Terral to the effect that he had given his property to George.   34
None of the testimony singled out a specific transfer or conveyance; nor did it give the   35
exact or approximate dates on which James R. Terral was supposed to have made such state-   36
ments. This evidence could not have sustained the charge of simulation if the burden of   37
proof had been imposed upon petitioners.   38

However, the clause in the deed whereby the vendor James R. Terral reserved the right   39
to manage and remain on the property as long as he lived, and the stipulation binding George   40
Terral not to sell the land as long as James R. Terral lived, constituted a reservation of a   41
usufruct. This reservation vested in James R. Terral, the vendor, the right of enjoying the   42
land, the property of which was by the deed ostensibly in the vendee George, and, to   43
thereby draw from the same all the profit, utility and advantages it may produce. La.Civil   44
Code art. 533.   45

Where the seller has reserved to himself the usufruct, the case falls within the con-   46
templation of Article 2480 of the Civil Code.[1] And when the seller reserves the usufruct   47
'there is reason to presume that the sale is simulated, and with respect to third persons,   48
the parties must produce proof that they are acting in good faith, and establish the real-   49

---

1. La.Civil Code art. 2480 provides:
'In all cases where the thing sold remains in the possession of the seller, because he has reserved
to himself the usufruct, or retains possession by a precarious title, there is reason to presume that the
sale is simulated, and with respect to third persons, the parties must produce proof that they are acting in good faith, and establish the reality of the sale.'

ity of the sale.' There is, moreover, evidence which is essentially undisputed that James R. Terral remained upon the property in the family home until his death in 1957. His widow survived him and continued in residence there until two years prior to her death in 1967. In a sense, therefore, 'the thing sold remains in the possession of the seller.' La.Civil Code art. 2480.

As is usual in these cases the burden of establishing the reality of a sale many years after the fact is an onerous one. The burden is compounded when the party so charged must overcome a legal presumption that the purported sale is a simulation. Here the notary and witnesses were deceased; and George Terral possessed no checks, receipts, bank accounts or other documentation to support his contention that the price was in fact paid. His only evidence was the deed and his self-serving statements that he paid the price with funds he had saved and which he kept 'in his pocket.'

He is apparently a man of limited education. At the time of the trial he was 74 years of age. His income from a simple farming operation was meagre. His testimony, given on two occasions in contradictory and at times incoherent [sic].

His father, according to Martha Anderson's testimony, was supposed to have maintained records of his financial affairs. If we are to believe this testimony, since George was the only child of James R. Terral living and working on the home place, only he had access to these records. Although at the time his deposition was taken he was supposed to bring all records and documents dealing with the succession and the sale, he appeared empty handed, claiming that the only records were those 'in his head'. He depends upon his testimony and his assertion that there were no written records to rebut the presumption established by Article 2480.

[. . . .]

Forced heirs have the right to annul absolutely and by parol evidence the simulated contracts of those from whom they inherit, and shall not be restricted to the legitime. La.Civil Code art. 2239.

Charges of simulated contracts are principally governed by Article 2480 of the Civil Code. See footnote 1, supra.

Although these articles are somewhat explicit, there is no effort in the code to define the doctrine of simulation. And there are no articles in the French Civil Code on this subject save Article 1321,[2] which is not one upon which we can rely for a definition. There is, however, an elaborate doctrinal edifice of simulation long recognized by the French Courts and text writers. See Aubry et Rau, Cours de droit civil francais XII (5e ed. 1922), no 756 bis., p. 184: 'Il n'y a pas de contre-lettre la o u il n'y pas simulation.' Cf. also Baudry-Lacantinerie, Precis de droit civil II (12E ed 1921), nos 295–96, p. 299; Baudry-Lacantinerie et Barde, Traite de droit civil XV, Des Obligations III (3e ed 1908), nos 2385–2418, pp. 111–138; Demolombe, Traite des contracts IV (1878) nos 303–49, pp. 270–298.

Simulation, according to Planiol, is an understanding between the parties against third persons. Ordinarily one of the parties, by means of the simulated act, proposes to deceive someone, and the simulation is thus a means of fraud. Planiol, Traite Ele me ntaire de Droit Civil, Vol. 2-part 1, nos 1185–1208.

---

2. French Civil Code art. 1321 provides: 'Counter letters can only have effect between the contracting parties; they have no effect against others.'

To some extent our decisions have discussed simulation and a definition of sorts may
be derived from these expressions. For instance, in Viguerie v. Hall, 107 La. 767, 31 So.
1019 (1902) the Court said:

> 'It is no unusual occurrence for parties to place their property and rights in the
> name and under the control of others, without any consideration whatever, and
> without the intention of ownership being actually transferred. Such acts are per-
> missible, and cannot be gainsaid, unless they carry injury to some one. A sim-
> ulation is not necessarily a fraud. It is only so when injury to third persons is
> intended. Gravier's Curator v. Carraby's Ex'r, 17 La. 118, 36 Am.Dec. 608.'

Where the alleged sale is a mere simulation, it may be set aside as a nullity by the heirs
of the seller, for a simulated sale does not transfer the property. The fraudulent simulation, a mere pretense, without reality, conveys no title. Olivier, Voorhies & Lowrey v. Ma-
jors, 133 La. 764, 63 So. 323 (1913).

A simulated contract is one which, though clothed in concrete form, has no existence
in fact, and it may at any time, and at the demand of any person in interest, be declared
a sham and may be annulled by the heirs of the apparent vendor. Maddox v. Butchee,
203 La. 299, 14 So.2d 4 (1943); Hibernia Bank and Trust Co. v. Louisiana Ave. Realty
Co., 143 La. 962, 79 So. 554 (1918); Interstate Trust and Banking Co. v. Louisiana Ave.
Realty Co., 143 La. 971, 79 So. 557 (1918).

Each case involving simulation must be decided on its peculiar facts. And where
the issue is primarily dependent upon the credibility of a single witness, as here, the
decision of the trial judge is entitled to considerable weight. In this case the trial judge
was unimpressed by George Terral's testimony, and properly so. A legal presumption
established in law to shield the legitime of forced heirs from fraudulent transactions
must be rebutted by convincing evidence which preponderates in favor of the reality
of the sale. This has not been accomplished by George Terral's testimony; and the
judgment of the trial court nullifying the sale of December 2, 1943 as a simulation is
affirmed. The following described property is therefore ordered returned to the succession:

> 'S 1/2 of SW 1/4, Section 14, and beginning at the Northwest corner of Section
> 23, and run South 70 yards, thence East 210 yards, thence North 70 yards and
> thence West 210 yards to place of beginning. All in Township 13, North of Range
> 3 West, La.Mer., together with all improvements and appurtenances thereto be-
> longing, containing 83 acres more or less.'

[....]

Questions

1. Lines 6 *et seq.*: Is the purpose of an action in simulation to declare the nullity of a juridical act? Can you reconcile Louisiana Civil Code articles 2025 and 2028 on simulation with Louisiana Civil Code article 1983?

2. Lines 22 *et seq.*: Compare the stipulations in the deed with the Louisiana Civil Code
articles on usufruct, particularly La. Civ. Code arts. 535 and 550 *et seq.* Do you agree
with the Court that the reservation of a usufruct in a contract of sale is reason to
presume a simulation? Where does the Court find this presumption?

3. Lines 62–64: Does it appear from this *in concreto* description of the son that the
Court had its mind pretty much set on finding a simulation?

4. Line 74 *et seq.*: What important statements does the court make about "simulation and fraud" and "simulation and the legitime"?

J. B. OWEN et al.

v.

W. H. OWEN et al.

Supreme Court of Louisiana
June 21, 1976
336 So.2d 782

CALOGERO, Justice.

This is a lawsuit by six of the seven children of I. M. and Henrietta Owen, including one J. B. Owen, against their brother (the seventh child W. H. Owen) and his vendees (Wayne S. Bush and Charles Wayne Bush) to have two transfers from their father, I. M. Owen, one to W. H. Owen and the other to W. H. Owen and J. B. Owen jointly, declared simulations, or, alternatively, nullified because they were donations in disguise and donations Omnium bonorum, or, alternatively, to have such property collated in a partition.[1]

On March 22, 1957, I. M. Owen executed three separate deeds of sale covering tracts composed respectively of 40 acres, 40 acres, and 15 acres. He conveyed 40 acres to his son W. H. Owen for a stated consideration of $100, 40 acres to a second son J. B. Owen for a stated consideration of $720, and 15 acres to both W. H. Owen and J. B. Owen for a stated consideration of $300. The property descriptions are more fully given in the Court of Appeal opinion, Owen v. Owen, 325 So.2d 283 (La.App.2nd Cir. 1975), and are incorporated herein by reference. The properties are here referred to respectively as tracts one, two, and three. Ownership of tracts one and three are those at issue in this lawsuit.

In October 12, 1957, I. M. Owen died intestate, and on February 1, 1970 his widow, Henrietta Owen, died intestate. In 1972, following the deaths of Mr. and Mrs. Owen and, of course, subsequent to the execution of the three deeds mentioned above, one of the plaintiffs, J. B. Owen, conveyed all of his interest in tract three to his brother W. H. Owen for $1500. Thereafter, on January 29, 1973, W. H. Owen conveyed the acreage made up of tracts one and three in the following manner: twenty-seven and one-half acres comprising the western half thereof to defendant, Wayne S. Bush for $7,837.50, and twenty-seven and one-half acres comprising the eastern half thereof to defendant Charles Wayne Bush, Wayne S. Bush's son, for $7,837.50. Some nine months thereafter this suit was instituted by six of the Owen children against the seventh child, W. H. Owen, and his vendees Wayne and Charles Bush. Plaintiffs asked that the court set aside the transfers from I. M. Owen to his sons, and order the property returned to the decedent's estate or declare that each of the forced heirs own an undivided one-seventh interest in the property. Alternatively, plaintiffs asked that the property be collated under the provisions of Article 1227 Et seq. of the Civil Code.

[....]

We granted writs upon defendants' application. 326 So.2d 376 (La.1976). In this Court, defendants allege that the Court of Appeal erred in finding that the conveyances by I. M. Owen were donations in disguise and donations Omnium bonorum, that they erred in

---

1. Petitioners do not attack the transfers as being in derogation of Henrietta Owen's community rights (see C.C. art. 2404), presumably because she signed the deeds along with her husband.

concluding that a donation Omnium bonorum is an absolute nullity, and that they erred in decreeing that the seven heirs of Mr. and Mrs. I. M. Owen were owners each of an undivided one-seventh interest in the subject property.

The following facts are borne out by the record and are not seriously contested. In March 1957, at the time I. M. Owen purported to sell the land in question to his sons, he sold tract number three, comprising 15 acres, for $300, although the property was worth $45 per acre, or $675.[2] On that same date he purported to sell tract one, comprising 40 acres, for a stated consideration of $100, although it was worth $45 per acre, or $1800.

In 1970 the fifty-five acres owned by W. H. Owen were valued at $10,725. He sold the land to the Bushes in 1973 for approximately $16,000. In 1975, that same property was worth $18,700. Although neither of the courts below reached this issue, it is clear that the Bushes purchased the disputed property for a fair price.

The acts of sale by which I. M. Owen conveyed the three tracts in 1957 identified the vendor as I. M. Owen and the vendees as W. H. Owen and J. B. Owen. The deeds, in authentic form, recite that the properties were sold to the respective vendees for the stated consideration 'cash in hand paid, the receipt of which is hereby acknowledged.' The deeds do not indicate that I. M. Owen was the father of W. H. and J. B., nor that these three properties constituted all of the property owned by Mr., or by Mr. and Mrs., Owen.

The only contested issue of fact in the case is whether the sons actually paid their father for the property. J. B. judicially confessed that he paid nothing for the property. W. H. claimed that he did pay for the property which was transferred to him, but could produce no evidence to support his assertion. The trial court found that nothing was paid by either brother for the land, a finding the Court of Appeal upheld. There is no error in this finding, and we agree with the courts below that the March 22, 1957 sales of tracts one and three to W. H. Owen and to J. B. Owen and W. H. Owen, respectively, were not sales but were disguised donations under Article 2444 of the Civil Code.[3]

It was established at the trial that before the Bushes purchased the property in question from W. H. Owen they were told by J. B. Owen that there was some question as to whether W. H. Owen could transfer a 'clear deed,' but they were given no reason for J. B.'s assertion. Wayne Bush also learned from W. H. Owen that he had bought the property from his father. However, there is no evidence that the Bushes ever had any knowledge of Mr. and Mrs. I. M. Owen's financial condition (at any time) nor any knowledge of the value of the property in March of 1957, some fifteen years before their purchase of the property.

The plaintiffs established at trial that at the time of the transfers in question Mr. and Mrs. Owen were living on social security and welfare payments, and that they owned no immovable property other than the three tracts transferred; but there was no evidence as to the amount of income they were receiving, nor was there any evidence as to what their living expenses were. It was established that I. M. Owen had $600 when he died in late 1957, a sum W. H. Owen kept in an account 'for his mother.'[4]

---

2. The property values quoted here were established by expert evidence at the trial and were uncontroverted.

3. Article 2444 provides in full that: 'The sales of immovable property made by parents to their children, may be attacked by the forced heirs, as containing a donation in disguise, if the latter can prove that no price has been paid, or that the price was below one-fourth of the real value of the immovable sold, at the time of the sale.'

4. W. H. Owen also testified that he put aside $1400 for his mother, money he received from a mineral lease, presumably sometime after his father's death in 1957.

81   The plaintiffs contend, and the courts below found, that when I. M. Owen sold
82 these two tracts he had divested himself of all of his property without reserving to him-
83 self enough for subsistence. Article 1497 prohibits such a donation in the following
84 language:

85   'The donation Inter vivos shall in no case divest the donor of all his property; he
86   must reserve to himself enough for subsistence; if he does not do it, the dona-
87   tion is null for the whole.'

88   In order to sustain an attack on a gift as a donation Omnium bonorum, the heirs must
89 prove conclusively that the donation divested the donor of all of his property. Whitman
90 v. Whitman, 206 La. 1, 18 So.2d 633 (1944); Potts v. Potts, 142 La. 906, 77 So. 786 (1918);
91 Hearsey v. Craig, 126 La. 824, 53 So. 17 (1910); Hinton v. May, 241 So.2d 583 (La.App.2nd
92 Cir. 1970). In light of the stringent requirements set forth in the aforementioned cases,
93 we are not as certain as were the lower courts that the requirements of Article 1497 were
94 met so as to brand I. M. Owen's disguised donations as donations Omnium bonorum.
95 We nonetheless accept the finding of the lower courts, for, even assuming the donations
96 were Omnium bonorum, the decision of the Court of Appeal in our view must be re-
97 versed for the reasons we relate thereinafter.

98   The plaintiffs allege first that the transfers from parent to sons were simulations. In our
99 law, a simulation is a transfer of property which is not what it seems. Simulations are of
100 two types: pure simulations, and disguised transfers.[5] In a pure simulation, sometimes
101 called a non-transfer, the parties only pretend to transfer the property from one to the
102 other, but in fact both transferor and transferee intend that the transferor retain owner-
103 ship of the property. When this type of simulation is successfully attacked, the true in-
104 tent of the parties is revealed, which was that no transfer had in fact taken place. In a
105 contest between a vendor and vendee in this situation the true intent of the parties is ef-
106 fectuated and the courts hold that no transfer took place because the simulated sale is an
107 absolute nullity. Successions of Webre, 247 La. 461, 172 So.2d 285 (1965); Schalaida v. Gon-
108 zales, 174 La. 907, 142 So. 123 (1932); Milano v. Milano, 243 So.2d 876 (La.App.1st Cir.
109 1971). The other type of simulation is a disguised transfer which seems on its face to be
110 a valid sale, but which is intended by the parties to be a gift rather than a sale. When this
111 sort of simulation is attacked successfully, as it has been here under Article 2444, the true
112 intent of the parties is likewise effectuated by the law. A valid transfer has taken place,
113 but its form is a donation rather than a sale and the Code articles on donations apply to
114 the transfer. Stevens v. Stevens, 227 La. 761, 80 So.2d 399 (1955); Carter v. Bolden, 13
115 La.App. 48, 127 So. 111 (La.App.2nd Cir. 1930); 35 La.L.Rev. 192 (1974); 25 La.L.Rev. 313
116 (1965).

117   However, when the property is no longer held by the original vendee but has passed
118 into the hands of an innocent third party who has purchased for value and in reliance
119 on the public records, the result is much different. In the case of Chachere v. Superior Oil
120 Co., 192 La. 193, 187 So. 321 (1939), this Court upheld the rights of third party pur-
121 chasers to retain the land in question even though the transfer to their vendor had been
122 a disguised donation. The Court held that because the transfer from the original vendor
123 (the parent of the plaintiff-forced heirs) to the original vendee (who in turn sold to the
124 defendant-third party purchasers) was on its face a valid sale, the plaintiffs were not al-
125 lowed, after the property had passed into the hands of third parties, to introduce evi-
126 dence that the transfer was not a sale. The Court stated that:

---

5. For discussions of the legal concept of simulations, See Lemann, Some Aspects of Simulations
in France and Louisiana, 29 Tul.L.Rev. 22 (1954) and 35 La.L.Rev. 192 (1974).

'It is the well settled jurisprudence of this state that third persons dealing with immovable property have a right to depend upon the faith of the recorded title thereof and are not bound by any secret equities that may exist between their own vendor and prior owners of the land.' 187 So. 321.

In the case of Thompson v. Thompson, 211 La. 468, 30 So.2d 321 (1947), this Court reaffirmed Chachere and held that, when a third person acquires title to land prior to the assertion by forced heirs of their rights to have the disguised donation annulled, and third party who had purchased for value on the strength of the public records will defeat the claim of the forced heir. The Court stated that:

'(W)hereas our system of law has protected the forced heirs against acts designed to deprive him of his legitimate portion, the rights granted to such forced heir cannot be extended so as to defeat the subsequently acquired rights of third persons who have bought property on the faith of the public records and under the belief that their vendor acquired a valid title by purchase. In fine, considerations of public policy, respecting a stability of titles, makes it necessary that innocent third parties prevail over the forced heir even though it results in the denial of the heir's right which our law has so carefully guarded.' 30 So.2d at 329.

Likewise, when immovable property which has been the subject of a 'pure' simulated sale is later sold to third persons who rely on the public records, in a case where the records show that the transfer was a proper sale, and where the records reveal no counterletter, the rights of the third party cannot be affected by subsequent proof that the original transfer was a pure simulation. Beard v. Nunn, 172 La. 155, 133 So. 429 (1931); Jackson v. Creswell, 147 La. 914, 86 So. 329 (1920); Vital v. Andrus, 121 La. 221, 46 So. 217 (1908); Gordon v. Culbertson, 296 So.2d 401 (La.App.2nd Cir. 1974); Redmann, The Louisiana Law of Recordation: Some Principles and Some Problems, 39 Tul.L.Rev. 491 (1965); 35 La.L.Rev. 192 (1974); 17 Tul.L.Rev. 457 (1943). It is clear then from the jurisprudence that in the situation where the original transfer was a pure simulation (and Not therefore effective to pass title) And in the situation where the original transfer was a disguised donation (and Did therefore effectively pass title to the transferee) that the rights of a third party are protected if he purchased on the basis of a public record evidencing an apparently valid sale. Since the third party purchasers here, the Bushes, did purchase for value and in reliance on public records which evidenced a valid sale, they are protected against the claims of the plaintiff forced heirs notwithstanding the fact that the transfer was actually a donation in disguise.

However, plaintiffs urge alternatively that the transfer was a disguised donation which purported to give away all that the donor (I. M. Owen) had, without retaining enough for his subsistence, in contravention of Article 1497, and therefore 'null for the whole.' Plaintiff argues that if the vendee received only a null title, one that was ineffective to transfer title, he could not validly pass title on to the Bushes.

We find, however, that even if the title which passed to the sons could be declared absolutely null while the property remained in their hands,[6] when the property passed into the hands of an innocent third party purchasing in reliance on the public records, the claimants could no longer recover the property. In the case of Rocques v. Freeman, 125 La. 60, 51 So. 68 (1909), a widow transferred to her children through a partition her undivided interest in her community property. The children subsequently sold the prop-

---

6. For discussions of the area of donations Omnium bonorum, see 34 Tul.L.Rev. 228 (1974); 23 La.L.Rev. 433 (1963); and 6 La.L.Rev. 98 (1944).

172 erty to third parties. The mother later attempted to nullify her transfer as a donation in
173 disguise and as a donation Omnium bonorum, but this Court affirmed the dismissal of
174 her petition. The Court found that her transfer was null because it was a donation in dis-
175 guise and a donation Omnium bonorum, but held that the nullity could be asserted only
176 against the donees, not against innocent third parties who had dealt with the property on
177 the faith of the public records.

178   The Court stated:

179   'The act which is sought to be annulled in this case as a donation does not ap-
180   pear on its face to possess that character. On its face, it is a partition between
181   Charles F. Metoyer and his sister (plaintiffs' children). It was no more calculated
182   to put innocent third parties on their guard against defects in the title than would
183   have been a donation in the form of a sham sale. *And we do not imagine any one*
184   *would say that a donation in the form of a sham sale could be annulled to the detri-*
185   *ment of innocent third persons who had dealt with the property in the faith of the*
186   *public records.*' 51 So. at 70. (emphasis added)

187   We hold, therefore, that where there is nothing of record to indicate that the transfer
188 to the original vendee could have been annulled as a donation Omnium bonorum and
189 when an innocent party has purchased the land for valuable consideration relying upon
190 the public records, the third party takes the property free of these unrecorded and secret
191 equities.

192   Plaintiffs, however, claim that the Bushes were not innocent third party purchasers
193 because they had certain actual knowledge about the original transfers, namely, that the
194 transfers were from father to children and that one of the brothers felt there was some doubt
195 as to whether they (the Bushes) could get a 'clear deed.'

196   It is uncontroverted that the Bushes were arms length purchasers who were buying
197 the property for value, and that they were not participants or co-participants in any at-
198 tempt at fraud. The legal issue here is whether the actual knowledge which they had of
199 the previous transfer placed them in such a position that they could not rely on the pub-
200 lic records. We hold that it did not.

201   A third party purchaser can rely on the public records so long as he does not par-
202 ticipate in fraud. Jackson v. Creswell, 147 La. 914, 86 So. 329 (1920); Kinchen v.
203 Kinchen, 244 So.2d 316 (La.App.1st Cir. 1970), writ not considered, 257 La. 854, 244
204 So.2d 608; Dugas v. Talley, 109 So.2d 300 (La.App.1st Cir. 1959). Even if he has some
205 actual nonrecord knowledge of a preceding transfer which might have made him sus-
206 picious of a deed's validity, he may still rely on the public records if they reveal an ap-
207 parently valid sale. In the case of Prather v. Porter, 176 La. 324, 145 So. 675 (1933),
208 this Court upheld the dismissal of a suit by the forced heir of the original vendor on
209 defendants' exception of no cause of action (defendants were third party purchasers)
210 where the plaintiff contended that defendants were chargeable with knowledge that
211 the transfer was a donation, because the defendants knew the following things: the
212 original vendees were stated in the recorded instrument to be the daughter-in-law and
213 grandson of the vendor; the consideration was stated to be 'whatever amount'; and
214 the transfer actually divested the transferor of all of his property. The Court held that
215 these allegations were insufficient to charge the defendants with bad faith because, as
216 it stated:

217   'the conveyance records are the only things to which one dealing with real es-
218   tate or real rights needs to look. Notice or knowledge dehors the public records
219   on the part of a third person is not equivalent to registry.' 145 So. at 677.

As to plaintiffs' contentions as to the family relationship and the price, the Court stated: 220

> 'There is no law prohibiting the owner of real property from selling the property   221
> to his daughter-in-law and grandson. The price as finally expressed in an act of   222
> sale represents the stated consideration for the sale. And a vendee who has paid   223
> an adequate price cannot be dispossessed of his property because a prior vendor   224
> has chosen to part with his title for an inadequate consideration.' Id.   225

The actual knowledge which the Bushes had of the transfer to their vendor was far less   226
than the Court in Prather assumed that the defendants had there. Of record, defendants   227
Bush knew only that the vendor and vendee had a common surname, and that fifteen acres   228
had been sold ostensibly for $300 and forty acres ostensibly for $100. Although the price   229
of the forty-acre tract might have seemed unusually low (had the Bushes known the land   230
values some fifteen years before), the stated consideration of the smaller tract was later es-   231
tablished as a full 44% Of its true fair market value,[7] and, as this Court stated in Prather,   232
'a vendee who has paid an adequate price cannot be dispossessed of his property because   233
a prior vendor has chosen to part with his title for an inadequate consideration.' Beyond the   234
record, the Bushes were aware that the original vendor-vendees were father and sons, and   235
that one of the sons felt they could not get a clear deed. However, no suggestion has been   236
made that the Bushes had any reason to believe that the sons had not paid for the property   237
or that the sales in March of 1957 comprised all that the father had for his subsistence. It   238
can therefore hardly be said that the Bushes were put on notice, either by the record or in   239
fact, that the sales in question were donations, much less donations Omnium bonorum.   240

Therefore we conclude that a third party, who is not participating in fraud, and who   241
plans to purchase for value property which according to the public records was properly   242
Sold to his prospective vendor, may rely on those records even though he has some ac-   243
tual knowledge on which he could speculate that a timely prosecuted legal attack upon   244
his vendor's title might be successful.   245

[....]

Questions

1. Lines 8–97: What is a donation omnium bonorum? *See* La. Civ. Code art. 1498. Why is it reasonable to prohibit this type of donation?

2. Lines 98 *et seq.*: Where does the court find the adjective "pure" in "pure simulation"? Is it proper for the court to state that "simulations are of two types" and to refer only to a pure simulation and to refer to what should have been another adjective for the second type of simulation as being actually a "disguise transfer"? Look at the adjectives used in the 1984–85 version of Louisiana Civil Code articles 2025 to 2028. Has a disguise transfer become a relative simulation?

3. Lines 104–107: Is the court going too far in declaring that "the simulated sale is an absolute nullity"? Is it really an issue of nullity or one of a juridical act which, because it is simulated, can have no effect against third parties (*see* La. Civ. Code art. 2028)? Do you see the difference between nullity of a juridical act and lack of effect against third parties?

4. Lines 98–177: What do you think of this public record doctrine? What goals do you think it is meant to achieve? Can you think of any possible unfairness, particularly

---

7. It is not a matter of record in this case as to which twenty-seven and one-half acre tract encompasses the fifteen acres.

when third parties had knowledge outside of the public records (*see* below lines 166–169)? On lines 166–167, the Court refers to the title as "absolutely null" and, yet, third parties would be protected. Can you identify any inconsistency in the court's choice of words (*see* question 3 above)?

LONDON TOWNE CONDOMINIUM HOMEOWNER'S ASSOCIATION

v.

LONDON TOWNE COMPANY, et al.

Supreme Court of Louisiana
Oct. 17, 2006
939 So.2d 1227

VICTORY, J.

We granted this writ application to resolve a split among the circuits as to the correct interpretation of Louisiana Civil Code Article 2041, which provides the prescriptive and peremptive periods for bringing a revocatory action. After reviewing the record and the applicable law, we reverse the judgment of the court of appeal and hold that, where the obligee seeks to annul an act of the obligor, the relevant date for prescriptive purposes is the date the obligee knew or should have known of the act, and that the date of recordation of the act does not, standing alone, commence the running of prescription.

FACTS AND PROCEDURAL HISTORY

On August 28, 2001, the London Towne Homeowner's Association (the "Association") filed suit against the London Towne Condominiums (the "LTC") in the 24th Judicial District Court to collect amounts due for association dues and for defects in the condominiums (the "Lawsuit"). On May 24, 2004, the 24th Judicial District Court signed a judgment in favor of the Association and against LTC in the principal amount of $281,899.16, plus legal interest, expert witness fees and attorney's fees. LTC did not appeal the judgment, which has not been satisfied.

On August 19, 2000, LTC acquired Unit 9 of 1201 Chartres Street in New Orleans for $202,000.00. On February 1, 2002, after the Lawsuit was filed, but prior to the entry of judgment against LTC, LTC executed an Act of Sale by which it purportedly sold the property to Millennium Group I, LLC ("Millennium") for $202,000.00. The February 1, 2002, Act of Sale was recorded in the Orleans Parish conveyance records on February 19, 2002.

The Association alleges that shortly after obtaining its judgment against LTC, the Association learned of the 2002 transfer of the Chartres Street property. Believing that the transfer was part of a scheme to place LTC's assets out of the reach of its creditors, the Association filed a Petition for Declaratory Judgment in Orleans Parish on November 18, 2004, challenging the transfer under both the revocatory action and simulation articles of the Civil Code,[1] and seeking to have the transfer adjudged either an absolute or relative nullity. On June 2, 2005, Millennium filed peremptory exceptions of no cause of ac-

---

1. In support of its claims, the Association alleged that the transfer by LTC to Millennium was made for less then the amount stated in the Act of Sale or for no consideration at all, that the parties to the transfer intended for different effects to flow from the transaction than those stated in the Act of Sale or for the transaction to produce no effects between them, and that the transfer caused or increased LTC's insolvency. The Association also alleged that the purported transfer was made to place the Chartres Street property beyond the reach of LTC's creditors.

tion and no right of action in response to the action in simulation and a peremptory exception of prescription in response to the revocatory action. Millennium argued that the Association's revocatory action was prescribed on its face under La. C.C. art.2041 because it was filed more than one year after the date the document evidencing the transfer was recorded.

By judgment dated July 13, 2005, the trial court denied Millennium's exceptions. LTC sought supervisory review of the denial of its exception of prescription. The court of appeal granted LTC's writ and reversed the judgment of the trial court, holding that "Millennium met its burden of proof to show that the Association's revocatory action had prescribed, since over a year has passed from the date on which the Association received constructive notice of the sale," which the court of appeal ruled was the date the Act of Sale was recorded. *London Towne Condominium Homeowner's Association v. London Towne Company, et al.,* 05-1243 (La.App. 4 Cir. 1/18/06). We granted this writ application to resolve a split in the circuits as to commencement of prescription of a revocatory action under La. C.C. art.2041. *London Towne Condominium Homeowner's Association v. London Towne Company, et al.,* 06-0401 (La.5/5/06), 927 So.2d 298.

DISCUSSION

Louisiana Civil Code articles 2036–2043 provide the rules applicable to the revocatory action, pursuant to which "[a]n obligee has a right to annul an act of the obligor, or the result of a failure to act of the obligor, made or effected after the right of the obligee arose, that causes or increases the obligor's insolvency."[2] La. C.C. art.2036. These code articles dictate the type of relief to which an obligee is entitled and the procedures which must be followed in a revocatory action.[3] Civil Code article 2041 provides as follows:

> The action of the obligee must be brought within one year from the time he learned or should have learned of the act, or the result of the failure to act,[4] of

---

2. "An obligor is insolvent when the total of his liabilities exceeds the total of his fairly appraised assets." La. C.C. art.2037.

3. La. C.C. art.2038 provides:

An obligee may annul an onerous contract made by the obligor with a person who knew or should have known that the contract would cause or increase the obligor's insolvency. In that case, the person is entitled to recover what he gave in return only to the extent that it has inured to the benefit of the obligor's creditors.

An obligee may annul an onerous contract made by the obligor with a person who did not know that the contract would cause or increase the obligor's insolvency, but in that case that person is entitled to recover as much as he gave to the obligor. That lack of knowledge is presumed when that person has given at least four-fifths of the value of the thing obtained in return from the obligor.

La. C.C. art.2039 provides:

An obligee may attack a gratuitous contract made by the obligor whether or not the other party knew that the contract would cause or increase the obligor's insolvency.

La. C.C. art.2040 provides:

An obligee may not annul a contract made by the obligor in the regular course of his business.

La. C.C. art.2042 provides:

In an action to annul either his obligor's act, or the result of his obligor's failure to act, the obligee must join the obligor and the third persons involved in that act or failure to act.

A third person joined in the action may plead discussion of the obligor's assets.

La. C.C. art.2043 provides:

If an obligee establishes his right to annul his obligor's act, or the result of his obligor's failure to act, that act or result shall be annulled only to the extent that it affects the obligee's right.

4. "The expression, '... the result of a failure to act of the obligor' contemplates situations in which an obligor becomes insolvent, or his insolvency increases, because of his failure to act, or when the

the obligor that the obligee seeks to annul, but never after three years from the date of that act or result.

[....]

In reversing the judgment of the trial court, the court of appeal relied on its prior holding in *Allied Shipyard, Inc. v. Edgett*, 03-1315 (La.App. 4 Cir. 2/11/04), 868 So.2d 189, *writ granted*, 04-0503 (La.4/23/04), 870 So.2d 281 (case settled after writ grant). *Allied Shipyard* held that prescription under La. C.C. art.2041 begins to run when the obligee-creditor knew or should have known of the donation which they alleged created or increased the insolvency of the debtor, which is when the donation sought to be set aside was recorded in the public record. 868 So.2d at 192. Based on *Allied Shipyard*, the court of appeal held:

> La. C.C. art.2041 clearly provides for constructive notice to trigger the running of prescription based on its express provision that a revocatory action shall be brought within one year from the time the creditor learned or **should have learned of the act.** Although the Association argues and the trial court reasoned that prescription should not commence until the Association learned that it had been damaged by the transfer, we find nothing in the record supporting an alternative date from which the Association claims that prescription should have run. Millennium met its burden of proof to show that the Association's revocatory action had prescribed, since over a year has passed from the date on which the Association received constructive notice of the sale.

London Towne Condominium Homeowner's Ass'n, 95-1243, p. 3.

The court in *Allied Shipyard* made clear its disagreement with the view of the Third Circuit, which has held that prescription does not begin to run until the creditor has constructive knowledge of the damage caused by the act which increases the insolvency of the debtor, rather than the date of the act itself. *First Federal Savings & Loan Ass'n of Lake Charles v. Jones*, 620 So.2d 408 (La.App. 3 Cir.), *writ denied*, 629 So.2d 347 (La.1993); *Jeme, Inc. v. Gold Coast Carpets, Inc.*, 94-182 (La.App. 3 Cir. 10/5/94), 643 So.2d 898. The Third Circuit reasoned in *First Federal* that "before First Federal could exercise its right to the revocatory action, it first had to be able to prove that it had been damaged by its debtor's actions." 620 So.2d at 411. Thus, "[t]he trial court's reliance on the recordation date of the trust instrument in the public records as the date prescription began to run was clearly misplaced." *Id.*

The First Circuit has reached yet another conclusion as to the interpretation of La. C.C. art.2041. In *Parish Nat. Bank v. Wilks*, 04-1439 (La.App. 1 Cir. 8/3/05), 923 So.2d 8, 15, a case with essentially the same facts for prescription purposes as the case *sub judice*, the court "decline[d] to find that the time of the filing of the act of donation in the conveyance records was the date when [the creditor] knew or should have known of the act of donation, so as to commence the prescriptive period on its revocatory action." In so holding, the First Circuit correctly relied on our holding in *Phillips v. Parker*, 483 So.2d 972 (La.1986), which explained the public records doctrine as follows:

> The fundamental principle of the law of registry is that any sale, mortgage, privilege, contract or judgment affecting immovable property, which is required to be recorded, is utterly null and void as to third persons unless recorded. When the law of recordation applies, an interest in immovable property is effective

---

obligor fails to defend himself in a lawsuit, and the resulting judgment creates or increases his insolvency." La. C.C. art. 2036, Official Revisions Comment (e) (1984).

against third persons only if it is recorded; if the interest is not recorded, it is not effective against third persons, even if the third person knows of the claim....

Thus, the law of registry does not create rights in a positive sense, but rather has the negative effect of denying the effectiveness of certain rights unless they are recorded. The essence of the public records doctrine is that recordation is an essential element for the effectiveness of a right, and it is important to distinguish between effectiveness of a right against third persons and knowledge of a right by third persons. An unrecorded interest is not effective against anyone (except the parties). A recorded interest, however, is effective both against those third persons who have knowledge and those who do not have knowledge of the presence of the interest in the public records. From the standpoint of the operation of the public records doctrine, knowledge is an irrelevant consideration. *Any theory of constructive knowledge which imputes knowledge of the contents of the public records to third persons forms no part of the public records doctrine.* (Emphasis added.)

Phillips, 483 So.2d at 975–76 (footnotes and citations omitted). Thus, based on our holding in *Phillips*, the court of appeal in *Parish Nat. Bank* held:

Since the public records doctrine allows the parties to rely on the absence of documents in the public records and does not impute knowledge of the contents of the public records to third persons, the public records doctrine cannot be used to charge an obligee (creditor) with constructive knowledge of documents in the public records for purposes of determining whether he knew or should have known of the act so as to commence the prescriptive period under La. C.C. art.2041.

Parish Nat. Bank, supra at p. 15. In that case, because the defendant's motion for summary judgment was supported only by the recordation of the donation in the public records on March 4, 2002, and the plaintiff admitted in its petition that it learned of the donation on January 16, 2003, the court held that prescription began to run on January 16, 2003. *Id.*

We have consistently held that the starting point in interpreting any statute is the language of the statute itself. *Touchard v. Williams*, 617 So.2d 885, 888 (La.1993); *Theriot v. Midland Risk Ins. Co.*, 95-2895 (La.5/20/97), 694 So.2d 184, 186. In reading the clear language of La. C.C. art.2041, it is evident that there are two possible prescriptive dates and one peremptive date for bringing a revocatory action. An action must be brought: (1) within one year from the time the obligee learned or should have learned of the act of the obligor that the obligee seeks to annul; (2) within one year from the time the obligee learned or should have learned of the result of the failure to act of the obligor that the obligee seeks to annul; or (3) never after three years from the date of the act or the result of the failure to act.

In this case, what we have is an *act*, i.e., the sale of Unit 9 of 1201 Chartres Street in New Orleans, that the obligee seeks to annul. La. C.C. art.2041 clearly states that under these circumstances, the relevant date is one year from the time the obligee learned or should have learned of the act. The result of the act, or the harm caused as a result of the act, is not a relevant consideration because a result is only significant when there has been a failure to act.[5]

---

5. The Revision Comments to this article state:
   (a) This Article is new. As "insolvency" is substituted from "fraud" as the criterion for availability of the revocatory action, the prescriptive period should be one year from the day the obligee learned of the harm. Otherwise, a devious obligor could prejudice his obligee's claim and conceal his actions for a year, thereby escaping liability altogether.
   La. C.C. art.2041, 1984 Revision Comments (a). In light of the clear wording of the statute, which provides a different commencement date depending on whether the obligee is seek-

147 Therefore, where an obligee is seeking to annul an *act* of an obligor, the relevant date
148 is when the obligee learned or should have learned of the act. Granted, an obligee only
149 has the right to bring an action to annul an act "that causes or increases the obligor's in-
150 solvency." La. C.C. art.2036. However, according to the clear language of La. C.C. art.2041,
151 prescription begins to run from the date the obligee learned or should have learned of the
152 act, not the date the obligee knows the act has caused or increased the obligor's insolvency.
153 While this may, in theory, result in a cause of action prescribing before the obligee has the
154 right to bring the action, we do not believe this was contrary to the intent of the legisla-
155 ture, as they have cut off the right to file a revocatory action by setting a peremptive pe-
156 riod, regardless of the obligee's knowledge or lack thereof, three years from the date of the
157 act or the result. As we held in *Reeder v. North*, 97-0239 (La.10/21/97), 701 So.2d 1291,
158 1296, in interpreting the legal malpractice prescriptive and peremptive period under La.
159 R.S. 9:5605, "while the terms of the ... statute of limitations statute may be unfair in that
160 a person's claim may be extinguished before he realizes the full extent of his damages, the
161 enactment of such a statute of limitations is exclusively a legislative prerogative." Just as in
162 *Reeder,* the legislature has clearly stated the terms of this prescriptive/peremptive statute of
163 limitations and we are bound to interpret it as written.

164 Thus, the remaining issue is whether the date of recordation in the public records *ipso*
165 *facto* constitutes constructive notice to the obligee of the act itself. Based on our expla-
166 nation of the public records doctrine in *Philips v. Parker, supra*, we reject that legal con-
167 clusion. As we stated in *Philips*, "[a]ny theory of constructive knowledge which imputes
168 knowledge of the contents of the public records to third persons forms no part of the
169 public records doctrine." 483 So.2d at 975–76. Therefore, recordation in the public records
170 does not constitute constructive notice to third parties under La. C.C. art.2041.

171 In light of the above, we need to determine if the trial court was manifestly erroneous
172 in denying Millennium's exception of prescription. [....] As our holding indicates, the
173 date of recordation does not, standing alone, prove actual or constructive knowledge of
174 the act. Constructive knowledge sufficient to trigger the running of prescription exists
175 when a party has sufficient information or notice to excite inquiry regarding a possible
176 claim. *Id.* at 510–11. Such information or knowledge as ought to reasonably put the vic-
177 tim on notice is sufficient to start the running of prescription. *Id.* The date upon which
178 an obligee learned or should have learned of the act is a factual determination to be made
179 by the trial court considering all the facts and circumstances of the case.[6]

180 In its petition, the Association alleged in its Second Supplemental and Amended Pe-
181 tition for Declaratory Judgment that "[t]he Act of Sale was recorded on February 19, 2002
182 under Instrument No. 231488, and a copy of said act is attached hereto as Exhibit B."
183 Millennium did not introduce any evidence in the trial court to prove actual or con-

ing to annul an act of the obligee or the result of a failure to act on the part of the obligee,
we reject the Comment's blanket statement that "the prescriptive period should be one year
from the day the obligee learned of the harm." Clearly, this is not true where the obligee is
seeking to annul an act of the obligor. As clearly expressed by the legislature, prescription
begins to run in that case when the obligee learned or should have learned of the act.

6. The date of recordation may be a relevant consideration if, based on the facts and circumstances of the case, the obligee knew or should have known of the recordation. Further, if it is found
that the obligee knew about the recordation, the date he found out about the recordation would commence the running of prescription. Thus, while the date of recordation is not the determinative factor in ascertaining the commencement of prescription, it may be a relevant factor depending upon
the facts and circumstances of the case. One example of an act that would provide constructive notice where an transfer has been recorded would be a judgment debtor examination where the creditor learns of the debtor's property but fails to investigate whether it has been transferred to a third party.

structive knowledge of the transfer. Instead, it relied on the Association's statement in its   184
petition that the transfer was recorded on February 19, 2002 as proof that the revocatory   185
action has prescribed. However, as we have held today that the date of recordation does   186
not provide constructive notice of the transfer, that statement in the petition does not   187
prove that the Association learned or should have learned of the transfer on that date.   188
Therefore, the burden of proof did not shift to the Association, but instead remained   189
with Millennium; thus it was incumbent upon Millennium to introduce such evidence   190
at the trial of its exception. Millennium failed to do so; therefore, it failed to satisfy its bur-   191
den of proof.   192

CONCLUSION   193

Under the clear wording of La. C.C. art.2041, prescription on a revocatory action be-   194
gins to run from (1) the time the obligee learned or should have learned of the act of the   195
obligor that the obligee seeks to annul, or (2) the time the obligee learned or should have   196
learned of the result of the failure to act of the obligor that the obligee seeks to annul. How-   197
ever, in all cases, a revocatory action is perempted three years from the date of the act or   198
the result of the failure to act. The date the obligee learned or should have learned of the   199
act or the result of the failure to act is determined by considering all the relevant facts and   200
circumstances of the particular case. Where the obligee is seeking to annul an act of the   201
obligor, the act of recordation in the public records, does not, standing alone, provide con-   202
structive knowledge of the act. In this case, Millennium bore the burden of proving that   203
one year had passed since the Association learned or should have learned of the transfer of   204
the Chartres Street property. Because the only evidence it presented in support of its ex-   205
ception was the date of recordation of the transfer, it did not carry its burden of proof.   206

[....]

Questions

1. Lines 10–51: Why is the plaintiff Association bringing a revocatory action in con-
    junction with an action in simulation? Are the grounds of the two actions the same?
    Are the grounds for a revocatory action met in the facts of the case? We have seen in
    the *Owen v. Owen* case the importance of the public records doctrine and its effects
    as regards third parties. How does the court's statement on lines 11–15 fit with that
    doctrine? What is the difference between "prescription" and "peremption"? *See* La. Civ.
    Code arts. 3447 and 3458.

2. Lines 53–107: Because the Louisiana Supreme Court must resolve a split among the
    circuits as to the correct interpretation of Louisiana Civil Code article 2041, notice
    that in its "Discussion", the Supreme Court starts with a list of the Louisiana Civil Code
    articles, as the binding sources of law, to turn then to the jurisprudence. How many
    different interpretations of the same article 2041 were co-existing? *See* question below.

3. Lines 150–152: How can the Louisiana Supreme Court speak of "the clear language
    of La. C. C. art. 2041 ..." when the courts of appeal had different interpretations of
    that article?

4. Lines 147–192: Do you see the distinction that the Louisiana Supreme Court makes
    between "the date of recordation" of an act, "constructive notice or knowledge of the
    act", and "imputed knowledge of the act"?

5. Lines 194–206: Can you restate in your own words the "Conclusion" given by the
    Court? Consider footnote 6: does it make "the clear wording of La. C.C. art.2041"

clearer? Did the Court spend its time making clearer the public records doctrine or the determination of that time (knowledge) that triggers the computation of the prescriptive or peremptive period of the revocatory action? Or were the two intimately tied together?

Section V—Of the Interpretation of Agreements

Louisiana Sources of Law

Louisiana Civil Code

Art. 2045. Determination of the intent of the parties.

Interpretation of a contract is the determination of the common intent of the parties. (Acts 1984, No. 331, § 1, eff. Jan. 1, 1985.)

Art. 2046. No further interpretation when intent is clear.

When the words of a contract are clear and explicit and lead to no absurd consequences, no further interpretation may be made in search of the parties' intent. (Acts 1984, No. 331, § 1, eff. Jan. 1, 1985.)

Art. 2047. Meaning of words.

The words of a contract must be given their generally prevailing meaning.

Words of art and technical terms must be given their technical meaning when the contract involves a technical matter. (Acts 1984, No. 331, § 1, eff. Jan. 1, 1985.)

Art. 2048. Words susceptible of different meanings.

Words susceptible of different meanings must be interpreted as having the meaning that best conforms to the object of the contract. (Acts 1984, No. 331, § 1, eff. Jan. 1, 1985.)

Art. 2049. Provision susceptible of different meanings.

A provision susceptible of different meanings must be interpreted with a meaning that renders it effective and not with one that renders it ineffective. (Acts 1984, No. 331, § 1, eff. Jan. 1, 1985.)

Art. 2050. Provisions interpreted in light of each other.

Each provision in a contract must be interpreted in light of the other provisions so that each is given the meaning suggested by the contract as a whole. (Acts 1984, No. 331, § 1, eff. Jan. 1, 1985.)

Art. 2051. Contract worded in general terms.

Although a contract is worded in general terms, it must be interpreted to cover only those things it appears the parties intended to include. (Acts 1984, No. 331, § 1, eff. Jan. 1, 1985.)

Art. 2052. Situation to which the contract applies.

When the parties intend a contract of general scope but, to eliminate doubt, include a provision that describes a specific situation, interpretation must not restrict the scope of the contract to that situation alone. (Acts 1984, No. 331, § 1, eff. Jan. 1, 1985.)

Art. 2053. Nature of contract, equity, usages, conduct of the parties, and other contracts between same parties.

A doubtful provision must be interpreted in light of the nature of the contract, equity, usages, the conduct of the parties before and after the formation of the contract, and of other contracts of a like nature between the same parties. (Acts 1984, No. 331, § 1, eff. Jan. 1, 1985.)

Art. 2054. No provision of the parties for a particular situation.

When the parties made no provision for a particular situation, it must be assumed that they intended to bind themselves not only to the express provisions of the contract, but also to whatever the law, equity, or usage regards as implied in a contract of that kind or necessary for the contract to achieve its purpose. (Acts 1984, No. 331, § 1, eff. Jan. 1, 1985.)

Art. 2055. Equity and usage.

Equity, as intended in the preceding articles, is based on the principles that no one is allowed to take unfair advantage of another and that no one is allowed to enrich himself unjustly at the expense of another.

Usage, as intended in the preceding articles, is a practice regularly observed in affairs of a nature identical or similar to the object of a contract subject to interpretation. (Acts 1984, No. 331, § 1, eff. Jan. 1, 1985.)

Art. 2056. Standard-form contracts.

In case of doubt that cannot be otherwise resolved, a provision in a contract must be interpreted against the party who furnished its text.

A contract executed in a standard form of one party must be interpreted, in case of doubt, in favor of the other party. (Acts 1984, No. 331, § 1, eff. Jan. 1, 1985.)

Art. 2057. Contract interpreted in favor of obligor.

In case of doubt that cannot be otherwise resolved, a contract must be interpreted against the obligee and in favor of the obligor of a particular obligation.

Yet, if the doubt arises from lack of a necessary explanation that one party should have given, or from negligence or fault of one party, the contract must be interpreted in a manner favorable to the other party whether obligee or obligor. (Acts 1984, No. 331, § 1, eff. Jan. 1, 1985.)

Précis: Louisiana Law of Conventional Obligations — §§ 10.1.1 to 10.2.2

A contract being, presumably, the outward manifestation of the parties' intent, the Code Articles which lay down the "rules" of interpretation of contracts can only have for their purpose to provide guidelines to ascertain and extract the intent of the parties out of the contract. This is the whole meaning of Art. 2045: "Interpretation of a contract is the determination of the common intent of the parties." ...

The majority of the Code Articles on this issue of interpretation focus on the words of the contract and the provisions of the contract. **Art. 2046, Art. 2047, Art. 2048.**

The words of a contract must be read also within the context of the provisions of the contract....

Articles 2049, 2050, 2051 and 2052....

It remains however, that in relating a provision of a contract to another provision in the same contract the courts must strive to **"determine the common intent of the parties." Art. 2045.** Ascertaining that "common intent" should be the goal to reach.

This is particularly important in those instances where one party to a contract is in a weaker bargaining position than the other party. The civil Code gives the courts two special rules to use for the purpose of protecting that party presumed to be the weaker of the two in any one of two situations contemplated in Articles 2056 and 2057....

Whenever the performance of the obligations created by a contract spreads over any length of time there exists the risk that the actual performance of the obligations may not match the performance as expected or as anticipated by the common intent of the parties when they entered their contract. The many different kinds of "surrounding circumstances" that prevailed at the time the contract was entered into may or, rather, are likely to be different from the circumstances that will surround the actual performance of the obligations created by the contract....

The question then raised is: what of the situation of the party negatively affected by a subsequent change in the circumstances? Can a court "re-write" the contract to adapt it to present day surroundings and claim, still, to "interpret" the contract as per the presumed "common intent" of the parties as it was at the time of formation of their contract?...

A few specific Articles in the civil Code invite the judge to "re-write" a contract in specific circumstances. Such is the case of Art. 1861(2), Art. 1877, Articles 1951 and 1952. However, in all other circumstances, a contract being the "law" between the parties it should not be revised by a court under the guise of "interpretation".

Cases

Charles Ray SANDERS, et al.
v.
ASHLAND OIL, INC., et al.

Louisiana Court of Appeal
First Circuit
June 20, 1997
696 So.2d 1031

CARTER, Judge.

[....]

BACKGROUND

On December 8, 1990, employees of Protech Environmental Services, Inc. (Protech) were performing asbestos abatement services in connection with the renovation of Grandison Hall dormitory at Southern University in Baton Rouge, Louisiana. A fire began in the dormitory where two Protech employees, Charles Ray Sanders and Jesse Wayne Bickford, were removing mastic tile adhesive from the floors. As a result of the fire, Charles Ray Sanders sustained serious injuries, and Jesse Wayne Bickford was killed. The fire also caused substantial damage to the dormitory.

On December 6, 1991, Charles Ray Sanders and Bobbie O. Bickford, individually, as administratrix of the Estate of Jesse Wayne Bickford, and as tutrix of the minor children, Brian Wayne Bickford and Travis Dan Bickford, filed the instant action **for personal in-**

juries and punitive damages, under docket number 376,039. Numerous defendants were named in the petition, including the State of Louisiana, through the Office of Risk Management, Division of Administration, Office of the Governor, and Southern University (the State); Protech; Roy Eschette, President of Protech; and Aetna Life and Casualty Company (Aetna Life), the liability insurer of Protech. Aetna Casualty and Surety Company (Aetna Casualty), the workers' compensation insurer of Protech, subsequently intervened in the action to exercise its right of subrogation.

In a separate action, the State filed suit against Protech and its building loss insurer, Great American Insurance Company (Great American), under docket number 376,088, for **property damages** sustained to the dormitory. This suit was subsequently settled, and the State entered into a "General Release and Indemnity Agreement" with Protech and Great American for the sum of $10,000.00.

On June 29, 1995, in the action for personal injuries and punitive damages, Eschette, Protech, Aetna Life, and Aetna Casualty (hereafter collectively referred to as Protech) filed a cross-claim and third-party demand against the State. Protech alleged that, under the second paragraph of the "General Release and Indemnity Agreement" executed in the property damage suit, the State agreed to indemnify Protech for any amounts for which it may be cast, together with legal interest and costs. Additionally, Protech alleged that Aetna Casualty had paid substantial sums to defend and protect Eschette and Protech in connection with the claims for which the State agreed to provide indemnity, and, therefore, it was entitled to reimbursement by the State.

The State answered, contending that, in entering into the release and indemnity agreement, the parties intended to settle *only* those claims arising out of the State's suit for property damage, not claims arising out of the suit for personal injuries and punitive damages.

On September 26, 1995, the State filed a motion for summary judgment on the cross-claim/third-party demand, contending that the release and indemnity agreement did not grant Protech indemnification by the State because the parties to the agreement did not intend for the indemnification to extend to any suit other than the State's suit for property damage. [....]

On October 23, 1995, a hearing was held on the State's motion for summary judgment. At the conclusion of the hearing, the trial court, for oral reasons assigned, granted the motion for summary judgment, dismissing, with prejudice, Protech's contractual indemnity claims against the State and assessing costs to Protech. A judgment was signed on November 16, 1995.

Protech appealed, assigning the following specifications of error:

1. The trial court erred in interpreting the agreement contrary to the clear and unambiguous meaning of its terms.

2. The trial court erred in considering parol evidence purporting to show the parties' intent.

[....]

CONTRACT INTERPRETATION

Generally, legal agreements have the effect of law upon the parties, and, as they bind themselves, they shall be held to a full performance of the obligations flowing therefrom. *Belle Pass Terminal, Inc. v. Jolin, Inc.*, 92-1544, 92-1545, p. 16 (La.App. 1st Cir. 3/11/94); 634 So.2d 466, 479, *writ denied*, 94-0906 (La.6/17/94); 638 So.2d 1094; *Spohrer v. Spohrer*,

610 So.2d 849, 851–52 (La.App. 1st Cir.1992). In other words, a contract between the parties is the law between them, and the courts are obligated to give legal effect to such contracts according to the true intent of the parties. LSA-C.C. art.2045; *Martin Exploration Company v. Amoco Production Company*, 93-0349, p. 4 (La.App. 1st Cir. 5/20/94); 637 So.2d 1202, 1205, *writ denied*, 94-2003 (La.11/4/94); 644 So.2d 1048; *Spohrer v. Spohrer*, 610 So.2d at 852. This intent is to be determined by the words of the contract when they are clear, explicit, and lead to no absurd consequences. LSA-C.C. art.2046; *Woodrow Wilson Construction Company, Inc. v. MMR-Radon Constructors, Inc.*, 93-2346, p. 3 (La.App. 1st Cir. 4/8/94); 635 So.2d 758, 759, *writ denied*, 94-1206 (La.7/1/94); 639 So.2d 1167; *Belle Pass Terminal, Inc. v. Jolin, Inc.*, 634 So.2d at 479.

When the words of a contract are clear and explicit and lead to no absurd consequences, no further interpretation may be made in search of the parties' intent. LSA-C.C. art.2046; *Belle Pass Terminal, Inc. v. Jolin, Inc.*, 634 So.2d at 479; *Stafford v. Jennings-Norwood Farm and Irrigation Company, Inc.*, 586 So.2d 735, 737 (La.App. 3rd Cir.1991), *writ denied*, 590 So.2d 590 (La.1992); *Investors Associates Ltd. v. B.F. Trappey's Sons Inc.*, 500 So.2d 909, 912 (La.App. 3rd Cir.), *writ denied*, 502 So.2d 116 (La.1987). The rules of interpretation establish that, when a clause in a contract is clear and unambiguous, the letter of that clause should not be disregarded under the pretext of pursuing its spirit. LSA-C.C. art.2046, comment (b); *Cashio v. Shoriak*, 481 So.2d 1013, 1015 (La.1986); *Belle Pass Terminal, Inc. v. Jolin, Inc.*, 634 So.2d at 479; *Spohrer v. Spohrer*, 610 So.2d at 852.

In such cases, the meaning and intent of the parties to the written contract must be sought within the four corners of the instrument and cannot be explained or contradicted by parol evidence. LSA-C.C. art. 1848; *Belle Pass Terminal, Inc. v. Jolin, Inc.*, 634 So.2d at 479; *Investors Associates Ltd. v. B.F. Trappey's Sons Inc.*, 500 So.2d at 912. Contracts, subject to interpretation from the instrument's four corners without the necessity of extrinsic evidence, are to be interpreted as a matter of law, and the use of extrinsic evidence is proper only where a contract is ambiguous after an examination of the four corners of the agreement. *Martin Exploration Company v. Amoco Production Company*, 637 So.2d at 1205; *Investors Associates Ltd. v. B.F. Trappey's Sons Inc.*, 500 So.2d at 912.

When the terms of a written contract are susceptible to more than one interpretation, or there is uncertainty or ambiguity as to its provisions, or the intent of the parties cannot be ascertained from the language employed, parol evidence is admissible to clarify the ambiguity or show the intention of the parties. *Martin Exploration Company v. Amoco Production Company*, 637 So.2d at 1205; *Belle Pass Terminal, Inc. v. Jolin, Inc.*, 634 So.2d at 480. In cases in which the contract is ambiguous, the agreement shall be construed according to the intent of the parties. LSA-C.C. art.2045. Intent is an issue of fact which is to be inferred from all of the surrounding circumstances. *Kuswa & Associates, Inc. v. Thibaut Construction Co., Inc.*, 463 So.2d 1264, 1266 (La.1985); *Commercial Bank & Trust Company v. Bank of Louisiana*, 487 So.2d 655, 659 (La.App. 5th Cir.1986). A doubtful provision must be interpreted in light of the nature of the contract, equity, usages, the conduct of the parties before and after the formation of the contract, and other contracts of a like nature between the same parties. LSA-C.C. art.2053; *Allen v. Burnett*, 530 So.2d 1294, 1301 (La.App. 2nd Cir.1988).

Whether a contract is ambiguous or not is a question of law. *Spohrer v. Spohrer*, 610 So.2d at 853; *Myers v. Myers*, 532 So.2d 490, 494 (La.App. 1st Cir.1988); *Aycock v. Allied Enterprises, Inc.*, 517 So.2d 303, 309 (La.App. 1st Cir.1987), *writs denied*, 518 So.2d 512, 513 (La.1988). However, where factual findings are pertinent to the interpretation of a contract, those factual findings are not to be disturbed unless manifest error is shown. *See G/O Enterprises, Inc. v. Mid Louisiana Gas Company*, 444 So.2d 1279, 1286 (La.App. 4th

Cir.), *writ denied*, 446 So.2d 318 (La.1984); *Universal Iron Works, Inc. v. Falgout Refrigeration, Inc.*, 419 So.2d 1272, 1274 (La.App. 1st Cir.1982). When appellate review is not premised upon any factual findings made at the trial level, but instead is based upon an independent review and examination of the contract on its face, the manifest error rule does not apply. *Spohrer v. Spohrer*, 610 So.2d at 853; *Conoco, Inc. v. Tenneco, Inc., Tennessee Gas Pipeline Company*, 524 So.2d 1305, 1312 (La.App. 3rd Cir.), *writ denied*, 525 So.2d 1048 (La.1988). In such cases, appellate review of questions of law is simply whether the trial court was legally correct. *Spohrer v. Spohrer*, 610 So.2d at 853.

In the instant case, the trial court, in oral reasons for judgment, stated, in pertinent part, as follows:

> The court finds that [the State] was referring to the suit for building damages, suit number 376,[0]88, when it signed the release indemnity agreement for $10,000.[00]. The court is also of the opinion that Pro-Tech could not possibly believe that the State would release them from a wrongful death [or] a personal injury action for this small amount. The second paragraph clarifies the language in the first paragraph, and this court interprets the language aforesaid to mean the State or Southern University and claims they may have means the State and Southern University. Furthermore, this is the standard release and indemnity agreement, and it's [*sic*] purpose is to protect Pro-Tech from the claims of those who are subrogated to the rights of the releasor, in this case the State. Clearly, the State did not sign this agreement to protect Pro-Tech from any and all claims made by anyone and everyone. Furthermore, this court feels that had the parties intended to included [*sic*] the pending personal injury suit 376,039, it would have been referenced. However, there's [*sic*] ample facts, I believe, before this court to render summary judgment....

From these reasons, it is unclear whether the trial court looked only at the four corners of the agreement and found it to be unambiguous or whether he found it to be ambiguous and then reviewed the parol evidence to determine the intent of the parties. Regardless of what the trial court reviewed, the threshold issue on appeal is whether the terms of the agreement are clear and unambiguous. If the language of the agreement is explicit and unambiguous, the contract must be enforced as written. However, if the language of the agreement is unclear and ambiguous, the contract must be construed in light of the intent of the parties.

A. Ambiguity

The "General Release and Indemnity Agreement" at issue in this case provides, in pertinent part, as follows:

> That WE, THE STATE OF LOUISIANA THROUGH THE OFFICE OF RISK MANAGEMENT, DIVISION OF ADMINISTRATION, OFFICE OF THE GOVERNOR, AND SOUTHERN UNIVERSITY, for the sole consideration of the sum of $10,000.00, the receipt whereof is hereby acknowledged, do hereby release and forever discharge PRO-TECH ENVIRONMENTAL SERVICES, INC. AND GREAT AMERICAN INSURANCE COMPANY, and any related and/or affiliated company of and from any and all claims or demands of whatsoever kind or nature, including strict liability, for or because of any matter or thing done, omitted or suffered to be done by any officer, agent, employee, successor or assigns of said parties, prior to and including the day hereof, and particularly on the [*sic*] account of any and all claims which they may have for personal injuries, smoke damage, cost of clean-up, removal of asbestos, air monitoring services,

165 construction costs, painting, damage to terrazzo floors in Grandison Hall, as a
166 result of a[*sic*] explosion/fire on December 8, 1990, at Grandison Hall, SOUTH-
167 ERN UNIVERSITY Campus, Baton Rouge, Louisiana.

168 **We do hereby further agree to indemnify and hold harmless said parties, to-**
169 **gether with all employees, agents, officers, or assigns thereof of and from any and**
170 **all further claims and/or punitive damage claims that may be made or asserted**
171 **by the aforesaid or by anyone because of the aforesaid injuries, damages, loss**
172 **or expenses suffered as a result of the aforesaid explosion/fire, whether such**
173 **claim is made by way of indemnity, contribution, subrogation or otherwise.**

174 The foregoing payment is also received in full compromise and settlement of any
175 and all claims that we have or may have against the insurers under any policy of
176 insurance issued to any defendant, whether under the liability, medical payment
177 or any other portion of said policy as a result of the aforesaid accident.

178 We further recognize that the injuries may be worse than they now appear to be,
179 or may grow worse later, and that we accept this settlement with said knowl-
180 edge. (Emphasis added.)

181   The first paragraph of the agreement is a release clause, wherein the State agreed to re-
182 lease Protech and Great American and any related and/or affiliated company from any
183 and all claims resulting from the actions or inactions of Protech or Great American (or
184 any officer, agent, employee, successor, or assign of Protech or Great American), partic-
185 ularly, any and all claims which they (the State) may have for personal injuries, smoke dam-
186 age, cost of clean-up, removal of asbestos, air monitoring services, construction costs,
187 painting, or damage to terrazzo floors in Grandison Hall, resulting from the December
188 8, 1990 fire.

189   The second paragraph of the agreement is an indemnity clause, wherein the State
190 agreed to indemnify Protech, Great American, and their employees, agents, officers, or
191 assigns from any and all *further* claims which may be asserted by the "aforesaid" (the
192 State) or by "anyone" because of the aforesaid injuries, damages, loss or expenses suf-
193 fered as a result of the "aforesaid" fire.

194   After carefully reviewing the agreement, we conclude that it is neither explicit nor un-
195 ambiguous. Initially, we note that the agreement is poorly drafted and that the use of
196 legalese, such as "aforesaid," makes the meaning of the contract terms unclear. The agree-
197 ment fails to reference the suit which is affected by the agreement and is signed by only one
198 party to the agreement, the State. The indemnity clause utilizes the term "parties," but it fails
199 to specify which "parties" are indemnified, i.e., the parties to the contract or the parties to
200 the lawsuit. Additionally, we find that the indemnity clause, as written, is subject to more
201 than one reasonable interpretation. It could be interpreted to provide indemnity for **all**
202 claims arising from the fire filed by **anyone**, including those for personal injuries suffered
203 by the petitioners in the personal injury suit filed against Protech. On the other hand, it could
204 be interpreted to provide indemnity for only those claims listed in paragraph one to which
205 the release was applicable. Because the agreement is neither explicit nor unambiguous, we
206 will review the extrinsic evidence to determine whether the parties intended for the in-
207 demnity to extend to claims besides those involved in the State's suit for property damage.

208 **B. Intent**

209   The extrinsic evidence in this case consists of various pleadings, correspondence be-
210 tween counsel for Protech and counsel for the State, and the transcript of a stipulation
211 to settle between the State and Protech.

In answers to a request for admissions propounded by the State, Protech admits that a series of letters exchanged between counsel (its attorney and counsel for the State) constitute the entirety of the settlement negotiations in suit number 376,088, the property damage suit. A review of those letters reveals that none of the letters discussed suit number 376,039, the suit for personal injuries. A November 23, 1993 letter from Protech's attorney to counsel for the State, states that "[o]ur client contacted us recently and requested that we obtain a reasonable settlement demand from you in hopes that we can close the *State of Louisiana versus Pro Tech Environmental* portion of this case." The letter then discussed figures relevant to the damage to Grandison Hall. A January 21, 1994 letter from Protech's attorney to the State's counsel states "[w]e confirm our telepone conversation on Wednesday, January 19, 1994 wherein you past [*sic*] along a settlement demand on behalf of the State of Louisiana as [a] result of its suit against Great American Insurance Company for a total of $32,552.98." On January 27, 1994, Protech's attorney wrote to counsel for the State, indicating as follows:

> After reviewing the entire file in this matter, it is apparent that there was no damage to the physical structure itself as a result of the fire since the building had been completely gutted prior to the fire taking place....
>
> Accordingly, we ask that you pass along our settlement offer of $9,500.00, each party to bear its own expenses....

On February 4, 1994, the attorney for Protech wrote to counsel for the State, offering to settle the property damage suit for $10,000.00. Moreover, the exchange of letters resulted in an oral stipulation to settle which was transcribed by the court reporter at the May 26, 1994 deposition of George Bigelow. The stipulation provides as follows:

> [Counsel for Protech]:
>
> This is a matter entitled *State of Louisiana through the Office of Risk Management versus Pro-Tech and Great American Insurance Company.* We were here today for the deposition of the State of Louisiana through its representative George Bigelow.
>
> Prior to the start of the deposition, we had some discussions and are in a position to settle **this matter** on the following terms and conditions:
>
> Great American Insurance Company and Pro-Tech will pay to the State of Louisiana the total sum of $10,000.[00], each party to bear some expenses, in full and final settlement of **this case.** (Emphasis added.)
>
> Agreed?
>
> [Counsel for the State]: Agreed.

Based on the foregoing evidence, we conclude that the State showed that there is no genuine issue of material fact concerning the parties' intent that the State provide indemnification only for the claims set forth in suit number 376,088, the suit for property damage. The correspondence and the stipulation show that the settlement would encompass **only** that part of the case dealing with the State's suit for property damage against Protech. There is nothing to indicate that any other suit was to be included. The agreement does not reference any particular suit, and there is no caption on the agreement. Additionally, in the release portion of the agreement, the State releases Protech, Great American, and their employees, agents, officers, or assigns for the damages it (the State) sustained; there is no reference to anything else. In opposition to the motion for summary judgment, Protech failed to submit any affidavits or other documentation to contradict the State's evidence regarding intent and, thus, failed to raise a genuine issue of material fact as to the intent of the parties. There is not one scintilla of extrinsic evidence to sup-

259 port Protech's position. Therefore, we conclude that the trial court appropriately granted
260 summary judgment in favor of the State.

[....]

Questions

1. What types of persons are involved in this case? Are they pretty much on a par level to negotiate with each other? Should this be relevant if some disagreement occurs between them? Are they professionals in the same line of business? Is a "State" or "state institution" in a somewhat unusual or different negotiating position vis-à-vis the other party whether it be a legal entity or a physical person? Could the State, in the "General Release and Indemnity Agreement", have waived its delictual liability? Could it have waived its contractual liability?

2. Lines 97–110: Is this paragraph a logical consequence of the Court's statement in lines 88–90 above, i.e. that the meaning of a contract must be sought within the four corners of that contract even when parol evidence is admissible?

3. Line 111: Why is it a question of law whether a contract is ambiguous or not?

4. Lines 209 *et seq.*: Since Louisiana Civil Code article 2046 does not allow the court to search for the parties' intent unless there is ambiguity, absurd consequences, etc..., isn't a court rather free to decide whether or not to search for the common intent of the parties under Louisiana Civil Code article 2045? Do Louisiana Civil Code articles 2045–2057 give the courts any guidance as to how to determine the common intent of the parties? Where does the word and concept of equity mentioned in Louisiana Civil Code articles 2053–2055 fit in the four corners of a contract, its words, or in the parties intent?

1 ## Kathy PREJEAN

2 v.

3 ## Walter GUILLORY, et al.

4 Supreme Court of Louisiana
5 July 2, 2010
6 38 So.3d 274

7 [....]

8 On February 15, 1995, by written contract, the Broussard Housing Authority (BHA)
9 hired [Kathy] Prejean as executive director of its Section 8 Housing Program[1] for an ini-
10 tial five-year term, with an extension period of another five years.[2] [....] [A susbsequent
11 addendum to her employment contract,] provided, in pertinent part:

12   1—That the [BHA] hereby retains and employs Kathy Prejean to be its Execu-
13   tive Director for a term of four (4) years commencing with the *1st* day of *Janu-*
14   *ary, 2002* and expiring *January 1, 2006*. In addition, it is further agreed by the
15   parties hereto that this contract shall be extended for an additional four (4) years
16   (the "extension period") upon the same terms and conditions at the option of

---

1. Section 8 housing is a tenant-based program financed with vouchers consisting of federal funds through the Department of Housing and Urban Development (HUD) to provide suitable housing for tenants in homes offered by approved homeowners/landlords.

2. Prejean actually began working for the BHA without contract in October of 1994.

[Prejean], unless the [BHA] gives [Prejean] by *October 1, 2005,* notice in writing that it will not extend the contract due to the inadequate performance of [Prejean]. The Board may make a finding of inadequate performance, after providing [Prejean] with written notice and an opportunity to be heard, upon a determination that a significant adverse audit finding (or adverse management review) by federal or state funding agencies has gone uncorrected for more than sixty (60) days due to action or inaction by [Prejean].

2 — That [Prejean] hereby accepts employment and hereby agrees that for the consideration hereinafter set forth, he/she shall perform the duties as the Executive Director in conducting the business of said [BHA] and perform the duties of Secretary to the Board Members at their regular, special and annual meetings.

In early 2004, without Prejean's knowledge, the BHA decided to transfer its Section 8 Housing Program to the LHA. [....]

Immediately following the adjournment of the BHA meeting, members of the BHA and LHA, along with Guillory, proceeded to the BHA office in Broussard. There a confrontation occurred between Guillory and Prejean concerning the keys to the office, which Prejean refused to relinquish to Guillory, for the purpose of securing the building to commence a final audit of the BHA's financial records. Eventually, Prejean and her staff left the building. That evening Prejean contacted the HUD offices in New Orleans. Upon returning to the BHA office the next morning, Prejean discovered the locks had been changed. After a phone conversation in which HUD officials, Prejean, and Guillory participated, Guillory gave Prejean the new keys to the building and left. Prejean then had the locks re-changed.

[....]

On October 5, 2004, Prejean filed suit against Guillory and the LHA for damages resulting from the "hostile takeover" of the BHA by the LHA. In her petition, Prejean sought [....] [**among other things,**] "a declaratory judgment that her employment contract with [BHA] is valid and enforceable and will become the lawful obligation of the [LHA][, according to its terms] after any formal consolidation occurs."

By November 2004, with HUD's approval of the transfer, Guillory assigned Tim Declouet to head the Broussard office. That same month, Prejean was diagnosed with cancer of her right breast, for which she underwent a mastectomy. By note dated November 2, 2004, Prejean's physician stated Prejean was scheduled for surgery on November 3, and excused her from work until November 22, 2004. By note dated November 11, 2004, Prejean's physician explained Prejean was scheduled for surgery on November 17, 2004, and would return to work after four weeks. Prejean was released to work on January 10, 2005, by noted dated December 9, 2004. In February 2005, Prejean was diagnosed with cancer of the left breast, for which she underwent a second mastectomy. By note dated February 10, 2005, Prejean's physician excused her from work for eight weeks following her surgery scheduled for February 16, 2005. Prejean was released to work on May 2, 2005, by her physician's note dated March 29, 2005, but that release date was extended to July 25, 2005, as stated in her physician's note dated April 25, 2005.

On May 16, 2005, Prejean was called by her staff to the Broussard office regarding the presence of IRS agents inquiring about the BHA's third quarter 941 Form, which should have been filed in late December of 2004 or early January of 2005. By May 17, 2005, Prejean had remedied the situation by filing the necessary form with the IRS.[3]

---

3. On the facsimile transmittal letter, Prejean wrote the following note of explanation for the late filings:

62 During that same month, Guillory, with knowledge of Prejean's illness, looked into
63 the Prejean's medical file with the LHA's human resources department, which contained
64 her physician's notes, and discovered Prejean was excused from work until July 25, 2005.
65 He then brought her absenteeism to the attention of the LHA's Board of Commissioners.
66 On May 17, 2005, the LHA passed a resolution to terminate Prejean due to excessive ab-
67 sences and sent Prejean a letter informing her of her termination effective May 31, 2005.
68 The letter, dated May 17, 2005, stated:

69   RE: Permanent Termination

70   Please be advised that the Lafayette Housing Authority Board of Commission-
71   ers voted unanimously in favor of terminating your employment for failure to
72   perform effective May 31, 2005. Enclosed you will find a copy of the resolution,
73   background, and a check for May 2005.[4]

74   The Board's decision is based on your being absent from your position of em-
75   ployment for over sixty (60) continuous days and uninterrupted days after ex-
76   hausting all sick and annual leave days. During your absence you did not contact
77   this Board to make any type of arrangements concerning your continued and
78   interrupted absence from work.

79   In her First Supplemental and Amending Petition filed on February 22, 2008, Prejean
80 sought damages for the LHA's breach of her employment contract by its wrongful ter-
81 mination of her employment.

82   [....]

LAW AND DISCUSSION

84   "[W]hen a contract can be construed from the four corners of the instrument with-
85 out looking to extrinsic evidence, the question of contractual interpretation is answered
86 as a matter of law." *Sims v. Mulhearn Funeral Home, Inc.,* 07-0054, p. 10 (La.5/22/07),
87 956 So.2d 583, 590. "Interpretation of a contract is the determination of the common
88 intent of the parties." La. Civ.Code art. 2045. The reasonable intention of the parties to
89 a contract is to be sought by examining the words of the contract itself, and not assumed.
90 *Sims,* 07-0054 at p. 7, 956 So.2d at 589; *McConnell v. City of New Orleans,* 35 La. Ann. 273
91 (1883). "When the words of a contract are clear and explicit and lead to no absurd con-
92 sequences, no further interpretation may be made in search of the parties' intent." La.
93 Civ.Code art. 2046. Common intent is determined, therefore, in accordance with the gen-
94 eral, ordinary, plain and popular meaning of the words used in the contract. *Louisiana
95 Ins. Guar. Ass'n v. Interstate Fire & Cas. Co.,* 93-0911, p. 5 (La.1/14/94), 630 So.2d 759,
96 763. Accordingly, when a clause in a contract is clear and unambiguous, the letter of that
97 clause should not be disregarded under the pretext of pursuing its spirit, as it is not the
98 duty of the courts to bend the meaning of the words of a contract into harmony with a
99 supposed reasonable intention of the parties. *See Maloney v. Oak Builders, Inc.,* 256 La.
100 85, 98, 235 So.2d 386, 390 (1970); *McConnell,* 35 La. Ann. at 275. Most importantly, a

---

Yesterday I was told by IRS that the attach forms where [*sic*] not sent into there [*sic*] office. So this
morning I went and turned in the 941 forms to I.R.S. [*sic*]. I was the one to do them before Lafayette
Housing took over in Oct. 2004. But not a soul (person) ever gave them to me. At these times I was
into the hospital battling the cancer. So I took care of there [*sic*] work for them.

4. From April 2004 through May 2005, Prejean's salary was paid by check drafted from the BHA's
bank account. However, from around November 2004 and onward, the checks were signed by Guillory and Jonathan Carmouche. Prior to that time, the checks had been signed by Prejean and the
chairwoman of the BHA, Gertrude Batiste.

contract "must be interpreted in a common-sense fashion, according to the words of the   101
contract their common and usual significance." *Lambert v. Maryland Cas. Co.*, 418 So.2d   102
553, 559 (La.1982).   103

With these basic principles in mind, we examine the relevant provisions of the con-   104
tract at issue, particularly the extension provision, which as noted above provided in per-   105
tinent part: "That the [BHA] hereby retains and employs Kathy Prejean ... for a term of   106
four (4) years ... *expiring January 1, 2006*. In addition, ... this contract shall be extended   107
for an additional four ... *unless* the [BHA] gives [Prejean] by *October 1, 2005*, *notice in*   108
writing that it will not extend the contract due to the *inadequate performance* of [Pre-   109
jean]." (Emphasis added).   110

The language of Prejean's employment contract is explicit. Prejean's contract ex-   111
pired on January 1, 2006. However, the addendum also contained an extension period   112
of four years, which would take effect *unless* the BHA provided Prejean written notice   113
of its intent not to extend the contract due to her inadequate performance by October   114
1, 2005.   115

While the written notice provision posed no interpretative problems, the Court of Ap-   116
peal took exception with the ambiguity of the phrase "inadequate performance." However,   117
in accord with the longstanding rules of contractual interpretation, the general, ordinary,   118
plain and popular meaning of the words "inadequate performance" is insufficient fulfill-   119
ment of an obligation according to its terms. *See Webster's New International Dictionary*   120
Unabridged, "Inadequate" (2d Ed.1955); *Webster's,* "Performance"; *Black's Law Dictionary,*   121
"Inadequate" (6th Ed.1991); *Black's,* "Performance." Thus, under the terms of the con-   122
tract at issue, Prejean's employer could refuse to extend her contract due to her insuffi-   123
cient fulfillment of an obligation arising from her employment.   124

The Court of Appeal was further critical of the sentence directly succeeding the ex-   125
tension provision and found it could not even determine whether a finding by the   126
board of an adverse audit was the only form of inadequate performance justifying Pre-   127
jean's termination or whether the language was merely illustrative of inadequate per-   128
formance. Under our civilian tradition, however, "may" is permission. *Jacobs v. City of*   129
Bunkie, 98-2510, p. 6 (La.5/18/99), 737 So.2d 14, 19; *Underwood v. Lane Memorial*   130
Hosp., 97-1997, p. 4 (La.7/8/98), 714 So.2d 715, 717; La.Rev.Stat. § 1:3. Therefore, by   131
the general, ordinary, plain and popular meaning of the word, this provision should   132
be read as merely illustrative, not mandatory. Nevertheless, as the appellate court cor-   133
rectly noted, any ambiguity in a contract is construed against the drafter thereof. *See*   134
Robinson v. Robinson, 99-3097, p. 18 (La.1/17/01), 778 So.2d 1105, 1122; *Williams En-*   135
gineering, Inc. v. Goodyear, 496 So.2d 1012, 1018 (La.1986). Because Prejean drafted   136
the contract, inadequate performance by Prejean in any form would have justified her   137
termination.   138

Therefore, to prevent the activation of the extension period under the terms of the   139
contract, the LHA, as the BHA's successor, had to provide written notice of its intent not   140
to extend the contract due to her inadequate performance. Through its letter dated May   141
17, 2005, the LHA provided Prejean with written notice of its intent not to extend her con-   142
tract, clearly satisfying the addendum's written notice requirement well within the October   143
1 deadline.   144

Moreover, the record reflects three grounds upon which the LHA could have based its   145
finding of inadequate performance. First, the record definitively shows Prejean was med-   146
ically excused from work from November 2, 2004 through January 10, 2005, and from   147
February 16, 2005 through July 25, 2005, both of which periods far exceeded the LHA's   148

149 uncontested two-week paid sick leave policy.[5] Significantly, the only records of Prejean's
150 attendance were the medical excuses contained in her LHA medical file, and Prejean con-
151 ceded to "someone looking at [her] file the beginning of May, it would look like [she]
152 hadn't been at work from … February 16th … [a]nd [she wasn't] scheduled to come back
153 until July 25th."[6] Therefore, based on her attendance record, the LHA had grounds for its
154 finding of inadequate performance due to excessive absenteeism in that Prejean failed to
155 fulfill her basic employment obligation of attendance. Second, according to the adden-
156 dum's second paragraph, Prejean "shall … perform the duties of Secretary to the Board
157 Members at their regular, special and annual meetings." The record irrefutably shows Pre-
158 jean never attended any LHA board meeting from April 2004 through May 2005, and,
159 therefore, never performed her duties of secretary to the board at its meetings. Third,
160 Prejean testified she was responsible for filing the BHA's 941 Forms with the IRS, which
161 she failed to do in January 2005, prompting a visit from the IRS to the BHA office in May
162 of that year. Therefore, the record supports the LHA had grounds for finding inadequate
163 performance on the part of Prejean in failing to sufficiently fulfill her contractual oblig-
164 ations and did not breach her contract by its termination.[7]

165   Prejean, herself, testified she could not work full days during this period and admit-
166 ted she was not in contact on the days of her surgeries or the three to four days thereafter:

167   Two (2) weeks after my surgery in November, I was cutting the checks for the [BHA].
168   And I was doing my recertifications. And I was doing the input into the computer.
169   I may not have stayed the full eight (8) hours, but I was at the office.…

170   ⋆ ⋆ ⋆

171   The only time I was not in contact is when I was undergoing surgery or recouping
172   the three (3) to four (4) days after surgery.

173   Moreover, given the numerous surgeries, follow up procedures, treatments, and doc-
174 tors' visits Prejean endured and as documented in the medical excuses and records admitted
175 into evidence, even viewing the testimony in a light most favorable to Prejean, a reason-
176 able person could not find Prejean did not exceed her allotted sick leave time, at the very
177 least during the latter six-month period.

178   Additionally, LHA policy as testified to by both Prejean and Guillory required a per-
179 son medically excused from work not be allowed to work for liability reasons. Prejean
180 presented to the LHA numerous medical excuses in which her physicians ordered her not
181 to work over a period of six months with each excuse further extending the prescribed "no
182 work" period.

---

5. Contrary to the Court of Appeal's finding, the record contains no evidence Prejean did not exceed her two-week paid leave allotment. Of the three co-workers/employees, who testified on Prejean's behalf, only Linda Anderson was employed during the "excused from work" time period in
question, and although she testified Prejean came into work and work was delivered to Prejean's home,
she did not know what Prejean's duties were nor could she say when or for how long Prejean was in
the office during that period.

6. Notably, the record is silent concerning any contact between the LHA and Prejean regarding arrangements for her continued absences, although Prejean did testified she asked Guillory, during her November 2004 assessment meeting held at his request, "for some time because I knew I was fixing to
have another surgery." Both Guillory and Prejean testified, however, they never met in 2005 regarding her job performance, her ability to perform, or her illness and medically necessitated leave time.
The record is further silent regarding any discussion between Prejean, Guillory, or the LHA concerning her February diagnosis. Prejean admittedly did not seek extended leave under the federal
Family Medical Leave Act.

7. Finding no breach, we pretermit discussion of all other assignments of error.

We find, therefore, by its own terms, Prejean's contract expired on January 1, 2006, upon   183
written notice of the LHA of its intention not to extend her contract due to inadequate   184
performance. Consequently, Prejean is entitled to judgment awarding her seven months   185
of salary for June through December 2005, plus interest from the date of judicial demand.   186
We render judgment accordingly. Further, we render judgment dismissing Prejean's claims   187
against Walter Guillory with full prejudice. The judgment of the Court of Appeal contrary   188
to this holding is hereby reversed.   189

[....]

Questions

1. Lines 84–103: At the beginning of line 104, the court states: "with these basic prin-
    ciples in mind ..." Nowhere in the preceding paragraph, lines 84–103, does the court
    identify these principles. Can you identify them? Aren't they stated, after all, in some
    articles of the Louisiana Civil code? So why give the impression that without the cases
    these principles could not be taken from legislation?

2. Lines 111 *et seq.*: Can you describe the type of person "Prejean" is in relation to the
    other persons involved, BHA in particular? Do you know what a contract of adhe-
    sion is? What nominate contract was in existence between BHA and Prejean? What kind
    of obligations (give, do, not do) does such a contract create for Prejean for instance?

3. Lines 116–124: The issue revolves around performance and inadequate performance.
    Before looking into the particular named contract at issue here, couldn't the court have
    looked at the Louisiana Civil Code articles on "Obligations", such as 1756, 1758 and
    1759, as well as the articles on "Damages", articles 1994–1995 in particular? What
    about Louisiana Civil Code articles 2746–2750?

4. Lines 125 *et seq.*: Even though Kathy Prejean was a mere natural person, she "drafted
    the contract" and, therefore, "any ambiguity in a contract is construed against the
    drafter thereof". Do you think that Kathy Prejean contemplated such a ruling when
    she drafted the addendum to her employment contract? In the following paragraphs,
    how does the court read the contract and, particularly, Prejean's understanding of
    inadequate performance and the giving of adequate notice? Didn't LHA have suffi-
    cient grounds to justify an inadequate performance of her obligations by Prejean?
    Did the court give an objective interpretation of inadequate performance, in the sense
    that objective circumstances much beyond Prejean's control (medical reasons mostly)
    prevented her (or anybody else) from performing her obligations in an objectively ad-
    equate/inadequate manner? Or did the court give a subjective interpretation of in-
    adequate performance and blame Kathy Prejean as a person for not performing her
    obligations in an adequate manner? Thus, can you suggest any ground on which the
    Court of Appeal had ruled in favor of Kathy Prejean and against LHA?

Chapter Four

Of the Manner in Which Obligations May Be Transferred and Extinguished

Section I—Assumption of Obligations

Louisiana Sources of Law

Louisiana Civil Code

Art. 1821. Assumption by agreement between obligor and third person.

An obligor and a third person may agree to an assumption by the latter of an obligation of the former. To be enforceable by the obligee against the third person, the agreement must be made in writing.

The obligee's consent to the agreement does not effect a release of the obligor.

The unreleased obligor remains solidarily bound with the third person. (Acts 1984, No. 331, § 1, eff. Jan. 1, 1985.)

Art. 1822. Third person bound for amount assumed.

A person who, by agreement with the obligor, assumes the obligation of the latter is bound only to the extent of his assumption.

The assuming obligor may raise any defense based on the contract by which the assumption was made. (Acts 1984, No. 331, § 1, eff. Jan. 1, 1985.)

Art. 1823. Assumption by agreement between obligee and third person.

An obligee and a third person may agree on an assumption by the latter of an obligation owed by another to the former. That agreement must be made in writing. That agreement does not effect a release of the original obligor. (Acts 1984, No. 331, § 1, eff. Jan. 1, 1985.)

Art. 1824. Defenses.

A person who, by agreement with the obligee, has assumed another's obligation may not raise against the obligee any defense based on the relationship between the assuming obligor and the original obligor.

The assuming obligor may raise any defense based on the relationship between the original obligor and obligee. He may not invoke compensation based on an obligation owed by the obligee to the original obligor. (Acts 1984, No. 331, § 1, eff. Jan. 1, 1985.)

Précis: Louisiana Law of Obligations in General §§ 5.1.1 to 5.1.3

An assumption of an obligation is a juridical act which involves three parties at least. Two of these parties are already bound to each other when a third one agrees to take upon himself the debt or obligation of one of the original two parties....

The first paragraph of LSA-C.C. Art. 1821 provides that "an obligor and a third person may agree to an assumption by the latter of an obligation of the former. To be enforceable by the obligee against the third person, the agreement must be made in writing." ...

To be binding between the obligor and the third person, the juridical act of assumption must meet all the requirement for a valid contract....

Although the agreement of assumption is entered into between the obligor and the third person, it is necessary that the instrument be in writing so that the agreement of assumption can be submitted to the obligee to be enforceable by him against the third person....

LSA-C.C. Art. 1823 states that "[A]n obligee and a third person may agree on an assumption by the latter of an obligation owed by another to the former. That agreement must be made in writing. That agreement does not effect a release of the original obligor."

This form of assumption involves only two parties and, because it amounts to an agreement to pay the debt of another, it must be in writing as LSA-C.C. Art. 1823 emphasizes in this particular instance....

An assumption of the original obligor's obligation by an agreement between the obligee and the third person-assuming obligor is a unilateral onerous contract between the latter two parties. The involvement of the original obligor is not necessary and, actually, this form of assumption may take place without the original obligor's knowledge.

By such an agreement, the third person-assuming obligor binds himself towards the obligee to substitute his own performance to that which was to be rendered by the original obligor. This agreement must, therefore, meet all the requirements for a valid contract, the requirement of cause in particular....

Cases

Beverly B. McCrory, Wife of/and Gerard L. McCRORY
v.
TERMINIX SERVICE CO., INC., and XYZ Insurance Company

Louisiana Court of Appeal
Fourth Circuit
Nov. 13, 1992
609 So.2d 883

ARMSTRONG, Judge.

    The plaintiffs, Beverly and Gerard McCrory ("McCrorys"), filed suit against defendant, Terminix Service Co., Inc. ("Terminix"), and its insurer claiming property and personal injury damages.[1] On Terminix's motion, the trial court granted partial summary

---

1. The McCrorys' claim for personal injury damages, arising from Terminix's use/misuse of termiticides on the McCrorys' residence, is not relevant to this appeal.

judgment. The judgment limited the McCrorys' property damage claim to $5,000 in accordance with a provision in the parties' termite protection contract. The McCrorys appeal from that judgment, claiming the trial court erred in granting the partial summary judgment because the contractual provision interpreted by the court is ambiguous and because doubt exists as to the parties' intent to limit Terminix's liability to $5,000. We disagree.

In 1962, the McCrorys' predecessor in interest, W.D. Fowler, contracted with Terminix for termite protection for the residence and garage located at 4763 Marigny Street, New Orleans. (Bruce-Terminix Protection Contract No. 72PRO62208-5.) Under the terms of this contract, for an annual fee, Terminix obligated itself to perform annual re-inspections and future applications of termiticides necessary for the continued protection of the property against subterranean termites. Additionally, the contract provided that:

> The Terminix company further agrees that in the event of new subterranean termite damage to the structure or contents repairs will be performed with the approval and at the expense of the Terminix company. The liability of the Terminix company is not to exceed five thousand dollars ($5,000.00).

The McCrorys assumed the terms of this contract when they purchased 4763 Marigny Street from Fowler.

During a routine inspection of the McCrorys' residence in June of 1989, Terminix discovered termite activity and damage. Through this suit, the McCrorys contend that the termite damage to their home resulted from Terminix's failure to properly treat and/or annually inspect their property. They claim Terminix is liable for the full cost of repairing the property damage caused by the termites.

Terminix's motion for partial summary judgment claimed that, under the clear and unambiguous terms of the parties' termite protection contract, its obligation to the McCrorys for property damage caused by termites does not exceed $5,000. Terminix contended that the contract's provision which unambiguously limits its liability must be enforced as written and, under well-settled Louisiana law, cannot be varied because it was not procured by fraud, accident or mistake. As the contract has the effect of law as between the parties, Terminix further argued that its terms could not be repudiated for economic or imprudent reasons, citing LSA-C.C. arts. 1971 and 1983.[2]

[....]

On appeal, the McCrorys assert that the contractual provision which purports to limit Terminix's liability to $5,000 is ambiguous because it does not specifically state the liability limitation of $5,000 is for property damage. The McCrorys argue that the contract clearly states that in the event of new termite damage to the structure or contents of 4763 Marigny Street, repairs will be performed at the expense of Terminix. They further claim that the contract does not place a dollar limit on those structure and contents repairs. Alternatively, the McCrorys assert that doubt exists as to the parties' intent regarding the contract provision. They claim that because Terminix has written post-1962 termite protection con-

---

2. The cited Civil Code articles provide as follows:
    Art. 1971. Freedom of parties
    Parties are free to contract for any object that is lawful, possible, and determined or determinable.
    Art. 1983. Law for the parties; performance in good faith
    Contracts have the effect of law for the parties and may be dissolved only through the consent of the parties or on grounds provided by law. Contracts must be performed in good faith.

tracts for other clients, providing them with property damage liability limits of $25,000,   52
Terminix intended to increase the liability limitation in their contract.   53

Subject to the limits imposed by law, parties are free to contract as they choose. *Zei-*   54
gler v. Pleasant Manor Nursing Home, 600 So.2d 819 (La.App. 3d Cir.1992). The terms of   55
the contract then have the effect of law on the parties. LSA-C.C. art. 1983 (former C.C.   56
art. 1901). Interpretation of a contract is the determination of the parties' common in-   57
tent. LSA-C.C. art. 2045 (former C.C. arts. 1945, 1950). When the words of a contract   58
are clear and explicit and lead to no absurd consequences, no further interpretation may   59
be made in search of the parties' intent. LSA-C.C. art. 2046 (former C.C. arts. 13, 1945).   60
However, when the terms of a contract are susceptible to more than one interpretation,   61
it is ambiguous, and parol evidence may be used to show the true intent of the parties.   62
LSA-C.C. art. 2045, *et seq.; Dixie Campers, Inc. v. Vesely Co.,* 398 So.2d 1087 (La.1981);   63
Carter v. BRMAP, 591 So.2d 1184 (La.App. 1st Cir.1992). Words susceptible of different   64
meanings must be interpreted as having the meaning that best conforms to the object of   65
the contract. LSA-C.C. art. 2048 (former C.C. art. 1952).   66

Whether a contract is ambiguous or not is a question of law. *Carter v. BRMAP, supra.;*   67
Borden, Inc. v. Gulf States Utilities Co., 543 So.2d 924 (La.App. 1st Cir.1989), *writ den.,* 545   68
So.2d 1041 (La.1989). When a contract is to be interpreted by the court as a matter of   69
law, a motion for summary judgment is the proper procedural vehicle to present the ques-   70
tion to the court. *Carter v. BRMAP, supra.* Appellate review of the question(s) of law, is   71
simply whether the trial court's interpretive decision is legally correct. *O'Neill v. Louisiana*   72
Power & Light Co., 558 So.2d 1235 (La.App. 1st Cir.1990).   73

The McCrorys urge the trial court erred by determining that the contract they have sued   74
upon limits Terminix's liability for property damage to $5,000. We disagree. The terms   75
of this liability provision, taken as a whole, are not susceptible to more than one inter-   76
pretation. The rule of strict construction does not authorize perversion of a contract's   77
language or the creation of ambiguity where none exists. *Ransom v. Camcraft, Inc.,* 580   78
So.2d 1073 (La.App. 4th Cir.1991). The contract's provisions clearly and explicitly sug-   79
gest that in the event of new subterranean termite infestation, Terminix's maximum lia-   80
bility for property damage, structure and/or contents repairs, is limited to $5,000.   81

When the McCrorys purchased Fowler's residence and assumed the terms of his ter-   82
mite protection contract, they became bound by its terms. See LSA-C.C. arts. 1764, 1765,   83
1821 *et seq.* The contract became the law between them. The McCrorys cannot be given   84
relief merely because they assumed a bad and/or outdated bargain. *Groom v. W.H. Ward*   85
Lumber Co., Inc., 432 So.2d 984 (La.App. 1st Cir.1983); *Louisiana Power & Light Co. v. Mecom,*   86
357 So.2d 596 (La.App. 1st Cir.1978). Hence, the McCrorys' initial claim of error is with-   87
out merit.   88

As the parties' contract is clear and unambiguous, there is no need to go outside the   89
document to discover the parties' intent. *American Waste and Pollution Control Co. v. Jef-*   90
ferson Davis Parish Sanitary Landfill Com'sn, 578 So.2d 541 (La.App. 3d Cir.1991), *writ*   91
den., 581 So.2d 694 (La.1991). The McCrorys are not entitled to present extrinsic, parol   92
evidence on the issue of intent. It is therefore not consequential that their neighbor has   93
a termite protection contract with Terminix, dated 1968, providing property damage li-   94
ability limits of $25,000. The letter of the McCrorys' contract clause cannot be disre-   95
garded under the pretext of pursuing its spirit. LSA-C.C. art. 2046, comment b (former   96
C.C. arts. 13 and 1945(3)); *O'Neill v. Louisiana Power & Light Co., supra.* Thus, the Mc-   97
Crorys' second claim of error is also without merit.   98

[....]

Questions

1. Lines 9–98: Identify clearly the number of parties and kinds of parties involved in this case. Identify the legal or types of relationships (if any) between these parties; are they legal, contractual, delictual, etc … ? Identify the kinds of obligations that were created; are they personal or heritable? Is this form of identification of obligations important? How many relationships do you come up with and how do they relate one to the other, particularly if they are contractual in nature? Is there any type of relationship between the contract of sale of the house and the contract for services between the seller and Terminix? Is there any direct relationship between the buyer and Terminix? In the negative, how could a relationship between the buyer and Terminix be created? Are the dates of these relationships somewhat or very relevant? Remember the principles which govern contracts?

2. Lines 54–81: Which rules of interpretation of contracts are relied on here? Remember the previous questions on the number of legal relationships existing here and the types of these relationships? Do you see, now, any justification for asking the above preliminary questions?

3. Lines 82–98: The court uses the verb "assumed" (after "purchased") on line 82 and the court refers to Louisiana Civil Code articles 1765 & 1821 *et seq.* Are the two sets of articles intimately tied together? Are they stating one and the same thing? If assumption there is, what type of assumption took place? Notice that the court does not name the type of assumption that occurred in this case, whereas the Louisiana Civil Code mentions two types of assumption: so?

1

Linda BROWN

2 v.

3 ### CONNECTICUT GENERAL LIFE INSURANCE COMPANY,
4 ### ABC Contractor, and DEF architect

5 Louisiana Court of Appeal
6 Fourth Circuit
7 March 7, 2001
8 793 So.2d 211

9 LOVE, Judge.

10 Third Party Defendant, CIGNA, appeals a summary judgment granted in favor of the
11 defendants, Mervyn's Department Store of California, Inc. For the following reasons, we
12 find that the trial court judgment granting the defendant's Motion for Summary Judgment
13 was in error.

FACTS AND PROCEDURAL HISTORY

15 Linda Brown ("Ms. Brown") was employed by Mervyn's Department Store of California,
16 Inc. ("Mervyn's"), located in the Lake Forest Shopping Center in New Orleans, Louisiana.
17 On November 14, 1994, while in the course and scope of her employment, Ms. Brown fell
18 down a flight of stairs. Ms. Brown filed a claim against Mervyn's under the Louisiana Worker's
19 Compensation Act, seeking payment for medical treatment and weekly indemnity benefits.

20 As a result of her worker's compensation claim, Mervyn's paid Ms. Brown compensa-
21 tion benefits and medical expenses in the amount of twenty-six thousand eight hundred
22 twenty-four dollars and twenty-six cents ($26,824.26).

On September 1, 1995, Ms. Brown filed a petition for damages against CIGNA Corporation, which is the owner of the land leased by Mervyn's, Audubon Construction Company and Sizeler Architects. In response to the lawsuit, on September 29, 1997, CIGNA Corporation filed a Third Party Demand against Mervyn's alleging that in the lease agreement, Mervyn's agreed to defend and indemnify CIGNA against claims such as Ms. Brown's.

On or about May 7, 1998, Mervyn's filed a Motion for Summary Judgment alleging that CIGNA's Third Party Demand should be dismissed because as Ms. Brown's employer, Mervyn's is statutorily immune from suit under LSA-R.S. 23:1032.

[....]

DISCUSSION

In this appeal, the defendant argues that Louisiana's Worker's Compensation statute, La. R.S. 23:1032, bars the claim filed by CIGNA. In response, CIGNA argues that, although La. R.S. 23:1032 does provide statutory immuny [*sic*] from tort claims filed by an employee for on the job injuries, the statute does not preclude an employer from contractually agreeing to indemnify another party for claims brought by employees.

In part, Louisiana's worker's compensation statute, La. R.S. 23:1032, provides as follows:

A. (1)(a) Except for intentional acts provided for in Subsection B, the rights and remedies herein granted to an employee or his dependent on account of an injury, or compensable sickness or disease for which he is entitled to compensation under this Chapter, shall be exclusive of all other rights, remedies and claims for damages, including but not limited to punitive or exemplary damages, unless such rights, remedies and damages are created by a statute, whether now existing or created in the future, expressly establishing same as available to such employee, his personal representatives, dependents, or relations, as against his employer, or any principal or any officer, director, stockholder, partner or employee of such employer or principal for said injury, or compensable sickness or disease.

(b) The exclusive remedy is exclusive of all claims, including any claims that might arise against his employer, or any principal or any officer, director, stockholder, partner or employee of such employer or principal under any dual capacity theory or doctrine.

In applying La. R.S. 23:1032, Louisiana case law is clear that an employee may not sue his employer in tort for non-intentional injuries sustained during the course and scope of employment. See *Chase v. La. Riverboat Gaming P'ship*, 31610 (La.App. 2 Cir. 9/22/99), 747 So.2d 115, 120. An employee's exclusive remedy for on the job injuries is limited to worker's compensation, in exchange for which, the employer is immune from any other liability arising out of the injury. See *Haley v. Calcasieu Parish ch. Bd.*, 99-883 (La.App. 3 Cir. 12/8/99), 753 So.2d 882, 888 *writ denied*, 2000-0054 (La.2/24/00), 755 So.2d 242. As the court in *Roberts v. Orpheum*, 610 So.2d 1097 (La.App. 4 Cir.1992) articulated in describing the concept of worker's compensation:

> [E]ach party has surrendered certain rights to gain others. The employer has given up immunity under tort law to which he would be entitled if he were not at fault; the employee has given up the right to full compensation in order to collect some compensation for any injury sustained on the job.

Id. at 1101 (citing *Ducote v. Albert*, 521 So.2d 399, 403 (La.1988)).

In this case, pursuant to the terms of the lease, the employer/lessee agreed to indemnify the building owner/lessor for any claims due to defects on the property. In Louisiana, the general rule is that the owner/lessor bears responsibility for the condition of the leased

premises. See *La. Civ.Code Ann., Arts. 2695, 2317, 2322*; *Roberts*, 610 So.2d at 1100. However, the Louisiana legislature enacted an exception to this rule, which enables the lessee
to assume responsibility for the condition of the premises in the lease contract. *La. R.S.
9: 3221*; *Mendoza v. Seidenbach*, 598 So.2d 404, 405 (La.App. 4 Cir. 3/31/92); *Dorion v.
Eleven Eleven Building*, 98-3018 (La.App. 4 Cir. 5/12/99), 737 So.2d 878. Specifically, La.
R.S. 9:3221 provides:

> The owner of premises leased under a contract whereby the lessee assumes re-
> sponsibility for their condition is not liable for injury caused by any defect
> therein to the lessee or anyone on the premises who derives his right to be
> thereon from the lessee, unless the owner knew or should have known of the
> defect or had received notice thereof and failed to remedy it within a reason-
> able time.

The issue that this Court must decide is, when an employee is injured in the course and
scope of employment and asserts a worker's compensation claim against his employer, is
his employer immune from all other liability arising out of such injuries, even if the employer has agreed to indemnify the owner/lessor of the employment premises.

This Court addressed this precise issue in *Norfleet v. Jackson Brewing Market, Inc.*, 99-
1949 (La.App. 4 Cir. 11/17/99), 748 So.2d 525. In *Norfleet* an employee was injured during the scope of her employment, due to alleged dangerous conditions on leased premises.
The employee brought a personal injury action against the owner of the property from
whom the employer leased the premises. In turn, the property owner and its liability insurer filed a third party demand against the employer and the employer's liability insurer,
seeking indemnity pursuant to the terms of the lease. Thereafter, the employer filed an
exception of no cause of action against the third-party demand, arguing that under
worker's compensation laws, it was statutorily immune against non-intentional tort claims
of its employee. The trial court granted the employer's exception of no cause of action.
However, on application for supervisory writ, this Court reversed the trial court and
found that the petition did state a cause of action.

In the writ application, the employer argued that if forced to indemnify the building
owner, then he was being held "indirectly" liable for the non-intentional tort claims of his
employee that he could not be held directly liable for under worker's compensation laws.
Norfleet, 748 So.2d at 526. In response to this argument, this Court stated:

> Perhaps it is true in a sense, but the short answer to this argument is that Pre-
> mier Concepts contractually agreed to such "indirect" liability in its lease with Jack-
> son Brewery. In other words, having voluntarily obligated itself to indemnify
> Jackson Brewery, Premier Concepts cannot renege upon that obligation to Jack-
> son Brewery simply because the claim against Jackson Brewery was made by a Pre-
> mier Concepts employee. *The exclusive remedy provision of the worker's
> compensation laws, which regulate liability as between employer and employee, do
> not strip Jackson Brewery, a stranger to the employment relation of Premier Con-
> cepts and Norfleet of its contracted-for right to indemnify.* [Emphasis added]

Id. at 526.

Similarly, in this case, Mervyn's contractually assumed responsibility for liability resulting from defects in the leased premises. In Louisiana, parties may contract for any
lawful cause. *La. Civ.Code art. 1971*. This provided, Louisiana courts have held that an
employer is not prohibited from entering into an indemnification agreement with a potential third party tortfeasor, such as a lessor. See *Miller v. Louisiana Gas Serv. Co.*, 95-874
(La.App. 5 Cir. 6/25/96) 680 So.2d 52, 55; *Berninger v. Georgia-Pacific Corp.*, 582 So.2d

266, 267 (La.App. 1 Cir.1991). Thus, there is no Louisiana statute which prohibits the   117
indemnification agreement entered into between Mervyn's and the building owner. As   118
such, the indemnification provision contained in the lease contract is lawful. See *La.Civ.Code*   119
art. 1971.   120

Additionally, it is well settled that the provisions of a lease can affect third parties and   121
govern the rights between the parties. See *Roberts*, 610 So.2d at 1100. Consequently, the   122
lease agreement constitutes the law between the parties. See *K & M Ent. Slaughter, Inc. v.*   123
Pennington, 99-0930 (La.App. 1 Cir. 5/12/00, 764 So.2d 1089), *writ denied*, 766 So.2d 548   124
(La.2000). Therefore, in this case, the lease contract dictates the rights between Mervyn's,   125
the building owner and third parties. In the lease contract, Mervyn's agreed to indemnify   126
and defend the building owner for all claims filed by third parties injured on the leased   127
premises. As the Court in *Norfleet* determined, Mervyn's cannot relinquish this obligation   128
solely because the third party who made the claim against the building owner happened   129
to be a Mervyn's employee. See *Id.*, 748 So.2d at 526. Admittedly, the indemnification   130
agreement contained in the lease exposes Mervyn's to liability in excess of its' [*sic*] worker's   131
compensation obligation. However, as in *Norfleet*, since Mervyn's voluntarily agreed to this   132
arrangement, it is bound to honor this commitment.   133

[....]

Questions

1. Go through the same general questions asked above in Question 1 under the *Mc-Crory* case.

2. In the *McCrory* case, a principal contract of sale had been entered into; in this case what was the name of the contract (if any) between CIGNA and Mervyn's Department Store? Read the relevant Louisiana Civil Code articles, particularly articles 2696 *et seq*. What kinds of obligations are created by this kind of contract? What are the sources of liability of both the lessee, Mervyn's Store, and the lessor, CIGNA? If under the law (Louisiana Civil Code articles and Louisiana Revised Statutes), delictual liability cannot be waived, can contractual liability be waived or limited? *See* La. Civ. Code art. 2004. In this case again, the Court lays down one very important principle of the law of contract: can you identify it? How is this principle relevant to the outcome of the case? The court writes that "Mervyn's contractually assumed responsibility for liability resulting from defects in the leased premises." What kind of contractual assumption is the court referring to? Are the conditions for this kind of assumption as listed in the Louisiana Civil Code met in this case?

Section II — Of Payment with or without Subrogation

Louisiana Sources of Law

Louisiana Civil Code

Art. 1825. Definition.

Subrogation is the substitution of one person to the rights of another. It may be conventional or legal. (Acts 1984, No. 331, § 1, eff. Jan. 1, 1985.)

Art. 1826. Effects.

A. When subrogation results from a person's performance of the obligation of another, that obligation subsists in favor of the person who performed it who may avail himself of the action and security of the original obligee against the obligor, but is extinguished for the original obligee.

B. An original obligee who has been paid only in part may exercise his right for the balance of the debt in preference to the new obligee. This right shall not be waived or altered if the original obligation arose from injuries sustained or loss occasioned by the original obligee as a result of the negligence or intentional conduct of the original obligor. (Acts 1984, No. 331, § 1, eff. Jan. 1, 1985; Acts 2001, No. 305, § 1.)

Art. 1827. Conventional subrogation by the obligee.

An obligee who receives performance from a third person may subrogate that person to the rights of the obligee, even without the obligor's consent. That subrogation is subject to the rules governing the assignment of rights. (Acts 1984, No. 331, § 1, eff. Jan. 1, 1985.)

Art. 1828. Conventional subrogation by the obligor.

An obligor who pays a debt with money or other fungible things borrowed for that purpose may subrogate the lender to the rights of the obligee, even without the obligee's consent.

The agreement for subrogation must be made in writing expressing that the purpose of the loan is to pay the debt. (Acts 1984, No. 331, § 1, eff. Jan. 1, 1985.)

Art. 1829. Subrogation by operation of law.

Subrogation takes place by operation of law:

(1) In favor of an obligee who pays another obligee whose right is preferred to his because of a privilege, pledge, mortgage, or security interest;

(2) In favor of a purchaser of movable or immovable property who uses the purchase money to pay creditors holding any privilege, pledge, mortgage, or security interest on the property;

(3) In favor of an obligor who pays a debt he owes with others or for others and who has recourse against those others as a result of the payment;

(4) In favor of a successor who pays estate debts with his own funds; and

(5) In the other cases provided by law. (Acts 1984, No. 331, § 1, eff. Jan. 1, 1985; Acts 1989, No. 137, § 16, eff. Sept. 1, 1989; Acts 2001, No. 572, § 1.)

Précis: Louisiana Law of Obligations in General §§ 5.2.1 to 5.2.3
CONCEPT OF SUBROGATION.

Article 1825 of the civil Code defines subrogation in these terms: "**Subrogation is the substitution of one person to the rights of another. It may be conventional or legal.**"

Subrogation can then be described as a legal device meant to cause a person to be placed in the shoes of another. A legal fiction is thus created whereby an obligation is declared to survive in a person other than the original party and despite the performance of the original obligation. This is why "subrogation" amounts to the transfer of an obligation. For example, an obligee-creditor called subrogee-solvens (**subrogee** because he is subrogated and **solvens** because he has performed an obligation) can be substituted to another creditor, the original obligee-accipiens, (**accipiens** because he has received the benefit of the performance of an obligation), so that the obligor is now indebted to the subrogee—solvens who extinguished the obligation owed the accipiens by performing in the place of the original obligor. Subrogation is, therefore, both a mode of extinction of an obligation and a method of transfer of that same obligation....

The *raison d'être* and justification for this concept of subrogation are to be found in the shifting of the rights of action available to an obligee—accipiens to the benefit of the subrogee—solvens against the obligor. Whenever a third person pays the debt of another, unless that third person was motivated by a gratuitous intent (*animus donandi*) and meant, therefore, to make a gift to the obligor by extinguishing his debt, the third person will have a right of action for reimbursement against the obligor....

Article 1825 of the civil Code states that **"Subrogation is the substitution of one person to the rights of another. It may be conventional or legal."** ...

A conventional subrogation can result from a contract between the obligee-accipiens and the third person-solvens. Such a conventional subrogation granted by the obligee or creditor is known as *ex parte creditoris* (on the part of the creditor). The second type of conventional subrogation can be the outcome of a contract between the obligor-debtor and the third person; in this case the subrogation is described as *ex parte debitoris* (on the part of the debtor)....

Article 1827 ..."**An obligee who receives performance from a third person may subrogate that person to the rights of the obligee, even without the obligor's consent. That subrogation is subject to the rules governing the assignment of rights."** ...

Article 1828 ..."**An obligor who pays a debt with money or other fungible things borrowed for that purpose may subrogate the lender to the rights of the obligee, even without the obligee's consent.**

The agreement for subrogation must be made in writing expressing that the purpose of the loan is to pay the debt." ...

Article 1829 of the civil Code lists four specific instances of subrogation by operation of law and adds a fifth catch all category....

There are two essential effects attached to a payment with subrogation: a) a transfer of the obligee-creditor's right to the third person-solvens and b) limitations on the extent of that right....

According to civil Code **Article 1826**, the **"obligation subsists in favor of the person who performed it who may avail himself of the action against the obligor and security on the assets of the same obligor that the original obligee had against the obligor ..."** Thus the action and the security as a whole are transferred with their particular modalities be they a term, a condition etc....

The second paragraph of civil Code **Article 1826** states, in part, that: "B. **An original obligee who has been paid only in part may exercise his right for the balance of the debt in preference to the new oblige ...**" It follows that subrogation takes place only up to the amount of the debt paid by the third person-subrogated solvens to the original obligee in discharge of the obligation of the obligor....

This same limitation applicable to conventional subrogation governs also subrogation by operation of law as stated in **Article 1830**: "**When subrogation takes place by operation of law, the new obligee may recover from the obligor only to the extent of the per-**

formance rendered to the original obligee. The new obligee may not recover more by invoking conventional subrogation." …

Cases

STANDARD MOTOR CAR COMPANY et al.

v.

STATE FARM MUTUAL AUTOMOBILE INSURANCE COMPANY

Louisiana Court of Appeal
First Circuit
Oct. 4, 1957
97 So.2d 435

TATE, Judge.

Plaintiffs appeal from judgment dismissing their suit upon exception of no right and cause of action.

The petition alleges: A car left by a customer of the plaintiff, Standard Motor Car Company, Inc. ('Standard'),[1] for servicing was involved in an intersectional collision while being road-tested by Standard's employee in the course and scope of his employment. The negligence of a driver insured by defendant, State Farm Mutual Insurance Company, was the sole proximate cause of the accident. Standard paid for repair of the damages and by this tort suit seeks recovery of same from the insurer of the tortfeasor.

Defendant contends that, in the absence of a conventional subrogation by the Owner of the damaged car in favor of Standard, Standard as Possessor has no right or cause of action for the damage caused to its customer's car, even though Standard paid for the repair of same. This contention is based upon the doctrine that 'subrogation will not generally be decreed in favor of a mere volunteer or intermeddler who, without any duty, moral or otherwise, pays the debt or discharges the obligation of another,' 50 Am.Jur. 696, 'Subrogation', Section 21. See also 83 C.J.S., Subrogation s 9, p. 601. See LSA-Civil Code Article 2161, especially 2161(3).

Able counsel for defendant argues that Standard was a 'volunteer' since, as depositary or bailees of its customer's car, it was not legally liable to its customer for damages caused through the negligence of another and without fault on its own part. See cases such as Niagara Fire Insurance Co. v. Shuff, La.App. 1 Cir., 93 So.2d 325. 'The depositary is only bound to restore the thing in the state in which it is at the moment of restitution. Deteriorations, not effected by an act of his, are to the loss of the depositor.' Article 2945, LSA-C.C. (Italics ours.)[2]

Plaintiffs urge most forcefully that the garageman is at least under a moral duty to repair the cars of his customers injured while in his custody. It is argued that the garage-

---

1. Standard's collision insurer is co-plaintiff for the portion of the damage paid by it.

2. Of course, had Standard alleged fault on its own part so as to entitle it to subrogations as of right, then the pleaded contributory negligence would likewise subject this tort suit to dismissal, save possibly as a suit for contribution by a co-obligor or joint tortfeasor.

man cannot morally or as a matter of sound business practice return his customer's car to the latter in a damaged condition with the observation that it is up to the customer to collect for the loss from an allegedly negligent third party. We are reminded that the garageman, as depositary or bailee, is under a duty to return the car deposited with him in the same condition as received, and that—as between him and his customer, the depositor—injury to the car during the garageman's custody establishes a prima facie case in favor of the customer against the garageman. Hazel v. Williams, La.App. 2 Cir., 80 So.2d 133; Articles 1908, 2937, 2938, 2944, 2945, LSA-Civil Code. The garageman thus has at least a prima facie duty to repair the vehicle damaged while in his custody before returning it to his customer. Furthermore, should be refuse to repair the vehicle on the ground that the damages resulted from the negligence of a third party tortfeasor, the prescriptive period applicable to his customer's action against him for the damages to the car, while in the garageman's custody is that of ten years, Article 3444, LSA-C.C., Reehlman v. Calamari, La.App.Orleans, 94 So.2d 311; far longer than the peremptive one year for tort actions during which either party must seek to hold the negligent third person.

The contentions of the plaintiffs-appellants are sustained by the jurisprudence; although in fairness we must add that the authorities cited below were not called to the attention of the learned trial judge.

The identical legal question was before our brethren of the Orleans Court of Appeal in Douglas v. Haro, 32 So.2d 387. Their opinion at 32 So.2d 387 contains a scholarly review of the applicable authorities. As against third persons misappropriating or damaging same, the possessors (such as an administrator, depositary, or consignee) of property damaged or stolen while in their possession, although not owned by them, have been permitted to recover the property or for the damages thereto, irrespective of their non-ownership thereof. Lannes v. Courege, 31 La.Ann. 74; Johnson v. Imboden, 7 La.Ann. 110; Johnson v. Imboden, 4 La.Ann. 178; Fowler v. Cooper, Carathers & Co., 3 La. 215; Morgan v. Bell, 4 Mart., O.S., 615; McGrew v. Browder, 2 Mart., N.S., 17, 20; Klein v. Anderson, 4 Orleans App. 262. But based upon Article 15, C.P., the Orleans Court held in Douglas v. Haro that the depositary or bailee was without interest to institute suit to recover damage to property in his possession, when the sole cause of such damage was the negligence of a third party defendant, who under these circumstances was held to be liable solely to the owner (unless of course a conventional subrogation had been secured).

The Orleans court's decision was, however, reversed by our Supreme Court, 214 La. 1099, 39 So.2d 744, which opinion, in the words of the Supreme Court in a later decision, Holley v. Butler Furniture Co., 217 La. 8, 45 So.2d 747, at page 748,[3] 'held that inasmuch as the depositor had ten years in which to file a suit against the plaintiff under the provisions of the Civil Code, and the right of action to recover damages from the defendant was one which prescribed in one year, that the plaintiff was deemed to have an interest to bring such action—but inasmuch as the depositor had not been made a party remanded for such purpose'.

In Douglas v. Haro, above cited, a strong argument had been made by the defendant that there was no allegation that the plaintiff-garageman had paid the owner for the dam-

---

3. In this Holley case, the depositor (i.e., bailee or possessor) of property was not allowed to recover as plaintiff, because in his petition he had alleged he was the owner of the property damaged. At the trial it developed that the damaged car was actually owned by his father, who had paid for said damages; and the plaintiff-son was not permitted to amend his petition, as this would have changed the nature of the cause of action from one by the owner of property, to one by the possessor of property damaged by another.

78 age to the automobile or that the owner had demanded payment of same from the garage-
79 man. In response to this argument, the Supreme Court remanded the case to implead
80 the owner-depositor as a necessary party to settle the rights of all three parties and to
81 prevent the possibility of the garageman being unjustly enriched by recovering the dam-
82 ages to the customer's car although such damages were not demanded of him by the cus-
83 tomer. Thus the cited decision might be interpreted so as to require our reversal, but also
84 to require on the remand the impleader of the owner of the damaged automobile as a
85 party to the suit. However, we feel that under the pleadings in this particular case, this
86 requirement would be a useless technicality, since herein (unlike in Douglas v. Haro) the
87 garageman-plaintiff has specifically pleaded that he himself has paid the claim for the
88 damages sustained by the car while deposited with him.

89   The result we have reached is consistent with the common law principles surround-
90 ing a 'bailment', which is quite similar in many respects to a civil law 'deposit'. 'A bailee
91 may recover from a third person for the latter's wrongful injury to bailed property or dis-
92 turbance of his possession thereof,' 8 C.J.S. Bailments s 39 b, p. 317. 'Every bailee or per-
93 son clothed with the exclusive right of possession has a temporary or qualified ownership
94 in the property to the extent of enabling him to maintain actions in respect thereof against
95 third persons, as has been shown in s 39, and he may sue for the protection of his own
96 interest, or for the benefit of his bailor, or he may sue for both interests and recover full
97 damages,' 8 C.J.S. Bailments s 56, p. 371.[4] See also 6 Am.Jur. 430.

98   The jurisprudence specifically pertaining to deposit and bailment has thus readily fur-
99 nished a rationale for this decision. But it is not inappropriate to note that although the
100 garageman in this case may be not subrogated to rights of the customer against the tort-
101 feasor nevertheless he may have acquired by the payment to the creditor (i.e., the owner
102 of the car) a right of action to recover the payment from the person legally obligated for
103 the debt (i.e., the tortfeasor). This arises under Article 2134, LSA-C.C., which provides
104 that the obligation is discharged by payment by another party 'no way concerned in it' (i.e.,
105 the garageman), even if the latter 'act in his own name', although it also provides that the
106 latter 'be not subrogated to the rights of the creditor'.

107   While there are no Louisiana cases on the subject the equivalent article of the French
108 Civil Code, CN 1236, was explained in the report of Monsier Jaubert presented to the Tri-
109 bunal (8 Fenet, Discussions, p. 341-342), in part as follows: 'Quoique le tiers qui offre le
110 paiement n' ait pas un intérêt direct et civil à l'acquittement de l' obligation, le créancier
111 ne pourra non plus refuser de recevoir, puisqu'en dernière analyse le créancier n' a d'autre
112 intérêt que d'être payé; mais dans ce cas le tiers ne peut forcer le créancier a le mettre a son
113 lieu et place pour les privilèges, les hypothèques et la contrainte par corps. La loi ne veut
114 pas, avec raison, que contre le gré du créancier un tiers vienne s' interposer pour acquérir
115 le droit de vexer le debiteur; *le tiers que paie qui paie n'acquiert alors qu'une action simple*
116 *contre le débiteur qui entièrement libre de l'obligation primitive.*'[5]

---

4. 'It is now an almost universal rule that for a conversion of, or damage to, bailed goods by a
third person, the bailee is entitled to recover the full value of the goods or the full extent of the damage inflicted,' Brown, The Law of Personal Property (2nd Edition; 1955) 390, Section 90. Quoting
with approval from the English reports, this treatise points out that 'the root principle of the whole
discussion is that, as against a wrongdoer, possession is title' (p. 392), and that 'to allow the defendant, in an action in which his wrongful conduct is in question, to raise doubts as to the plaintiff's
title to the property, would raise collateral issues sharply interfering with the principal point in the
case—the defendant's wrongdoing' (p. 393).

5. Roughly translated: 'Although the third person who offers the payment has not a direct civil interest in extinguishing the obligation, the creditor cannot refuse to receive it, for in the last analysis

As was recently stated by one of the main treatises on French Civil law: 'Celui qui a effectué un paiment pour le compte d'un tiers sans ne lui ayant donné aucun mandat a cette fin, ne saurait en réclamer le remboursement audit tiers qu'à la condition de prouver l'obligation de celui-ci dans la dette ainsi acquitté par lui,'[6] IV Aubry et Rau, Droit Civil Francais (Supplement permanent, p. 1. 1957) Section 316, citing Cass. civ. 13 novembre 1939 (Gaz.Pal.1940, 1, 8 Sir.1940, 1, 27; J.C.P. 40, II, 1956).

Or as stated in Planiol et Ripert, Droit Civil Francais, Tome VII (2, 2 ed, 1954), Section 1150, p. 352: '* * * (U)n tiers quelconque, même non intéressé et agissant de son proper gré, a qualitè pour payer. Mais le tiers qui paie ne peut exiger à son profit le bénéfice de la subrogation de la part du créancier (art. 1236); il ne pourra exercer contre le debiteur que la recours fonde sur la gestion d'affaires ou l'enrichisement sans cause.'[7] The footnote to this sentence in the French text is the citation to the decision of the Civil Chamber of the Court of Cassation, Feb. 12, 1939 (D.He 1929 180), in which the court reversed a lower court judgment which had held that the stranger or volunteer could not recover in the absence of a legal or conventional subrogation. See also Cass. req. Feb. 3, 1879 (S.79.1.365; D.79.1.231), in which by way of dictum, remarking that 'Ce principle est incontestable', the court of cassation said: 'Le tiers qui a payé la dette d'autrui de ses propres deniers, a, bien que non subroge aux droits du créancier, un recours contre le debiteur (c. civ. 1236.).'[8]

See also 2 Baudry-Lacantinerie, Précis De Droit Civil, II (13e Ed.) 149, Section 324 'Recours du tiers qui a payé.'

Furthermore, the civil law does not share the hostility of the Anglo-American common law to the 'volunteer', and as stated above quite possibly recovery in the present case is allowable under the theory of negotiorum gestio, Articles 2295–2300, LSA-Civil Code, see Comment, 'Negotiorum Gestio in Louisiana', 7 Tulane Law Review 254, the quasi-contractual obligation arising from the situation where a person voluntarily manages the business of another without any authorization whatsoever.

The action of the garageman in repairing the damage to its customer's automobile might be considered to be in satisfaction of the third party tortfeasor's obligation to the customer for the damage to the latter's car, and therefore an act of negotiorum gestio as to said third party defendant tortfeasor herein. For all that is required for an instance of negotiorum gestio is that one person (the gestor) manage, of his own accord, the 'affair' of another (the principal) LSA-Civil Code, Article 2295. The garageman attended to the

---

the creditor has no other interest than to be paid; but in this case, the third (party) cannot force the creditor to put him in his (the creditor's) place with regard to the privileges and mortgages he may have or to his right to cause the arrest of the debtor. The law rightly does not allow a third party to interpose himself against the will of the creditor in order to acquire the right to harass the debtor; *the third party who pays then acquires only a simple action for reimbursement against the debtor who is then entirely free of the original obligation.*' (Italics ours.)

6. Roughly translated: 'He who has effected a payment for the account of a third person without having been given any authority for that purpose, will be allowed to demand reimbursement from the said third person only on the condition of proving that the latter was bound to pay the debt thus discharged by him.'

7. Roughly translated: 'Any third person whatever, even though not interested and acting of his own inclination, has the capacity to pay (the debt of another). But the third person who thus pays cannot demand subrogation to the creditor's interest (art. 1236); he can exercise against the debtor only the remedy founded on negotiorum gestio or unjust enrichment.'

8. Roughly translated: 'The principle is incontestable * * * (that) The third person who pays the debt of another from his own funds has, although not subrogated to the rights of the creditor, a remedy against the debtor (CN 1236).'

150 'affair' of the defendant herein when he fulfilled defendant tortfeasor's obligation to the
151 owner of the car existing by reason of his negligently damaging said vehicle. LSA-Civil Code,
152 Article 2316.[9]

153   For the above and foregoing reasons the judgment of the District Court herein sus-
154 taining defendant's exceptions of no right and cause of action is reversed, and the cause
155 is remanded for further proceedings according to law. The costs of this appeal are as-
156 sessed against defendant-appellee; all further costs to await final disposition of this
     matter.

157 Reversed and remanded.

Questions

1. Lines 12–17: Identify clearly all the parties involved in this case. Identify, in legal terms, the relationships existing between sets of parties; is each based in contract, delict/tort, etc…? Can you phrase precisely the issue raised in the case?

2. Lines 18–25: How strong is the defendant's argument that the plaintiff was not subrogated into the rights of the car owner? What kind of subrogation is the defendant referring to? Is the word or the concept of "intermeddler" in the Louisiana Civil Code? Notice the references given by the Court: are they persuasive sources of law in Louisiana?

3. Lines 26–50: Why is the defendant arguing that plaintiff is a "depositary"? After you have read the Louisiana Civil Code articles on deposit (*see* La. Civ. Code arts. 2926–2940), is it possible for the plaintiff to fit the legal profile of a depositary? Is it in the plaintiff's interest to argue the existence of a "moral duty" to repair cars of his customers? Would a "natural obligation" have been a better legal argument? Could the concept of moral duty be, here, a borrowing from the common law which does not know of natural obligations? How would the different prescriptive peri-

---

9. In this regard, it is of no consequence that the plaintiff garageman herein must have intended to favor its customer, the car owner, or to preserve or foster his own business good will in fulfilling the defendant tortfeasor's obligation to the owner of the car damaged through its negligence. Although the institution of Negotiorum gestio is often associated with an act Motivated by the desire to render a Service to the principal whose affair is managed, this motivation is said not to be an essential of its application. All that is required is that the gestor be aware of the fact that he is attending to another's business, in this case the defendant tortfeasor's obligation to repair the damage caused to the owner of the car, and his motive may be to benefit (a) another or even (b) himself. For instance, the Italian Civil Code of 1942, the newest of the major Codes, specifically reflects this thought with the formula requiring no more than that the gestor act Knowing he is managing or attending to another's affair. Italian Civil Code, Article 2028; Pandolfelli, Codice Civile illustrato con i lavori preparatori (Libro d lle Obligazaioni) (1942) 658, 659. And Negotiorum gestio is often used in France (according to the jurisprudence and doctrine) and in Germany (under German Civil Code, Article 679) to permit recovery by a person (the gestor) who supplies food, clothing, or money to dependents of the principal. Certainly in these cases the motive is to help the dependent rather than the principal. On the French law, see Picard, La gestion d'affaires dans la jurisprudence contemporaine, Revue Trimestrielle de Droit Civil (1942) 419, 446 seq. Besides, the mere fact that one protects his own interest or even advances his own welfare does not of itself take the action out of the scope of Negotiorum gestio. Thus French jurisprudence admits that a seller, whose buyer could not take delivery of grain because of the rise of a war, could sell the grain both in his own and his buyer's interests and still be a gestor. (Req. 19 juin 1872, Dalloz Periodique 1872.1.471.) Similarly, a co-owner may be a gestor in repairing property or attending to a common obligation; and the surety and co-debtor who pay to fulfill their own obligations as well as those of the principal are treated as negotiorum gestors. See generally on the matter of motive, Picard, La gestion d'affaires dans la jurisprudence contemporaine, Revue Trimestrielle de Droit Civil (1922) 5, at 23; Gore, L'enrichissement sans Cause (1949) No. 261.

ods (10 years for deposit compared to 1 year for torts/delicts) affect (negatively) the plaintiff? On line 49, is the Court really meaning "peremptive one year for tort actions...."?

4. Lines 98–152: Judge Tate makes a distinction between subrogation and payment of the debt of another: is this the proper distinction to make? Are these two concepts two different ways/modes of paying another's debt? Read the Code articles on "Payment" or "Performance" (*see* La. Civ. Code arts. 1854 *et seq.*) and on "Subrogation" (*see* La. Civ. Code arts. 1825–1830) carefully. Judge Tate cites then to Louisiana Civil Code article 2134 (now La. Civ. Code art. 1855) and refers extensively to French doctrine. Is this a legitimate and proper approach for a Louisiana court? Pay particular attention to the text translated from French into English in footnote 8. Is the second sentence particularly relevant to the case? Keep this sentence in mind as you read Judge Tate's opinion to come. Compare the Louisiana Civil Code articles on payment (article 1855 particularly) with the Louisiana Civil Code articles on the Management of the Affairs of Another (*see* La. Civ. Code arts. 2292–2297). Do you see any difference?

5. Lines 138–143: What do you think of the statement made here by Judge Tate? Is he finding this feature of the civil law in some *ratio juris* (reason for the Law) which is then incorporated in some institutions of the civil law, such as the Management of the Affairs of Another, Unjust Enrichment, or Louisiana Civil Code article 1855? What about the concept of good faith which is different at civil law from what it is at common law?

ST. PAUL FIRE & MARINE INSURANCE COMPANY

v.

Verry GALLIEN et al.

Louisiana Court of Appeal
First Circuit
April 27, 1959
111 So.2d 571

LANDRY, Judge ad hoc.

Plaintiff, St. Paul Fire and Marine Insurance Company, subrogee of its assured Willard L. Calloway, has taken this appeal from the judgment of the lower court rejecting plaintiff's demand against said assured Calloway and one Verry Gallien for the sum of $597.50 paid Calloway pursuant to a policy of collision insurance covering a 1954 Plymouth Tudor automobile belonging to Calloway and which said vehicle was totally destroyed in a collision with a 1956 Ford pickup truck owned and being operated by Gallien. The accident in question occurred March 1, 1957.

Following said accident, plaintiff insurance company, on March 25, 1957, paid its assured Calloway the sum of $597.50 (the value thereof less an amount obtained for its salvage and the sum of $50 deducted from its value according to the policy provisions), and obtained from its said assured a subrogation agreement wherein Calloway subrogated plaintiff to all his rights against the third party, Gallien.

Subsequent to signing the subrogation agreement in favor of plaintiff, Calloway granted Gallien a release on a form provided by the Department of Public Safety, Responsibility Division, State of Louisiana, discharging Gallien from responsibility for all claims arising from said accident, said release from Calloway to Gallien being dated April 19, 1957.

1
2
3
4
5
6
7
8
9
10
11
12
13
14
15
16
17
18
19
20
21
22
23
24

Plaintiff's claim against the third party Gallien is predicated on the theory that the release from Calloway is null and void considering Calloway had previously subrogated plaintiff to all his rights against Gallien and Gallien's negligence being the sole cause of the accident, plaintiff is entitled to recover from him the amount paid plaintiff's assured Calloway.

As against its assured Calloway, plaintiff's demand is founded on the principle that the subrogation agreement executed by Calloway prohibits his releasing from liability anyone who may be responsible in damages for destruction of the insured vehicle and, granting of such discharge by Calloway constitutes an active breach of plaintiff's antedated subrogation contract thereby conferring upon plaintiff the right to recover from Calloway the amount paid him.

[....]

The law of our state relative to subrogation is found in Articles 2159–2162 L.S.A. Revised Civil Code. The term subrogation has been defined by the courts of this state as the right of a person secondarily liable for a debt or obligation which he is compelled to discharge, to assume all the rights of the principal creditor against a third party who may be legally responsible for the amount paid. Motors Insurance Corporation v. Employers' Liability Assurance Corporation, La.App., 52 So.2d 311.

Although it possesses some attributes and characteristics of a sale, an act of subrogation is not a sale, transfer or assignment but rather a substitution of one claimant for another. As between an insurer and its assured, subrogation takes place by operation of law in those instances in which the insurer pays its assured a sum of money pursuant to a policy covering damages to property of the assured. Motors Insurance Corporation v. Employers' Liability Assurance Corporation, supra.

Travelers Fire Ins. Co. v. Ackel, 29 So.2d 617 (relied upon by the court below) was decided by the Court of Appeal, Second Circuit, and held that a release granted by an assured to a third party prior to execution of an act of subrogation to his insurer, operates as a valid cancellation and discharge of all rights which the assured possessed against the third party thereby extinguishing the obligation of the third party to both insurer and assured. This case further held that an assured who executes a release to a third party prior to subrogating his rights to his insurer, violates his contractual obligation to the insurer thereby rendering the assured liable to the insurer for any amount paid.

For reasons hereinafter set forth, we deem it unnecessary to consider either the applicability of the Ackel case, supra, or the validity of the release herein relied upon by plaintiff as the basis of its suit against its assured Calloway.

The purpose of a contract of subrogation is to afford the subrogee the opportunity of a day in court to seek recovery from the third party allegedly answerable for such loss as the subrogee has been called upon to pay. Under the terms of the policy issued Calloway and the subrogation agreement received from him, plaintiff acquired the right and privilege of seeking reimbursement from Gallien of the amount paid Calloway. Among the rights thus acquired by plaintiff was that of instituting legal action against Gallien to seek to establish his liability to plaintiff for the amount plaintiff has been compelled to pay its assured Calloway.

A determination of this case does not require decision on the issue of whether the release by Calloway constituted an active breach of his contractual obligation to plaintiff. Assuming arguendo the release to Gallien was valid (an issue upon which we refrain from ruling herein), plaintiff has in no way been aggrieved thereby considering Gallien has not urged said release as a defense to plaintiff's claim against him.

In the case at bar, both the assured and third party were sued in a single action. The   72
third party, Gallien, has not resisted plaintiff's demand against him despite his holding   73
a release from plaintiff's assured. Said third party has not offered or urged the release in   74
opposition to plaintiff's claim. No substantive or procedural right of plaintiff arising from   75
the policy and subrogation agreement between plaintiff and its assured has been denied   76
or adversely affected in any manner whatsoever.   77

[....]

Questions

1. Lines 9–48: What type of subrogation was created between the assured Calloway and
   its insurer St. Paul? Was that subrogation conditioned upon the occurrence of some
   event or was it always vested in the insurer regardless of any prior event occurring (*see*,
   in this respect, lines 30–35)? Under the collision insurance contract, since the insurer St. Paul was bound to pay its insured, Calloway, isn't the insurer, St. Paul, paying the debt of another, the tortfeasor, Gallien? If that is the case, how are St. Paul
   and Gallien bound together, if at all? Could that relationship fit under any one of
   the five instances of "subrogation by operation of law", per Louisiana Civil Code article 1829 (*see* lines 43–48)? What important legal consequences would flow from
   this legal subrogation? What impact would it have on the release? What particular type
   of a legal/contractual relationship does the insurance contract create between the insured and its insurer? How are these two parties bound vis-à-vis a tortfeasor? Can one
   party do whatever it wants without thinking about the other party's rights?

2. Lines 37–66: Do these two paragraphs answer some of the questions asked above? Do
   you understand the true meaning of subrogation, as distinguished from an assignment of rights, for example? *See* La. Civ. Code arts. 2642–2654.

PRINGLE-ASSOCIATED MORTGAGE CORPORATION   1
v.   2
Ernest R. EANES, Jr., et al.   3
Supreme Court of Louisiana   4
Feb. 24, 1969   5
226 So.2d 502   6

ON REHEARING   7

SANDERS, Justice.   8

Because of the importance of this case, we granted a rehearing to reconsider the fol-   9
lowing question: Is a subcontractor who pays wages to his employees as they become due   10
for labor on a building project subrogated under Article 2161 of the Louisiana Civil Code   11
to the superior privilege granted laborers by LSA-R.S. 9:4801 and LSA-R.S. 9:4812?   12

The facts are clearly and completely stated in our original opinion, and we condense   13
them here: In 1965, Ernest R. Eanes, Jr. purchased a lot in East Baton Rouge Parish, for   14
the purpose of subdividing the property and constructing apartment buildings. To se-   15
cure funds for the construction, Eanes executed a promissory note for $335,000 in favor   16
of plaintiff mortgage corporation, secured by a collateral mortgage affecting the land   17
upon which the development project was to be erected. Eanes also entered into an agree-   18
ment with Buddy Eanes Homebuilders, Incorporated, of which he was president, to con-   19

struct apartments on the mortgaged property. Pursuant to this agreement, Buddy Eanes Homebuilders let variou [*sic*] subcontractors to other firms to supply the labor and material necessary for construction. Although it did considerable work, Buddy Eanes Homebuilders defaulted as prime contractor. At the time of the default, plaintiff had advanced Eanes $263,615.70 for the project.

On April 20, 1966 plaintiff sued Eanes in this proceeding on his promissory note and was awarded judgment for the amount then due. A writ of fieri facias issued under which the property subject to the collateral mortgage was seized and sold and, on June 8, 1966, plaintiff purchased the property at the sheriff's sale. This sale was made subject to certain previously recorded privileges.

Now competing with the mortgage holder, the claimants to these privileges are Livingston Roofing & Sheet Metal Company, Inc. for $2,961.74, representing wages paid by it for labor; J. R. McFarland, d/b/a United Masonry Company, for $5,606.86, representing wages paid to his employees ($3,214.24) and wages of $2,396.62 for labor personally performed by McFarland, as subcontractor of the masonry work involved; and Capitol Detective Agency, Inc. for $1,446.26, representing salaries paid two night watchmen who were assigned to protect the project during its construction.

The parties concede that no laborer, except McFarland, filed a lien or privilege, but the subcontractors timely filed a claim for the privilege of their laborers.

The Court of Appeal, rejecting the subcontractors' right of subrogation under Article 2161, LSA-C.C., held plaintiff's mortgage primed all liens filed by the subcontractors, except the lien for labor personally performed by J. R. McFarland for $2,396.62. On original hearing, we upheld the subcontractors' right of subrogation under our decision in Tilly v. Bauman, 174 La. 71, 139 So. 762 (1932), and reversed the holding of the Court of Appeal.

Subrogation is an ancient concept, having its origin in Roman law. It was more fully developed and refined in France and became part of the Code Napoleon of 1804.[1] The Louisiana Civil Code Articles on this subject are almost identical to the corresponding articles of the French Civil Code. See Comment, 25 Tul.L.Rev. 358, 359.

As to legal subrogation, Article 2161 of the Louisiana Civil Code provides:

'Art. 2161. Subrogation takes place of right:

'1. For the benefit of him who, being himself a creditor, pays another creditor, whose claim is preferable to his by reason of his privileges or mortgages. * * *

'3. For the benefit of him who, being bound with others, or for others, for the payment of the debt, had an interest in discharging it.'

The foregoing article enumerates exceptions to the general rule of Article 2134, that when a third person pays the debt of another, no subrogation takes place and the debt is extinguished. Under familiar principles of statutory construction, these exceptions should be strictly construed. Succession of Andrews, La.App., 153 So.2d 470, cert. denied 244 La. 1005, 156 So.2d 57; 50 Am.Jur., Statutes, s 431, pp. 451–452; 82 C.J.S. Statutes s 382, pp. 891–894.

Subparagraph 1 of Article 2161 declares that subrogation takes place 'for the benefit of him who, being himself a creditor, pays another creditor, whose claim is preferable to his by reason of his privileges or mortgages.'

---

1. Arts. 1249–1252.

The subcontractors in the present case, of course, are creditors of the prime contractor, Buddy Eanes Homebuilders, and we can assume they are creditors of the owner. For subrogation to occur, however, the laborers must also be creditors of the owner at the time their wages are paid.

When this litigation arose, LSA-R.S. 9:4812 provided:

> 'The effect of the registry ceases, *even against the owner* of the property or the property itself, if the inscription has not been renewed within one year *from the date of the recordation*. Any person furnishing service or material or performing any labor on the said building or other work to or for a contractor or sub-contractor, when a contract, oral or written has been entered into, but no contract has been timely recorded, *shall have a personal right of action against the owner for the amount of his claim for a period of one year from the filing of his claim*, which right of action shall not prescribe within one year of the date of its recordation, or the reinscription thereof. This shall not interfere with the personal liability of the owner for material sold to or services or labor performed for him or his authorized agent. The said privilege shall be superior to all other claims against the land and improvements except taxes, local assessments for public improvements, a bona fide mortgage, or a bond fide vendor's privilege, whether arising from a sale or arising from a sale and resale to and from a regularly organized homestead or building and loan association, if the vendor's privilege or mortgage exists and has been duly recorded before the work or labor is begun or any material is furnished. *The wages of a laborer for work done by him in any building, shall, when properly presented and recorded by him in accordance with the provisions of this Sub-part, create in his favor a privilege on the land and improvements which will prime the right of mortgagees or vendors.*' (Italics ours).

Since the laborers had no contractual relation with the owner, they can be the owner's creditors only if they are accorded that status by the foregoing statute. The statute provides, however, that a laborer shall have a personal right of action against the owner 'from the filing of his claim.' Until the laborer files this claim, he never achieves the status of creditor. At best, he has only an inchoate right to become a creditor of the owner. Concededly, the laborers in the present case never filed an affidavit under the statute; their employers, the subcontractors, paid their wages as they became due. Hence, the laborers cannot be considered creditors of the owner to fulfil [sic] the conditions of subrogation.

Another equally valid principle bars application of the first Subparagraph of Article 2161. No subrogation takes place under this provision when the creditor and potential subrogee acquits a debt for which he is primarily liable.

In New Orleans Nat. Bank v. Eagle Cotton Warehouse & Compress Co., 43 La.Ann. 814, 9 So. 442, this Court recognized the principle:

> 'It is the essence of the legal subrogation which is defined in the foregoing paragraph that the person making payment should be a third person in respect to the obligee of the debt he is seeking to prime by making the payment, and also that such payor should himself be a creditor of inferior rank of the common debtor whose debt he pays.

> 'But Lallande was not only not a third person in respect to the obligee of the debt he sought to prime, but he was himself the original obligor, and more recently the plaintiff's pledgor.'

The modern French authorities support this principle. See 2 Aubry and Rau, Obligations, s 321, pp. 187, 203 (English Translation by the Louisiana State Law Institute, 1965);

112 2 Planiol Civil Law Treatise, No. 491, Footnote 27, p. 278 (English Translation by the
113 Louisiana State Law Institute, 1959); 2 Baudry-Lacantinerie, Obligations, s 1560, pp.
114 670–671 (3d ed. 1907).

115   The basic theory of this type of subrogation is that payment must be made by another
116 creditor for the beneit [*sic*] of the debtor. When such a payment is made, the debtor is not
117 liberated. Instead, the credit paid is in effect transmitted to the paying creditor, who as-
118 sumes the preferred status of the creditor who has been paid. A creditor who pays his
119 own debt has done no more than he was obligated to do. He has given nothing for the
120 benefit of the debtor. Hence, subrogation is normally disallowed.

121   To permit the subcontractors to invoke legal subrogation for the payment of their em-
122 ployees' wages would in effect award them a first ranking privilege for their own credit against
123 the owner.

124   We conclude subrogation must be rejected under Subparagrah 1 of Article 2161.

125   The subcontractors maintain, however, they fulfil [*sic*] all requirements for subroga-
126 tion under Subparagraph 3, declaring that subrogation takes place of right in favor of
127 him, who 'being bound with others' pays the debt that he had an interest in discharging.

128   Clearly this language presupposes the existence of a solidary obligation. If no solidary
129 obligation exists, subrogation does not take place.

130   In denying subrogation under this clause, the Court of Appeal held:

131   '(T)he subcontractors and owners were not and indeed could not have been
132   solidarily liable to the laborers whose claims are herein asserted. Under the
133   circumstances herein the owner was never liable to the laborers as no liens
134   were filed by any party occupying such status. Under the lien law, no liability
135   arises on the part of the owner until the lien is recorded. Since the owner was
136   never liable to the laborers, it necessarily follows he was not liable for such
137   wages, solidarily or otherwise, with those priamrily [*sic*] obligated for the wages
        earned.

138   'In the instant case when the subcontractors herein involved paid the wages for
139   which they now claim subrogation, said subcontractors were the sole debtors
140   and prime obligors of the laborers concerned.'

141   After reconsideration, we conclude the Court of Appeal correctly disposed of this issue.
142 It is now apparent we erred in holding the owner became a debtor of the laborers 'as soon
143 as the services are performed.' As we have demonstrated, the personal liability of the
144 owner comes into existence only when laborers file their claim. Since the owner was no
145 debtor, there can be no solidary obligation.

146   In holding the owner a debtor of the laborers on original hearing, we relied upon Al-
147 fred Hiller Co. v. Hotel Grunewald Co., 138 La. 305, 70 So. 234, and Rathborne Lumber
148 & Supply Co. v. Falgout, 218 La. 629, 50 So.2d 295. A reexamination of these cases dis-
149 closes a lien affidavit was filed in them as a basis for personal liability under the statute.
150 Hence, they are inapposite.

151   We hold, as did the Court of Appeal, that subrogation is unavailable to the subcontractors
152 for their wage payments.

153   Concededly, the 1932 decision of this Court in Tilly v. Bauman is in direct conflict
154 with our present holding. That decision stands alone in the jurisprudence and has been
155 criticized as a 'strained' construction of the pertinent statutes. See Steeg and Meyer, 'When

is a Security Not A Secured Right?' 39 Tul.L.Rev. 513, 516. The decision is unsound and   156
must yield to the legislative will embodied in the statutes and code articles.   157

The clash of economic interests in this litigation has not escaped our attention. When   158
asserted under the present circumstances, a laborers' privilege protects no laborers. They   159
receive their wages in full as they accrue. On the other hand, the construction lender may   160
be deprived of reasonable security for money already advanced.   161

Our present holding converges with a salutary policy: the optimum protection of   162
recorded mortgages from the intrusion of later claims, unrecorded when the funds are dis-   163
bursed. Our holding safeguards the security of the recorded mortgage—a catalytic force   164
in the state's economy.   165

For the reasons assigned, the judgment of the Court of Appeal is affirmed. The right   166
of the unsuccessful litigants to apply for a rehearing is reserved.   167

Questions

1.   Lines 110–120: Read carefully these two paragraphs. Of particular importance is the
statement in lines 115–116: "The basic theory of this type of subrogation (legal subrogation) is that payment must be made by another creditor for **the benefit of the debtor**".
(Emphasis ours.)

2.   Lines 121–124: Notice how the Court justifies (explains on legal grounds) its ruling:
"subrogation must be rejected...." for the reasons here given. Does this case explain
the foundation and purpose of subrogation?

Charles W. COX   1
v.   2
W. M. HEROMAN & CO., INC., and   3
American Employers Insurance Co.   4
Supreme Court of Louisiana   5
June 10, 1974   6
298 So.2d 848   7

TATE, Justice.   8

A subcontractor ('Cox') sues his general contractor ('Heroman') for the balance due   9
on the subcontract. The general contractor claims a credit for a payment made directly   10
by Heroman to a supplier ('Reulet') of the subcontractor. [....]   11

The issue before us is two fold: 12

(1) Was Heroman entitled to pay Cox's creditor Reulet directly, over Cox's pro-   13
tect, thus (under Civil Code Article 2134) extinguishing Cox's debt to Reulet as   14
to the extent of the payment and also giving Heroman a right to receive reim-   15
bursement of this payment from Cox?;   16

(2) If Heroman was Not entitled to pay Cox's debt to Reulet, nevertheless was not   17
Heroman (by his payment and express agreement with Reulet) subrogated to re-   18
cover Reulet's debt against Cox (Article 2159), thus entitling Heroman in the   19
present suit to reduce the balance due by Heroman to Cox under the subcon-   20
tract to the extent that it is extinguished (through the compensation of two debts,   21
Article 2207) by the subrogated (Reulet) debt due by Cox to Heroman?   22

Facts

Heroman as general contractor entered into a construction contract with a university in the amount of over five hundred thousand dollars. Heroman and Cox entered into a subcontract by which Cox agreed to perform the electrical work for $37,590.00.

In the course of construction, progess [*sic*] payments were made by Heroman to Cox totalling [*sic*] $27,681.27. (An additional ten percent of the total of the progress estimates was retained by Heroman, in accordance with the subcontract agreement, for payment upon final acceptance.)

As the completion of both the general contract and the subcontract neared, the present controversy arose. Heroman was informed by several suppliers of Cox on the job that Cox had not paid them, and Reulet (Cox's principal supplier) informed Heroman that it would lien the job.

The facts forming the basis of the litigation occurred when on April 14, 1971 Heroman paid Reulet directly $4,349.74 to credit against Cox's debt due Reulet for supplies on the job. This sum was the total balance then due by Heroman to Cox. (It did not include the ten percent retained per the contract.) The payment was specifically made for the account of Cox due for supplies on the present contract. Cox was sent a carbon copy of the letter by which payment was made.

Prior to this payment of April 14, 1971, Reulet had conferred with Heroman about an unpaid amount of $8,360.55 due for supplies furnished Cox for the contract. Heroman had then sent to Cox a check for $4,439.74, payable to Cox and Reulet jointly. (This was the same amount later paid Reulet directly, being the then total unpaid balance due by Heroman to Cox.)

Cox returned the check to Heroman. He stated that he considered this direct payment improper and unacceptable. He alleged that there were considerable overcharges claimed by Reulet amounting to over twenty-five hundred dollars.[1]

Reulet then wrote Heroman that it would place a lien on the job unless the amount due was paid at this time. Reulet's letter concluded, that, if Heroman would pay the unpaid invoices due by Cox, Heroman 'is subrogated to all rights that we have against Cox in connection with this job and such payment.'[2]

Upon receipt of this letter, Heroman immediately paid Reulet the full balance then due Cox ($4,349.74) by progress estimates, as stated above. Reulet accepted this payment, credited Cox's account, and did not lien the job.

Cox then on April 22, 1974 filed a lien for the unpaid balance due on the job. Correspondence introduced by Cox shows that unsuccessful negotiations were subsequently conducted between Cox, Reulet, and other suppliers in an effort to allocate the remaining amount due by Heroman to Cox to unpaid accounts of Cox resulting from his performance of his subcontract.

---

1. Cox, in failing circumstances, was at this point claiming that all his suppliers had overcharged him.

2. Reulet's letter to Heroman provides: 'We enclosed herewith our unpaid invoices for materials purchased by Mr. Cox and installed on the above captioned job. The total amount of these unpaid invoices is $8,360.55. I hereby certify that the amounts shown on these invoices are true and correct.' As we have previously told you, we have been unable to collect the $8,360.55 from Mr. Cox. Accordingly, we have no alternative buy to place a lien on this job unless the amount due us is paid at this time. You have told us that under the circumstances you will pay our unpaid invoices on this job, and this is to acknowledge that *upon receipt of said payment from you, your Company is subrogated to all rights that we have against Cox in connection with this job and such payment.'* (Italics ours.)

On December 27, 1971, Cox filed the present suit against Heroman and its surety (American Employers) to recover $10,016.62, then allegedly due under the contract, together with ten percent statutory attorney fees. The suit alleged that the unpaid balance included the sum of $4,349.74 which had been paid by Heroman to Reulet. In the suit, Cox specifically alleges that he was contesting the total amount claimed by Reulet ($8,360.55) because he estimates 'Reulet overcharges and errors in the amount of $2,500.00' See Art. 9 of petition.

Cox alleged that Heroman owed him: $5,448.99 representing the final draw and retainage (which Heroman in its answer conceded owing, except for back charges of $304.45), an alleged add-on due of $107.89 (which both previous courts found not owing), and the $4,349.74 previously paid by Heroman to Reulet.

Heroman's answer pleaded the facts of the dispute, and acknowledged liability for only the final draw and retainage of $5,254.54.

The trial court held that Heroman was not entitled under its contract to pay Reulet, Cox's creditor, directly. It therefore disallowed credit to Heroman for such payment and awarded Cox judgment for that sum, plus the amount due for the final draw and retainage, for a total amount of $9,908.73.[3]

As earlier noted, the court of appeal concluded that the trial court was in error in refusing to allow Heroman credit against Cox's claim for the amount paid by Heroman to extinguish pro tanto Reulet's claim against Cox for supplies furnished for the present job. The court of appeal essentially held that Heroman was entitled to pay the debt due by Cox to Reulet and to be reimbursed by Cox for this payment, by reason of Civil Code Article 2134.[4] See Standard Motor Car Company v. State Farm Mutual Automobile Insurance Co., 97 So.2d 435 (La.App.1st Cir. 1957).

1. 'Payment' under Article 2134

We granted certiorari primarily because of our doubt that, under the circumstances here shown, the debtor Heroman could extinguish a debt due to its creditor Cox by paying, not Cox, but Cox's creditor. We entertained this doubt because: (a) Cox expressly opposed such payment by Heroman of His debt due Reulet; instead, Cox expressly desired to receive amounts due him by Heroman for purposes of negotiating the payment due by him to Reulet in connection with certain disputed items; (b) The subcontract between Heroman and Cox expressly provided for Heroman's remedy, in the event of Cox's non-payment of suppliers on the job, namely, Heroman was to withhold payments due Cox until the grounds for non-payment were removed.

Article 2134 (quoted in full in Footnote 5) provides that an 'obligation may even be discharged by a third person in no way concerned in it', provided that, 'if he act in his own name, he be not *subrogated* to the rights of the creditor.' (Italics ours.)

Although not subrogated to the rights of the creditor (such as to receive a stipulated interest or attorney's fees in the event of non-payment), a third person acting in his own

---

3. We may say at this point that the questions of the disallowance of the ten percent attorneys fees for nonpayment when due of the subcontract price, and of the $107.89 add-on, as well as of Heroman's claim that the final draw and retainage was subject to a credit for $304.45 back charges, are not before us. The parties apparently accepted the determinations of the previous courts as to them, and they did not and do not seek further review of them.

4. Article 2134 provides: 'An obligation may be discharged by any person concerned in it, such as a coobligor or a surety.' The obligation may even be discharged by a third person no way concerned in it, provided that person act in the name and for the discharge of the debtor, or that, if he act in his own name, he be not subrogated to the rights of the creditor.'

name is entitled to be reimbursed by the debtor for the sum used to discharge the latter's debt. See Article 2299; Roman v. Forstall, 11 La.Ann. 717, 720 (1856); Standard Motor Car Company v. State Farm Mutual Automobile Insurance Co., 97 So.2d 435 (La.App.1st Cir. 1975). See also Hutchinson v. Rice, 105 La. 474, 29 So. 898 (1901); Weil v. Enterprise Ginnery & Mfg. Co., 42 La.Ann. 492, 7 So. 622 (1890); Gernon v. McCan, 23 La.Ann. 84 (1871); Nicholls v. His Creditors, 9 Rob. 476 (1845). The creditor cannot even refuse to receive the payment tendered by the third person, State ex rel. John Klein & Co. v. Pilsbury, 29 La.Ann. 787 (1877), unless perhaps the creditor has some special interest in having the obligation fulfilled by the debtor himself, Article 2136.[5]

Articles 2134 and 2136, literal translations of French Civil Code Articles 1236 and 1237, are in accord, as thus interpreted, with traditional civilian obligations theory. 1 Litvinoff on Obligations, Section 27, p. 47, and Section 49 (Louisiana Civil Law Treatise, Vol. 6; 1969); Planiol, Civil Law Treatise, Vol. 2, Section 401 (LSLI translation, 1959); 1 Civil Law Translations (Aubry & Rau, Obligations), Sections 315, 316 (1965).

As summarized in the last-cited translation of Aubry & Rau, at pp. 156–58: 'In general, the creditor cannot refuse payment offered by a third person whether or not interested in the extinction of the obligation ... A payment made by a third person and accepted by the creditor extinguishes the obligation as definitively as one effected by the debtor personally, Except where the third person is legally or contractually subrogated to the rights of the creditor. In the last case, the debtor is discharged toward the original creditor, but the obligation continues to exist in favor of the third person who has been subrogated thereto.' (The italics are supplied to emphasize a legal distinction between 'payment' under Article 2134 and 'subrogation' under Articles 2159–2161, a distinction which is of decisional importance in this case.)

The right of the third person to pay the creditor in his own name, and the obligation of the creditor to receive such payment for the benefit of the debtor's account, is not unqualified:

Where, for instance, it is done to harm the debtor's interest, it may be an abuse of the third person's right to make the payment. See Comment, Abuse of Rights in Louisiana, 7 Tul.L.Rev. 426 (1933). Further, when the debtor opposes the payment, some decisions hold that the third person's payment, In the absence of subrogation, cannot be recovered, since the third person cannot conceptually be held to have acted on behalf of the debtor.[6] Woodlief & Legendre v. Moncure, 17 La.Ann. 241 (1865). See also Succession of Mulligan v. Kenny, 34 La.Ann. 50 (1882). See Comment, 7 Tul.L.Rev. 253, 256 (1933). Finally, where the third person and the debtor have a contractual relationship which regulated the former's right to pay the debts due by the debtor to others,[7] this contractual right

---

5. Article 2136 provides in full: 'The obligation of doing can not be discharged by a third person against the will of the creditor, when it is the interest of the latter that it be fulfilled by the debtor himself.' This article literally refers to an obligation to Do, as distinguished from an obligation to Give (which includes an obligation to Pay.) Articles 1883, 1905. The French interpretations of French Civil Code Article 1237 (of which Louisiana's Article 2136 is a literal translation) are in disagreement whether the provision permits the creditor to reject Payment as distinguished from Doing tendered by a third person. See 1 Civil Law Translations (Aubry & Rau, Obligations), Section 316 at footnote 2 (1965).

6. Here, however, the principle of unjustified enrichment may permit the third person to recover for benefits received by the person enriched. Police Jury v. Hampton, 5 Mart., N.S., 389 (1827).

7. The subcontract between Heroman and Cox provided that, when the subcontractor (Cox) failed to pay his suppliers on the job as required by the contract, then the general contractor (Heroman) had the right to withhold payments due Cox until Cox paid his suppliers. This might be regarded as a

may limit the third person's right to extinguish such debt due by the debtor to another. 136
See Civil Code Article 1901: 'Agreements entered into have the effects of laws on those 137
who have formed them. * * *.' Cf. Hardin v. Federal Rice Mill Co., 164 La. 49, 113 So. 760 138
(1927).[8] 139

Without at this time attempting to determine what weight, if any, shall be accorded to 140
any of these particular factors, it is sufficient for us to hold that, by reason of the total- 141
ity of circumstances (including the contractual relationship between Heroman and Cox), 142
Heroman did not have the right under Article 2134 to Extinguish Cox's debt to Reulet by 143
directly paying Reulet despite Cox's opposition to such payment. 144

2. Subrogation under Articles 2159, 2160 145

This does not end our inquiry, however. Heroman argues that, even though it was not 146
entitled to entinguish Cox's debt and to receive reimbursement under Article 2134, it was 147
by its payment expressly subrogated to recover from Cox this amount paid by it and to 148
receive credit against its liability due Cox under the subcontract. For the reasons to be 149
stated, we find this last contention to be well-founded. 150

To recapitulate: 151

On the date of the April 14, 1971 payment, Two debts were involved: (a) that 152
between Heroman and Cox, by which Heroman owed Cox $4,349.74, payable im- 153
mediately, but subject to Heroman's contractual right to withhold payment to Cox 154
until Cox paid his debt due Reulet (see debt B); and (b) Cox's debt due Reulet 155
for supplies received on the Heroman-Cox job, which totalled [sic] $8,360.55 by 156
Reulet's invoices, of which amount Cox contested $2,500 as overcharges. 157

If Heroman's payment to Reulet did not entitle Heroman to extinguish pro tanto 158
Heroman's debt to Cox, then as (at least) of the date of the trial court judgment 159
of June 20, 1972 there are also Two debts at issue in this litigation, both equally 160
liquidated and demandable: (a) the debt due Cox by Heroman in the amount of 161
$9,908.73, being due for the final progress estimate and the retainage; (b) the 162
debt due Heroman by Cox for $4,349.74, Heroman's expressly subrogated right 163
to recover this amount of the debt previously due by Cox to Reulet. 164

For reasons we will set forth, debt (b) exists as well as debt (a). The debts being equally 165
due and demandable, at least as of the time of the judgment, they are mutually extin- 166
guished by the compensation. See Articles 2207–2209.[9] 167

---

contractual substitution limiting the right of Heroman under Article 2134 to extinguish by direct payment any debt owed by Cox to his suppliers.

8. A rice broker paid the freight-charges on rice shipped by the owner-consignor. The rice had
been sold upon the express agreement that the Purchaser would be liable for shipping costs. The broker paid the freight charges and then, when the purchaser became insolvent, sued the seller-consignor.
He was denied recovery. Although the consignor-sellor was ordinarily primarily liable, under the contract the shipping charges became the debt of the purchaser. Whatever the broker's rights against the
purchaser, he was not entitled to recover the shipping charges from the seller because, under the contract, the shipping charges were to be paid otherwise than by it.

9. These articles provide: 'Art. 2207. When two persons are indebted to each other, there takes
place between them a compensation that extinguishes both the debts, in the manner and cases hereafter expressed.' 'Art. 2208. Compensation takes place of course by the mere operation of law, even unknown to the debtors; the two debts are reciprocally extinguished, as soon as they exist simultaneously,
to the amount of their respective sums.' 'Art. 2209. Compensation takes place only between two debts
having equally for their object a sum of money, or a certain quantity of consumable things of one
and the same kind, and which are equally liquidated and demandable. The days of grace are no obstacle to the compensation.'

The subrogated debt of $4,349.74 is due by Cox to Heroman, for the following reasons:

> Article 2159 provides: 'Subrogation to the right of a creditor in favor of a third person who pays him, is either conventional or legal.' Article 2160(1) provides that a conventional subrogation shall take place, 'When the creditor, receiving his payment from a third person, subrogates him in his rights, actions, privileges, and mortgages against the debtor; this subrogation must be expressed and made at the same time as the payment.'

In urging that an express conventional subrogation took place, Heroman relies upon: (a) the offer by Reulet to receive payment of invoices due it by Cox and 'upon receipt of said payment, your Company (i.e., Heroman) is subrogated to all rights that we have against Cox in connection with this job and such payment',[10] Cox further offering not to lien the job if Heroman would make such direct payment; (2) Heroman's acceptance of such offer by paying all the money then due Cox to Reulet, whereupon Reulet ratified the qualified acceptance by crediting Cox's account with payment and desisting from liening the job.

Heroman's contention is well founded. By the acceptance of the offer, Heroman was subrogated to Reulet's right to recover Reulet's debt against Cox. A third person 'having agreed to pay the debt only on condition that he should be subrogated, he was ipso facto subrogated when he made the payment. The thing having been understood and agreed upon, it was not necessary to have any further agreement on the subject at the time of payment. The payment was made in accordance with the agreement; that is to say, with subrogation.' Cooper v. Jennings Refining Co., 118 La. 181, 183, 42 So. 766 (1907).

A creditor (Reulet) has the right to receive payment on a debt owed him and, by contract, to subrogate his payor (Heroman) to his claim. The debtor (Cox) cannot, by prohibiting the payor (Heroman) to make such payment, thus limit the creditor's legal right to make such a contract in order for the latter to receive payment. Subrogation is thus permitted in the interest of the creditor rather than of the debtor. This is distinguishable from a payment made by a third person under Article 2134, which theoretically is an act done in the debtor's interest; the debtor, by prohibiting the act, can deny the third-person payor the right to act allegedly in the former's interest.

Cox argues that subrogation is not at issue and did not occur because [**among other things**]: [....] partial subrogation is not permitted without the consent of the debtor.

[....]

[....] In contending that partial Subrogation is not permitted, as dividing the debt without the consent of the debtor, Cox relies upon a line of decisions holding that partial assignment is not permitted without the consent of the debtor.[11] There is a substantial conceptual difference between, on the one hand, an 'assignment', which has the nature

---

10. The letter is quoted in full at Footnote 2. It was introduced in evidence as D-1 without objection in connection with Reulet's testimony. The pre-trial order previously noted Heroman's intention to offer this letter in evidence.

11. Red River Valley Bank & Trust Co. v. Louisiana Petrolithic Const. Co., 142 La. 838, 77 So. 763 (1918); Meyer v. Vicksburg, Shreveport & P. Railway Co., 35 La.Ann. 897 (1883); LeBlanc v. Parish of East Baton Rouge, 10 Rob. 25 (1845); Cantrelle v. LeGoaster, 3 Rob. 432 (1943); Miller v. Brigot, 8 La. 533 (1835); King v. Havard, 5 Mart., N.S., 193 (1826); Stein v. Williams Lumber Co., 36 So.2d 62 (La.App.Orl.Cir. 1948); Lane v. Deas Co., 12 La.App. 382, 125 So. 514 (1929). All of these cases involved Assignments rather than subrogation. Stein, however, itself an assignment case, included the dictum that subrogation, as well as assignment, was prohibited without the debtor's consent, erroneously citing the other above-noted assignment cases as authority.

of the sale and acquisition of a credit so as to permit its enforcement of the assignee, and, on the other hand, a conventional 'subrogation', which has for its primary purpose the negotiated discharge of a debt due to the creditor. Civil Law Translations (Aubry & Rau, Obligations), Section 321 b (1965); Comment, 25 Tul.L.Rev. 358, 368–69 (1951). Thus, in a subrogation the interest of a creditor (here, Reulet) in receiving payment of his debt in return for subrogating the third party to his right to recover it, outweighs the interest of the debtor (here, Cox) in avoiding the division of the debt he owes into multiple claims, the policy preventing partial assignments (see decisions cited in Footnote 4 above).

No authority is cited to us which prevents partial subrogation. The Civil Code, in fact, recognizes that a partial subrogation can take place in the case of a legal subrogation, Article 2161, and that, in the case of both legal and conventional subrogation, a partial subrogation may take place, Article 2162.[12]

Planiol notes: 'Subrogation by consent of (the) creditor … is always possible. The creditor, on receiving payment from a person other than the debtor, can always accord to him a subrogation to assure his recourse, and he is also free to refuse it.' Vol. 2, Section 479. 'The subrogation, resulting exclusively from the creditor's will, may, at his pleasure, be total or partial.' Section 482. 'When the creditor has received from the subrogee a partial payment only, the credit is divided between them; the original creditor remains creditor for the unpaid portion and the subrogee becomes creditor to the extent of the payment he has made.' Section 515. Planiol also notes that the only conditions required to effect a conventional subrogation are that it be express and that the creditor should consent to it, at the latest, at the time that the creditor receives his payment. Section 480.[13]

We could find no decisions which held that the consent of the debtor was necessary for the creditor to subrogate part of the debt due by receiving payment from a third person. On the other hand, we found decisions such as R. M. Walmsley & Co. v. Theus, 107 La. 417, 31 So. 869 (1901) and numerous collision insurer subrogation cases which without discussion allowed a partial subrogation by the creditor unconsented—to by the debtor.

We therefore find valid the partial subrogation to Heroman resulting from the express agreement of Reulet at the time Heroman made payment to Reulet upon Cox's debt.

When a subrogor sues the debtor, the latter has the right to raise all defenses available. Here, the evidence is uncontradicted that Cox owed Reulet in excess of the amount paid to Reulet by Heroman, the claim against Cox to which Reulet was expressly subrogated to such payment. If Cox seriously contended he did not owe Reulet the amount to which Heroman was subrogated, Cox had the right under the pleadings to prove such opposition to Heroman's claim of credit for such amount.

3. Conclusion

In summary, we hold that Heroman is entitled to reason of compensation to receive a credit against the debt Heroman owes Cox arising out of the equally liquidated and demandable debt due Heroman by Cox by reason of Heroman's subrogated claim.

---

12. Article 2162 in full provides: 'The subrogation established by the preceding articles, takes place as well against the sureties, as against the debtors. It can not injure the creditor, since, if he has been paid but in part, he may exercise his right for what remains due, in preference to him from whom he has received only a partial payment.'

13. We should note that there is a difference between a subrogation by the creditor, Article 2160(1), and a subrogation by the debtor, Article 2160(2)—the latter requiring the consent of the creditor affected. See Planiol, Vol. 2, Sections 484–490.

At the time Heroman made the payment to Reulet, it was not entitled to credit against its debt due Cox, by reason of the stipulations in the contract between Cox and Heroman and of Cox's expressed opposition to such payment. However, whatever right Cox may have had under its contract to secure penalties from Heroman for non-compliance with the contract terms, this issue has passed out of the case (see Footnote 4).

The only issue thus before us is whether, when both claims are equally liquidated and demanded, Heroman is entitled to compensate its subrogated claim owed by Cox against its debt owed to Cox. We hold that it is.[14] We thus reach, for different reasons, the same result as the court of appeal.

Accordingly, for the reasons assigned, we affirm the court of appeal decree.

Court of appeal decree affirmed.

DIXON, J., dissents with reasons.

DIXON, Justice (dissenting).

I respectfully dissent. The Code provides that the subrogation agreement must be made at the same time as the payment.

C.C. 2160 provides:

'The subrogation is conventional:

1. When the creditor, receiving his payment from a third person, subrogates him in his rights, actions, privileges, and mortgages against the debtor; this subrogation must be expressed and made at the same time as the payment. * * *'

This provision requires that the subrogation be clear, definite and that the subrogation be made at the time of payment. The French article is the same. (C.N. 1804, Art. 1250).

Translations of French commentators that are available to us are even more specific. Planiol says the subrogation 'must be conferred at the same time as payment.' Planiol, Civil Law Treatise, Vol. 2, No. 480 (Louisiana State Law Institute Translation 1959). Aubry and Rau say the subrogation 'must be made simultaneously with the payment.' Aubry and Rau, Cours de Droit Civil Francais, s 321, Vol. I, Civil Law Translations, La.Law Inst. 1965.

From the meager resources at hand, it appears that the modern French view has not departed from the very explicit codal provisions.

Carbonnier says:

'Condition de temps: la subrogation doit e tre consentie au moment mem du paiement (en pratique, dans la quittance me me, quittance subrogatoire).' Droit Civil, Vol. 2, No. 130 (1956).

A report of the most recent jurisprudence states:

'La date de la subrogation doit e tre contemporaine du paiement (Com. 14 de c. 1965, Rec. Gaz. Pal. 1966. 1. 278).' Repertorie De Droit Civil (Mise A Jour 1974).

For whatever reason, conventional subrogation agreements in anticipation of payment are not sanctioned by our statutes. The subrogation must be consented to at the time of payment.

---

14. If we were to hold otherwise, then Heroman would have to sue Reulet to recover back the money paid to it in error, and Reulet would have to sue Cox to recover such amount, which until now it has credited on its unpaid claim for supplies against Cox.

Dicta in Cooper v. Jennings Refining Co., 118 La. 181, 42 So. 766 is contrary. That case, however, did not necessarily involve conventional subrogation, in spite of the discussion of conventional subrogation in the opinion. The claimant guaranteed payment for a load of pipe—the debt of another—and became a surety. C.C. 3035. Upon payment, the surety had recourse against the debtor (C.C. 3052) and, in addition, was subrogated to the rights of the creditor by operation of law. C.C. 2161(3). 283 284 285 286 287 288

The Court was distracted in Cooper v. Jennings, Supra, because the surety did not agree In writing to pay the debt of another. C.C. 2278. Nevertheless, when the surety recognized his obligation and paid the debt, that problem of proof no longer existed. See C.C. 2133. 289 290 291

The case before us could be decided with less violence to the law under C.C. 2161(3) as a legal subrogation. In spite of toobroad [sic] language in Pringle-Associated Mtg. Corp. v. Eanes, 254 La. 705, 226 So.2d 502, the contractor is obligated to pay the materialman if the subcontractor does not. (In Pringle, the subcontractor did not pay the debt of another. He paid his own debt, for which he was primarily liable-wages of his workmen-and sought legal subrogation to their lien rights.) 292 293 294 295 296 297

Nevertheless, there is something fundamentally wrong in allowing a debtor (Heroman) to pay another person instead of his creditor (Cox) over the strong protest of the creditor. 298 299 300

The unqualified statement by the majority that a non-subrogated third party acting in his own name is entitled to be reimbursed by the debtor for the sum used to discharge the latter's debt is of doubtful validity. The authorities cited to support such a proposition were, in the main, concerned with other issues. In Roman v. Forstall, 11 La.Ann. 717 (1856), there was a valid subrogation of the third party to the rights of the creditor; however, the court found that the third party was entitled to recover the sum paid from the debtors under a theory of negotiorum gestio. Weil v. Enterprise Ginnery & Mfg. Co., 42 La.Ann. 492, 7 So. 622 (1890) holds that mere payment of a note by a third party does not subrogate that person to the rights of the creditor. The opinion then states as dicta, in reliance on a head-note from Nicholls v. His Creditors, Infra, that such circumstances would constitute the party who paid an ordinary creditor of him for whose benefit the payment was made. Gernon v. McCan, 23 La.Ann. 84 (1871), has nothing to do with the proposition for which it is cited. Nicholls v. His Creditors, 9 Rob. 476 (1845), holds that mere payment of a note by one not bound for it does not subrogate the one who pays to the rights of the creditor. 301 302 303 304 305 306 307 308 309 310 311 312 313 314

The preferred solution to the problem in the case before us is to allow the creditor Cox to prevail, and collect from his debtor Heroman, reserving to Heroman whatever rights he might have to reimbursement from Reulet. 315 316 317

Questions

1. To attempt to understand this case as clearly as possible, we suggest that, after you have read the "Facts", you draw a diagram of the relationships created between the three major parties involved here; identify and name the contracts that may exist in the case. Since several 'bilateral' contracts exist here, be sure to single out which 'party' may be a 'third party' to a particular contract between two other parties. This exercise will be essential to an understanding of the Court's opinion. In addition, you should read the Louisiana Civil Code article on Performance/Payment (La. Civ. Code arts. 1854–1863), Subrogation (La. Civ. Code arts. 1825–1830), Assumption (La. Civ. Code arts. 1821–1824), and Assignment of Rights (La. Civ. Code arts. 2642–2654, particularly La. Civ. Code art. 2653).

2. Lines 85 *et seq.*: On line 101, how can the Court bring in former Louisiana Civil Code article 2299 (now articles 2292–2293) when Heroman is bound by a contract with Cox? On the basis of Louisiana Civil Code article 2134, shouldn't Heroman be denied subrogation if he pays Reulet "in his own name" and against the will of Cox? Would the law be the same today under Louisiana Civil Code articles 2292–2293 and 1855?

3. Lines 124–126: How do these limitations to the right of a third person to pay for the benefit of his debtor's account apply to the case at hand? To the extent that a subrogation is a transfer of a right and, thereby, has much in common with an assignment of rights, of what relevance is Louisiana Civil Code article 2653? Could Cox's objections be equal to a prohibition under Louisiana Civil Code article 2653?

4. Lines 146–150: Heroman acknowledges that he was not entitled to extinguish Cox's debt; thus was the payment lawful? Either Heroman had a "right" to pay Cox's debt to Reulet or he didn't, right? Under the facts of the case, Reulet claimed to be Cox's obligee, but didn't Cox claim that he had been overcharged and, therefore, was himself possibly an obligee to some extent of Reulet? So if Reulet is Cox's creditor and if Cox is, in turn, Reulet's creditor, how can these two reciprocal debts be extinguished up to the amount of the lesser? *See* La. Civ. Code arts. 1893–1902 on Compensation. Notice that on line 148–149 the court refers to Heroman "receiving credit against its liability due Cox...." In other words, from Heroman's debt to Cox the amount of Heroman's payment to Reulet (on behalf of Cox) will be deducted. The Court imposed on Cox the method of payment called compensation (*see supra*). Could compensation be a legal obstacle to Heroman paying Cox's debt to Reulet? *See* La. Civ. Code art. 1824–2 by analogy or on the basis of a reasoning *ubi eadem ratio idem jus*, "where the reason is the same the law must be the same." What about Cox's objections, which could be based on redhibitory defects (*see* La. Civ. Code arts. 2520–2548) or disproportionate price (*see* La. Civ. Code art. 2464)? In an action between Cox and Reulet, Cox could raise such defenses. What happened to these defenses, once the Court allowed compensation to take place in the relationship between Heroman and Cox? Could Cox still raise against Heroman the same defenses he could have raised against Reulet? If Cox could prove that he had been overcharged by Reulet in the amount of $X (or that there were defects of that amount), does it mean that Cox could get that amount from Heroman who would then have to pay that $X dollars amount on top of the balance of his debt to Cox? If that is so, could Heroman then turn against Reulet for having paid too much to the latter when subrogation took place?

5. Lines 190–197: From the above, Heroman's payment of Cox's debt to Reulet by way of compensation should not be allowed because Heroman should not have the right to make that payment. What then is the Court saying in the sentence: "A creditor (Reulet) has the right ... claim"? And the Court continues with this statement: "The debtor (Cox) cannot ... limit the creditor's legal right to make such a contract (of subrogation)...." In conclusion the Court states: "Subrogation is thus permitted in the interest of the creditor rather than of the debtor. This is distinguishable from a payment made by a third person under Article 2134, which ... interest." Is the Court saying that Heroman was not a third party to the contract between Cox and Heroman? Where does the Court finds this law? Do you agree with the Court's statement in lines 209–212 on subrogation: "Thus, in a subrogation the interest of a creditor (here, Reulet).... outweighs the interest of the debtor...."? Is the Court really finding this kind of holding or statement of the law of the case in the Louisiana Civil Code? Is this issue of partial division of the debt for the benefit of the creditor that important as to justify, in a sense, subrogation? Remember your diagram above:

where did you place Heroman in relation to the contract between Cox and Reulet? Was "Heroman" a third party or not to that contract?

6. On this issue of the simultaneous timing of a payment of a debt with subrogation, do you agree with the majority or with the dissenting opinion.... and the doctrine quoted here? Considering the foundation and raison d'être of subrogation, which opinion makes more sense?

Bruce MARTIN

v.

LOUISIANA FARM BUREAU CASUALTY INSURANCE COMPANY, et al.

Supreme Court of Louisiana
July 5, 1994
638 So.2d 1067

WATSON, Justice. [...]

The issue is whether a health and accident insurer, which pays its insured's medical expenses after an automobile accident, is entitled to legal subrogation against the tortfeasors.

FACTS

On October 27, 1987, guest passenger Bruce Martin was injured in a two-vehicle collision. Martin sued the drivers, the owners, and the insurers of both vehicles. Golden Rule Insurance Company, Martin's health and accident insurer, paid his medical expenses and intervened to recoup the sums paid under Martin's policy.

[...]

LAW AND DISCUSSION

Golden Rule's claim for legal subrogation rests on Civil Code article 1829(3), which provides:

Art. 1829. Subrogation by operation of law.

Subrogation takes place by operation of law:

* * *

3) In favor of an obligor who pays a debt he owes with others or for others and who has recourse against those others as a result of the payment.

Article 1829(3) is an exception to the general rule that subrogation does not take place when a third person pays the debt of another. LSA-C.C. art. 1855 states the general rule that "... performance rendered by a third person effects subrogation only when so provided by law or by agreement." Legal subrogation derogates from the principle that no one may acquire another's right without that person's concurrence. 1 Saul Litvinoff, Obligations, § 11.51, at 289–90 (5 Louisiana Civil Law Treatise 1992); 7 Planiol & Ripert, *Traité Pratique de Droit Civil Français* nos. 632–33 (2e ed. 1954). Due to the exceptional nature of subrogation by operation of law, the right is strictly construed. *Pringle--Associated Mortgage Corporation v. Eanes*, 254 La. 705, 226 So.2d 502 (1969).

The initial inquiry under article 1829(3) is whether Golden Rule is bound "with ... or for others."

An obligor is bound with others when the obligation is solidary. LSA-C.C. art. 1794. Obligors are also bound with others when the obligation is indivisible. LSA-C.C. art. 1815; LSA-C.C. art. 1818. Co-sureties of the same debt are bound with each other. LSA-C.C. art. 3056. Sureties for debtors, who bind themselves or their property to secure performance, are subsidiary obligors and bound for others. LSA-C.C. art. 3048; LSA-C.C. art. 3295. These applications are supported by leading civil law commentators. *See* 2 Planiol & Ripert, *Traité Elémentaire de Droit Civil*, pt. 1, no. 501, at 282 (La.St.L.Inst. trans., 11th ed. 1959); Aubry & Rau, *Droit Civil Français*, in 1 Civil Law Translations § 321, at 202 (1965); 1 Saul Litvinoff, Obligations, § 11.54-56, at 297–301 (5 Louisiana Civil Law Treatise 1992); 12 Duranton, *Cours de Droit Français* no. 166-70 (3e ed. 1834); 7 Toullier, *Droit Civil Français* no. 147-153 (5e ed. 1839). Comments of French authors interpreting articles adopted from the French Civil Code are entitled to great weight. *Orleans Parish Sch. Bd. v. Pittman Construction Co.*, 261 La. 665, 260 So.2d 661 (1972); *Rials v. Davis*, 212 La. 161, 31 So.2d 726 (1947).

None of these relationships are present in this case. First, Golden Rule is not solidarily bound with the defendants. An obligation is solidary among debtors when they are obliged to the same thing, so that either may be compelled to perform the whole obligation, and payment by one exonerates the other. LSA-C.C. art. 1794; *Hoefly v. Government Employees Ins. Co.*, 418 So.2d 575 (La.1982). Solidary liability is never presumed and arises only from a clear expression of the parties' intent or from the law. LSA-C.C. art. 1796. An insurer bound to repair the damage caused by a tortfeasor is solidarily liable with the tortfeasor because both are obliged to the same thing—repair of the tort damage. *Fertitta v. Allstate Ins. Co.*, 462 So.2d 159 (La.1985). See LSA-R.S. 22:1406(D)(1)(a); LSA-R.S. 22:655(B)(1). Medical insurers are not obligated to repair tort damages. A medical insurer contracts to pay stipulated medical expenses, regardless of whether there is a tortfeasor and tort liability. The medical insurer thus pays its own debt, not that of the tortfeasor, and the two are not obligated to "the same thing." *See Fertitta*, 462 So.2d at 164, n. 7; 2 Planiol & Ripert, *Traité Elémentaire de Droit Civil*, p. 1, no. 491 n. 27, at 278 (La.St.L.Inst. trans. 11th ed. 1959).

Golden Rule's obligation is not indivisible. An obligation is indivisible when the object of performance is not susceptible of division, for example an obligation to deliver a specific thing. LSA-C.C. art. 1815. The obligation to pay money at issue here is susceptible of division and thus provides no basis for legal subrogation.

A health and accident insurer is principally liable for the insured's medical expenses within the policy limits. Golden Rule is therefore not a subsidiary obligor or surety whose purpose is to secure the tortfeasors' debt.

Aetna Ins. Co. v. Naquin, 488 So.2d 950 (La.1986), allowed the insurer of rental property subrogation recovery against a negligent roofing contractor. In *Naquin*, both the insurer and the negligent roofer were bound for payment of the leaky roof damages. *Naquin* was a property damage exception to the general rule, which should not be extended to health and accident insurance. See the *Naquin* dissent by Dixon, C.J.

Golden Rule argues that legal subrogation should obtain because a contrary result would produce dual recovery. The possibility of a plaintiff's dual recovery alone does not overcome the weight of authority against legal subrogation. A tortfeasor is barred from raising collateral sources as a defense. See e.g., *American Indemnity Co. v. New York F. & M. Under. Inc.*, 196 So.2d 592 (La.App. 1 Cir.1967); *Peacock's, Inc. v. Shreveport Alarm Co.*, 510 So.2d 387 (La.App. 2 Cir.), writ denied, 513 So.2d 826, 827, 828 (La.1987); *Dixie Trucks, Inc. v. Davis*, 530 So.2d 107 (La.App. 2 Cir.1988); *Brannon v. Shelter Mut. Ins.*

Co., 520 So.2d 984 (La.App. 3 Cir.1987); *Weir v. Gasper*, 459 So.2d 655 (La.App. 4 Cir.1984), writ denied, 462 So.2d 650 (La.1985); *Teague v. Barnes*, 519 So.2d 817 (La.App. 5 Cir.1988). Consequently, plaintiffs will occasionally have insurance reimbursements for certain elements of damages and recover some of the same elements from tortfeasors. 84 85 86 87

Legal subrogation would bestow a windfall on Golden Rule, which did not bargain for that benefit. Health and accident insurers can readily protect themselves by stipulating reimbursement rights or conventional subrogation in their policy contracts. See, for example, *Miller v. Sauseda*, 611 So.2d 831 (La.App. 3d Cir.1992), writ denied, 614 So.2d 1254 (La.1993). 88 89 90 91 92

CONCLUSION 93

A health and accident insurer is not "bound with ... or for" a tortfeasor whose actions give rise to medical expenses. Consequently the insurer does not become legally subrogated to its insured's cause of action simply by making the medical payments called for in its insurance contract. 94 95 96 97

[....] 98

LEMMON, J., concurs and assigns reasons. 99

MARCUS, J., dissents and assigns reasons. 100

MARCUS, Justice (dissenting). 101

I disagree with the majority's holding that a health and accident insurer does not become legally subrogated to its insured's cause of action against a tortfeasor by making medical payments. La.C.C. art. 1829(3) provides for legal subrogation: 102 103 104

in favor of an obligor who pays a debt he owes with others or for others and who has recourse against those others as a result of the payment. 105 106

Golden Rule, as the insurer, is responsible for plaintiff's medical expenses. Defendants are also liable for those expenses as a result of the accident. This is sufficient to satisfy the requirement in art. 1829(3) that the obligor owe a debt "with others." It is not necessary to examine the nature of the relationship between the obligors as the article does not require solidarity. *See Aetna Insurance Co. v. Naquin*, 488 So.2d 950, 954 (La.1986) (interpreting similar language in old La.C.C. art. 2161(3), the predecessor of art. 1829). Since the tortfeasor has not yet paid the plaintiff, the insurer still has recourse against the tortfeasor, thus satisfying the second requirement of art. 1829(3). Therefore, the insurer should be legally subrogated to the rights of the plaintiff against the tortfeasor for the medical expenses it has paid. Accordingly, I respectfully dissent. 107 108 109 110 111 112 113 114 115 116

Questions

1. Describe, in legal terms, and identify properly the relationships therein created before and after the accident. Describe the obligations resulting from these relationships. For example, was there any condition? Was there any heritable or personal obligation? Was there any joint or solidary obligation?

2. Read the Louisiana Code articles on "Subrogation" and contrast the distinctive features of the two forms of subrogation. On the basis of those articles, which form of subrogation, if at all, could take place in the case?

3. Lines 50–64: How do the statements of the Court fit with your description of the legal relationships (Question 1 above)? How important, and even determinant, is the Court's emphasis on "the same thing"?

4. Lines 65–68: Why is the Court referring to indivisible obligation? Is there any con-
    nection between solidarity and indivisibility? Could either one lead to an instance of
    legal subrogation?

5. Lines 72–76: What do you think of the Court rejecting here an *a pari ratione* rea-
    soning? Does it make sense?

6. Lines 77–92: Would Golden Rule really be bestowed a windfall? About what kind of
    windfall is the Court talking? According to the Court, "Golden Rule did not bargain
    for that benefit". With whom should Golden Rule have bargained?

Lionel Lorio SMITH

v.

Kathleen Hebert SMITH

Louisiana Court of Appeal
First Circuit
Dec. 20, 1996
685 So.2d 649

PARRO, Judge.

[....]

Facts and Procedural History

[This case involves the partition of the community property. More specifically, it addresses, among other issues, the husband's claims of reimbursement due to his use of
separate funds to purchase the first family home, which was later sold, whereupon the proceeds of that sale were deposited by husband into an account and later used to purchase
the family's replacement home.]

[....]

Applicable Law

Under Louisiana law, property is generally characterized as either community or separate. LSA-C.C. art. 2335. The classification of property as separate or community is fixed
at the time of its acquisition. *Terry v. Terry*, 565 So.2d 997, 999 (La.App. 1st Cir.1990).
In proving whether an asset is community or separate, the parties are guided by the following principles.

LSA-C.C. art. 2338 provides that community property comprises: property acquired
during the existence of the legal regime through the effort, skill, or industry of either
spouse; property acquired with community things or with community and separate things,
unless classified as separate property under Article 2341; property donated to the spouses
jointly; natural and civil fruits of community property; damages awarded for loss or injury to a thing belonging to the community; and all other property not classified by law
as separate property. Things in the possession of a spouse during the existence of the
community are presumed to be community, but either spouse may prove that they are separate property. LSA-C.C. art. 2340.

Regarding the classification of property as separate, LSA-C.C. art. 2341 provides, in
part, that a person's separate estate comprises: property acquired by a spouse prior to the
establishment of a community property regime; property acquired by a spouse with separate things or with separate and community things when the value of the community things

is inconsequential in comparison with the value of the separate things used; and property acquired by a spouse by inheritance or donation to him individually. In order to transfer separate property to the community with the stipulation that it shall be part of the community, a transfer by onerous title must be made in writing or a transfer by gratuitous title must be done by authentic act. LSA-C.C. art. 2343.1.

Lionel's Claims for Reimbursement

Lionel contended the trial court erred in failing to recognize his right to reimbursement for the use of his separate funds to make a down payment on the first family home [...] following the termination of the marriage.

A. Down Payment on the First Family Home

Kathleen admitted Lionel had used his separate funds in the acquisition of their first home, which was community property. Even the trial court believed Lionel had sold his separate stock and used the proceeds for the down payment on the first home. Although Lionel claimed in his detailed descriptive list that he expended approximately $50,000 of his separate funds toward the purchase of the home, his list of reimbursements introduced at trial itemized the amount expended at only $11,000, which coincided with the amount withdrawn from Lionel's separate passbook savings account on May 28, 1975 (the date the first home was purchased). Although no other specific evidence of this amount was introduced at trial, there is nothing in the record to indicate the parties disputed the amount of separate funds expended.

Following the sale of the first home, the proceeds were placed into an account and later used to acquire the family's replacement home. The trial court concluded that the sale of the community asset resulted in a contribution to the community of the separate funds used in acquiring the first home.[1] Such a finding presupposes the separate identity of the funds expended in acquiring the first home was reestablished after the sale of the first home. We disagree. Under the principle of real subrogation, which is applicable to both separate and community property, the funds derived from the sale of the first home remained community property.[2] *See* LSA-C.C. art. 2341, comment (c); *Albert v. Albert*, 625 So.2d 765, 768 (La.App. 1st Cir.1993).

The parties do not dispute that the first home belonged to the community and that Lionel's separate funds were used for the acquisition of this community property. Since Lionel used his separate funds in acquiring community property, obviously, he would have had a claim for reimbursement for the use of his separate funds pursuant to LSA-C.C. art. 2367. Thus, the issue presented to this court is whether Lionel's right to reimbursement was affected as a result of the subsequent sale of the first home. We think not.

Under LSA-C.C. art. 2367, a spouse is entitled to reimbursement upon proof that his or her separate property was "used for the acquisition, use, improvement, or benefit of community property." The right to reimbursement is not peculiar to any particular prop-

---

1. There is no evidence that the requirements of LSA-C.C. art. 2343.1 were ever satisfied. Therefore, the separate funds of Lionel were never given to the community. *See Landry v. Landry*, 610 So.2d 1045, 1047 (La.App. 3rd Cir.1992).

2. There is no codal authority to support a finding that the funds derived from the sale of a community asset is part community and part separate based on the original classification of the things used to acquire the community asset.

74 erty or its proceeds. Thus, Lionel's right to reimbursement was not affected by the sale
75 of the first home. Therefore, the trial court was legally incorrect in denying Lionel's right
76 to reimbursement under LSA-C.C. art. 2367 for the use of his separate property in the ac-
77 quisition of community property. Accordingly, Lionel is entitled to reimbursement from
78 Kathleen in the amount of $5,500.[3]

[....]

Questions

1. What kind of 'subrogation' is occurring in this case? What is the root of the word 'real'? What is the opposite?

2. Lines 56–64: What is the source of this form of subrogation? Does the Court refer specifically to a Louisiana Civil Code article as is the case of personal subrogation (*see* La. Civ. Code arts. 1825–1830)? What is a principle of law? Where and how do you find it (or them)? Can you think of some other form of real subrogation? Aren't monetary damages a substitute thing for the destruction of the principal object of a contract of sale, for example? Isn't this a form of real subrogation?

1 **SAFEWAY INSURANCE COMPANY OF LOUISIANA**
2 **v.**
3 **STATE FARM MUTUAL AUTOMOBILE INSURANCE**
4 **COMPANY**

5 Louisiana Court of Appeal
6 Second Circuit
7 March 5, 2003
8 839 So.2d 1022

9 KOSTELKA, Judge Pro Tempore.

10 State Farm Mutual Automobile Insurance Company ("State Farm") appeals a judg-
11 ment by the Shreveport City Court against it in the amount of $1,394.99 and in favor
12 of Safeway Insurance Company of Louisiana ("Safeway"). For the following reasons,
we affirm.

13 ### FACTS

14 On November 2, 2000, Jopawnna Baines ("Baines") borrowed, with permission, the
15 vehicle of her friend, Jackie Holloway ("Holloway") while Baines' vehicle was being re-
16 paired. Holloway's vehicle was insured by an insurance policy issued by Safeway (the
17 "Safeway policy"). Baines' vehicle was insured by a policy of insurance issued by State
18 Farm (the "State Farm policy").

19 As Baines was operating Holloway's vehicle in Shreveport, Louisiana, the vehicle came
20 in contact with a child, Tori Ladd, who was walking along the street upon which Baines
21 was traveling. As a result of the accident, the child was injured and received medical treat-

---

3. However, Kathleen's liability for one-half of the funds used would be limited to the value of her share in the community after deduction of all community obligations. LSA-C.C. art. 2367.

ment for which medical expenses were incurred. Safeway (Holloway's insurer) paid Ladd's parents, $1,394.99 in full and final settlement of any and all claims for the injuries and expenses incurred on behalf of their child as a result of the accident.

Subsequently, Safeway filed its Petition of Subrogation against State Farm, asserting that the State Farm policy which covered Baines' vehicle, provided primary liability coverage for the accident. Safeway further claimed that it was subrogated for the amount of $1,394.99 it paid in settlement. [....]

After issuing its written Opinion, which included its findings and reasons for judgment, the trial court rendered Judgment in favor of Safeway and against State Farm in the amount of $1,394.99. This appeal by State Farm ensued.

DISCUSSION

The minimal monetary amount at issue in this appeal truly belies the interesting and complex issues of law before us. [....]

[....]

Safeway's Subrogation Claim

Concluding that State Farm was primarily obligated to the Ladds despite Safeway's payment to them, we must next ascertain whether Safeway had a valid claim against State Farm for the amount of the payment made to the Ladds.

Subrogation is the substitution of one person or entity to the rights of another. La. C.C. art. 1825. As stated by the Louisiana Supreme Court in *A. Copeland Enterprises, Inc. v. Slidell Memorial Hosp.*, 94-2011 (La.06/30/95), 657 So.2d 1292, "[S]ubrogation is the legal fiction established by law whereby an obligation, extinguished with regard to the original creditor by payment which he has received from a third person, or from the original debtor but with funds that a third person has provided, is regarded as substituting in favor of this third person who in essence steps into the shoes of the original debtor and is entitled to assert, in the measure of what he has paid, the rights and actions of the former creditor." Subrogation may be either conventional or legal. La. C.C. art. 1825. It may result from either the agreement of the obligor or the obligee or both with a third person (i.e., conventional subrogation), or directly from the operation of law (i.e., legal subrogation). Thus, the intention of subrogation is to protect such persons who perform certain acts. *A. Copeland Enterprises, Inc., supra.*

When subrogated to the rights of the insured, the insurer stands in the shoes of the insured and thereby acquires the independent right to assert the actions and rights of the insured. *Barreca v. Cobb*, 95-1651 (La.02/28/96), 668 So.2d 1129; La. C.C. arts. 1825 and 1826; *Bailsco Blades & Casting, Inc. v. Fireman's Fund Ins. Co.*, 31,876 (La.App.2d Cir.05/05/99), 737 So.2d 164.

In its Petition of Subrogation, Safeway alleged to be subrogated to the rights of Holloway, its insured, as a result of its payment of settlement proceeds to the Ladds. Clearly, its policy provides such. It did not claim any other rights of subrogation as to Baines or the Ladds. After a hearing [....], the trial court ruled in favor of Safeway, noting that Safeway could be potentially subrogated to (1) "its insured's rights against State Farm for not paying the claim" or (2) the Ladds. We determine that Safeway properly made a subrogation claim; however, it was neither subrogated to the rights of Holloway, as claimed, or the Ladds, as the trial court determined. Instead, we determine that Safeway is subrogated to the rights of Baines, for the following reasons.

Although not specifically claimed by Safeway, it clearly would be subrogated to the rights of Baines in the case *sub judice*. Baines operated Holloway's vehicle with permission, which, under the clear terms of the Safeway policy, made Baines its insured.[1] State Farm concedes that Baines was also Safeway's insured under the Safeway policy. The Safeway policy further provides "[I]n the event of any payment under this policy, [Safeway] shall be subrogated to all the insured's rights of recovery therefor against any person or organization...."[2] Thus, Safeway had the right to assert any claim of Baines arising from the collision with the Ladd child—another fact conceded by State Farm.

However, State Farm argues in brief that Safeway could not assert subrogation rights as to Baines, because she had no rights or claims against State Farm as a result of her collision in Holloway's vehicle, as she suffered no damages to her person or property. However, State Farm overlooks the rights Baines has against it arising from the contractual relationship between her and State Farm vis-à-vis the State Farm policy issued to Baines. Obviously, she had a right to assert a claim against State Farm in the event it failed to provide coverage as stated in the policy. See, La. C.C. art.1994.[3] So considering, Safeway, as subrogee of Baines, and under La. R.S. 22:1406(F), clearly has a subrogation claim against State Farm in this proceeding.

Moreover, we are not constrained by the fact that Safeway failed to specifically claim that it was subrogated to the rights of Baines in this case. The appellate court shall render any judgment which is just, legal, and proper upon the record on appeal. La. C.C.P. art. 2164. The purpose of this article is to give the appellate court complete freedom to do justice on the record regardless of whether a particular legal point or theory was made, argued, or decided by the court below. Id., Comment (a); see also, Rachal v. Rachal, 35,074 (La.App.2d Cir.10/12/01), 795 So.2d 1286. Considering the record before us, including the policy of insurance issued by Safeway and La. R.S. 22:1406(F) making State Farm primary insurer, it is clear that Safeway was subrogated to the rights of Baines against State Farm. It is only fair and equitable that Safeway be able to recoup the monies paid to the Ladds, which, under the statute, were primarily owed by State Farm.

Direct Action Statute

Finally, State Farm argues that the trial court erred in allowing a cause of action by Safeway directly against State Farm. It argues that pursuant to La. R.S. 22:655 (the "Direct Action Statute"), there is no provision therein that would allow Safeway to proceed directly against State Farm. However, as determined by the Louisiana Supreme Court in *Cacamo v. Liberty Mut. Fire Ins. Co.*, 1999-3479 (La.06/30/00), 764 So.2d 41, 43:

> The Direct Action Statute is designed to grant a procedural right of action against an insurer where the plaintiff has a substantive cause of action against the insured. It was enacted to give special rights to tort victims, not to insureds with contract claims against a defendant. In this case, plaintiffs do not purport to file their claims under the Direct Action Statute and have no need to do so.... (Citations omitted).

Here, as discussed, Safeway;s claim against State Farm is as subrogee of Baines—whose own rights against State Farm derive from the terms of the State Farm policy of insurance.

---

1. The Safeway policy defines "Persons Insured" as "(1) the named insured" or "(2) any other person using such automobile to whom the name insured has given permission, provided the use is within the scope of such permission."

2. Notably, the right of subrogation is not limited to the "named insured."

3. Also, La. R.S. 22:1220(A) imposes a duty of good faith and fair dealing in performance of the insurance contract. See also, La. C.C. art.1983; *Williams v. Louisiana Indem. Co.*, 26,887 (La.App.2d Cir.06/21/95), 658 So.2d 739, 742. Breach of this particular duty by the insurer renders it liable for any damages, foreseeable or not, that are a direct consequence of its failure to perform. La. C.C. art.1997; La. R.S. 22:1220(A). No allegations of bad faith were made against State Farm by Safeway; however, the statute is illustrative to show that Baines potentially had rights against State Farm.

Just as the *Cacamo* plaintiffs, any right of action Baines had against State Farm was in   107
contract, giving her and Safeway, as subrogee, the right to make claims directly against   108
State Farm. So considering, State Farm's reliance on the Direct Action Statute is mis-   109
placed, and the trial court was not in error finding that the Direct Action Statute was in-   110
applicable in this particular proceeding.   111

[....]

Questions

1. Identify clearly the sources and the types of legal relationships therein created between all of the parties involved. In the final analysis, where do the two insurance
   companies stand in relation one vis-à-vis the other?

2. Lines 40–56: Notice how the Court introduces the concept of subrogation. The Court
   cites the Louisiana Civil Code article first and illustrates its application by the jurisprudence in the second place. Notice the sentence on lines 47–48. Is it in the nature of a policy statement? How does the next sentence (lines 48–51) fit in the nature
   of the previous sentence?

3. Lines 57–73: Into whose rights is Safeway subrogated? Does your analysis of the
   sources and types of obligations created here fit with the Court's ruling on Safeway's
   right of subrogation?

4. Lines 74 *et seq.*: How important do you think is the statement made by the Court in
   lines 74–82? Is the Court saying that whoever has a lawful right to be compensated, no
   procedural hindrance should stand in the way of that right? In fact, isn't the court saying, in its own words, what Louisiana Civil Code article 2298 states: "A person who has
   been enriched without cause at the expense of another person is bound to compensate
   that person"? Thus, shouldn't a Court find a way to make whole someone who, otherwise, would be unjustly or unfairly (i.e. without cause/reason) impoverished? Is subrogation in the law of contract (conventional subrogation) or under the law (legal
   subrogation) somewhat the equivalent of what a direct action would be in torts?

Section III—Imputation of Payment

Louisiana Sources of Law

Louisiana Civil Code

Art. 1864. Imputation by obligor.

An obligor who owes several debts to an obligee has the right to impute payment to the
debt he intends to pay.

The obligor's intent to pay a certain debt may be expressed at the time of payment or
may be inferred from circumstances known to the obligee. (Acts 1984, No. 331, §1, eff.
Jan. 1, 1985.)

Art. 1865. Imputation to debt not yet due.

An obligor may not, without the obligee's consent, impute payment to a debt not yet due.
(Acts 1984, No. 331, §1, eff. Jan. 1, 1985.)

Art. 1866. Payment imputed to interest.

An obligor of a debt that bears interest may not, without the obligee's consent, impute a payment to principal when interest is due.

A payment made on principal and interest must be imputed first to interest. (Acts 1984, No. 331, § 1, eff. Jan. 1, 1985.)

Art. 1868. Imputation not made by the parties.

When the parties have made no imputation, payment must be imputed to the debt that is already due.

If several debts are due, payment must be imputed to the debt that bears interest. If all, or none, of the debts that are due bear interest, payment must be imputed to the debt that is secured.

If several unsecured debts bear interest, payment must be imputed to the debt that, because of the rate of interest, is most burdensome to the obligor.

If several secured debts bear no interest, payment must be imputed to the debt that, because of the nature of the security, is most burdensome to the obligor.

If the obligor had the same interest in paying all debts, payment must be imputed to the debt that became due first.

If all debts are of the same nature and became due at the same time, payment must be proportionally imputed to all. (Acts 1984, No. 331, § 1, eff. Jan. 1, 1985.)

Précis: Louisiana Law of Obligations in General §§ 7.1.2

When an obligor owes his obligee several obligations bearing on fungible things or when he owes several debts of money to the same obligee-creditor, it is important to determine which one of the many obligations or debts he owes the obligor wishes to extinguish when making a payment. Such is the purpose of the codal provisions outlining the regime of imputation of payment....

The parties to an obligation may, by common agreement, decide which one of the debts owed by the obligor will be extinguished first when a payment is made. Unless the law raises an obstacle of public order to the goal pursued by the parties, a conventional imputation agreed upon by the parties should be fully enforceable.

When the parties involved have not specifically provided for this situation, preference of choice will then be given to the obligor since he is the party bearing the burden of the obligation. This preference is expressed in a principle stated in **Article 1864** ...

In the event that neither the obligor nor the obligee have exercised their right to state which debt is to be discharged by imputation, the law lays down rules which supplement the wills of the parties by providing different ways in which that imputation of payment is to take place. These different ways are listed in civil Code **Article 1868** ...

Cases

Gilbert M. PORCHE and Theresa Landry Porche
v.
Thomas S. WALDRIP, et al.

Louisiana Court of Appeal
First Circuit
March 6, 1992
597 So.2d 536

SHORTESS, Judge.

Gilbert Porche (plaintiff) was injured in an automobile accident. He sued the other motorist, Thomas Waldrip; Waldrip's employer, Forshag; Forshag's insurer, United States Fidelity & Guaranty Company (USF & G); and his own uninsured motorist carrier, Louisiana Farm Bureau Mutual Insurance Company (Farm Bureau). Prior to trial, plaintiff settled with USF & G for $100,000.00, and Farm Bureau tendered $50,000.00.

The trial court found plaintiff's damages totaled $426,917.42.[1] The court imputed the payments made by USF & G and Farm Bureau to the principal due and entered judgment in favor of plaintiff against Farm Bureau in the sum of $276,917.42, together with legal interest on that sum from date of judicial demand. The court also awarded plaintiff interest on the $50,000.00 tendered by Farm Bureau from date of judicial demand until the date of tender.

Plaintiff's appeal is limited [**for purposes herein to**] [...] whether the $50,000.00 tendered made by Farm Bureau prior to trial should have been imputed first to principal rather than interest.

[....]

Plaintiff contends the trial court erred in applying the tender made by Farm Bureau prior to trial to the principal sum due plaintiff for damages rather than to accrued interest. The trial court subtracted $150,000.00 (the tender plus USF & G's payment) from the total damages awarded of $426,917.42 and entered judgment in that amount. At the time of judgment, accrued interest exceeded $50,000.00. Plaintiff contends the court should have entered judgment for $326,917.42, together with legal interest from date of judicial demand until paid, subject to a credit of $50,000.00, to be applied first to accrued interest.

Plaintiff bases this contention on Louisiana Civil Code article 1866 and the case of *Payton v. Colar*, 518 So.2d 1104 (La.App. 4th Cir.1987). Article 1866 provides:

An obligor of a debt that bears interest may not, without the obligee's consent, impute a payment to principal when interest is due.

A payment made on principal and interest must be imputed first to interest.

Payton involved a post-judgment tender. In that case, the court held a "tort judgment bearing judicial interest" is a "debt that bears interest" within the meaning of article 1866. 518 So.2d at 1106.

In this case, however, we have a pre-judgment tender. At the time the tender was made, there was no "debt that bears interest" within the meaning of article 1866. In *McElrath v.*

---

1. The trial court also awarded plaintiff's wife $7,500.00 for loss of consortium.

41 *Dupuy*, 2 La.Ann. 520 (1847), the court held that when the debt was not yet due at the
42 time of payment, this article did not apply.[2] The court stated that the credit was to be ap-
43 plied "to that part of the debt which the debtor had the greatest interest in discharging,
44 which was the principal, as upon that interest was accruing." 2 La.Ann. at 523.

45 We note article 1865 provides a creditor may not impute payment to a debt not yet
46 due without the debtor's consent. In this case, the plaintiff accepted Farm Bureau's ten-
47 der and thus consented to imputation of payment to the debt. Since the debt was not yet
48 due, the payment must be imputed to the principal, the part of the debt Farm Bureau had
49 the greatest interest in discharging. Thus, the trial court properly credited the pre-trial ten-
50 der by Farm Bureau to the principal due.

[....]

Questions

1. The focus of your attention should be on the court's statements on lines 20–22, i.e.
    whether the $50,000.00 paid (tendered: *see* La. Civ. Code arts. 1869–1872) by Louisiana
    Farm Bureau *"prior to trial"* should have been imputed to the principal rather than
    to the interest (emphasis ours). What is the nature of an obligation before a trial on
    that obligation? Does it exist and if it does, what is its nature? How would you qual-
    ify or describe in legal terms a judgment in conclusion of a trial? Is it a term and if
    so, what kind? Is it a condition and if so, what kind? Does it matter to assign a legal
    qualification or description to such an event as judgment?

2. Lines 31–50: Read all of the Louisiana Civil Code articles on "imputation" (La. Civ.
    Code arts. 1864–1868). What is the purpose of imputation? Which party should it
    benefit and under what circumstances? *See* La. Civ. Code arts. 1864 and 1867. As far
    as imputation is concerned, how relevant was the question above about the proper
    legal qualification of a judgment as a term or as a condition? Likewise, as concerns
    imputation, was it relevant (as asked above) to make a distinction between a princi-
    pal obligation and a secondary obligation? Do you see a difference between the word
    "due" used by the Court in the statement in lines 45–50, and the word "owed"? Which
    one should the Court have used?

---

2. At the time of this decision, the court was interpreting article 2160 of the 1825 Civil Code,
which contained substantially the same language as current article 1866, as follows:
    The debtor of a debt, which bears interest or produces rents, can not, without the consent
    of the creditor, impute to the reduction of the capital any payment he may make, when
    there is interest or rent due.
Every payment which does not extinguish both the principal and the interest must be imputed first
to the payment of the interest.

Andrew PAYTON

v.

Wendell COLAR, et al.

Louisiana Court of Appeal
Fourth Circuit
Dec. 15, 1987
518 So.2d 1104

GULOTTA, Chief Judge.

Plaintiff appeals from a judgment dismissing his rule to calculate and compel the payment of the remaining balance due on a partially paid personal injury judgment. The issue to be decided is whether funds deposited as partial payment by a judgment debtor are to be first applied to principal or interest. Because LSA-C.C. Art. 1866 provides that, in the absence of the obligee's consent, the obligor of an interest bearing debt may not impute payment to the principal when interest is due, we conclude that partial payments by the judgment debtor must be applied first to reduce outstanding judicial interest before they can reduce the principal amount of the judgment.

In October, 1984, plaintiff recovered a personal injury judgment against Wendell A. Colar, New 77 Club, Inc., and Insurors Indemnity and Insurance Company, in solido, in the sum of $711,000.00 plus costs and interest from date of judicial demand (February 21, 1979). On February 4, 1985, the defendant insurer delivered to plaintiff's attorney a check for $305,610.00. This check was offered under the terms of "payment in full" and represented the insurance policy limits plus post judgment interest on the total judgment. Plaintiff's attorney rejected the amount as full settlement and returned the check. On March 1, 1985, defendant deposited $305,610.00 in the registry of the court. On April 9, 1985, plaintiff filed a "Motion to Withdraw the Funds from the Registry of the Court", stating that there was a substantial dispute about other funds being due in excess of the amount deposited. Pursuant to an order on April 12, 1985, plaintiff withdrew the funds.

On May 12, 1986, in *Payton v. Colar*, 488 So.2d 1271 (La.App. 4th Cir.1986), writ denied 494 So.2d 332 (La.1986), this court held that Insurors Indemnity was liable in solido with other defendants to the plaintiff for the full amount of the judgment of $711,000.00, plus interest from the date of the judicial demand and all costs. After writs were denied by the Supreme Court, the defendant insurer tendered $931,586.30 to plaintiff, who refused to accept this amount as full satisfaction. On October 15, 1986, defendant filed a motion to deposit the funds in the registry of the court, and on that same day plaintiff withdrew the funds.

On October 28, 1986, plaintiff filed a "Rule to Compel Satisfaction of Judgment and Calculate and Assess Interest". In this rule, plaintiff disputed the "calculation and application of funds" paid by the insurer, and asked for the principal amount of $56,735.93, plus interest, which plaintiff contended was the remaining balance still unpaid. Without written reasons, the trial judge dismissed the rule with prejudice.

Appealing, plaintiff contends that under LSA-C.C. Art. 1866 all payments made to an interest bearing debt must first be applied to interest unless otherwise agreed to by the obligee. According to plaintiff, when defendant deposited the $305,610.00 into the registry of the court on March 1, 1985, the amount of judicial interest due at that time was $444,335.98. Plaintiff argues that the $305,610.00 payment should have first been applied to satisfy the interest, leaving $138,725.89 in interest and the entire $711,000.00 principal still unpaid after the partial payment. As a result, plaintiff contends that until defendant deposited

$931,586.30 in the court registry, interest continued to be calculated on the $711,000.00 judgment. Furthermore, according to plaintiff, after the $931,586.30 payment was made, the full amount of interest owed at the time of payment was satisfied, and the principal was reduced to $56,735.93. Plaintiff thus argues that defendant still owes that judgment balance plus interest from date of judicial demand, costs, and attorney's fees.

On the other hand, defendant contends that when a debtor makes a good faith tender of an undisputed portion of a judgment to a plaintiff, the plaintiff is not entitled to recover legal interest on the amount tendered after it has been either presented to plaintiff or deposited in the court's registry. Because the insurer never disputed that it was liable for at least $300,000.00 of the judgment principal, plus post judgment interest, defendant argues that its initial tender of $305,610.00 was in good faith, and that the deposit of that amount in the court registry reduced the judgment principal to $411,000.00 and the interest by $5,610.00. Defendant contends that after the March 1, 1985 deposit, interest is calculated on $411,000.00 of the judgment principal. According to defendant, the subsequent payment of $931,586.30 fully satisfied all outstanding principal and interest, and the trial judge properly dismissed plaintiff's rule for additional interest. We disagree.

LSA-C.C. Art. 1866, relied on by plaintiff, provides as follows:

> An obligor of a debt that bears interest may not, without the obligee's consent, impute a payment to principal when interest is due.

> A payment made on principal and interest must be imputed first to interest.

This article is found in Title III of Book III of the Civil Code, which is entitled "Obligations in General". LSA-C.C. Art. 1757, which is also included in Title III, provides that obligations can arise from contracts as well as from the law, as in instances of wrongful acts.[1] Thus, an offense or quasi offense under LSA-C.C. Arts. 2315 et seq. creates an obligation on the part of the wrongdoer in favor of the injured party.

It is well settled that an obligation, when reduced to judgment, is merged therein and no longer exists as a distinct obligation, but it is deemed as having acquired the status of the thing adjudged. *Sailing Wiping Cloth Co. v. Sewell, Inc.*, 419 So.2d 112 (La.App. 2nd Cir.1982); *Glazer Steel Corp. v. LaRose Shipyard, Inc.*, 372 So.2d 250 (La.App. 1st Cir.1979); *Agricultural Enterprises, Inc. v. Morgan*, 147 So.2d 40 (La.App. 2nd Cir.1962); *Mackee v. Cairnes*, 2 Mart., M.S. 599 (1824); *Abat v. Buisson*, 9 La. 417 (1836); *West Feliciana Railroad Co. v. Thornton*, 12 La.Ann. 736 (1857); *The Citizens Bank of Louisiana v. Hancock*, 35 La.Ann. 41 (1883); *Lalanne v. Payne*, 42 La.Ann. 152, 7 So. 481 (1890); *Cassiere v. Cuban Coffee Mills*, 225 La. 1003, 74 So.2d 193, (1954). Likewise, a debt reduced to a judgment also acquires the status of the thing adjudged. *Cassiere v. Cuban Coffee Mills*, supra; *Mackee v. Cairnes*, supra; *Abat v. Buisson*, supra; *West Feliciana R. Co. v. Thornton*, supra; *Citizens Bank of Louisiana v. Hancock*, supra; *Lalanne v. Payne*, supra. LSA-C.C. Art. 2924, which is also found in Book III of the Civil Code, defines "judicial interest" as legal interest on a sum that is the object of a judicial demand.[2]

---

1. LSA-C.C. Art. 1757 provides:
Obligations arise from contracts and other declarations of will. They also arise directly from the law, regardless of a declaration of will, in instances such as wrongful acts, the management of the affairs of another, unjust enrichment and other acts or facts.
2. LSA-C.C. Art. 2924 provides, in pertinent part:
A. Interest is either legal or conventional.
B. (1) Legal interest is fixed at the following rates, to wit:
(a) At twelve percent per annum on all sums which are the object of a judicial demand, whence this is called judicial interest; and * * * *
(2) The rate of judicial interest resulting from a lawsuit pending or filed during the indicated

Reading these codal provisions *in pari materia*, we conclude that a tort judgment bearing judicial interest is a "debt that bears interest" within the meaning of LSA-C.C. Art. 1866 and that a judgment debtor may not, without the obligee's consent, impute a payment to principal when interest is due. Thus, a partial payment on a tort judgment must be imputed first to judicial interest before it can be applied to reduce the principal amount of the judgment.

In *Lambert v. Cronvich*, 373 So.2d 554 (La.App. 4th Cir.1979), writ denied 376 So.2d 960 (La.1979), we applied former LSA-C.C. Art. 2164, the precursor to present LSA-C.C. Art. 1866, to a money judgment rendered on promissory notes that contained specific provisions for interest and attorney's fees. In *Lambert*, the trial judge applied partial credits to reduce the principal amount of the judgment. Although we agreed with the application of certain credits, we amended the judgment after concluding that the credits should be applied in accordance with LSA-C.C. Art. 2164,[3] i.e., if the payment does not extinguish both interest and principal, it should be applied to the interest first. Thus implicit in *Lambert* was a conclusion that a money judgment containing interest is a debt bearing interest within the meaning of the codal article. Applying the *Lambert* rationale, we conclude that LSA-C.C. Art. 1866 applies to the money judgment in our case, even though we are dealing with a tort judgment rather than a judgment on a promissory note.

Having determined that LSA-C.C. Art. 1866 applies in the instant case, we conclude that the payment made by defendant on March 1, 1985 should have first been applied to satisfy the interest owed, and the remainder, if any, applied to reduce the principal. According to our calculations set out below, the $305,610.00 did not reduce the principal but merely reduced the interest owed on March 1, 1985. Consequently, Insurors Indemnity still owes plaintiff the remaining judgment principal of $57,538.60 plus judicial interest until paid. [....]

Although the cases[4] relied on by defendant do apparently stand for the proposition that judicial interest ceases to run upon an amount tendered in partial payment of a judgment, none of the cited opinions discusses LSA-C.C. Art. 1866 or its precursor, former LSA-C.C. Art. 2164, which specifically provides that a partial payment must be credited first to interest before it can be applied to reduce the principal.

In *Schmidt v. Holmes*, 487 So.2d 577 (La.App. 4th Cir.1986), one of two solidary judgment debtors forwarded a check for his one half virile share of the tort judgment including interest and costs. The plaintiffs in *Schmidt* refused to accept the payment on the grounds that they were entitled to full satisfaction of the judgment from either or both

---

periods shall be as follows:

(a) Prior to September 12, 1980, the rate shall be seven percent per annum.

(b) On and after September 12, 1980, until September 11, 1981, the rate shall be ten percent per annum.

(c) On and after September 11, 1981, the rate shall be twelve percent per annum.

3. LSA-C.C. Art. 2164 provides that:

"The debtor of a debt, which bears interest or produces rents, cannot, without the consent of the creditor, impute to the reduction of the capital any payment he may make, when there is interest or rent due.

"Every payment which does not distinguish both the principle and the interest must be imputed first to the payment of the interest."

4. *Schmidt v. Holmes*, 487 So.2d 577 (La.App. 4th Cir.1986); *Williams v. Hanover Insurance Company of New York*, 351 So.2d 858 (La.App. 2nd Cir.1977); *Boudreaux v. Riley Buick, Inc.*, 415 So.2d 970 (La.App. 2nd Cir.1982); *Carlyon v. Aetna Casualty and Surety Company*, 413 So.2d 1355 (La.App. 3rd Cir.1982), and *Mamou Farm Service, Inc. v. Hudson Insurance Company*, 488 So.2d 259 (La.App. 3rd Cir.1986).

of the solidary judgment debtors and that the acceptance would prejudice their rights to the full satisfaction of the judgment. The debtor then sent a letter to the plaintiff stating that it was not its intention that plaintiffs should waive any rights to ultimately collect the full judgment against them in the event the other debtor would not be able to pay. Two months later, after the second solidary debtor tendered its one-half of the total judgment principal plus costs and interest, the plaintiffs then accepted the earlier tender by the first obligor. Because the first debtor's tender did not include the interest accrued from the original date of that tender to the date of the second debtor's tender, plaintiffs thereafter filed a "Rule to Compel Satisfaction of Judgment and To Assess Interest against Defendant". The trial court in *Schmidt* dismissed plaintiffs' claims for the additional interest, and we affirmed the trial court's decision.

By allowing a solidary debtor to pay less than the full amount of a judgment and thereby interrupt the accrual of interest on the amount paid, *Schmidt* and the cases there directly conflict with our interpretation and application of LSA-C.C. Art. 1866 in the instant case. The *Schmidt* opinion is silent as to LSA-C.C. Art. 1866, however, and an argument based on this codal article was apparently not presented to the court. Nonetheless, to the extent that our earlier opinion conflicts with our reasoning in the instant case, we hereby overrule Schmidt.[5]

[....]

BARRY, J., concurs and would distinguish Schmidt v. Holmes from Payton v. Colar.

KLEES, J., dissents in part from the Court's En Banc decision to overrule the Schmidt opinion.

LOBRANO, J., dissents in part for the reasons expressed by KLEES, J.

KLEES, Judge, dissenting in part and concurring in part.

I do not agree that our decision in the instant case necessitates the overruling of *Schmidt v. Holmes* and accordingly dissent from that part of the opinion. In *Schmidt*, one of two solidary debtors tendered payment of one-half the total principal, costs and interest due on the date of the tender. Plaintiffs refused to accept this amount until six weeks later, at which time they received a check from the other debtor for one-half the total judgment, costs and interest due on the date of the second tender. After accepting both checks, plaintiffs filed a Rule against the debtor who had made the initial tender seeking to recover the interest that had allegedly accrued on his half of the principal from the date of the original tender until the date that plaintiffs actually accepted the payment. We held that plaintiffs were not entitled to the additional interest because they could have accepted the initial tender without prejudicing their rights to collect the entire judgment from either defendant. *Schmidt, supra* at 578.

Schmidt is distinguishable from the instant case because the plaintiffs in *Schmidt* did not contend that the initial payment should have been imputed to interest before principal, but rather that they were entitled to additional interest because they chose not to accept the payment until six weeks after it was originally tendered.

Civil Code article 1866, upon which the majority relies, states that "[t]he obligor of a debt that bears interest may not, *without the obligee's consent*, impute a payment to principal when interest is due." (Emphasis added). In *Schmidt*, the plaintiffs and defendants were in agreement as to which portion of each payment constituted principal and which

5. In accordance with our internal rules, our opinion in the instant case has been submitted to all judges of this court, and a majority of them have voted to overrule the *Schmidt* decision.

portion constituted interest; at issue was the date at which the interest ceased to accrue. [165]
By not making an argument under article 1866, the *Schmidt* plaintiffs tacitly consented [166]
to the defendants' allocation of the funds. Accordingly, the court's interpretation of arti- [167]
cle 1866 in the instant case does not conflict with *Schmidt*. [168]

While I agree with the majority's holding in this case, I can foresee potential problems [169]
with the application of C.C. Art. 1866 to solidary obligations which this case does not [170]
address. [171]

ON APPLICATION FOR REHEARING [172]

PER CURIAM. [173]

In a petition for rehearing, the defendant insurer contends that LSA-C.C. Art. 1866 ap- [174]
plies only to debts bearing "conventional interest", i.e., a charge by an obligee for the [175]
obligor's right to use the obligee's money over a period of time. According to defendant, [176]
legal interest on a judicial demand is a form of "moratory" damages or penalty that is a [177]
separate debt from the principal amount of the judgment, and a judgment debtor can [178]
therefore choose to apply his partial payment toward either the judgment principal or [179]
the judicial interest pursuant to LSA-C.C. Art. 1864.[6] [180]

In support of this contention, defendant cites the 18th Century French legal scholar, [181]
Pothier, as follows: [182]

> "The rule which we have established, that the application ought to be made to [183]
> the interest before the principal, does not hold with regard to interest due by a [184]
> debtor, from the time of a judicial demand being made, as a penalty for his delay; [185]
> such interest is awarded by way of damages, and forms a distinct debt from the [186]
> principal; and what the debtor pays is applied rather to the principal than to this [187]
> interest.... This is established by an arrêt [decision] of 1649 and another of [188]
> 1706."[7] [189]

Although Pothier's works are influential as a source of the Code Napoleon, we do not [190]
find this passage persuasive in our case. Article 1254 of the Code Napoleon of 1804, which [191]
is the French counterpart to our present LSA-C.C. Art. 1866, makes no exception for [192]
moratory interest in stating the rule for imputing payments.[8] The 19th Century com- [193]
mentators Aubry and Rau have noted that the French redactors did not adopt Pothier's [194]
distinction between the two types of interest: [195]

> "Pothier (No. 571) teaches that this rule [of applying payment to interest before prin- [196]
> cipal] applied in the past to compensatory interests only and not to moratory interests. [197]

---

6. LSA-C.C. Art. 1864 provides:

"An obligor who owes several debts to an obligee has the right to impute payment to the debt he intends to pay.

"The obligor's intent to pay a certain debt may be expressed at the time of payment or may be inferred from circumstances known to the obligee."

7. Pothier, *A Treatise On The Law of Obligations, or Contracts*, trans. William David Evans (Philadelphia: 1826).

Although the passage cited by defendant is numbered "534" in the Evans translation, it is numbered "571" in the French edition of Pothier's works. See II *Oeuvres De Pothier*, Nouvelle Edition (Paris: 1821).

8. C.N. 1804, Art. 1254 provides:

"The debtor of a debt which bears interest or produces arrearages, cannot, without the consent of the creditor, impute the payment which he makes on the capital, in preference to the arrearages or interest; a payment made on the capital and interest but which is not integral, is first imputed to the interest."

198 Since Article 1254, however, did not reproduce this distinction it seems that it should not
199 be admitted today. Delvincourt, II, p. 556; Favard, *Rép.*, Imputation, § 3; Larombière,
200 III, Art. 1254, No. 4; Zachariae, § 320, note 5. But see: Duranton, XII, 192; Marcadé, on
201 Art. 1254, No. 3."9

202   In addition to this authority, we note that Jean Domat, another French legal scholar
203 whose writings influenced the redactors of the Code Napoleon and the Louisiana Civil Code,
204 has recognized that interest can arise from four causes: by contract, by the nature of an
205 obligation, by law, or " ... as a punishment of the debtor who defers payment after the
206 creditor has made his demand in a court of justice, both of his principal, and of the in-
207 terest due for default of payment."10 Unlike Pothier, Domat notes that a payment on a
208 debt should be applied first to the discharge of the interest, even if the interest is "due by
209 a sentence of a court of justice":

210   "If a debtor makes a payment to discharge debts which of their nature bear interest,
211 such as that of a marriage portion, or what is due by virtue of a contract of sale, *or the*
212 *same be due by a sentence of a court of justice,* and the payment be not sufficient to acquit
213 both the principal and the interest due thereon; the payment will be applied, in the first
214 place, to the discharge of the interest, and the overplus to the discharge of a part of the
215 principal sum. [Emphasis ours]."11

216   Based on these authorities, we reaffirm our interpretation of LSA-C.C. Art. 1866 as ex-
217 pressed in our initial opinion. As we have noted, LSA-C.C. Art. 1866 is found in Title III
218 ("Obligations in General") of Book III of the Louisiana Civil Code. LSA-C.C. Art. 1866
219 makes no distinctions between contractual debts or judgment debts, or between con-
220 ventional interest and judicial interest. Pothier's observations of early French law on this
221 issue have not been incorporated in either the Code Napoleon or the Louisiana Civil
222 Code, and do not persuade us to reach a different result in our case.

223   We further distinguish *Lone Star Industries v. American Chemical*, 480 So.2d 730
224 (La.1986), and on rehearing 491 So.2d 1333 (La.1986), cited by defendant. In *Lone Star*,
225 $62,678.94 was deposited in the registry of the court by American Chemical's surety at the
226 beginning of trial. After trial, a judgment was rendered against American Chemical for
227 $132,785.31 plus interest and costs. On appeal, a second defendant, Strickland, was cast
228 solidarily liable with American Chemical for $100,000.00 of the judgment debt.

229   The only issue in the *Lone Star* case was the proper allocation of the $62,678.94 pay-
230 ment: should it (1) be first applied to satisfy the $32,785.31 amount for which American
231 Chemical was solely liable, or (2) should the entire amount of the payment be applied to
232 the $100,000.00 obligation owed by both defendants *in solido*. The Supreme Court held
233 that the payment should first be applied to cancel completely American Chemical's sole
234 liability for $32,785.31, and the remaining $29,893.63 of the payment should then be ap-
235 plied to reduce the $100,000.00 solidary liability of American Chemical and Strickland,
236 leaving a balance of $70,106.37, plus interest and costs due from the defendants.

237   Because *Lone Star* involved only the respective liabilities of two obligors for different
238 portions of a single judgment debt, the cited case did not address our problem of allo-
239 cating a partial payment between judgment interest and principal. Furthermore, because

---

9. Aubry and Rau, *Cours de Droit Civil Français*, § 320, Footnote 4, trans. Louisiana State Law Institute (1965). See also Fuzier-Herman, *Code Civil*, Art. 1254, Footnote 2, (Paris: 1896), citing similar authorities on this issue.
10. Domat, *The Civil Law in Its Natural Order*, § 1958, trans. by William Strahan (Boston: 1850).
11. Domat, § 2284.

the payment was made during trial in the *Lone Star* case, the Supreme Court was not   240
confronted with accrued interest after a post-judgment delay as in our case. The *Lone*   241
Star decision, therefore, is inapposite to the instant case, and does not compel us to change   242
our interpretation of LSA-C.C. Art. 1866 as set forth in our original opinion.   243

Accordingly, defendant's petition for a rehearing is denied.   244

[....]

Questions

1. Design a diagram of all the relationships existing in this case and describe in legal terms the obligations created. Identify, for example, any principal obligor v. secondary obligor, sources of obligations (contract v. tort)?

2. Lines 41–52: What are the legal arguments made by plaintiff as regards the different amounts of money he claims are owed to him? As regards the interest that plaintiff claims is owed to him, how does plaintiff look upon this interest? Does he look upon it as an additional compensation for his inability to have used the principal amount of money? Does he look upon it as damages for some loss?

3. Lines 53–63: What do you think of defendant's statement that "when a debtor makes a good faith tender of an undisputed portion ... the plaintiff is not entitled to recover legal interest...."? Isn't 'good faith' a strong argument? How does defendant look at the interest he claims he should not pay? Does he look at it as a penalty? Does he look at it as damages not due because there was no loss or prejudice suffered by plaintiff?

4. Lines 64 *et seq.*: Note that the Court first states the law in the form of Louisiana Civil Code articles 1866, 1757, and 2315. In the first part of the sentence on line 73, "It is well.... judgment", is the Court saying that the judgment *creates* the obligation or it only acknowledges the existence of an obligation as arising from the sources of law mentioned at the outset by the Court? On line 75, what does the phrase "thing adjudged" mean? Does it mean case-law jurisprudence constante?

5. Lines 186 *et seq.*: Remember the questions 1 and 2 asked above? What are the defendant's views on the legal nature of interest, particularly conventional interest, and moratory damages? What do you think of the Court searching for support in comparative law? Should it look to "any" comparative law?

Don J. CHAISSON and Diane Chaisson   1

v.   2

Matthew CHAISSON   3

Louisiana Court of Appeal   4
Second Circuit   5
Feb. 26, 1997   6
690 So.2d 899   7

STEWART, Judge.   8

Matthew Chaisson appeals a judgment of the Shreveport City Court finding that his   9
parents, Don and Diane Chaisson, were entitled to repayment, in the amount of $10,006.12,   10
plus legal interest from the date of judicial demand, on money advanced to Matthew for   11
a car, college expenses, furniture, etc. Matthew assigns five errors. For the following rea-   12
sons, we affirm.   13

FACTS

From March, 1989, through December, 1991, Mr. and Mrs. Chaisson advanced money to their youngest son Matthew for a car, college expenses, furniture, etc. When Matthew graduated Louisiana Tech University and obtained full-time employment, he began making payments to his parents in the amount of $300.00 per month from September, 1991, through September, 1992. In July, 1993, the amount of the payments were [*sic*] reduced to $200.00 per month by agreement between Matthew and his parents. Matthew made five payments in the amount of $200.00. After November, 1993, all payments from Matthew ceased.

Mr. and Mrs. Chaisson retained counsel who wrote Matthew demanding repayment on the money lent him by the Chaissons. Once Matthew obtained counsel, all further contact regarding the debt was made with Matthew's attorney. Matthew disputed that any money was owed his parents, except on the loan with which Matthew purchased a car.

Thereafter, on May 19, 1995, Mr. and Mrs. Chaisson filed suit in Shreveport City Court to recover the amount they allegedly loaned Matthew for a car and college expenses. Trial was held on January 18, 1996. At trial, Mr. and Mrs. Chaisson introduced a handwritten document listing money loaned to Matthew for numerous reasons, including summer school tuition, rent, furniture, housewares, spending money, etc. That document also indicated several payments made by Matthew and included a detailed repayment schedule. At trial, Matthew's siblings testified as to their agreement with their parents regarding payment of college expenses. Matthew's sister, Audra, did not owe her parents any amount when she graduated college. However, Matthew's brother, Peter, did owe his parents some amount of money and made payments until he had paid his parents back on those loans. A family friend, Anna Ratcliff, testified regarding her personal knowledge of Mr. and Mrs. Chaisson's policy of advancing money to their children for various reasons and of requiring repayment of those advances.

On April 1, 1996, the trial court rendered written reasons and found that there was an oral agreement between Matthew and his parents to repay the advances of money, that, upon his securing full-time employment after graduation, Matthew did begin making payments "without imputation as to which of these debts would be paid first," and that, as the debts were of the same nature and were due at the same time, payment was proportionally imputed to all debts pursuant to La.C.C. art. 1868. The court further found that the debts had not prescribed nor had Mr. and Mrs. Chaisson violated the Fair Debt Collection Act. The court rendered judgment in favor of Mr. and Mrs. Chaisson in the amount of $10,006.12 plus legal interest from the date of judicial demand. Judgment was prepared by counsel for Mr. and Mrs. Chaisson, approved by counsel for Matthew Chaisson, and signed on April 15, 1996.

DISCUSSION

Assignment of Error #1

Matthew asserts that the trial court erred in finding that an agreement existed between he [*sic*] and his parents concerning the repayment of money advanced by Mr. and Mrs. Chaisson, except for the amount advanced for purchase of a car.

[....]

In any action based on contract, three elements must be proven: 1) an offer, 2) an acceptance, and 3) the consent of the parties. *La.C.C. art. 1927.* Absent any formalities as may required by law, an offer and acceptance may be made "orally, in writing, or by action or inaction that under the circumstances is clearly indicative of consent." *La.C.C. art. 1927.*

Matthew contends that Mr. and Mrs. Chaisson failed to prove that they made an offer   61
to Matthew which he accepted and that, therefore, there was never any consent or "meet-   62
ing of the minds" regarding the terms of the alleged loan agreement. See *Eagle Plumbing,*   63
Heating and Air Conditioning, Inc. v. Ragusa, 517 So.2d 280 (La.App. 1 Cir.1987).   64

Included in the evidence adduced at trial was a hand written document listing the ad-   65
vances of money made to Matthew for various reasons, indicating any payments made by   66
Matthew and the balance owed, and including computation of a monthly payment amount   67
and a payment schedule. Further, the testimony of Mr. and Mrs. Chaisson, Audra, and Peter   68
clearly established that Mr. and Mrs. Chaisson advanced money to their children during   69
their college years for personal needs and that Mr. and Mrs. Chaisson intended these ad-   70
vances to be loans which would be repaid by the individual child upon graduation and   71
obtaining full-time employment. Matthew also testified that this was the family policy   72
and admitted that he and his parents had discussed, on more than one occasion, the money   73
advanced to him and their intention that the advances were to be considered a loan.   74

Although Matthew, by his own admission, understood his parents' intent, he contends   75
that he did not explicitly agree to their terms but that he merely took the money. The   76
trial court questioned Matthew extensively concerning this aspect of his testimony and whether   77
Matthew considered any options for funding his college education other than his parents,   78
such as student loans, National Guard, etc. The colloquy between the trial court and   79
Matthew clearly establishes that Matthew knew that his parents intended the advances to   80
be loans which he was responsible for repaying upon obtaining full-time employment   81
after graduation and that, although the specific details of the agreement, i.e., interest rate   82
and term of repayment were not determined at the time he accepted the loans, he knew   83
there would be a term for repayment of the balance of the money advanced plus interest.   84

Contrary to Matthew's contention, we find an offer and an acceptance under the cir-   85
cumstances of this case. Matthew's parents made him a standing offer to lend him money   86
for his tuition and other things during his college years on the understanding that he   87
would be obligated to pay the loans in installments once he was out of college and gain-   88
fully employed. He accepted their offer from time to time by accepting from them spe-   89
cific amounts of money for particular purposes for which he needed money. An offer   90
may be accepted other than by sacramental words such as "I accept your offer." *North*   91
Louisiana Milk Producers Ass'n, Inc. v. Southland Corp., 352 So.2d 293 (La.App. 2 Cir.1977).   92

Based on the evidence and testimony presented, we do not find that the trial court   93
was clearly wrong or manifestly erroneous in finding that an agreement existed between   94
Matthew and his parents concerning repayment of money advanced for college expenses   95
by Mr. and Mrs. Chaisson to Matthew. This assignment is without merit.   96

[....]   97

Assignments of Error #3 and #4   98

Matthew contends that his parents failed to file suit for repayment timely. He asserts   99
that the money advanced was not "of the same nature" as found by the trial court and that   100
a three year prescriptive period applied so that his parents should have filed suit within   101
three years of his graduation from college on May 18, 1991.   102

Mr. and Mrs. Chaisson argue that the trial court did not err in finding that the money   103
advanced Matthew were loans "of the same nature" and that the debts had not prescribed   104
because Matthew made payments by check with no reference to payment on the car loan.   105

La.C.C. art. 1868 provides, in pertinent part, that "if all debts are of the same nature   106
and became due at the same time, payment must be proportionally imputed to all." An   107

108 action on money lent is subject to a three-year prescriptive period which commences to
109 run from the day payment is exigible. *La.C.C. art. 3494; La.C.C. art. 3495.*

110   The record establishes that the loans were used to purchase such items as a car, gifts,
111 and household necessities and to pay such expenses as rent, utilities, and insurance pre-
112 miums. All these loans were for expenses incurred during the time Matthew attended
113 college and were related to his college attendance. We find that the trial court was not
114 clearly wrong in finding that, pursuant to *La.C.C. art. 1868*, the debts were of the same
115 nature and became due at the same time and that, therefore, payment on one debt must
116 be imputed proportionally to all.

117   As previously discussed, the agreement between Matthew and Mr. and Mrs. Chaisson
118 provided that Matthew was not obligated to begin repaying the amounts advanced for
119 his college expenses until he obtained full-time employment after graduation. Matthew
120 graduated on May 18, 1991. Matthew made payments sporadically until November 6,
121 1993. Each payment was made by check referenced only as a monthly payment such as
122 "June payment" or "August payment." Mr. and Mrs. Chaisson filed this lawsuit on May
123 19, 1995.

124   Prescription is interrupted by acknowledgment of the debt. *La.C.C. art. 3464.* Payment
125 on the debt constitutes an acknowledgment which interrupts prescription. *Marr v. John-*
126 *son*, 204 So.2d 806 (La.App. 2 Cir.1967). As we agree with the trial court that these debts
127 are of the same nature and due at the same time and that payment must be proportion-
128 ally imputed to all the debts, Matthew's payments on these loans interrupted prescription
129 until the last payment on November 6, 1993. Clearly, Mr. and Mrs. Chaisson timely filed
130 this action within three years of that date. We find that the trial court was not clearly wrong
131 in finding that the debts had not prescribed. Therefore, this assignment is without merit.

[....]

Questions

Note: To better prepare to discuss this case, you should read the Louisiana Civil Code articles on "donations" (particularly arts. 1467–1567 and most particularly arts. 1526–1567)
and "Loan" (arts. 2891–2912).

1. Lines 9–13: Describe in legal terms the nature of things for which money was ad-
    vanced to Matthew. Was graduating from college any kind of condition for the par-
    ents advancing money to Matthew or Matthew paying it back? What about securing
    employment?

2. Lines 15–22: Does the Court identify the source or sources of Matthew's payments
    to his parents? What name, if any, could or should the court have given to the (legal?)
    relationship between Matthew and his parents? Was there a legal duty on the part of
    the parents to advance money to Matthew?

3. Lines 27–39: what 'name' is the Court giving to the bond of law created between the
    parents and Matthew? Is there any legal reason or ground for Matthew to refer to his
    sister Audra, "who did not owe her parents any amount ..."?

4. Lines 61 *et seq.*: Do you have any comment on whether or not there was a meeting
    of the minds? What would have been the effect of having a writing?

5. Lines 106 *et seq.*: After you have read the Code articles on "Imputation", what is your
    comment on the Court's application of the requirements for imputation, particu-
    larly under Louisiana Civil Code article 1868?

Section IV — Tender & Deposit

Louisiana Sources of Law

Louisiana Civil Code

Art. 1869. Offer to perform and deposit by obligor.

When the object of the performance is the delivery of a thing or a sum of money and the obligee, without justification, fails to accept the performance tendered by the obligor, the tender, followed by deposit to the order of the court, produces all the effects of a performance from the time the tender was made if declared valid by the court.

A valid tender is an offer to perform according to the nature of the obligation. (Acts 1984, No. 331, § 1, eff. Jan. 1, 1985.)

Art. 1870. Notice as tender.

If the obligor knows or has reason to know that the obligee will refuse the performance, or when the object of the performance is the delivery of a thing or a sum of money at a place other than the obligee's domicile, a notice given to the obligee that the obligor is ready to perform has the same effect as a tender. (Acts 1984, No. 331, § 1, eff. Jan. 1, 1985.)

Art. 1872. Sale of a thing and deposit of proceeds.

If performance consists of the delivery of a perishable thing, or of a thing whose deposit and custody are excessively costly in proportion to its value, the court may order the sale of the thing under the conditions that it may direct, and the deposit of the proceeds. (Acts 1984, No. 331, § 1, eff. Jan. 1, 1985.)

Précis: Louisiana Law of Obligations in General § 7.1.3

Although an obligor may be willing and ready to perform, it is still conceivable that his obligee might refuse to receive the performance offered. Whether the obligee's objections to the performance are valid or unreasonable, it remains that the obligor who is in a position to perform might suffer a prejudice should he have no alternative means of carrying through with his performance.

Taking into account the concerns and interests of both the obligee and the obligor, the law has devised the institution of *tender and deposit* as a means of providing a temporary solution to the conflicting rights of the two parties involved....

The civil Code provides for two forms of *tender and deposit* at the same time it outlines the effects, both general and particular, of each one....

In the event an obligee has, unequivocally and without apparent justification, refused to accept the performance offered by his obligor, the latter may, thereafter, make a *tender* followed by a *deposit* to the order of the court....

A *tender and deposit* is meant to amount to the performance of the object or item of the obligation involved rather than be a substitute for it....

It is possible that the thing tendered and deposited be a perishable product to be consumed or used within a relatively short period of time. A long storage might lead to the destruction of that thing despite all the diligence exercised by the obligor. To prevent such a useless outcome, **Article 1872** offers the depositor, and the court, an alternative solution which will protect the interest the obligee has in the performance....

The second form of tender available to an obligor is outlined in **Article 1870**....

The importance of this rule of law is that it makes a mere notice of readiness to perform equivalent to a tender and vests in it the same legal effects....

Section V—Impossibility of Performance

Louisiana Sources of Law

Louisiana Civil Code

Art. 1873. Obligor not liable when failure caused by fortuitous event.

An obligor is not liable for his failure to perform when it is caused by a fortuitous event that makes performance impossible.

An obligor is, however, liable for his failure to perform when he has assumed the risk of such a fortuitous event.

An obligor is liable also when the fortuitous event occurred after he has been put in default.

An obligor is likewise liable when the fortuitous event that caused his failure to perform has been preceded by his fault, without which the failure would not have occurred. (Acts 1984, No. 331, § 1, eff. Jan. 1, 1985.)

Art. 1875. Fortuitous event.

A fortuitous event is one that, at the time the contract was made, could not have been reasonably foreseen. (Acts 1984, No. 331, § 1, eff. Jan. 1, 1985.)

Art. 1876. Contract dissolved when performance becomes impossible.

When the entire performance owed by one party has become impossible because of a fortuitous event, the contract is dissolved.

The other party may then recover any performance he has already rendered. (Acts 1984, No. 331, § 1, eff. Jan. 1, 1985.)

Art. 1877. Fortuitous event that has made performance impossible in part.

When a fortuitous event has made a party's performance impossible in part, the court may reduce the other party's counterperformance proportionally, or, according to the circumstances, may declare the contract dissolved. (Acts 1984, No. 331, § 1, eff. Jan. 1, 1985.)

Précis: Louisiana Law of Obligations in General §§ 7.2.1 to 7.2.2

Whenever a legal relationship requires that a performance be undertaken in the future, be it a day, a month or a year, or when the performance itself spreads over a period of time, there always exists the danger that the expectations of the parties will be upset, betrayed or altered in one way or another. Events may occur which will interfere with the proper planning and anticipation of the parties....

Civil Code Article 1875 defines a fortuitous event in these terms:

"A fortuitous event is one that, at the time the contract was made, could not have been reasonably foreseen."

The simplicity of this definition is misleading, in particular when one is asked to weigh the meaning of the requirement of *reasonableness*....

To ensure the stability of contracts, the security of business transactions and the reliability of the promises given, the courts should make use of certain criteria to test the reasonableness of the parties' failure to foresee a fortuitous event and plan accordingly their contractual obligations....

The legal effects resulting from the occurrence of a fortuitous event that affects an obligor's performance will vary in extent with the time of that occurrence and its factual impact. In this respect one can distinguish between an absolute impossibility for the obligor to perform and a partial impossibility to do so....

Civil Code **Article 1873-1** formulates the general principle as follows:

"An obligor is not liable for his failure to perform when it is caused by a fortuitous event that makes performance impossible."....

The legal consequence of this absolute impossibility to carry out an entire performance because of a fortuitous event is that **"the contract is dissolved"** and **"the other party may then recover any performance he has already rendered."** ...

Civil Code **Article 1877** formulates an equitable rule in these terms:

"When a fortuitous event has made a party's performance impossible in part, the court may reduce the other party's counterperformance proportionally, or, according to the circumstances, may declare the contract dissolved."

Cases

CITY OF NEW ORLEANS; Blake G. Arata et al., representatives, etc.; and New Orleans Public Service, Inc.

v.

UNITED GAS PIPE LINE COMPANY.

LOUISIANA POWER & LIGHT COMPANY

v.

UNITED GAS PIPE LINE COMPANY and Pennzoil Company

Louisiana Court of Appeal
Fourth Circuit
April 30, 1987
517 So.2d 145

REDMANN, Chief Judge.

United Gas Pipe Line Company appeals from judgments for breach of contract damages in favor of Louisiana Power and Light Company for $40,309,142 and New Orleans Public Service, Inc. (and the class of persons paying the latter's electric rates during the breach) for $44,403,106. LP & L and NOPSI were obliged by the contracts to buy, and United was obliged to supply to them, their requirements (or part-requirements) of natural gas

18   for electric power plants over periods of up to 25 years. United raises many issues[...]
19   [**but its**] principal argument is that a national gas shortage and governmental distribu-
20   tion orders reduced or excused its contractual delivery obligations, both because the con-
21   tracts so provide in cases of gas shortage, governmental orders, or force majeure, and
22   because of a variety of other defenses.

23   [....]

24   We conclude that the record supports the trial judge's factual conclusion that United
25   did not prove its affirmative defenses for its conceded failure to deliver the contracted
26   gas. United did not prove that, if it had not released gas reserves that it already had (and
27   had acted with reasonable diligence to acquire additional available gas reserves to meet
28   its already existing contractual commitments and had not further committed itself to
29   new sales of gas), the shortage would still have occurred (or to what extent) on its inter-
30   state and New Orleans area intrastate pipelines. United did not prove that its actions did
31   not cause its shortage and were not, at the least, a breach of its implied contractual oblig-
32   ations under its contracts to provide gas. We reason that the contractual impairment of
33   deliveries clause does not purport to exonerate United from liability; that the govern-
34   mental orders would not have been necessary as to United but for United's self-caused short-
35   age; and that the force majeure clause is inapplicable because United did not prove that
36   the shortage was not within its control. [....]

37   It is undisputed that United did not supply the gas that, unless somehow excused, it
38   was obliged to supply for LP & L's and NOPSI's power plants under the long-term con-
39   tracts. United is therefore liable for the damages caused by its failure to deliver the con-
40   tracted gas, unless it proves that its delivery obligation is reduced or excused by one of its
41   several defenses.

42   Essentially, all of United's defenses partake of the nature of impossibility of perfor-
43   mance because of a nationwide gas shortage and federal commission and court orders
44   adopted because of that shortage. Essentially, the trial court's response, which we deem
45   not manifestly erroneous but supported by the evidence, is that United bound itself to
46   perform its contracts with LP & L and NOPSI, and that United did not prove that it
47   did perform those contracts reasonably and in good faith: did not prove that it acted
48   reasonably, in view of its performance obligations, to acquire and maintain sufficient
49   gas reserves to satisfy its contractual obligations. The trial court's reasoning is that
50   United itself brought about its shortage, which therefore does not exonerate United
51   from liability.

52   UNITED'S APPEAL

53   [**Among other things, United argues that ...**] liability was imposed on United with-
54   out any consideration of the effect of the well-recognized gas shortage of the 1970s on United's
55   ability to serve its customers and without reasoned analysis of the prudence of United's
56   management of its gas supplies [... **and that ...**] damages were awarded for reductions
57   in deliveries brought about entirely by federal order rather than by United's shortage of
58   gas[.] [....]

59   [....]

60   III. THE GAS SHORTAGE AS EXONERATION

61   That gas in ample quantity was unavailable from 1970 or so is not gainsaid. Begin-
62   ning in 1968 and continuing through the 1970s, nationwide gas reserves declined as usage
63   exceeded additions. But the shortage did not produce the results United claims by its
64   many defenses, some of which overlap (as do this opinion's discussions).

III(a). INDUSTRY CONDITIONS AND UNITED'S ACTIONS

United's basic contention is that it did seek to perform, reasonably and in good faith, its contractual commitments; that its purportedly imprudent or improvident management decisions were in fact reasonable and blameless, given the conditions existing at the time and the knowledge available at the time, including the expectations regarding the size and accessibility of underground reserves of natural gas. The genuine shortage of natural gas during the 1970s in Louisiana and throughout the nation, United claims, was unforeseeable and beyond the control of any individual pipeline company.

The trial court concluded that United's management of its gas supplies, including releases, acquisitions and sales, was imprudent and constituted the sole cause of its shortage. United claims that the trial court's evaluation of United's conduct was flawed because the court did not identify what was imprudent, based its findings on a purely retrospective analysis, and ignored the practices and expectations of the pipeline industry.

United claims that its expectations about the future availability of natural gas were reasonable and consistent with industry expectations; that it had no reason to believe in the period of 1960–66 that it faced a possible shortage. United asserts that it first became aware of possible peak-day shortages in 1969, and that its maintenance of its gas reserve inventory was reasonable and responsive to changing supply and market conditions.

United contends that it could not reasonably maintain the reserves it had because its contracts obliged it to take certain proportions of production annually or else pay for them, and that increasingly high levels of penalty payments for failure to take the contracted gas, caused by its inability to increase sales meaningfully until 1965, coupled with the continual increase in proved reserves in take-or-pay fields boding yet higher penalties, made it impossible for United to maintain existing reserves or make major new gas acquisitions for its interstate system until after 1965. In late 1965 and early 1966, as its system-wide oversupply problems were in the process of being resolved, United contends it recommended the acquiring of major new reserves.

United asserts that it was not until 1970, when it began to experience a sudden unavailability of new reserves, combined with continued delays in the construction of an ambitious offshore project and unforeseen downward revisions of estimates of its remaining reserves, that United realized that it would not be able to get sufficient new reserves to avoid some system-wide curtailments.

Another element contributing to United's predicament was that customers varied their level of takes during the year, at differing percentages of their maximum contract levels. The ratio of actual deliveries to the maximum contract limit is known as the annual load factor. The load factor of United's pipeline customers increased from 81% in 1965 to 94% in 1969. United's power plant customers also increased their load factors. United claims that the increases within existing maximum daily quantities under contracts were not predicted by customers or by United. According to United, new or enlarged commitments entered into after Jan. 1, 1968, account for less than 1% of total sales (excluding sales by facilities transferred to Pennzoil) during 1968–1970, and, by comparison with increasing load factors and other problems (increased sales on prior contracts were 14% of total sales), new sales were not, as the trial judge had found, a significant factor in its ultimate curtailment of deliveries.

In short, United contends that when considered in light of the problems it had to address, the information available to it at the time, and the accepted industry custom and practice, United's business decisions regarding the management of its gas supplies were reasonable and designed to ensure adequate supplies for United's customers.

We conclude, as amplified in the discussion below of United's more particularized defenses, that United's actions, however reasonable in other contexts, were not reasonable in the context of firm requirements contracts, because they did not constitute a reasonable effort to perform those contracts, especially in their implied obligations to have and maintain, or to acquire, at whatever cost, the gas necessary to fulfill the explicit delivery obligations.

On its New Orleans intrastate line, which supplied LP & L's Ninemile Point plant and NOPSI, for example, in the years 1962 through 1969, United released massive reserves of gas under contract. These releases were the result of United's contractual attempts (some allowing the producer the right to cancel United's rights) to avoid costly and escalating penalty payments, under "take or pay" contracts, for failure to take gas as United had contracted to do. By these releases, United lost reserves of some 2,063 billion cubic feet (Bcf) between 1962 and 1969 (and in 1967 shifted another 269 Bcf to an interstate system) from its New Orleans intrastate line. Annual sales from that pipeline in 1968 and 1969 were about 150 Bcf. The released reserves would have provided gas at that rate for over 13 years. (NOPSI's claim covers only about five years. While LP & L's Ninemile contract extended some 17 years at determinable prices, the delivery obligation actually decreased from 100% of requirements for the existing three generators to a third of requirements for those plus a planned fourth, once the fourth began operation. This decrease reduced the contractual daily maximum from 125,000 to 80,000 thousand cubic feet (Mcf). 17 years of reduced delivery would have roughly equalled 13 years of the original delivery.) The primary reason gas was not provided to Ninemile and NOPSI—the reason there was a "shortage"—was that United released those reserves notwithstanding its contractual obligations to supply gas.

The releases of those reserves (over half to Humble Oil as a result of an "omnibus agreement" of October 1, 1962) had business considerations as their purpose, and in that sense may well be described as reasonable. United's contract for one of the largest fields enabled the producer to cancel if United did not take 25% of the field's production capacity for two years, and United did not take that quantity despite a price reduction aimed at increased consumption. Other contracts included "take or pay" provisions that obliged United to pay for specified minimums based on reserves even if not taken. Those provisions cost United $754,702 in 1960 and $6,776,068 in 1961 (and were expected to cost more as additional reserves in the contracted fields were discovered). United argues that its releases of reserves were reasonable responses to problems such as these. One may well accept that reserve releases were reasonable for United's purposes, but the releases, and the intrastate system shortage they caused, simply were not beyond United's control—as is required for the applicability of the contract's force majeure provision and the Civil Code's impossibility defense.

United's conversion of the New Orleans intrastate system into part of the interstate system (by injecting interstate gas), United argues plausibly, was more beneficial than harmful to intrastate system customers, in that the gas that had been still attached to the former intrastate system (after the releases) was used in that lower-pressure ("locked-in") system only, which also received additional gas from the higher-pressure remainder of the interstate system. Also plausible is that United's sales to new intrastate system customers would, by themselves, not have created any problem for old customers (had the releases not occurred).

Even so, United's efforts as a whole to deal with (to escape) increasing costs of performance do not constitute good faith performance of its obligations, explicit and implicit, under its gas delivery contracts.

Thousands of times greater by absolute count, although less dramatic in proportion   162
to usage, were the releases affecting United's interstate system, which served LP & L's Ster-   163
lington plant near Monroe. That system's annual usage was about 1,300 to 1,500 billion   164
cubic feet between 1960 and 1968, with a growth trend of over 3% a year and with a total   165
usage during that period of about 12,454 Bcf. During that period United released almost   166
4,590 Bcf while adding only about 4,083 Bcf. Thus, over that nine-year period, that sys-   167
tem suffered a continuing and increasing decline of reserves of over 1,300 Bcf a year from   168
usage plus a slight further decline because additions to reserves were more than offset by   169
releases of reserves. Had reserves simply been maintained at the 1960 level, United could   170
have met its delivery obligations under its contracts for well beyond another nine years.   171
LP & L's Sterlington contract only ran about eight years from the first curtailment. The   172
record shows that there was no gas shortage in the early 1960s, and the trial judge's con-   173
clusion was therefore reasonable that United could have acquired additional reserves that,   174
coupled with the reserves it released, would have maintained its reserve position and its   175
ability to fulfill its contractual obligations over the lives of the contracts at issue. United   176
does show that take-or-pay costs and other considerations prompted its business deci-   177
sions, but increased costs to perform do not excuse nonperformance of contracts. In per-   178
spective, penalty pre-payments for gas of $7,000,000 a year (or their balance of $15.3   179
million by 1963 or even $21.3 million by 1965) to assure ability to comply with its con-   180
tracts, although truly a substantial amount of money, are not so excessive a "prepayment   181
[of] working capital" (as the Federal Power Commission deemed them) as to justify non-   182
performance by an enterprise whose annual sales of 1,300,000,000 thousand cubic feet of   183
gas, if all sold at a minimum price of $.175 per Mcf (its 1956 contract prices for LP & L   184
were from $.175 to .745) would bring annual gross income of $227,500,000.   185

III(b). CONTRACT CONSTRUCTION   186

United argues (and the trial court agreed) that the contracts authorize certain curtailments,   187
and that those curtailments would therefore not constitute a breach of the contracts. United   188
argues that the trial court erred, however, by improperly identifying the circumstances au-   189
thorizing curtailments and by finding that those circumstances were not present.   190

In particular, United argues that the "impairment of deliveries" clause should operate   191
to allow curtailments without liability if a shortage exists, provided only that the shortage   192
was not brought about through United's bad faith. The trial court ruled that in addition   193
to there being a shortage, the shortage has to be the result of force majeure and United has   194
to have "prorated its gas supplies between its customers in the order of priorities enu-   195
merated," before the impairment of deliveries clause would reduce or suspend United's   196
delivery obligations. United argues that its curtailment priorities differed from those enu-   197
merated only because federal commission curtailment orders required curtailment prior-   198
ities as mandated under the Natural Gas Act and that those orders superseded contract   199
priorities because of the contracts' "duly constituted authorities" clause. Furthermore,   200
United claims that the impairment of deliveries clause is not dependent on the "force ma-   201
jeure" clause, but is intended to be operative with respect to any system-wide shortages that   202
would impair deliveries. Finally, United argues that the trial court erred in determining and   203
applying the appropriate fault standard under the impairment of deliveries clause.   204

[....]   205

Force Majeure   206

The contracts also contained force majeure clauses, which suspended the obligations   207
of a party when "rendered unable wholly or in part by force majeure to carry out its oblig-   208
ations...." The contracts define force majeure as   209

"acts of God, strikes, lockouts or other industrial disturbances, acts of public enemy, wars, blockades, insurrections, riots, epidemics, landslides, lightning, earthquakes, fires, storms, floods, washouts, arrests and restraints of governments and people, civil disturbances, explosions, breakage or accident to machinery or lines of pipe, the necessity for making repairs or alterations to machinery or lines of pipe, freezing of wells or lines of pipe, partial or entire failure of wells, and any other causes, whether of the kind herein enumerated or otherwise, not within the control of the party claiming suspension and which by the exercise of due diligence such party is unable to prevent or overcome....."

The trial judge's factual conclusion, reasonably supported by the record, was that by the exercise of due diligence, in not releasing reserves, in acquiring reserves when it could have done so, and in not committing itself to further deliveries by added sales atop its preexisting contractual obligations, United could have prevented the shortage that its own actions caused. In such a factual situation, the force majeure clauses by their own definition do not apply and therefore did not suspend United's obligations.

[....]

III(d). LOUISIANA CODE DEFENSES

United also argues that the trial judge erred in rejecting its separate defenses, under the Louisiana Civil Code, of fortuitous event or irresistible force, failure of cause, error as to motive, and implied condition.

Fortuitous Event

United contends that the nationwide gas shortage was a "fortuitous event or irresistible force" within C.C. 1933(2) (1870). United cites cases of performance excused by flood (*Viterbo v. Friedlander,* 120 U.S. 707, 7 S.Ct. 962, 30 L.Ed. 776 (1887)) and very heavy rainfall (*Davis v. Tillman*, 370 So.2d 1323 (La.App. 2 Cir.1979)). But those were not cases in which, for example, a contractor was held not liable for the failure of a flood-wall or roof because of flood or rain—that is, was exonerated by the occurrence of the risks that his contract undertook to protect against. United's contracts undertook to provide gas requirements over specified periods of many years and, by necessary implication, to do what was necessary to have the gas to be able to provide it. Had United done the necessary, there would have been no "fortuitous" shortage on its lines here involved. United's fortuitous event or irresistible force defense, C.C. 1933(2) (if applicable despite United's arguably "active" breach, C.C. 1931, by release of reserves), is not different in substance or in result from its contractual force majeure defense.

Lack or Failure of Cause; Error; Condition

United also argues that there was a lack or failure of cause in the contracts in question and therefore they can have no effect; that the error of the parties in assuming the continued availability of natural gas was an error as to the principal cause, thereby vitiating consent to the contracts; and that the availability of gas was at least an implied condition of the contracts.

United argues that civil law "cause," C.C. 1893 (1870) (largely analogous to common law consideration), for United's obligation to deliver LP & L's and NOPSI's requirements was lacking or failed. United cites art. 1897' s declaration that a contract is without cause "when the consideration for making it was something which, in the contemplation of the parties, was thereafter expected to exist or take place, and which did not take place or exist." Art. 1897 itself exemplifies its meaning: "A gift in consideration of a future marriage is void by this rule, if the marriage do not take place." The record suggests that

United, in failing to put itself into a position of ability to perform its long-term contracts, may have relied on a "contemplation" that gas would always be available; but it does not suggest that LP & L and NOPSI, in obtaining firm 20-year contracts for requirements, relied on that contemplation. That is not the tenor of the contracts. United did not contract only that, as long as gas were freely available, it would transport it through its pipelines to LP & L and NOPSI. United's argument from art. 1897 would transform United's obligation from one to supply requirements into one to supply what it might have available, and that was not the intent of the contracts. The utility companies did not commit themselves to buy the contracted requirements exclusively from United for 20 years for the "principal cause" that gas was assumed to be readily available, nor in exchange for a conditional obligation that United would sell if gas were available. The utilities committed themselves to buy exclusively from United for the described contract prices in exchange for United's commitment that it would have and deliver gas. The utilities' commitment was the cause for United's obligation (not conditioned on the availability of gas), just as United's commitment was the cause for the utilities' obligation. The contracts were ordinary requirements contracts that are not invalid for lack or failure of cause or consideration.

[....]

Questions

1. *City of New Orleans* was decided prior to the Revision of the law of force majeure/ "impossibility of performance". Which part(s) of new Louisiana Civil Code article 1873 seem(s) to you to be the most pertinent to disputes of the kind presented in this case? The first paragraph, which states the "general principle" of impossibility of performance, is, of course, pertinent. But isn't there another, one that's even more directly "on point"? Explain.

2. Was the supposed "fortuitous event" on the basis of which United sought to exonerate itself—an acute shortage of natural gas—truly "fortuitous"? Why or why not? *See* La. Civ. Code art. 1875.

3. In order for an obligor to be relieved of liability due to impossibility of performance, the fortuitous event must render performance "truly" or, as it is sometimes said, "absolutely" impossible. *See* La. Civ. Code art. 1873. Did the acute natural gas shortage of which United complained in fact have that effect?

HANOVER PETROLEUM CORPORATION
v.
TENNECO INC.
Louisiana Court of Appeal
Third Circuit
March 2, 1988
521 So.2d 1234

GUIDRY, Judge.

In this suit, Hanover Petroleum Corporation (hereafter Hanover) seeks relief from Tenneco Inc.'s alleged breach of a Gas Purchase Contract (hereafter the "Kaplan Contract") relating to Hanover's interest in the production from three gas wells located in the Kaplan Field, Vermilion Parish, Louisiana. The trial court granted summary judgment in favor of Hanover finding that the Kaplan Contract is a valid and enforceable contract; the defenses raised by Tenneco in opposition to the motion for summary judgment are issues of law which have no merit; Tenneco breached its "take or pay" obligations under the contract; and, a separate evidentiary hearing should be held to determine the quantum of Hanover's damages and the availability of the remedy of specific performance. [....]

FACTS

The Kaplan Contract is dated June 8, 1981. The terms of the contract, as amended, obligate Hanover to sell and Tenneco to buy a quantity of "deep gas" produced from three wells in the Kaplan Field equal to 85% of the delivery capacity of the wells.[1] Under the terms of the contract, Tenneco agreed to annually take, or pay for if not taken, the aforementioned quantity of gas. Where gas is paid for but not taken, Tenneco is given the right, under the contract, to make up such volumes, during the term of the contract, by taking volumes of gas, at a later date, above the minimum contract volume without charge. The obligation assumed by Tenneco under the Kaplan Contract is commonly referred to in the industry as a "take or pay" obligation.

The record establishes that, for a considerable period of time prior to the institution of this suit, and continuing thereafter, Tenneco has not taken nor has it paid for the volume of gas which it is required to take or pay for annually under the terms of the Kaplan Contract. In fact, in the spring of 1983, Tenneco notified its producer-suppliers, including Hanover, in a document styled "Emergency Gas Purchase Policy" (EGPP), of its inability to, in substantial part, comply with its "take or pay" obligations under existing gas contracts because of events occurring subsequent to the contracts allegedly constituting force majeure. Hanover repudiated the EGPP announced by Tenneco as a unilateral breach of the Kaplan Contract and this suit followed.

On appeal Tenneco contends, as a basic proposition, that the trial court erred in granting summary judgment despite the presence of genuine issues of material fact with regard to the applicability of the affirmative defenses of Force Majeure, Commercial Impracticability, Imprevision, Mistake and Error, Failure of Cause or Consideration etc., all of which were urged by it at the trial level and all or any one of which, it suggests, would excuse its failure to perform under the Kaplan Contract. Stated another way, Tenneco urges that the trial court erred in striking the affirmative defenses urged by Tenneco without regard to the presence of genuine issues of material fact regarding their applicability. [....]

At the outset, we address a threshold issue before consideration of this appeal on its merits.

[....]

FORCE MAJEURE

The Kaplan Contract contains a force majeure provision which reads in pertinent part as follows: "In the event of either party being rendered unable, wholly or in part, by force majeure to carry out its obligations under this Contract, other than to make payments due for gas delivered prior to such force majeure, it is agreed that on such party giving notice and reasonably full particulars of such force majeure in writing or by telegraph to the other party within a reasonable time after the occurrence of the cause relied on, then

---

1. The contract covers only gas produced from a subsurface interval below 15,000 feet, i.e., gas classified as "deep gas" which was deregulated under Section 107 of the Natural Gas Policy Act of 1978 (NGPA).

the obligations of the party giving such notice, so far as they are affected by such force majeure, shall be suspended during the continuance of any inability so caused, but for no longer period, and such cause shall so far as possible be remedied with all reasonable dispatch. The term 'force majeure,' as employed herein, means act of God, strikes, lockouts or other industrial disturbances, acts of public enemy, wars, blockades, insurrections, riots, epidemics, landslides, lightning, earthquakes, fires, storms, floods, high water, washouts, arrests and restraints by government or persons, civil disturbances, explosions, breakage or accident to machinery, wells, or lines of pipe, the necessity for making repairs or alterations to machinery, wells or lines of pipe, freezing of wells or lines of pipe, partial or entire failure of any wells, and any other causes, whether of the kind herein enumerated or otherwise, not reasonably within the control of the party claiming suspension."

Tenneco principally contends that the following events, subsequent to the confection of the Kaplan Contract, constitute force majeure within the meaning of the quoted clause and excuses their failure to fully perform the contract: the economic recession; the pricing scheme of the Natural Gas Policy Act of 1978; the abundance of and the drop in the price of competitive fuels; the mild 1982–1983 winter; the increase in deliverability of fields committed to Tenneco under gas purchase contracts; and, the delivery by producers of greater quantities of higher cost gas rather than lower cost gas under contracts which involve the sale of gas in more than one price category. Additionally, Tenneco contends that, at the very least, the meaning of the force majeure clause, particularly the catch-all provision "any other causes, whether of the kind herein enumerated or otherwise" and the intent of the parties in adopting same constitute genuine issues of fact which preclude the rendition of summary judgment. The trial court determined otherwise, presumably finding no ambiguity in the force majeure clause and Tennecos affirmative defense based thereon a meritless issue of law.

Our research discloses that these issues are res nova at the state appellate level. See *Universal Resources Corporation v. Panhandle Eastern Pipe Line Company,* 813 F.2d 77 (5th Cir.1987). However, these precise issues have been considered at the trial level by both the State and Federal Judiciary. Judge Parker in *Koch v. Columbia Gas Transmission Corporation,* No. 83990-A (M.D.La.1985); Judge Duhe in *Exxon Corporation v. Columbia Gas Transmission Corporation,* 624 F.Supp. 610 (W.D.La.1985); and, Judge Brunson in *The Stone Petroleum Corporation et al v. Tenneco, Inc.,* No. 84-5072, Div. "F", 15th Judicial District Court, Parish of Lafayette, Louisiana (Jan. 1987), respectively, refused to grant summary judgment on the contractual force majeure issue concluding that (1) the scope of force majeure in the contracts is considerably broader than the statutory concept of force majeure; and, (2) genuine issues of fact as to whether the events cited actually prevented performance and are encompassed by the force majeure clause existed which precluded summary judgment. On the other hand, Judge Dirosa in *Amoco Production Company v. Columbia Gas Transmission Corporation,* No. 83-11570, Div. "L", Civil District Court for the Parish of Orleans, Louisiana (June 1985), and Judge Gonzales in *Preston Oil Company v. Transcontinental Gas Pipeline Corporation,* No. 294491, Div. "L", 19th Judicial District Court, Parish of East Baton Rouge, Louisiana (Dec. 1986), decided otherwise, as did the learned trial judge in the instant case. We find the analysis in *Preston* by Judge Gonzales of the force majeure issue compelling and persuasive and take the liberty of quoting same:

"In light of this *broad* language and in response to their apparent breach of the contract, the defendant adopts several of the same "force majeure"-type factual defenses used by other defendants to this kind of litigation involving 'take-or-pay' contracts. The three most significant are: 1) increased capacity of Preston

105 to deliver gas; 2) reduced market demand for defendant's product; 3) funda-
106 mentally changed governmental regulations transforming the industry from a
107 regulated to an unregulated one.

108   However, shifting supply and demand and changing governmental regulations are nor-
109 mal factors considered in any business transaction. By the clear and unambiguous terms
110 of the remainder of the contract, the plaintiff accepts the supply risk, the defendant ac-
111 cepts the market risk, and both parties adopt the risk of changed governmental regula-
112 tions. These three factual defenses certainly do not constitute the same type of catastrophic
113 events enumerated in the first part of the 'force majeure' article. Although these are forces
114 or events beyond the defendant's control, no court has ever brought them within the
115 ambit of the 'force majeure' defense.

116   The defendant would have the court interpret the clause 'whether of the kind herein
117 enumerated or otherwise' which modifies the phrase 'or any other cause,' to mean any
118 other cause *whatsoever* beyond the control of the defendant in addition to the specifically
119 named ones. If this interpretation were correct, the contract would state that either party
120 could escape responsibility if events beyond the party's control made performance either
121 difficult or unprofitable. An obscure, modifying phrase, buried in an exhibit, would be
122 the most important writing in the entire contract. However, a party would never sign a
123 contract, if this interpretation were correct, because the remainder of the contract would
124 become meaningless. Instead, the court unequivocally interprets the 'or otherwise' phrase
125 to not include the specific promises and provisions in other parts of the contract. In other
126 words, the remainder of the contract clearly and unambiguously states that the plaintiff
127 assumes the supply risk while the defendant assumes the market risk, and these are not
128 the events contemplated by the 'force majeure' escape valve. The basis commitments of
129 the other parts of the contract remain in force despite the 'or otherwise' phrase. The con-
130 tract must be interpreted consistently; otherwise, defendant's interpretation would ren-
131 der the bulk of the contract meaningless.

132   Moreover, defendant's strained interpretation of the obscure 'force majeure' clause can-
133 not mean that changed governmental policy or regulation will suspend obligations under
134 the contract. There are absolutely no criteria in the 'force majeure' provisions by which to
135 judge when or how such changes would affect the contractual obligations. What degree of
136 shifting governmental policy is required? Must the change be unfavorable? The 'force ma-
137 jeure' provisions do not address these issues because they were never intended to do so.
138 Modifications in governmental policy and regulation are economic facts of life and are not
139 a basis for suspending a contract. *Superior Oil Co. v. Transco Energy Co.* [616 F.Supp. 98] C.A.
140 No. 84-2138, mem. (W.D.La., Feb. 13, 1985); *Universal Resources Corp. v. Panhandle East-*
141 *ern Pipeline Co.,* mem. (N.D.Tex., April 1, 1986). Finally, because a contract is law between
142 the parties, this court believes that interpretation of a contract is solely a matter of law, and
143 thus, no material issue of fact must be decided in reaching the conclusions outlined above."

144   In a similar vein, the learned trial judge in the instant case stated:

145   "Tenneco claims that due to prevailing economic conditions resulting in a dra-
146 matic drop in natural gas prices it was necessary to repudiate its contracts with
147 natural gas producers-suppliers. Tenneco, accordingly, instituted its Emergency
148 Gas Purchase Policy (EGPP), thereby unilaterally modifying the quantity and
149 pricing provisions of its purchase contracts effective May 1, 1983, and the take
150 or pay provisions effective January 1, 1983. Hanover filed this suit for specific per-
151 formance seeking to invalidate the EGPP and to enforce the original quantity,
152 pricing and take or pay provisions of the contract.

Historically Louisiana jurisprudence has recognized these type [*sic*] of requirements contracts which have been viewed as a veritable constitution between the parties to govern future sales. See 6 S. Litvinoff, Louisiana Civil Law Treatise § 119 n. 32, § 284 n. 47 (1969); Hopkins, 49 Tulane Law Review 605 (1975). In fact, take-or-pay provisions are commonplace in the natural gas industry and are not unconscionable or unfair. *Sid Richardson Carbon & Gasoline Co. vs. Internorth, Inc.*, 595 F.Supp. 497 (N.D.Tex.1984). The seller's obligation is twofold: (1) insuring that the buyer receives all the goods he requires and (2) supplying the goods at the fixed contract price regardless of market fluctuations. The buyer thereby is assured of his supply and is insulated from increases in the market price. In return, he assures the seller a ready market for his goods at a fixed price. 'Under such a provision, the buyer must assume the market risk; that is, that it may not find a market for all the gas it is obligated to purchase under the contract. If the gas does, in fact, expire during the pendency of the contract, the buyer would then have an action against the seller for its failure to perform under the contract. The buyer thus takes the market risk, while the seller takes the supply risk ... The market risk implicit in take-or-pay provisions is the burden of the [buyer], which must be accepted along with the benefits of the contract. Changing market conditions cannot rewrite an unambiguous and evenly negotiated contract.' *Universal Resources Corporation vs. Panhandle Eastern Pipeline Company*, No. CA 3-85-0723-R (April 1, 1986); see also *Sid Richardson Carbon & Gasoline vs. Internorth*, supra."

Our careful consideration of this issue prompts us to conclude that the events relied on by Tenneco as excusing its failure to fully perform the Kaplan Contract do not constitute force majeure within the meaning of the force majeure clause of the contract and no issue of fact material to this determination exists.

It is a cardinal rule that in construing a contract, it must be considered as a whole, and all clauses of the agreement are to be interpreted in reference and relation to each other giving to each that meaning which results from the entire act. *Farrell v. Hodges Stock Yards, Inc.*, 343 So.2d 1364 (La.1977). As noted by Judge Gonzales in *Preston*, the construction of the force majeure clause advocated by Tenneco cannot be squared with the other provisions of the contract and, in particular, the mutual obligations assumed by the parties under the take or pay provisions thereof. Although the circumstances relied upon by Tenneco are forces or events beyond its control, adverse economic conditions and modifications in governmental regulations and policy which tend to render performance burdensome and unprofitable do not constitute force majeure. As stated in *Northern Indiana Public Service Company v. Carbon County Coal Company*, 799 F.2d 265 (7th Cir.1986):

> "The whole purpose of a fixed-price contract is to allocate risk in this way. A force majeure clause interpreted to excuse the buyer from the risk he expressly assumed would nullify a central term of the contract."

For these reasons, we conclude that Tenneco's reliance on force majeure is without merit as a matter of law.

WHETHER TENNECO'S PERFORMANCE IS EXCUSED BECAUSE OF THE AFFIRMATIVE DEFENSES OF COMMERCIAL IMPRACTICABILITY AND IMPREVISION

Tenneco first urges that, under Texas law, commercial impracticability excuses its failure to perform under the contract. We previously concluded that Louisiana law rather than Texas law governs this proceeding. The common law doctrine of commercial impracticability has no application under Louisiana law. See *The Superior Oil Company v. Transco Energy Company, et al.*, supra.

We reject Tenneco's defense of imprevision for the same reason. This essentially French doctrine which permits judicial reformation of contracts whenever a drastic change in circumstances renders performance for one of the parties harsh has not been recognized or accepted by the courts of this state. Although reference to this doctrine appears in *Armour v. Shongaloo Lodge No. 352, Etc.*, 342 So.2d 600 (La.1977), the doctrine is not discussed and the result reached in that case would indicate that if considered our Supreme Court rejected same.

THE DEFENSE OF ERROR

Tenneco urges that the unforeseen collapse of the natural gas market and governmental restructuring of the industry has rendered its performance under the contract untenable. From this premise, it argues that the doctrine of mutual or unilateral error requires the voidance of the contract. In effect, what Tenneco argues is that, had it anticipated the mentioned events, it would never have agreed to the terms of the Kaplan Contract, therefore its consent was the result of error.

The language of the Kaplan Contract is plain and unambiguous. Tenneco's claim of error is founded on nothing more than an error in judgment founded upon its own evaluation of future market conditions.

Our Civil Code declares that consent may be vitiated by error only when it concerns the principal cause or motive and that cause or motive was known or should have been known to the other party. La.C.C. arts. 1948 and 1949. In *Caddo Parish School Board v. Cotton Baking Company*, 342 So.2d 1196 (La.App. 3d Cir.1977), our brethren rejected a claim of error based upon a change in market conditions stating: "The alleged error is not an error in mathematical calculation, but an error in judgment which does not entitle [the seller] to rescind the agreement. In addition, Article 1825 requires both parties to be aware of an error before a contract can be voided. There is no evidence that the [plaintiff] had any knowledge of the effect the Russian wheat sales would have on the price of bread products. The fact that [the seller's] bid on the item was much less than the other bid is not in itself sufficient to impute knowledge of an error to the [plaintiff]. 342 So2d at 1198."

It is not within the province of the courts to relieve parties of their bad bargains. *Kenny v. Oak Builders, Inc.*, 256 La. 85, 235 So.2d 386 (1970). The principal cause of the Kaplan Contract was the sale and concommittant purchase of a certain volume of gas at a fixed price. There is no error alleged in regard thereto. The expectations of the parties as to the profitability of the contract are irrelevant to a determination of error. As stated by Judge Duhe in *Superior Oil Company*, supra. "Undoubtedly, Pipeline [Transcontinental Gas Pipeline Company] was in error as to its motive for entering into this obligation. The market has simply not evolved in the manner anticipated. But this error is far from an error in the obligation itself. And Pipeline has failed to establish an issue of fact as to whether there was error as to the principal cause of the contract, i.e., a certain price for a certain quantity of gas. *The Superior Oil Co., supra*, p. 109."

For these reasons we reject Tenneco's claim of error.

FAILURE OF CAUSE OR CONSIDERATION

Tenneco argues that the consideration for its obligation to pay for gas not taken was the ability to make up the gas at a later time and, since make up is no longer possible because of changes in market conditions, there is no cause or consideration for Tenneco's take or pay obligation. In this connection, Tenneco argues alternatively that its inability to make up the gas at a later time renders the take or pay obligation an unlawful stipu-

lated damage clause rather than an alternative obligation. We find merit in neither of   248
these contentions.   249

The Kaplan Contract specifically mandates that for each contract year Tenneco will ei-   250
ther take and pay for, or pay for if not taken, a specified quantity of gas. The contract es-   251
tablishes a limited makeup period after which Tenneco loses its right to make-up.   252
Take-or-pay obligations are common-place in the natural gas industry and are not un-   253
conscionable or unfair. *Sid Richardson Carbon & Gasoline Co. v. InterNorth, Inc.*, 595   254
F.Supp. 497 (N.D.Tex.1984). Tenneco and Hanover bargained for a certain allocation of   255
risks. Tenneco cannot now be heard to complain of lack of cause based on its projections   256
of future market conditions which apparently turned out to be incorrect.   257

The take or pay obligation assumed by Tenneco is not an unlawful stipulated damage   258
clause but an alternative obligation. We so held in *Pogo Producing Co. v. Sea Robin Pipeline*   259
Co., 493 So.2d 909 (La.App. 3rd Cir.1986), writ denied, 497 So.2d 310 (La.1986).   260

[....]

Questions

1. As the *Hanover Petroleum* court explained, the "take or pay" contract into which the parties entered obligated Tenneco either (1) to buy a certain amount of gas per term ("take") or (2) to pay a certain sum of money representing a percentage of the price of that gas ("pay"). In terms of "classification of obligations", how should the kind of obligation that Tenneco undertook be described? Hint: *see* La. Civ. Code art. 1807 *et seq.*

2. The *Hanover Petroleum* court concludes that, in the end, the force majeure clause in the contract under examination provided no greater protection for the parties than did the "law" of force majeure (now called the law of impossibility of performance). Does that seem plausible to you? Why or why not?

3. *Hanover Petroleum* was decided prior to the Revision of the law of force majeure/ "impossibility of performance". Which part(s) of new Louisiana Civil Code article 1873 seem(s) to you to be the most pertinent to disputes of the kind presented in this case? The first paragraph, which states the "general principle" of impossibility of performance, is, of course, pertinent. But isn't there another, one that's even more directly "on point"? Explain.

4. Did the "shifting supply and demand and changing governmental regulations" of which Tenneco complained in fact render the performance of its obligations "truly" or "absolutely" impossible? *See* La. Civ. Code art. 1873.

Comparative Law Perspective

Alain Levasseur, COMPARATIVE LAW OF CONTRACTS
165–84 (2008)

[B]etween the time the contract is negotiated and entered into on the basis of the circumstances that exist at that time and the time specified for the performances to be carried out, many different, unexpected or unforeseen events may occur in such a manner
as to upset and disrupt the parties' plans as laid down in the contract....

These events may fit under a variety of adjectives: 'political', 'economic', 'financial',
'natural'... Yet, they all have in common the fact that they may serve as a justification for

a party not to perform her side of the bargain, or carry out a modified and adjusted performance of the original obligation....

Civil Law

See La. Civ. C. Articles: 1873—1877

Art. 1137(1): An obligation to preserve the thing, whether the contract has for its object the benefit of one party only, or whether it has for its object the common interest of the parties, imposes on the party in charge of preserving the thing the duty to act as a prudent administrator (bon pere de famille).

Art. 1147: Should it be the case, an obligor is liable to pay damages either on account of his failure to perform, or on account of his delay in performing, whenever he is unable to prove that the non-performance was caused by a fortuitous event for which he cannot be held liable, or that he did not act in bad faith.

Art. 1148: No damages are owed when, because of force majeure or a fortuitous event, an obligor was prevented from giving or doing what he was bound to give or do, or when he did what he was forbidden from doing.

Art. 1302: When a certain and identified thing which was the object of an obligation, has perished, is out of commerce, or is lost in such a manner that one absolutely cannot know of its existence, the obligation is extinguished is the thing has perished or has been lost without the obligor's fault and before he had been put in default ... The obligor must prove the fortuitous event he alleges.

BGB

Section 275. Exclusion of the duty of performance.

(1) A claim for performance cannot be made in so far as it is impossible for the obligor or for anyone else to perform.

(2) The obligor may refuse to perform in so far as performance requires expenditure which, having regard to the subject matter of the obligation and the principle of good faith, is manifestly disproportionate to the obligee's interest in performance. When determining what may reasonably be required of the obligor, regard must also be had to whether he is responsible for the impediment to performance.

(3) Moreover, the obligor may refuse to perform, if he is to effect the performance in in person and, after weighing up the obligee's interest in performance and the impediment to performance, performance cannot be reasonably required of the obligor.

C. C. Q.

Art. 1693: A debtor is released where he cannot perform an obligation by reason of a superior force and before he is in default, or where, although he was in default, the creditor could not, in any case, benefit by the performance of the obligation by reason of that superior force, unless, in either case, the debtor has expressly assumed the risk of superior force.

The burden of proof of superior force is on the debtor.

Art. 1694: A debtor released by impossibility of performance may not exact performance of the correlative obligation of the creditor; if the performance has already been rendered, restitution is owed.

Where the debtor has performed part of his obligation, the creditor remains bound to perform his own obligation to the extent of his enrichment.

Ph. Malaurie, L. Aynès, Ph. Stoffel-Munck, Droit Civil, Les Obligations, Defrénois 2003

§ 3. Grounds for exoneration

[…] An obligor cannot be held liable when the non-performance of his obligation can be imputed to a 'foreign cause' (fortuitous event), unless the obligor was held to an obligation of warranty. The most typical is force majeure, to which are assimilated the 'fact' of the obligee and the fact of a third person. These 'causes' (grounds) exonerate the obligor, unless they have only a temporary effect, in which case they merely suspend the contract.

I. — Force majeure

952. Reasonable. — […]. Just as the English theory of *frustration* is now used in reference to the notion of a 'reasonable person', in France force majeure tends to be defined by an event which is reasonably irresistible, unforeseeable and exterior which, most often requires a case by case appraisal.

953. Irresistible. — The event must be irresistible; it is the main requirement; if it could have been overcome, even though the performance would have been more difficult and onerous, the obligor would still be held liable for not having performed; there does not exist any financial force majeure.… […] The difficult question is to determine at which point in time there is 'irresistibility'. It is obvious that law is not absolute and cannot expect the obligor to be a 'superman', Tarzan … Rambo … All is necessarily relative. The real question to ask is the following: should irresistibility be evaluated *in abstracto* or *in concreto*? There are cases on both sides.…

955. Unforeseeable. — … the event … must have been unforeseeable at the time of perfection of the contract. If the obligor could have foreseen the event, he will be at fault for non having taken the necessary measures.… (same comment with respect to "absolute" unforeseeability as for "irresistibility" above); as with respect to irrestibility, unforeseeability depends on the circumstances …

956. Exterior. — The event must be 'exterior' to the obligor, otherwise he should be liable. Exteriority is implied by the expression of "a cause (source) foreign to the obligor" so that the event cannot be imputed to the obligor.…

II. — Fact of the creditor, of a third person or of the prince

958. F act of the creditor. — The fact of the creditor (the victim) exonerates the obligor. This is a rational view: if the damage was caused by the victim, it cannot be held against the obligor.…

959. Fact of a third person or the prince. — (there is there also a ground for not holding the obligor liable) if the fact was irresistible, unforeseeable and if the obligor was not to be held liable in one way or another. It is a type of force majeure.…

Common Law

Common Law in the UK

William Blackstone, Commentaries on the Laws of England

Chapter XXII. *Of Proceedings in the Courts of Equity.*

3. With respect to the mode of *relief.* […] A court of equity will compel them [executory agreements] to be carried into strict execution, unless where it is improper or impossible; instead of giving damages for their non-performance …

G. H. Treitel (opus cited)

Chapter 20 Frustration

(7) Impossibility and impracticability

(a) IMPRACTICABILITY DISTINGUISHED FROM IMPOSSIBILITY. The doctrine of frustration originated in cases where performance was said to have become "impossible".

That, in itself, is something of a relative term. What is "impossible" depends partly on the current state of technology, and partly on the amount of trouble and expense to which one is prepared to go to achieve it.[...] For this reason the current trend in the United States is to abandon the very words "impossible" and "impossibility" and to use instead the terms "impracticable" and "impracticability" ...

(b) IMPRACTICABILITY GENERALLY NO EXCUSE. [...] it appears that "impracticability" is not generally sufficient to frustrate a contract in English law ... Lord Radcliffe said: "It is not hardship or inconvenience or material loss itself which calls the principle of frustration into play. There must be as well a change in the significance of the obligation that the thing undertaken would, if performed, be a different thing from that contracted for ..." Where performance would, in view of changed circumstances, cause not merely extra expense but acute personal hardship to one party, it has been said that "equitable relief may ... be refused because of an unforeseen change of circumstances not amounting to legal frustration." But in such cases the contract is not discharged: the defendant remains liable in damages even though specific performance is refused on the ground of severe hardship. [...]

2. Frustration of Purpose

Frustration of purpose is, in a sense, the converse of impracticability. The two ideas resemble each other in that neither is concerned with cases in which performance has become impossible. Impracticability is said to arise when a *supplier* of goods, services or other facilities alleges that performance of his own promise has become so burdensome to him that he should no longer be bound to render it. The argument of frustration of purpose, on the other hand, is put forward by the recipient of the goods, services or facilities: it is that supervening events have so greatly reduced the value to him of the other party's performance that he should no longer be bound to accept and to pay the agreed price ...

The more recent authorities show that "the frustrated expectations and intentions of one party to a contract do not necessarily, or indeed usually, lead to the frustration of that contract". They make it difficult to establish the defence of frustration of purpose; but they do not make it impossible ...

Common Law in the USA

Restatement, 2d

§261. Discharge by Supervening Impracticability

Where, after a contract is made, a party's performance is made impracticable without his fault by the occurrence of an event the non-occurrence of which was a basic assumption on which the contract was made, his duty to render that performance is discharged, unless the language or the circumstances indicate the contrary.

§265. Discharge by Supervening Frustration

(1)Where, after a contract is made, a party's performance under it is impracticable without his fault because of a fact of which he has no reason to know and the non-existence of which is a basic assumption on which the contract is made, no duty to render that performance arises, unless the language or circumstances indicate the contrary.

(2) Where, at the time a contract is made, a party's principle purpose is substantially frustrated without his fault by a fact of which he has no reason to know and the non-existence of which is a basic assumption on which the contract is made, no duty of that party to render performance arises, unless the language or circumstances indicate the contrary.

UCC

§ 2-613. Casualty to Identified Goods.

Where the contract requires for its performance goods identified when the contract is made, and the goods suffer casualty without fault of either party before the risk of loss passes to the buyer, or in a proper case under a "no arrival, no sale" term (Section 2-324) then

(a) if the loss is total the contract is avoided; and

(b) if the loss is partial or the goods have so deteriorated as no longer to conform to the contract the buyer may nevertheless demand inspection and at his option either treat the contract as avoided or accept the goods with due allowance from the contract price for the deterioration or the deficiency in quantity but without further right against the seller.

§ 2-614. Substituted Performance.

(1) If without fault of either party the agreed berthing, loading, or unloading facilities fail or an agreed type of carrier becomes unavailable or the agreed manner of performance otherwise becomes commercially impracticable but a commercially reasonable substitute is available, the substitute performance must be tendered and accepted.

§ 2-615. Excuse by Failure of Presupposed Conditions.

Except to the extent that a seller may have assumed a greater obligation and subject to section 2-614:

(a) Delay in performance or nonperformance in whole or in part by a seller that complies with paragraphs (b) and (c) is not a breach of the seller's duty under a contract for sale if performance as agreed has been made impracticable by the occurrence of a contingency the nonoccurrence of which was a basic assumption on which the contract was made or by compliance in good faith with any applicable foreign or domestic governmental regulation or order whether or not it later proves to be invalid.

E. Allan Farnsworth

C. IMPRACTICABILITY AND FRUSTRATION

§ 9.5. Growth of Impossibility as an Excuse. The common law was slow to give effect to the maxim *impossibilium nulla obligatio est* ("there is no obligation to do the impossible"). Courts were less receptive to claims of excuse based on events occurring after the making of the contract than they were to claims of excuse based on facts that existed at the time of the agreement. [...]

§ 9.6. A New Synthesis: The Doctrine of Impracticability. The common law development ... is synthesized in UCC 2-615, Excuse by Failure of Presupposed Conditions. [...]

Under the new synthesis, the party that claims that a supervening event or "contingency" prevented performance must meet four requirements. First, the event must have made "performance as agreed ... impracticable." Second, the nonoccurrence of the event must have been "a basic assumption on which the contract was made." Third, the impracticability must have resulted without the fault of the party seeking to be excused. Fourth, that party must not have assumed a greater obligation than the law imposes. Although these requirements involve questions of fact, courts have sometimes been reluctant to entrust the granting of excuse on this ground to a jury. [...]

§ 9.9. **Effects of Impracticability and Frustration.** The effect of *supervening* impracticability or frustration on the excused party is usually to discharge that party's remaining duties of performance. The effect of *existing* impracticability or frustration on the excused party is usually to prevent any duty of performance on that party's side from arising. [...]

A prospective failure of performance due to impracticability or frustration has a similar effect. The fact that one party's anticipated failure to perform will be excused on the ground of impracticability or frustration does not prevent the other party from justifiably suspending performance and from terminating the contract. But the other party cannot recover damages for breach. [...]

UNIDROIT

Article 6.2.1 (Contract to be observed)

Where the performance of a contract becomes more onerous for one of the parties, that party is nevertheless bound to perform its obligations subject to the following provisions on hardship.

Article 6.2.2 (Definition of hardship)

There is hardship where the occurrence of events fundamentally alters the equilibrium of the contract either because the cost of a party's performance has increased of because the value of the performance has increased or because the value of the performance a party receives has diminished, and

(a) the events occur or become known to the disadvantaged party after the conclusion of the contract;

(b) the events could not reasonably have been taken into account by the disadvantaged party at the time of the conclusion of the contract;

(c) the events are beyond the control of the disadvantaged party; and

(d) the risk of the events was not assumed by the disadvantaged party.

Article 6.2.3 (Effects of hardship)

(1) In case of hardship the disadvantaged party is entitled to request renegotiations. The request shall be made without undue delay and shall indicate the grounds on which it is based.

(2) The request for renegotiation does not in itself entitle the disadvantaged party to withhold performance.

(3) Upon failure to reach agreement within a reasonable time either party may resort to the court.

(4) If the court finds hardship it may, if reasonable,

(a) terminate the contract at a date and on terms to be fixed, or

(b) adapt the contract with a view to restoring its equilibrium.

Article 7.1.7 (Force majeure)

(1) Non-performance by a party is excused if that party proves that the nonperformance was due to an impediment beyond its control and that it could not reasonably be ex-

pected to have taken the impediment into account at the time of the conclusion of the contract or to have avoided or overcome it or its consequences.

(2) When the impediment is only temporary, the excuse shall have effect for such period as is reasonable having regard to the effect of the impediment on the performance of the contract.

(3) The party who fails to perform must give notice to the other party of the impediment and its effect on its ability to perform. If the notice is not received by the other party within a reasonable time after the party who fails to perform knew or ought to have known of the impediment, it is liable for damages resulting from such nonreceipt.

(4) Nothing in this article prevents a party from exercising a right to terminate the contract or to withhold performance or request interest on money due.

Section VI — Of Novation

Louisiana Sources of Law

Louisiana Civil Code

Art. 1879. Extinguishment of existing obligation.

Novation is the extinguishment of an existing obligation by the substitution of a new one. (Acts 1984, No. 331, § 1, eff. Jan. 1, 1985.)

Art. 1880. Novation not presumed.

The intention to extinguish the original obligation must be clear and unequivocal. Novation may not be presumed. (Acts 1984, No. 331, § 1, eff. Jan. 1, 1985.)

Art. 1881. Objective novation.

Novation takes place when, by agreement of the parties, a new performance is substituted for that previously owed, or a new cause is substituted for that of the original obligation. If any substantial part of the original performance is still owed, there is no novation.

Novation takes place also when the parties expressly declare their intention to novate an obligation.

Mere modification of an obligation, made without intention to extinguish it, does not effect a novation. The execution of a new writing, the issuance or renewal of a negotiable instrument, or the giving of new securities for the performance of an existing obligation are examples of such a modification. (Acts 1984, No. 331, § 1, eff. Jan. 1, 1985.)

Art. 1882. Subjective novation.

Novation takes place when a new obligor is substituted for a prior obligor who is discharged by the obligee. In that case, the novation is accomplished even without the consent of the prior obligor, unless he had an interest in performing the obligation himself. (Acts 1984, No. 331, § 1, eff. Jan. 1, 1985.)

Art. 1885. Novation of solidary obligation.

A novation made by the obligee and one of the obligors of a solidary obligation releases the other solidary obligors.

In that case, the security given for the performance of the extinguished obligation may be retained by the obligee only on property of that obligor with whom the novation has been made.

If the obligee requires that the other co-obligors remain solidarily bound, there is no novation unless the co-obligors consent to the new obligation. (Acts 1984, No. 331, § 1, eff. Jan. 1, 1985.)

Art. 1886. Delegation of performance.

A delegation of performance by an obligor to a third person is effective when that person binds himself to perform.

A delegation effects a novation only when the obligee expressly discharges the original obligor. (Acts 1984, No. 331, § 1, eff. Jan. 1, 1985.)

Précis: Louisiana Law of Obligations in General §§ 7.3.1 to 7.3.4

Novation is one of these legal devices meant, at the same time, to extinguish and to transfer an obligation....

As a general rule, a novation is a juridical act, the creation of the wills of two parties at least, which brings about **"the extinguishment of an existing obligation by the substitution of a new one."** (LSA-C.C. Art. 1879). It follows necessarily that a new obligation is substituted to a previously existing one through a change in one of the *essential* requirements constitutive of an obligation. There takes place then a true legal metamorphosis of obligations.

A novation amounts, actually, to a merger into one legal concept, that of novation, of two separate juridical acts: one juridical act extinguishes an existing obligation while the other juridical act creates a new obligation. This dual effect of novation requires that some conditions be met for novation to take place and carries with it some important practical consequences....

Two fundamental conditions must be met for a novation to take place under whatever form it might appear....

The first condition required is that of a succession of obligations and the second is that of the intent to novate (animus novandi)....

A novation is the outcome of a change in an *essential* component part of an obligation (parties, cause, object) or in the substitution of a modality which affects the very existence of an obligation....

An objective **"novation takes place when, by agreement of the parties, a new performance is substituted for that previously owed, or a new cause is substituted for that of the original obligation. If any substantial part of the original performance is still owed, there is no novation.**

Novation takes place also when the parties expressly declare their intention to novate an obligation." ...

LSA-C.C. **Art. 1882** provides expressly for one form of subjective novation by substitution of an obligor to another....

Novation of obligees. LSA-C.C. **Art. 1882** does not mention this form of subjective novation as a possibility open to parties to an obligation....

In a novation of obligees, the obligation which is created is a new one and none of the accessory rights attached to the former obligation are transferred to the new obligee. In addition, because the obligation is new, it will be subjected to its own (and new) prescriptive period....

"The immediate effects of novation are two, essentially: 1) extinction of an existing obligation and 2) its replacement by a new one." ...

LSA-C.C. Art. 1879 states unequivocally that "**novation is the extinguishment of an existing obligation by the substitution of a new one.**" It follows from the creation of a <u>new</u> obligation that all the accessory rights which ensured the performance of the <u>original</u> primary obligation are also extinguished as is suggested, furthermore, by LSA-C.C. Art. 1884: "**Security given for the performance of the extinguished obligation may not be transferred to the new obligation without agreement of the parties who gave the security.**" ...

The new obligation which emerges from the juridical act of novation is free of all the rights of action and exceptions which were attached to the former and original obligation. The new obligation takes on its particular legal features and a legal existence of its own....

[A] delegation is a juridical act whereby the debtor-obligor instructs another, the third person or delegated debtor, to become a debtor and perform an obligation for the benefit of the obligee. Under these circumstances the consent of the obligee is not necessary as his right of action against his original obligor is preserved....

[A] personal obligation on the part of the obligor cannot be delegated as long as the obligee has not agreed to make that same obligation personal on the part of the delegated obligor....

On the order or request of the original obligor, the delegated obligor binds himself *vis-à-vis* the obligee and, thereby, creates an obligation which is totally independent and distinct from the obligation still binding the original obligor towards the obligee....

[A] delegation does not create a bond of solidarity between the original obligor and the delegated obligor as an assumption of obligations between an obligor and a third person would establish....

A perfect delegation amounts to a novation when the obligee expressly discharges the original obligor....

An imperfect delegation does not amount to a novation because the oblige does not wish to discharge the original obligor....

Cases

POLK CHEVROLET, INC.
v.
Vince J. VICARO
Louisiana Court of Appeal
First Circuit
April 6, 1964
162 So.2d 761

LANDRY, Judge.

This appeal is by defendant, Vince J. Vicaro, from a deficiency judgment rendered against him, as co-maker of a promissory note, in favor of appellee, Polk Chevrolet, Inc.,

11 in the sum of $1,010.32, together within interest at the rate of 8% Per annum from April
12 1, 1961, until paid, plus the additional sum of 25% On both principal and interest, as at-
13 torney's fees, and costs.

14   The note in question, dated April 30, 1959, was signed by present defendant, Vince J.
15 Vicaro, and his son, Samuel J. Vicaro, and represented the balance due on the sale price
16 of an automobile purchased by said Samuel J. Vicaro which said vendee simultaneously
17 granted a chattel mortgage on the vehicle as security for the note. Appellee subsequently
18 transferred the note to General Motors Acceptance Corporation (sometimes hereinafter
19 referred to simply as 'GMAC'), said transfer being by full or special endorsement.

20   On December 29, 1960, Samuel J. Vicaro executed another promissory note made
21 payable to the order of GMAC, the primary purpose of which was to effect a rearrange-
22 ment of the installments due under the prior note of April 30, 1959. The latter note,
23 which was not signed by defendant herein, expressly provided that the terms of the for-
24 mer instrument, except as to the modification and rearrangement of installments, were
25 to remain in full force and effect.

26   Subsequently, plaintiff herein obtained judgment against Samuel J. Vicaro in a suit
27 brought on both said notes for the unpaid delinquent balance due on the indebtedness.
28 In execution of said judgment plaintiff caused the mortgaged property to be sold, with
29 appraisement, and instituted the present action against defendant as co-maker of the ini-
30 tial note, for the aforesaid deficiency.

31   Although defendant, for all practical purposes, concedes the correctness of the perti-
32 nent facts as hereinabove set forth, [**presents the defense, among others, that plaintiff has**]
33 [...] no cause of action predicated upon the alleged extinguishment of the note sued upon
34 by novation[.] [....]

35   Novation is a contract consisting of two stipulations; one to extinguish an existing
36 obligation, the other to substitute a new one in its place. To constitute a novation there
37 must simultaneously occur both the cancellation of a present or outstanding obligation
38 and the substitution in its place of a new obligation with the consent of the parties con-
39 cerned. LSA-C.C. Article 2185.

40   It is clear that defendant's obligation on the note, being that of co-maker, was in solido.
41 Therefore, if, as contended by defendant, execution of the second note by his solidary
42 obligor, Samuel J. Vicaro, operated as a novation of the first note, defendant was released
43 and discharged from all obligation thereon. LSA-C.C. Article 2198.

44   Novation, however, is never presumed. Johnson v. Johnson, 235 La. 226, 103 So.2d 263;
45 Hayes v. Claterbaugh, La.App., 140 So.2d 737. For novation to result the discharge of the
46 original debtor or obligor must be express. LSA-C.C. Articles 2185, 2187, 2190, Hayes v.
47 Claterbaugh, supra.

48   It is equally well settled that modification of an obligation does not effect a novation
49 unless the intention of the parties to novate the obligation is clear and explicit. Rex Fi-
50 nance Co. v. Cary, La.App., 145 So.2d 672 (affirmed on other grounds, 244 La. 675, 154
51 So.2d 360). The taking of a new note in partial renewal of an old one, does not operate
52 a novation or extinguish the original debt or the pledge securing same. Davis v. Welch,
53 128 La. 785, 55 So. 372.

54   In the case at bar there was patently no intention to novate the preexisting indebt-
55 edness by the execution of the second note by Samuel J. Vicaro alone. On the contrary,
56 the latter instrument, in referring to the mortgage of April 30, 1959, states "the terms
57 and provisions of which document except as modified by this rearrangement of in-

stallments, remain in full force and effect." Such language clearly refutes an intention to novate the original indebtedness. Inasmuch as there was no intention on the part of either obligor or obligee to cancel the existing indebtedness, execution of the second note did not operate as a novation. The asserted defense of release by novation is therefore without merit.

[....]

Questions

1. Describe clearly and in legal terms the many relationships involved here, particularly the relationship between Vince Vicaro and his son, Samuel, as co-makers of the promissory note.

2. Lines 20 *et seq.*: After you have read the Code articles on "Novation" (La. Civ. Code arts. 1879–1887) compare the contents of the two notes, the 1959 note and its transfer with the 1960 note. Do you have any comment? Is the Court's statement on lines 22–25 of any importance? What fundamental distinction does it make between the types of requirements for a contract to exist? Does the distinction between essential requirements versus accessory requirements mean anything to you?

3. Lines 31 *et seq.*: What do you think of the defendant's arguments, particularly (1), (3), and (4)?

4. Lines 35 *et seq.*: Can you see any difference between former Louisiana Civil Code article 2185, as cited by the Court, and new Louisiana Civil Code article 1879? How does the Court's statement on lines 44–47 match your description of the legal relationships above? On lines 48 *et seq.*, to what kind of novation is the Court referring (subjective or objective)? How relevant is the third paragraph of Louisiana Civil Code article 1881? What is a partial renewal? Is there a danger in using renewal next to novation? Isn't novation creating a new obligation? *See* La. Civ. Code art. 1879.

5. Lines 59–61: How does this statement fit your distinction between essential requirements versus accessory requirements in Question 2 above?

CRESCENT CIGARETTE VENDING CORPORATION
v.
Alvin J. TOCA

Louisiana Court of Appeal
Fourth Circuit
Dec. 19, 1972
271 So.2d 53

BOUTALL, Judge.

This is a suit on a promissory note made by the defendant, Alvin Toca, in the principal sum of $1,000.00, alleging a balance due of $507.95. The defendant filed his answer pleading extinguishment of the obligation. He alleged that the obligation was extinguished by the delivery of a new note executed by a third party in the amount of the balance due at that time, pursuant to an agreement between the parties. The trial court rendered judgment in favor of the defendant, and from this adverse judgment, plaintiff appeals.

The record shows that the defendant admitted making the note and further admits that he did not make all of the payments thereon. He contends, however, that he is not obligated to make any further payments because of the following facts. Defendant was the operator of a lounge called "Laura's Playroom", and in connection with that business had installed in the premises a cigarette machine belonging to plaintiff. Defendant needed some money for stock and other purposes, and as a consequence borrowed from the plaintiff $1,000.00 for which he signed the note in question. The note was payable out of the defendant's commission received from the operation of the cigarette machine plus $10.00 weekly. The defendant on or about October 17, 1969, sold the business "Laura's Playroom" to a certain Sam Jones without benefit of the Bulk Sales Act.

The defendant contends that at the time he sold the business to Sam Jones, there was an agreement between Jones, Crescent Cigarette, and himself that Jones would assume the outstanding obligation on the note by signing another promissory note in which Jones alone was responsible. In effect, defendant is contending that a novation has taken place and is relying on LSA-C.C. art. 2185 which states:

"Art. 2185. Novation, definition

"Art. 2185. Novation is a contract, consisting of two stipulations; one to extinguish an existing obligation, the other to substitute a new one in its place."

In the present situation we should also observe LSA-C.C. art. 2192 which states:

"Art. 2192. Discharge of original debtor

"Art. 2192. The delegation, by which a debtor gives to the creditor another debtor who obliges himself towards such creditor, does not operate a novation, unless the creditor has expressly declared that he intends to discharge his debtor who has made the delegation."

Express declaration of intent to discharge the defendant is denied by the representative of plaintiff, and Jones was not a party to the suit, nor was he called as a witness. The issue in the case thus becomes one of preponderance of evidence, burden of proof, and credibility of witnesses. In Midlo & Lehmann v. Katz, 195 So.2d 383 (La.App.4th Cir., 1967), the court stated that a novation is never presumed, and the burden of proof to establish a novation is on the person who claims it. The court also stated in Midlo that the intention of parties to substitute a new obligation for the original one may be shown by the character of the transaction and the facts and circumstances surrounding the transaction, as well as by the terms of the agreement itself.

The only evidence in the case is the testimony of the representative of Crescent Cigarette and the testimony of the defendant. The testimony of the representative of Crescent Cigarette is that Jones did not make a promissory note to be substituted for the note in question, but that Jones borrowed some money from Crescent Cigarette in an independent transaction and executed a note for the money borrowed. The conditions or terms of the note are not in evidence. The representative of plaintiff testified that he handled the transaction personally and that the new note signed by Jones had nothing to do with the note sued upon. As opposed to this, the defendant testified that he talked to Jones about buying the business, but because Jones did not have as much money as defendant wanted, Jones agreed to assume defendant's note with plaintiff; that defendant then contacted Crescent Cigarette and spoke to a person known only as "Tommy" who told him that he had to get "the OK from Mr. Moore." Defendant then testified that he never heard any further from Crescent until the building burden down in March, 1971.

The trial judge rendered judgment in favor of the defendant with the following statements:

"The defendant impresses the court as being a fundamentally honest and good man. He probably did the very best he could for his situation in life. Plaintiff's suit is dismissed at plaintiff"'s cost."

While the reasons given by the trial judge would indicate that this is a question simply of credibility of the witnesses, such is not the situation here. If it were simply a question of credibility of the witnesses, it would appear that the statement of the trial judge quoted above would indicate that he believed one witness and disbelieved the other witness, and hence, we would not interfere with his judgment in such a matter. However, this is a suit on a promissory note and a special affirmative defense of extinguishment of the obligation is set forth in the answer in accordance with LSA-C.C.P. art. 1005. Our jurisprudence has consistently held that a person pleading an affirmative defense bears the burden of proving such a defense, and of course it must be established by a preponderance of the evidence. B. F. Goodrich Company v. Ryan Tire Service, Inc., 203 So.2d 863 (La.App.1st Cir., 1967); Barbari v. Fireman's Insurance Co., 107 So.2d 480 (La.App.1st Cir., 1958). In B. F. Goodrich, the court stated that novation is an affirmative defense and the party claiming it must establish it by positive proof.

It is noted in the case at bar that along with the testimony of the parties, there is in evidence the promissory note itself, which contains nothing upon it to show that it was cancelled or in any other way extinguished or modified. Under the facts as related by the defendant, he did not establish that there was another promissory note signed by Jones, relating to the same debt, nor that Jones bound himself for the debt, nor that Crescent consented to release him from the obligation. Except for the reference to a conversation with a clerk named 'Tommy', who announced to him that transferring the debt would require approval of Mr. Moore, defendant's testimony is devoid of any conversation or agreement with any representative of Crescent that approval was granted or a binding contract was entered into. In this regard it is noteworthy that although he alleges that he sold the place to Jones and that Jones assumed the obligation of the note, Jones was not called to testify. While it may be presumed that Jones could just as easily have been called by the plaintiff as well as the defendant, we must note that the burden is upon the defendant of establishing the affirmative defense. The record does not disclose to us the preponderance of evidence necessary for the defendant to overcome the plaintiff's demand, and we are of the opinion that the judgment should be reversed.

For the foregoing reasons, it is ordered that there is judgment herein in favor of appellant annulling and reversing the judgment appealed from. It is further ordered that there is now judgment rendered in favor of plaintiff-appellant, Crescent Cigarette Vending Company, and against defendant-appellee, Alvin Toca, in the full sum of $507.95, together with 8% Per annum interest from date of demand until paid, plus 25% Of said amounts as attorney's fees. Appellee to pay all costs of these proceedings.

[....]

Questions

1. Establish and describe in legal terms the relationships existing in this case.

2. Lines 25 et seq.: Jones "would assume the outstanding obligation on the note...." What is an assumption of obligation? See La. Civ. Code arts. 1821–1824. On line 28, the court states: "In effect ...", and it refers to then Louisiana Civil Code article 2185 (current Louisiana Civil Code article 1879) on novation. Are novation and assumption one and the same thing? On lines 34 et seq., the Court refers to then Louisiana

Civil Code article 2192 (current Louisiana Civil Code article 1886) on delegation. What are the differences between a novation and a delegation?

3. On the basis of the evidence considered by the Court, in your legal opinion, was the right decision reached by the Court? What kind of novation did the defendant fail to establish (subjective or objective)?

FIRST NATIONAL BANK OF ABBEVILLE
v.
Donald GREENE, et al.
Louisiana Court of Appeal
Third Circuit
Dec. 21, 1992
612 So.2d 759

STOKER, Judge.

This is an appeal from a judgment recognizing certain in rem collateral mortgages on defendants' property which secure two collateral mortgage notes. The main issues in this case are whether there was a proper pledge of the collateral mortgage notes to secure a hand note and whether the hand note was novated without a repledging of the collateral mortgage notes. We affirm.

FACTS

In 1984, Hardy Tractor of Gueydon, Inc. sought financing for the construction of a new building. Ruby Linscomb Hair LeBlanc and Delores Hair Dietz were relatives of the company's president in 1984, Keith Hair. LeBlanc and Dietz owned the tract of land which Hardy Tractor leased for its business operations. LeBlanc and Dietz agreed to put in rem collateral mortgages on their property in order to secure two loans to Hardy Tractor from First National Bank of Abbeville. Dietz, who lived out of state, executed two powers of attorney in favor of LeBlanc for the sole purpose of confecting the collateral mortgages to secure the two loans to Hardy Tractor (for $100,000 and, later, an additional $20,000).

The collateral mortgage for $100,000 was executed on January 11, 1984 and signed by Keith Hair on behalf of Hardy Tractor and by Ruby Linscomb (now LeBlanc) on behalf of herself and Dietz. However, the collateral mortgage note and the collateral pledge agreement were signed only by Keith Hair for Hardy Tractor. The pledge agreement states that the collateral is pledged by the borrower (Hardy Tractor).

On June 1, 1984, a collateral mortgage for $20,000 was executed and signed by Keith Hair for Hardy Tractor and by Ruby Linscomb for herself and Dietz. Again, the collateral mortgage note and the collateral pledge agreement were signed only by Keith Hair for Hardy Tractor. The pledge agreement states that the collateral is pledged by the borrower (Hardy Tractor).

The debtors delivered both of these notes to the First National Bank of Abbeville (Bank), and these two collateral mortgage notes have remained in the Bank's possession at all times pertinent to the lawsuit.

Hardy Tractor executed five hand notes in 1984 up to the $120,000 total limit, against which the collateral mortgage notes were pledged as security. The hand notes each matured in sixty or ninety days. Subsequently, the hand notes were consolidated and renewed in one note for $120,000, with eleven monthly payments plus a final balloon payment due in August 1985. This note stated that it was also secured by the original pledges. It was signed by Keith Hair and Donald Greene for Hardy Tractor. Donald Greene was a director of Hardy Tractor.

In September 1985, the hand note was again renewed for the balance due of $113,463.96, payable in eleven monthly installments plus a final balloon note due in September 1986. This note was signed for Hardy Tractor by Wayne Zaunbrecker, Donald Greene and Burton Hardy, all directors of Hardy Tractor. A new collateral pledge agreement was drawn up, pledging the two 1984 collateral mortgage notes to secure the new hand note. The 1985 pledge agreement states that it does not have the effect of releasing the original 1984 pledge agreements. The 1985 pledge agreement is signed by Wayne Zaunbrecker, on behalf of himself, Hardy Tractor and three other principals in Hardy Tractor, and by Donald Greene and Burton Hardy. Also, Wayne Zaunbrecker, Donald Greene and Burton Hardy signed a continuing guaranty for the Hardy Tractor note on September 30, 1985.

Sometime in 1986, Hardy Tractor of Gueydon, Inc. became defunct. Donald Greene, Wayne Zaunbrecker and Burton Hardy agreed to divide and personally assume the corporate debts. Donald Greene assumed the debt owed to First National Bank of Abbeville.

In February 1987, First National Bank accepted a new hand note signed by Donald Greene for $108,339.55, for which it renewed the loan for the balance due on the 1985 Hardy Tractor hand note. The new note was payable in eleven monthly installments with a balloon payment due in February 1988. The note stated, "Collateral securing other loans with us may also secure this loan." Also, on February 17, 1987, Burton Hardy and Wayne Zaunbrecker signed a continuing guaranty on the note given by Donald Greene.

Finally, in July 1988, the Bank made the last renewal of the loan on the basis of a note given by Donald Greene for $104,920.92, payable on demand or on January 25, 1989, plus one quarterly interest payment on October 25, 1988. The note states that it is secured by the two 1984 collateral mortgage notes. It is signed by Donald Greene.

Donald Greene became delinquent in payment of the 1988 hand note. The Bank placed him in default and sent a notice of the default to LeBlanc and Dietz, as required by the collateral mortgage. On June 22, 1989, the Bank filed this suit against Donald Greene, Delores Hair (Dietz) and Ruby Linscomb (LeBlanc) for the balance due on the 1988 hand note plus accrued interest ($112,301.83), plus interest until paid, attorney fees and costs, and for recognition of the two 1984 collateral mortgages.

TRIAL COURT ACTION

[**After losing on an exception of no cause of action,...**] Dietz and LeBlanc then answered with a general denial.

At trial, the Bank introduced evidence of the debt, the in rem collateral mortgages, and the pledges. The loan officer who handled the loan, Steve Griffin, testified that Donald Greene personally took over Hardy Tractor's debt after Hardy Tractor went out of business. Donald Greene testified that neither he nor Hardy Tractor ever released the collateral mortgages on the property which secured the debt.

Dietz, LeBlanc, and their attorney failed to appear at trial, due to having overlooked the notice of the trial date which was sent to them.

The trial judge held in favor of the Bank, granting a judgment against Greene for $113,759.29 and recognizing the collateral mortgages and the in rem collateral mortgage notes pledged to the Bank.

[....]

ASSIGNMENTS OF ERROR

On appeal, Dietz and LeBlanc [...] argue[, **among other things**,] that the hand note issued to Hardy Tractor was extinguished by novation. Therefore, the new hand note to Donald Greene was not secured by the pledge securing the Hardy Tractor note.

[....]

Novation

Appellants argue that the hand notes executed by Hardy Tractor were novated, thereby extinguishing the ancillary obligation of pledge with the discharge of the principal obligation. This argument is founded on the contention that the collateral mortgage notes were only pledged as security for the original $120,000 loan to Hardy Tractor.

Appellants further argue that the hand notes executed by Hardy Tractor were novated either by the creation of a new debt and coincidental payment of the original debt, through the 1987 hand note executed by Donald Greene or by the substitution of Donald Greene as the debtor on the hand note after Hardy Tractor had become defunct.

The principles of novation are well settled and understood. The Louisiana Supreme Court has set forth an excellent discussion of these principles in *Scott v. Bank of Coushatta*, 512 So.2d 356 (La.1987). As provided in LSA-C.C. art. 1882, novation takes place when a new obligor is substituted for a prior obligor who is discharged by the obligee. The facts and circumstances of a given case must clearly evidence an intent by the creditor to release the prior debtor. See the 1984 Revision Comments under LSA-C.C. art. 1882 and the discussion in *Scott*.

In the case before us, we find no evidence that the parties to the loan contract intended to extinguish existing debt and substitute a new one in its place. The Bank permitted one of the guarantors of Hardy Tractor's debt to assume responsibility for its continued payment. No new obligation was created by accepting payment from one of Hardy Tractor's guarantors. The Bank merely renewed Hardy Tractor's loan as it had done annually since the loan was originated. It is not reasonable to believe the Bank intended to substitute an unsecured debt for one secured by collateral mortgage notes and personal guarantees. Therefore, the debt was not novated by payment.

Moreover, we do not find that the Bank intended to release Hardy Tractor when it accepted payment by Donald Greene and renewed the loan in his name. Such an intention was never discussed by the parties to the loan, nor was it expressed by the Bank. Since Donald Greene was one of the guarantors of the Hardy Tractor loan, we cannot justifiably assume that the Bank intended to release Hardy Tractor from liability when it accepted payments by Donald Greene.

Therefore, we hold that the hand notes executed by Hardy Tractor were not novated.

[....]

CONCLUSION

Therefore, we hold that the trial judge did not err in rendering a judgment in favor of the Bank, recognizing the collateral mortgage notes secured by the collateral mortgages on the property of Dietz and LeBlanc.

[....]

Questions

Note: Before focusing on novation, it is essential, once again, to ascertain the number, the sources and the kinds of relationships created in this case.

1. Consider the "FACTS": Assuming obligations have been created, identify the legal component parts of these obligations. For example, is an obligation personal or real? Is one obligation a principal obligation and another a secondary obligation? How are the parties bound if they are obligors? How are they bound if they are obligees? What are the sources of these obligations: the law or a contract or more than one contract? Is the contract or are the contracts nominate contracts?

2. Lines 91 *et seq.*: How would you phrase the novation issue? Would you phrase it in terms of subjective novation? If so, what are the requirements for such a subjective novation to take place? Isn't a note a thing? Could the novation, if there is one, be an objective novation (*see* lines 100–103)? On what particular requirement of a novation is the Court focusing?

3. Lines 110 *et seq.*: In the sentence starting with "In the case before us ..." and ending with "... in its place", is the Court listing the requirements for a type of novation? Which are these requirements and to what type of novation is the Court referring? On line 114, the Court uses the verb" renewed": is there any difference, in terms of effects, between a renewal and a novation? What weight would you give to the fact that the loan had been renewed annually since it originated? If you had to take the side of Rubly H. LeBlanc and Delores H.Dietz who signed the collateral mortgage notes, could you make an argument (strong?) on the basis of Louisiana Civil Code article 1884?

Comparative Law Perspective

Robert J. Pothier, A Treatise on the Law of Obligations or Contracts
vol. 1, nᵒˢ 546–565, at 380–94 (William David Evans trans., 1806)

Of the Nature of a Novation and its Several Kinds

[546] A Novation is a substitution of a new debt for an old. The old debt is extinguished, for which reason, a novation is included amongst the different modes, in which obligations are extinguished.

[547] A novation may be made in three different ways, which form three different kinds of novations. The first takes place, without the intervention of any new person, where a debtor contracts a new engagement with his creditor, in consideration of being liberated from the former. This kind has no appropriate name, and is called a novation generally.

[548] The second is that which takes place by the intervention of a new debtor, where another person becomes a debtor in my stead, and is accepted by the creditor, who thereupon discharges me from it. The person thus rendering himself debtor for another, who is in consequence discharged, is called expromissor; and this kind of novation is called *expromissio.*

The expromissor differs entirely from a surety, who is sometimes called in law, *adpromissor.* For a person by becoming a surety does not discharge, but accede to, the obligation of his principal, and becomes jointly indebted with him.

[549] The third kind of novation takes place by the intervention of a new creditor, where a debtor, for the purpose of being discharged from his original creditor, by the order of that creditor, contracts some obligation in favour of a new creditor.

There is a particular kind of novation called delegation, which frequently includes double novation....

[550] It results from the definition which has been given, that there can be no novation without two debts being contracted, one of which is extinguished by the substitution of the other.

It follows that if the debt, of which it is proposed to make a novation by another engagement, is conditional, the novation cannot take effect until the condition is accomplished.

Therefore, if there is a failure in the accomplishment of the condition, there can be no novation, because there is no original debt to which the new one can be substituted.

Also, if the conditional debt, of which it is intended to make a novation by a new engagement, is a specific thing, which has been destroyed or perishes, before the condition is accomplished, there will be no novation even if the condition should exist; for, since the accomplishment of the condition cannot confirm a debt of a thing which has no existence, there is no original debt to which the new one can be substituted....

§ II. *Of the Intention to make a Novation.*

[559] In order to constitute a novation, the consent of the creditor, or of some person having authority from him, or a quality to make a novation for him, is requisite....

The reason of this law is, that a person should not easily be presumed to abandon the rights which belong to him. Therefore, as a novation implies an abandonment by the creditor of the first claim, to which the second is substituted, it ought not to be easily presumed, and the parties ought expressly to state it....

[563] The effect of a novation is, that the former debt is extinguished in the same manner as it would be by a real payment.

Where one of several debtors in solido alone contracts a new engagement with the creditor, as a novation of the former debt, the first debt being extinguished by the novation, in the same manner as it would have been by a real payment, all his co-debtors are equally liberated with himself. And as the extinction of principal obligation induces that of all accessary obligations, the novation of the principal debt extinguishes all accessary obligations, such as those of sureties.

If the creditor wished to preserve the obligations of the other debtors and sureties, it would be necessary for him to make it a condition of the novation, that the co-debtors and sureties should accede to the new debt; in which case, in default of their acceding to it, there would be no novation, and the creditor would preserve his ancient claim....

Of Delegation.

[564] Delegation is a kind of novation, by which the original debtor, in order to be liberated from his creditor, gives him a third person, who becomes obliged in his stead to the creditor, or to the person appointed by him....

It results from this definition, that a delegation is made by the concurrence of three parties, and that there may be a fourth.

There must be a concurrence, 1st, of the party delegating, that is, the ancient debtor who procures another debtor in his stead.

2d, Of the party delegated, who enters into an obligation, in the stead of the ancient debtor, either to the creditor or some other person appointed by him.

3d, Of the creditor, who, in consequence of the obligation contracted by the party delegated, discharges the party delegating.

Sometimes there intervenes a fourth party, *viz.* the person indicated by the creditor, and in whose favour the person delegated becomes obliged, upon the indication of the creditor, and by the order of the person delegating....

[565] A delegation includes a novation, by the extinction of the debt from the person delegating, and the obligation contracted in his stead by the person delegated. Commonly, indeed, there is a double novation; for the party delegated is commonly a debtor of the person delegating, and in order to be liberated from the obligation to him, contracts a new one with his creditor. In this case there is novation both of the obligation of the person delegating, by his giving his creditor a new debtor, and of the person delegated, by the new obligation which he contracts....

Robert Pothier, Traité Des Obligations
n° 594 (1761), in 2 Œuvres de Pothier 65–66 (nouv. ed. 1825).

Unless it appears clearly that the oblgiee has had the intention of making a novation, novation is not presumed.... It is so if, since the debt was contracted, some act has been passed between the obligee and the obligor [i] whereby a term for payment has been granted; or [ii] whereby they have agreed on a new place for the performance; or [iii] whereby the obligor has been accorded the privilege [a] of rendering performance to someone other than the obligee or [b] of giving a thing in lieu of the money that was due [i.e., a *dation en paiement*]; or [iv] even whereby the obligor obligates himself to pay a larger or a smaller sum than that to which the obligee would have wanted to restrain himself. In all these cases, and in others like them, it is necessary to decide, on the basis of our principle-novation is not presumed—, that there has been no novation and that the parties have wanted only to modify, diminish, or augment the debt rather than to extinguish it so as to substitute another for it, if they have not explained themselves.

Section VII — Remission of Debt

Louisiana Sources of Law

Louisiana Civil Code

Art. 1888. Express or tacit remission.

A remission of debt by an obligee extinguishes the obligation. That remission may be express or tacit. (Acts 1984, No. 331, § 1, eff. Jan. 1, 1985.)

Art. 1890. Remission effective when communication is received by the obligor.

A remission of debt is effective when the obligor receives the communication from the obligee. Acceptance of a remission is always presumed unless the obligor rejects the remission within a reasonable time. (Acts 1984, No. 331, § 1, eff. Jan. 1, 1985.)

Art. 1892. Remission granted to sureties.

Remission of debt granted to the principal obligor releases the sureties.

Remission of debt granted to the sureties does not release the principal obligor.

Remission of debt granted to one surety releases the other sureties only to the extent of the contribution the other sureties might have recovered from the surety to whom the remission was granted.

If the obligee grants a remission of debt to a surety in return for an advantage, that advantage will be imputed to the debt, unless the surety and the obligee agree otherwise. (Acts 1984, No. 331, § 1, eff. Jan. 1, 1985.)

Précis: Louisiana Law of Obligations in General §§ 7.4.1 to 7.4.2

A remission of debt can be defined as a bilateral juridical act or contract, gratuitous or onerous, whereby an obligee gives up the right to demand the performance of an obligation owed by his obligor. Civil Code **Article 1888** states that "**A remission of debt by an obligee extinguishes the obligation. That remission may be express or tacit.**" ...

For a remission to be valid two wills must coexist, the obligor in particular must agree to the remission offered to him by his obligee. **LSA-C.C. Art. 1890** states, in part, that "**acceptance of a remission is always presumed, unless the obligor rejects the remission within a reasonable time.**" ...

An obligor who would want to reject a remission of his debt would have to expressly manifest his opposition or rejection. One cannot be forced to accept a "gift," a "gratuity," which is often the case of a remission of debt. In a sense, the obligee "forgives" the debt owed by his obligor. ...

The effectiveness of a remission of debt, its binding effect and its proof are contingent upon the obligor receiving the communication of the obligee's intent. As **LSA-C.C. Art. 1890** states: "**A remission of debt is effective when the obligor receives the communication from the obligee. Acceptance of a remission is always presumed unless the obligor rejects the remission within a reasonable time.**" The selection of the *receipt theory,* as the time of effectiveness of the remission, is quite reasonable since it assumes that the obligor will accept the benefit of the remission of debt. ...

Besides this tacit acceptance by the obligor, the law has provided for instances of presumption of remission of debt. One such example is referred to in **LSA-C.C. Art. 1889** in these terms: "**An obligee's voluntary surrender to the obligor of the instrument evidencing the obligation gives rise to a presumption that the obligee intended to remit the debt.**" ...

Once an obligor has had his obligation remitted, he is discharged of any performance. The extinction of the primary obligation will carry with it the discharge of any accessory obligation by virtue of the principle *accessorium sequitur principale.* ...

When obligors are joint obligors each one owes a share of the whole performance. ...

The remission of debt benefits only the joint obligor who was offered, and who accepted, the discharge granted to him. ...

Departing from the law of solidarity as it existed before 1984, the new Code Articles have opted for a rational principle by providing that "**Remission of debt by the obligee in favor of one obligor, or a transaction or compromise between the obligee and one obligor, benefits the other solidary obligors in the amount of the portion of that obligor.**" (LSA-C.C. Art. 1803-1. ...

In its first paragraph, **Article 1892** states that "**A remission of debt granted to the principal obligor releases the sureties.**" This rule is but an application of the principle that the accessory follows the fate of the principal (*accessorium sequitur principale*).

However, "A remission of debt granted to the sureties does not release the principal obligor." (LSA-C.C. Art. 1892-2)....

The third paragraph of LSA-C.C. Art. 1892 states that "Remission of debt granted to one surety releases the other sureties only to the extent of the contribution the other sureties might have recovered from the surety to whom the remission was granted." ...

Lastly "If the obligee grants a remission of debt to a surety in return for an advantage, that advantage will be imputed to the debt, unless the surety and the obligee agree otherwise." (LSA-C.C. Art. 1892-4)....

Cases

Frank ARENDER, d/b/a Farm Realty Company

v.

Jess Carr GILBERT

Louisiana Court of Appeal
Third Circuit
March 4, 1977
343 So.2d 1146

CULPEPPER, Judge.

This is a suit filed by Frank Arender, a real estate broker, to enforce the bonus clause of a 30-day 'exclusive listing agreement' between him and defendant, Jess Carr Gilbert. The exclusive listing agreement provided that plaintiff would receive a commission of $35,000 plus a bonus of one-half of any amounts received in excess of the price set by Gilbert for the sale of certain woodland and timber on the 'Black Hawk Plantation'. Defendant reconvened against plaintiff seeking return of a $35,000 payment which he made to plaintiff for his services. The basis of the reconventional demand is that plaintiff allegedly breached his fiduciary duty to defendant by representing and having an ownership interest in Three Rivers Farm, Inc., the corporation which purchased the subject property. The trial judge rendered a judgment rejecting the claims of both parties, and both parties appealed.

The litigation arises from a very complex land sale transaction. The trial record and briefs of counsel suggest several issues. The decisive issue, however, is whether the following letter from Arender to Gilbert dated 8/18/1973 constitutes and 'accord and satisfaction' which estops Arender from claiming any futher [sic] compensation under the terms of the July 11, 1973 exclusive listing agreement:

> 'RE: Agreement between you and myself dated 7/11/73 relative to sale of Black Hawk Plantation-land and timber 'Dear Sir: 'I acknowledge my fee to be in the sum of $35,000.00 as a result of the sale to Three Rivers Farm, Inc. dated 8/17/73. 'I hereby accept a note from you in the amount of $35,000.00 to be paid 1/10/1974 (one line of type is marked out at this point) and is full compensation for my services.
>
> /s/ Frank L. Arender'

This letter was introduced into evidence without objection.

The record shows that Gilbert purchased Black Hawk Plantation for approximately $1,200,000 in February of 1973. It consisted of 9,615 acres of woodland and cleared land situated in the southern part of Concordia Parish along the Mississippi River.

On July 11, 1973, Gilbert entered into an 'exclusive listing agreement' with Arender to secure a purchaser for the woodland and timber on Black Hawk Plantation. The agreement specified that 7,532 acres of woodland were to be sold at $140 per acre. The standing timber on Black Hawk Plantation was to be sold for an additional $650,000. The total proposed selling price, therefore, was $1,704,480.

The listing agreement set the credit terms of the sale at '29% Down and the balance in January, 1974.' The agreement provided further that Arender was to receive a commission of $35,000, to be paid in January, 1974. Also, the following bonus clause was contained in the listing agreement: 'In the event the selling price is more than the above figure, Frank (Arender) is to receive one-half of all over this figure.' The agreement was to run 30 days from July 11, 1973.

After securing the exclusive listing, Arender immediately began contacting potential purchasers. One of these, Dale Rogers, was interested in purchasing only a portion of the plantation for use in his farming operation. He was not interested in purchasing the entire tract offered.

Arender also contacted a Lake Providence attorney, Captan Jack Wyly. Wyly, as Rogers, was interested in purchasing only portions of the land offered. Through the efforts of Arender, Wyly and Rogers met and formed a corporation to purchase the subject property. The corporation was formed on July 19, 1973 under the name Three Rivers Farm, Inc. Its president was Dale Rogers. A total of 300 shares of stock were issued on three certificates. 100 shares were issued to Rogers, 100 shares to his wife, and 100 shares to Wyly's secretary, who held the shares for him. Arender owned no stock in the corporation.

A round of negotiations between Wyly, Gilbert, Rogers and Arender followed. Gilbert's attorney, George Griffing, was also involved in these negotiations. Wyly and Rogers trusted Arender, and often Arender acted as 'middle man' between representatives of Three Rivers and Gilbert. Offers and counteroffers were communicated to both parties through Arender. Finally, on July 26, 1973, Three Rivers and Gilbert executed a contract whereby Three Rivers acquired an option to purchase a certain portion of Black Hawk Plantation (about 7,100 acres) for the total sum of $1,798,560. The option price, $50,000, was paid by Three Rivers on July 26, and applied toward the purchase price.

The option agreement stated that the act of sale was to be passed on August 17, 1973, at which time an additional $450,000 was to be paid in cash to Gilbert. The remainder of the purchase price, $1,298,560, was to be represented by a promissory note due on January 5, 1974.

The property described in the option to purchase was not the same property described in the exclusive listing agreement between Gilbert and Arender. During the course of negotiations, Rogers stated that in order to secure financing for the purchase, some cleared land would have to be included in the property sold. In response to Rogers' financing difficulties, Gilbert added about 550 acres of cleared land, but in return, Gilbert retained several hundred additional acres of woodland which he originally intended to sell.

The act of sale was passed on August 17, 1973 substantially in accordance with the terms of the 'Option To Purchase.' The $450,000 cash payment was in the form of a check drawn on the account of J. E. Jones Lumber Company payable to Three Rivers, which was endorsed to Gilbert by Three Rivers. J. E. Jones Lumber Company stopped payment on its check, however, when its attorney discovered a notice of lis pendens affecting the subject property had been filed by Ricks Lumber Company on August 17. In its petition, Ricks alleged that Arender, acting as Gilbert's agent, had promised to sell certain timber located on Black Hawk Plantation to Ricks for a specified price. The Ricks' suit was even-

tually dismissed on an exception of no cause of action, but the stop payment order on the   82
check brought the subject sale transaction to a halt.   83

All of the parties were concerned about the future course of the transaction. On the   84
day after the act of sale was passed, August 18, 1973, Arender, Rogers, Gilbert and his   85
attorney, George Griffing, met at Gilbert's house to determine what course of action   86
they should follow. The initial purpose of the meeting was to determine how the Ricks   87
suit could be dismissed and the notice of lis pendens removed from the record. Other   88
types of negotiations also took place at the meeting, including some negotiations con-   89
cerning Arender's fee. It is the negotiations regarding Arender's fee that we are con-   90
cerned with.   91

Prior to the meeting, Gilbert had become dissatisfied with Arender. Apparently, he   92
thought that Arender was not entitled to his fee. For example, Gilbert testified he consid-   93
ered the listing agreement to be terminated because the land actually sold was not the land   94
described in the listing agreement. The credit terms of the final sale were also different   95
from those specified in the listing agreement. Additionally, Gilbert testified that shortly   96
after the option to purchase was executed, Arender told him that he had an ownership in-   97
terest in Three Rivers. (The evidence shows, however, that Arender had no such interest   98
in Three Rivers.) Gilbert testified, and the trial judge concluded, that shortly after the op-   99
tion agreement was executed, Gilbert began negotiating for himself and no longer con-   100
sidered Arender his agent. In summary, Gilbert entered the August 18 negotiations with   101
Arender and others believing that Arender had not fulfilled the terms of the listing agree-   102
ment, had represented Three Rivers to Gilbert's detriment, and was not entitled to his fee.   103

The atmosphere at the August 18 meeting was tense. Gilbert testified, and the trial   104
judge concluded, that Arender demanded payment of his $35,000 commission at this   105
meeting. The listing agreement of July 11, 1973 provided that the commission was not   106
due until January, 1974. Gilbert and his attorney, George Griffing, drafted the letter   107
quoted at the outset of this opinion in response to Arender's demand. By way of review,   108
Arender acknowledged in the letter that his fee for the sale of Three Rivers was $35,000.   109
Arender further stated in the letter that he accepted a note from Gilbert in the amount   110
of $35,000 to be paid 1/10/74, the note being 'full compensation for my services.' The let-   111
ter made specific reference to the exclusive listing agreement of 7/11/73, but did not men-   112
tion the 'one/half over' bonus provision. The question before us is whether this letter   113
constitutes an 'accord and satisfaction', which would bar Arender's claim to any further   114
compensation under the terms of the July 11 exclusive listing agreement.   115

Our courts have adopted the common law doctrine of accord and satisfaction. Each of   116
these three conditions must be present for its application: (1) An unliquidated or dis-   117
puted claim. (2) A tender by the debtor. (3) An acceptance of the tender by the creditor.   118
Young v. White Stores, Inc., 269 So.2d 266 (La.App.3rd Cir. 1972) and cases cited therein.   119
An additional prerequisite to settlement by accord and satisfaction is that the creditor   120
must understand that if the reduced payment is accepted his claim will have been paid in   121
full. Antoine v. Elder Realty Company, 255 So.2d 625 (La.App.3rd Cir. 1971). If the ten-   122
der itself clearly sets forth that the lesser sum is offered in full payment of the disputed or   123
unliquidated debt, however, acceptance of the tender constitutes acceptance of the debtor's   124
offer. Charles X. Miller, Inc. v. Oak Builders, Inc., 306 So.2d 449 (La.App.4th Cir. 1975).   125

The August 18 letter executed by Arender, accompanied by Arender's acceptance of   126
the tendered note for $35,000, constitutes an accord and satisfaction. The requirements   127
of tender of payment by the debtor and acceptance by the creditor are obviously satisfied.   128
The further requirement that the debt be unliquidated or disputed is also satisfied.   129

130 The debt was, in fact, unliquidated and disputed. Though there is some question as
131 to whether Gilbert informed Arender of all of the reasons that he felt would prevent Aren-
132 der from receiving the full amount of the fee contemplated by the listing agreement, there
133 is no doubt that the fee was disputed.

134 The fee was the subject of negotiations between Gilbert and Arender at the August 18
135 meeting. It was Arender who first brought up the subject by demanding payment of the
136 $35,000 commission at the meeting. By the terms of the exclusive listing agreement, the
137 commission payment was not due until January, 1974. Apparently, Arender opted to take
138 a $35,000 note as full compensation for his services rather than risking both his com-
139 mission and his 'one-half over' on successful resolution of the transaction in accordance
140 with the terms of the original listing agreement. In other words, Arender bargained away
141 his chances to collect a commission plus a bonus by accepting a $35,000 note tendered
142 as full compensation before any compensation was due under the terms of the listing
143 agreement. The note was paid at maturity.

144 The present case is not one of those where the debtor scrawls 'in full settlement' or
145 other similar words on his check and sends it off to the distant creditor, hoping that the
146 creditor will unwittingly cash it and effect an accord and satisfaction. Arender and Gilbert
147 were literally negotiating at arms' length when the tender was made. The tender was ap-
148 parently the subject of some discussion between the two. The bargaining process was op-
149 erative. Its end product was the accord and satisfaction agreement.

150 Arender argues that no dispute as to the amount of money owed to him existed when
151 Gilbert tendered the $35,000 note as full compensation for his services. The record supports
152 this argument to the extent that there was no discussion as to the 'one-half over' provision
153 of the contract at the August 18 meeting. There was, however, a dispute as to whether any
154 portion of Arender's fee, either the commission or the one-half over bonus, was due.

155 Even if we assume that Arender was not aware of any dispute concerning the amount
156 of his fee before August 18, he would have been put on notice that such a dispute existed
157 by the very terms of the letter which he signed on that day. The letter made specific ref-
158 erence to the exclusive listing agreement of July 11, 1973. In unambiguous terms, Aren-
159 der acknowledged in the letter that his Fee as a result of the sale to Three Rivers Farm, Inc.
160 was $35,000. It is significant that he acknowledged his Fee to be in the amount of $35,000
161 rather than acknowledging his Commission to be in that amount. The term 'fee' is much
162 broader than the term 'commission'. 'Fee' can reasonably be deemed to include all of the
163 compensation to be earned by Arender as a result of the sale, including the 'one-half over'
164 bonus stipulated in the listing agreement. The broad scope of the letter and its intended
165 effect become even clearer when the second paragraph of the letter is considered along with
166 the first paragraph. In the second paragraph, Arender acknowledges acceptance of the
167 note as 'full compensation' for his services.

168 Though the letter does not mention the 'one-half over' provision, its intent could hardly
169 be more clearly expressed. The letter was intended as an 'accord and satisfaction' to bar any
170 future claim for compensation based upon the terms of the July 11 exclusive listing agreement.

171 In the Charles X. Miller case, supra, the court quoted from 1 C.J.S. Accord and Satis-
172 faction s 6, P. 479, to explain that an accord and satisfaction could be effected even though
173 the creditor may have acted under a misapprehension as to the legal effect of his accep-
174 tance or may not have understood or believed that it would have the effect of accord and
175 satisfaction, provided that the creditor acted knowingly or with knowledge of all the per-
176 tinent facts. Arender was intimately involved in all aspects of the transaction and had
177 knowledge of all of the pertinent facts. Furthermore, any fact or opinion unknown to

him could have been easily ascertained by simply asking one of the parties present at the August 18 meeting.

The question of whether a debt is 'disputed' is a factual one which must be decided on a case by case basis by reference to the record as a whole. In the present case, we determine a dispute existed. Under a similar factual situation in Hancock v. Lincoln American Life Insurance Company, 278 So.2d 561 (La.App.1st Cir. 1973), the court determined that no dispute existed and held the doctrine of accord and satisfaction was inapplicable. In Hancock, the court quoted at length from the decision of our Supreme Court in Pontchartrain Park Homes v. Sewerage & Water Board, 246 La. 893, 168 So.2d 595. A portion of the quotation from Pontchartrain Park dealing with the requirement of a 'dispute' for accord and satisfaction follows: 'Unquestionably the creditor must have knowledge, actual or imputed, of the existence of a dispute regarding the amount due. It is not necessary, however, that there be haggling over a fixed contract price to either constitute a dispute or impute knowledge thereof to the creditor. It suffices that actual knowledge be shown *or circumstances demonstrated from which knowledge may reasonably be inferred.*' (Emphasis added) 278 So.2d 561 at 564[.]

In the present case, it was Arender who provoked the dispute concerning his fee by demanding its payment four months before it would have been due. There was no haggling over the exact amount due, but Arender had knowledge of the facts upon which Gilbert based his contention that Arender was not entitled to a fee. Furthermore, the contents of the letter signed by Arender on August 18 charged him with imputed knowledge that some dispute concerning the amount of his fee existed. The answers to any questions he may have had were within his grasp. He failed, either intentionally or unintentionally, to avail himself of these answers.

'Accord and satisfaction' is an affirmative defense which must be pleaded in the answer. LSA-C.C.P. Art. 1005 and Official Comment E to that article. Defendant pleaded facts constituting the basis for the defense of accord and satisfaction in paragraphs 4 and 15 of his answer, though he did not label the defense 'accord and satisfaction.' Furthermore, the letter which affected the accord and satisfaction was introduced into evidence without objection, thereby enlarging the pleadings to include the defense. LSA-C.C.P. Art. 1154; Conques v. Hardy, 337 So.2d 627 (La.App.3rd Cir. 1976); Edwards v. Edwards, 282 So.2d 858 (La.App.1st Cir. 1973), writ refused, 284 So.2d 777 (La.1973). Therefore, Arender's assertion that Gilbert cannot urge the affirmative defense of accord and satisfaction because he failed to plead it in his answer is without merit.

The same result could be reached through application of the provisions of our Civil Code dealing with voluntary remission of debt. LSA-C.C. Art. 2199, et seq. The application of the principle of remission in cases such as the present one is explained in Obligations, J. Denson Smith, 26 La.L.Rev. 497 and 498. There, Professor Smith explains that under the common law theory, the significance of the 'dispute' requirement for accord and satisfaction lies in the fact that in the absence of a dispute, the receipt by the creditor of less than the amount due will not serve as consideration to discharge the remainder. In our civilian system, however, although a disputed claim may be compromised by way of settlement, an undisputed claim may also be discharged in whole or in part by voluntary remission. No consideration is required and the absence of a dispute is wholly unimportant. All that is required under the remission articles is a finding that the creditor intended to remit his claim or that he estopped himself to claim the contrary.

In the present case, the letter of August 18 shows a clear and convincing intent to effect a voluntary intentional remission of any part of the debt (broker's fee) beyond the acknowledged total fee of $35,000.

226 Having disposed of Arender's claim, we move now to Gilbert's reconventional demand
227 for return of the $35,000 fee paid to Arender pursuant to the terms of the August 18 ac-
228 cord and satisfaction agreement. The alleged grounds for the reconventional demand are
229 that (1) Arender breached his fiduciary duty to Gilbert by representing Three Rivers in
230 negotiation preceding the July 26 'Option To Purchase', and (2) Arender allegedly ac-
231 quired an ownership interest in Three Rivers prior to execution of the option to purchase.
232 The evidence in the record supports neither of these assertions. To the contrary, the ev-
233 idence shows that Arender had no ownership interest in Three Rivers and received no
234 compensation from them.

235 The most conclusive answer to Gilbert's reconventional demand is that he is also barred
236 by the accord and satisfaction between the parties stated in the August 18, 1973 letter
237 quoted above.

238 We conclude there is no merit to Gilbert's reconventional demand for return of the $35,000
239 fee which he paid to Arender.

[....]

Questions

1. The *Arender* court, without explanation, notes that the Louisiana courts had long
    ago "adopted the common law doctrine of accord and satisfaction". *See* line 116. By
    what authority did they do so? Regardless whether what the courts did was autho-
    rized, was it needed? Did the civil law of Louisiana not already possess an analo-
    gous institution, one through which interested parties could have obtained the same
    effects as those that arise from accord and satisfaction? *See* La. Civ. Code art. 3071
    et seq.

2. Since *Arender* was decided, Louisiana's "law" of accord and satisfaction has been cod-
    ified. *See* Civ. Code art. 3079. Would the "accord and satisfaction" issue presented in
    Arender be decided any differently under the codified law?

3. The *Arender* court states that "[n]o consideration is required" for a valid remission
    of debt. *Arender* was decided under the old law of remission. Is the *Arender* court's
    statement consistent with the new law? *See* La. Civ. Code art. 1888. If consideration
    is not required for a valid remission, then what kind of juridical act is a remission?
    Hint: *see* La. Civ. Code arts. 1909 & 1910; then *see* La. Civ. Code art. 1888.

1 ## Alvin J. ARLEDGE as Administrator of the Succession of
2 ## Joseph Alton Arledge
3 ### v.
4 ## Arlen C. BELL
5 Louisiana Court of Appeal
6 Second Circuit
7 Jan. 23, 1985
8 463 So.2d 856

9 SEXTON, Judge.

10 Arlen C. Bell appeals a declaratory judgment finding that he is indebted to the succession
11 of Joseph Alton Arledge in the amount of $9,000, representing the unpaid balance of a
12 loan from decedent to defendant. We reverse and remand for a new trial.

Decedent, Joseph Alton Arledge, was a single man with no children who died intestate on November 17, 1982. One sister, Willie Travis Arledge Bell, predeceased Joseph. He was survived by one brother, Alvin Julius Arledge, the duly qualified administrator of this succession. Defendant herein is one of the three children born to Willie Bell and is therefore a nephew to the decedent.

The administrator of the succession brought suit for declaratory judgment separately against defendant, and his sister Charlotte Bell, seeking declarations of the amounts of their respective indebtedness to the succession. Arlen Bell's answer alleged that the transaction was a gift and, in the alternative, that if the initial transaction was characterized as a loan, the debt was extinguished by remission in a long distance telephone call between Arlen C. Bell and the decedent. In interrogatories which were admitted into evidence, appellant conceded that the money was originally advanced from his uncle as a loan. The cases were consolidated for trial. Judgment was rendered in favor of the succession and against both defendants. Only Arlen C. Bell has appealed.

At trial Arlen Bell testified that in 1980 he borrowed $10,000 from his uncle in order to place a down payment on a home for his family. He subsequently paid ten installments of $100 each on the loan, reducing the unpaid balance to $9,000.

On appeal, defendant urges the applicability of LSA-C.C. Art. 1888, et seq.,* claiming that the debt had been remitted by his uncle.

All that is required under the remission articles is a determination that the creditor intended to remit his claim or that he has estopped himself to claim the contrary. *Cowley Corporation v. Shreveport Packing Co.*, 440 So.2d 1345 (La.App. 2d Cir.1983), writ denied, 444 So.2d 122 (La.1984). While the remission of a debt cannot be revoked by a creditor, remission is never presumed unless it clearly appears that the creditor intended it. The burden of proving remission, express or tacit, rests with those claiming the benefit. *Cowley, supra; Succession of Martin,* 335 So.2d 494 (La.App. 2d Cir.1976), writ denied, 337 So.2d 516 (La.1976). No particular form for remission is necessary and the remission may either occur by oral declaration or in writing. *Gulf States Finance Corporation v. Moses,* 56 So.2d 221 (La.App. 2d Cir.1951).

At trial, defendant's attorney attempted to elicit testimony concerning the substance of the long distance telephone conversation. Counsel for the succession objected on hearsay and relevancy grounds. The objection was sustained, and the evidence was admitted by proffer. Appellant contends that the trial court erred in refusing to admit and consider this evidence.

In regard to his relevancy argument, appellee contends that LSA-C.C. Art. 1536 precludes the admission of this evidence. Appellee claims that the alleged conversation relative to forgiveness of Arlen Bell's debt constituted a gift of a credit, an incorporeal thing. Thus, he asserts that LSA-C.C. Art. 1536, which stipulates formal requirements for the donation of incorporeal movables, is controlling, thus rendering appellant's evidence irrelevant.

Our initial inquiry, then, must be directed to the character of the transaction here involved to determine whether the formal requirements of Article 1536 are pertinent. It is clear from the testimony and answers to interrogatories of the defendant Arlen C. Bell that this transaction was originally intended to be a loan and not a donation. Therefore, if the deceased acted as the defendant asserts, that action forgave an existing obligation.

While the forgiveness of a debt may in some respects appear to be a donation because of the gratuitous intent manifested by the act of forgiveness, in specific terms it is the remission of a previous obligation. It therefore must be considered within the context of our law on remission.

As Professor Levasseur explains:

When remitting a debt, the creditor is usually motivated by a gratuitous intent (animus donandi). Such a gratuitous juridical act is tantamount to a donation and should, therefore, be subjected to the conditions of substance applicable to liberalities (collation, reduction, revocation …). However, the conditions of form pertaining to donations are not applicable (LCC 1536 et seq).

A. Levasseur, *Précis in Conventional Obligations: A Civil Code Analysis*, at 84 (1980). Accord, S. Litvinoff, 6 *Louisiana Civil Law Treatise: Obligations*, § 371 (1969). See also *Hicks v. Hicks*, 145 La. 465, 82 So. 415 (1919).

The redactors comment (b) to the new Article 1888 is succinctly in accord with Professor Levasseur: (b) Although *remission* is an act gratuitous in principle, it *is considered a sort of indirect liberality not subject to the requirements of form prescribed for donations.* See 4 Aubry et Rau, Cours de droit civil francais-Obligations 223 (Louisiana State Law Institute trans. 1965); 2 Colin et Capitant, Cours elementaire de droit civil francais 403 (10th ed. 1953); 7 Planiol et Ripert, Traité pratique de droit civil français 716 (2nd ed. 1954); 1 Litvinoff, Obligations 627–628 (1969). See also *Hicks v. Hicks,* 145 La. 465, 82 So. 415 (1919); *Reinecke v. Pelham,* 199 So. 521 (La.App.Orl.1941). [Emphasis ours]

Therefore, while a remission may involve a donative intent on the part of the creditor, the authentic form requirements of LSA-C.C. Art. 1536 do not apply. A remission may be perfected by an oral agreement and appellant's evidence which sought to establish an oral remission was relevant.

[….]

Question

1. As the *Arledge* case correctly notes, a remission, though it is a donation, nevertheless is excepted from the ordinary "form" requirements for donations. But why should that be so? Does Louisiana Civil Code article 1888 help? Can you think of any other kinds of "indirect liberalities" that may be excepted from the donative form requirements? *See* La. Civ. Code arts. 1243 & 1248.

Comparative Law Perspective

Remission of Debt/Renunciation of Solidarity

Passive Solidary: Distribution of Loss Caused by Post-Release[1] Insolvency

Victor Marcadé, EXPLICATION THÉORIQUE ET PRATIQUE DU CODE CIVIL
vol. 4, n° 802, at 642 (7th ed. 1873)

When the obligee … declares that he is remitting the debt of a co-obligor only *for his part* or *while conserving his rights against the other obligors*, he always has an action against

---

1. There are two distinct kinds of "release" with which we are concerned here: (i) a remission *of the debt* and (ii) a renunciation of solidarity, formerly called "discharge from solidarity" or, even more confusingly, "remission *of solidarity*." The distinction turns on the *intent of the parties to the release,* in particular, on precisely *from what* the obligee intends to release the obligor. If the obligee intends to release the obligor from any further liability whatsoever, so that the obligee could not thereafter demand anything else from that obligor, then the release is a "remission of debt." If the obligee intends to release the obligor only from solidarity, in other words, to relieve him of the unique burdens associated with being a *solidary* obligor, thereby transforming him into an "ordinary" obligor (that is,

the others, but only with a deduction for the part of the first. If, for example, the debt was 12,000 francs, with four solidary obligors, the credit, after a remission had been given to one of them, would thereafter be only 9,000 francs and there would thereafter be solidary among the other three only for these 9,000 francs. And if one of these three became insolvent, the portion that the discharged co-obligor would have had to bear of this insolvency would find itself, too, as a necessary consequence, lost for the obligee, and it could not be recovered from the other two. It is obvious, then, that a remission made to one of the co-obligors can never aggravate the position of the others.

But if the obligee had declared that he was remitting not the *debt* (whether absolutely and without restriction or only for the part of one obligor), but simply *solidarity* [i.e., if the obligee had merely "renounced" solidarity], he would then conserve his action for the totality of the 12,000 francs against each of the three others and for 3,000 francs against him as to whom solidarity had been remitted [i.e., renounced] [La. Civ. Code art. 1806].

Jacques Mestre & Marie-Ève Tian, *Solidarité Passive*

nn° 126–127, at 28 (1995), *in Contrats et Obligations: Obligations Conjointes et Solidaires: Solidarité* fasc. 2, Art. 1197 à 1216, fasc. 20, Juris-Classeur Civil (1998)

126.—Solidarity continues to weigh on the other co-obligors for the ensemble of the debt, with a deduction made for the contributive part of the beneficiary of the remission [renunciation] of solidarity. The contribution of each to the debt will be fixed according to the principles exposed ... [above] and the following. Suppose, for example, a debt of 60,000 francs that must be repaid in parts that are equal among four obligors A, B, C, and D. If A ... benefits from a remission [renunciation] of solidarity, each of the three others is exposed to paying 60,000 − 15,000 = 45,000. But he who pays that sum can exercise an action in contribution against the two others, for 15,000 from each of them.

127.—The exercise of the contribution action can become complicated by the insolvency of one of the co-obligors. This hypothetical case is provided for in article 1215 of the Civil Code [La. Civ. Code art. 1806]....

Taking up again the previous example, one supposed that the ... obligee has granted A an individual remission [renunciation] of solidarity; that the obligor B, having been pursued by the obligee, paid the 45,000 francs that constituted the balance of the debt; and that the obligor D finds himself in a state of insolvency. The question is onto whom, at the end of the day, the charge of 15,000 francs that represents the contributive part of the insolvency falls.

... [U]pon remitting [renouncing] the solidarity of one of the obligors, the obligee did not have the intention of assuming the risk of the insolvency of another obligor. He should never bear the consequences of that insolvency.... The result, in the same example, is that the obligor B, having been condemned to pay 45,000, can exercise his contribution action against C not only for 15,000, by also for a third of the contributive part of the insolvency (5,000), that is, for 20,000. An[other] third of the contributive part of the insolvency will be reclaimed from the obligor who was discharged from solidarity.

---

a *joint* obligor), then the release is a "renunciation of solidarity." *See* 1 Saúl Litvinoff, The Law of Obligations §7.83, at 189–90, *in* 5 Louisiana Civil Law Treatise (1992).

It is imperative not to confuse these two types of release. As you will see, in Louisiana and France, each has profoundly different effects from the other.

And the paying obligor B will retain a final charge of 15,000 + 5,000 = 20,000. This interpretation is altogether conformed to the text of article 1215 [La. Civ. Code art. 1806].

Section VIII — Of Compensation

Louisiana Sources of Law

Louisiana Civil Code

Art. 1893. Compensation extinguishes obligations.

Compensation takes place by operation of law when two persons owe to each other sums of money or quantities of fungible things identical in kind, and these sums or quantities are liquidated and presently due.

In such a case, compensation extinguishes both obligations to the extent of the lesser amount.

Delays of grace do not prevent compensation. (Acts 1984, No. 331, § 1, eff. Jan. 1, 1985.)

Art. 1897. Compensation extinguishes obligation of surety.

Compensation between obligee and principal obligor extinguishes the obligation of a surety.

Compensation between obligee and surety does not extinguish the obligation of the principal obligor. (Acts 1984, No. 331, § 1, eff. Jan. 1, 1985.)

Art. 1898. Compensation between obligee and solidary obligor.

Compensation between the obligee and one solidary obligor extinguishes the obligation of the other solidary obligors only for the portion of that obligor.

Compensation between one solidary obligee and the obligor extinguishes the obligation only for the portion of that obligee.

The compensation provided in this Article does not operate in favor of a liability insurer. (Acts 1984, No. 331, § 1, eff. Jan. 1, 1985.)

Art. 1899. Rights acquired by third parties.

Compensation can neither take place nor may it be renounced to the prejudice of rights previously acquired by third parties. (Acts 1984, No. 331, § 1, eff. Jan. 1, 1985.)

Art. 1901. Compensation by agreement.

Compensation of obligations may take place also by agreement of the parties even though the requirements for compensation by operation of law are not met. (Acts 1984, No. 331, § 1, eff. Jan. 1, 1985.)

Art. 1902. Compensation by judicial declaration.

Although the obligation claimed in compensation is unliquidated, the court can declare compensation as to that part of the obligation that is susceptible of prompt and easy liquidation. (Acts 1984, No. 331, § 1, eff. Jan. 1, 1985.)

Précis: Louisiana Law of Obligations in General §§ 7.5.1 to 7.5.3

LSA-C.C. Art. 1893 describes compensation by operation of law in these terms: "Compensation takes place by operation of law when two persons owe to each other sums of money or quantities of fungible things identical in kind, and these sums or quantities are liquidated and presently due.

> In such a case, compensation extinguishes both obligations to the extent of the lesser amount.

> Delays of grace do not prevent compensation."

Compensation by operation of law is circumscribed, however, by a series of four conditions which limit its scope of application....

The first condition is that the two persons must be indebted to each other in the same capacity as principal obligors and entitled to claim a performance from each other in the same capacity as principal obligees. Thus each part must be, at the same time, principal obligor and principal obligee....

Compensation by operation of law may occur only between obligations of sums of money or between obligations bearing on things which are fungible and of the same kind. This form of compensation by operation of law is, therefore, circumscribed to obligations to give things which are fungible ...

A debt is liquidated when it is certain and its amount determined. A debt which is contested, as when it is being litigated, is not liquidated and, in addition, its amount is not fixed or determined.

An obligation is due whenever it is demandable so that the creditor can obtain its immediate performance....

LSA-C.C. Art. 1894-2 lists two important exceptions to the right of compensation by operation of law: "Compensation does not take place, however, if one of the obligations is to return a thing of which the owner has been unjustly dispossessed, or is to return a thing given in deposit or loan for use, ..."

Occurrence by operation of law means simply that, in this case, compensation takes place automatically even unbeknownst to the parties. As soon as the requirements for compensation by operation of law are met, the two obligations involved are extinguished either entirely or *pro tanto;* "Compensation extinguishes both obligations to the extent of the lesser amount." (LSA-C.C. Art. 1893-2)....

There exists this paradox that, although compensation takes place by operation of law, still it must be demanded, claimed or pleaded. Under LSA-C.C. Art. 1900,

> An obligor who has consented to an assignment of the credit by the obligee to a third party may not claim against the latter any compensation that otherwise he could have claimed against the former.

> An obligor who has been given notice of an assignment to which he did not consent may not claim compensation against the assignee for an obligation of the assignor arising after that notice....

Once compensation has occurred as a result of all its conditions being met, the parties, or a party, may renounce it....

LSA-C.C. Art. 1901 lays down a very reasonable rule which is but an illustration of the general principle of freedom of contracts: "Compensation of obligations may take place also by agreement of the parties even though the requirements for compensation by operation of law are not met." ...

The third form of compensation is the judicial compensation.

A court may allow compensation to take place despite the non existence of all the conditions required for compensation by operation of law. **"Although the obligation claimed in compensation is unliquidated, the court can declare compensation as to that part of the obligation that is susceptible of prompt and easy liquidation." (LSA-C.C. Art. 1902)** ...

Cases

In re CANAL BANK & TRUST CO.
Intervention of WAINER

Louisiana Supreme Court
Jan. 2, 1934
152 So. 578

LAND, Justice.

On December 27, 1932, H. Wainer & Co. borrowed from Canal Bank & Trust Company $20,000, for which H. Wainer & Co. gave its promissory note indorsed by H. Wainer, individually, payable ninety days after date.

H. Wainer & Co. is a trade-name under which H. Wainer, individually, is doing business.

The note is made payable at the Canal Bank & Trust Company, New Orleans, La.

There is a provision in the note that: 'At the maturity of this note, or when otherwise due, as above provided, any and all money, stocks, bonds or other securities or property of any nature whatsoever on deposit with, or held by, or in the possession of, said bank as collateral or otherwise, to the credit or for account of the makers, endorsers or other parties hereto, or any of them, shall be and stand applied forthwith to the payment of this note, or any other indebtedness due said bank by said parties hereto, or any of them. * * *'

On March 1, 1933, H. Wainer & Co. had on deposit with the Canal Bank & Trust Company the sum of $18,490.45, and H. Wainer, individually, had on deposit with that bank the sum of $5,551.02.

From March 1, 1933, until March 20, 1933, the Canal Bank & Trust Company remained closed and did no business, except that on Friday March 3, 1933, pursuant to a resolution adopted by the New Orleans Clearing House Association, with the approval of the state banking commissioner and the acting Governor of the state, permitted withdrawals by its depositors not exceeding 5 per cent. of the balance to the credit of the depositors as of March 1, 1933. During this period the Canal Bank & Trust Company remained closed, except as above stated, acting under the orders of the state authorities and the Proclamations of the President of the United States, of date March 6 and March 9, 1933 (see 12 USCA § 95 note), declaring and extending a national banking holiday.

On March 10, 1933, the President by Executive Order (see 12 USCA § 95 note) authorized the Secretary of the Treasury, under such regulations as he may prescribe, to permit any member bank of the Federal Reserve System to perform any and all of its usual banking functions.

The President in this Executive Order further directed that all banks who are members of the Federal Reserve System, desiring to reopen for the performance of all of their usual or normal banking functions, should apply for a license therefor to the Secretary of the Treasury.

The Canal Bank & Trust Company was at that time a member of the Federal Reserve System, and promptly applied for a license to be permitted to reopen for the performance of all its usual and normal banking functions, but was refused a license by the Treasury Department.

On March 18, 1933, the Secretary of the Treasury issued and promulgated a regulation, designated as No. 27, in which he authorized any bank which was a member of the Federal Reserve System, and which was not licensed to reopen for the purpose of its usual banking functions, to permit withdrawals by depositors and payments to creditors of such percentage of amount due to them, not exceeding 5 per cent., as it may determine with the approval of the appropriate state authorities.

Thereafter the Canal Bank & Trust Company, with the approval of the state banking commissioner, permitted withdrawals by depositors not exceeding 5 per cent. of the amount to their credit as of the close of business on March 1, 1933.

Prior to March 27, 1933, H. Wainer & Co. withdrew all of the 5 per cent. balance to its credit as of March 1, 1933, $924.52.

The Canal Bank & Trust Company notified its depositor that it would not permit the withdrawal of the remaining 95 per cent. of its balance, $17,537.85.

On March 27, 1933, the Canal Bank & Trust Company made available and permitted H. Wainer, individually, to withdraw 5 per cent. of the balance to his credit as of March 1, 1933, namely, $277.50. All of this amount the depositor withdrew, except the sum of $57.65.

The remaining 95 per cent. to his credit as of March 1, 1933, $5,273.47, the Canal Bank & Trust Company notified him he could not withdraw.

On the date on which the note of H. Wainer & Co., indorsed by H. Wainer, fell due, March 27, 1933, H. Wainer & Co. sent the Canal Bank & Trust Company two checks, one for the sum of $2,500 and the other for the sum of $17,500, claiming that they were entitled to pay, compensate or offset the note with these checks. The offer of H. Wainer & Co. and H. Wainer was refused, and the checks were subsequently returned to them without prejudice to the rights of either party.

At no time during the period beginning March 2, 1933, and ending May 20, 1933, did the Canal Bank & Trust Company pay out more than 5 per cent. to any depositor of the balance to the credit of such depositor as of March 1, 1933, and did not pay out any gold or gold certificates whatever.

The bank did not lend any money, but did collect on notes and extend notes and did borrow cash on its assets from the Reconstruction Finance Corporation for the purpose of setting up the fund to pay the 5 per cent. due depositors and creditors.

The amount borrowed from the Reconstruction Finance Corporation is as follows:

$1,000,000 on March 3, 1933.

$2,300,000 on March 20, 1933.

$1,100,000 on March 22, 1933.

The Canal Bank & Trust Company was placed in liquidation on May 20, 1933, and it is not now and has not been since May 20, 1933, in a position to pay all creditors and depositors in full in cash, and the amount that will ultimately be paid to creditors and depositors, or the time at which payment or payments will be made, is indefinite and not capable of ascertainment.

The facts above stated are in accordance with the statement of facts agreed upon by counsel, and found at pages 24 to 27, inclusive, in the transcript in this case.

At the date of the maturity of the note, H. Wainer & Co. had a balance in the Canal Bank & Trust Company of $17,537.85, and H. Wainer a balance of $5,331.12, a total balance of $22,868.97, or $2,868.97 over and above the amount due the bank on the note, in which it is expressly stipulated that the deposits of intervener in the bank, at the maturity of the note, 'shall be and stand applied forthwith to the payment of this note.'

The Canal Bank & Trust Company having refused on March 27, 1933, when the note fell due, to accept the check of H. Wainer & Co. for $17,500 and the check of H. Wainer for $2,500 in compensation or offset of the note, the intervener, H. Wainer, filed the present suit against the liquidators of the bank to compel them to deliver to him as paid and canceled the note for $20,000 and also a dividend of $842.70 on the balance of deposit remaining in the bank.

The trial judge held that the Canal Bank & Trust Company was solvent on March 27, 1933; that the note for $20,000 was compensated on that date, when it fell due, by virtue of the waiver provision therein that the deposit should be applied to the discharge and extinguishment of the debt evidenced by the note; and that the proclamations and orders of the President of the United States and the regulations of the Secretary of the Treasury did not affect plaintiff's right to compensate and offset the note with his deposits in the bank.

[....]

From this judgment intervener has appealed.

[....]

3. The general law as to compensation or set-off, as it prevails in this state, is found in the following articles of our Civil Code:

Article 2207. 'When two persons are indebted to each other, there takes place between them a compensation the extinguishes both the debts, in the manner and cases hereafter expressed.'

Article 2208. 'Compensation takes place of course by the mere operation of law, even unknown to the debtors; the two debts are reciprocally extinguished, as soon as they exist simultaneously, to the amount of their respective sums.'

Article 2209. 'Compensation takes place only between two debts, having equally for their object a sum of money, or a certain quantity of consumable things of one and the same kind, and which are equally liquidated and demandable.

'The days of grace are no obstacle to the compensation.'

There can be no doubt that the bank was indebted to intervener in the amount of the deposits, and that intervener was indebted to the bank in the amount of the note.

These debts existed simultaneously on March 27, 1933, when the note fell due, and they were equally liquidated and demandable on that day.

The two debts, therefore, became reciprocally extinguished at that date, 'by the mere-operation of law, even unknown to the dobtors.'

The general American rule is that: 'Where a depositor is indebted to the bank and his indebtedness is due, he may set off his deposit against his indebtedness * * * and this right of set-off exists without any previous demand being made for the deposit.' Ruling Case Law, vol. 3, par. 157, p. 529.

Colin and Capitant, in discussing this subject, say:

'C'est en matière commerciale que la compensation trouve ses plus importantes applications. Cela se comprend sans peine. Il est rare que des rapports réciproques d'obligations se forment entre personnes non commercantes. Au contraire, ces rapports mutuels entre deux négociants, par exemple entre un commercant et son banquier, entre unfabricant et un commissionnaire, sont de tous les jours. Or, le commerce vit surtout de crédit; ilévite le plus possible l'emploi du numéraire, il a besoin de simplifier le plus possible les paiements.

'De là est né l'usage du compte courant dont nous avons déjà parlé et qui est fondé sur le principe de la compensation. Toutes les opérations commerciales qui se font entre les deux parties, viennent se fondre dans le compte courant, et le solde constaté lors la clôture de ce compte fait seul l'objet d'un paiement effectif. * * *'

The translation of the above is as follows: 'It is in commercial matters that compensation finds its most important applications. That is easily understood. It is rare that reciprocal accounts of obligations are formed between persons who are not merchants. On the contrary, these mutual accounts between two merchants, for example, between a merchant and his banker, between a manufacturer and an agent, occur every day. Now, commerce subsists above all on credit; it avoids as much as possible the use of cash, it needs to simplify payments as much as possible.

'From this was born the custom of the account *current*, of which we have already spoken, and which is founded on the principle of compensation. All the commercial operations which occur between the two parties become blended in the account current, and *the established balance* at the time of the closing of this account *alone* is the object of a *real payment.* * * *' (Italics partly ours.) Colin & Capitant, Cours Élémentaire De Droit Civil Francais, Tome II, Septième Édition (1932), pp. 319, 325, n° 336, 346.

No *real* payment being necessary as the basis of the right of intervener to compensate the note with his deposits, the contention of the liquidators of the bank that intervener in this case cannot plead compensation, because he could not draw more than 5 per cent. of his deposits in bank, an amount insufficient to pay the note, is not sound in law.

Compensation, at all events, is but a *fictitious* payment, the balancing of accounts, the extinction of one debt by another, by mere operation of law.

We are not impressed, therefore, with the contention of the liquidators in this case that the universal law of compensation, or set-off, prevailing in the various states of the Union was set aside, either by the prohibition in the President's promulgations against 'paying out' bank deposits after the national banking holiday had been declared, or by the limitation in Regulation No. 27 of the Secretary of the Treasury of payment of 5 per cent. to depositors and creditors.

The reasons for the promulgations of the President and the resolution of the Secretary of the Treasury are made apparent by the following preamble in the promulgation made by the Chief Executive of the Nation, of date March 6, 1933:

'Whereas there have been heavy and unwarranted withdrawals of gold and currency from our Banking institutions for the purpose of hoarding; and

'Whereas continuous and increasingly extensive speculative activity abroad in foreign exchange has resulted in severe drains on the Nation's stocks of Gold; and

'Whereas it is in the best interests of all Bank depositors that a period of respite be provided with a view to preventing further hoarding of coin, bullion or currency or speculation in foreign exchange and permitting the application of appropriate measures to protect the interests of our people.'

It is clear, therefore, that 'the paying out of deposits' prohibited by federal action is leveled solely at the paying out of actual money, and not at such fictitious payments as

176 arise from settlement of accounts between banker and depositor by the universal law of
177 compensation, or set-off, which takes place by mere operation of law, and not by the
178 withdrawal of actual funds from the banks.

179 Neither the proclamations of the President, nor the regulation of the Secretary of
180 the Treasury changed, or could change, the indisputable fact that mutual indebted-
181 ness between the bank and intervener existed simultaneously on March 27, 1933, when
182 the note of intervener fell due, and that this indebtedness on that date was equally liq-
183 uidated and demandable. Necessarily, the law of compensation or set-off applies to
184 the case.

185 4. The Secretary of the Treasury, under the authority conferred upon him by the Presi-
186 dent's proclamations declaring and continuing the national bank holiday, issued on March
187 18, 1933, Regulation No. 27, which provides that 'Any State Banking Institution which is a
188 member of the Federal Reserve System and which is not licensed by the Secretary of the
189 Treasury to reopen for the performance of usual Banking functions may, with the approval
190 of the appropriate State authority having immediate supervision of such Banking institu-
191 tion, permit withdrawals by depositors and make payments to creditors of such percentage
192 of the amounts due to them (not exceeding 5%) as it may determine, provided that at or
193 before the time of such withdrawal or payment it shall set aside and make available for such
194 purpose a fund sufficient to pay all depositors and creditors the percentage so determined.'

195 Intervener contends that, to claim that this order defeated intervener's right to com-
196 pensate his note, by such part of his deposit as was necessary for that purpose, would de-
197 prive him of his private property, his right of compensation under the law, and 'his
198 contract' with the bank to have his deposits applied on the note, in violation of article 5
199 of the Amendments to the Federal Constitution.

200 This contention on the part of the intervener, in our opinion, is without merit for two
201 reasons. In the first place, we are not of the opinion that the regulation of the Secretary
202 of the Treasury has, or was intended to have, such effect, for reasons already assigned.

203 In the second place, the provision in the note applying intervener's deposits on the
204 note is not a contract, but is a mere waiver by the intervener of the obstacle of article
205 2210 of our Civil Code, in providing that compensation does not take place where one
206 of the demands is for the restitution of a deposit.

207 The exception provided by article 2210 of the Civil Code as to irregular deposits is in
208 favor of the depositor and not of the bank.

209 In France, where the Code contains articles similar to ours, it is universally recongized
210 [*sic*] that, where the obstacle preventing compensation is in favor of one of the parties,
211 that similar to ours, it is universally recognized this kind of compensation being desig-
212 nated by the French commentators as 'facultative compensation.'

213 In discussing this subject Planiol says. 'Définition et Utilité-La compensation faculta-
214 tive est celle qui s'opère *par la volonté des parties*, quand l'une d'elles lève un obstacle ré-
215 sultant des dispositions de la loi. Une des conditions manque pour la compensation légale:
216 par exemple, l'une des deux dettes n'est pas liquide, ou bien elle est suspendue par un
217 terme, ou bien encore il s'agit d'une créance née d'un dépôt: si les parties sont d'accord pour
218 accepter en compensation la dette non liquide, ou si celle qui y avait droit renonce au béné-
219 fice du terme, ou enfin si le déposant consent á être réglé par compensation, leur volonté
220 doit être respectée et la compensation s'opérera (Cass. 25 nov. 1891, D. 92, 1 296).'

221 The translation of the above is as follows: 'Facultative Compensation is that which
222 operates by the will of the parties, when one of them removes an obstacle resulting

from the dispositions of the law. One of the conditions is lacking for legal compensa- 223
tion: for example, one of the two debts is not liquidated or perhaps it is suspended by 224
a term, or perhaps it involves a credit arising out of a deposit: if the parties agreed to 225
accept in compensation the non liquidated debt, or if the one who had the right, re- 226
nounces the benefit of the term, or finally, if the depositor agrees to be governed by com- 227
pensation, there will ought to be respected and compensation will operate (Cass. Nov. 228
25, 1891, D. 92. 1 296).' M. Planiol, Droit Civil, vol. 2, Troisième Édition (1905) n. 229
594, pp. 194, 195. 230

5. Article 2215 of our Civil Code also provides that: 'Compensation can not take place 231
to the prejudice of the rights acquired by a third person; therefore, he who, being a debtor, 232
is become creditor since the attachment made by a third person in his hands, can not, in 233
prejudice to the person seizing, oppose compensation.' 234

This article is a literal reproduction of article 1298 of the Code Napoleon, and has no 235
application to the present controversy. 236

It refers to the case where a third person 'acquires' rights to one of the obligations, by 237
attachment, assignment, or in any other legal way, before the other claim comes into ex- 238
istence, or before it has become demandable. See in this connection Colin & Capitant, Cours 239
Élémentaire De Droit Civil Français, Tome II Septième Édition (1932) p. 325, n. 346. 240

[....]

Questions

1. In order for a debt to be compensable, it must be "presently due". *See* La. Civ. Code
    art. 1893. After the Secretary of the Treasury, implementing the President's Execu-
    tive Order, effectively prohibited Canal Bank from paying out any more than 5% of
    what it owed to Wainer, was Canal Bank's obligation to refund Wainer's deposit truly
    "due"? What does it mean for a debt to be "due"? Is "due" something different from
    "payable"?

2. At the time at which Canal Bank was decided, there was no legislation in place in
    Louisiana that in so many words recognized the French doctrinal principle of "fac-
    ultative compensation". Is that true under the Revision? *See* La. Civ. Code art. 1901;
    see also La. Civ. Code art. 1894.

FIRST NATIONAL BANK OF COMMERCE   1

v.   2

Arthur DUFRENE[1] and Kim Dufrene d/b/a Dufrene Super Market   3

Louisiana Court of Appeal   4
First Circuit   5
April 19, 1988   6
525 So.2d 298   7

CARTER, Judge.   8

This is an appeal from the judgment of the trial court in favor of First National 9
Bank of Commerce (Bank) and against defendant Kim Dufrene d/b/a Dufrene Super 10

---

1. On October 13, 1986, Arthur Dufrene was dismissed as a party defendant pursuant to a motion to dismiss.

Market (Dufrene) awarding the Bank $3,100.00 and denying set-off and/or compensation.

FACTS

The Louisiana Grocers' Co-Operative, Inc. (Co-op) was a cooperative of grocery stores organized as a Louisiana corporation. Its purpose was to purchase items in volume for resale to its various members. There were two primary sources of financing, i.e., "members' buying deposit" and loans by the Bank. The Co-op owed the Bank several million dollars in loans, which were secured by an assignment of accounts receivable and a mortgage affecting the inventory of the Co-op. The Co-op subsequently filed for relief under Chapter 11 of the United States Bankruptcy Code, and the United States Bankruptcy Court authorized the Bank to collect the accounts receivable due the Co-op.

Defendant was a member-stockholder in the Co-op and had a balance in the "members' buying deposit," as defined by the bylaws, in the amount of $9,954.00. Dufrene was also indebted to the Co-op for $3,100.00 in receivables. Dufrene did not give notice of withdrawal from membership in the Co-op, in accordance with the bylaws, until after his receipt of the notification of the assignment of his account to the Bank by the Co-op.

Thereafter, the Bank filed suit against Dufrene for the $6,387.63 in receivables owed to the Co-op. After trial, the trial judge rendered judgment in favor of the Bank and against Dufrene for $3,100.00, but denied the Bank's claim for attorney's fees. From this adverse judgment, Dufrene appeals.

ISSUE

The primary issue raised is whether Dufrene is entitled to the legal defense of compensation or set-off. Dufrene reasons that any indebtedness to the Co-op should be set-off against the funds in Dufrene's "members' buying deposit," which was stipulated to have been $9,954.00 as of the date Dufrene received notice of the assignment of accounts receivable from the Bank.

DISCUSSION

The trial court found as follows, and we agree that:

This matter involves the claim of First National Bank of Commerce to collect the indebtedness of Kim Dufrene, doing business as Dufrene's Supermarket, due to Louisiana Grocers Cooperative, Incorporated. The facts have been stipulated to and filed as a joint exhibit by both the plaintiff and defendant. No witnesses were presented to the Court due to the stipulations. The Court has considered the arguments of counsel and the brief submitted by plaintiff's attorney. The Court notes for the record that defendant's attorney did not submit a pre-trial memorandum as ordered by the Court.

The parties argue Article 1893 of the Civil Code which states in pertinent part that compensation takes place by operation of law when two persons owe to each other sums of money or quantities of fungible things identical in kind, and these sums or quantities are liquidated and presently due. The key language in that Article seems to be "liquidated and presently due."

In this case there's no question that Mr. Kim Dufrene was a member of Louisiana Grocer's Cooperative, Incorporated and that he had established a buying deposit account with the corporation which amounted to $9,954. The Court does not feel that that account is a "liquidated and presently due" account since the bylaws set forth certain prerequisites before a member can withdraw that money. Furthermore, Article 1894 of the Civil

Code states in pertinent part that compensation does not take place, however, if one of the obligations is to return a thing given in deposit or loan for use.

In this case there seems to be no question in this Court's mind that the members' buying deposit is exactly what it says it is and that's a deposit, or, as counsel for the defendant argues, a loan for use. In either case, it's covered by Article 1894 of the Civil Code (it seems to this Court) and therefore, compensation does not take place by operation of law.

In light of this Court's oral reasons and the reasons set forth in the plaintiff's pre-trial memoranda, the Court will render a judgment in this matter in favor of First National Bank of Commerce against Kim Dufrene, doing business as Dufrene's Supermarket, in the sum of $3,100. [....]

From the above, it is clear that the financial purpose of the "members' buying deposit" was to provide operating capital for the Co-op and not to pay receivables due the Co-op from its members. The "members' buying deposit" represented part of the "members' equity" in the corporation (along with Class A and Class B stock, patronage dividends, and retained earnings) rather than a current liability or a short term debt. Since the "members' buying deposit" was an equity of the Co-op and not a current liability of the corporation, compensation and/or set-off are not available to Dufrene.

We further note that the burden of proof is upon Dufrene to establish by a preponderance of the evidence his right to set-off or compensation. *See Coburn v. Commercial National Bank*, 453 So.2d 597 (La.App. 2nd Cir.1984), *writ denied*, 457 So.2d 681 (La.1984).

LSA-C.C. art. 1893 provides as follows:[2]

Compensation takes place by operation of law when two persons owe to each other sums of money or quantities of fungible things identical in kind, and these sums or quantities are liquidated and presently due.

In such a case, compensation extinguishes both obligations to the extent of the lesser amount.

Delays of grace do not prevent compensation.

In the instant case, at the time of the notice, the "members' buying deposit" did not constitute an equally demandable debt of the Co-op, and compensation was not available. *See Beninate v. Licata*, 473 So.2d 94 (La.App. 5th Cir.1985), *writ denied*, 477 So.2d 1124 (La.1985). Dufrene had not withdrawn from the Co-op at the time of his receipt of notice of the assignment to the Bank. According to Article 4.4.2 of the bylaws, Dufrene was not entitled to receive any funds from the "members' buying deposit" until he withdrew from the Co-op. Therefore, the debt was not liquidated and presently due at the time of the assignment.

Therefore, compensation and/or set-off were not available to Dufrene for three reasons: the "members' buying deposit" was not liquidated and presently due since the bylaws provided certain prerequisites before a member could withdraw the money; secondly, the "members' buying deposit" represented an equity contribution of the respective mem-

---

2. *See also* LSA-C.C. art. 1900 which deals with an assignment of an obligation and provides that an "obligor who has been given notice of an assignment to which he did not consent may not claim compensation against the assignee for an obligation of the assignor arising after that notice."

bers of the Co-op; and compensation is precluded under LSA-C.C. art. 1894[3] in that the "members' buying deposit" was a deposit or loan for use.

[....]

Questions

1. The *First National Bank* court concludes that the Co-op's obligation to pay out Dufrene's deposit was not "due" because, under the terms of the agreement between the Co-op and Dufrene, he was not yet entitled to "withdraw" any of the deposited funds. And yet the Canal Bank court concluded that, notwithstanding that Wainer, thanks to the federal Treasury Department's order, he was not entitled to "withdraw" but 5% of his deposited funds, Canal Bank's obligation to pay out Wainer's deposit was fully "due". Is it possible to reconcile these conclusions?

2. What do you think of the *First National Bank* court's argument that compensation was unavailable to Dufrene because Co-op's debt to him was "to return a thing given in deposit"? What of the *Canal Bank* court's assertion that the rule that compensation does not take place if one of the debts of this kind "is in favor of the depositor and not of the bank" (or other depositary) (*see* lines 207–208)? If that is true, then shouldn't the depositor, in this case Dufrene, be able to "waive" the benefit of the rule unilaterally? *See Canal Bank*, lines 227–229 ("if the depositor agrees to be governed by compensation, there [sic: their] will ought to be respected and compensation will operate") (quoting Planiol). And wasn't that precisely what he tried to do when he claimed that compensation had taken place?

3. The *First National Bank* court states that the "deposit" arrangement between the Co-op and Dufrene could be classified as a "loan for use". Given that the deposit consisted of money, which is a "consumable" thing, *see* La. Civ. Code art. 536, is this classification correct?

A CONFIDENTIAL LIMOUSINE SERVICE, INC.

v.

LONDON LIVERY, LTD.

Louisiana Court of Appeal
Fourth Circuit
Jan. 8, 1993
612 So.2d 875

ARMSTRONG, Judge.

This case involves a suit on an open account.

Plaintiff, A Confidential Limousine Service, Inc. ("A Confidential") filed suit against London Livery, Ltd. ("London Livery") for money due for certain limousine services rendered on an open account. The petition asked for $13,565. The record reflects that Lon-

---

3. LSA-C.C. art. 1894 provides as follows:
   Compensation takes place regardless of the sources of the obligations.
Compensation does not take place, however, if one of the obligations is to return a thing of which the owner has been unjustly dispossessed, or is to return a thing given in deposit or loan for use, or if the object of one of the obligations is exempt from seizure.

don Livery had contracted with A Confidential to provide limousine services to it in January 1990. A Confidential alleged that London Livery refused to pay for these services after amicable demand.

London Livery answered the petition pleading defenses of failure and/or want of consideration and setoff. It also filed a reconventional demand against A Confidential raising factual allegations under the Louisiana Unfair Trade Practices Act, LSA-R.S. 51:1401, *et seq*, and the Uniform Trade Secrets Act, LSA-R.S. 51:1431, *et seq*. [....]

After various discoveries took place, A Confidential filed a motion for summary judgment contending that based upon its original petition[1] its attached documents and the sworn affidavit of its owner, Jamie Obermeyer, no genuine issue of material fact existed and it was entitled to summary judgment on the open account as a matter of law. LSA-C.C.P. arts. 966, 967. A Confidential contended that London Livery had not contested that services were rendered and its claims are for unliquidated damages and/or do not constitute a defense to a liquidated claim. In support of its argument A Confidential cited *Gulf Fed. Sav. and Loan Ass'n v. Nugent*, 528 So.2d 782 (La.App. 3d Cir.1988), *writ den.*, 533 So.2d 19 (La.1988), for the position that London Livery is not entitled to set off and/or compensation since it does not occur when two debts are not equally liquidated and contemporaneously demandable.

In its opposition to the motion, London Livery argued that A Confidential was not legally entitled to summary judgment since it was contesting the correctness of the quantum of the debt and did not admit it. London Livery contended that the affidavit of Alan B. Fisher, its president, contains an analysis of A Confidential's invoices, and reveals billing errors totalling $1,410. On those grounds, it claimed the debt was not liquidated.

After a hearing, the trial court granted partial summary judgment in favor of A Confidential in the amount of $10,835 plus legal interest from date of judicial demand. London Livery appeals.

[....]

[....] **London Livery claims summary judgment should not have been granted because the quantum of A Confidential's claim is disputed and therefore not liquidated. Since it proved overbilling, it contends A Confidential's claim is not liquid. Therefore, summary judgment should not have been granted and London Livery's claims should have offset A Confidential's after both were liquidated and demandable.**

We disagree. While the trial court did not provide its rationale for entering judgment for $10,835, an amount $1,410 less than was prayed for in the petition, the parties' memoranda, written contract and A Confidential's computerized trip sheets favor the explanation that the amount of the judgment reflects the portion of the debt which was certain and liquid. A liquid debt is one whose existence is certain and its quantity determined. *American Bank v. Saxena*, 553 So.2d 836 (La.1989), citing 4 Aubry & Rau, Cours de Troit Civil Francais, s. 326 (6th ed. 1965); Litvanoff, The Law of Obligations in Louisiana Jurisprudence (1979), p. 646. The portion of the debt which was capable of ascertainment by mere calculation in accordance with accepted legal standards was therefore liquid. *American Bank v. Saxena, supra.*; *Sims v. Hays*, 521 So.2d 730 (La.App. 2d Cir.1988).

For a debt to be liquidated, acknowledgment by the debtor is not required. Litvanoff, *supra*. Nevertheless, we note that London Livery has not denied receiving the limousine services for which it was billed. The documents corroborate that the disputed $1,410 cor-

---

1. In response to an exception filed by London Livery, A Confidential filed a first amending and supplemental petition adding Jamie and Kurt Obermeyer as parties plaintiff.

relates to the parties' varied interpretations of the contractual term "daily rental rate" and not to billings for services which were not rendered. Thus, the trial court did not err in finding $10,835 of the debt liquid and determinable.

London Livery's claim for offset and/or compensation was not sufficient to prevent summary judgment of this liquidated debt. The statutory requirements of setoff, or compensation as it is called in the Civil Code, are set forth in LSA-C.C. art. 1893 as follows:

Art. 1893. Compensation extinguishes obligations

Compensation takes place by operation of law when two persons owe to each other sums of money or quantities of fungible things identical in kind, and these sums or quantities are liquidated and presently due.

In such a case, compensation extinguishes both obligations to the extent of the lesser amount.

Delays of grace do not prevent compensation.

For compensation to apply, two distinct debts equally liquidated and demandable must exist contemporaneously. *American Bank v. Saxena, supra.*; *Hartley v. Hartley*, 349 So.2d 1258 (La.1977); *Rauch v. Rauch*, 535 So.2d 1317 (La.App. 5th Cir.1988); *Gulf Fed. Sav. & Loan Ass'n v. Nugent, supra.* Louisiana jurisprudence has barred the application of compensation to tort claims. *American Bank v. Saxena, supra.* Thus, at the time judgment was entered, London Livery's reconventional demand did not constitute an equally demandable debt of A Confidential. *Cf. First Nat. Bank of Commerce v. Dufrene*, 525 So.2d 298 (La.App. 1st Cir.1988), writ den., 530 So.2d 567 (La.1988); *Van Hoosen v. First Nat. Bank of St. Martin*, 583 So.2d 106 (La.App. 3d Cir.1991); *Project Square 221 v. Salles*, 557 So.2d 345 (La.App. 4th Cir.1990), *writ den.*, 560 So.2d 12 (La.1990). But see *Rosenthal v. Oubre*, 504 So.2d 1102 (La.App. 5th Cir.1987) [applied/defined terms of "mutuality of obligors" and "equally liquidated and determinable debt" very loosely.] London Livery's unliquidated claim for tort damages could not be pleaded in compensation against A Confidential's liquidated claim based on an open account. *Cf. American Bank v. Saxena, supra*; *Gulf Fed. Sav. & Loan Ass'n v. Nugent, supra.* London Livery's second assignment is also without merit.

[....]

The trial court entered partial summary judgment in favor of A Confidential in the amount of $10,835, the portion of the obligation which was liquid and determinable. As the judgment is in accord with the above cited provisions and the intent of the summary judgment statutes, it was not error for the trial court to grant summary judgment on that portion of the debt.

For the foregoing reasons, the judgment of the trial court is affirmed. Costs of this appeal are assessed against appellant.

[....]

Question

1. The *Confidential Limousine* court rules, in the end, that though the debt that London Livery owes A Confidential is liquidated in part and, therefore, is to that extent compensable, nevertheless compensation cannot take place because the debt that A Confidential owes back to London Livery—a "tort" debt—is entirely unliquidated. Does that mean that a delictual obligation can never be subject to compensation, not even in part? What if the tort victim in a personal injury case were to claim, say, $50,000

in lost wages and the tortfeasor were to acknowledge, first, that he was liable for the tort and, second, that the tort victim's lost wages damages amounted to at least $40,000?

Comparative Law Perspective

Marcel Planiol, Treatise on the Civil Law
Vol. 2, pt. 1, nᵒˢ 562–567, at 314–315, at 322, & nᵒˢ 594–597, at 324–325 (Louisiana State Law Institute tr., 11th ed. 1939)

562. Definition

When two persons mutually owe each other similar objects, it is not necessary that each of them pay to the other that which he owes; it is more simple to consider them both liberated up to the amount of the lesser of the two debts, so that the excess of the greater alone can become the object of an effective enforcement (Art. 1289). Compensation may therefore be defined as a special mode of extinguishing reciprocal obligations, which mutually dispense the two debtors of effective performance. Thus each one of them possesses at the same time (1) a means of liberating himself by renouncing his credit; (2) a guaranty for his credit, in refusing to pay what he owes....

566. Definition

Compensation is legal when it operates by effect of the law and under conditions fixed by it. It is the only one with which the Code is concerned.

567. Enumeration

Five conditions, of which three only are indicated by the law (Art. 1291) are necessary: (1) reciprocity of obligation; (2) fungible nature of their objects; (3) liquid estate of the two debts; (4) exigibility of the credit opposed in compensation; (5) seizability of the right extinguished by the compensation.

588. Extinction of the Two Debts

Compensation is equivalent to a double payment: it extinguishes the two debts, up to the amount of the lesser. The two debts are extinguished with all their accessories, mortgages, sureties, etc. Interest ceases to run.

If there are several debts owing by one of the parties to the other, the rules as to imputation of payments are followed in determining which will be extinguished by compensation.

594. Definition and Usefulness

Facultative compensation is that which operates by the will of the parties, when one of them raises an obstacle resulting from the provisions of the law. One of the conditions for legal compensation may be lacking: for example, one of the debts may be unliquidated, suspended by a term, or created by virtue of a deposit; if the parties agree to accept the unliquidated debt in compensation, or if the party who is entitled to the term renounces the benefit thereof, or if the depositor consents to a settlement by compensation, there is no reason why their wishes should not be respected and no reason why the compensation should not take place.

595. Effects

Facultative compensation being the work of the will of the parties, naturally cannot exist and produce its effects except from the day it was agreed upon. It is not endowed with any retroactivity.

597. Definition

There is judicial compensation when a debtor who is sued for the execution of a debt files a reconventional demand against the plaintiff pleading a credit in opposition to the original demand, which credit does not have or fulfill the conditions required for legal compensation....

Section IX — Of Confusion

Louisiana Sources of Law

Louisiana Civil Code

Art. 1903. Union of qualities of obligee and obligor.

When the qualities of obligee and obligor are united in the same person, the obligation is extinguished by confusion. (Acts 1984, No. 331, § 1, eff. Jan. 1, 1985.)

Art. 1904. Obligation of the surety.

Confusion of the qualities of obligee and obligor in the person of the principal obligor extinguishes the obligation of the surety.

Confusion of the qualities of obligee and obligor in the person of the surety does not extinguish the obligation of the principal obligor. (Acts 1984, No. 331, § 1, eff. Jan. 1, 1985.)

Art. 1905. Solidary obligations.

If a solidary obligor becomes an obligee, confusion extinguishes the obligation only for the portion of that obligor.

If a solidary obligee becomes an obligor, confusion extinguishes the obligation only for the portion of that obligee. (Acts 1984, No. 331, § 1, eff. Jan. 1, 1985.)

Précis: Louisiana Law of Obligations in General §§ 7.6.1 to 7.6.2

Confusion is the merging in the same person of the qualities of obligee and principal obligor with respect to the same obligation. As **Article 1903** states: "**When the qualities of obligee and obligor are united in the same person, the obligation is extinguished by confusion.**"

For confusion to occur one must assume the existence of an obligation and a party who is, at the same time, obligee and obligor of that obligation. A typical example of confusion would occur in matters of succession where an obligee could inherit from his obligor....

Confusion thus creates an obstacle to a legal action by the party involved against himself....

LSA-C.C. Art. 1904-1 provides another illustration of the principle according to which the fate of an accessory obligation is determined by the fate of the principal obligation: "**Confusion of the qualities of obligee and obligor in the person of the principal obligor extinguishes the obligation of the surety.**" When the principal obligation is extinguished by confusion the accessory obligation will also disappear....

A confusion may be only partial where a part of an obligation is not susceptible of performance. Such could be the case in the event an obligation involves solidary obligors or solidary obligees. **LSA-C.C. Art. 1905**....

Cases

Noah DESHOTEL

v.

TRAVELERS INDEMNITY COMPANY

Supreme Court of Louisiana
Jan. 18, 1971
243 So.2d 259

BARHAM, Justice.

We granted certiorari in this case to review a judgment of the Third Circuit Court of Appeal. 231 So.2d 448. Subsequently we granted certiorari in the case of Laddie J. Bennett v. Employers' Liability Assurance Corporation, Ltd., to review a judgment of the First Circuit Court of Appeal involving the same issue. 238 So.2d 206. We consolidated the two cases for argument. See Bennett v. Employers' Liability Assurance Corporation, Ltd., this day decided, 257 La. 575, 243 So.2d 262.

The precise question presented in each of these cases is whether a father injured through his minor son's negligence may bring a direct action for his damages against his insurer, which, under the policy's omnibus clause, is also the insurer of the minor son.

The plaintiff in this case, Noah Deshotel, was injured in an accident while riding in a car owned by him and driven by his unemancipated minor son, Ronald. It is conceded in this court that Ronald's negligence caused the injuries suffered by his father. The father has sued his insurer, Travelers Indemnity Company, under the direct action statute, R.S. 22:655, because his son is an insured under the omnibus clause of the policy. The trial court gave judgment for the policy limits, $5000.00, with legal interest and costs, and the Court of Appeal affirmed.[1]

The principal contention of the defendant is that under Article 2318 of the Civil Code the negligence of the minor son must be imputed to the father, who is thus effectively barred from recovery.

If the father has a cause of action against his minor son for his personal damages resulting from the son's delicts, it is found under Civil Code, Article 2315: 'Every act whatever of man that causes damage to another obliges him by whose fault it happened to repair it.' Article 2318 makes the father, or after his death the mother or the tutor, of the minor responsible for the damage occasioned by the minor's delicts. However, Article 2318 does not relieve the minor of his responsibility for his tortious conduct, and other codal provisions expressly recognize the minor's responsibility for his own delicts. Article 1785 provides: 'The obligation arising from an offense or quasi offense, is also binding on the minor.' Article 1874 reads: 'He (the minor) is not relievable against obligations resulting from (his) offenses or quasi offenses.' This same provision is found in Article 2227. Additionally, our jurisprudence has recognized that there is a cause of action in others against the minor for his delicts. The procedure for exercising this cause of action is through suit against the minor's legal representative.

---

1. On rehearing by per curiam that court noted the conflict with Funderburk v. Millers Mutual Fire Insurance Company of Texas, 228 So.2d 169, decided by that same circuit on October 30, 1969, only a few months previously, writs refused 255 La. 158, 229 So.2d 735; 255 La. 159, 229 So.2d 736.

Since others have a cause of action against a minor for his offenses and quasi-offenses, the question then arises as to whether the father of a minor child is excepted and denied a cause of action for his personal damage resulting from the delicts of that minor. Article 2315 makes no exception as to those who are entitled to recompense for the damages occasioned them by others. There is no article in the Civil Code, no article in the Code of Civil Procedure, and no statutory provision which deprive the father of a Cause of action against his minor child for the child's delicts which cause damage to the father.

Moreover, nowhere is there any provision of law which deprives the father of the Right of action against the child for his delicts. However, R.S. 9:571 (formerly Article 104 of the Code of Practice) bars a suit by an unemancipated minor child against either parent during their marriage, and R.S. 9:291 prohibits a suit by a wife against her husband during marriage except for certain specified purposes. These Code ancillaries necessarily recognize the existence of a Cause of action but deny the Right of action during the existence of the particular familial relationship. We have allowed a child to sue the estate of his deceased father for the wrongful death of his mother resulting from the negligence of the father. Ruiz v. Clancy, 182 La. 935, 162 So. 734. Although as between husband and wife during marriage there is no right of action, we have repeatedly held that the wife has a cause of action against the husband for his delicts which cause her damage, and we have held under the direct action statute that the defense against the accrual of a right of action during marriage is personal to the husband and is not a defense available to the husband's insurer. Edwards v. Royal Indemnity Co., 182 La. 171, 161 So. 191; Le Blanc v. New Amsterdam Casualty Co., 202 La. 857, 13 So.2d 245.

From all this legislation and jurisprudence we conclude that the father has a Cause of action against his minor son for damages resulting from the minor's delictual acts. Moreover, there now exists no bar, either legislative or jurisprudential, to a Right of action in the father during the minority of the child.[2] If the child has a defense of no right of action, it would be personal to him and could not be relied upon by his insurer. Edwards v. Royal Indemnity Co., and LeBlanc v. New Amsterdam Casualty Co., both cited above.

As previously stated, the defendant's principal contention is that Article 2318 is applicable to the case at hand and bars a father's recovery from his son for the minor's negligent acts because those negligent acts are imputed to the father. The Court of Appeal correctly concluded that Article 2318 is inapplicable here, and that it determines only the responsibility of the father for the delicts of the minor child in relation to third parties. Article 2318 does not create negligence in the father because of the minor's negligent acts; it merely attaches financial responsibility to the father for the delicts of his minor child. See Williams v. City of Baton Rouge, 252 La. 770, 214 So.2d 138; Johnson v. Butterworth, 180 La. 586, 157 So. 121; Barham, Liability Without Fault, XVII La.Bar. J. 271 (1970). Article 2318 has no application to the instant case in which the father's claim is against the insurer of his son for damages which inure directly and only to his own benefit as compensation for his personal losses.

---

2. We express no opinion at this time on whether public policy would deny the father a right of action directly against a minor son. Since the present suit is against the insurer, that question is not presented. We are cognizant of a problem in semantics in using 'right of action', the exception which raises absence of interest in the plaintiff. 'Immunity from suit' is more descriptive and precise. Regardless of terminology, the issue would be raised by a peremptory exception and not by the dilatory exception of lack of procedural capacity. We use 'right of action' advisedly here since Code of Civil Procedure Article 927 allows the court, on its own motion and at all levels, to note failure to disclose a right of action. If this defense is available here, it should be accorded this legal dignity.

It has also been urged that the father becomes here both debtor and creditor, and that when the qualities of debtor and creditor are united in the same person, confusion extinguishes the obligation; that where confusion takes place in the person of the principal debtor, it also avails the surety. La.Civ.Code, Arts. 2217, 2218. In the instant case, under Article 2315 the debtor is the minor son, and the damage sued for is a debt due only to the father. There is one debtor, and one creditor; they are separate entities.[3]

[....]

Question

1. The *Deshotel* court's assertion that the father is only a creditor of, not a debtor to, his son rests on the court's conclusion, stated earlier in the opinion, that the father has no liability to the son under Louisiana Civil Code article 2318. What, then, should be the result in a case in which that article would impose liability on the father? Consider this example: a minor child, through his negligence, injures a third person who, it so happens, is already obligated to repay to the child's father a sum of money that the father had previously loaned to him. Let's ignore the fact that the third person's tort claim is unliquidated, a fact that, by itself, would preclude compensation. Under these circumstances, could compensation take place between the tort victim's loan debt to the father, on the one hand, and the father's tort debt to the tort victim under Louisiana Civil Code article 2318, on the other? Does Louisiana Civil Code article 1905 help you to answer this question?

HIBERNIA NATIONAL BANK
v.
CONTINENTAL MARBLE AND GRANITE COMPANY, INC., et al.

Louisiana Court of Appeal
Fifth Circuit
March 17, 1993
615 So.2d 1109

GRISBAUM, Judge.

This appeal concerns a dation en paiement. From the trial court's judgment recognizing defendant Doyle Coulon's judicial mortgage against defendant Continental Marble and Granite Company, Inc. (Continental), Hibernia National Bank (Hibernia) appeals. We affirm.

---

3. This suit does not involve a claim for a debt which could inure to the benefit of the negligent child, such as a debt for that child's medical expenses for which the father is responsible. In such a case we might be concerned with derivative negligence rather than with imputed negligence. To avoid confusion, we note that in Funderburk v. Millers Mutual Fire Insurance Company of Texas (La.App.3rd Cir. 1969), 228 So.2d 169, the father was suing for his damages which were the medical expenses of One of his minors incurred because of the negligence of Another of his minors. The principles laid down in this opinion are applicable to Funderburk, and that case is specifically overruled.

ISSUES

We are called upon to determine [...] [**among other things [w**]]hether the trial court erred in holding Hibernia's collateral mortgages on the subject immovable property were extinguished by confusion as the result of the dation.

FACTS

The facts are basically undisputed.

From 1982 to 1984, Hibernia lent Continental various sums of money, evidenced by 12 promissory notes. As a part of the security therefor, Continental granted Hibernia two collateral mortgages on certain movable and immovable property owned by Continental. In 1987, Continental, because it experienced difficulties paying its debt to Hibernia, entered into a partial dation with Hibernia. In consideration for its agreement to relieve Continental of part of the financial obligations owed, Hibernia bargained to receive from Continental the transfer, conveyance, and delivery of certain movable and immovable property "free from any lien, mortgage or encumbrance whatsoever" other than the two mortgages in favor of Hibernia. The parties (Hibernia and Continental) executed the dation on August 3, 1987. Hibernia recorded the dation in the conveyance records in Jefferson Parish at 10:50 a.m. on August 5, 1987. It is undisputed by either party that, at the time the dation was executed, no liens, mortgages, or other encumbrances were recorded against the immovable property other than Hibernia's two collateral mortgages. Unbeknownst to either party, at 10:01 a.m. on August 5, 1987, shortly before Hibernia recorded the dation, defendant Doyle Coulon recorded a civil judgment in Jefferson Parish against Continental.

[....]

Hibernia claims the trial court erred in holding Hibernia's mortgages were extinguished by confusion when Hibernia did not receive unencumbered title to the immovable as bargained.

The Civil Code articles concerning confusion read as follows:

Art. 1903. **Union of qualities of obligee and obligor**

When the qualities of the obligee and obligor are united in the same person, the obligation is extinguished by confusion.

Art. 3411. **Methods of extinction**

Art. 3411. Mortgages are extinguished:

1. By the extinction of the thing mortgaged.

2. By the creditor acquiring the ownership of the thing mortgaged.

3. By the extinction of the mortgagor's right.

4. By the extinction of the debt, for which the mortgage was given.

5. By the creditor renouncing the mortgage.

6. By prescription.

In light of our finding regarding the initial issue, we commonsensibly conclude that when the dation was executed, Hibernia, the creditor, received unconditioned ownership of the property. Thus, by operation of law, the two collateral mortgages were extinguished by confusion.

For the reasons assigned the trial court's judgment is hereby affirmed. All costs of this appeal are to be assessed against the appellant.

[....]

Questions

1. What, precisely, is a dation en paiment (in English, "giving in payment")? *See* La. Civ. Code art. 2655 *et seq.*

2. According to Louisiana Civil Code article 1933, confusion takes place "[w]hen the qualities of obligee and obligor are united in the same person". In what sense does this "union" of the qualities of "obligee" and "obligor" take place when the mortgagee acquires ownership of the mortgaged thing? In other words, what is the "obligation" as to which the mortgagee is now, at once, supposedly both obligee and obligor? *See* La. Civ. Code art. 3279.

Section X — Dissolution and Nullity

Louisiana Sources of Law

Louisiana Civil Code

Art. 2013. Obligee's right to dissolution.

When the obligor fails to perform, the obligee has a right to the judicial dissolution of the contract or, according to the circumstances, to regard the contract as dissolved. In either case, the obligee may recover damages.

In an action involving judicial dissolution, the obligor who failed to perform may be granted, according to the circumstances, an additional time to perform. (Acts 1984, No. 331, § 1, eff. Jan. 1, 1985.)

Art. 2014. Importance of failure to perform.

A contract may not be dissolved when the obligor has rendered a substantial part of the performance and the part not rendered does not substantially impair the interest of the obligee. (Acts 1984, No. 331, § 1, eff. Jan. 1, 1985.)

Art. 2015. Dissolution after notice to perform.

Upon a party's failure to perform, the other may serve him a notice to perform within a certain time, with a warning that, unless performance is rendered within that time, the contract shall be deemed dissolved. The time allowed for that purpose must be reasonable according to the circumstances.

The notice to perform is subject to the requirements governing a putting of the obligor in default and, for the recovery of damages for delay, shall have the same effect as a putting of the obligor in default. (Acts 1984, No. 331, § 1, eff. Jan. 1, 1985.)

Art. 2017. Express dissolution clause.

The parties may expressly agree that the contract shall be dissolved for the failure to perform a particular obligation. In that case, the contract is deemed dissolved at the time it provides for or, in the absence of such a provision, at the time the obligee gives notice to the obligor that he avails himself of the dissolution clause. (Acts 1984, No. 331, § 1, eff. Jan. 1, 1985.)

Art. 2018. Effects of dissolution.

Upon dissolution of a contract, the parties shall be restored to the situation that existed before the contract was made. If restoration in kind is impossible or impracticable, the court may award damages.

If partial performance has been rendered and that performance is of value to the party seeking to dissolve the contract, the dissolution does not preclude recovery for that performance, whether in contract or quasi-contract. (Acts 1984, No. 331, § 1, eff. Jan. 1, 1985.)

Art. 2019. Contracts for continuous or periodic performance.

In contracts providing for continuous or periodic performance, the effect of the dissolution shall not be extended to any performance already rendered. (Acts 1984, No. 331, § 1, effective January 1, 1985.)

Art. 2021. Rights of third party in good faith.

Dissolution of a contract does not impair the rights acquired through an onerous contract by a third party in good faith.

If the contract involves immovable property, the principles of recordation apply to a third person acquiring an interest in the property whether by onerous or gratuitous title. (Acts 1984, No. 331, § 1, eff. Jan. 1, 1985; Acts 2005, No. 169, § 2, eff. Jan. 1, 2006; Acts 2005 1st Ex. Sess., No. 13, § 1, eff. Nov. 29, 2005.)

Art. 2022. Refusal to perform.

Either party to a commutative contract may refuse to perform his obligation if the other has failed to perform or does not offer to perform his own at the same time, if the performances are due simultaneously. (Acts 1984, No. 331, § 1, eff. Jan. 1, 1985.)

Art. 2023. Security for performance.

If the situation of a party, financial or otherwise, has become such as to clearly endanger his ability to perform an obligation, the other party may demand in writing that adequate security be given and, upon failure to give that security, that party may withhold or discontinue his own performance.

A contract of unspecified duration may be terminated at the will of either party by giving notice, reasonable in time and form, to the other party. (Acts 1984, No. 331, § 1, eff. Jan. 1, 1985. Art. 2024. Contract terminated by a party's initiative.) (Acts 1984, No. 331, § 1, eff. Jan. 1, 1985.)

Art. 2029. Nullity of contracts.

A contract is null when the requirements for its formation have not been met. (Acts 1984, No. 331, § 1, eff. Jan. 1, 1985.)

Art. 2030. Absolute nullity of contracts.

A contract is absolutely null when it violates a rule of public order, as when the object of a contract is illicit or immoral. A contract that is absolutely null may not be confirmed.

Absolute nullity may be invoked by any person or may be declared by the court on its own initiative. (Acts 1984, No. 331, § 1, eff. Jan. 1, 1985.)

Art. 2031. Relative nullity of contracts.

A contract is relatively null when it violates a rule intended for the protection of private parties, as when a party lacked capacity or did not give free consent at the time the contract was made. A contract that is only relatively null may be confirmed.

Relative nullity may be invoked only by those persons for whose interest the ground for nullity was established, and may not be declared by the court on its own initiative. (Acts 1984, No. 331, § 1, effective January 1, 1985.)

Art. 2032. Prescription of action.

Action for annulment of an absolutely null contract does not prescribe.

Action of annulment of a relatively null contract must be brought within five years from the time the ground for nullity either ceased, as in the case of incapacity or duress, or was discovered, as in the case of error or fraud.

Nullity may be raised at any time as a defense against an action on the contract, even after the action for annulment has prescribed. (Acts 1984, No. 331, § 1, eff. Jan. 1, 1985.)

Art. 2033. Effects.

An absolutely null contract, or a relatively null contract that has been declared null by the court, is deemed never to have existed. The parties must be restored to the situation that existed before the contract was made. If it is impossible or impracticable to make restoration in kind, it may be made through an award of damages.

Nevertheless, a performance rendered under a contract that is absolutely null because its object or its cause is illicit or immoral may not be recovered by a party who knew or should have known of the defect that makes the contract null. The performance may be recovered, however, when that party invokes the nullity to withdraw from the contract before its purpose is achieved and also in exceptional situations when, in the discretion of the court, that recovery would further the interest of justice.

Absolute nullity may be raised as a defense even by a party who, at the time the contract was made, knew or should have known of the defect that makes the contract null. (Acts 1984, No. 331, § 1, eff. Jan. 1, 1985.)

Art. 2035. Rights of third party in good faith.

Nullity of a contract does not impair the rights acquired through an onerous contract by a third party in good faith.

If the contract involves immovable property, the principles of recordation apply to a third person acquiring an interest in the property whether by onerous or gratuitous title. (Acts 1984, No. 331, § 1, eff. Jan. 1, 1985; Acts 2005, No. 169, § 2, eff. Jan. 1, 2006; Acts 2005 1st Ex. Sess., No. 13, § 1, eff. Nov. 29, 2005.)

Précis: Louisiana Law of Conventional Obligations §§ 9.1.1 to 9.2.2

"Dissolution", in the civil Code, is the "undoing" of an existing bond of law such as a contract, for example. The essence of the word "dissolution" means that something that exists or has existed is or was "dissolved" and, thus, ceases or has ceased to exist.

The word "dissolution" is not the only one used in the civil Code to convey the same meaning that the word "dissolution," in a legal sense, carries....

Words such as "termination", "extinction", or "rescission" are also often used in the place of 'dissolution' to mean the same thing as dissolution....

All this to say that a variety of words are used, unfortunately not consistently, in the civil Code to instruct us that some existing legal relationships come to an end for reasons provided by law or as per the intent of parties. What is essential and most important to state here is that these different words, whichever one is selected, are all to be contrasted with, and differentiated from, the concept and word "nullity". As will be discussed below, "nullity" prevents the coming into existence of a juridical act because an essential requirement for that act is lacking or because the act is against public order.

The concept of "dissolution" and, therefore, the legal meaning of the word itself is that a legal bond has been created and has been in existence and that, most likely, it has had effects or could have had effects. However, because of circumstances that have occurred during the existence of the bond of law, the latter must now be dissolved or considered as having been dissolved. For example, **Art. 2013** provides that **"When the obligor fails to perform, the obligee has a right to the judicial dissolution of the contract ..."**

One can identify two different sets of grounds that justify the dissolution of a contract. One set includes grounds which are outside the control of the obligor to bring about or not and the other set includes grounds which are within the control of the obligor to bring about or not. Obviously, the consequences of a dissolution resulting from one set of grounds will be different from the consequences resulting from the other set of grounds....

[A]n obligor who cannot perform his contractual obligation because of some circumstance outside his control, will be relieved of any performance because of the dissolution of the contract; the contract has ceased to exist....

The legal nature or identity of a contract may give either party the right, when exercised in good faith, to 'terminate' the contract. Art. 2024 ... Art. 2747 ... Art. 3025.

The fact that the obligor may have contributed to the breach of his own principal obligation will have consequences for that obligor. **Art. 2013**....

[A] failure to perform by the obligor may also result from the breach of performance of a secondary obligation in such a manner that the future performance of the principal obligation will be endangered. **Art. 2023**....

An obligor who fails to perform, besides being granted, may be, an additional time to perform, may have a lawful reason not to perform at all as explained in **Art. 2022**....

Dissolution can be "judicial" when declared by a court of law, or it can be left to the parties to a contract.

Judicial dissolution may be declared by a court **"when the obligor fails to perform"** because **"the obligee has a right to the judicial dissolution of the contract ..."** and he **"may recover damages."** Art. 2013(1)....

Dissolution can be claimed by the obligee to have occurred "automatically", "of right", where, **"according to the circumstances"** he may **"regard the contract as dissolved."** Art. 2013. This same Article goes on to say that **"the obligee may recover damages."** It is obvious that the obligor will be somewhat reticent to pay, willingly, 'damages' to the obligee in addition to having to accept that the contract "is" dissolved. It is most likely that only a court will be in a position to grant damages to the obligee....

The situation that is most likely to occur is described in **Art. 2015**....

The effects of dissolution between the parties are governed by one principle and some exceptions to that principle.

The principle is that the parties must be returned to the situation they were in before the contract was entered into. To state the principle otherwise, the parties must be returned to the *status quo ante*. There are exceptions to that principle on account of an impossibility or impracticability to restore the parties to their pre-contract situation....

The principle is stated in the first sentence of **Art. 2018 "Upon dissolution of a contract, the parties shall be restored to the situation that existed before the contract was made...."** It follows that the contract is 'retroactively' undone, erased, as if it had never existed....

The second sentence of this first paragraph of Art. 2018 takes into consideration the fact that the 'restoration in kind' is not always, actually very seldom, possible. Damages will be awarded by the court to prevent one party from being enriched at the expense of the other....

As regards **Art. 2019**, it addresses another situation in which 'restoration' is impossible, impractical or simply useless. **"In contracts providing for continuous or periodic performance, the effect of the dissolution shall not be extended to any performance already rendered."** ...

Article 2021 ... states that **"Dissolution of a contract does not impair the rights acquired through an onerous contract by a third party in good faith. If the contract involves immovable property, the principles of recordation apply to a third person acquiring an interest in the property, whether by onerous or gratuitous title."** ...

Nullity of a juridical act is the sanction resulting from the non existence or the failure in the integrity of an essential requirement <u>at the time the juridical act is entered into</u>. As **Art. 2029 states very clearly: "A contract is null when the requirements for its formation have not been met."** ...

There lies the distinction between *"nullity"* and *"caducity"*....

"Caducity", operates only in the future, it *has no retroactive* effect; it does not erase the past of a juridical act. The consequences of "caducity" are simply that the legacy or donation will have no effect in the future....

There are two broad kinds of Nullity, absolute or relative, depending on the type of cause or ground that justifies the nullity of a juridical act....

LCC Art. 2030 describes an absolute nullity in these words: **"A contract is absolutely null when it violates a rule of public order, as when the object of a contract is illicit or immoral. A contract that is absolutely null may not be confirmed. Absolute nullity may be invoked by any person or may be declared by the court on its own initiative."** Article 2031 describes a relative nullity as follows: **"A contract is relatively null when it violates a rule intended for the protection of private parties, as when a party lacked capacity or did not give free consent at the time the contract was made. A contract that is only relatively null may be confirmed. Relative nullity may be invoked only by those persons for whose interest the ground for nullity was established, and may not be declared by the court on its own initiative."**

Article 2030 suggests that a juridical act is absolutely null when the violation of the law is of great concern and so major that it is "absolutely" necessary to protect, by the absolute nullity of the juridical act, the general interest or public order of the societal group at the expense of the private interest of the parties involved in the unlawful juridical act....

The lesser effects of relative nullity are explained by the fact that the 'nullity' of the juridical act occurs in the relation between the parties because only their private interest, as opposed to 'public', is at stake; that private interest of the parties deserves some degree of protection. It follows that, because of the private nature of this kind of nullity, the relative nullity of a juridical act can be 'waved' by the party or parties or it can be 'cured' by the party protected by the nullity. In addition, whereas an action to have a juridical act declared absolutely null does not prescribe, an action in relative nullity does prescribe....

In some instances, the courts are guided in their evaluation of the nature of a nullity and, therefore, in the amount of discretion they may have.... **Art. 94 ... Art. 1965.**

Art. 2034 limits the "presumptive" nullity of a contract to one provision of a contract: **"Nullity of a provision does not render the whole contract null unless from the nature**

of the provision or the intention of the parties, it can be presumed that the contract would not have been made without the null provision." ...

[A] relative nullity can be claimed only by that party whose interest is meant to be protected. Such is the case in the most common instance of relative nullity, i.e. vices of consent in the formation of a contract. Because a private interest is at stake, the party protected by the relative nullity can "cure" the ground of nullity by such juridical acts as "confirmation" and "novation"....

As regards the absolute nullity of a juridical act, it is obvious that more plaintiffs should be granted the right of action than only those who may seek the relative nullity of a juridical act. The protection of the public interest needs for the circle of potential plaintiffs to be enlarged to include anyone who has a "legitimate interest" because of some legal relationship he or she has with the parties to the absolutely null juridical act....

Art. 2032 speaks for itself: "**Action for annulment of an absolutely null contract does not prescribe.**

Action of annulment of a relatively null contract must be brought within five years from the time the ground for nullity either ceased, as in the case of incapacity or duress, or was discovered, as in the case of error or fraud.

Nullity may be raised at any time as a defense against an action on the contract, even after the action for annulment has prescribed." ...

It is important to point out here that if an action may prescribe, particularly for a relative nullity, the defense or exception of nullity itself never prescribes. Such is the meaning of the third paragraph of Art. 2032....

A principle common to both kinds of nullity is that of the retroactive effect of the nullity. The first sentence of the first paragraph of **Art. 2033** is very clear: "**An absolutely null contract, or a relatively null contract that has been declared null by the court, is deemed never to have existed....**" If the contract is *deemed never to have existed*, it follows that anything that has been done "in the past", any of the performances that have been carried out by a party or the parties have to be erased, wiped out, as if nothing had ever occurred. The problem is practical: how to restore the past to what it was before the parties entered their contract and performed, in toto or in part, their obligations. Somewhat of an answer is given in Arts. 2033 and 2035 which draw a distinction between the effects of retroactivity between the parties themselves, on the one hand, and vis-à-vis third persons, on the other hand....

As regards the principle of the retroactive effect of nullity, whether relative or absolute, it has the same effects as the retroactivity of a resolutory condition the purpose of which is to wipe out the effects of whatever performance may have occurred. Thus, each party must return to the other the performance received because that performance has become "undue"....

The exception described in **Art. 2033-2**, is a standard application of the civil law maxim: *Nemo auditur suam propriam turpitudinem allegans.* This maxim is somewhat equivalent to the common law maxim of "clean hands"....

[T]he nullity of a contract between two parties should not have detrimental effects against good faith third persons, i.e. persons who did not know and could not have known of the ground of nullity of a contract to which they were not parties. "Good faith" once again will protect those third persons who can claim its benefit. Hence Art. 2035: "**Nullity of a contract does not impair the rights acquired through an onerous contract by a third party in good faith. If the contract involves immovable property, the principles** of recordation apply to a third person acquiring an interest in the property whether by onerous or gratuitous title." ...

Cases

Opal MENNELLA
v.
KURT E. SCHON E.A.I., LTD., et al.
United States Court of Appeals
Fifth Circuit
Dec. 2, 1992
979 F.2d 357

1
2
3
4
5
6
7

POLITZ, Chief Judge.

8

In these consolidated appeals, the parties dispute the ownership of a masterpiece painted by Sir Anthony Van Dyck. Mrs. Opal Mennella complains of the district court's summary judgment dismissal of her claim of conversion and denial of sanctions; Kurt E. Schon, E.A.I., Ltd., et al., complain of the court's award to Mrs. Mennella of certain payments she made on the painting and of the dismissal of their claim of defamation. Concluding that the question of ownership is controlled by basic principles of property and contract law as adopted and codified in the Louisiana Civil Code, and concluding that Schon's defamation suit is without merit, we affirm the district court except as relates to recovery of interest by Mrs. Mennella.

9
10
11
12
13
14
15
16
17

Background

18

This *mise en scene* began in the Spring of 1988 when Mrs. Mennella agreed to purchase a painting from Schon's New Orleans art gallery. She previously had purchased two paintings from Schon and had admired this piece on previous visits. The painting, entitled "Princess Mary, Eldest Daughter of King Charles I, Mother of King William III" by the Flemish Master Sir Anthony Van Dyck, was more than 300 years old.[1] Princess Mary married William of Orange; it is their names which identify one of America's first and finest colleges. The purchase price was $350,000. Motivated to purchase, she paid Schon $50,000 with the $300,000 balance, according to the invoice, to be paid on June 1, 1988.

19
20
21
22
23
24
25
26
27

The painting never left Schon's possession. Mrs. Mennella, experiencing cash-flow problems, amicably secured an agreement to pay the balance over a six-month period. By Christmas of 1988, however, she had managed to pay only an additional $90,000. At that point she demanded authentication of the painting to be used to secure a loan to pay the balance of the purchase price. Schon sent an expert's appraisal stating that the portrait was "one of five copies by Sir Anthony Van Dyck."[2] Concerned that the portrait might be a counterfeit, Mrs. Mennella enlisted the aid of her attorneys who moved

28
29
30
31
32
33
34

---

1. Van Dyck is, after Rubens, the most prominent Flemish painter of the 17th Century. Under the appointment of King Charles I he served as "principal paynter in ordinary of their Majesties." It was during this period that Van Dyck was Knighted and presumably painted the portrait in question.

2. The appraisal was conducted in January of 1989. The conclusion was confirmed by a Dr. Erik Larsen in March and reduced to writing in April of 1989.

35 to void the sale and recover the sum paid. Acting through counsel, Mrs. Mennella re-
36 pudiated the painting's value, refused to make further payments, and demanded re-
37 turn of the $140,000 paid.

38   Schon responded by letter on April 25, 1989, a full year after the ostensible sale,
39 that Mrs. Mennella should be satisfied with the authenticity of the painting after re-
40 ceiving a second appraisal. In that letter Schon demanded performance within five
41 days, absent which he would be forced to place the painting back in the active sale
42 stock of the gallery. Mrs. Mennella made no apparent effort to reply or to enforce her
43 rights under the contract. She did not make or tender the agreed price or object to the
44 time period in which Schon demanded payment. Instead, she and her attorneys in-
45 sisted on referring to the contract as "an agreement to purchase" rather than as a sale,
46 obviously seeking to distance her from ownership and the obligation to pay the balance
47 of the purchase price.

48   On May 2, 1989, Schon wrote Mrs. Mennella, informing her that he regarded her si-
49 lence and inaction as a default and that he considered the sale canceled. No money was re-
50 funded. Instead, in September Schon offered to either refund $95,000, representing the
51 consideration paid less $45,000 for the cost of authentication and commission paid to
52 Schon's salesman, or to give Mrs. Mennella $140,000 in store credit. Mrs. Mennella re-
53 jected both offers.

54   Without Mrs. Mennella's knowledge, the painting was shipped to Christie's in Lon-
55 don where, in November 1989, it sold for more than $1.4 million.

56   The following month, unaware of the London sale, Mrs. Mennella filed the instant
57 suit seeking recision [*sic*] of the sale and damages, claiming that she only agreed to buy
58 the painting upon "proper authentication and verification." She complained that the
59 painting she agreed to purchase was a fraud and was worth far less than she had agreed
60 to pay.[3] Schon answered and counterclaimed, alleging defamation. Informed of the Lon-
61 don sale, Mrs. Mennella's attitude markedly changed. Her lawyers, presumably some-
62 what chagrined, amended the complaint, claiming that the sale was complete from the
63 start and, as a result, the painting was Mrs. Mennella's and the London sale constituted
    a conversion.[4]

64   Based on the pleadings, depositions, and affidavits, the district court concluded that
65 Mrs. Mennella, though entitled to her payments and interest from the day of her de-
66 mand, was not entitled to the proceeds of the London sale. Schon's counterclaim for
67 defamation was rejected. Mrs. Mennella apparently thought this claim to be frivolous
68 and moved for sanctions against Schon for presuming to advance it. The district court de-
69 nied the motion for sanctions. Both parties timely appealed.

70   *Analysis*

71   [....]

72   The controlling principles of Louisiana law are neither complex nor mysterious. This
73 dispute is readily resolved by resort to its chronology. That the parties formed some man-
74 ner of contract on April 5, 1988 is not disputed. Rather, the dispute concerns the more
75 remote question of whether the painting belonged to Mrs. Mennella so as to lend cre-

---

3. In her original complaint, Mrs. Mennella claimed that she "made verbal demands in early 1989 which were followed by written demand ... for the return of [her $140,000]."

4. The amended complaint sought to "amend her [complaint] to state that: Plaintiff is and has been the owner of the [portrait]."

dence to her claim that Schon's sale of the painting constituted conversion.[5] We must first decide whether the contract supports her claim to ownership.[6]

1. The nature of the obligation

Whether the contract provided for a present transfer of title depends on the objectively determined intentions of the parties.[7] If the sale was intended to be contingent on adequate authentication and verification, as Mrs. Mennella originally claimed, or on the payment of the purchase price and tender of delivery, as the district court determined, then the obligation would have been "suspensive" under the Louisiana Civil Code. The Code defines a suspensive obligation as one which is "dependent on an uncertain event."[8] Article 2471 of the Code provides: "A sale, made with a suspensive condition, does not transfer property to the buyer, until the fulfillment of the condition." If, on the other hand, the sale was not conditioned "on an uncertain event," then title would pass under article 2456 of the Code which provides:

> The sale is considered to be perfect between the parties, **and the property is of right acquired to the purchaser** with regard to the seller, as soon as there exists an agreement for the object and the price thereof, although the object has not yet been delivered, nor the price paid [emphasis added].

After reviewing all relevant indicia of the parties' intentions, we conclude that they did not intend to create a suspensive obligation.

Because we do not have the luxury of a fully comprehensive written contract[9] we must glean the intention of the parties from other sources. The Civil Code commands our consideration of the "nature of the contract, equity, usages, the conduct of the parties before and after the formation of the contract, and of other contracts of a like nature between the same parties."[10] We find the conduct of both parties, before and after April 5, 1988, to be instructive.

It is clear that Schon regarded the transaction as a perfected sale, one not contingent on authentication or anything else. The day after Mrs. Mennella paid the gallery $50,000, Kurt Schon wrote to congratulate her on the "purchase of the painting." Equally telling, Schon immediately paid his salesman a substantial sales commission.[11] The invoice was straightforward; it described the transaction as a sale without reference to any condition.

---

5. Conversion is a common-law tort recognized by Louisiana courts as a quasi-offense under Civil Code article 2315. *See, e.g., Holley v. Singletary*, 464 So.2d 410 (La.App.1985).

6. Mrs. Mennella's claim to the proceeds flows from her right to the painting. That right is defined by the Civil Code and the contract. One must recall the boundaries of common-law conversion before applying it to the unique relation created by Civil Code sales. Conversion, as the action has evolved, is predicated on (1) the plaintiff's right to possession, and (2) the defendant's exercise of dominion or control over the goods which is in fact inconsistent with the plaintiff's rights. W. Page Keeton, et al., *Prosser and Keeton on the Law of Torts*, § 15, at 92, 104–05 (5th ed. 1984). If the April contract transferred title and Schon was not within his rights to sell the painting, only then would he be liable in damages under a conversion theory. The key is whether Schon, based on Mrs. Mennella's conduct, had the right to sell the painting.

7. La.Civ.Code art. 2045 (West 1987); *M.O.N.T. Boat Rental Serv., Inc. v. Union Oil Co. of Cal.*, 613 F.2d 576 (5th Cir.1980); *Kuswa & Assoc., Inc. v. Thibaut Constr. Co., Inc.*, 463 So.2d 1264 (La.1985).

8. La.Civ.Code art. 1767.

9. A written contract is not required to accomplish a sale of a movable. La.Civ.Code art. 2441. Where the price or value exceeds $500, however, proof of the contract must be proved by at least one witness and other corroborating circumstances. La.Civ.Code art. 1846. The summary judgment record contains ample proof of the making of the contract.

10. La.Civ.Code art. 2053.

11. Schon later sought to withhold this commission from the refund of Mrs. Mennella's payments.

There was only the notation of the initial payment, amount and due date of the balance, and identification of the portrait.

Similarly, Mrs. Mennella never made any claim to a right to authentication until December, when she was facing financial difficulties and already had paid $140,000 for the painting. We are mindful of and consider significant the fact that the parties had executed two similar contracts without any authentication requirement. Though the present efforts to reverse an earlier position may be the cause of uplifted eyebrows, it appears consistent with the original understanding and prior dealings.

The district court found the sale to be conditioned on both the delivery of the painting and the payment of the purchase price. We find that this reading creates unnecessary tension with the literal language of article 2456 and fails to comport with the accepted civilian rubrics.

Article 1767 defines a conditional obligation as "one dependent on an uncertain event." If the anticipated performance were treated as an uncertain event virtually every bilateral contract would be a conditional obligation and venerable article 2456 would be rendered meaningless. Indeed, if the performance was so "uncertain" as to create a conditional obligation, it would be nigh impossible to treat the exchange of promises as a contract. Louisiana courts long have recognized that the Civil Code does not allow the parties to condition the transfer of title on the payment of the purchase price.[12] Instead, in credit sales, Louisiana courts consistently have held that when the parties consent and agree as to the price and the thing, title passes instanter. So sayeth article 2456.

Therefore we are compelled to hold that title to the painting passed to Mrs. Mennella in April of 1988. We must now consider whether that title was divested prior to the London sale.

2. The execution of the duties under the contract

In support of her claim of ownership of the painting, Mrs. Mennella seizes upon the transfer of title and would ignore all of her subsequent actions. Legal title is not so barren a concept. The Civil Code clearly portends a transfer of title subject to the execution of the contract. For example, the seller may wrongfully sell and deliver the object to an innocent third party who would acquire title, provided he has paid fair value.[13] The seller retains a security interest in the property[14] pending tender of the purchase price and has the concomitant duty of due care towards the object.[15] The seller has the right to put the buyer in default and to dissolve the contract upon the buyer's failure to perform, and under certain conditions to simply regard the contract as dissolved.[16] That divestment is the principal issue presented by this appeal.

Mrs. Mennella was obliged to carry her end of the bargain, timely payment, just as Schon was obliged to care for and ultimately deliver the painting. Mrs. Mennella's er-

---

12. *Haymon v. Holliday*, 405 So.2d 1304 (La.App.1981).

13. The Code explicitly accommodates such a result: "The sale is considered to be perfect and the property is of right acquired to the purchaser **with regard to the seller**...." La.Civ.Code art. 2456. *See also* La.Civ.Code art. 518 ("when possession has not been delivered, a subsequent transferee to whom possession is delivered acquires ownership provided he is in good faith"); Yiannopoulos, 2 *Louisiana Civil Law Treatise* § 354 (1991).

14. La.Civ.Code art. 3227; *C & A Tractor Co. v. Holland American Ins. Co.*, 445 So.2d 1286 (La.App.), *cert. denied*, 449 So.2d 1348 (La.1984).

15. La.Civ.Code art. 2468.

16. La.Civ.Code art. 2013. *See e.g.*, *Texala Oil & Gas Co. v. Caddo Mineral Lands Co.*, 152 La. 549, 93 So. 788 (1922); *Hay v. Bush*, 110 La. 575, 34 So. 692 (1903). Comment (a) of the 1984 addition of article 2013 cites both opinions.

roneous conclusion that the painting was not authentic caused her to repudiate the
transaction, demand a return of her partial payment, and refuse to pay the balance due.
This is a course of action she would have been entitled to follow had she been correct
in her assumption.[17] That assumption was not correct, however. Indeed, in forming her
belief that the painting was a fraud she relied on an appraisal which clearly indicated that
the painting was executed by Van Dyck. She received repeated assurances from the seller
that he would perform, accompanied by repeated demands for her performance. Further, from January to May she made no effort whatever to authenticate the painting or
to investigate the credentials of the experts from whom she had received appraisals. Instead, through counsel, Mrs. Mennella made manifest that she had no intention of performing[18] and demanded a return of her money, refusing a "net" refund or a full store
credit.

Whether she claims to have been exercising her right to receive adequate authentication under the contract, or an effort to enforce a warranty, there is no excusing Mrs. Mennella's express repudiation and continued refusal to perform after receiving two appraisals.
Mrs. Mennella comes before the courts burdened with the troublesome albatross of her
repudiation. We may not ignore it.

Mrs. Mennella now offers a somewhat tortured explanation of the legal significance
of her failure to perform. Essentially, the argument turns on what she characterizes as
Schon's failure to formally accept her offer to rescind the contract. Such obfuscation
need not long detain us. That argument ignores the fact that Mrs. Mennella was in
default by January of 1989, at the very latest, when the voluntary extension expired.
The communication from counsel refusing to proceed and demanding a refund cannot be construed as anything but a definitive refusal to perform. The lamb of her so-
called "offer to rescind" cannot lie peacefully beside the lion of her refusal to perform.
The fact that she may have based her actions on a mistaken belief that the painting
was not genuine[19] does not change the character of her actions; failure to perform
does not presuppose a fraudulent intent, only an inexcusable failure to do that which
was promised.[20]

If accepted at face value, the argument by counsel for Mrs. Mennella would stand the
law of contracts on its ear. Contracts bind persons to the assigned risks and benefits. Mrs.
Mennella would blithely shift the benefits and the corresponding burdens as best suits
her most immediate interests. She may not do so.[21]

We conclude that Mrs. Mennella's written communication through counsel refusing
to perform may justly be treated as an anticipatory repudiation[22] and that her failure to

---

17. When both parties to a contract share a mistake of fact involving the essence of a party's consent "the granting of relief presents no problem." La.Civ.Code art. 1949, cmt. (d); *see generally*,
La.Civ.Code arts. 1948–50.

18. Counsel for Mrs. Mennella concedes that this is the weakest part of their argument: "that it
appears as though she didn't want it."

19. Neither may her failure to receive what, by her estimation, was sufficient evidence of authentication—a right she did not have—serve as an adequate excuse for her failure to perform.

20. *See generally, Robertson v. Buoni*, 504 So.2d 860 (La.1987).

21. La.Civ.Code art. 2055; *see also Douglas Oil Tools, Inc. v. Demesnil*, 552 So.2d 77 (La.App.1989)
(representations which are relied upon to a party's detriment give rise to estoppel). *See also Ranger
Nationwide Ins. v. American Cas. Co.*, 658 F.Supp. 103, 108 (D.Del.1987) ("A party who breaches a contract may not rely on the benefits of that same contract."), aff'd, 833 F.2d 307 (3d Cir.1987).

22. Litvinoff, *Law of Obligations in the Louisiana Jurisprudence*, 371 (2d ed. 1985) ("[A] situation
that could be characterized as an anticipatory breach at common law can be regarded as an active violation of the contract in Louisiana.").

pay the balance in the extended period allowed for same constituted an active repudiation of the contract.

3. Dissolution

Dissolution of the contract would terminate Mrs. Mennella's property rights in the painting. Indeed, this was the prayer of Mrs. Mennella's initial lawsuit. The final question before us is whether Schon secured a dissolution before the London sale.

When faced with Mrs. Mennella's refusal to perform Schon had three choices. He could: (1) sue to enforce performance or to secure a judicial dissolution; (2) continue to seek performance albeit in an untimely manner; and/or (3) put Mrs. Mennella in default and, if she failed to correct same, regard the contract as dissolved.

Initially, Schon opted for the second choice; he invited untimely performance. Seeking to accommodate Mrs. Mennella's cash-flow problems, he agreed to a modification of the contract, extending the $300,000 payment from June until the following January. He then provided two appraisals to assuage her voiced concerns regarding the painting's origin.[23] Schon informed Mrs. Mennella she had five additional days to perform; otherwise he would have to consider the sale dissolved. Finally, when Mrs. Mennella made clear that she would not perform, Schon gave her notice that he was treating the sale as canceled and was returning the painting to the active stock for sale.

Recently, revisions to the Civil Code formally adopted a practice the Louisiana courts have long recognized: extrajudicial dissolution.[24] Schon's letters were sufficient to put Mrs. Mennella in default, a prerequisite to dissolution by notice.[25] We find them sufficient, under the circumstances, to dissolve the contract.

The Civil Code provides that the obligee has a right, in certain cases, to treat the contract as dissolved.[26] The "unilateral, non-judicial dissolution provided for in the revised articles is not a novelty."[27] Under the civilian tradition, the obligor must be notified of his default, given a certain time to perform, and warned that the contract will be considered dissolved if performance is not rendered.[28] The time set must be reasonable according to the circumstances,[29] and the breach must be substantial to justify the dissolution.[30]

The Civil Code is not exhaustive in its description of the circumstances that will entitle the obligee "to regard the contract as dissolved" without litigation. Because the pertinent articles are relatively new, the Louisiana courts have not yet expounded on the issue. Whether a repudiation is sufficiently clear to allow dissolution without litigation un-

---

23. There is some dispute as to when the Larsen appraisal was sent. It is clear, however, that it was sent by April when Schon still demanded performance. Mrs. Mennella complains that this communication by Schon included a demand for two different prices, one which included interest and one for the contract price. In either event she refused to perform at any price and then waited, saying nothing after receiving Schon's next letter which informed her that the sale was dissolved; indeed, she was still seeking dissolution and disavowing ownership, as late as March, 1990.

24. Mrs. Mennella cites cases from the 1940s and 1950s suggesting that judicial dissolution was Schon's exclusive remedy. In light of much earlier precedents and the recent amendments to the Civil Code, we can hardly view those decisions as persuasive. *See* n. 16, *supra*.

25. La.Civ.Code art. 1991. "An obligee may put the obligor in default by a written request of performance … or by filing suit for performance…."

26. La.Civ.Code art. 2013.

27. Litvinoff, *supra*, at 389.

28. Id.

29. La.Civ.Code art. 2015.

30. La.Civ.Code art. 2014.

doubtedly will pose a difficult question in some cases. Fortunately for this *Erie* court, this   210
is not one of those cases. Schon prudently waited until Mrs. Mennella unequivocally re-   211
fused to perform and demanded the return of her money before notifying her of the de-   212
fault and dissolution.[31] Article 2013, when read in harmony with related articles, such as   213
articles 2014[32] and 2018,[33] allows extrajudicial dissolution where the obligee has received   214
partial payment. The Code makes clear, however, that the obligee is liable for the return   215
of any partial payments unless he has a right to retain them.[34]   216

Schon's notice is not rendered ineffective by his failure to simultaneously return the par-   217
tial payments. Article 2018 provides the obligor in default with an action to recover par-   218
tial payments to the extent they exceed the damages incurred. Article 2013[35] states that   219
the obligee who regards the contract as dissolved has the right to pursue a remedy in dam-   220
ages. The comments to article 2015 (non-judicial dissolution by notice) likewise state that   221
"[a]fter such notice is given, the obligor will be liable for any delay damages that accrue."   222
At the same time, the obligee is duty bound to mitigate his damages.[36] We conclude that   223
article 2013, when read *in pari materia* with other articles,[37] allows the seller to regard   224
the contract as dissolved and temporarily retain partial payments when the buyer is in   225
breach. The seller, of course, is limited in his actions by operation of article 1759, which   226
provides that "Good faith shall govern the conduct of the obligor or obligee in whatever   227
pertains to their obligation."[38] Thus he may hold only the funds necessary to compensate   228
for the loss he reasonably believes he will suffer. Under the prevailing circumstances, we   229
conclude that Schon's actions were reasonable and that they were executed in good faith.   230

We hold that Schon validly dissolved the contract by notice of default after it became   231
obvious that Mrs. Mennella would not perform. Consistent therewith, we therefore hold   232
that Schon had legal title to the painting when it was sold in London.   233

[....]

Questions

1.   The part of the *Manella* opinion in which the court addresses the question whether
Schon was entitled to regard the sale contract as dissolved once Manella refused to
pay the balance of the purchase price, *see* lines 199–230, displays an impressive interpretative methodology. Can you identify the various interpretative methods/tech-
niques that the court employed?

2.   The *Manella* court assumes, without much explanation, that the "notice to perform"
that Schon gave Manella, an essential prerequisite to extra-juridical dissolution in most

---

31. If extrajudicial dissolution were not appropriate in this case we have difficulty conceiving of
a case in which it would be. Such a result would be intolerable as litigation would have to result from
every failed sales agreement to clear title.

32. The article allows dissolution where the obligor has partially performed but the part not rendered substantially impairs the obligee's interest.

33. That article provides: "If partial performance has been rendered and that performance is of
value to the party seeking to dissolve..., the dissolution does not preclude recovery for that performance, whether in contract or quasi-contract."

34. *See, e.g.*, La.Civ.Code art. 2018.

35. "In either case [judicial or non-judicial dissolution] the obligee may recover damages."
La.Civ.Code art. 2013.

36. La.Civ.Code art. 2002.

37. La.Civ.Code art. 13.

38. *See also* La.Civ.Code art. 1983.

cases, was adequate under Louisiana Civil Code article 2015. What, precisely, does that article require of such a notice? What is meant in the second paragraph of the article by "the requirements governing a putting … in default"? *See* La. Civ. Code art. 1989 *et seq.*

3. What is the "source" (in the sense of La. Civ. Code art. 1757) of Schon's obligation to refund to Manella the payments she had made of the sale price? Is it a "contract"? Or is it something else? *See* La. Civ. Code art. 2018, par. 2; *see also* La. Civ. Code art. 2298.

See, *Marek v. McHards, supra* p. 431

Kenneth David JONES
v.
Ezeb CHEVALIER
Louisiana Court of Appeal
Third Circuit
May 22, 1991
579 So.2d 1217

FORET, Judge.

Plaintiff and appellant, Kenneth David Jones, appeals from a judgment in favor of Ezeb Chevalier, defendant and appellee herein.

Jones brought this action, alleging that Chevalier was liable to him for what appears to be a claim for breach of an illegal contract. Jones claims that Chevalier was responsible for his arrest and ensuing damages because Chevalier did not warn him of the police investigation into his activities, as agreed.

Chevalier filed an exception of no cause of action in response to Jones' petition, which was granted by the trial court.

By this appeal, Jones contends that he was not given notice of the hearing, and an opportunity to present evidence at the hearing on the exception of no cause of action. The record supports his contention. Although the record contains a notice of the hearing on the exception, the record does not reflect that Jones was personally served pursuant to La.C.C.P. art. 1314 and 1231, et seq.

Jones was not prejudiced by the lack of notice because evidence may not be introduced to support or controvert the exception of no cause of action. La.C.C.P. art. 931. Nor was Jones entitled to notice as a matter of constitutional due process: the failure to disclose a cause of action is a peremptory objection which may be noticed by either the trial or the appellate court on its own motion. La.C.C.P. art. 927. When either the trial or the appellate court notices the failure to disclose a cause of action, no hearing is required. Conversely, when notice is not given and no hearing is conducted, it must be presumed that the court, in granting the exception, has acted on its own motion.

Moreover, a contract which violates a rule of public order, as does this alleged agreement, is absolutely null, and unenforceable. La.C.C. art. 2030. The absolute nullity of such a contract may be declared by the court on its own initiative. *Id.*

The trial court's judgment was proper.

[....]

Question

1. In the *Jones* case, the disappointed party—Jones—had not yet rendered his performance (paying of money) as of the time at which the other party—Chevalier—breached the contract. But what if Jones had done so, that is, what if he had paid Chevalier for his services "in advance"? Under those circumstances, would Jones have been entitled to recover this performance? Why or why not? *See* La. Civ. Code art. 2033, pars. 1 & 2.

M. Robert VOITIER, Sr.

v.

ANTIQUE ART GALLERY, et al.

Louisiana Court of Appeal
Third Circuit
April 6, 1988
524 So.2d 80

GUIDRY, Judge.

On May 15, 1984, plaintiff, M. Robert Voitier, Sr., filed this suit seeking rescission of a contract of sale of a painting entitled "Wooded Farmland Glade", supposedly an original work of art by George Inness. Voitier purchased the painting, which was owned by Fred Rotondaro, on June 26, 1982 at an auction sale conducted by Morton's Auction Exchange, Inc., in New Orleans, Louisiana. Plaintiff seeks a rescission of the sale and a return of the sale price because of an error of fact which he alleges was the principal cause for making the contract, i.e., the painting is not an original work of art by George Inness. Plaintiff, in addition, sought the recovery of attendant damages.

[....]

After a trial on the merits, [...] **found, among other things, that ... t**]he painting owned by Rotondaro which was sold to Voitier was not an original George Inness.

[T]he trial court rendered judgment in favor of plaintiff [...] for the sum of $23,610.93, which included a return of the purchase price of $17,500.00 and all damages sustained by the purchaser, Voitier. [....]

FACTS

In early 1982, Fred Rotondaro, a resident of the state of Maryland, purchased the painting at issue, which was reputed to be an original George Inness work of art from David Harrison, d/b/a Antique Art Gallery. Prior to the purchase, Rotondaro had the painting authenticated and was satisfied that it was an original George Inness painting. [....]

[....]

[...] [**Subsequently, at an auction**], M. Robert Voitier, Sr. was the successful bidder on the painting at issue which was alleged to be an original work of art by the early American artist, George Inness. The bid price was $17,500.00. Voitier had seen the painting prior to the auction and on the day of sale made his bid telephonically. In addition to the purchase price, Voitier paid a 10% hammer fee, $1,750.00, and 3% sales tax. He was also required to pay freight and insurance fees to transport the painting to his residence. Upon delivery to his residence, Voitier noticed the absence of the letter of authenticity which he had been assured would accompany the painting. [**He immediately requested**] [...] and was eventually sent a letter of authenticity written by a Rosalyn Mikesell, owner/director of the Webberly Galleries in Chicago, Illinois. Voitier was not satisfied with Mikesell's letter of authenticity and engaged the services of Nicolai Cikovsky, an expert on the works of George Inness. Cikovsky, after studying the painting, rendered a written opinion to Voitier stating that the painting was not a George Inness original. [**After unsuccessful attempts to recover the purchase price,**] [...] Voitier then instituted this suit.

[....]

SUFFICIENT CAUSE FOR RESCISSION OF SALE [....]

The trial court determined that the painting in question was not an original George Inness work of art. Appellants do not seriously question this fact determination. They contend that this fact determination will not support a cause of action for rescission on the ground of error. [....]

Our brethren of the Fourth Circuit in *Deutschmann v. Standard Fur Company, Inc.*, 331 So.2d 219 (La.App.1976), succinctly stated the law regarding the invalidation of contracts for unilateral error as follows:

> "Our jurisprudence is well settled that a contract may be invalidated for a unilateral error as to a fact which was the principal cause for making the contract, where the other party knew or should have known it was the principal cause. LSA-C.C. art. 1845; *Savoie v. Bills*, 317 So.2d 249 (La.App. 3d Cir.1975); *West Esplanade Shell Service, Inc. v. Breithoff*, 293 So.2d 595 (La.App. 4th Cir.1974). Error as to the nature or object of a contract may be with regard to either the substance or the object of the agreement, or substantial quality of the object, or some other quality of the object if such quality is the principal cause of making the contract. *Jefferson Truck Equipment Co. v. Guarisco Motor Co.*, 250 So.2d 211 (La.App. 1st Cir.1971)."

The record discloses that the painting in question was advertised [...] as a George Inness original work of art. The record establishes that Voitier had previously purchased an original George Inness painting and was anxious to add another original to his collection. In other words, the record makes crystal clear that Voitier was not interested in just any painting but rather that his principal motive was to acquire a George Inness original. In furtherance of this desire, Voitier paid the substantial price of $17,500.00 for the painting. It is equally clear from the record that [**the seller**] [...] was fully aware of plaintiff's motive. Before submitting a bid, Voitier viewed the painting and exacted assurances [from **Morton's**], albeit made in good faith, that the painting was an authentic original and that a letter of authenticity would accompany the painting. Under the circumstances present in this case and considering the applicable legal principles, we have little difficulty concluding that plaintiff has established his right to a rescission of the contract on the basis of unilateral error.

[....]

Questions

1. The *Voitier* court, curiously enough, did not cite any legislative authority in support of its conclusion that Voitier was entitled to recover the purchase price that he had paid. Can you find any such authority? *See* La. Civ. Code art. 2033.

2. Though the *Voitier* opinion is silent on the matter, one must suppose that Antique Art Gallery sustained damages of some sort as a result of this sale-gone-bad, e.g., costs of appraisement of the painting. If Antique Art Gallery had, in fact, sustained

such damages, should it have been entitled to recover them from Voitier? Why or why not? *See* La. Civ. Code art. 1952.

Chapter Five

Of the Proof of Obligations and of That of Payment

Louisiana Sources of Law

Louisiana Civil Code

Art. 1831. Party must prove obligation.

A party who demands performance of an obligation must prove the existence of the obligation.

A party who asserts that an obligation is null, or that it has been modified or extinguished, must prove the facts or acts giving rise to the nullity, modification, or extinction. (Acts 1984, No. 331, § 1, eff. Jan. 1, 1985.)

Art. 1832. Written form required by law.

When the law requires a contract to be in written form, the contract may not be proved by testimony or by presumption, unless the written instrument has been destroyed, lost, or stolen. (Acts 1984, No. 331, § 1, eff. Jan. 1, 1985.)

Art. 1833. Authentic act.

A. An authentic act is a writing executed before a notary public or other officer authorized to perform that function, in the presence of two witnesses, and signed by each party who executed it, by each witness, and by each notary public before whom it was executed. The typed or hand-printed name of each person shall be placed in a legible form immediately beneath the signature of each person signing the act.

B. To be an authentic act, the writing need not be executed at one time or place, or before the same notary public or in the presence of the same witnesses, provided that each party who executes it does so before a notary public or other officer authorized to perform that function, and in the presence of two witnesses and each party, each witness, and each notary public signs it. The failure to include the typed or hand-printed name of each person signing the act shall not affect the validity or authenticity of the act.

C. If a party is unable or does not know how to sign his name, the notary public must cause him to affix his mark to the writing. (Acts 1984, No. 331, § 1, eff. Jan. 1, 1985; Acts 2003, No. 965, § 1, eff. Jan. 1, 2005.)

Art. 1835. Authentic act constitutes full proof between parties and heirs.

An authentic act constitutes full proof of the agreement it contains, as against the parties, their heirs, and successors by universal or particular title. (Acts 1984, No. 331, § 1, eff. Jan. 1, 1985.)

Art. 1836. Act under private signature duly acknowledged.

An act under private signature is regarded prima facie as the true and genuine act of a party executing it when his signature has been acknowledged, and the act shall be admitted in evidence without further proof.

An act under private signature may be acknowledged by a party to that act by recognizing the signature as his own before a court, or before a notary public, or other officer authorized to perform that function, in the presence of two witnesses. An act under private signature may be acknowledged also in any other manner authorized by law.

Nevertheless, an act under private signature, though acknowledged, cannot substitute for an authentic act when the law prescribes such an act. (Acts 1984, No. 331, § 1, eff. Jan. 1, 1985.)

Art. 1837. Act under private signature.

An act under private signature need not be written by the parties, but must be signed by them. (Acts 1984, No. 331, § 1, eff. Jan. 1, 1985.)

Art. 1842. Confirmation.

Confirmation is a declaration whereby a person cures the relative nullity of an obligation.

An express act of confirmation must contain or identify the substance of the obligation and evidence the intention to cure its relative nullity.

Tacit confirmation may result from voluntary performance of the obligation. (Acts 1984, No. 331, § 1, eff. Jan. 1, 1985.)

Art. 1843. Ratification.

Ratification is a declaration whereby a person gives his consent to an obligation incurred on his behalf by another without authority.

An express act of ratification must evidence the intention to be bound by the ratified obligation.

Tacit ratification results when a person, with knowledge of an obligation incurred on his behalf by another, accepts the benefit of that obligation. (Acts 1984, No. 331, § 1, eff. Jan. 1, 1985.)

Art. 1846. Contract not in excess of five hundred dollars.

When a writing is not required by law, a contract not reduced to writing, for a price or, in the absence of a price, for a value not in excess of five hundred dollars may be proved by competent evidence.

If the price or value is in excess of five hundred dollars, the contract must be proved by at least one witness and other corroborating circumstances. (Acts 1984, No. 331, § 1, eff. Jan. 1, 1985.)

Art. 1848. Testimonial or other evidence not admitted to disprove a writing. [*Amended*]

Testimonial or other evidence may not be admitted to negate or vary the contents of an authentic act or an act under private signature. Nevertheless, in the interest of justice, that evidence may be admitted to prove such circumstances as a vice of consent or to prove that the written act was modified by a subsequent and valid oral agreement. (Acts 1984, No. 331, § 1, eff. Jan. 1, 1985; Acts 2012, No. 277, § 1.)

Art. 1853. Judicial confession.

A judicial confession is a declaration made by a party in a judicial proceeding. That confession constitutes full proof against the party who made it.

A judicial confession is indivisible and it may be revoked only on the ground of error of fact. (Acts 1984, No. 331, § 1, eff. Jan. 1, 1985.)

Précis: Louisiana Law of Obligations in General § 6.1.1 to 6.1.3

An authentic act is defined as a writing executed before a notary public or an officer **"authorized to perform that function, in the presence of two witnesses and signed by each party who executed it, by each witness and by each notary public before whom it was executed."** (LSA-C.C. Art. 1833)....

Although a notary is the most likely officer who will preside over the formalities of the act, other public officers are authorized to stand in the place of a notary to perform the latter's functions. As illustrations, the laws allows commissioned officers in the active service of the Armed Forces or the Coast Guard of the U.S. [R.S. 35:7] as well as ambassadors, consuls [R.S. 35:9] or recorders [R.S. 44:101] to perform the functions of a notary....

The role played by the written instrument itself *[instrumentum]* in the prerequisites of a valid authentic act explains why the contents of such an act are given a binding force which admits of few exceptions. Oral evidence, if freely admitted, could so tamper with the contents of an authentic act as to deprive the latter of any value, at the same time it would seriously discredit the role and authority of notaries or other qualified public officers....

An act under private signature is defined as an act **"which need not be written by the parties, but must be signed by them."** (LSA-C.C. Arts. 1837).

The legal weight attached to such an act rests, as a consequence, upon the validity of the signatures of the parties, or party to it. It follows that a party against whom an act under private signature is asserted may attempt to deny his signature by any available means of proof. Conversely, any means of proof may be used to establish that the signature belongs to that party....

An act under private signature facilitates the burden of proof of the party who claims its benefit even though the evidentiary weight of such an act is limited....

"Confirmation is a declaration whereby a person cures the relative nullity of an obligation." (LSA-C.C. Art. 1842-1). Confirmation is, therefore, a unilateral juridical act, express or tacit, enabling a person to make *retroactively* valid a juridical act which was defective when first entered into....

"Ratification is a declaration whereby a person gives his consent to an obligation incurred on his behalf by another without authority." (LSA-C.C. Art. 1843)....

Ratification is, therefore, a unilateral juridical act, express or tacit, enabling a person to give her consent to a juridical act entered into on her behalf by another who had no authority to do so. In a sense, to ratify another person's juridical act is to vest power and authority in that person after the juridical act has been carried out [ex *post facto*] or retroactively in a sense....

The difference between confirmation and ratification is, therefore, that confirmation erases a ground for nullity of a contract whereas ratification adds to a juridical act a necessary requirement for its validity....

A juridical act which is confirmed or ratified is fictitiously considered to have been perfect, and therefore valid, as of the time it had been entered into [*ex tunc* or "as of then"], since it is cured retroactively of its defect....

Whenever a written instrument is required, or where written proof is prescribed, an exception to these legal dispositions can be found in civil Code **Article 1853** which provides for a judicial confession....

Section I — Of Literal Proof

Cases

SUNRAY SERVICES, INC.

v.

The CITY OF MINDEN

Louisiana Court of Appeal
Second Circuit
Feb. 28, 1997
690 So.2d 970

GASKINS, Judge.

FACTS

[Plaintiff, garbage hauler, who had provided commercial and industrial garbage hauling services under exclusive contract with city brought action against the city for breach of contract. The city council motioned to extend the plaintiff's contract for an additional seven years. The mayor vetoed the action as being contrary to the provisions of the statute dealing with city trash collection contracts and sent the plaintiff written notice of the city's intent to terminate the contract. The plaintiff contended that its contract was still in effect because the mayor was not authorized by the city council to act alone in terminating contract. The city asserted that by its subsequent actions in receiving bids and awarding the contract to another company, it ratified the mayor's letter of termination.]

RATIFICATION

Law

As a general rule, a mayor acting alone is without power to execute a contract binding on the city in the absence of an ordinance or resolution by the governing council authorizing him to do so. *Smith v. Town of Vinton*, 209 La. 587, 25 So.2d 237 (1946); *Daspit v. City of Alexandria*, 342 So.2d 683 (La.App. 3d Cir.1977), writ denied, 344 So.2d 1056 (La.1977).

Ratification is a declaration whereby a person gives his consent to an obligation incurred on his behalf by another without authority. An express act of ratification must evidence the intention to be bound by the ratified obligation. Tacit ratification results when a person, with knowledge of an obligation incurred on his behalf by another, accepts the benefit of that obligation. La.C.C. Art. 1843.

An unauthorized contract of an agent may be ratified by the subsequent action or inaction of the principal upon being apprised of the facts. *Louisiana Consumer's League, Inc. v. City of Baton Rouge*, 431 So.2d 35 (La.App. 1st Cir.1983), writ denied, 435 So.2d 431 (La.1983). The general theory of ratification of the unauthorized acts of an agent is that the principal, with full knowledge of the facts, consents to the unauthorized actions

36 and adopts the contract as if it had been previously authorized. *Everett v. Foxwood Prop-*
37 *erties*, 584 So.2d 1233 (La.App.2d Cir.1991).

Discussion

39   In late 1989, the Minden City Council appointed a committee to study the privatiza-
40 tion of both residential and commercial trash collection. Although the 1982 contract with
41 Sunray functionally privatized commercial collection, there was an apparent consensus
42 that opening commercial collection to a free market would allow bidders on the resi-
43 dential collection to offer better prices if they had the chance to offer both types of col-
44 lection. According to the testimony of Councilman Starkey, even Mr. McFarland agreed
45 with this position. Furthermore, the need to open up commercial collection to the free
46 market was frequently discussed at the sanitation committee meetings, many of which
47 Mr. McFarland attended. Certainly, Mayor Brown's internal memo dated February 9,
48 1990, a copy of which was received by Mr. McFarland, demonstrated that this was a se-
49 rious consideration on the issue of trash collection and that Sunray's exclusive contract
50 was going to expire at the end of August 1990.

51   When the city council voted at its April 2, 1990 meeting to accept the recommenda-
52 tion of the sanitation committee, it specifically referred to privatizing both residential
53 *and* commercial sanitation. In his testimony, Mr. McFarland, who attended that meeting,
54 attempted to dismiss the inclusion of the commercial collection as merely "negligent."
55 Also, Sunray makes much of the fact that the bid packages sent out to prospective bid-
56 ders pertained only to residential collection. However, the evidence taken as a whole
57 amply demonstrates that it was well understood by all parties—including Mr. McFar-
58 land—that a consideration in privatizing residential collection was the termination of
59 the exclusive franchise on commercial collection. The testimony of members of the city
60 council and/or the sanitation committee reveals that they understood that the termina-
61 tion of the Sunray contract flowed from their decision to privatize both residential and
62 commercial collection and that they approved the contents of the mayor's notice letter
63 to Sunray. They were fully aware of the termination notice, and no effort was ever made
64 to repudiate it. To the contrary, the city council proceeded ahead and awarded the con-
65 tract for the residential collection to Waste Management.

66   Inasmuch as we find that Mayor Brown's termination notice was tacitly ratified by
67 the Minden City Council, we find no basis for rendering judgment against the City of
68 Minden. Accordingly, we reverse the trial court judgment awarding damages in favor of
69 Sunray.

[....]

Questions

1. Did Sunray involve a case of "ratification", properly so called, as that term is defined
    in Louisiana Civil Code article 1843? Why or why not? If not, was it proper for the
    court to apply the principles established in that and related articles in order to re-
    solve the dispute before it? In doing so, what kind of "methodology" was the court
    employing?

2. Problems of ratification most commonly arise in connection with the nominate con-
    tract of "mandate" (comparable to Anglo-American "agency"), *see* La. Civ. Code art.
    2989 *et seq.*, to be more specific, in cases where the mandatary ("agent") "exceeds"
    the "authority" that has been conferred on him by his principal. As a general rule, the
    principal is not bound to perform contracts that the mandatary, acting in excess of

his authority, makes for him, *see* La. Civ. Code art. 3020, and, in such a case, the principal is not liable to the mandatary for any loss he may sustain, *see* La. Civ. Code art. 3008, unless the principal thereafter "ratifies" the contract.

STATE ex rel. HEBERT

v.

RECORDER OF MORTGAGES et al.

Louisiana Supreme Court
May 23, 1932
143 So. 15

ST. PAUL, Justice.

Relator was the owner of certain real estate on which there was a homestead mortgage of $4,000. He made a nominal sale thereof to one Thiberville for the recited consideration of $1,500 cash and the assumption of said mortgage, which deed was duly recorded. In point of fact, this sale was simulated and made for convenience only. The supposed purchaser paid no cash and paid nothing on the mortgage which he nominally assumed, nor was he expected to do so. The vendor remained in possession of the property and continued to make his payments to the homestead. The supposed purchaser at once gave relator a counter letter acknowledging that he had no interest in the property and that same belonged to relator. But this counter letter was not registered.

I.

For some three years and more the property stood on the public records as belonging to Thiberville, who then retransferred it to relator, reciting the circumstances as above stated.

But in the meanwhile, certain creditors of Thiberville had obtained judgments against him and had recorded same as judicial mortgages against all his property.

It is not shown that Thiberville's creditors gave him credit or took judgments against him and recorded them with actual knowledge that the property stood in his name, or that they had any other knowledge than that which the law presumes from the fact that it stood as his upon the public records.

II.

This is a proceeding to cancel and erase from the records the inscription of said judicial mortgages in so far as they affect this property on the ground urged by relator that "recorded judgments against a simulated transferee of property do not operate as judicial mortgages against the property in the absence of circumstances creating an estoppel against the owner"; which seems to be an established principle in courts of equity and common law, but which the defendants contend is not the law of this state.

The trial judge held with the defendants, and the relator appeals.

III.

Rev. Civ. Code, article 2239, reads as follows: "Counter letters can have no effect against creditors or bona fide purchasers. * * *"

Rev. Civ. Code, article 2266, reads as follows: "All sales, contracts and judgments affecting immovable property, which shall not be so recorded [i.e. in the proper office], shall be utterly null and void, except between the parties thereto. The recording may be made at any time, but shall only affect third persons from the time of the recording. * * *"

The creditors meant in Rev. Civ. Code. article 2230, are, of course, the creditors of the party giving the counter letter, and in whose name the property stands.

And a counter letter relating to immovable property is, of course, a contract affecting immovable property, since it is the immovable property, since it is the acknowledgment of a natural obligation to restore the property to its true owner and a promise, express or implied, to do so.

IV.

Articles 2239 and 2266, Rev. Civ. Code, must therefore be read together. Counter letters duly recorded affect all persons even creditors from the time of the recording. Counter letters not recorded are "utterly null and void" except between the parties thereto.

In Slark v. Broom, 9 La. Ann. 69, this court held that a counter letter (unrecorded) acknowledging that the price of a ship had not been paid in full, though the bill of sale so recited, could not be opposed to other creditors of the purchaser, or avail to claim a vendor's lien on the ship.

In Tulane v. Levinson, 2 La. Ann. 787, this court held that the creditors of the vendor of an immovable could, by recording their judgment against him, obtain a valid judicial mortgage against the property, and could validly seize, sell, and buy in the property, although knowing that the property had been sold to another who had failed to record his deed in the proper office.

In Harang v. Plattsmier, 21 La. Ann. 426, this court overruled Swan v. Moore, 14 La. Ann. 833, wherein it had been held that actual knowledge of an unrecorded title on the part of a creditor is equivalent to knowledge or notice resulting from the registry of such title; and, referring to Acts of 1855, p. 335 (now Rev. Civ. Code, art. 2266), held that: "The lawgiver, it would seem, was determined to settle the vexed question, whether knowledge was equivalent to registry in Louisiana, and he declared that it was not." In First Nat. Bank v. Ft. Wayne Artificial Ice Co., 105 La. 133, 29 So. 379, 381, this court said: "We take it to be well settled under our law that, while a sale of immovable property may be good as between the parties by virtue of their agreement, it is void as to third persons until registered."

In McDuffie v. Walker, 125 La. 152, 51 So. 100, this court held, that as to third persons, unrecorded acts affecting immovable property were so far nonexistent, that they might be deliberately ignored with entire good faith; for "It cannot, however, be said that a third person perpetrates a fraud merely by treating as void, as to himself, a contract which the law in terms declares 'shall be utterly null and void, except between the parties thereto;'" (just as had actually been done, and approved of by the court, in Tulane v. Levinson, supra). "To hold such doctrine is necessarily to hold that one who knows a particular contract to be denounced by the law as utterly void is bound in spite of the law to respect it as valid and binding, a paradox to which a court of justice would be unwilling to commit itself as an interpretation of law." And the court said further: "It is evident that whether a person acquires an interest in real estate to the extent of its value or part of its value as a mortgagee or as a vendee the principle involved in the application of the law of registry is the same; and hence if it be true that one may acquire a valid first mortgage, though he know at the time that as between the mortgagor and another there already exists an unrecorded mortgage upon the same property, it must also be true that one may acquire a valid title to such property, though he know that as between his vendor and another an unrecorded title has already been passed. The law makes no distinction between mortgages and sales or between creditors and vendees or mortgagees; nor does it discriminate between those who acquire property with knowledge of unrecorded

contracts and those who acquire without such knowledge. Its purpose is to establish and   89
enforce as a matter of public policy upon the subject of the most important property   90
right with which it deals the rule that unrecorded contracts affecting immovable property   91
"shall be utterly null and void, except between the parties thereto." No language could be   92
plainer or more emphatic, and the courts have no more power to read into the rule es-   93
tablished by it an exception, not contained in it, than they would have to read such an ex-   94
ception into the rule that a verbal sale of immovable property shall not affect third persons."   95

V.   96

We have cited these few cases out of the very large number holding to the same effect,   97
because these case show that in this state registry is not a mere matter of notice alone, but   98
a matter of public policy upon a "most important property right"; and that considerations   99
of equity cannot prevail against it. "With us, those laws [of registry] are considered as   100
founded on public policy, and the want of registry cannot be supplied. In the other States   101
they are viewed differently, and notice in any form is held to be equivalent to registry."   102
Lockett v. Toby, 10 La. Ann. 713, 715.   103

The only case in which the contrary was held, to wit, that registry was only a matter   104
of notice and not of public policy (Swan v. Moore, supra), was emphatically repudiated   105
by legislative act in 1855 (Harang v. Plattsmier, supra), and by the uniform jurisprudence   106
of this court ever since that time.   107

Hence, all consideration of equity being banished, the creditors of a vendor who record   108
judgments against him after he has sold the property but before the purchaser records   109
his deed may not only ignore the purchaser with the unrecorded title, but acquire a ju-   110
dicial mortgage superior in rank to that of all judgment creditors of the purchaser with-   111
out exception; since "there can be no actual owner of immovable property, so far as third   112
persons are concerned, other than the owner of record; for, except as between the par-   113
ties thereto, an unrecorded conveyance is 'utterly null and void,' and conveys no title."   114
Baker v. Atkins, 107 La. 490, 32 So. 69, 70.   115

VI.   116

The equity doctrine on which relator relies is that a judgment creditor acquires no lien   117
against property standing in the name of his judgment debtor, but in which that debtor   118
has no beneficial interest, unless the judgment creditor can successfully plead an estop-   119
pel in pais against the actual owner of the property.   120

But, as we have endeavored to show, registry is a matter of public policy in this state,   121
against which considerations of equity cannot prevail; and "there can be no actual owner   122
of immovable property, so far as third persons are concerned, other than the owner of record."   123

It is true there are a few cases apparently out of harmony with the otherwise uniform   124
jurisprudence of this court.   125

Peters v. Toby, 10 La. Ann. 408, was decided in 1855 on a state of facts existing, and   126
in litigation which had begun, long before the legislative act of that year. It is not au-   127
thority under that legislation.   128

The other cases (Broussard v. Le Blanc, 44 La. 880, 11 So. 460; Succession of Manson,   129
51 La. Ann. 130, 25 So. 639; Douglass v. Douglass, 51 La. Ann. 1455, 26 So. 546) were ex-   130
amined and distinguished in Baker v. Atkins, 107 La. 490, 32 So. 69, 72, in which it was   131
said: "There is, no doubt, some language in these opinions which sustains the views which   132
have been here considered [substantially those herein urged by relator], but we are of opin-   133
ion that its application should be confined to the cases in which it was used, it being much   134
safer at times to reason from general propositions to particular cases than the reverse."   135

136   This case is governed by articles of the Louisiana Civil Code as they existed before the
137 Civil Code revision of 1984, as all acts pertinent to this case occurred before the revision.

Questions

1. Line 11: The *Hebert* court states that the sale out of which the case arose was "simulated". We studied the concept of "simulation" earlier in the course. *See supra* pp. 356. Which kind of simulation was involved in Hebert? What is the significance of that classification?

2. Lines 43–46: The *Hebert* court states that a counter-letter signed by the ostensible buyer of a simulated sale constitutes an "acknowledgment of a natural obligation to restore the property to its true owner", that is, the ostensible seller. We studied the concept of "natural obligation" earlier in the course. *See supra* pp. 5. What do you think of the *Hebert* court's statement regarding the ostensible buyer's "natural obligation" to restore the property to the ostensible seller? Is this among the examples of natural obligations listed in Louisiana Civil Code article 1762? Does this supposed natural obligation conform to the account of natural obligations provided in Louisiana Civil Code article 1760?

3. The *Hebert* case concerns what is known as the "public records doctrine", a body of principles to which you have already been exposed in this course, *see supra* pp. 377. [The public records doctrine is an important aspect of the law of "Sales and Leases".] (Since *Hebert* was decided, this body of principles has been codified. *See* La. Civ. Code art. 3338 *et seq.*) Looking at the *Hebert* case, what would you say that the "public records doctrine" has to do with the topic that you are presently studying, that is, "proof of obligations"? Is it that, when juridical acts involving immovable property are involved, proof of the existence of rights and duties pertaining to that property requires that there be some written evidence of their existence in the public records? Cf. La. Civ. Code art. 1839, par. 2.

SUCCESSION OF Mrs. Allena Rogers MONTGOMERY

1

2   Louisiana Court of Appeal
3   Second Circuit
4   May 6, 1987
5   506 So.2d 1309

6 LINDSAY, Judge.

7   On January 9, 1984, William Johnson, executor of the Succession of Allena Rogers
8 Montgomery, filed with the succession a descriptive list of assets and liabilities. Listed
9 under the liabilities is an unsecured note in the original amount of $128,525 executed by
10 Allena Montgomery in favor of Thomas Montgomery. The amount of liability for the
11 aforementioned note was recorded in the descriptive list as $0.00.

12   On December 17, 1985, Thomas Montgomery filed a motion to traverse the descriptive list, seeking to have the descriptive list amended to include the amount allegedly remaining due on the note. The executor filed an opposition to the motion to traverse, claiming that the promissory note was issued without consideration. A hearing was held on January 2, 1986. At the conclusion of the hearing, the trial judge denied Thomas Montgomery's motion to traverse, and dismissed the action with prejudice, ruling that the note had been issued without consideration.

Mr. Montgomery has appealed, raising the issues of whether the trial court properly admitted certain parol and documentary evidence, whether the evidence supported the conclusion of the trial court and whether the trial court erred in rendering a judgment dismissing plaintiff's motion to traverse "with prejudice." For the following reasons, we affirm the trial court judgment.

The record reveals that at the hearing on the motion to traverse the descriptive list, counsel for Mr. Montgomery introduced into evidence the promissory note in question, and an attached affidavit which had been executed by the decedent. In the affidavit, the affiant, Allena Montgomery, states that she has executed a promissory note in favor of her son, Thomas Montgomery, in the amount of $128,525 and that the consideration for the note is the money, groceries and other items furnished by her son since the death of her husband in 1959. Additionally, the affidavit recites that her son has also paid her accounts, paid taxes on real estate, provided transportation and managed her affairs. The notary before whom the affidavit was executed testified that the affidavit expressed the desires of the affiant. Mr. Montgomery did not testify, nor was he present at the hearing.

William Johnson, the executor of the succession and the grandson of the deceased, testified that the note should not be listed in the descriptive list because he felt there was no real debt involved; i.e., there was no consideration for the note. To substantiate his belief, Mr. Johnson testified that Mrs. Allena Montgomery and her previously deceased husband donated land and a store to Thomas Montgomery in 1959 to compensate him for services rendered and to be rendered in caring for Mrs. Allena Montgomery. Mrs. Allena Montgomery's husband died five days after the act of donation was passed. Furthermore, on January 3, 1981, eight lots in Benton, Louisiana were sold by Mrs. Allena Montgomery to Thomas Montgomery for $2,000. Mr. Johnson felt that this price was substantially inadequate. Likewise, on June 6, 1981,[1] Allena Montgomery sold approximately 130 acres of land in Bossier Parish to Thomas Montgomery for $37,650. Mr. Johnson also felt that this was a substantially inadequate price. Certified copies of the various transactions were filed in evidence.

Appellant contends that copies of the documents and the testimony of William Johnson were inadmissible. [....] [A]ppellant contends that the affidavit and note together constitute an act under private signature duly acknowledged which, at the time of execution, was equivalent to an authentic act and therefore full proof of its contents against the parties, their heirs or assigns. Thus, any evidence presented which would contradict the facts as established in the authentic act should be excluded as parol evidence.

I. ADMISSIBILITY OF EVIDENCE

[....]

[....] [**Appellant contends, among other things,**] that the note and affidavit constitute an act under private signature, duly acknowledged, and therefore other evidence cannot be admitted to contradict this "authenticated document."

Under former Civil Code Article 2242,[2] an act under private signature, duly acknowledged has, between those who have subscribed to it, and their heirs and their assigns, the same credit as an authentic act. An authentic act is full proof of the agreement contained in it, against the contracting parties and their heirs or assigns, unless it be declared and proved a forgery. LSA-C.C. Art. 2236.[3]

---

1. Allena Montgomery's will and the note at issue are also dated June 6, 1981.
2. This case is governed by articles of the Louisiana Civil Code as they existed before the Civil Code revision of 1984, as all acts pertinent to this case occurred before the revision.
3. Id.

63   However, appellee contends that evidence of simulation and failure of consideration were
64 admissible by virtue of former LSA-C.C. Art. 2239.[4] That article of the Code provides that
65 forced heirs shall have the right to annul absolutely and by parol evidence the simulated
66 contracts of those from whom they inherit, and they shall not be restricted to the legitime.

67   Appellee is correct in asserting that LSA-C.C. Art. 2239 allows him, as executor of the
68 succession and a forced heir, to attack an act of the deceased, even though in authentic
69 form, by parol evidence to prove that the act is a simulated contract. *Smelley v. Ricks*, 174
70 La. 734, 141 So. 445 (1932); *Succession of Broussard*, 306 So.2d 399 (La.App. 3rd Cir.1975).

71   The evidence was also admissible to show that the deceased has acted to deplete her
72 estate through the use of a simulation to defeat the forced heirship laws of this state. *Smith
73 v. Smith*, 239 La. 688, 119 So.2d 827 (1960).

74   For the foregoing reasons, we conclude that the trial court correctly admitted Mr. John-
75 son's testimony concerning a lack of consideration, as well as the evidence of the other
76 donations which the deceased made to Thomas Montgomery.

[....]

Questions

1.   Throughout its opinion, the *Montgomery* court proceeds on the assumption that
   what it calls "lack of consideration" is an adequate "defense" to the enforcement of a
   "promissory note". Was that assumption correct? *See* La. Civ. Code art. 1966 & art.
   1967. If not, that is, if "lack of consideration" was not a per se defense to the enforcement of the note, does it not, nevertheless, lay the basis for another attack on
   the enforceability of the note, for example, that the note was not in "proper form"?
   If the promissory note was not given "for consideration", then what kind of contract
   did it represent? Hint: *see* La. Civ. Code arts. 1909 & 1910. What does one call a gratuitous contract that transfers a thing? *See* La. Civ. Code art. 1468. What form is required for such a contract? *See* La. Civ. Code art. 1541.

2.   *Montgomery* was decided under the "old law" of "proof of obligations". Under the "new
   law", may one still use parol evidence in an effort to show that a juridical act that has
   been documented in an authentic act was simulated? *See* La. Civ. Code art. 1848.

1 **Lane N. MELTZER**

2 **v.**

3 **Sarah A. MELTZER**

4 Louisiana Court of Appeal

5 Fourth Circuit

6 Sept. 28, 1995

7 662 So.2d 58

8 WALTZER, Judge.

[....]

10 *STATEMENT OF FACTS*

11   [In connection with their divorce proceedings, Lane M. Meltzer (Lane) and Sarah
12 Allen Meltzer (Sarah) litigated the validity of a marriage contract entered into by the par-

---

4. Id.

ties prior to their marriage and later recorded. In this marriage contract, Lane and Sarah   13
rejected the community property regime. The litigation is based on Sarah's denial] [...   14
] that it was executed in the presence of a notary public and two witnesses.   15

[....]   16

At the hearing on 26 July 1994, the parties to the contract, the notary public before whom   17
it was executed and the two witnesses testified.   18

Louis G. Shushan, the notary and Lane's first cousin, testified that he has practiced   19
law for forty-one years. He recognized the contract when it was shown to him, but had   20
no independent recollection of the contract from the time of its execution, eighteen years   21
previous. He identified his signature, and identified witness Linda Condon as Lane's sec-   22
retary at the time the contract was executed and identified witness Carol Lazaro as his   23
own secretary for the last twenty-eight years. He recalled that Sarah was represented at   24
the time by attorney, now United States District Judge Martin L.C. Feldman. He did not   25
recall whether all parties were in his office at the time the contract was executed. He said   26
it was not unusual at the time for all the parties not to be present at the same time when   27
acts were executed. He testified that if he signed this act, all of the signatories came into   28
his office and signed it. He testified that he had no reason to believe that he did not fol-   29
low the requisite procedure of having each party and witness sign before him.   30

Sarah testified that Lane presented the contract to her about two weeks before their wed-   31
ding date, and suggested she take it to a lawyer to "have him check it out." Sarah testified   32
that she took the contract to Feldman, whom she described as her lawyer and a friend.   33
She admitted having had the opportunity to obtain legal advice in connection with the   34
contract. She admitted having signed the contract, but testified that she did so outside the   35
presence of Mr. Shushan, in "Shepard's office"[1] on the 31st floor 1010 Common Street in   36
New Orleans. She testified that Mr. Shushan's office was on the 5th floor of the same   37
building, but that her first visit to Mr. Shushan's office occurred after her marriage to   38
Lane in conjunction with the sale of a parcel he had acquired with his first wife. Sarah de-   39
nied that Linda Condon was present when she signed the contract, and denied ever hav-   40
ing met Carol Lazaro.   41

Sarah testified that during her marriage to Lane she maintained a separate account   42
into which she deposited the income she received from her property, and to which Lane   43
had no access. It is uncontroverted that during the entire seventeen year existence of their   44
marriage, Lane and Sarah conducted their financial affairs in conformity with the terms   45
of the Matrimonial Agreement.   46

Lane testified that the contract was prepared by Mr. Shushan's office. He gave it to   47
Sarah, to be reviewed by her attorney. Sarah told him she had talked to her attorney about   48
the contractual provisions and was prepared to sign it. It was Lane's understanding that   49
the contract provided that his and Sarah's properties were separate, and what was his re-   50
mained his, and what was hers would remain hers. Lane could not recall who was pre-   51
sent when the contract was signed, and recalled that it was signed in Shepard's office.   52
Lane testified, and Sarah admitted, that she eventually left him. He testified that he had   53
feared she would leave him as she had left her two former husbands.   54

Linda Condon testified that in 1976 she was secretary of a partnership in which Lane   55
had an interest. Her recollection was that she signed the Marriage Contract in Lane's of-   56
fice. She did not recall if Mr. Shushan or Ms. Lazaro were present, although she did re-   57

---

1. The reference is to Shepard Latter. According to Mr. Shushan, Latter died in 1973.

call Mr. Shushan's coming to Lane's office from time to time. She testified that Mr. Shushan's office was on the 15th floor and Lane's office was on the 31st floor of the 1010 Common Street Building.

Carol Lazaro testified that she has been Mr. Shushan's legal secretary for twenty-seven years, and had no recollection of the actual signing of the Marriage Contract. She testified that she was sure she met Sarah when the contract was signed. Ms. Lazaro testified that she believed the Marriage Contract was executed by the parties in front of the witnesses. According to Ms. Lazaro, Mr. Shushan was careful that all requisites for a notarial act were met, particularly after his involvement in the Louis Johnson case in late 1975 or early 1976 wherein Mr. Shushan was required to prove in court that he had met the codal requirements for the execution of an authentic act.

In its Reasons for Judgment, the trial court found:

> Of the five [witnesses], Mrs. Meltzer was the only one to claim that she recalled the circumstances surrounding the execution of the document nearly seventeen years ago. She stated that she signed the document in the office of Shepard Latter at 1010 Common Street with only Lane Meltzer present. However, this testimony was weakened by her failure to recall another incident which occurred soon after the execution of the Marriage Contract.

SPECIFICATION OF ERROR: The trial court was clearly wrong in finding that Sarah Meltzer did not prove the Marriage Contract was null.

Sarah contends that she offered sufficient proof that the execution of the Marriage Contract did not comply with the formal requisites set forth in La.C.C. art. 2328, which provided in 1976 that every matrimonial agreement must be made by an act before a notary and two witnesses.

Plaintiff's burden of disproving the validity of an authentic act is indeed heavy. Planiol wrote:

> The person who produces an authentic act, regular in appearance, does not need to prove its authenticity. The act comes accompanied by exterior signs difficult to imitate ... These exterior signs suffice. As Dumoulin said in speaking of this kind of writing: "*Scripta publica probant se ipsa.*" As a result, the public act which is regular in appearance, enjoys a presumption of authenticity, which reverses on this point the burden of proof: if the attribution of the act to its apparent author is contested, the latter who offers it has nothing to prove; it is for his adversary who denies the authenticity to demonstrate the falsity of the act, and he *cannot make this proof except by the perilous means of the "inscription de faux" (above Nos. 83–85).*[2] Planiol, *Traité Elémentaire de Droit Civil*, Vol. 2, No. 88. (Emphasis added.)

In the case at bar, Sarah does not contend that the Matrimonial Agreement was forged. Neither does she contend that she or Lane or the witnesses or the notary did not sign the document, nor that it was procured through any vice of consent such as duress, fraud or error. She admits that she had two weeks within which to consult with her own able counsel, Judge Feldman, and to determine whether she would renounce during this, her third marriage, the benefits and responsibilities of the community property regime then in effect in Louisiana. Sarah's only basis for reversing seventeen

---

2. The "*inscription de faux*" is the name of a special procedure which serves to establish that an instrument has been forged. Planiol, *supra*, Vol. 2, No. 83.

years of financial activity based upon a separate property regime is not that any signature, including her own, on the document is forged or fraudulently obtained or otherwise not authentic, but rather that she signed the document in the presence only of her then fiance.

Historically, the reason for the requirement of execution of the marriage contract before a notary and for its recordation was to protect the sanctity of the agreement from the danger that a contract under private signature, not recorded, could easily be destroyed and the matrimonial agreement inevitably changed through the obligatory application of statutory community. Planiol, *supra*, Vol. 3, No. 806.[3]

Planiol notes the significance of predictability in his discussion of the effect of these contracts on third parties dealing with married persons. Absent a recorded contract, "people were afraid to deal with married persons who claimed they had marriage contract [sic]; thus even spouses in good faith had their credit jeopardized." Planiol, *supra*, Vol. 3, No. 809. In the instant case, where the parties owned, bought and sold substantial real estate holdings, this aspect, the immutability of the marriage contract, is most significant.

The Louisiana Civil Code defines an authentic act:

> An authentic act is a writing executed before a notary public ... in the presence of two witnesses, and signed by each party who executed it, by each witness, and by the notary public before whom it was executed.

To be an authentic act, the writing need not be executed at one time or place, or before the same notary public or in the presence of the same witnesses, provided that each party who executes it does so before a notary public, ... and in the presence of two witnesses and each party, each witness, and each notary public signs it.... La.C.C. art. 1833.[4]

This Court interpreted these formal requirements in the context of an antenuptial marriage contract, holding:

> All that the law requires [for the validity of an authentic act] is that the notary and witnesses be present, C.C. 2328, when each contracting party signs the act, C.C. 2234, and that notary and witnesses themselves also sign the act, although not necessarily at the time that any party signs it. Accordingly, the act before us is not invalid because of the simple facts that the husband and wife in this case did not execute the act in the presence of each other, and that the notary and witnesses did not sign the act at the time that one (or either) party signed it.

> Our basic reasoning is that substance should prevail over form unless the law unmistakably requires a contrary result. Here the mature spouses-to-be must be presumed to have desired and consented to the exact agreement contained in the written instrument. The law only requires that the agreement be "made by an act before a notary and two witnesses," C.C. 2328: such an act is an authentic act, C.C. 2234, "executed before a notary public..., in the presence of two witnesses...." Nowhere does the law expressly require that the notary and the witnesses sign the act in the presence of the parties,....

---

3. This immutability of the matrimonial agreement in French law was a fundamental principle: the will of the parties expressed prior to the marriage was regarded as sacred and worthy of protection against subsequent assault by a party seeking institution of the statutory community system. *See*, Planiol, *supra*, Vol. 3, Nos. 813–814.

4. Acts 1984, No. 331, sec. 1, effective 1 January 1985. According to Comment (a) to the present article, this Article reproduces the substance of C.C. Art. 2234 (1870), and does not change the law.

Rittiner v. Sinclair, 374 So.2d 680, 685 (La.App. 4th Cir.1978). *See also, Nunez v. Nunez*, 436 So.2d 682, 683 at footnote 1 (La.App. 4th Cir.1983).

An authentic act in Louisiana, as under the French Code, is presumed to be valid, and this presumption is established in the interest of public order, to maintain peace among men and to prevent contestations concerning the proof or evidence of their conventions. *Succession of Tete*, 7 La.Ann. 95, 96 (La.1852).

Where, as here, the memories of the signatories are blurred by the passage of time, one seeking to invalidate an apparently authentic act must present strong and convincing proof of such magnitude as to overcome the presumption of verity of notarial acts. *DiVincenti v. McIntyre*, 611 So.2d 140, 142 (La.App. 1st Cir.1992), *writ denied* 614 So.2d 1264 (La.1993).

Sarah does not contend that any of the five signatories failed to sign the Marriage Contract or that any of the signatures were obtained by fraud, mistake or duress. Neither did she offer any proof that Lane's signature was not signed in the presence of the notary and two witnesses. As to her own signature, only Sarah testified to an exact recollection of the signing process, and her testimony standing alone, even if accepted by the trier of fact, would be insufficient to overcome the presumption of validity. *See, DiVincenti*, 611 So.2d at 141–143.

We are mindful that a marriage contract should be maintained if possible. *Id.* At the time of the execution of the Marriage Contract, Sarah was thirty-seven years old, twice divorced, and represented by able independent counsel. Lane, seventeen years her senior, was likewise represented. The notary was an experienced practitioner who had recently been required to offer proof in court that another of his notarial authentic acts had been properly executed. The record is devoid of any proof, even were we to consider Sarah's testimony, which was rejected by the trial court, that the Rittiner standard was not met.

The trial judge, who observed the witnesses, chose not to accept Sarah's testimony. This credibility determination can virtually never be manifestly erroneous, and we find it to have been within the sound discretion of the trier of fact. *Stobart v. State of Louisiana, through Dept. of Transp. and Development*, 617 So.2d 880, 882 (La.1993); *Rosell v. ESCO*, 549 So.2d 840, 844 (La.1989). We will not disturb that credibility choice.

Sarah's testimony having been rejected by the trial court, we turn to the testimony of the remaining witnesses. The trial court accepted Mr. Shushan's testimony that he had no reason to believe he did not follow the requisite procedure in the execution of the Marriage Contract, and found support in Ms. Lazaro's testimony that she was sure that the parties and other witness came to Mr. Shushan's office to execute the document because it was his practice to have everyone present in his office when notarized documents were executed. The trial court found this testimony to have been bolstered by Mr. Shushan's participation in prior litigation concerning the validity of an authentic act. The trial judge found that Ms. Condon did not recall the circumstances of the execution. We find these conclusions to be supported by the record taken as a whole. Sarah relies on Lane's testimony that he could not refute her testimony as an admission by Lane of the truth of her version of the signing; however, a careful reading of the record shows that Lane testified that he had no specific recollection of the signing, and, therefore, could not conscientiously say that her testimony was incorrect. We cannot equate a failure to remember with corroboration of an adverse party's testimony.

The trial court concluded that the evidence offered by Sarah as a whole did not support by a reasonable preponderance of the evidence that the Marriage Contract was not an authentic act. We find this conclusion to be supported by the record as a whole, and find no manifest error in the trial court's determination.

We affirm the trial court's judgment finding that Sarah A. Meltzer failed to prove by   190
a reasonable preponderance of the evidence that the Marriage Contract executed by and   191
between Lane Meltzer and Sarah Allen on 10 November 1976 was invalid.   192

AFFIRMED.   193

Questions

1.   From the point of view of the *Meltzer* court, what was the fundamental "problem"
     with Sarah's case? Was it (1) that the "defect" in the creation of the act that she alleged—
     that she had not signed the act in the presence of the notary and the witnesses—was
     not, by itself, sufficient to render the act invalid or (2) that she simply lacked suffi-
     cient proof of this alleged defect? If it is the latter, then what is one to make of the
     court's repeated statements that Sarah alleged neither "forgery" nor "vice of consent"?

2.   The *Meltzer* court seems to have assumed that an act that purports to be in authentic
     form carries with it a presumption that the process whereby the act was produced
     was, in fact, "regular", that is, that it was signed by each party before the notary and
     the witnesses, etc. Does the applicable legislation support this assumption? Consider,
     in particular, Louisiana Civil Code article 1835, which provides that an authentic act
     constitutes "full proof of the agreement it contains". Is the process for preparing an au-
     thentic act part of "the agreement" the act contains? If not, then what is the basis for
     the court's assumption? Is it "doctrine", as represented by Planiol? Prior jurisprudence?

Section II — Of Testimonial Proof

Case

SNOW-WHITE ROOFS, INC.   1
v.   2
Frank BOUCHER and Robert Coppage   3
Louisiana Court of Appeal   4
Fourth Circuit   5
Feb. 7, 1966   6
182 So.2d 846   7

SAMUEL, Judge.   8

[Plaintiff contractor sued owners of residence for, among other things, the contract price.   9
Defendant denied liability and asked, alternatively, for a reduction of the contract price   10
for roof repair work not completed by the plaintiff.] [....]   11

[....]   12

The fact that in performing its work under the contract plaintiff did "snow white" the   13
roof (a process discussed later in this opinion) and did not repair the leaks is undisputed.   14
The appeal is based on plaintiff's contention that under the terms of the contract it was not   15
obligated to repair leaks in the roof, that the contract must be enforced as written and that   16
the trial judge was in error in admitting parol evidence which had the effect of placing plain-   17
tiff under that added obligation. Plaintiff had made timely objections to that evidence.   18

19   Under our Civil Code and jurisprudence parol evidence cannot be admitted against or
20   beyond what is contained in a written contract; such evidence is inadmissible to vary,
21   alter or add to the contract's terms. LSA-C.C. Art. 2276; Dufrene v. Tracy, 232 La. 386,
22   94 So.2d 297; Rosenthal v. Cauthier, 224 La. 341, 69 So.2d 367; Reuter v. Reuter's Suc-
23   cession, 206 La. 474, 19 So.2d 209. However, where there are ambiguities in a written
24   contract, parol evidence is admissible to clarify those ambiguities by showing the inten-
25   tion of the parties. See Rosenthal v. Gauthier, supra; Rudman v. Dupuis, 206 La. 1061,
26   20 So.2d 363; Holloway Gravel Co. v. McKowen, 200 La. 917, 9 So.2d 228.

27   The contract in the instant case is on one of plaintiff's printed forms. It does state that
28   "Snow-White is not a water proofing" and it does make reference to a plaintiff brochure
29   which accompanied the contract. The brochure sets out the work to be done in connec-
30   tion with the "Snow White Service". The repair of roof leaks is not included as part of the
31   work as set out in the brochure. There appears in handwriting (all unprinted portions of
32   the contract are in handwriting) on the first page of the contract, immediately below the
33   name of the defendant-agent and the address of the premises upon which the work was
34   to be done, the phrase "Residence to be Repaired and Snow White Coated". The approxi-
35   mate area to be covered by the work is stated as being the "Entire Roof Area". The con-
36   tract was signed by the defendant-agent, a realtor, and by a representative of the plaintiff.

37   The president of the plaintiff corporation, that party's only witness, testified relative
38   to the purposes of "snow whiting" a roof and that testimony appears to be consistent with
39   the printed terms of the contract and brochure. His testimony was to the effect that the
40   process beautifies, reduces the cost of air conditioning, and secures gravel on the type of
41   roof here involved; it does not waterproof or repair leaks. However, this witness also tes-
42   tified that the plaintiff corporation occasionally did do other types of roofing work, in-
43   cluding the repairing of leaks, when called for by the contract.

44   Clearly the contractual phase, "Residence to be Repaired and Show White Coated",
45   calls for more than the snow whiting process. The word "Repaired" is in addition to that
46   process and is ambiguous in that the type of repair is not specified. This case therefore
47   falls under the exception to the rule we have set out above and parol evidence was prop-
48   erly admitted to explain the repairs intended by the parties.

49   The evidence admitted for this purpose consisted only of testimony given by witnesses
50   on behalf of the defendants. Those witnesses were the defendant-agent, his secretary, and the
51   tenant who occupied the premises. The plaintiff"s representative, who had negotiated and
52   signed the contract on behalf of plaintiff, was deceased at the time of trial. The testimony thus
53   adduced establishes the fact that the parties intended to enter into a contract which included
54   repairing leaks in the roof. In short summary that testimony was to the following effect:

55   The defendant-agent was informed by the tenant that the roof was leaking and needed
56   repairs. He contacted several roofing contractors asking for bids or prices. He also con-
58   tacted plaintiff, obtaining his information as to that corporation from the classified sec-
59   tion of the local telephone directory and eventually entered into the contract here involved.
60   At the time he discussed the matter with plaintiff's representative he informed that per-
61   son he wished to have the leaks repaired and was told by the representative that the leaks
62   would be repaired as a part of the contract. The leaks were not repaired and the roof con-
63   tinued to leak after plaintiff's work had been completed. The leaks were later repaired by
64   another contractor at a cost of $165.

65   Our conclusion is that, insofar as plaintiff's appeal is concerned, the judgment must
66   be affirmed.

[....]

Question

1. Does the jurisprudential rule on which the *Snow-White* court based its analysis—
   "where there are ambiguities in a written contract, parol evidence is admissible to
   clarify those ambiguities by showing the intention of the parties", see lines 23–25—
   constitute an "exception", properly so called, to the general legislative rule that "[t]es-
   timonial or other evidence may not be admitted to negate or vary the contents of
   an authentic act or an act under private signature" (*see* La. Civ. Code art. 1848, sent.
   1)? If so, then why is it not included among the legislative exceptions to that general rule that are collected in second sentence of that same article? If not, then what
   is the nature of the relationship between the jurisprudential rule and the general
   legislative rule?

Section III — Of Presumptions

Case

Lloyd JACKSON, Sr., et al.
v.
GULF INSURANCE COMPANY et al.

Louisiana Supreme Court
June 5, 1967
199 So.2d 886

SANDERS, Justice.

This action for damages Ex delicto poses the question of whether the disserving testimony of a plaintiff as to the circumstances of an automobile accident bars his recovery
as a judicial confession or conclusive admission, despite other preponderating evidence
supporting the liability of the defendant. [....]

On November 3, 1962, Lloyd Jackson, Sr., Lena Porea, and Kathleen Lee, plaintiffs
herein, were guest passengers in an automobile driven by Lloyd Jackson, Jr. and insured
by Gulf Insurance Company. The automobile collided with a pickup truck owned by H.
A. Folse Sons and insured by Maryland Casualty Company. At the time of the accident,
a Folse employee was driving the truck. He was accompanied by two boys, who were distributing circular advertisements.

[....]

Lloyd Jackson, Sr. and Kathleen Lee, who were riding in the front seat of the automobile, testified they first saw the truck approaching when the two vehicles were about
a block apart. At that time each vehicle was moving at a reasonable speed in its proper
lane. After the vehicles were very close to each other, so they testified, the truck suddenly
swerved across the center of the highway, striking the automobile in its lane of travel.

The testimony of plaintiff Lena Porea corroborated that of the other plaintiffs in some respects, but her testimony failed to completely absolve the automobile driver from negligence.

The three occupants of the truck testified at the trial. Having been injured in the collision, one of the delivery boys was unable to recall the details of the accident. But the

28 combined testimony of the driver and the other delivery boy was to the effect that at the
29 time of the collision the truck was stopped partially off the highway on the proper side,
30 while one of the delivery boys picked up some circulars that had blown off the truck.
31 The approaching automobile drove across the highway and hit the stopped truck. The
32 record contains other testimony showing that after the collision there were skid or tire
33 marks running from the automobile's travel lane to the impact point on the truck's side
34 of the road.

35   The trial court found that the automobile crossed the highway and hit the stopped
36 truck, as related by the truck driver and his corroborating witnesses. The court dismissed
37 the suit against the truck driver's insurer, Maryland Casualty Company. The court also
38 dismissed the plaintiffs' suit against the other defendant, Gulf Insurance Company, insurer
39 of the automobile driver, on the ground that the plaintiffs were "precluded from recov-
40 ery * * * because they testified to no acts of negligence" on the part of the automobile
41 driver. The court held that their testimony operated as a judicial confession under LSA-
42 C.C. Article 2291, barring recovery since it exonerated the automobile driver from neg-
43 ligence. The plaintiffs appealed.

44   In the Court of Appeal, the plaintiffs attacked the trial court judgment rejecting their
45 demands against Gulf Insurance Company, the insurer of the automobile driver. The
46 Court of Appeal partially reversed and granted recovery to plaintiff Lena Porea, finding
47 that her testimony did not completely exonerate the automobile driver from negligence.
48 The Court of Appeal affirmed the judgment insofar as it rejected the demands of the
49 other plaintiffs, finding that their testimony did exonerate their host driver from negli-
50 gence. The court held this testimony was a judicial confession under LSA-C.C. Article
51 2291, barring the plaintiffs' recovery despite a finding that the host driver was at fault in
52 the accident. See La.App., 188 So.2d 84. On application of the unsuccessful plaintiffs, we
53 granted certiorari to review the Court of Appeal judgment. See 249 La. 771, 191 So.2d 144.

54   We agree with the Court of Appeal's finding of fact and find the collision resulted from
55 the fault of the automobile driver. The Court of Appeal also found that plaintiffs-relators
56 testified that the truck suddenly swerved into the automobile's lane and struck the auto-
57 mobile, contrary to the court's finding. From our review of the testimony, we conclude
58 the plaintiffs testified to facts which, if accepted by the court, would exonerate their host
59 driver from fault.

60 Article 2291 of the Louisiana Civil Code provides:

61   "The judicial confession is the declaration which the party, or his special attor-
62   ney in fact, makes in a judicial proceeding.

63   "It amounts to full proof against him who has made it.

64   "It can not be divided against him.

65   "It can not be revoked, unless it be proved to have been made through an error
66   in fact.

67   "It can not be revoked on a pretense of an error in law."

68   The defendant-respondent contends that this Article applies to the present case and that
69 plaintiffs' factual testimony exonerating the automobile driver from fault is a judicial con-
70 fession which bars their recovery. The respondent relies upon a series of cases in the in-
71 termediate courts of appeal, including Thompson v. Haubtman, 18 La.App. 119, 137 So.
72 362 (1931); Stroud v. Standard Accident Insurance Co., La.App., 90 So.2d 477 (1956);
73 Bowers v. Hardware Mutual Casualty Co., La.App., 119 So.2d 671 (1960); and Franklin
74 v. Zurich Ins. Co., La.App., 136 So.2d 735 (1962).

The plaintiffs-relators contend Article 2291 is inapplicable to an automobile accident suit. They assert the Article applies only to proof of conventional obligations, or contracts, since it is found in Title IV of the Civil Code relating to conventional obligations and in a chapter entitled, "Of the Proof of Obligations and of That of Payment." Alternatively, they assert that the disserving testimony of the plaintiffs does not bar their recovery, because the court found the host driver was in fact guilty of negligence causing the accident.

The initial question framed by these contentions is whether LSA-C.C. Article 2291 applies to a suit for damages arising from a delict, or tort.

The Article, of course, is in Title IV of the Louisiana Civil Code dealing with conventional obligations. It forms part of Chapter 6, entitled, "Of the Proof of Obligations and of That of Payment." This chapter, however, contains a number of articles of general application. For example, Article 2282 deals with the competency of witnesses; Article 2283, with the attorneyclient privilege; Article 2284, with legal presumptions; and Article 2286, with res judicata. See, generally, Saundes" Lectures on the Civil Code (Bonomo ed., 1925) p. 460.

Article 2291 contains no language delimiting it to proof of conventional obligations. The Article refers generally to "a judicial proceeding." This Court has long recognized that the Article applies to judicial proceedings other than those involving the proof of a contractal [*sic*] obligation. See, e.g., Penn v. Burk, 244 La. 267, 152 So.2d 16 (suit to enjoin executory process); D'Antoni v. Geraci, 224 La. 818, 70 So.2d 883 (divorce action); and Sanderson v. Frost, 198 La. 295, 3 So.2d 626 (petitory action). We conclude that Article 2291 applies to the present delictual action.

More difficult is the question of whether the disserving factual testimony of a party-witness is a judicial confession under Article 2291, barring recovery despite a contrary judicial finding of facts consistent with the defendant's liability.

Some appellate decisions, without analyzing the history and purpose of the Article, have assumed that a party's disserving factual testimony amounts to a judicial confession, inexorably binding the party irrespective of preponderating evidence to the contrary. The underlying notion seems to be that a party who has testified incorrectly against himself should lose his case. See Franklim v. Zurich Insurance Co. and Thompson v. Haubtman, supra. This Court has never passed upon the question, though in the recent case of Reynolds v. Hardware Mutual Casualty Company, 249 La. 268, 186 So.2d 588, we expressed serious doubt that Article 2291 applies to a party's testimonial recitation of facts.

The codal text relating to the judicial confession (l'aveu judiciaire) emanates from Article 1356 of the Code Napoleon. Imported from that code, the text became part of Louisiana's first Civil Code, See C.C.1808, p. 314, Art. 257. Succeeding codes retained the test without substantial change.

Like the Code Napoleon, the Louisiana Codes classified the judicial confession as a distinct method of proof. C.N. 1804, Art. 1316; C.C.1808, p. 304, Art. 216; C.C.1825, Art. 2230; C.C.1870, Art. 2233. Article 2233 of the present Code classifies the methods of proof as the literal proof, the testimonial proof, the presumption, and the confession of the party.

Under the original Code Napoleon, only a witness could give Testimony. A party litigant could offer proof only by Admissions and Oaths. 2 Planiol, Civil Law Treatise (Translation by Louisiana State Law Institute) No. 17.

The judicial admission, or confession, was a party's express acknowledgement of the correctness of "the fact or the act charged against him" by his adversary. 2 Planiol, supra,

No. 24. In practice, the judicial confession was incorporated in a formal act. See 20 Laurent, Droit Civil Francois, s 166, p. 196 (3d ed. 1878). Such a confession amounted to full proof and dispensed with testimony. 2 Planiol, supra, Nos. 22–29.

Party oaths under the Code Napoleon represented a formal system designed to test the truth when the testimony was unsatisfactory. Planiol, supra, Nos. 31–35. This system was never fully adopted in Louisiana.

At the time Louisiana adopted the judicial confession principle, the Civil Code disqualified a party litigant as a witness, because of his interest in the cause. C.C.1808, p. 312, Art. 248; Pugh, Evidence, 23 La.L.Rev. pp. 407–408. The Code restricted proof by party oath to interrogatories on facts and articles. C.C.1808, p. 316, Art. 258. Article 259 of the Louisiana Civil Code of 1808 specifically defined the interrogatory on facts and articles as written questions propounded to the opposite party endeavoring to obtain from the party's avowals (les aveux) some proof respecting the object of the litigation. Article 263 provided that the answer, that is, the avowal elicited by this formal procedure, formed complete proof against the responding party. Thus, the avowal dispensed with the production of evidence.

The disqualification of a party litigant as a witness continued in Article 2260 of the Civil Code of 1825. See Beer v. Word, Asher & Co., 13 La.Ann. 467 (1858); Baudoin v. Nicholas, 12 Rob, 594 (1846); and Brander v. Ferriday, Bennett & Co., 16 La. 296 (1840). By 1867, witness disqualification because of interest in the cause had been removed through amendment of the Code Article. See Act 71 of 1867 and Act 204 of 1868.

The Civil Code of 1825 omitted Articles 258 to 264 of the 1808 Code, dealing with proof by oath of a party through interrogatories on facts and articles. The codifiers relegated this series of articles to a code of evidence then being prepared. See Volume I, Louisiana Legal Archives, p. 290. At the same time, they retained in the Civil Code the judicial confession article, which immediately preceded the articles suppressed. See C.C.1825, Art. 2270.

This historical analysis clearly points to a conclusion that the judicial confession is distinct from a party's factual testimony. The Louisiana codes have distinguished the confession of a party from testimonial proof. Furthermore, during the formative period of the confession rule, a party litigant was generally incompetent to testify as a witness.

As a legal concept, the judicial confession is designed to dispense with evidence. It has the effect of withdrawing the subject matter of the confession from issue. See Sanderson v. Frost, 198 La. 295, 3 So.2d 626 and Farley v. Frost-Johnson Lumber Co., 133 La. 497, 63 So. 122, L.R.A.1915A, 200. In the landmark case of Frost-Johnson Lumber Co., supra, this Court pointed out that Article 2291 refers only to the confession made in the suit, that is, in the pleadings or note of evidence, "for the purpose of dispensing from taking evidence * * *."

As noted in Coleman v. Jones & Pickett, 131 La. 803, 60 So. 243, it is of the nature of this kind of admission that it be, by intention, an act of waiver relating to the opponent's proof and not merely an assertion made for some independent purpose, such as a statement made for the purpose of giving testimony.

See also Pugh, Evidence, 23 La.L.Rev. 406–408. For the common-law view of this subject, see McCormick On Evidence, ss 239, 243 (1954) and 9 Wigmore, Evidence, ss 2588, 2594A (3d ed. 1940).

A judicial confession under Article 2291 is a party's admission, or concession, in a judicial proceeding of an adverse factual element, waiving evidence as to the subject of the admission. A party's testimony is offered as evidence, not as a waiver of it. To be an effective agency of truth, the trier of fact must be allowed to weigh the disserving testimony of a party, as well as other evidence. When the truth is found elsewhere, the party's disserving testimony must yield in order to achieve the ends of justice. Hence, we reject as unsound the several expressions of the Courts of Appeal tending to equate a party's disserving factual testimony with a judicial confession.[1]

We hold that the plaintiffs' disserving testimony is not a judicial confession or conclusive admission. Hence, they are entitled to recover.

Heretofore, we have remanded cases to the Court of Appeal to fix damages when that court has failed to pass upon the issue. See Felt v. Price, 240 La. 966, 126 So.2d 330, and the cases therein cited. We will remand this case to permit the Court of Appeal to fix damages.

For the reasons assigned, the judgment of the Court of Appeal is reversed. Judgment is rendered in favor of the plaintiffs against the defendant, Gulf Insurance Company, in such sums as may hereafter be fixed, and the case is remanded to the Court of Appeal, Fourth Circuit, for the assessment of damages according to law. The defendant is condemned to pay all costs of court.

Questions

1. Regarding the first issue presented in *Jackson*—whether the rule of former Louisiana Civil Code article 2291 (*see* current La. Civ. Code art. 1853) applied to proof of delictual obligations ... (a) The plaintiffs, who contended that the article did not so apply, constructed an argument based on the structural arrangement of the Code: (1) premise: this article appears in the part of the Code that pertains to "conventional obligations"; (2) conclusion: therefore, this article applies only to conventional, as opposed to delictual, etc., obligations. What kind of argument (methodologically speaking) is this? (b) *Jackson* was decided under the old law of proof of obligations. Under the new law, which side—the plaintiffs or the defendants—would the structure-of-the-code argument favor? In what part of the Code is the new article situated?

2. Regarding the second issue presented in Jackson—whether a party's "disserving" testimony my constitute a judicial confession against him ... (a) How would you characterize (methodologically speaking) the first argument that the *Jackson* court makes in support of its answer to this question, *see* lines 101–152? (b) Once again, *Jackson* was decided under "old law". Would the case be decided the same way under "new law"?

---

1. These cases include *Thompson v. Haubtman*, 18 La.App. 119, 137 So. 362 (cert. denied 1932); *Stroud v. Standard Accident Ins. Co.*, La.App., 90 So.2d 477; *Bowers v. Hardware Mutual Casualty Co.*, La.App., 119 So.2d 671; and *Franklin v. Zurich Ins. Co.*, La.App., 136 So.2d 735 (cert. denied 1962). The results reached in these cases are not necessarily erroneous.

Index